From Breakpoint To Advantage

A Practical Guide to Optimal Tennis Health and Performance

Babette Pluim, M.D., Ph.D.
Marc Safran, M.D.

Racquet Tech Publishing
An Imprint of the USRSA
Vista, California, USA

USRSA
330 Main St.
Vista, California 92084
www.racquettech.com

Library of Congress Control Number: 2004093133

This book is written strictly for informational purposes, and the ideas, suggestions, and treatments presented are not to be used as a substitute for consulting a physician. Consult with a physcian before beginning any of the exercise programs in this book. Neither the authors nor publisher shall be liable or responsible for any loss, injury or damage allegedly arising from any information or suggestion in this book.

Cover design: R. Christian Anderson, Ph.D.
Photography: Frank de Jongh, Henk Koster, Frans Bosch,
          Bert Andree, Gordon Gillespie
Illustrations: Frans Bosch

Printed in the United States of America

ISBN 0-9722759-1-6

Praise for *From Breakpoint to Advantage*

"Babette Pluim and Marc Safran are true pioneers in the field of tennis medicine. Tennis coaches, parents, exercise physiologists, physiotherapists and physicians should have two copies of this book: one for the office, and one for the traveling bag. *From Breakpoint To Advantage* is a definitive tennis medicine resource "

> — *Brian Hainline Chief Medical Officer, US Open Tennis Championships; Chair, ITF Sports Medicine Commission*

"It is seldom that a book includes an appropriate mix of theory and practice. The book *From Breakpoint To Advantage* is written in such a manner by two world renown tennis medicine specialists. While medical issues are well covered, other areas of tennis science are also presented in an easy to read manner. A very useful book for the player, coach, and tennis enthusiast."

> — *Bruce Elliott, Professor of Biomechanics, The University of Western Australia, Australia; coeditor, Biomechanics of Advanced Tennis*

"This is an excellent practical and comprehensive book, one I wish I had a long time ago! Doctors Pluim and Safran have created an invaluable reference for anyone working with racquet sports. Coming from their expert backgrounds and experiences, they have edited and synthesized the many scientific and medical disciplines involved. This book will be a lasting contribution in the field and an essential resource."

> — *Carol L. Otis, M.D. FACSM, Former WTA medical advisor*

iii

"This book is the ultimate guide to sports medicine and physical training in tennis. Doctors Pluim and Safran have provided an exhaustive compilation of information on injury management, prevention and performance enhancement strategies for tennis players, coaches, and those who care for them. A great source of information for any tennis player, coach or sports medicine professional."

> — *Todd S. Ellenbecker, MS, PT, SCS, OCS, CSCS; Chairman, USTA Sport Science Committee; Clinic Director, Physiotherapy Associates Scottsdale Sports Clinic*

"Forty years of experience and ten years on the ATP Tour have taught me that players are careless with their bodies. The take-home message of this book is to take better care of your body, because you only have one!"

> — *Jan Naaktgeboren, physiotherapist, Dutch Davis Cup Team*

"Your body is like a bicycle chain. The weakest link determines the strength of the whole. This book will help to reveal and strengthen your weak points."

> — *Jurgen Roordink, physiotherapist, Dutch Davis Cup Team*

"Reading this book confirmed once again my conviction that prevention is more important than treatment. If you do need treatment, make sure you have a very good medical staff, like we have with the Dutch Davis Cup Team!"

> — *Tjerk Bogtstra, Dutch Davis Cup Captain*

"It was about time a book like this appeared on the market! It gives an excellent overview of all the possible injuries in tennis and good tips of what to do. I particularly like the exercises in the rehabilitation chapter."

> — *Juan Reque, PT, ATP Sports Medicine Trainer, Physiotherapist of the Spanish Davis Cup and Fed Cup Teams*

"Coming back after injury is a very tough road for every tennis player. I know this from personal experience. If you are injured, reading this book will make life easier, both for you and your coach!"

> — *Goren Ivanisevic, Wimbledon Champion, former #1 ATP Tour*

"This book is a must for everyone who starts playing intense tennis at a young age."

  — *Richard Krajicek, Wimbledon Champion*

"At the top levels, I need to be faster and more accurate than the other guy. Any injury is an obstacle on my way to the top. This book is a good tool to better prevent and treat injuries. Every coach, therapist, player, and parent should know what's inside it."

  — *Juan Carlos Ferrero, French Open Champion*

"Injury prevention is a key to a longer career. Read this book and make sure you look after your body."

  — *Mahesh Bhupathi, former #1 ATP Doubles, Doubles Champion French Open, Wimbledon, US Open*

"I am in the fortunate circumstance that I have been able to make a (rather successful!) career out of what I love doing most: playing tennis. One of the keys to my success was that I spent as much time on court as off-court to optimize my performance and to stay healthy. Reading this book might help you find your way to success!"

  — *Jonas Björkman, Doubles Champion Australian Open, Wimbledon, US Open*

"Consistent performance at the elite level is only possible if one combines high-intensity exercise with high-quality recovery. This book will give you excellent practical tips to enhance recovery and prevent injuries."

  — *Martin Verkerk, top-twenty ATP player, French Open finalist*

Contents

PART 2: A COMPLETE INVENTORY OF TENNIS INJURIES

Contents **ix**

X   Contents

Foreword

For most of my life, I have been a tennis player and, fortunately, a healthy one. That passion changed my life as I worked in tennis administration, first as a volunteer, on the national, regional and international level and, through that vantage point, my awareness of the health issues facing tennis players has grown. Clearly there is much more for all of us to learn about this field.

So you can imagine how pleased I was to welcome this timely new book, *From Breakpoint to Advantage: A Practical Guide to Optimal Tennis Health and Performance*. It is a great addition to our sport as it takes a look at ways to treat and prevent tennis injuries and to improve performance. Everyone from players and coaches to trainers and doctors will benefit from this volume written by two eminent doctors and sports scientists, Babette Pluim and Marc Safran.

Babette has been a valuable member of the ITF's Sports Medical Commission for many years and we are well aware of her expertise in this field. We are fortunate that her enthusiasm and dedication to tennis have resulted in this outstanding book of practical advice for the tennis family. We congratulate both Babette and her co-author, Marc Safran, on this excellent effort that we know will be a great contribution to the long term health of our sport.

Francesco Ricci Bitti
President, ITF (International Tennis Federation)

♦♦♦

Tennis is a wonderful sport enjoyed by millions of people of all ages, from 3 to 103 years old around the world. The sport of tennis provides an all-round game with quick starts and stops, repetitive overhead motions, and involvement of all the muscles of the body. A tennis match results not only in stimulating and exciting competition but also in conditioning and other general health benefits. Regular tennis improves the body's general functional capacity, and promotes both coordination and balance, which is of special importance for older tennis players.

At the top competitive levels, tennis can be a very demanding sport, both physically and mentally. During the last ten to twenty years, the game of tennis has developed enormously as facilitated by the new designs for rackets and other equipment and new playing techniques, with special reference to serving. The game is much more intense and demanding as compared to ten years ago.

A major concern for the sport is the extended length of the season for top-level tennis players. Another risk factor may be the conduct of tournaments on different surfaces, including hard court, clay, and grass. The increasing intensity of the game and the associated physical demands also involve an increased risk for injury and other medical problems.

The top level tennis players are offered excellent medical service as the ATP, WTA, and ITF provide outstanding medical services by assigning well-educated and specialized physiotherapists and/or athletic trainers to all major tournaments around the world. Well-qualified medical doctors are also available at all the tournaments for top players. The medical services provided in tennis on a world wide basis are probably the best any international sport can offer. The ITF has founded a medical and science committee that reviews and coordinates the medical and scientific concerns in tennis. The Society for Tennis Medicine and Science (STMS) provides education and disseminates information through journals and conferences in cooperation with the other international organizations.

Tennis is a wonderful game but as in all sports there is a rather limited risk for injury and other medical problems. More information and more education about how to manage these problems is needed. With this in mind this book represents a valuable contribution to help everybody who loves tennis and wants to enjoy the wonderful game while minimizing the risk for injury and other medical problems.

Per Renström, MD, PhD
Past President STMS
ATP Medical Director
Member ITF Sports Medical Commission

◆◆◆

Preface

A book like this does not just "happen" from one day to the next. Many steps need to be taken before the final product can be found on the bookstore shelves. And we never realized how many steps actually need to be taken, until we started writing this book ourselves.

Babette started working as a sports physician for the Royal Netherlands Lawn Tennis Association in 1990. One of the aspects of the job she very much enjoyed was writing short articles. The first article she wrote was called "Ten Ways to Prevent Tennis Elbow," which included ten practical tips for tennis players. The article was well received, so she decided to use that same concept with other topics as well. Later, she started extending the articles somewhat by including first aid and treatment, in addition to prevention. These articles became so popular that the Royal Netherlands Lawn Tennis Association decided to make "Injury Cards" of them. Each A4-sized laminated card discusses one tennis-related medical topic as it relates to coaches and players. The popularity of the cards showed us that practical medical information on tennis-related issues was very much needed and desired!

Marc worked in private practice and with an HMO before joining the full time faculty at the University of California, San Francisco as the director of sports medicine in the department of Orthopaedic Surgery in 2001. He studied junior tennis injury rates, patterns, and gender differences as he noticed the game of tennis was changing for boys, girls, men and women. He served as the medical director for the WTA tournament in La Costa (San Diego, California) and as the neutral site physician for several Davis Cup ties. As such, he had much experience dealing with the recreational, competitive and professional tennis player and had always tried to educate players, coaches and others in tennis injury treatment, prevention and return to play guidelines. He noted a lack of scientific data to help guide these recommendations, but noted that many of those with experience in treating players recommended similar procedures. By the time he was approached by Babette about writing this book, he was nearly finished writing a general sports medicine book for patients with sports medicine problems. But that book was not specific for tennis.

In 1991, the Society of Tennis Medicine and Science (STMS) was founded, with Ben Kibler and then Per Renström as the first presidents. Babette was thrilled to attend the first congress at Yale, in August 1991. What a great opportunity to be able to interact with an international group of sports medicine experts, working in close co-operation with the ITF, ATP and WTA Tour, dedicated to generating and disseminating knowledge of tennis medicine and science.

Marc joined the society in 1995, seeing the same wonderful things about the society that so enthralled Babette. This is where we found that many clinicians (surgeons, medical doctors, therapists and trainers) had similar practice ideas and results with regard to treating tennis players, but this was mostly based on their experience. Since then, we have both attended many meetings, sharing our knowledge with others and learning a lot in the process as well.

Marc organized a very successful STMS congress in Indian Wells, in March 1999. We got on very well, and started working together on projects within the STMS. And slowly the idea of writing a book emerged, with Babette initiating and driving the idea. We had noticed there are many books on the market on general sports medicine, but relatively few on tennis medicine, and fewer still written for non-physicians. And even though the knowledge in this field had steadily increased, the information was still not very accessible to the coach and player. So...why not write a book to fill the gap? But since writing a book is definitely more difficult and much more work than writing an article, it took us two years of thinking and playing with the idea before anything happened. If we were going to write this book, we really had to be sure we were writing a practical book for players, coaches, trainers and so forth.

The final impetus came at a conference in London where Babette discussed the idea of the book with a sport science colleague, Paul Roetert. Paul had written a great tennis book on strengthening and conditioning and was in the process of finishing another book. "How did you do that," Babette asked. "I just sat down and started writing," he told Babette. That did it! We could do that! And so the project began.

When we started writing this book, we had three goals in mind. First, we wanted to provide the reader with state-of-the-art information on tennis injuries and illnesses, and include both prevention and treatment approaches, as well as how to return to play. We knew from our experience that this information was lacking to the people who most need it. Secondly, we wanted to present this information in a very practical way, so the book would not remain lying on a shelf. We wanted the reader (coach, player, therapist, athletic trainer) to take the book on court with them. And thirdly, we wanted the reader to really understand their injuries and be able to perform the exercises without having to read a sentence three times and without the need of a medical translator. Since a picture says more than a thousand words, we decided to include many drawings and photographs.

We organized in such a way that it allows for selective reading. The book starts with the basics of the game: the physiological and biomechanical aspects of tennis, equipment variables, shoes and surfaces, and the basic principles of injury prevention and rehabilitation.

The core of the book is formed by a complete inventory of tennis injuries. All injuries are discussed by first describing the nature of the injury, followed by the symptoms, the treatment principles and then finally by practical tips for the tennis player - making this a very unique book. The next sections are devoted to medical issues in tennis players, selected issues (e.g., heat stress, doping, jet lag, and nutrition), special tennis groups (women, junior, veteran, and wheelchair tennis players), and managing and delivering tennis medicine programs (by the certified athletic trainer, sports physiotherapist, and sports physician). The final chapter presents a strength training program for tennis players.

We hope that reading this book will help you to enjoy tennis more, longer, and with as few injuries as possible. We have both learned by experience that you really DO need to prepare for tennis if you want to remain injury free. It has been said that you should get into shape to play tennis, but do not use tennis to get into shape...this is how players can get injured. This book will give you plenty of useful tips. So go out there, and enjoy!

Babette M. Pluim
Marc R. Safran

Acknowledgements

Many people helped shape the final form of this book.

We thank the following experts for reviewing one or more chapters in their field of expertise:

André van Alphen, Maria Amato, Mark Andeweg, Peter Arnold, Enrique Arosemena Hidalgo, Per Basthold, Michael Bergeron, Tim Binkhorst, Roland van der Borgh, Ilse Bouman, Amy Chappell, Robert van Cingel, Miguel Crespo, Marlies van Dijk, Bruce Elliott, Dave Fairfield, Frank van Fraaijenhoven, Ton Gorgels, Brian Hainline, Leo Heere, Joris Hermans, Henk van der Hoeven, Guido Hornman, Hans Hunze, Miguel Janssen, Piet van Kalmthout, Frits Kessel, Ben Kibler, Harm Kuipers, Ellen de Lange, Leon van Leeuwen, Tom van Loenhout, Kathy Martin, Joachim Mester, Ton ten Napel, Harriet Op Den Oordt, Carol Otis, Nellie Overbeeke, Luuk van Paridon, Stefan Raatgever, Machar Reid, Juan Reque, Paul Roetert, Carel Roos, Thomas Rowland, Theo Schennink, David Sharnoff, Maaike Smit, Fred Six, Randy Snow, Kathleen Stroia, Michael Turner, Jan Uil, Jacques van Unen, Jules van de Veen, Claire Verheul, Pat Viroux, Edwin Visser, Niels Wildeman, Frank Wilschut, and Wart van Zoest.

We would like to thank the following people for their special input:

- Christine MacBrien, who spent her ski-vacation editing the English of the book, after sadly tearing her anterior cruciate ligament.
- Pally Leuw and Tora Harris, for patiently posing for the photographs.
- Frans Bosch, for his creative ideas and skillful drawings.
- Gary Windler, who spent a great many hours reading and meticulously correcting the orthopedic chapters of the book, despite his busy schedule.
- Luuk van Paridon and Jan Uil, for inventing 20 possible book titles, including the final one!
- Theo de Vaal and the KNLTB, for mental, moral and financial support of the book.
- Crawford Lindsey, for taking up the challenge and making this book come true.

And finally, Babette would like to give special thanks to:

- My aunt Lilian Six, who critically commented on every single chapter of the book. Being an avid tennis player herself, she has had personal experience with a wide range of injuries. She simultaneously motivated and challenged me by reminding me how useful a book like this would be, if only I would manage to write it in a more "user-friendly" way.
- My friend Dave Fairfield, for letting me see the recreational tennis player's point of view, and helping me translate rocket science into sensible sentences.
- My parents, for their endless faith in my dreams.

To Sakiko

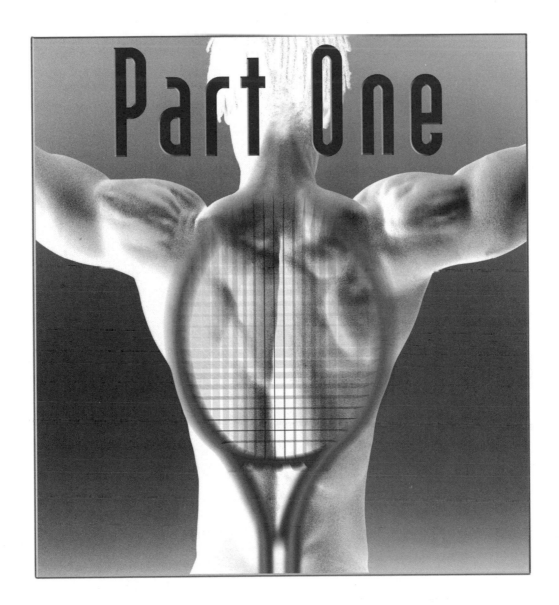

Part One

Fundamental Principles of Injury Prevention and Rehabilitation

1 The Biomechanics of Tennis

A movement analysis of the basic strokes in tennis is important, because a faulty technique is a major risk factor for injuries. Although there is no such thing as one best form for executing a stroke, there are several key motions that are common to all efficient stroke patterns. A basic understanding of the proper biomechanics of stroke production and movement patterns in tennis may help the player develop an effective and efficient technique, reduce injury risk, and improve his performance. In this chapter, we will take a closer look at the three basic strokes in tennis (service, forehand, and backhand) by means of a movement analysis (Figure 1.1 explains the terms necessary for such an analysis). This is followed by a discussion of the potential injury risk during the various phases of the strokes and the measures that can be taken to avoid these injuries. Although injuries may also occur when hitting overheads, volleys, half-volleys, drop shots, returns, or lobs, due to space limitations these were left out. However, these strokes may be referred to throughout the book, when applicable.

HOW TO HIT THE BALL WITH POWER

The game of tennis, as played currently, is described as a power game because of the high ball velocities and the explosive actions of the players needed to get to and hit the ball. In order to hit the ball both with power and precision without getting injured, players need to understand the basic principles of developing racquet speed and thus ball speed. A common misconception is that muscular strength determines how hard one can hit the ball. However, strength is only one factor, and not the most important one. That is why players with less muscular frames are sometimes able to hit the ball harder than players with stronger, more muscular builds. Other important factors, in addition to muscle strength, include good use of the stretch-shortening cycle of muscles, the length of the backswing, sufficient scapular and core stabilization, coordinated movements forming a "kinetic chain," and the right equipment (see Chapter 3).

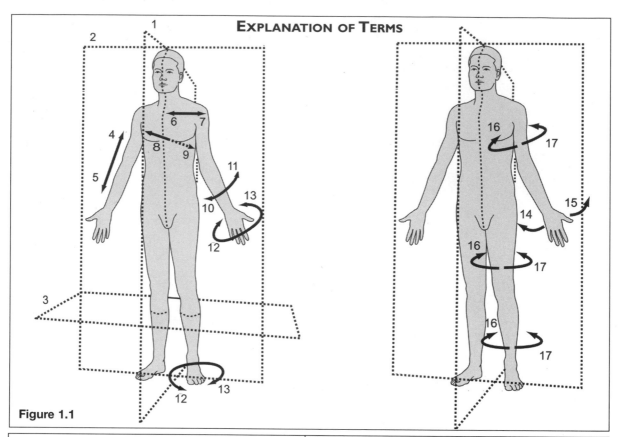

Figure 1.1

PLANES			JOINT ACTIONS		
1	*Sagital plane*	Longitudinal plane that divides body into right and left sections.	10	*Adduction*	Moving of a body part toward the central axis of the body.
2	*Frontal plane*	Vertical plane at right angles to the sagittal plane, dividing body into anterior and posterior sections.	11	*Abduction*	Moving of a body part away from the central axis of the body.
3	*Tranverse plane*	At right angles to both frontal and sagittal planes.	12	*Pronation*	Rotation of the hand or foot so the palm faces down or the inside of the sole is tilted down.
LIMB LOCATION			13	*Supination*	Rotation of the hand or foot so the palm faces up or the inside of the sole is tilted up.
4	*Proximal*	Means nearer to the center of the body.	14	*Ulnar deviation*	Moving the hand sideways toward the little finger.
5	*Distal*	Farther from the center or midline of the body.	15	*Radial deviation*	Moving the hand sideways toward the thumb.
6	*Medial*	Side of the body or body part that is nearer to the middle or center (median) of the body.	16	*Internal rotation*	Rotating inward of the shoulder, hip, or lower leg.
7	*Lateral*	Side of the body or body part that is farther from the middle or center of the body.	17	*External rotation*	Rotating outward of the shoulder, hip, or lower leg.
8	*Anterior*	In front or towards the front.	not num-bered	*Varus* *Valgus* *Inversion* *Eversion*	Angulation of bone toward midline. Angulation of bone from midline. Moving foot so sole faces inwards. Moving foot so sole faces outwards.
9	*Posterior*	Towards or at the back.			

Stretch-shortening cycle. Muscles can be compared with mechanical springs that are supported by biological reflexes. Muscles are able to contract more powerfully immediately following a stretch ("stretch-shortening cycle"), due to the release of the elastic energy that is stored during the stretch phase. In a tennis stroke, energy is stored when the stomach, shoulder, upper arm and forearm muscles are stretched during the preparation phase of the stroke, and part of this energy is recovered upon forward movement of the racquet, when the stretched muscles start contracting (Figure 1.2). However, this stored energy is lost after a very short period of time. For example, in the forearm muscles, this energy storage only lasts about 0.1 to 0.3 seconds. Thus, the muscle contraction should be well-timed and follow quickly after the stretch. This concept is similar to the principles involved in attaining maximum height while jumping. One can jump higher after bending the knees quickly, as compared to the situation where one stays squatted for a few sec-

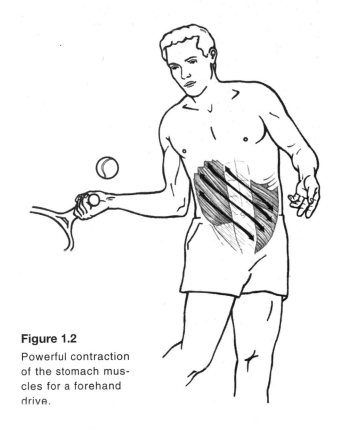

Figure 1.2
Powerful contraction of the stomach muscles for a forehand drive.

onds and then attempts to jump up. This is why timing is so important for a good split step. A stretching of the upper leg and calf muscles as the player is landing from his split step is rapidly followed by a contraction, enabling him to move away quickly.

Backswing. The function of the backswing is to increase the distance over which racquet speed can be developed. The more distance one has to accelerate the arm and racquet, the more speed and momentum can be attained at ball impact. The available time is usually limited by the high ball velocities used in top tennis, and a longer backswing for acceleration is not always possible. That is why a short and/or late backswing is often followed by an explosive "stretch-shortening cycle," enabling very high acceleration of the arm and the racquet. Thus, a player can develop greater racquet speed by reducing the time to move a certain distance (accelerate faster), but this also requires more force. Building the speed up more gradually would require less force, and may help to prevent injuries, but in modern top tennis this time is not always available. Therefore, the player must consider and train for the muscular requirements of such movements.

Scapular and core stabilization. The scapula is the base from which the arm works and includes the socket of the shoulder joint. The scapula must be firmly connected to the chest cage to provide a stable base for the arm, which provides most of the power. This is achieved by good coordination and strength of the scapular stabilizers (the muscles at the back of the shoulder). Also, the smaller and deeper lumbar spine and trunk muscles (the so-called "core" muscles) must be correctly coordinated and capable of working continuously, holding the lumbar spine in the neutral position. If the scapula and core are strong and stable, all other movements are more efficient and

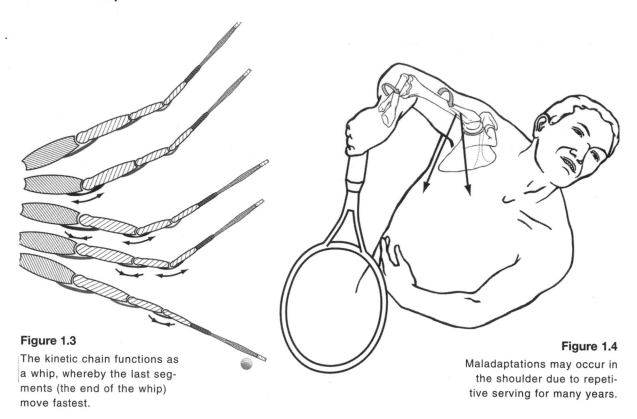

Figure 1.3
The kinetic chain functions as a whip, whereby the last segments (the end of the whip) move fastest.

Figure 1.4
Maladaptations may occur in the shoulder due to repetitive serving for many years.

effective. If there is lack of scapular and/or core stability, training should be geared toward solving these deficits (see Chapter 6).

Kinetic chain. The kinetic chain is defined as the coordinated activation of the segments of the body (legs, trunk, shoulder, arm, and hand), transferring force efficiently from the ground to the racquet and ultimately to the ball. Each successive body segment transfers more energy than the previous one, resulting in maximal racquet acceleration. The sequencing generally occurs in a proximal to distal order, with the larger and/or lower body parts moving first (feet, knees, hips), and the smaller and/or higher parts (shoulder, elbow, hands) moving later (Figure 1.3). Performance will improve and injury risk will reduce if this chain of movements is followed. Removal of a segment (e.g., not bending the knees, lack of trunk rotation) will detract from the ability to generate racquet speed and will increase the chance of getting injured.

Also, intense tennis practice for many years may lead to maladaptations in strength and flexibility such as loss of internal rotation of the dominant shoulder and of the dominant hip, and strength imbalances in the shoulder, with weakness of the posterior shoulder muscles (Figure 1.4). This may create abnormal biomechanics, kinetic chain segment drop out, loss of power and an increased injury risk. An individual training program should be aimed at preventing or correcting these deficiencies.

For a more detailed discussion of power generation in tennis, please refer to the book *Biomechanics of Tennis*, by Elliott, Crespo and Reid or to *World-Class Tennis Technique*, by Roetert and Groppel.

MOVEMENT ANALYSIS

Let us now take a look at the basic movement patterns of each stroke, and how these relate to (the prevention of) injuries.

THE SERVE

Research has shown that muscular activity in the shoulder and forearm muscles is higher during the service action than during any other stroke, indicating that the serve is the most strenuous stroke in tennis. The service is composed of motions that resemble throwing. The four major phases of serving are the wind-up, cocking, acceleration and follow-through.

Wind-up. The wind-up phase begins with the tennis player standing ready to serve and ends with the ball toss (Figures 1.5a-b). During the wind-up phase, the lower body prepares for the build up of power that occurs in the cocking phase and is transferred during the acceleration phase.

Cocking. The second phase, cocking, begins with ball release and ends with the racquet down and away from the back and the dominant shoulder (the one holding the racquet) in maximal external rotation (Figures 1.5c-e). This phase is characterized by a gradual building of power, a sort of coiling up that precedes the transfer and release of energy along the kinetic chain to the racquet and ball impact. Energy is stored by prestretching muscles all along the chain.

Acceleration. The third phase is the acceleration phase, which begins with the forward and upward movement of the dominant shoulder and ends with ball contact (Figure 1.5f-g). During this phase of the service motion, the accumulated power generated by the athlete's dynamic kinetic chain is released. The power, starting from ground reaction forces, is transferred from the legs to the hips/pelvis/trunk and then to the arm, racquet, and ball. Leaving one segment out (e.g., not bending the knees or not using the shoulder tilt), will lead to a loss of power. Upper arm internal rotation is particularly important, producing approximately 40 percent of racquet speed at impact.

Follow-through. The final serving phase is the follow-through. This stage starts just after ball contact and ends after the pronation of the hitting arm has been completed (Figure 1.5h-i). The internal rotation of the upper arm and pronation of the forearm ("long-axis rotation") during the early phase of the follow-through reduce the forces on the elbow. The predominant muscle activity in this phase is eccentric contraction of the posterior shoulder muscles, as the athlete is absorbing the energy and decelerating the racquet and upper limb.

INJURY RISK DURING SERVING

The peak velocity of a tennis racquet during a tennis serve can range from 62 to 83 miles per hour (100 to 130 km per hour) with ball velocities of 83 to 153 miles per hour (130 to 245 km per hour). This speed is achieved in 0.2 to 0.3 seconds from the end of the cocking phase until ball contact. The shoulder is observed to be internally rotating at 1,100 to 1,700 degrees per second during this phase. Forearm pronation has been recorded to be 350-900 degrees per second as measured 0.1 seconds prior to ball impact, and this increases to 1,300 degrees per second 0.1 seconds following impact.

Figure 1.5a   1.5b   1.5c

1.5d   1.5e   1.5f

1.5g   1.5h   1.5i

Shoulder. Shoulder pain is the most common complaint during serving. The pain is generally elicited during the acceleration phase, when high forces act on the shoulder joint, and pull the upper arm bone forward. In order to generate the necessary power without putting undue stress on the shoulder ligaments, tendons, and muscles, the kinetic chain should be used to full advantage. The best way to control the forces at the shoulder is to optimize the knee flexion and extension, use core muscle rotation to generate rotational momentum, strengthen the scapular muscles and rotator cuff, optimize the ball toss, and optimize the internal rotation and pronation of the arm.

Elbow. Elbow pain may occur during the acceleration phase, when the elbow is subjected to significant forces, or at impact. The elbow is flexed as much as 120 degrees at late cocking and extends to 15-20 degrees of flexion at ball impact. This results in an extension velocity of approximately 900 to 1,000 degrees per second during the acceleration phase. Strengthening of the biceps and triceps muscles improves control over the elbow and may help to reduce injury risk. Also, full pronation of the arm after impact will reduce excessive load and stress on the elbow.

Wrist. Wrist pain is commonly felt at impact. Wrist flexion has been recorded at more than 1,000 degrees per second at 0.1 seconds prior to ball impact. The range of motion of the wrist during the serve is an arc of 90 to 100 degrees of flexion/extension. Strengthening the elbow and reducing the wrist snap are important measures to prevent wrist injuries.

Abdominals. Abdominal muscle pain is usually felt at the start of the acceleration phase. At the end of the cocking phase, the lumbar spine is in hyperextension and the abdominal muscles are maximally stretched, storing elastic energy. On movement reversal, these abdominal muscles contract powerfully, using this stored elastic energy (stretch-shortening cycle). This is a high-risk moment for an abdominal muscle strain. When the ball is hit behind the body, such as with a kick service, the back is arched even more, resulting in more abdominal muscle stretch, increasing the risk for such a strain. Strengthening the abdominal muscles, reducing the number of kick serves, and taking adequate rest may help prevent this injury.

Knees. Knee pain may occur when extending the knees during the service action, or when landing on the leg after the serve, resulting in eccentric contraction of the upper leg muscles. Common mistakes are not bending the knees enough, and thereby not using the kinetic chain efficiently, or bending the knees too much, which may lead to overuse injury of the knees. An optimal knee bend and strong upper leg muscles may help prevent knee injuries.

Low back. Low back pain is generally felt during late cocking, when the trunk is rotated and hyperextended. Core stability exercises may help to protect the lumbar spine and reduce low back pain.

THE FOREHAND

Most forehands are hit with a semi-western or western grip, allowing for the easy production of topspin. This is particularly useful when playing on clay or slow hard courts. The eastern forehand is more suitable for slice and low balls, and may thus be preferred by serve and volley players on grass and carpet.

The forehand stroke can divided into three phases: stroke preparation, acceleration and follow-through.

Preparation. The stroke preparation phase starts with the rotation of the body and ends with the forward movement of the body (Figure 1.6a). The backswing is often a looped motion, though the degree of loop varies with player preference.

Acceleration. The second phase, acceleration, begins with forward racquet motion and ends at ball contact (Figure 1.6b-c). Depending on the foot position, the ball will be hit with a closed or with an open stance. Shown here is an open stance forehand. The traditional square stance takes longer to execute but generates more linear momentum (as the player steps forward) and angular momentum (from the rotation of the hips, legs and trunk) than the open stance forehand. Just before impact, the wrist trails behind in hyperextension, inducing stretch of the forearm muscles and thus preparing the spring-like action.

Follow-through. The third phase, follow-through, begins just after ball contact and ends at the completion of the stroke (Figure 1.6d-i). There is deceleration of the shoulder movement as the upper limb and racquet complete the upward and inward motion.

INJURY RISK DURING THE FOREHAND

Shoulder. Shoulder pain is generally felt during the acceleration phase and at impact, especially when hitting high topspin forehands. This places high demands on the anterior shoulder structures (e.g., biceps tendon, anterior shoulder joint capsule).

Elbow. Medial elbow pain may occur during the acceleration phase and at impact, particularly in players with a western grip, increasing valgus stress. Strengthening the forearm flexor muscles, reducing elbow extension, and full pronation of the arm after impact may help reduce injury risk.

Wrist. Wrist pain usually occurs at impact, due to contraction of the wrist flexors. The wrist should be thought of as the end of a whip. It gets most of its velocity and force from more proximal sources, because its muscles are too small to generate the forces seen at the wrist. Top players may accelerate the racquet within 100 ms, right before impact, from 6 m/s to 33 m/s. This acceleration can only be achieved if the proximal muscles have worked well. Using the full kinetic chain, strengthening the wrist muscles, and hitting the ball in front of the body are important preventative factors.

Knees. Medial knee pain may occur in players who drag their feet when hitting the forehand, forcing the knee into valgus. Pain may be prevented by better footwork and strengthening of the upper leg muscles.

Hips. Anterior hip pain is more common in players with an open stance than a closed stance forehand, as it forces the femoral head anteriorly creating shear forces on the anterior acetabular structures. The area of damage is characteristically found in the anterior labrum and the anterior articular surface of the acetabulum (hip socket). Core stability exercises are important to prevent hip injuries.

Figure 1.6a   1.6b   1.6c

1.6d   1.6e   1.6f

1.6g   1.6h   1.6i

THE BACKHAND

There are two common types of backhand strokes—the one-handed backhand and the two-handed backhand. Both types of backhand strokes are divided into three phases, similar to the forehand: stroke preparation, acceleration and follow-through.

Preparation. Stroke preparation begins with the first motion of the backswing and ends with the first forward motion of the racquet. In the one-handed backhand, the non-dominant hand is used to assist the backswing (Figures 1.7a-e). The racquet is brought back in a looped motion, but as with the forehand, the degree of loop is specific to each player. There is shoulder and trunk rotation, which is important to generate high racquet head speeds as part of the kinetic chain.

The two-handed backhand is characterized by a straighter backswing and less looped motion due to the constraints of the non-dominant hand holding the racquet (Figures 1.8a-b). The shoulders move in synchrony with trunk rotation.

Acceleration. The second phase, acceleration, begins with the forward motion of the racquet and ends with ball impact. The two-handed backhand (1.8c-e) is easier than the one-handed backhand, because the arms work as a unit and the stroke requires less strength. With the one-handed backhand (1.7f-g), the player has a slightly better reach and may find it easier to learn how to slice and hit a one-handed backhand volley. Contact point should be in front of the body.

Follow-through. The final phase, follow-through, begins at ball impact and ends with the completion of the swing (Figure 1.7h-i and 1.8f-i). Trunk rotation is more pronounced in the two-handed backhand because the back shoulder must rotate more completely with the follow-through. The follow-through on the two-handed backhand is more over the shoulder than the one-handed backhand.

INJURY RISK DURING THE BACKHAND

Elbow. Lateral elbow pain (tennis elbow) usually occurs at impact, with a higher incidence in novice players than in advanced players. An advanced player has his wrist extended an average 20 to 25 degrees just prior to ball impact and then extends his wrist further at impact. In contrast, novice players strike the ball with their wrist in 10 to 15 degrees of flexion with his wrist moving into further flexion at impact. Hitting the ball in front of the body will reduce injury risk. Another common problem with lateral elbow pain is not using the shoulder muscles enough, so that the player uses the elbow muscles to power the racquet. This is generally a technical problem that needs correction, but can also be due to weak posterior shoulder muscles.

Wrist. Wrist pain is commonly seen in the non-dominant hand of players with a two-handed backhand, due to excessive cocking (wrist extension) to try to "flick" the racquet through the hitting zone, rather than use trunk rotation. Taping of the wrist, wrist strengthening and correction of faulty technique are important preventative measures.

Lumbar spine. The two-handed backhand puts the lumbar spine at increased biomechanical risk when reaching for a wide ball. The obligatory trunk rotation with the two-handed backhand, coupled with a relatively fixed pelvis for hitting a wide ball, can cause a greater stress on the lumbar spine because forced rotation is applied to a rela-

Figure 1.7a

1.7b

1.7c

1.7d

1.7e

1.7f

1.7g

1.7h

1.7i

Figure 1.8a

1.8b

1.8c

1.8d

1.8e

1.8f

1.8g

1.8h

1.8i

tively fixed pivot point. Core stability exercises will help reduce the risk of low back pain.

Knees. Knee pain may be felt during the preparatory phase of the backhand, when the load is placed on the bent knee. Pain may also be felt during the follow-through, particularly if a player places his front knee parallel to the net, instead of pointing his feet in the direction he is hitting. This increases the rotational stress on the knee and may lead to meniscal or patellar (knee cap) problems. Good footwork with a correct stance, appropriate shoes with outsoles adapted to the surface and strengthening of the leg muscles are important preventative measures.

Ankles. Ankle injuries occur most commonly when hitting the backhand, because of the high forces on the lateral structures of the foot or when stepping on a ball. This may lead to an ankle sprain. Good footwork, removing balls from the court, taping or bracing of the ankle, and proprioceptive training and coordination exercises for the ankle will reduce injury risk.

SUMMARY

In this chapter the medical terms that are used throughout this book to discuss movements or injury localization in relation to the body are explained. Next, the factors that are involved in the production of racquet and ball speed are presented, including muscle strength, good use of the stretch-shortening cycle of muscles, the length of the backswing, sufficient scapular and core stabilization, coordinated movements forming a "kinetic chain," and the right equipment. The biomechanics and physical demands of the three basic strokes in tennis, the serve, forehand, and backhand, are described. This is followed by an analysis of the injuries that may occur during the various phases of the strokes, and how these injuries could be prevented.

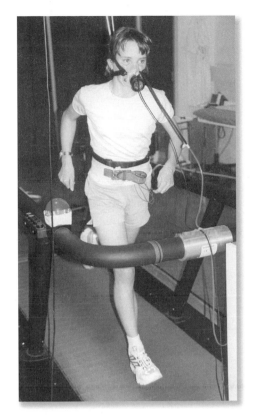

2

Physiological Demands of the Game

Tennis is an interesting sport from a physiological point of view. It is an intermittent high intensity exercise, and the energy demands differ from either pure sprinting or pure endurance running. Single rallies only last three to eight seconds, but complete matches may last longer than three hours. The physiological demands of tennis are quite complex and difficult to define, because of the stop-and-start nature of the game and its high technical and tactical demands. Over the course of a match, some 300 to 500 bursts of effort may be expended, with rest periods between points and games. The sport requires elements of quickness, endurance, strength, flexibility, reaction time and speed, agility, and co-ordination. In this chapter we will take a closer look at the three basic energy systems that come into play during the game of tennis: the immediate or phosphagen energy system; the short-term or glycolytic energy system; and the long-term or oxidative energy system.

ATP AND ENERGY

The energy systems are three ways that the body produces energy. Said another way, the three energy systems are different methods for manufacturing ATP (adenosine triphosphate), the so-called energy currency of the body. The three systems differ in how fast, how much, and under what conditions they can produce ATP.

ATP is a molecule composed of adenine, ribose sugar, and three phosphate groups. These phosphates are bound to the molecule by high energy bonds. When those bonds are broken by cell processes, that energy is released for use in muscle contractions and other bodily functions. The cells only store a small amount of ATP. In order for exercise, or any body function, to continue beyond a few seconds, there must be processes in the cell to continually replenish the ATP stores.

As previously noted, this replenishment occurs at different rates and utilizing different metabolic processes and raw materials. Each system is called upon depending on the intensity and duration of the activity. Each sport is characterized by its own combination of movements requiring speed, agility, strength, power, and endurance. Each sport therefore tends to utilize each of these three energy systems in different proportions. All three energy systems are always in play, but the sport's typical intensity and duration of movement will determine which energy system will provide the greatest amount of energy to the activity. That is why it is important for tennis players to understand which energy system is most important to them, what nutritional raw materials are necessary to the functioning of that system, and how to train that system to work more efficiently and at higher output levels.

The three energy systems are classified in terms of the immediacy of ATP production, the raw materials used, and whether or not oxygen is a necessary ingredient in the particular ATP generation process. Whether the energy system utilizes oxygen or not is referred to as aerobic and anaerobic, respectively. The immediate and short-term energy systems do not require oxygen to be present to produce ATP. Oxidative processes require more time to complete, and are therefore not large contributors to high intensity, noncontinuous, short duration activities. Tennis is primarily an anaerobic sport. However, the aerobic system is an important recovery and replenishment mechanism between points, sets, and matches.

THE IMMEDIATE ENERGY SYSTEM

The combined amounts of ATP and phosphocreatine (PCr) that are stored in the muscle cells are called the immediate, or phosphagen, energy system. A muscle cell has some amount of ATP floating around that it can use immediately, but only enough to last for about three seconds. To replenish the ATP levels quickly, muscle cells contain a high-energy phosphate compound called creatine phosphate. The phosphate group can be removed from creatine phosphate and be transferred to ADP (adenosine diphosphate) to form ATP. During exercise, the cell turns ATP into ADP, and the phosphagen rapidly combines with ADP to create ATP.

As the muscle continues to work, the creatine phosphate levels begin to decrease. The phosphagen system can supply the energy needs of working muscle at a high rate, but only for 8 to 10 seconds. In tennis, the ball is in play for about 10-30% of the time and out of play for about 70-90% of the time (i.e. 3-8 seconds of work with 15-25 seconds of rest per point). These data suggest that the immediate energy system is mainly used during tennis, with restoration of the PCr in the recovery periods during points and change of ends.

THE SHORT-TERM ENERGY SYSTEM

The immediate energy system can only supply energy for eight to ten seconds. For intense exercise longer than that, energy is produced using the short-term, or glycolytic, energy system. The glycolytic energy system produces energy thereby partially breaking down either blood glucose or muscle glycogen to a molecule called pyruvate. The term "glycolysis" refers to the breakdown of carbohydrate to form ATP. During this process, a relatively small amount of energy is produced.

The glycolytic energy system can take two different pathways, depending on the urgency of the energy requirements. If energy demand is urgent, then the cells will choose the "fast glycolytic" pathway, sometimes called "anaerobic glycolysis." If the exercise intensity is submaximal and there is plentiful oxygen present, then the "slow glycolytic" pathway will be chosen. Slow glycolysis is really just the first step in the long-term aerobic energy system and is therefore sometimes referred to as "aerobic glycolysis." In this process, the pyruvate is sent to the mitochondria in the cells to be utilized in the long-term energy system (see below).

Fast glycolysis occurs when oxygen demands exceed oxygen supply. In fast glycolysis, the pyruvate is not sent to the mitochondria for use in the aerobic energy system, but is instead converted to lactic acid and then to lactate. Lactic acid inhibits the very process that created it. Lactic acid in the muscle interferes with and diminishes the energy output of the glycolytic, short-term energy system. That is why it cannot be an energy source for long-term, sustained activity like a marathon. Lactic acid is converted into lactate and enters the blood stream to be transported to the liver where it is converted to glycogen to be used in future energy production. It is the lactic acid in the muscles that cause diminishing energy production. The lactate in the blood does not interfere with energy production itself, but it is an easily measurable indication of lactic acid levels in the muscle. Proper training will delay the onset of blood lactate accumulations to higher levels of exercise intensity. In other words, it allows one to play at higher intensities with less muscle fatigue. This is known as raising the lactate threshold.

Anaerobic glycolysis is a key contributor to total energy requirements for moderate to high intensity exercise lasting about one to two minutes. The glycolytic system comes into play during intense rallies that last longer than 10 to 15 seconds, or when recovery periods during practice or play are kept very short, such as often occurs in tennis drills with only one or two players ("suicide drills").

Anaerobic glycolysis causes an accumulation of lactic acid in the muscles and body fluids. In all-out sprint events lasting one to two minutes, such as 800 meter running, the demands on the glycolytic system are high, and muscle lactic acid levels can increase from a resting value of about 1 mmol per kilogram of muscle to more than 25 mmol per kilogram. Blood lactate values from 10 to 15 mmol per liter are common in tennis drills with high stroke intensity and short recovery periods.

However, this does generally not occur in a match situation. Lactate levels of tennis players in practice matches average around two mmol per liter, and reach slightly higher values in real match situations of around three mmol per liter (ranging from two to eight mmol per liter). Research has shown that the contribution of the anaerobic-lactic energy system to the total energy supply during practice matches is around 10%, increasing to around 20% in real match situations. There is a negative influence of lactic acid build up on performance, as has been shown in tennis under time pressure. The number of unforced errors increases significantly when the lactate level rises over three mmol per liter. Thus, if high technical skills are required during a training session, rally duration should remain short, with sufficient recovery periods.

THE LONG-TERM ENERGY SYSTEM

The long-term, or aerobic, energy system comes into play during any exercise lasting longer than one minute, and as duration of exercise goes beyond several minutes, aerobic energy production becomes increasingly more important. Aerobic energy production is much slower than both the phosphagen and anaerobic glycolytic energy systems, but it has benefit of being able to provide almost unlimited energy; as long as nutrients are available. The aerobic system is the end result of taking the slow, aerobic glycolytic pathway discussed above. It takes the pyruvate produced in glycolysis and produces more ATP through oxidation. This process can produce 12-13 times more ATP molecules than fast glycolysis, but it takes longer and requires that activity be submaximal so that plenty of oxygen can be supplied.

Because tennis matches played on clay may last up to five or more hours, particularly if the matches are best of five sets, the aerobic system is indeed used during tennis. The overall metabolic response in tennis resembles prolonged moderate-intensity exercise, even though tennis is characterized by intermittent periods of high-intensity exercise. During match play, there is an increased oxidation of fat and glucose, with a mean oxygen consumption around 50-60% of maximum at a heart rate of 140 to 160 beats per minute. During changeovers, oxygen consumption drops compared to the playing phases, but remains significantly elevated compared to the resting periods. Highest oxygen consumption values are found when two defensive players combat each other, leading to longer rally duration. In other words, even though ATP and PCr are used in order to play a rally (immediate energy system), the long-term energy system plays an important role in the recovery phase to replenish the depleted energy depots (during and between points).

MEASUREMENT OF ENERGY CAPACITIES

It may be helpful to know how well trained and developed the different energy systems of a certain player are. To that purpose several tests can be used.

Figure 2.1

The jumping-power test

TESTING THE IMMEDIATE ENERGY SYSTEM

Brief, all-out activities, such as sprints and power jumps, requiring an almost instantaneous energy release rely almost exclusively on the immediate energy system. The ATP-PCr (anaerobic alactic) energy system can thus be indirectly assessed by performance tests, such as a vertical jump (Figure 2.1.), 10m sprint, 20m sprint, spider run or stair climb, or more directly by supra-maximal bicycle tests.

TESTING THE SHORT-TERM ENERGY SYSTEM

Performances requiring substantial activation of the short-term energy system demand maximal exercise for up to three minutes. All-out runs and cycling have generally been used to assess anaerobic capacity, such as 200m and a 400m runs. A common test is the Wingate test, involving 30 seconds of all-out supra-maximal exercise performed on either an arm-crank or leg-cycle ergometer. Peak power is the highest mechanical power generated during any 3- to 5-second period of the test; average power is the average of the total power during the 30-second test period. The assumption underlying this test is that the peak power output represents the capacity of the high-energy phosphates, while the average power reflects glycolytic capacity.

Figure 2.2

The maximal exercise test on a treadmill.

TESTING THE LONG-TERM ENERGY SYSTEM

A reasonably accurate estimation of aerobic energy production can be made by measuring the amount of oxygen consumption by the lungs in an endurance test. The peak value is referred to as the aerobic capacity, maximal oxygen uptake, or VO_2 max. Maximal oxygen uptake is generally measured using treadmill running (Figure 2.2) and stationary cycling. The tests consist of progressive increments in effort (graded exercise) to the point at which the subject is no longer able to continue the exercise. Because individual needs for energy vary with body size, VO_2 max is generally expressed relative to body weight, in milliliters of oxygen consumed per kilogram of bodyweight per minute (milliliter per kilogram per minute). This allows a more accurate comparison of different sized individuals.

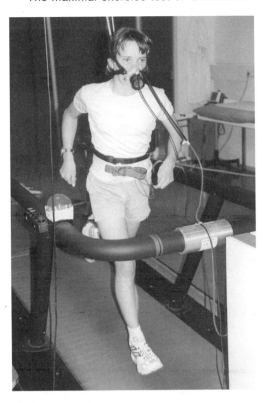

Normally active 18 to 22-year-old college students have average VO_2 max values of 38 to 42 ml per kilogram per minute for women and 44 to 50 ml per kilogram per minute for men. Values in elite tennis players are much higher, with a VO_2 max of 61-65 ml per kilogram per minute for contemporary top male players in Germany and Holland, and 53-57 ml per kilogram per minute for top female players in these countries. Maximal oxygen uptake will vary between 5 and 20% depending on "the physical shape" of a person at the time of measurement. Genetics, however, may have a larger influence than training. This should be taken into account when working with players.

An alternative to testing aerobic fitness in the laboratory is field testing. The so-called shuttle run is an appropriate test for tennis players. The test is easy to set up and to apply. The players run back and forth between two lines, 20 meters apart. The running speed is controlled by the sound of a beep, emitted at regular intervals by a cassette recorder. Advantages of this test are that one can test several players of different training levels at the same time and that it is reasonably tennis specific because of the stop-and-start nature of the test (Figures 2.3 and 2.4). However, the test is not as objective and reliable as measuring oxygen consumption, because running technique and motivation of the subject play a larger role.

Several specific field tests with the ball machine have been developed for tennis players (Figure 2.5). The ball is played alternately to the forehand and backhand during three minutes, followed by a minute rest. In this minute, blood is collected to determine the lactate level. The frequency is fifteen balls per minute, which is increased every four minutes by two balls per minute. Stroke rating may be added as well. This test, however, is relatively labor intensive and not very suitable for routine testing. It is not meant to replace the graded exercise test, but to be used as an additional diagnostic test. An even more specific test would be to perform 300 to 500 3-10 second sprints, but this test would take much too long to still be practical.

Figure 2.3

With the shuttle run test many players can be tested at the same time.

Figure 2.4

The stop-and-go nature of the shuttle run makes it tennis-specific.

Figure 2.5

The ball machine test.

Practical tips for the player

• Develop a strong aerobic fitness base and maintain this throughout the playing season. This can be accomplished by aerobic exercises two to three times per week for 30-40 minutes. Running, biking, skating, stair-climbing, steps, skipping, or rowing are all appropriate choices (Figure 2.6).

• For anaerobic training to occur, the dose must be of high intensity and performed to near exhaustion. Interval drills involving short work periods (<15 seconds) and short recovery periods (<30 seconds) and utilizing the established 1:2 work/recovery ratio are useful for this purpose. In a novice player, however, a 1:3 or 1:4 work/recovery ratio might be more appropriate.

• To improve tennis specific speed, choose exercises with a duration of four to six seconds, such as two sprint-stroke combinations over a distance of 8-16 meters. Examples of good exercises are series of four forehand winners, with four players per group; baseline drills with two players alternating; one sprint with eight players alternating, three repetitions.

• To improve technical skills under physical stress, it is recommended to stay below the lactate values that occur under match play conditions (seven to eight mmol per liter). Drills with series of four to six balls in a row are recommended. Examples are baseline drills with one player and series of six to eight forehand winners with four players per group.

- Lactate values over eight to ten mmol per liter lessen acceptance of the drill and disturb tennis specific coordination and running speed. Examples of drills leading to unacceptably high lactate values are: series of twelve forehand winner with four players per group; defensive baseline drills of long duration; two sprints in a row with only two players alternating; forehand/backhand drills all over the court with six consecutive strokes and four players per group.

SUMMARY

Tennis is defined as a non-cyclical anaerobic sport (10-30%), with an aerobic recovery phase (70-90%). Another way to define it would be a multiple sprint sport. All three energy systems of the human body, the immediate (ATP-PCr), the short-term (glycolytic), and the long-term (oxidative) energy system, come into play during a match. To evaluate the capacity of these systems, several laboratory and/or field tests can be used. This includes sprints and power jumps for testing of the immediate energy system; all-out runs and all-out cycling for the short-term energy system; and treadmill running and the shuttle run for the long-term energy system.

Figure 2.6
Skipping rope for aerobic fitness.

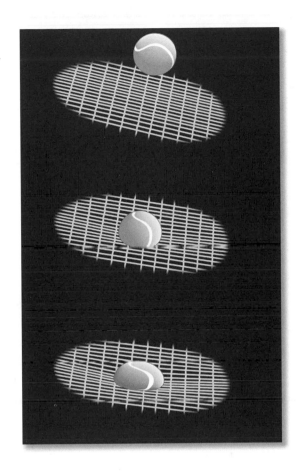

Racquets, Strings, and Balls

Over the years, changes and improvements in tennis equipment have influenced the way the game is played. With the development of space-age materials such as kevlar and boron, manufacturers were able to experiment with racquet designs and constructions in a way they could not with wood. Racquets are lighter, larger, stiffer, and more powerful than racquets in the past, enabling players to hit the ball harder and go for winners more often. In this chapter, we will take a closer look at various equipment variables, including racquets, strings, and tennis balls and their implications for power, control, and injury prevention.

MATERIAL AND COMPOSITION OF THE RACQUET

Tennis racquets can be constructed of wood, aluminum, fiberglass, boron, graphite, titanium, ceramic composite, and combinations of the above.

Wood racquets have good playing characteristics and damping qualities. However, because production is very labor intensive, and the racquets are not very durable and need to be relatively heavy, wood racquets are rarely manufactured today (Figure 3.1). Aluminum racquets are relatively cheap, light, strong, and easy to produce. Their biggest disadvantage is the almost unlimited transmission of vibrations to the hand and arm, which makes these racquets uncomfortable to play with.

Composite racquets generally consist of a combination of graphite and fiberglass, to which other materials such as kevlar, boron, ceramic or titanium are added. Mixing these materials results in a racquet with certain flexibility, strength, weight and other properties that no single material possesses. When racquets were made of wood, the strength-to-weight ratio determined many of the racquet characteristics. A stiff racquet,

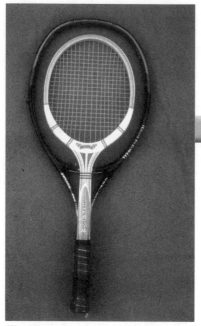

Figure 3.1

An old wood racquet versus a modern composite raccquet.

for example, had to be fairly heavy. Composite materials eliminate many of the structural limitations set by wood. Racquets can be longer, wider, stiffer, thicker, and still much lighter than the traditional wood frames. It is possible to manufacture composite racquets that produce less vibration when striking the ball by increasing the ratio of the matrix (nylon, epoxy resin) to fibers (fiberglass, graphite).

SIZE OF THE RACQUET HEAD

The size of the racquet head generally varies from midsize and midplus (85-105 sq. in.; 548-677 sq. cm) to oversize (105 to 117 sq. in.; 677-755 sq. cm). Standard size racquets (<85 sq. in.; < 548 sq. cm) have virtually disappeared from the market. The "sweet spot" is the area of the racquet where the shocks transmitted to the arm are minimal and where the ball rebounds with the highest velocity (Figure 3.2). The size and location of the sweet spot depends on the distribution of the weight over the racquet, the flexibility of the racquet, the size and shape of the head etc. In general, the larger the racquet head, the larger the sweet spot. Hitting the ball off-center results in loss of control and ball velocity and an increased load on the arm and hand. Also, the wider the racquet head, the less the racquet will twist and turn in the hand. The racquet will become more stable by increasing the mass at the edges, or by making the frame wider. The principle is the same as the figure skater performing a pirouette. If she wants to turn faster, she tucks in her arms. To slow down, she spreads her arms wide (Figure 3.3).

Figure 3.2

The sweet spots of a racquet.

Figure 3.3

A larger racquet head (supermid or oversize) is more stable than a smaller racquet head (midsize) on off-center hits.

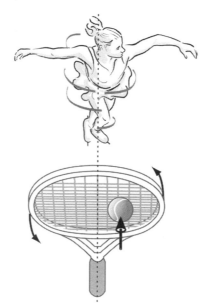
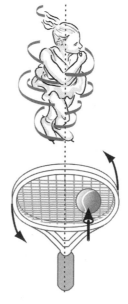

STIFFNESS

A flexible racquet bends more on impact. A racquet that bends little is described as "stiff". Although it has been suggested that a flexible racquet provides more power, as reflected in the slogan "Flex means power," the opposite is the case. If the ball hits a flexible racquet, the racquet head deforms considerably. The time taken for the racquet to deform and return to its original shape is approximately fifteen milliseconds. This is longer than the dwell time for the ball on the strings (about four to six milliseconds). Therefore, the ball has already left the strings before the frame has straightened again and the energy fed into racquet deformation is not transferred back to the ball (Figure 3.4). Consequently, there is a loss of kinetic energy. Thus, for more power, a stiff racquet is a better choice.

However, a flexible racquet is kinder to the arm, because the flexion will absorb some of the shock and spread it over a longer period. A compromise between power and shock absorption is a racquet with a stiff head and some degree of flexion in the shaft, since flexion in this location does not degrade the racquet's power as much as in the head. This is realized in a racquet with a so-called tapered profile: thin (and therefore flexible) in the shaft and wider (and therefore stiffer) in the racquet head, such as a widebody.

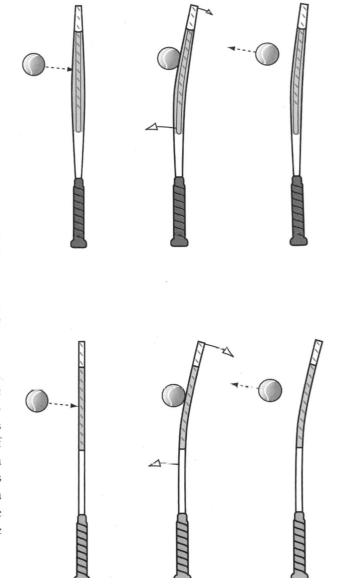

Figure 3.4

A flexible racquet loses more energy than a stiff racquet.

LENGTH

A conventional racquet is 27 inches (68.6 cm) long, but several years ago, longer racquets were introduced, with bodies of up to 29 inches (73.7 cm). Longbodied racquets increase the player's reach slightly. A longbody also enables a player to serve from a greater height, which decreases the risk of serving into the net. This will increase the power of the serve, because the player can take more risks. However, the longer racquet means that the angular momentum of the racquet increases, which will slightly increase the load on the arm.

WEIGHT

The weight of racquets currently on the market varies between about 240 and 360 grams. In recent years, the introduction of new materials, better design, and improved construction has led to a trend away from heavy racquets. Today it is possible to make a lightweight frame that is both stiff and durable—something that was impossible in the past. Both racquet weight and the speed of the racquet head are factors that determine the velocity of the ball. The extra racquet head speed that can be achieved with a lighter racquet head may more than compensate for its lighter weight and lead to higher ball velocity.

For a player with arm problems, however, a heavier racquet is preferable. Even though more effort is required to generate racquet speed, the shock transmitted to the hand and arm is less. The greater the mass of the racquet, the greater its ability to absorb shock. A heavier racquet also promotes better control, as it minimizes twisting and turning in the player's hand. Strokes therefore tend to be longer and more fluid.

BALANCE

The balance of a racquet depends on its weight distribution. The balance point, or center of gravity, is the point where the racquet remains in balance when resting on a sup-

Figure 3.5

The balance of a racquet.

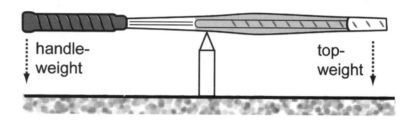

handle-weight   top-weight

port (Figure 3.5). A racquet that has its center of gravity at its geometrical center is balanced. A headheavy racquet has its balance point on the head side of the racquet's center. A headlight racquet has its balance point closer to the grip than to the head. Which type is best for a player with elbow problems? A headlight racquet feels lighter than a headheavy racquet, even if they actually weigh the same. This is because it is possible for the first moment of a headlight racquet (the weight of the racquet multiplied by the distance from the balance point to the location of the hand) to be less than that of a headheavy racquet. A headlight, low moment racquet is generally easier to maneuver than a headheavy, high moment racquet, and may therefore be more suitable to someone with elbow problems. But there is a trade-off. A light, maneuverable racquet puts less strain on the arm during the swing, but may cause more strain to occur during ball impact due to its lesser ability to absorb shock

Figure 3.6

Correct grip size.

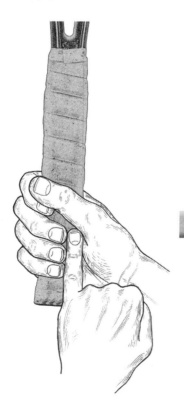

GRIP SIZE

Grips of most racquets range between 4-1/8 inches (10.5 cm) and 4-7/8 inches (12.4 cm) in circumference. The sizes are usually labeled from 1 to 7. In the past, players used thicker grips. Grip sizes 6 and 7, which used to be very common, are very difficult to find today. A grip that is too small or too large may cause problems. In both cases, the player may need to grip the racquet too tightly to prevent it from twisting, and high grip force may increase the risk of elbow injury. The largest comfortable grip size will control racquet torque best. Moreover, the larger the grip size, the greater the dorsal flexion of the wrist, the lower the tension on the origin of the forearm extensor muscles, and the less likely the chance of elbow injury. The little finger of the other hand should easily fit between the ends of the fingers and the fleshy part of the thumb (Figure 3.6).

GRIP MATERIAL

Some new racquets come with a leather grip. There are a number of materials that one can wrap around the leather grip to prevent the racquet handle from becoming slippery. Many types of synthetic materials are quite porous and can absorb a good deal of moisture. But the material of the grip is also important when it comes to the prevention of tennis elbow. A cushioned grip can increase racquet damping by up to 100% and may reduce the grip reaction force by 20%, which may be beneficial in preventing elbow problems.

STRINGING MATERIAL

In the past, all racquets were strung with gut produced from the intestines of cattle or sheep. The intestines of two cows were needed to manufacture one set of gut strings. The fabrication process is very labor intensive, and gut strings are therefore more expensive. They are also more fragile, less durable and less resistant to damage from moisture and humidity than synthetic strings. So, why play with gut? A comparison of gut and first grade synthetic gut strung at the same tension suggests that gut strings give slightly higher post-impact ball velocities, improved control and better racquet "feel." Gut strings also have greater resilience and better dampening qualities than synthetic strings.

What about the qualities of synthetic strings? There are basically two types of strings: monofilament and multifilament. Monofilament strings (made of nylon or polyester) are the cheapest, but also have the poorest playing qualities. They are hard to the touch, not very flexible, and uncomfortable to play with. The playing characteristics of multifilament strings resemble more closely those of gut. They are also cheaper and more durable than gut. Gut should be the choice if money is not a problem and it is possible to bring several extra racquets to the courts. A high quality multifilament synthetic string would be a good second choice.

STRING THICKNESS

The size of a tennis racquet string is measured in "gauges." Most strings are 16 to 18-gauge. A lower gauge (for example, 16) means a thicker string. The advantage of a thicker string is its durability. Thicker strings will last longer and will not break as quickly as a thinner string. However, thinner strings can be more elastic and consequently absorb more shock. Therefore, thinner strings are typically more comfortable to play with and take more pressure off the player's arm.

STRING TENSION

Tennis racquet strings are designed to return 90 to 95% of the energy they receive from the incoming ball. Balls themselves are much less efficient: they return only about half the energy when they bounce on a hard surface. If the ball is dropped on a racquet instead of the hard floor, it will bounce back to a considerably higher level, showing that less energy has been dissipated. Thus, the strings return almost all of the energy that they store when they deform, while the ball only returns about half the energy when it hits and deforms. Therefore, at the point of ball-string contact, the ideal situation requires the ball to be deformed as little as possible and the strings as much as possible (Figure 3.7). Lower string tensions encourage such a relationship, because the strings will deflect more, and the ball will deform less. Reducing the tension of the racquet strings also reduces the load on the arm, because less swing is needed for the same power output. Moreover, looser strings increase the dwell time of the ball on the

Figure 3.7
Deformation of ball and strings at contact.

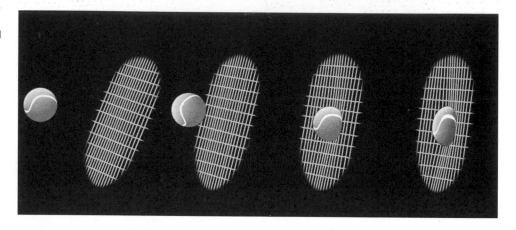

strings, which is better on the arm. Longer contact time ensures that the shock of the ball impact is spread over a longer period of time. However, the string tension should not be too low. If string tension is lower than 40 lbs., energy is lost because of excessive string movement.

VIBRATION STOPPERS (STRING IMPLANT DEVICES)

Vibration stoppers are small inserts made of rubber or plastic. They come in different shapes and sizes. According to the rules, they need to be placed between the two main longitudinal strings and the lowest horizontal string, close to the balance point of the racquet. Many players use this vibration absorbing material in their strings. However, because these damping devices only weigh one to two grams, and the racquet may weigh up to 360 grams, there is not a lot of mass available for shock absorption. It seems that these vibrations stoppers work quite well at damping down the high frequency vibrations of the strings. However, when the ball is hit off-center, the vibration stopper is not able to reduce the racquet vibrations transmitted to the hand and thus its role in injury prevention is unclear.

PRESSURIZED AND NONPRESSURIZED TENNIS BALLS

There are two types of balls—pressurized and nonpressurized. A nonpressurized ball bounces because of the thickness and suppleness of the rubber that is used. A pressurized ball bounces not only because of the rubber, but also because the internal air pressure is greater than the external air pressure. The bounce is a good indicator of the durability of a pressurized ball. Once the ball loses internal pressure, it does not bounce as well and feels dead. The height of the bounce remains constant for a longer period of time with a nonpressurized ball than with a pressurized ball. Therefore, the durability of a nonpressurized ball is generally longer than of a pressurized ball and is determined mainly by the wear of the fabric cover. However, players with elbow problems should use pressurized tennis balls in preference to nonpressurized ones. A nonpressurized ball has to be hit harder to acquire the same speed as with a pressurized ball, which will put more load on the arm. This is because nonpressurized balls have a lower so-called "coefficient of restitution." Furthermore, used balls have a slower rebound than new ones. Therefore, players suffering from elbow problems should preferably use new, pressurized, tennis balls.

THE SIZE AND DEFORMATION OF THE TENNIS BALL

Since January 1, 2002, two further types of tennis balls are used. The "fast type" ball will have less deformation than the regular "medium type" ball (i.e., it is stiffer and harder), and should only be used for play on slow pace surfaces. The ball rebounds less than the medium ball and slips across the surface more. This causes the ball to rebound shallower and faster, which means that less energy is lost as vertical momentum. Therefore, the forward velocity of the ball is higher than of a regular type tennis ball. Also, because there is less ball deformation, less energy is lost when the ball hits the strings. This allows the player to put in less effort, thereby reducing stress on the elbow.

The "slow type" ball is slightly larger than the regular ball, with a diameter of 2.750 inches (6.985 cm) to 2.875 inches (7.302 cm) compared to 2.575 inches (6.541 cm) and 2.700 inches (6.585 cm). The "slow type" ball should only be used for fast pace court surfaces. This ball is designed to have the same stiffness as the regular ball in compression tests. The peak force will likely be lower and the contact time longer when the ball hits the racquet, resulting in less peak load on the arm.

CHOOSING ARM FRIENDLY EQUIPMENT

These tips will help you to choose the material with the lowest risk of developing an arm injury.

Practical tips for the player

- Choose a composite racquet with good damping qualities.
- Use a racquet with a large "sweet spot", such as a midsize or oversize racquet.
- Choose a racquet with a stiff racquet head and a flexible shaft.
- Do not switch to a longbody if you have elbow problems.
- Choose the heaviest racquet you are able to handle without sacrificing technique.
- Go for a headlight racquet.
- Try the largest grip that is comfortable for you.
- Use a cushioned grip tape.
- Buy gut or high quality synthetic string.
- Choose a thinner string.
- String the racquet at a lower tension.
- Use new, pressurized tennis balls.
- On a fast pace surface, try the "slow type" ball. On a slow pace surface, try the "fast type" ball.

SUMMARY

In this chapter we have discussed the playing characteristics of the various equipment variables—racquets, strings and balls. The new composite materials and technical designs have made it possible to produce racquets that are lighter, more durable, bigger, stiffer and more powerful than racquets in the past. Also, attention is given to the characteristics of racquets, strings, and balls as they relate to upper extremity injuries, such as dampening characteristics and stress on the arm. A player with elbow problems would generally be advised to choose a flexible, headlight, composite racquet of standard length and with a large sweet spot. The grip should be cushioned and of correct size. The strings should be gut or thin, high-quality synthetic string, strung at a lower tension. It is recommended to use new, non-pressurized tennis balls.

4

Tennis Shoes and Playing Surfaces

Tennis is played on a wide variety of surfaces, including clay, carpet, grass, and hard court. These main surfaces are reflected by the Grand Slam tournaments, which are played on hard court (US Open and Australian Open), red clay (Roland Garros), and grass (Wimbledon). The various surfaces foster different playing styles, e.g. serve and volley on grass and carpet, baseline play on clay, and an all-court/aggressive baseline game on hard court. The shoes of the player need to suit the surface characteristics to reduce injury risk and to enhance performance.

Movements in tennis include sprinting, side-to-side running, cutting, twisting, sliding, and quick stops and starts. Frequently a player is forced to stop and start a movement during one action to prepare for the upcoming stroke. Throughout this deceleration process, as well as during movements such as jumping and lunging, high loads act on the joint system of the foot. A tennis player jumping eighteen inches (half a meter) to hit an overhead exerts a force upon landing about equal to four times the body weight. Both the playing surface and the tennis shoe have a significant influence on the kinematics of the foot and therefore the load on the lower extremities during fast movements in tennis. In this chapter we examine the effects of playing surfaces and footwear on injuries and performance in tennis.

PLAYING SURFACE

The various playing surfaces have been shown to significantly influence the occurrence and frequency of tennis injuries of the lower body. The sliding characteristics of the court surface are more important than the cushioning properties. Surfaces that permit some sliding (clay, synthetic sand), result in fewer injuries than surfaces that do not allow any sliding (hard court, grass). This is because sliding on a sandy surface results in a longer braking phase and thus generates less repetitive peak force (Figure 4.1).

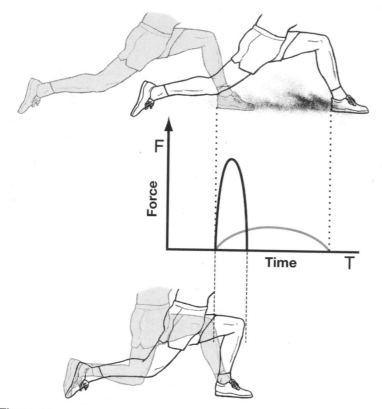

Figure 4.1

Sliding on a clay court (top) results in a longer braking phase and lower peak forces than playing on hard courts (below).

This was also shown in a study from the Association of Tennis Professionals (ATP). From 1995 to 1997, the ATP registered treatments of the lower body and back given to the players on the ATP Tour by the ATP sports medicine trainer (Table 4.1). On grass, 456 treatments were given during five tournaments, during which a total of 1092 matches were played. That results in a frequency of 0.42 treatments per match played. On hard court/carpet, 656 treatments were given during nine tournaments with a total of 1770 matches, resulting in a frequency of 0.37 treatments per match. On clay 475 treatments were given during nine tournaments, in which a total of 2361 matches were played. This gives a frequency of 0.20 treatments per match. In other words, the risk of having to receive treatment was 1.85 times higher on hard court compared to clay, and 1.14 times higher on grass compared to hard court. Although "treatment" is not the same as "injury," these results confirm that the ability to slide (clay) is more important than the cushioning effect (grass) for the reduction of load on the locomotor system of tennis players.

Table 4.1

Table demonstrating number of treatments to lower body and back of ATP players on different playing surfaces from 1995-1997.

	Grass court	Hard court	Clay court
Treatments	456	656	475
Matches	1,092	1,770	2,361
Frequency per match	0.42	0.37	0.20

THE TENNIS SHOE

It is appropriate to devote serious attention to the footwear used during the game of tennis because correct footwear will reduce injury risk. Important features of a tennis shoe are cushioning, stability, stiffness, and the design of the outsole.

CUSHIONING

The region of the foot that touches the ground first is most frequently the heel for the average player. Contact with the ball of the foot occurs only in about half of the times. In advanced players initial contact is made most frequently with the ball of the foot. Moreover, contact with the inner and outer edges occurs commonly. The tennis shoe must therefore be designed for landings on the heel, on the ball of the foot, and on the inner and outer edges. This is provided by a midsole with both sufficient cushioning and durability.

STABILITY

Tennis players need a shoe with a lot of stability for side-to-side motion. The foot of the player should not rotate inward too much (pronation), neither should the foot turn outward too much (supination) (Figure 4.2).

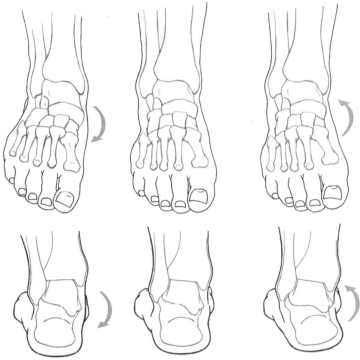

Figure 4.2

From left to right: a valgus foot (too much pronation), a neutral foot, and a cavus foot (too much supination). The top row shows the right foot from the front, the bottom row the left foot from behind.

The medial placing of harder density material in the midsole (anti-pronation), often used in running shoes, is generally not used in tennis shoes. However, a sturdy heel counter helps to keep the heel stable and to prevent rollovers as well as excessive pronation. It may also reduce the velocity of the inward turning of the foot and shoe. A shoe with good upper banding and a solid lacing system can prevent excessive supination. Also, choosing shoes that are cut a bit higher than the regular tennis shoe can be very effective in providing stability.

STIFFNESS

The shoe should neither be too soft, nor too stiff. Shoes that are too soft may result in problems in the region of the arch of the foot, whereas with hard shoes, the toes, ankles, and knees may be affected.

OUTSOLE

Although friction is more sensitive to the choice of playing surface than to the choice of the outsole of the tennis shoe, the friction value of the outsole is still important. There are many sole patterns, but the most popular design is the herringbone pattern or variations thereof (Figure 4.3, second from left). Higher friction values correspond to shoes with more pronounced and transverse sole profiles. During play on synthetic carpet a shoe with a smoother sole pattern should be used than during play on a clay surface, to avoid twisting of the knee or ankle (Figure 4.3, left). Carpets tend to have stronger grip than most other court surfaces and, thus, one needs a shoe with more freedom to twist and turn. Grass tends to be slippery, and dimples or nodules on the

Figure 4.3

Different types of tennis shoes with their outsole pattern. From left to right: smooth sole pattern for carpet, herringbone pattern for clay court, dimples for grass and a combined herringbone/dimple pattern for hard courts.

base of the shoe will provide this extra grip (Figure 4.3, second from right). On hard courts, a combination of the herringbone pattern and dimples is often used (Figure 4.3, right). The age, weight, strength, height, competitive level, and type of play may also influence the choice of the outsole, with younger, stronger, heavier, taller players with an attacking game generally choosing more grip.

Practical tips for the player (Figure 4.4)

- The shoes should fit and feel comfortable immediately. You should not have to break in a shoe before it feels good.
- Try on both shoes and walk around the store for a minute or so; stretch wide for an imaginary shot or stop quickly as if hitting a drop shot. The foot should not move inside the shoe.
- Wear the socks you normally wear when playing tennis when you try on the shoes, especially if you use thicker sport socks.
- You should be able to fully extend the toes when standing.
- The heel counter, supporting the heel, should fit close and be sturdy in order to correct the lateral movement of the heel.
- The midsole should have superior shock absorbing qualities and be firm.
- Check the flex point of the shoe. Hold the shoe firmly around the heel in one hand and press your other hand against the toe. The shoe should flex around the ball of the foot, its natural ending point, and not around the midfoot.
- The upper banding should be strong for side-to-side control.
- Bilateral and double lacing systems allow players to tighten or loosen one part of the shoe without affecting another. They are especially useful for players with low or high arched feet and those with chronic foot problems.
- Good inside (medial) support should generally be purchased separately (inlays).
- For soft, slippery surfaces such as clay or shale, wear shoes with softer outsoles for better traction than those worn on hard courts. Also,

Figure 4.4

The ideal tennis shoe. From left to right: sturdy heel counter, strong upper banding, midsole with medial support, high-topped shoe.

choose a wide herringbone pattern to keep clay from accumulating underneath.

- Use highly shock absorbent midsoles when playing on hard court.
- On synthetic carpet, try using a shoe that has a smoother sole pattern than you would use on a clay surface.
- For grass, there are shoes with dimples or nodules on the base of the shoes to avoid slip-sliding on the lush, hallowed lawns.

SUMMARY

The frictional characteristics of the playing surface are more important determining factors for injuries than are its cushioning properties. The higher the friction characteristics of the court, the less sliding it permits, resulting in a higher injury rate. Thus, from an injury prevention point of view, clay and synthetic sand are preferred over hard court or grass. It is important to adapt the friction value of the outsole of the shoe to the playing surface. Other important features of a tennis shoe are the fit, cushioning, stability for side-to-side motion, inside medial support, strong upper banding, and a sturdy heel counter.

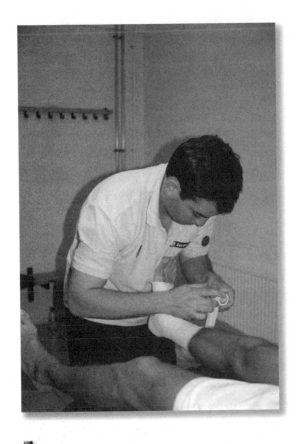

5

Injury Prevention

I njury risk is related to age, playing time per day, equipment, surfaces, and preventative exercises, and injury risk may be reduced by modifying these factors. In this chapter, the most important preventative measures in the game of tennis will be discussed, including the preparticipation physical examination, warming up and cooling down, stretching and strengthening exercises, protective devices, nutrition, equipment, shoes and surfaces, and recovery techniques.

Figure 5.1
Slipping on the court can lead to injury.

EPIDEMIOLOGY OF INJURIES

In tennis, a fairly even distribution of injuries over the upper and lower extremities is generally found, with a minority of injuries located in the trunk. A general population survey in the Netherlands from 1997-1998 showed an injury rate of 0.4 injuries per 1,000 hours of play in outdoor tennis, and of 1 injury per 1000 hours of play in indoor tennis. When all sports were ranked according to injury risk, indoor tennis was ranked 14 and outdoor tennis was ranked 19. In elite tennis players, injury rate is estimated to be higher, with 2 to 3 injuries per 1,000 hours of play. The majority of these injuries, especially those of the upper extremity, are caused by repetitive micro-traumata as a result of overuse, with losses in flexibility and strength. The remainder of injuries are caused by an acute, single major trauma, such as an ankle sprain (Figure 5.1).

In another study, all patients that received treatment in the casualty ward of a selection of hospitals in the Netherlands during 1998-2001 were registered. These hospitals formed a representative sample of all the teaching and general hospitals in the Netherlands with a casualty ward. In this study, primarily acute and more serious injuries were registered, while chronic and/or less serious injuries would have been reported less often. Injury risk was calculated as the number of injuries per 1,000 participants per year. Sports injuries were all afflictions that occurred during or as a result of sports participation. With the results of this study it is possible to compare injury risk in tennis to the injury risk in squash, badminton, and table tennis. Table 5.1 shows

Table 5.1
Yearly number of casualty ward treatments after a tennis, squash, badminton, or table tennis injury per 1,000 participants; age and gender.

	Total Number	Number per 1,000	Total Number	Number per 1,000	Total Number	Number per 1,000	Total Number	Number per 1,000
	6 to 80 years		16 years and older					
	Total		Total		Males		Females	
Tennis	5,300	4.4	4,800	4.7	2,700	4.5	2,200	4.9
Badminton	1,500	2.1	1,400	2.8	750	2.9	600	2.6
Squash	2,200	4.8	2,100	4.8	1,800	6.0	360	2.7
Table Tennis	260	0.56	180	0.67	130	0.69	40	0.52

Table 5.1
Yearly number of casualty ward treatments after a tennis, squash, badminton or table tennis injury per 1,000 participants; age.

	Total Number	Number per 1,000	Total Number	Number per 1,000	Total Number	Number per 1,000	Total Number	Number per 1,000
	16 to 35		35 to 50		50 to 65		65 years and older	
Tennis	1,400	3.3	1,800	5.3	1,400	6.5	280	5.3
Badminton	660	3.1	570	3.1	110	1.6	20	1.4
Squash	1,500	4.9	560	5.9	30	2.1	<10	2.8
Table Tennis	80	0.50	60	0.93	30	0.91	<10	0.68

Source: Letsel Informatie Systeem 1998-2001. Ongevallen tijdens racketsporten. Amsterdam: Consument en Veiligheid, 2003.

that injury risk in squash is highest (4.8 injuries per 1,000 participants per year), especially among adult male players (6.0 per 1,000 participants). In tennis, badminton, and squash, injury risk is fairly similar for males and females. In tennis the older age groups are affected most often, whereas in squash and badminton, the injury risk is higher among younger players (Table 5.2).

What then can be done to reduce this injury risk? We can divide preventative measures into those that we take before play, during play, and after play.

BEFORE PLAY

Good preparation may help reduce injury risk. Important preparatory measures include the pre-participation physical examination, stretching exercises, strengthening and conditioning, and a regular warm-up routine.

THE PRE-PARTICIPATION PHYSICAL EXAMINATION

The pre-participation physical examination is an important means to reduce injury risk in tennis players, especially in the maturing individual. The major purpose of a physical examination in youngsters is to identify predisposing physical factors to injuries, recommend rehabilitative measures, and advise on modification of training methods and equipment. A pre-participation examination generally consists of a medical history, a general medical evaluation, a specific examination of the musculoskeletal system, assessment of flexibility and strength, and an equipment review. Exercise testing for the evaluation of the cardiovascular system should be included if the player practices more than ten hours per week, and for those over 35 years of age. The emphasis in the growing individual should be on the musculoskeletal profile and physical deficits. By obtaining information on deviations in muscle endurance, strength, balance, and flexibility, the player can start working specifically on these areas in order to improve the capacity to withstand loads, reduce injury risk and enhance performance

Practical tips for the player
- The recommended frequency of the pre-participation examination is once a year, although injury prone individuals may benefit from a higher frequency.

WARM-UP

The warm-up is an important means to prevent injuries and should be performed before every workout. A gradual increase of the body temperature through the warm-up prepares the body for the upcoming hard work. Elevated temperature increases muscle blood flow, mechanical efficiency of smoothness of contraction, and the speed of nerve impulse, leading to more rapid and forceful muscle contractions. Moreover, the increase in temperature results in a greater force and length of stretch necessary to tear a muscle. Also, joint position appreciation is significantly more sensitive after warm-up. Thus, a proper warm-up may reduce the incidence and likelihood of musculoskeletal injuries and lead to improved performance. Sudden strenuous exercise may elicit subendocardial ischemia, which can also be prevented by performing a proper warm-up. Finally, there are psychological benefits of a warm-up, such as a better mental preparation for a match (increased focus and concentration), and release of anxiety.

A proper warm-up consists of both general and specific exercises. General exercises include jogging, skipping, hopping, calisthenics, and stationary bicycle riding. Specific exercises are meant to increase the temperature of those muscles that will be used during a game of tennis.

A specific warm-up for tennis may consist of swinging with the arms, shadow tennis, mini tennis, and playing tennis itself. The intensity and duration of the warm-up must be individualized according to the player's physical condition, the activity to follow, and environmental factors. A player should break into a light sweat without fatigue, and generally ten to fifteen minutes will be sufficient.

Practical tips for the player
- A longer warm-up is needed on a cold, windy morning than on a hot summer afternoon.
- When temperatures are low, adequate clothing (tracksuit) is advised to preserve the effects of the warm-up.
- A warm-up may help to ease the nerves. Thus, a brief 5-minute warm up period may be sufficient for an evening doubles match with friends, whereas the preparation for the singles finals of the club championships may include half an hour of warm-up play.

FLEXIBILITY AND STRETCHING

Flexibility allows a tennis player to move a joint freely through the entire range of motion with a low risk of muscular injury. For many years, stretching has been promoted as a way to increase flexibility, decrease the risk of injury, prevent muscle soreness, and improve performance. The theory behind it is that muscle tightness restricts range of motion, which in turn predisposes to muscle strain and tendon injuries. However, some of these concepts have been shown to be incorrect. Firstly, stretching is not the same as range of motion. Thus, different injury rates in athletes with different range of motion may be related to factors other than stretching (e.g. anatomy, strength etc). Secondly, the typical "more must be better" approach to stretching is incorrect. Both low and high levels of flexibility may increase the risk of injury compared to normal flexibility. Thirdly, stretching directly before exercise has a different effect than stretching at other times. Pre-exercise stretching does not prevent injury, and static stretching done in the period of 30-45 minutes prior to activity leads to substantial decreases in (5-30%) in muscular performance.

Stretching following physical activity, however, may be appropriate to maintain normal levels of range of motion. Stretching exercises may be performed in the cool-down following matches or conditioning, or at a time, separate from the training period, in order to maintain normal ranges of motion for all the major muscle groups.

TYPES OF STRETCHING

Various types of stretching can be identified, including active static stretching, ballistic (dynamic) stretching and proprioceptive neuromuscular facilitation (PNF) stretching. In active static stretching the muscle is slowly and gently stretched to the point of slight muscle discomfort and then held for an extended period of time. This type of stretching is used most widely, because it is a simple technique, has a low injury risk and does not require a partner. A survey of ATP Tour players showed that most of them performed static stretching exercises daily. In a ballistic stretch the muscle is stretched with repetitive bouncing motions. Some players use it right before play. However, these exercises may produce muscle soreness and should be used with caution. PNF stretching exercises require the help of a second person (Figure 5.2). An example of PNF stretching is the contract-relax technique, whereby the player first contracts the muscle, after which the muscle is actively or passively stretched. An advantage of PNF stretching is that it leads to large gains in flexibility. Disadvantages are that the player must be motivated and concentrated to perform these more complex stretching routines. In addition, the assisting person should be careful not to overstretch the muscles and joints because he can exert considerable force and does not feel the stretch himself.

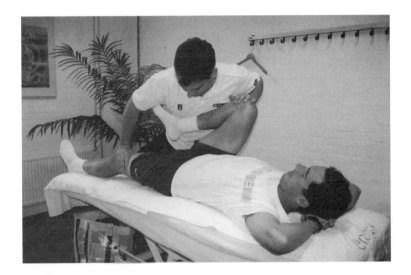

Figure 5.2
The ATP trainer assists the player with his stretches.

Practical tips for the player

- Figures 5.3 to 5.16 show a general stretching program for tennis players. Potential trouble areas that should be routinely stretched in tennis players are the hamstrings, low back, calf, hip adductors, internal rotators, flexors, and shoulder internal rotators. These stretches should be performed after a light warm-up or in the cool down period after play. Three to five static or PNF stretches should be performed for each muscle group. Each stretch should be held for 15- 30 seconds and repeated for both sides. Be careful not to stretch too much after a hard workout or eccentric muscle training, because this may lead to microscopic muscle tears and injury.

STRETCHING

Figure 5.3

Superficial calf muscle (gastrocnemius)

Lean against a wall or fence and step forward with one leg. Slowly flex the hips forward, keeping the back leg straight and the heel on the ground. Both feet should be pointed straight ahead. A stretch should be felt in the calf area.

Figure 5.4

Deep calf muscle (soleus)

Use the starting position as in the previous exercise and lower the knee of the back leg as far as possible. The stretch should now be felt further down the calf.

Figure 5.5

Front of the thigh (quadriceps)

In a standing position, pull the foot to the buttocks until a stretch is felt at the front of the thigh. Use a wall or fence to keep balance, if necessary.

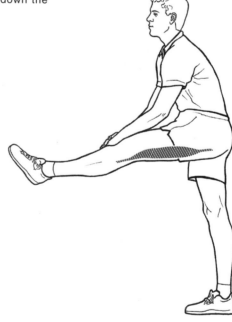

Figure 5.6

Back of the thigh (hamstrings)

In a standing position, raise one leg and rest it on a bench or some other object of comfortable height. Bend forward while keeping the back straight and the hips squared, thus try to bring your chin toward the foot resting on the bench. Hold the foot plantar flexed to avoid stretching of the sciatic nerve and to localize the stretch on the hamstrings.

Figure 5.7

Groin (long adductors)

Stand upright with the legs straddled about two to three feet apart. Place the hands on the hips or on the ground. Slowly lunge sideways, bending one knee, and pressing down on the hip. Keep the back straight.

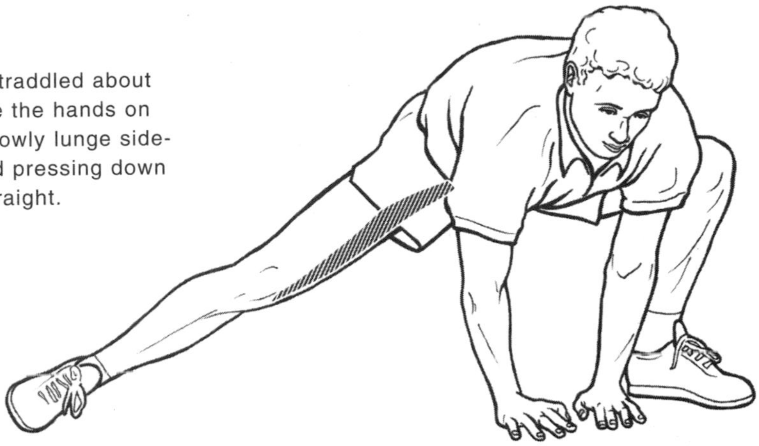

Figure 5.8

Groin (short adductors)

Sit on the floor with the knees flexed, soles of the feet together and the back straight. Gently push the knees towards the floor until a stretch is felt in the groin.

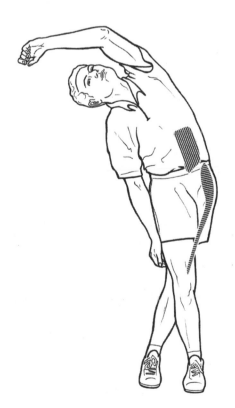

Figure 5.9

Outer thigh and waist (iliotibial tract, tensor fascialata, and transversus abdominis muscles)

For this stretch, make sure to stand upright, arms at the sides. Extend the left leg behind the right leg, while slowly bending the trunk to the right as far as possible. By simultaneously extending the left arm above the head, the transverse abdominal muscles are stretched as well.

Figure 5.10

Buttocks (gluteals and piriformis)

Sit on the floor with the right leg straight. Cross the left leg over the right leg, with the left knee bent. Hook the right elbow over the left knee and pull the knee towards the right shoulder.

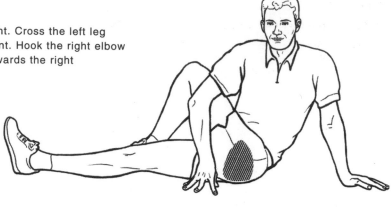

Figure 5.11

Hip flexors (iliopsoas)

From a standing position, take a big step forward with one leg. Then, while keeping the back as straight as possible, lower the knee of the other leg until it is a couple of inches off the ground, pressing the hip forward.

Figure 5.12

Lower back

Hold on to a table or stationary object. Squat down and lean back slowly and gently.

Figure 5.13

Posterior shoulder (external rotators)

Cross the arm in front of the body. Take the elbow with the other hand and pull.

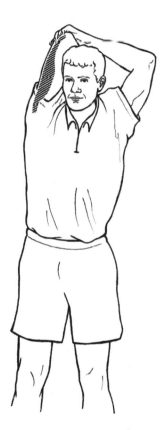

Figure 5.14

Triceps

Sit or stand upright with one arm flexed and raised overhead next to the ear. Grasp the elbow with the opposite hand and pull the elbow behind the head.

Figure 5.15

Forearm extensors

Extend the arm forward with the palm down and the elbow straight. The fingers point to the floor. Grasp the wrist and fingers with the other hand and bend the wrist, until tension is felt at the outside of the forearm.

Figure 5.16

Forearm flexors

Extend the arm forward with the palm facing up and the elbow straight. The wrist is extended, with the fingers pointing to the floor. Grasp the fingers and pull them backwards, until tension is felt at the inside of the forearm.

STRENGTHENING EXERCISES

Strengthening exercises incorporated into the daily training program may help decrease injury risk in tennis players. Strength training promotes growth and/or increases in strength of ligaments, tendons, tendon to bone, and ligament to bone junction, joint cartilage and the connective tissue within the muscle sheath. This makes these structures less susceptible to injury. Healthy, active muscle protects the joints from injury by improving the distribution of forces. Also, resistance training can increase bone mineral content and therefore may aid in prevention of skeletal injuries.

The muscle balance between agonists and antagonists at a particular joint is important in injury prevention. Tennis players have been shown to develop muscle imbalances, such as strength differences between the dominant and non-dominant arm, and abnormal ratios between antagonistic muscle groups. These imbalances are associated with injuries. For example, a hamstring/quadriceps strength ratio of the knee of lower than 60% and a external rotation/internal rotation strength ratio of the shoulder of lower than 40% have been associated with injuries. Strength training can normalize these muscle ratios and help prevent injuries. This has been shown in other joints as well. Functional strengthening of the adductor (groin) muscles has been shown to be an effective method for preventing adductor muscle strains, and strengthening of the vastus medialis (inner knee) muscle leads to reduced load on the knee. Also, participating in a structured core strengthening program, which emphasizes abdominal, back, and hip strengthening, has been shown to reduce the risk of low back pain. A preventative strengthening program for tennis players is described in Chapter 28.

DURING PLAY

During play, injury risk may be reduced by paying attention to the correct equipment and by wearing protective devices, if necessary. In addition, adequate fluids and nutrition will not only enhance performance, but will also help reduce the risk of cramps, heat stress and injuries.

RACQUETS, STRINGS AND BALLS

Players, especially those with arm and shoulder problems, should seek professional assistance when selecting a racquet and choosing string tension. For details on racquets, strings, and balls, see Chapter 3.

SHOES AND SURFACES

A good, well-fitting shoe, appropriate to the playing surface, will help prevent injuries to the lower extremities. Players should choose their shoes carefully, preferably with professional advice on the most appropriate shoe for their foot type and for the playing surface on which they mostly play (and use orthoses if recommended). Also, the choice of the surface influences injury risk. Surfaces that permit some sliding, such as clay and synthetic sand, result in fewer injuries than those surfaces that permit no sliding, such as hard courts. Shoes and surfaces are discussed in more detail in Chapter 4.

PROTECTIVE DEVICES

Protective devices commonly used by tennis players include taping, braces, and protective eyewear.

TAPING AND BRACING

Taping and bracing have an important role in the prevention of injuries in tennis. Taping and bracing are used to restrict undesired, potentially harmful motion, while allowing desired motion. The two main indications are prevention and rehabilitation. Taping or bracing can be used as a preventive measure in high risk activities, such as match play. It is also used as a protective mechanism during the healing and rehabilitation phase, to protect the healing area.

Taping to restrict undesired motion may be applied to almost any area of the body to treat a wide variety of muscular strains, tendon problems and joint instabilities. Adhesive, nonelastic tape is applied over joints where there is limited soft tissue surrounding the joint and sliding can be limited to one direction, such as the ankle, wrist, finger, acromio-clavicular joint, and the first metatarso-phalangeal joint. Tape is not as effective for use around the shoulder, elbow, knee and spinal joints. Complications of tape applications include reduced circulation or injury to the nerves from tight taping, skin irritation, and decreased effectiveness over time. Tape application requires practice to perfect. It enhances proprioception in addition to the mechanical support. The advantage of taping over bracing is that it can be fitted to the individual. Many professional tennis players use an ankle brace during practice, but choose an ankle tape (or tape and brace) during match play (Figure 5.17).

Figure 5.17a, b
Taping an ankle
before a match.

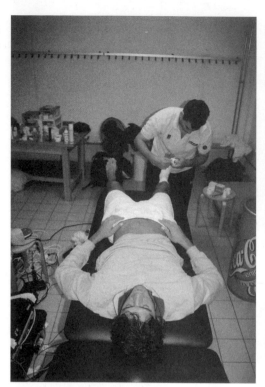
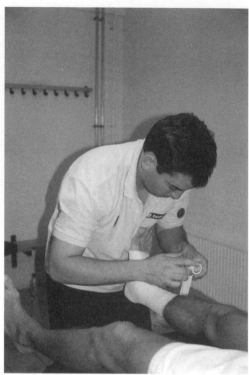

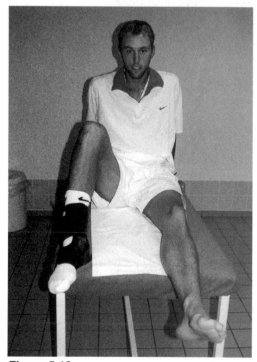

Figure 5.18
An ankle brace.

A brace is an appliance used to support or improve function of movable parts of the body (Figure 5.18). Bracing has a number of advantages over taping. It does not require the particular skill of the operator, and it may be more convenient, easier to remove and cost effective. However, bracing also has a number of disadvantages, which include possible slippage of the brace, the weight of the brace, problems with exact sizing, and playability of the brace. There are many types, such as sleeves, warm and comfortable, but with little mechanical support; custom-made braces which are made of various more rigid substances and have improved mechanical support; or medical braces with hinges and straps that limit joint motion in certain directions. In tennis, a brace or tape is used most often in connection with tennis elbow, wrist problems, anterior knee pain, or as a preventive measurement for ankle sprain.

PROTECTIVE EYEWEAR

Eye injuries may be prevented by wearing wrap-around polycarbonate lenses with eyeguard rims that are posterior to the orbital rim, antifog coated, and have secure stabilization to the back of the head. Glasses should have UV-A and UV-B protection. See for more details Chapter 11.

AFTER PLAY

Adequate recovery is essential for injury prevention and an optimal training effect. When planning the training program, it is important to provide adequate time for recovery. This should involve the inclusion of rest days in the weekly training cycle and easy weeks and vacation time in the longer training cycle. There are also a number of ways by which the player can speed up the recovery process. These include adequate cooling down, massage, yoga, spas and whirlpools, adequate sleep, and nutrition and rehydration.

COOLING-DOWN

Cooling-down consists of a period of milder activity, immediately after cessation of play. In tennis, cooling down may consist of baseline play, hitting the ball back and forth at an easy pace, or some light jogging, followed by stretching exercises. Cooling-down is felt to reduce the degree of muscle soreness and stiffness following intense exercise. Cooling-down has been shown to be more effective than passive recovery for removing blood lactate after intense exercise. A cooling-down combined with a massage is better than a cooling-down only to maintain maximal performance.

MASSAGE

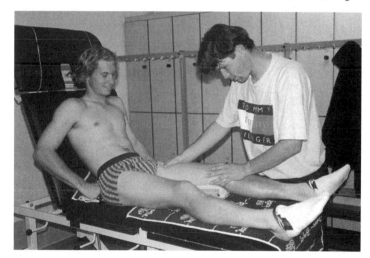

Figure 5.19
Post-match massage.

Massage consists primarily of palpation, rubbing, and kneading and is often used to enhance recovery from intense training (Figure 5.19). Studies show that massage therapy reduces delayed onset muscle soreness when administered two hours after the termination of eccentric exercise. This may be due to a diminished inflammatory response. Massage has not been shown to increase the circulation and nutrition to damaged tissue. Nonetheless, massage brings about symptomatic improvement and increases perceptions of recovery. It is a popular recovery measure among tennis players on the ATP and WTA tour.

WHIRLPOOL AND JACUZZI

The use of a whirlpool or Jacuzzi combines warmth with a hydromassaging effect to increase superficial skin temperature and decrease muscle spasm and pain. In the case of a heated whirlpool, the heat will completely surround the area. Add to this the jet massaging action of a Jacuzzi and you have an effective way to relax the muscles of the back.

SLEEP

A proper amount of rest and sleep is essential for adequate recovery after heavy training loads. It will help prepare the body and mind to function regularly at a high level. Sleep is different from just resting. The sleeper progresses from wakefulness to drowsiness to moderate sleep to deep, restorative sleep. Dream sleep, or rapid-eye-movement sleep, occurs about once every 90 minutes as part of the sleep cycle, and totals about 1.5 hours. Sleeping helps the storage, reorganization, and access of information. A person who does not get enough sleep may feel less alert and vigorous, or even confused and fatigued. Long-term sleep deprivation may result in persistent fatigue and contribute to the development of the overtraining syndrome. On average, an adult sleeps around 7-8 hours per night, but individual needs may vary. During heavy training periods players may require 10 or more hours each night.

Practical tips for the player
- Try to avoid stimulants late at night, such as caffeine (i.e. coffee, tea, cola, chocolate), nicotine, and alcohol.
- Try to avoid heavy, fatty meals two to four hours before going to bed.
- An empty stomach should also be avoided. A light evening snack may be effective.
- Do not try to tackle a difficult and demanding task, right before going to bed, because the mind will keep spinning in high gear.
- Try not to get nervous if sleep does not come right away. Sleeping pills should generally be avoided, particularly on the eve of an important match because there is the risk of a hang-over effect. There is no need to worry when on the day of a big match you have not slept as well and as long as you normally do. Olympic records have been set after sleepless nights.
- Reduce thinking and worrying in bed. Learn to switch off. When lying in bed, try to forget the problems and focus on pleasant thoughts that will help you fall asleep easily and provide for a peaceful night.
- Practice relaxation techniques to reduce stress: listen to relaxing music, follow a muscular relaxation routine, practice breathing exercises, use visualization, etc. Taking a hot shower or a warm bath, or reading a good book may also help.
- Rely on the routine: Go to bed and get up at the same time each day. If you go to bed and get up at the same time each day, the "internal clock" will be ready to wake up and go to bed following the routine.
- Choose the correct sleeping position. Try sleeping on one side with the knees bent upward and a pillow between them.
- A dark, silent, cool and ventilated room is usually most inductive to sleep. If this is difficult to achieve, use eye shades and ear plugs, particularly if you have a roommate who is prone to heavy snoring.
- The pajamas should be comfortable and made of soft fabrics. Clean, fresh linen sheets are preferable to cotton, because they feel different against the skin and disperse body heat better. The covers should be loose, to reduce the risk of cramping. An electric heating blanket helps to relax muscles and increases brain temperature. Use one with a timer, which shuts off just after falling asleep.

MUSCLE RELAXATION TECHNIQUES

Another way to improve the quality of the recovery time and thereby speed up recovery is by the use of muscle relaxation techniques. The goal is to relieve stress and reduce muscle tension. There are many different approaches to relaxation therapy. In autogenic training, one concentrates on self-suggestions of warmth and heaviness in the limbs. Jacobson's progressive muscle relaxation technique involves the conscious contraction and relaxation of various muscle groups throughout the body. The normal order of progression is from the large muscles of the legs up through the gluteals, abdominals, chest, back, shoulders, arms neck and finally the smaller muscles of the face.

Practical tip for the player
- For the progressive relaxation technique, lie supine, with the legs straight, arms at the sides, and eyes closed. The mind should be made as nearly blank as possible and the body allowed going limp. For each muscle group, the muscles are slowly contracted three times, and then slowly relaxed until the muscle is in a limp, calm position, with no trace of tension. The objective is to concentrate on the feeling of tension as it appears with each contraction and disappears when one consciously relaxes the muscle and allows it to go limp.

BREATHING EXERCISES

Deep breathing has a generally calming effect on the body. Correct breathing is performed from the diaphragm, with both the stomach and the chest expanding during inhalation and receding during expiration. When nervous or tense, many people will restrict or tighten the stomach while breathing, rather than relax it. This contributes to a faster and a more shallow breathing. Correct breathing is slow, calm, and rhythmical. The exhalation should be twice as long as the inhalation. Most yoga lessons and books include breathing exercises.

Practical tip for the player
- A good breathing exercise can be performed as follows. Lie supine with the knees pulled up and feet slightly apart. Inhale deeply and allow the stomach to relax and expand like an inflated balloon. Exhale and pull the stomach in so that the diaphragm rises and presses against the rib cage.

YOGA

Yoga is the Indian word for union. Union of self and the "Supreme Being" is sought through a state of complete awareness and tranquillity attained by certain physical exercises. Yoga consists of performing asanas, or postures, together with breathing control and meditation. Yoga differs from the routine stretching and strengthening programs in that it incorporates a "mind-body" approach. Muscular activity is coupled with an internally directed focus so that the participant produces a temporary self-contemplative mental state. Focusing the mind on each of the various postures and meditating their effects practices mental control, leading to relaxation.

PILATES

The Pilates method is a series of exercises performed on the mat and on equipment developed by Joseph Pilates which simultaneously strengthen the center, lengthen the spine, build muscle tone, and increase flexibility, while eliminating excess tension and strain on the joints.

The Pilates Method works the body in a systematic and organized way. First, the method builds core strength in the abdominal muscles and the muscles that surround and support the spine. Then, it balances strength and flexibility in the muscles surrounding all of the joints. Short muscles are stretched, and weak muscles are strengthened. As balance and stability are achieved, the Pilates Method adds more and more challenging exercises to the workout, bringing the whole body to a higher level of strength, flexibility and coordination.

NUTRITION

During work or exercise, there is always a "breakdown" of muscle protein, becausse protein degradation always exceeds protein synthesis during work. The recovery period (the rest period between a training session or match and the start of the next exercise session) is important, as this is when muscle tissue repairs itself by building and repair of muscle protein. Protein resynthesis and recovery is most efficient in the period immediately after exercise. After training, the net synthesis is about four times more efficient in the first four hours after exercise than during 12 to 16 hours after exercise. A combination of carbohydrates and protein seems to be most effective for such recovery. Consequently, intake of protein and carbohydrates soon after a tennis game or practice session is advisable for optimum recovery and repair of muscle tissue. See Chapter 18 for further details.

Practical tip for the player

- A glass of milk after a match is an ideal "sports drink" (milk contains protein). This could be combined with some fruit, sandwiches, or pasta (carbohydrates).

TENNIS FACILITIES

The checklist below can be a help to check if the facilities are safe and in good order. If not, appropriate action should be taken. The following questions should all be answered with a yes. An administrator of the tennis facilities should be made responsible for regularly going over the checklist.

FACILITY CHECKLIST

- Are the courts ready for play? The courts should be in good condition and neither too wet nor too dry. The lines should be clearly visible, firmly attached to the surface and should not stick out. The holes and pits of clay courts should be filled up and the surface smoothed. Synthetic surfaces should be free from moss and algae and swept once a week with a rough coconut matting, to get an even distribution of the sand.
- Are the materials in good condition and firmly attached? The playing material such as the nets and playing surface should be without defects to be able to tolerate the extreme demands of tennis. Irregularities may lead to injuries. There should be no open holes, slanting lids sticking out of the floor, or loose hooks or handles, because they may cause a player to stumble and fall.
- Is there enough space along the sidelines? In a safe situation there

should be enough space around the court. Behind the baseline there should be a minimum of 6.40 meters; along the sidelines there should be 3.66 meters.

- Is the vicinity of the courts free from dangerous obstacles? The space behind the courts and next to the sidelines should be free from obstacles. Superfluous training material should be stacked in the designated areas. There should be no bags, clothing, loose tennis balls, or other material along the sidelines that may form a hindrance for the players. There should be no wire sticking out from the fence. The nets to sweep the courts should be returned to their safe position after use. The poles for singles play should be attached to the net post if not in use.

- Is there a first aid kit present? Every tennis club should have a well-filled first aid kit. Know where to find it. The kit should not be locked or locked away in a closet. Trainers and coaches may bring their own small and simple first aid kit.

- Is there someone present who has a first aid certificate? In case there is an accident, first aid should be given immediately. The manager or other on-site employee of the complex should be certified.

- Are there ice cubes or cold packs available? Cooling is an important aspect of first aid treatment of sports injuries. Ice or cold packs are very convenient to this purpose. Cooling with cold, running water may also be effective.

- Is there a telephone line available for emergency situations? In case of emergency, a doctor or ambulance needs to be called. It is important that the telephone can be used at all times and does not need to be paid for with coins or cards. It is also of great importance that the telephone numbers of the doctors on duty, the first aid department, the hospital etc. are easily visible when using the phone. This list should be regularly checked for changes in the situation.

- Is the tennis complex freely accessible? The tennis club should be easily accessible for police, firemen and ambulance. The location of the park should be indicated with signs.

- Are the lockers rooms regularly cleaned? Regular cleaning of the locker rooms, showers, and toilets is important because of the risk of infections. Showers should be available. The courts and locker rooms should have wheelchair access. Dangerous situations should be avoided, such as broken hooks for the clothing in the locker room.

- Is the lighting functioning correctly? There should be no defective lamps. When the lighting is too low, players can make errors when trying to judge distances. Also, loose parts of lamps that hang too low can be dangerous. The recommended strength of the lighting is 400 lux.

- Is the temperature comfortable? The temperature on the court influences the speed at which players warm up and cool down. Avoid temperatures that are too high or too low. It should be between twelve and sixteen degrees centigrade. If not, adapt the training to the environmental conditions.

SUMMARY

Injury risk in tennis is fairly similar in males and females, and increases with age. Injury risk may be reduced by taking preventive measures. Preventive measures on an individual level that can be taken before play include a pre-participation medical examination, performing stretching and strengthening exercises, and warming up before play. During play, injuries may be avoided by wearing carefully selected shoes, playing with the right equipment, and choosing a forgiving surface. If necessary, protective devices such as taping, braces, or protective eyewear should be worn. After play, injury risk may be reduced by using recovery techniques, including performing a cooling down, massage, whirlpools, and Jacuzzis, adequate sleep, muscle relaxation techniques, breathing exercises, yoga, Pilates, and paying attention to nutrition. At a public level, injury risk may be reduced by ensuring tennis facilities are safe and "injury-proof."

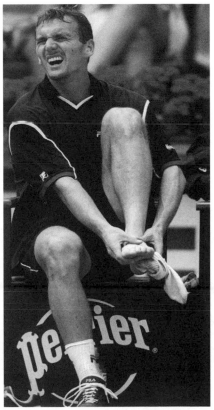

6

General Rehabilitation Principles

Figure 6.1
An acute injury of the left foot.

I n this chapter general rehabilitation principles of tennis injuries will be discussed. These basic principles apply to all the injuries that are discussed in this book. Many injuries in tennis take a long time to heal and have a high incidence of recurrence if not properly rehabilitated. The goal of rehabilitation after a tennis injury is to eliminate or minimize the disability experienced by the player and restore normal function. A well-structured rehabilitation program can result in a shortened recovery time, limitation of deconditioning, and reduced likelihood of re-injury. The goal is a quick, yet safe, return of the player to the tennis court. This chapter covers the basics of tissue healing and healing time and a description of the three phases of the rehabilitation process: the acute, intermediate and advanced phase. Therapeutic exercise programs for the knee, shoulder and lower back are presented.

PHASES OF TISSUE HEALING

A rehabilitation program is often divided into three phases, based upon the three stages of wound healing. These are the acute or inflammatory phase, the intermediate or repair phase, and the advanced or remodeling phase. The acute phase occurs immediately after injury and may last for up to 72 hours, depending on the severity of injury. Symptoms may include swelling, redness, warmth and pain (Figure 6.1). This initial inflammatory response is critical to the healing process. However, if it is excessive or prolonged, the extent of tissue damage may be increased and healing may be delayed. The intermediate or repair phase may begin by 48 to 72 hours and continue for up to six weeks. It is characterized by scar formation. Early controlled mobilization will enhance the healing process by increasing the deposition and strengthening of the scar tissue. The advanced or remodeling phase may begin after three weeks, depending on the tissue type, and continue for more than twelve months. During this period, the scar tissue undergoes remodeling and becomes stronger. There is considerable overlap of the repair and remodeling phase. Acute injuries will frequently require a greater emphasis on control of inflammation, while chronic injuries will require more emphasis on the repair and remodeling phases.

Table 6.1

Tissue type	Acute phase	Intermediate phase	Advanced phase	End result
Ligament	2-3 days	6 weeks	12- 50 weeks	Near-normal strength
Tendon	2-3 days	4-5 weeks	12- 50 weeks	85-95% normal strength
Muscle	2-3 days	2-3 weeks	3-6 months	90% normal strength
Cartilage	2 days	2 months	6 months	Small-normal healing Large- scar tissue
Bone	3-4 days	3-4 weeks (callus) 6 weeks (stable)	3-4 months	Near-normal strength

Source: Houglum, 2001

HEALING TIME OF SPECIFIC TISSUES

Healing time may vary, depending on the type of tissue that is injured, but each type of tissue goes through the different healing stages. Other factors that influence healing time include age, injury size, surgical repair, infection, nutrition, other diseases, muscle spasm, and tissue swelling.

Table 6.1 demonstrates that it may take a long time before normal strength can be regained. Typically, tendons, muscles, and cartilage are more vulnerable after having been injured previously. This is why a good rehabilitation program is very important.

ACUTE PHASE (FIRST AID)

The primary aim of the acute phase is to control and reduce swelling and bleeding, reduce pain, and avoid re-injury.

R.I.C.E.

The main treatment principles of the acute phase are summarized by the word RICE: Rest, Ice, Compression, and Elevation. When RICE is used during the "golden window" before swelling begins (immediately after injury), it can make a major difference in the amount of pain an athlete suffers and might also allow a quicker return to athletic participation.

Rest is important to avoid aggravating the injury further, although complete rest is seldom necessary. "Rest from offending activity" are the key words here, because it will help to limit bleeding, swelling, and the immediate risk of re-injury.

Ice decreases swelling, pain, and the inflammatory response, due to a local constriction of the blood vessels. Various methods can be used, including icepacks, ice towels, ice massage, gel packs, refrigerant gases, and inflatable splints (Figures 6.2a and b). Do not apply an icepack or gel pack directly on the skin, but use a towel underneath. The target temperature is reduction of 10-15 degrees C. Using repeated, rather than continuous, ice applications for periods of ten minutes help sustain reduced muscle temperature without compromising the skin and allow the superficial skin temperature to return to normal while deeper muscle temperature

Figure 6.2a, b
Cooling with ice.

remains low. Also, cold temporarily reduces pain by decreasing nerve conduction velocity and regional muscle spasm.

Compression stops the bleeding, helps to limit swelling, and provides some support. In this respect, immediate compression is more important than the immediate application of ice, although ice still has a function for the control of pain.

Elevation of the injured limb to the level of the heart also helps to decrease swelling. In the post-acute phase, elevation may be more beneficial than compression in reducing edema.

THERAPEUTIC MODALITIES

Several therapeutic modalities can be used in the acute stage of an injury. Electrical stimulation may be applied in the early management of injuries. It enhances protein synthesis, which promotes healing and increases the strength of tendons and ligaments. It can also be applied to muscles to relax muscle spasm. When facilitating muscle contraction, is can be used to activate the muscle pump to control swelling. Transcutaneous electrical nerve stimulation (TENS) can be used to manage pain and retard muscle atrophy. Pulsed ultrasound may be used, as it is believed to promote healing. In the acute phase, heat and continuous ultrasound should be avoided.

MEDICATIONS

Medications that are commonly used in the treatment of sports injuries are non-steroidal and steroidal anti-inflammatory medications (NSAID's and corticosteroids).

NSAIDs, such as aspirin, ibuprofen, diclofenac, naproxen, celebrex, and viox, are used for control of pain and swelling. They give indeed pain relief, which may (indirectly) allow earlier motion. However, they also have blood-thinning properties, which carry the theoretical risk that they may lead to more swelling in the acute phase of the injury. Also, it has been shown that their use may lead to a (slight) delay in healing. So the general advice is to use NSAIDs for the control of pain, if necessary, but to limit their use to three to seven days. The lowest dose should be used that is effective for relieving pain and inflammation. Patients who have liver or kidney damage, an allergy to aspirin, or gastritis or peptic ulcer disease, should generally not use NSAIDs. Adding a drug that blocks the acid production of the stomach (H2 acid blockers, such as famotidine or ranitidine hydrochloride) can help prevent NSAID-associated ulcers.

In the past, corticosteroid injections were used extensively for the treatment of musculotendinous injuries. Nowadays a more restricted regiment is generally recommended. Corticosteroids are powerful anti-inflammatory medications, leading to a markedly reduced initial inflammatory response at the injury site. This may lead to increased strength of affected muscles, ligaments and tendons during the early phases, leading to high short-term (weeks to months) success rates. However, because corticosteroids are known to inhibit collagen synthesis, there is retardation of the normal healing response, resulting in long-term decreased tendon weight and strength, and a high recurrence rate. Also, there is an increased risk of tendon rupture with intra-tendinous injections. Thus, it appears that corticosteroid injections may have a beneficial effect in the short term on muscle, ligament and tendon healing, but may be detrimental in the longer run. Use of injectable corticosteroids for the treatment of bursitis and nerve compression syndromes is less controversial.

INTERMEDIATE PHASE

The objective of this phase is to promote the healing process and restore normal range of motion and flexibility, muscular strength and endurance, cardiovascular fitness, and proprioception and coordination.

EARLY MOBILIZATION

Immediately after the injury, a short period of immobilization is needed to limit swelling and pain. Long-term immobilization, however, is to be avoided. Early mobilization is required for the correct orientation of the regenerating muscle fibers, formation of new vessels, and resorption of the connective tissue scar. Another important aim of early mobilization is to minimize loss of muscle size, length, and strength.

RANGE OF MOTION AND FLEXIBILITY

Muscle spasm, immobilization, pain, swelling, and stiffness may all limit joint range of motion and flexibility. Restoration of full joint range of motion and flexibility is an essential step early in the rehabilitation process. This can be achieved through a progressive program of passive techniques (e.g., continuous passive motion and passive mobilization), followed by active-assisted and then active exercises. Soft tissue treatments and massage therapy may help relieve muscle spasm, facilitate stretching, and flexibility. Gentle, slow stretching exercises in muscle or tendon injuries can be included, using static stretches or proprioceptive neuromuscular facilitation techniques (see Chapter 5). Ballistic stretches are generally to be avoided because of the increased risk of re-injury. Flexibility is increased with tissue warming, so heat packs and aerobic exercise can also be used to increase range of motion.

MUSCULAR STRENGTH AND ENDURANCE

Strengthening exercises play a greater role than merely increasing muscle performance. Resistance training promotes an increase in strength of ligaments, tendons, tendon to bone and ligament to bone interfaces, joint cartilage, and the connective tissue sheaths within muscles.

Restoration of muscular strength and endurance may begin with isometric (static) exercises as soon as they can be performed without pain. This means just holding the muscle tension against resistance, without movement. Dynamic exercises can then be initiated with active range of motion, manual resistive techniques and rhythmic stabilization techniques to improve strength and neuromuscular control. The next step is the use of isokinetic, isotonic, and/or variable resistance devices (Figure 6-3). Elastic bands are especially useful in designing home exercise programs or when traveling

Figure 6.3

Isokinetic strengthening exercises for the knee.

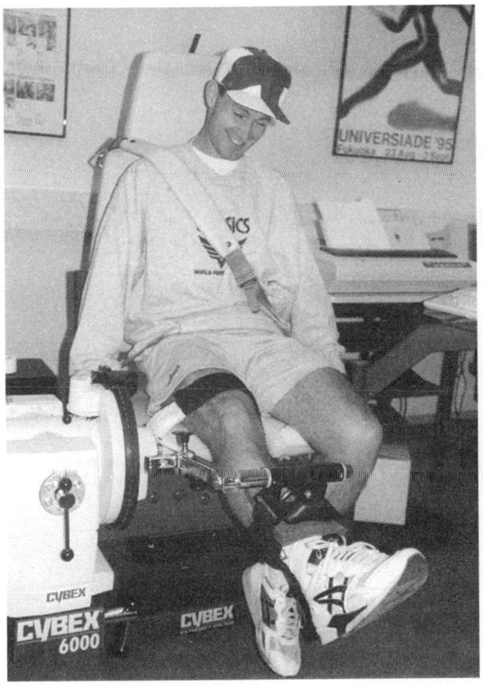

Figure 6.4

Strengthening exercises for the shoulder with an elastic band.

(Figure 6-4). The athlete should work in the pain free range of motion. For a more detailed overview of strengthening exercises that can be used for the rehabilitation of shoulder, knee, and lower back injuries, refer to pages 64 to 74.

ALTERNATIVE TRAINING METHODS

Alternative training methods should be resumed as soon as possible in the rehabilitation program, to prevent loss of physical conditioning. Aerobic exercise can be incorporated, which involves using the large muscles of the body in a cyclical fashion at intensities of 50 to 80% of maximum heart rate for more than 15 to 20 minutes. Sprints and anaerobic training—30 seconds to 2-minute bouts of exercise at 80-90% of maximum heart rate—can be included as well. Alternative exercises include jogging, swimming, rowing, stair climbing, bicycling, cross-country skiing, aqua jogging, and roller skating. An athlete may be progressed through different exercises. For example, a player with an Achilles tendon injury may initially be placed on a swimming program, and progress to aqua jogging and cycling before returning to running exercises.

PROPRIOCEPTIVE TRAINING

Proprioceptive training refers to the training of the sensorimotor system, the awareness and control of the positioning and movement of the body and limbs in space. After injury, there are proprioceptive deficits that make the player more vulnerable to re-injury. Proprioceptive training can reduce these deficits and should be initiated as soon as adequate range of motion and strength are present. Classical lower extremity proprioceptive exercises include the tilt board and the trampoline (Figure 6-5). Balance

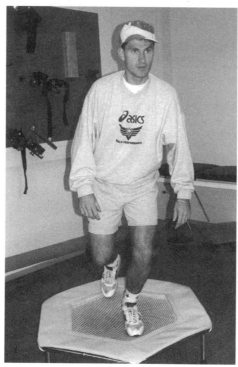

Figure 6.5

Proprioceptive training for the lower extremity on a trampoline.

Figure 6.6

Proprioceptive training as part of the regular conditioning program.

exercises should progress from simple to complex tasks; from static to dynamic movement patterns; from double to single leg stance; from stable to unstable surfaces; and from open to closed eyes. Gradually more distracting stimuli (ball forces) and external forces (e.g. light push) should be incorporated.

THERAPEUTIC MODALITIES

In the intermediate and advanced stage of an injury, different therapeutic modalities may be used than in the acute stage. In the later stages of an injury, in addition to cold, heat may be used as an adjunct to treatment. It may help reduce pain and decrease muscle spasm. Heat can be applied several ways, e.g. in the form of hot packs or paraffin baths. Phonophoresis and iontophoresis can be used to drive topically applied cortisone (decreases inflammation) or histamine (increases blood flow) deeper into underlying tissues. Phonophoresis uses ultrasound to deliver the medication, while iontophoresis uses electrical current. Extracorporal shock wave therapy (ESWT) is a non-invasive method for the treatment of localized musculoskeletal pain. Pneumatically or electromagnetically generated energy is used to generate a shock wave transmitted to the area being treated. This is believed to cause microtrauma, which encourages revascularization and faster healing. Electrical stimulation can be used for muscle control, reeducation, and strengthening.

MEDICATIONS

Intra-articular injections of hyaluronic acid have been advocated for the treatment of (osteo-) chondral injuries and osteoarthritic pain. Hyaluronic acid is considered a chondroprotective agent that acts as a shock absorber and lubricant in synovial fluid. Possibly, it promotes cartilage synthesis, but further studies are needed to evaluate its mechanism of action.

ADVANCED PHASE

In the last phase of rehabilitation the focus is on a safe return to playing tennis. Prior to return to play, the athlete must be capable of performing all the strokes and activities required in tennis, the cause of the injury should have been addressed and corrected if possible and appropriate preventive measures should have been installed. Basic functional activities that should be mastered before returning to tennis are running, starting, stopping, jumping, pivoting, and cutting for a lower extremity injury; twisting and turning for an injury of the trunk, and throwing and catching for an upper extremity injury.

STRENGTHENING AND AGILITY EXERCISES

Therapeutic exercises in the advanced stage are aimed at improving functional muscle strength, power, and endurance. In addition to isotonic and isokinetic exercises, plyometric exercises may be included. Plyometrics can be defined as brief, explosive exercises that involve an eccentric (lengthening) muscle contraction that is rapidly followed by a concentric (shortening) contraction. This eccentric-concentric muscle contraction has been referred to as the stretch-shortening cycle and leads to more powerful muscle contractions. Plyometrics can be progressed from simple, two-footed, in-place jumps to complex, one-footed agility drills and depth jumps. For the upper body, plyometric exercises can be performed using a medicine ball.

RETURN TO PLAY

Return to play should be built up gradually. An example of a progressive tennis training program after injury is presented. Depending on the localization of the injury, more time should be spent on building up a specific part of the program (e.g. foot work exercises after lower extremity injury, overheads and serves after an upper extremity injury).

- Start against the practice wall or with mini-tennis (playing within the service lines). Gradually increase the area of play and move back toward the baseline. Make sure you use small steps to position your-self correctly for the ball.

- A start can now be made with volley exercises.
- The next step is easy hitting from the baseline.
- In the course of the following days to weeks, gradually incorporate exercises that require running longer distances to the ball (tennis drills from side to side).
- Next, include low volleys, overheads, and serves. Start hitting easy serves from the service line and gradually increase distance, speed, and number of serves.
- When you can hit a jump smash without problems, you can start playing practice matches.
- Start playing points, then games, and then a full practice match. Once practice matches have been completed for two to four successive weeks without problems, you are ready for match play.

THERAPEUTIC EXERCISE TRAINING FOR THE KNEE

A progressive strengthening program for the knee is shown below. The exercises shown are just some examples. More and different exercises can be included. It can be divided into the three stages of the healing process: acute, intermediate, and advanced. The first stage consists of quadriceps setting and static strengthening exercises. The second stage includes more dynamic concentric and eccentric strengthening exercises and balance drills. In the final stage functional exercises are included, such as jogging, jumping, sprinting, and agility exercises. In general, try to build up to three to five series of ten to fifteen repetitions.

Stage 1
- **Static quadriceps strengthening.** Sit down on the floor with your legs straight. Place a rolled-up towel under your knee. Try pushing the towel into the floor by contracting your quadriceps muscles. Hold for three seconds and relax.

Figure 6.7
Static quadriceps strengthening.

- **Straight leg raise.** Sit down on the floor with your legs straight. Now tighten the muscles of the affected knee and point your toes towards the ceiling. Lift your leg ten to fifteen inches (25-40 cm), keeping the leg straight. Hold for two seconds and return to the starting position.

Figure 6.8
Straight leg raise.

Stage 2

- **Double leg squat.** See Figure 28.61 for instructions.

- **Leg raises.** See Figure 28.55 for instructions.

- **Step ups.** See Figure 28.63 for instructions.

- **Co-ordination exercises.** See Figure 8.12 for further instructions.

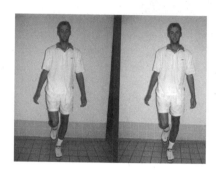

- **Single leg squat.** See Figure 28.62 for instructions.

Stage 3
- Take small, quick steps on the spot, alternating the left and the right leg. If this goes well, you can begin jogging. Start with an easy jog, and gradually increase the pace.
- **Perform two-foot ankle hops.** Stand with feet shoulder width apart. Using only the ankles for momentum, hop continuously in place. Extend the ankles to their maximum range on each hop. Land with knees slightly bent. Then include jumps forward, backward, and sideways.
- **Jump running.** Simply run in "slow motion" landing on alternate feet. Try to achieve as much height and distance with each stride as possible. For every right and left foot strike, count one repetition.
- **Single leg hops.** Stand on one foot and bend your knee slightly. Staying on the same foot try to gain as much height and distance with each hop. Keep ground contact time as short as possible. Hop for the desired number of repetitions and repeat with the other leg (See Figure 28.66).
- The next step is to include some forward and lateral sprints.

- This is followed by quick turns, starts, stops, and jumps. Now you are ready for play again!

THERAPEUTIC EXERCISE TRAINING FOR THE SHOULDER

The following is an example of a progressive strengthening program for the shoulder. Shoulder rehabilitation should generally progress from scapular stabilization exercises to rotator cuff strengthening, followed by plyometrics and throwing exercises. The exercises shown are just some examples. Different exercises can be included. Try to build up to two to three sets of twelve to twenty repetitions.

Stage 1
Scapulo-thoracic stabilization. The scapula must be firmly connected to the thorax to provide a firm base for the arm. This can be achieved by strengthening the scapular stabilizers.

- **Shrugs.** See Figures 28.9 and 28.10 for instructions.

- **Supine punches.** See Figures 28.3 and 28.4 for instructions.

- **Scapular retraction.** See Figure 28.2 for instructions.

- **Rolling a ball over the wall.** Stand facing the wall with a ball (Swiss or other) held up on the wall at head height. Step back so you are leaning towards the ball. Set scapula. Make small circles on the wall with the outstretched hand on the ball.

Figure 6.9

Rolling a ball over the wall.

- **Dumbbell rowing.** See Figures 28.31 and 28.32 for instructions.

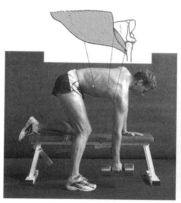

- **Shoulder extension.** See Figure 28.1 for instructions.

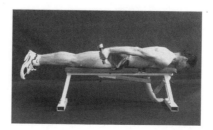

Stage 2

After proficient scapular stabilization is restored rotator cuff exercises can
be included.

- **External rotation.** See Figures 28.6 and 28.7 for instructions.

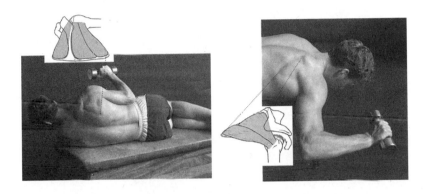

- **Internal rotation.** See Figure 28.8 for instructions.

- **Lat pull down.** See Figure 28.33 for instructions.

- **Rotator cuff circles.** See Figures 28.17 and 28.18 for instructions.

Stage 3

- **Power drops.** See Figures 28.14 and 28.15 for instructions.

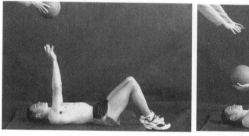

- **Catch and throw backhands.** See Figure 28.16 for instructions.

- **Push up plus.** See Figure 28.12 and 28.13

- Throw a tennis ball overhead against the wall and catch it again.

THERAPEUTIC EXERCISE TRAINING FOR THE LOWER BACK

One of the main developments in treating lower back pain has been the understanding that the smaller and deeper lumbar spine and trunk muscles (transversus abdominis, multifidus and internal oblique, the so-called "core" muscles) play an important role in protecting and supporting the spine. "Core stability training" refers to programs aimed at stabilizing these muscles to protect the spinal column from repetitive micro-trauma, recurrent pain, and degenerative lesions. The aim of core stability training is to effectively recruit the core muscles and then learn to control the position of the lumbar spine during dynamic movements. The core muscles work in concert with the abdominals, paraspinal muscles, hip flexors, gluteal muscles, and upper back muscles. The core muscles do not need to be very strong, but they must be correctly co-ordinated and capable of working continuously, holding the lumbar spine in the neutral position. If the core is strong and stable, all other movements are more efficient and effective. The following is an example of a progressive rehabilitation program for the lower back. Other exercises could be included as well.

Stage 1

Stage 1 includes basic exercises to recruit core stabilizers and exercise stomach and low back muscles.

- **Core stabilization (supine).** Start by lying on your back with the knees bent. Your lumbar spine should be neither arched up nor flattened against the floor, but aligned normally with a small gap between the floor and your back. This is the "neutral" lumbar position. Breathe in deeply and relax all your stomach muscles. Breathe out and, as you do so, draw your lower abdomen inward as if your belly button is going back towards the floor. Hold the contraction for ten seconds and stay relaxed, allowing yourself to breathe in and out as you hold the tension in your lower stomach area. Repeat 5-10 times.

Figure 6.10
Core stabilization (supine).

- **Core stabilization (supine, lifting legs).** Lie on your back with your knees bent, ensuring your back is in neutral position. Breathe in and relax. Breathe out and, as you do so, draw in lower abdomen (abdominal hollowing). Once you have established some transversus abdominis tension, slowly slide your left leg out along the floor until it is straight, then slide it back. Repeat for the other side, 10 times each leg.

Figure 6.11

Core stabilization (supine, lifting legs).

- **Spinal extensions.** See Figure 28.43 for instructions.

Stage 2
- **Bridging.** See Figures 28.47 and 28.48 for instructions.

- **The plank.** Lie on your front resting on your elbows. Go up on your toes forming one straight line from your feet to your elbows.

Stage 3

Exercises with the gym ball. The principle of unstable surfaces can be incorporated into all sorts of exercises with the gym ball. Below are three examples, but use your creativity to come up with more.

- **Gym ball balance (sitting).** See Figures 28.44 and 28.45 for instructions.

- **Gym ball balance (prone).** See Figure 28.46 for instructions.

- **Gym ball balance (bridge).** See Figure 28.54 for instructions.

SUMMARY

In this chapter we discussed the three phases of the rehabilitation process. These are the acute or inflammatory phase, the intermediate or repair phase, and the advanced or remodeling phase. The main treatment principle of the acute phase is RICE: Rest, Ice, Compression, and Elevation. In the intermediate phase, emphasis is placed on range of motion, flexibility, aerobic training, strength and endurance, and proprioception and coordination. In the advanced phase, emphasis is on a safe return to playing tennis, with the exercises aimed at improving functional muscle strength, power, and endurance. Therapeutic exercises programs for the knee, shoulder and back are presented.

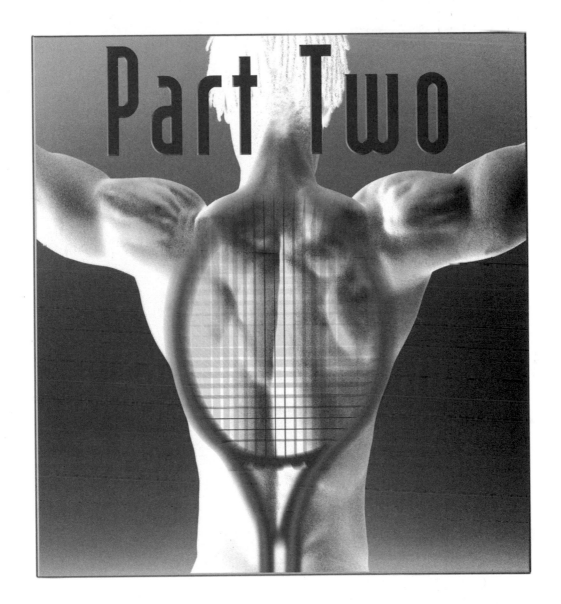

A Complete Inventory of Tennis Injuries

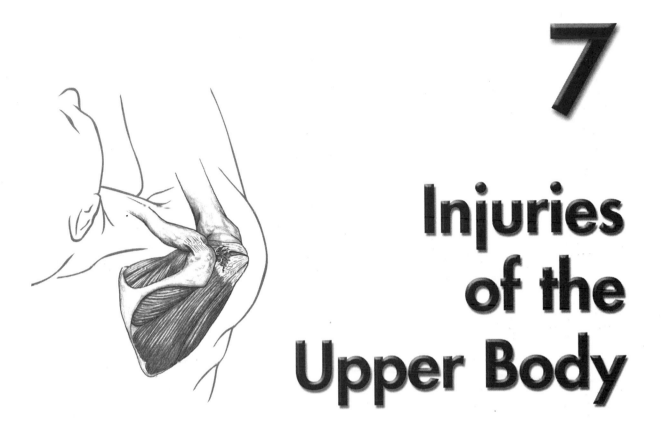

7

Injuries of the Upper Body

In this chapter, we discuss common injuries of the shoulder, elbow, wrist and hand in tennis. Overuse injuries to the soft tissues, including muscles, tendons, and ligaments, occur frequently in tennis, due to the repetitive motion of the serve and ground strokes. Acute traumatic injuries to the upper extremity may result from a fall onto the arm or hand, but are much less common in tennis.

BUMP ON THE HAND OR WRIST (GANGLION CYST)

Description. A ganglion cyst is a fluid-filled sac arising from an adjacent joint or tendon (Figure 7.1). Although ganglions can develop in many areas including the shoulder, elbow, knee, ankle and foot, ganglions in the wrist and the hand are the most common. It is thought that ganglions form as a result of either a single traumatic injury or repetitive stress, resulting in production of a thick gelatinous fluid. The cyst arises from accumulation of this fluid in a sac outside the joint or tendon sheath.

Symptoms. A ganglion appears as a rubbery, rounded swelling. The cyst may get bigger and smaller intermittently. Usually, the more active one is, the larger the ganglion becomes; during rest periods, the ganglion decreases in size. The cyst may be completely painless. However, large cysts tend to cause mild pain or a feeling of fullness. Ganglion cysts can become more bothersome when they interfere with joint motion or compress nerves in the area. Diagnosis of a ganglion cyst in the wrist can usually be made on physical examination alone. Because ganglion cysts do not show up on X-ray, small cysts or those located in unusual places around the wrist may require ultrasound or MRI to confirm the diagnosis (Figure 7.2).

Figure 7.1

A ganglion cyst is a fluid-filled sac arising from an adjacent joint or tendon.

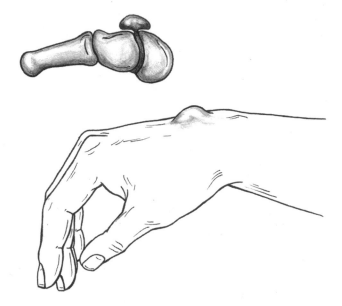

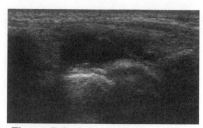

Figure 7.2

An ultrasound image of a ganglion cyst.

Treatment. Approximately half of the cysts around the wrist disappear without any treatment at all. Nonoperative treatment may include removing fluid from the cyst with a needle, injecting the cyst with a cortisone type medication, and/or the wearing of a splint to rest the wrist. Surgical excision can be done on an outpatient basis (day surgery) either through a small incision and sometimes arthroscopically. After surgery, a splint may be worn for a short period of time before wrist motion and rehabilitation is started. Following surgical excision of a ganglion cyst, there is a small risk of reoccurrence of the cyst.

Practical tips for the player
- Support the wrist during play, e.g, by using a wrapped elastic bandage, tape, or brace.

SNAPPING WRIST (SUBLUXATING EXTENSOR CARPI ULNARIS TENDON)

Description. A subluxating extensor carpi ulnaris tendon is characterized by a painful snapping over the back of the small finger side of the wrist, particularly on forearm rotation. It results from a tear or stretching of the retinaculum (roof) of the extensor carpi ulnaris tunnel. This allows the tendon to slide back and forth, in and out of its normal position in the groove of the tunnel. The injury may result from a single sudden movement or repetitive movements of the wrist, with the palm of the hand turning upwards and sideward, such a when hitting a slice forehand, low volleys, and topspin serves (Figure 7.3).

Symptoms. There may be painful snapping over the backside of the wrist, on the side of the little finger, usually with rotation of the forearm and wrist. There may be weakness of the wrist and swelling, tenderness and bruising at the injury site. One can see the tendon move from its normal position and slide sideward when the supinated wrist

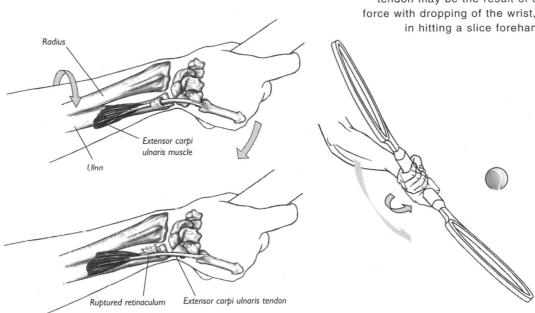

Figure 7.3
A luxation of the extensor carpi ulnaris
tendon may be the result of a sudden
force with dropping of the wrist, such as
in hitting a slice forehand volley.

(palm up) is moved from side to side. On pronation (turning the palm down), the tendon relocates into its normal position. Ultrasonography and/or MRI may be helpful in establishing the diagnosis when it is in question.

Treatment. If the injury is acute, treatment may consist of immobilization in a long cast for six weeks. If nonoperative treatment fails, or if the symptoms have been present for a long time, surgery may be necessary to repair the retinaculum. If the tendon is also torn, repair is necessary to restore its function.

Practical tips for the player

- Use a firm wrist when hitting volleys.
- When returning to play, start with flat strokes. Gradually build up hitting slice shots, topspin serves and reflex volleys.
- Wrist supportive devices, such as wrapped elastic bandages, tape, or braces may be helpful.
- Strengthen the muscles that stabilize the wrist at ball contact. Recommended exercises include wrist curls, wrist extensions, ball squeezes, and rotation exercises. See Figures 28.26-28.30 for instructions.

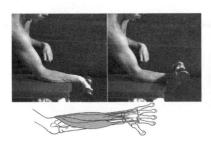
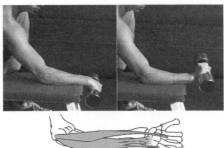

CLICKING, PAINFUL WRIST (TRIANGULAR FIBROCARTILAGE TEARS)

Description. The triangular fibrocartilage complex (TFCC) is a small disc-like structure between the end of the forearm and the wrist bones (Figure 7.4). The TFCC serves as a point of connection of ligaments as well as a stabilizer and shock absorber between the wrist bones and forearm. The TFCC may tear as a result of traumatic injury, such as falling on an outstretched hand, or degenerate with time and age. Tennis players may develop a tear of this cartilage due to repetitive twisting and hyperextension motions at the wrist, particularly hitting slice forehands and backhands, and slice and topspin serves. Particularly high-risk groups are players with an ulna that is longer than the radius bone at the wrist. The longer ulna causes pinching of the triangular fibrocartilage between the end of the ulna and the wrist bones; this is called ulnocarpal impaction. This may also lead to degeneration of the cartilage that lines the bones.

Symptoms. Symptoms are generally pain, which may be associated with an uncomfortable "click" on the little finger side of the wrist. Painless "clicking" in the wrist is generally not considered as concerning. There may be pain when bending the wrist toward the little finger side or extending the wrist such as with push ups or with gripping the racquet. The wrist will generally hurt during play. The pain may or may not persist after play is finished.

Treatment. The torn cartilage may gradually heal with rest by immobilizing the wrist. A splint, brace or cast is usually recommended for several weeks, followed by initiation of hand therapy to regain strength and motion once healing has occurred. If symptoms persist, surgery may be required. Arthroscopy can usually be used to repair or remove a torn fibrocartilage. Occasionally, the type and location of the tear may make an open procedure necessary. If the ulna is particularly long, an open procedure to shorten the

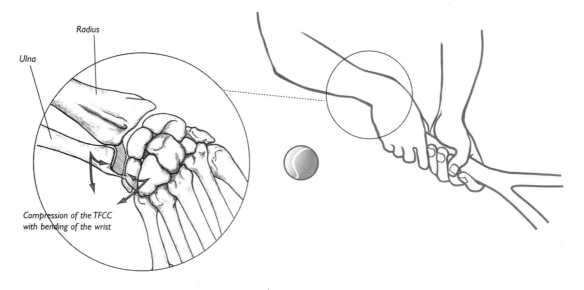

Radius

Ulna

Compression of the TFCC
with bending of the wrist

Figure 7.4
Degenerative triangular fibrocartilage tears may be due to repetitive twisting and
hyperextension motions at the wrist

ulnar bone may also be recommended. If ulnar shortening is required, return to sports may be attempted after three to six months.

Practical tips for the player

- Functional braces may be effective in preventing re-injury by reducing forceful bending of the wrist.
- Adjust your swing. A tennis swing that is too "wristy" with twisting motion will make the symptoms worse.
- When initially returning to play after injury, start with hitting flat strokes. Gradually build up slice serves, topspin serves, and slice and topspin ground strokes. Hitting with a Western grip may contribute to developing this problem.
- Wrist strengthening exercises should be performed following healing, before going back to hitting balls again. Recommended exercises include wrist rotationss, wrist curls, wrist extensions, and ball squeezes. See Figures 28.24-28.30 for instructions.

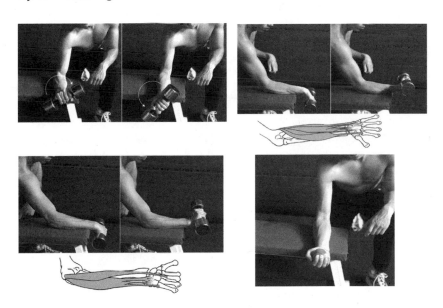

WRIST SPRAIN

Description. A wrist sprain is an acute over-stretching or tearing of one or more ligaments in the wrist, the tough bands of fibrous tissue that connect the bones to one another that help make up the wrist joint. Although we generally speak of the wrist as a single joint between the bones of the forearm and hand, the wrist actually contains many joints that link fifteen separate bones. Any twist, bend or impact that suddenly forces the wrist into a position beyond its normal range of motion can tear the ligaments that connect these bones. This can occur from a fall on the tennis court. Athletes with a wrist sprain complain of severe pain at the time of injury, and may recall a popping or tearing sensation at the time of the injury.

Symptoms. Symptoms include tenderness and swelling in the wrist, initially over the area of injury. The pain and swelling may progress over several hours or days to involve the whole wrist and occasionally the hand. Some bruising may gradually develop depending on the severity of the injury. The ability to use the hand and wrist may be impaired due to the pain and swelling. X-rays may be recommended to rule out a fracture. In some circumstances special testing such as MRI, with or without the injection of dye, may help identify the extent of the injury.

Treatment. Initial treatment at the time of injury consists of ice, rest, a compressive elastic bandage and elevation (RICE) to help reduce swelling and discomfort. This is generally followed by a cast, splint or brace to provide support to the joint for varying lengths of time depending on severity of injury. Proper care and sufficient healing time before resuming activity usually allows complete healing. After immobilization, therapy to increase range of motion and strength are important to reduce pain and recurrence of injury. Healing time may vary from two to twelve weeks, depending on the severity of the sprain. The need for surgical treatment is uncommon except in specific instances when key wrist ligaments are completely torn.

> *Practical tips for the player*
> * Provide the wrist with support, such as a tape, brace, wrist splint, or protective strapping during play after recovering from a wrist sprain until you are completely pain-free.

WRIST PAIN IN YOUNG PLAYERS (WRIST EPIPHYSITIS)

Description. This condition is characterized by inflammation of the growth plate (epiphysis) of the wrist, usually the radius (the bone on the thumb side). The growth plate of the radius or ulna at the wrist becomes inflamed due to repetitive stress injury such as with repeated hyperextension (bending the wrist up) and rotation of the wrist, which occurs often in tennis. Repeated stress or injury interferes with bony development, causing inflammation and eventually premature closure of the growth plate, resulting in shortening of the bone. The growth plate is an area of relative weakness and injury susceptibility as a result of repeated stress. It is a temporary condition of the wrist that is uncommon after age sixteen. Those at increased risk include adolescents who overtrain, especially attempting to hit with as much topspin as possible on their groundstrokes, at a time that they are undergoing rapid skeletal growth.

Symptoms. The wrist is often quite tender to direct palpation over the distal radius epiphysis. There may be a swollen, warm and tender bump on the wrist. Pain increases with activity, especially serving, bending the wrist or bearing weight on the wrist (push ups). X-rays may be helpful in establishing the diagnosis.

Treatment. Mild cases of wrist epiphysitis can be resolved with slight reduction of activity level (no push ups, no topspin strokes), while moderate to severe cases may require significantly reduced activity or even immobilization with casting.

Surgery is necessary if a fracture occurs (uncommon) and the growth plate separates. Surgery may further be necessary in an older athlete if the growth plate of the radius or ulna closes prematurely and one bone is significantly shorter than the other. Gradual return to sports is allowed after inflammation is resolved and wrist motion and strength are fully restored. Follow up at least one year after injury and in some cases until all the growth plates are closed, is necessary.

> *Practical tips for the player*
> * If you have had this injury, avoid push-ups. There are many other

ways to strengthen your arm, chest and shoulder muscles.
- When initially returning to play, flatten your strokes to avoid topspin.

TENDINOPATHY (TENDINITIS) AROUND THE WRIST

Description. Tendinopathy (tendinitis) of the wrist is the result of repeated over-stretching of a tendon, caused by the sudden deceleration as the racquet strikes the ball. Any tendon of the wrist may be affected. The extensor tendons (on the back of the wrist) are affected most on the backhand, while the flexor tendons (on the front of the wrist) are affected more on forehands (Figure 7.5 and 7.6). These injuries may result from playing with a new racquet, higher string tension, new stroke mechanics, or simple overuse due to an increase in frequency of play. Women appear to get these injuries more often than men.

Symptoms. Symptoms include pain and tenderness over the involved tendon. Swelling, warmth and/or redness may also be present. Injury of the flexor or extensor carpi ulnaris tendons leads to pain on the ulnar (pinky) side of the wrist, while tendinopathy of the flexor carpi radialis causes pain on the radial (thumb) side of the wrist. Injury of the extensor carpi ulnaris tendon occurs more frequently in the nondominant hand of players with a double-handed backhand and pain is felt when hitting backhands. Pain can be elicited by extending the wrist again resistance or bending toward the little finger. Pain of the flexor tendons is more often felt during the snap of the serve and when hitting forehands. Pain can be elicited by bending of the wrist against resistance or turning the palm down against resistance. Diagnosis can usually be made on clinical examination but occasionally ultrasound or MRI scanning may be helpful.

Treatment. Treatment consists of ice, rest and anti-inflammatory medication. This is followed by strengthening exercises once the pain has subsided.

Figure 7.5

Shown here are the tendons of the flexor carpi ulnaris, the flexor carpi radialis (front), and the extensor carpi ulnaris (back).

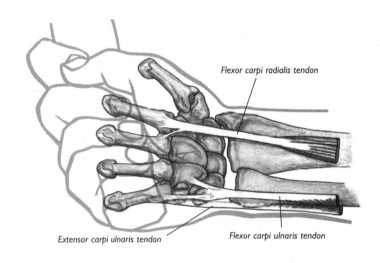

Flexor carpi radialis tendon

Extensor carpi ulnaris tendon

Flexor carpi ulnaris tendon

Figure 7.6

De Quervain's stenosing tenosynovitis and the intersection syndrome

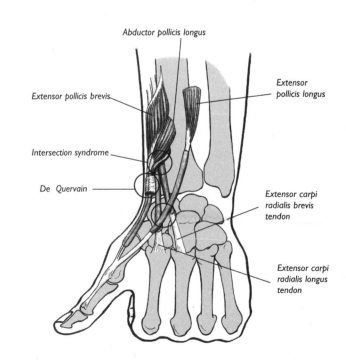

Abductor pollicis longus

Extensor pollicis brevis

Extensor pollicis longus

Intersection syndrome

De Quervain

Extensor carpi radialis brevis tendon

Extensor carpi radialis longus tendon

Occasionally a cast, brace, or splint to reduce motion off-court helps to reduce symptoms. An injection of cortisone to the area around the tendon is generally not recommended, because this may lead to weakening of the tendon. Surgery is rarely necessary for this condition.

Practical tips for the player

- Strengthen the muscles that stabilize the wrist at ball contact. Recommended exercises include wrist curls, wrist extensions and ball squeezes. Players with a two-handed backhand should strengthen both wrists. See Figures 28.26-28.30 for instructions.

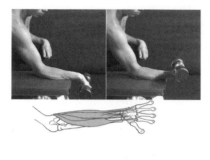 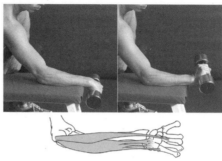 

- Try using a wrist brace or taping during play. The purpose is to stabilize the wrist so that the tendons do not get over-stretched.
- Use a larger grip or use grip overwrap to increase the size of the grip of the racquet.
- Avoid doing push ups with the hand flat on the floor, because this may worsen wrist problems. The best way to perform a push up is on the knuckles (with the wrist straight) or by holding onto parallel bars (Figure 7.7).
- With an extensor tendon injury, try to limit hitting topspin backhands, especially short angle cross-court topspin backhands. Try hitting one-handed backhands or slice backhands for a while, if the nondominant hand is affected, to give the injury time to heal.
- With an injury of the flexor tendon, avoid excessive snapping of the wrist on your serve and flatten your stroke to limit wrist action when hitting topspin forehands.

Figure 7.7

In order to prevent wrist problems, the push up can be performed using parallel bars

PAIN WHEN MOVING THUMB (DE QUERVAIN'S STENOSING TENOSYNOVITIS)

Description. De Quervain's stenosing tenosynovitis occurs at the level of the radial styloid as the two tendons to the thumb pass across the wrist through a canal just beneath the base of the thumb (Figure 7.6). One tendon straightens the thumb, while the other tendon moves the thumb away from the index finger. When these tendons become swollen or inflamed (from overuse or shear trauma), there is pain as the tendons pass through the tight canal. Individuals who suddenly increase their activity or change their activity involving the thumb (including gripping the racquet) are at increased risk to this problem. Women are also more likely to develop this problem than men.

Symptoms. Patients with De Quervain's tenosynovitis usually complain of pain, tenderness, swelling, and warmth over the base of the thumb and thumb side of the wrist. The pain is worse with straightening the thumb or moving it away from the index finger against resistance as well as with pinching or gripping. Enclosing the thumb within a fist of the same hand and bending the wrist away from the thumb causes pain (Finkelstein's test). The athlete with this problem may have limited motion of the thumb. Occasionally, the affected individual will note a catching or locking sensation with attempted movement of the thumb or crepitation (a crackling sound) when the tendon or thumb is moved or touched.

Treatment. Initial treatment consists of rest and ice. Splinting of the thumb and wrist may be recommended to relieve symptoms. A less restrictive figure-8 taping of the thumb to limit thumb movements may be tried instead. If immobilization alone is not effective, an injection of cortisteroid around the tendon may be given to reduce tendon swelling and inflammation. If injection therapy fails, surgery to release the inflamed tendon lining may be necessary. This surgery is performed as an outpatient procedure and may be done with local, regional (whole arm), or general anesthesia. Anticipated return to tennis may be eight weeks following decompression.

Practical tips for the player
- Try to limit extreme ulnar deviation (dropping the racquet) during inition of (slice) forehands and backhands.
- Perform preventative strengthening exercises for the wrist after healing, including wrist curls, wrist extensions, and tennis ball squeezes. See Figures 28.26-28.30 for instructions.

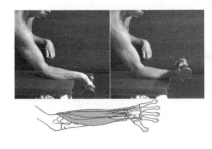
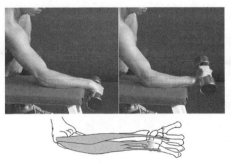

Squeaker's Wrist (intersection syndrome)

Description. Squeaker's wrist, also called intersection syndrome or peritendinitis crepitans, is inflammation of the tendon sheath of the two radial wrist extensors. The condition also affects the two muscles that move the thumb, causing pain and swelling of their muscle bellies. It is characterized by pain, crepitus, and swelling in the forearm, on the thumb side, four to eight cm proximal to the wrist (Figure 7.6). The injury usually occurs when there is a sudden change or increase in activity, requiring repetitive wrist flexion and extension, such as attempting to put more topspin on shots.

Symptoms. There is pain and discrete swelling on the back of the forearm, on the thumb side, close to the wrist. The pain is worse when moving the wrist or thumb against resistance. There may be limited motion of the thumb or wrist, due to the pain. Active or passive movement of the wrist produces a characteristic "wet leather" crackling sound. This crackling, which in some instances may be more like a squeak, may be audible and/or palpable. Diagnosis can be made in clinical examination.

Treatment. Initial treatment consists of activity modification and cooling with ice (ten to fifteen minutes every couple of hours) to relieve the pain and reduce the inflammation. Occasionally, a cast, brace, or splint for one or more weeks may be used to limit motion to help reduce inflammation. An injection of cortisone may be attempted to the area around the tendon. Surgery to release and/or remove the inflamed tendon lining may be necessary if the condition does not respond to nonoperative treatment.

Practical tips for the player
- Proper stroke mechanics are important in the prevention of this problem, especially to prevent recurrence. Flatten your strokes to avoid excessive topspin forehands when first returning to play. Try to limit wrist action when hitting the ball.
- Wrist extensor strengthening exercises should be incorporated into the training program to prevent a recurrence. Use a light weight. See Figures 28.28 and 28.29 for instructions.

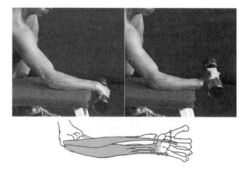

Hamate (hook) Fractures

Description. Fracture of the hook of the hamate is a complete or incomplete break of a part of the hamate bone, a small bone of the wrist. The hamate bone has a bony protuberance, the hook, which is susceptible to injury. This injury usually occurs as a result of a direct force of the butt end of the racquet repeatedly exerting pressure on the hook during the swing (Figure 7.8). The risk of hamate fracture is increased by previous wrist immobilization that has resulted in weakening of the bones.

Symptoms. There is pain and/or soreness in the palm, on the side of the little finger. There may be some swelling and bruising. The player will complain of pain when gripping or swinging the racquet. Occasionally, there may be associated numbness and/or coldness in the fingers, caused by pressure on the blood vessel or nerve that run adjacent to the hook of the hamate. Fractures of the hook of the hamate may be difficult to detect on X-rays. If physical examination suggests the possibility of this injury and X-rays do not show it, a CT scan, bone scan or MRI may be necessary to detect the fracture.

Treatment. The hamate bone may heal with immobilization in a cast. However, because there is a high risk of the fracture not healing with immobilization, surgery is often recommended. Surgery involves either removal of the broken piece or fixing it with pins or screws. Following cast immobilization or surgery, stretching and strengthening exercises for the wrist and hand should be initiated.

Practical tips for the player
- Protective equipment such as padded gloves or a padded tip (butt) of the racquet may help reduce the risk of this injury, particularly if the athlete has had a previous wrist or hand injury.
- A brace or splint may be recommended initially when returning to play.
- Injury risk is increased if you hold the racquet at the outer end, supporting the butt of the handle with the palm of the hand.
- Recommended exercises after surgery include wrist curls, wrist extensions, and tennis ball squeezes (see Figures 28.26-28.30).

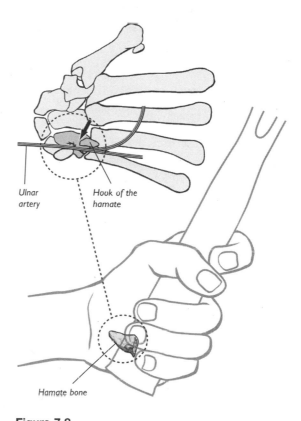

Ulnar artery

Hook of the hamate

Hamate bone

Figure 7.8
Fractures of the hook of the hamate may occur due to direct impact with the racquet.

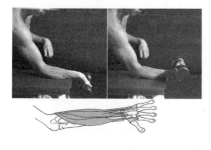
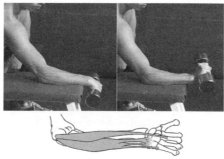

TENNIS ELBOW (LATERAL EPICONDYLITIS)

Description. Tennis elbow is the most common elbow injury in tennis players. Almost half of all tennis players will suffer from tennis elbow in the course of their career. The incidence in tennis players (new cases per year) is about 10%, and the chance of a recurrence varies between 12 to 20%. Players aged over the age of 35 are particularly at risk. Tennis elbow is an overuse injury of the tendon portion of the muscles that extend the wrist. Pain and tenderness are felt at the attachment of the tendon at the bony protuberance on the outer side of the elbow (lateral epicondyle of the humeral bone) (Figure 7.9). The injury usually develops gradually, as a result of multiple microruptures and the resulting degenerative tissue that develops at the tendon attachment. The injury may also occur suddenly, as a result of miss-hitting the ball, or lunging for a backhand, resulting in an acute tear or aggravating an already damaged tendon. Simple day to day activities such as lifting, gripping, shaking hands, washing dishes, or opening a door may all be very painful. During tennis, hitting backhands usually provokes the pain. Tennis elbow is more common in novice than in advanced players. This is probably due to the fact novice players tend to strike the ball with a more flexed wrist than advanced players do. In addition, the extensor muscles of novice players may not be as strong and flexible. Therefore, at ball impact, this leads to stretching of an already lengthened extensor muscle, with a high risk of tendon damage.

Figure 7.9

Tennis elbow is a common affliction among tennis players.

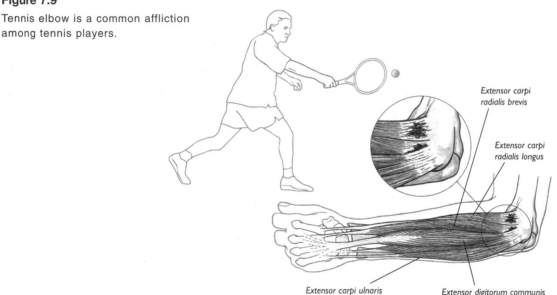

Extensor carpi radialis brevis

Extensor carpi radialis longus

Extensor carpi ulnaris

Extensor digitorum communis

Symptoms. Symptoms are pain and tenderness at the outside of the elbow, along with pain and/or weakness with gripping activities. During play, pain is generally felt at ball impact, mainly on backhand groundstrokes and volleys. The pain may radiate into the arm, wrist, and fingers. On examination, the pain can be reproduced by attempting to extend the wrist against resistance. X-rays of the elbow are typically normal except in long-standing cases, when a bone spur may develop at the tendon attachment site. Ultrasound or MRI are generally not necessary to make the diagnosis, but in certain cases may be helpful in determining the severity of the injury.

Treatment. Initial treatment consists of rest and cooling with ice. If the condition is relatively mild, avoidance of only the pain producing strokes (generally backhands) is necessary to allow adequate healing. In more severe cases, complete cessation from any tennis may be required. The key is to pay attention to the pain. Any activity which causes pain may be interfering with the damaged tendon's ability to heal. Unfortunately, due to the poor blood supply to this area of the tendon, it may take weeks to several months for healing to occur. Physiotherapy (friction massage, electrical stimulation, and a standardized exercise program aimed at the mobility of the elbow and the wrist, stretching exercises, and strengthening of the muscles of the forearm, upper arm and hand, and manual therapy often have good effects. Extracorporeal shockwave therapy may be tried. A brace worn around the upper forearm (counterforce brace) is helpful in protecting the tendon during the healing process. The brace should be worn only during tennis or other activities which involve gripping or lifting with the affected hand, as prolonged use of the brace can cause other problems such as nerve compression within the forearm.

A corticosteroid injection into the area around the damaged tendon may result in considerable pain relief within 48-72 hours. However, it is now generally accepted that such an injection has no significant effect on tendon healing. Therefore, it is important to note that the pain relief following an injection does not signify tendon healing, and return to tennis based upon the pain relief will result in further damage to the tendon and recurrence of symptoms. Since corticosteroids can weaken the tendon tissue, it is generally recommended that no more than three injections are given into the area within one year. Injection of corticosteroids for tennis elbow in competitive tennis players should be avoided when possible, due to the deleterious effect on the tendon. Surgery may be recommended if symptoms persist despite therapy and an appropriate period of rest, generally at least six months. Surgery involves removal of the damaged tissue from the tendon, with shaving or drilling of the bone at the attachment site to stimulate healing. Following surgery, an appropriate rehabilitation program is initiated to regain range of motion and restore flexibility and strength. Return to light hitting is usually allowed in two to three months. Full recovery may take six months or longer.

Practical tips for the player

- Stretch the wrist extensor muscles daily, strengthen the wrist extensors, and increase grip strength. See Figures 5.15, and 28.28-28.30 for instructions.

 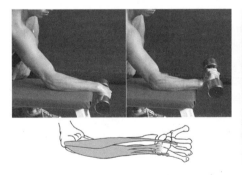 

- Choose a flexible racquet with a large sweet spot, such as a mid-size or oversize racquet. Even though a stiff racquet gives the player more power and control, a flexible racquet is gentler on the arm with off-center hits, because the flexion will absorb some of the shock and spread it over a longer period.
- Relatively low string tension is better for the arm because it increases the dwell time of the ball on the strings. The longer contact time means that the shock of the ball impact is spread over a longer period of time. Thinner strings are more elastic and have better shock-absorbing capacities, and are therefore better for the arm than thicker strings.

- Choose new, pressurized tennis balls. Avoid old, wet, and pressure-less tennis balls.
- Avoid using an extreme grip size. A grip that is too small or too large may cause problems. In both cases, the player may have to grip the racquet too tightly to prevent it from twisting, and high grip force may increase the risk of elbow injury. An easy way to determine the correct grip size is by looking at the space between the finger and muscular area at the base of the thumb while gripping the racquet (Figure 3.6). One finger from the other hand should fit snugly into this space.
- Try an elbow counterforce brace if you start to develop symptoms of tennis elbow.

How to build up play

- Gradually build up play, progressing from mini-tennis (within the service court), to baseline tennis, hitting only forehands and double-handed backhands. If possible, start on a slow court (clay or Har-tru), because on fast courts there is less time available to perform the strokes well.
- Now gradually introduce the flat and slice backhand, volleys, over-heads and service, and finally the topspin backhand.
- When hitting backhands, try to hit the ball in front of the body, so it is easier to fully use the shoulder and trunk and to stabilize the wrist. When the ball impacts the racquet, the wrist should be straight. The forearm extensor muscles are better able to handle the shock when the wrist is straight than when it is flexed. Try to use the forearm for control instead of strength. The application of strength should come mainly from the shoulder and trunk muscles, which are much stronger than the forearm muscles.
- Try to use the other arm for balance when hitting a one-handed back-hand. The function of the balance arm is to ensure a smooth stroke (supporting the racquet in the starting position, enabling a change of grip, improving the shoulder turn, etc).
- If you cannot develop sufficient strength or co-ordination during the one-handed backhand stroke, consider hitting a double-handed backhand.
- The frequency, duration, and intensity of play should be increased very gradually.

GOLFER'S ELBOW (MEDIAL EPICONDYLITIS)

Description. Medial epicondylitis, also known as golfer's elbow, is seen more frequently in high-level tennis players than lateral epicondylitis (tennis elbow). The ratio tennis elbow to golfer's elbow is about 3 to 7: 1. Golfer's elbow is hallmarked by pain on the inner side of the elbow, where muscles and tendons that flex the wrist attach to the bone (Figure 7.10). The injury is usually due to chronic repetitive stress and strain to the flexor muscles and tendons of the wrist and forearm, and is usually associated with the wrist snap when serving or hitting heavy topspin with the forehand.

Symptoms. Symptoms are pain and tenderness on the inner side of the elbow, pain and/or weakness with gripping activities, serving, or hitting forehands. There is also

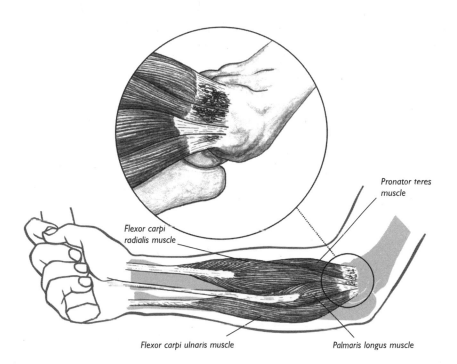

Pronator teres muscle

Flexor carpi radialis muscle

Flexor carpi ulnaris muscle

Palmaris longus muscle

Figure 7.10
Medial epicondylitis

pain with twisting motions of the wrist, such as using a screwdriver, playing golf, and bowling. Weight-lifting, especially biceps curls, also aggravates the pain.

Treatment. Initial treatment consists of activity modification and cooling with ice. Treatment is fairly similar to treatment for tennis elbow. Physiotherapy may include friction massage, stretching exercises and strengthening of the muscles of the forearm, upper arm and hand. A corticosteroid injection may be attempted but, as with lateral tennis elbow, a more conservative approach is taken with this therapy today than in the past. A counterforce brace may be used to reduce the forces to the damaged tendon. Extracorporal shockwave therapy may be tried. Surgery is not very often recommended. Surgery is only recommended if the condition does not respond to nonoperative measures and the persistent symptoms interfere with tennis or day to day activities. As with tennis elbow, the surgery involves removal of the damaged tissue.

Practical tips for the player
*   Stretch the wrist flexor muscles daily and strengthen the forearm flexor muscles. See Figures 5.15 and 28.26-28.27 for instructions.

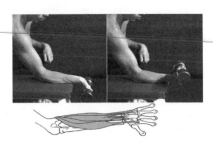

- When using ice, be sure to put a towel between the ice and the arm to prevent injury to the nerve on the inner part of the elbow.
- Decrease wrist motion with forehands, serves and overheads.
- When playing with an extreme forehand grip (Western), try to modify it into a semi-Western.
- Choose elbow-friendly racquets, strings, and balls (see Chapter 3).

ELBOW PAIN IN YOUNG CHILDREN (PANNER'S DISEASE)

Description. Panner's disease or avascular necrosis of the capitellum is a bony condition of the elbow in children, in which death of the bone and cartilage of the end of the arm bone at the outer portion of the elbow is followed by regeneration and recalcification. It is a benign condition, and is found in children five to ten years of age.

Symptoms. Symptoms include intermittent pain and stiffness around the elbow joint that can last for several months. There may be local swelling and pain on compression of the lateral (outer) side of the elbow. Extension of the elbow may elicit pain and extension may be slightly (20 to 30 degrees) limited. Radiographs show fragmentation of the epiphysis of the capitellum. When in doubt, MRI may be used to confirm the diagnosis. In a later stage, recalcification takes place, resulting in a normal bony contour of the elbow at the end of the growth period. Loose bodies have not been described with this disease.

Treatment. It is important to reduce elbow activities, particularly those that strain the joint. This means no tennis, or at least no serving and overheads for a while. The use of a long arm or cast or splint for three to four weeks may be necessary until pain, swelling, and local tenderness subside. Long term outlook is excellent, but a slight loss of elbow extension may persist in some players, though usually without loss of tennis function or ability.

Practical tips for the player
- Hit the forehand with a bent (not a straight or overextended) arm.
- Switch to a double handed backhand.

OSTEOCHONDRITS DISSECANS OF THE ELBOW

Description. Osteochondritis dissecans is a localized injury affecting the joint surface. It usually affects adolescents and young adults. It involves the separation of a segment of cartilage and bone from the underlying bone. This can occur in any joint, though it occurs most commonly in the knee, followed by the ankle, elbow (6% of all cases), and shoulder. The cause of osteochondritis dissecans is unknown, though many theories exist including traumatic injury (direct force to the joint), repetitive stress (overuse), loss of blood supply to the bone and cartilage and abnormal bone formation. It occurs more frequently in males than in females, in athletes than in nonathletes, and in those with a family history of osteochondritis dissecans than in those without.

Symptoms. Symptoms include swelling, pain (which often comes and goes), aching, giving way, and locking or catching of the elbow. There may be a crackling sound within the joint with motion. Maximal extension of the elbow, such as may occur with serving, may be painful. X-rays and MRI may be used to establish the diagnosis.

Treatment. Best success of treatment is after early detection and in young patients. Once the diagnosis has been made, the initial treatment is rest and avoiding tennis practice and play until the fragment heals naturally or with surgery. If the overlying cartilage is intact, nonoperative treatment is more likely successful when the affected player is still growing. Once fully grown, there is a greater likelihood of it not healing and more often may require surgery (especially if the piece breaks off and becomes loose within the joint). Surgery is usually recommended for those with persistent pain after conservative treatment or loose fragments within the joint. Surgery may include arthroscopy to remove the loose fragments, procedures to stimulate healing into the space left empty by the loose fragment, and when possible, procedures to reattach the fragment (if large enough and not deformed). Chronic symptoms with repetitive pain and swelling carry an increased risk of premature osteoarthrosis of the affected joint.

Practical tips for the player

- Reduce serving, overheads, and forehands. Try to avoid maximal extensions when hitting forehands and serves.
- Avoid heavy loads on the elbow, such as push-ups.
- Consider switching to a double handed backhand.
- Strengthen the muscles around the elbow. Recommended exercises are the biceps curl (both with palm up and down) and triceps kickback. See Figures 28.21-28.23 for instructions. Build up to two to three series of ten to fifteen repetitions.

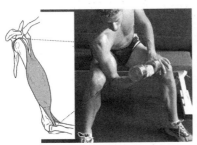

MEDIAL EPICONDYLAR APOPHYSITIS

Description. Medial epicondylar apophysitis is an overuse injury of the growth plate of the inner elbow. Growth plates, which persist until skeletal maturity, are areas of relative weakness. Injury may occur as a result of the repeated stress of muscular contraction of the forearm and wrist flexor muscles during ball contact, especially with serving and forehands. This injury is most common in males between the ages of eleven and eighteen. Those at higher risk include those undergoing rapid skeletal growth, have recently changed their strokes, or increased their training intensity and duration.

Symptoms. A common symptom is a slightly swollen, warm, and tender bump of the inner elbow. Affected players note pain with activity, especially bending the wrist against force (curls, lifting, serving, throwing) and/or following an extended period of vigorous exercise in an adolescent. They will also complain of an inability to serve at full speed and inability to fully straighten the elbow. X-rays and ultrasound can be used to establish the diagnosis. Occasionally, MRI is necessary.

Treatment. Mild cases can be resolved with a slight reduction of activity level, while moderate to severe cases may require significantly reduced activity for three to four months. Occasionally, the affected elbow may need to be immobilized for a few weeks (brace, cast, or splint). A counterforce brace (tennis elbow brace) may help relieve symptoms. Surgery is rarely needed (if conservative treatment fails) in the growing patient. However, surgery is necessary if the growth plate separates completely and moves away from where it should be. Cortisone injections are to be avoided. Sometimes, repeated injury may result in persistent loss of full function of the elbow.

Practical tips for the player

- This is an overuse injury that can be prevented by exercising (including play and practice) moderately, avoiding extremes, and resting appropriately after vigorous exercise.
- Muscular fatigue may put undue stress on the growth plate as well, which means that warming-up and stretching before practice or competition in addition to maintaining adequate forearm and wrist strength are important in preventing this problem.
- Wrist curls and extensions. See Figure 28.26-28.29 for instructions. Gradually build up to two to three series of ten to fifteen repetitions.

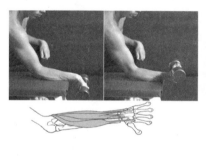 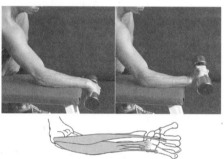

- Serving, overheads, throwing, and heavy lifting should be temporarily reduced.
- Use a composite racquet with good dampening characteristics, an oversized head, light head, and a stiff head and flexible shaft. Use a regular length racquet that is heavy, but comfortable (not too heavy) and the largest cushioned grip that is comfortable.
- The strings should be thin caliber gut or high quality synthetic strings with low tension.
- Play with new, pressurized tennis balls and avoid old, pressureless tennis balls.

POSTERIOR IMPINGEMENT SYNDROME OF THE ELBOW

Description. This injury is due to overuse and repetitive throwing forces. During forced maximal extensions, such as the serve, the olecranon (the bony tip of the elbow, which is the end of the ulnar bone of the forearm) is jammed into the fossa at the end of the humerus, which may result in injury of the cartilage and bone. Bone spur formation may lead to further injury and soft tissue impingement. There is an increased risk of impaction and injury when there are shearing forces that occur as a result of valgus strain (strain that "opens up" the inner side of the elbow), such as during serving and hitting topspin forehands with an extreme Western grip.

Symptoms. Symptoms are pain and tenderness about the elbow, especially when trying to throw or straighten the elbow, as well as locking or catching of the elbow. There may be swelling of the elbow and inability to serve at full speed. There may be some elbow stiffness and inability to fully straighten the elbow. X-rays, CT, and MRI may be used to establish the diagnosis.

Treatment. Posterior impingement syndrome is often treatable with nonoperative management. A rehabilitation program to improve strength, flexibility, and elbow range of motion may be helpful. Conservative treatment consists of mobilization of the elbow and gentle stretching and strengthening exercises. If there is locking or catching due to loose bone fragments within the joint, arthroscopic surgery is recommended to remove them. Surgery may also be performed to remove bone spurs which can cause pain or limit elbow motion. Return to sports after surgery may take three months.

Practical tips for the player
- An extreme Western forehand in combination with a fully extended arm when hitting the forehand should be avoided.
- Avoid leaning on the elbow.
- Recommended strengthening exercises are the biceps curl, triceps extension, wrist rotation, curl, and extension exercises. See Figures 28.21, 28.24-28.29 for instructions.

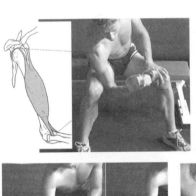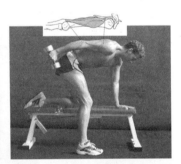
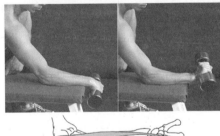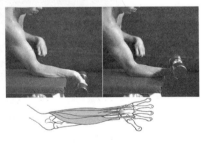

- Stretch the extensors and flexors of the wrist. See Figures 5.15 and 5.16 for instructions.
- When returning to play, with or without surgery, initially avoid serves and overheads, .

SPRAIN OF THE ULNAR COLLATERAL LIGAMENT

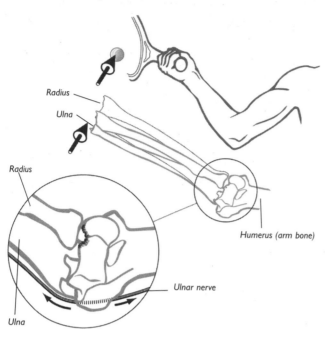

Radius

Ulna

Radius

Humerus (arm bone)

Ulnar nerve

Ulna

Figure 7.11

Repetitive valgus stress may result in strain of the ulnar collateral ligament, stretching of the ulnar nerve and injury to the cartilage at the outer elbow.

Description. The ulnar collateral ligament on the inner side of the elbow is a structure that helps keep the normal relationship of the humerus (arm bone) and the ulna (one of the forearm bones). This ligament may be stretched over time with repeated hard serving or poor forehand mechanics. The stretching of the ligament results in gapping apart of the inner side of the elbow (Figure 7.11). In rare circumstances, the ligament may be torn. This can be determined by an MRI scan done following injection of the elbow with a contrasting fluid.

Symptoms. Symptoms are pain on the inside of the elbow during the acceleration phase of a throw and during impact. Because the ligament ensures a normal relationship between the humerus and the elbow, a partial rupture may result in secondary injury because of valgus overload, such as loose bodies, osteophytes, and osteochondral injury.

Treatment. Ulnar collateral ligament sprain is often treatable with nonoperative management, though may require surgery to alleviate symptoms. Conservative treatment consists of physiotherapy (electrotherapy, friction massage, ice, and strengthening exercises). A completely torn ulnar collateral ligament requires reconstruction (replacement with another tendon) in most cases in order to return the player to competitive tennis.

Practical tips for the player
- Proper form and technique may help to prevent this injury. An extreme Western forehand in combination with a fully extended arm when hitting the forehand should be avoided.
- When using ice to reduce inflammation, make sure the ice is not placed on the skin directly over the nerve.
- Recommended strengthening exercises are the biceps curl, triceps extension, wrist curl, wrist extension, and rotation exercises. See Figures 28.21, 28.26-28.29, and 28.24-28.25 for instructions.

Cubital Tunnel Syndrome (Ulnar Neuritis)

Description. Cubital tunnel syndrome is a disorder in the elbow and upper arm that causes pain on the inner side of the elbow, as well as symptoms such as numbness and tingling in the hand, particularly the ring and little fingers. There is pressure, compression, or stretching of the ulnar nerve at the inner side of the elbow, in the arm and/or forearm by muscles or ligament-like tissues or due to loose ligaments at the elbow. In tennis, the repetitive valgus strain that occurs during serving and hitting topspin forehands with an extreme Western grip may lead to overstretching and injury of the nerve. Furthermore, the nerve has little tissue protecting it at the elbow, resulting in bruising by a direct blow to the nerve. Ulnar nerve dysfunction or inflammation may greatly decrease tennis performance, because strong hand and wrist action are needed. Other injury to the inner elbow, including medial epicondylitis (golfer's elbow) and loose inner elbow ligaments may make the nerve irritated. Athletes with diabetes mellitus and hypothyroidism (underactive thyroid gland) are at increased risk for this problem.

Symptoms. Those with cubital tunnel syndrome may complain of tingling, numbness, or burning in part of the hand or fingers (little finger and/or ring finger) and inside of the forearm. The athlete may also have sharp pains that may shoot from the elbow to the wrist and/or hand, as well as hand weakness, clumsiness, and heaviness. Occasionally, the athlete will complain of poor dexterity (fine hand function), and weak pinch and grip, especially power grip. The pain may be increased with forced full elbow bending. Tennis players often note reduced performance, power, and accuracy.

Treatment. Treatment usually begins with ruling out and treating other causes of nerve inflammation, including muscle, tendon, and ligament injury. Rest, anti-inflammatory medications and physical therapy are often curative. Sometimes wearing an elbow pad rotated to the front of the elbow to reduce prolonged elbow bending at night may help reduce the numbness that occasionally awakens the players from their sleep. Surgery is recommended if symptoms of nerve damage do not respond to nonoperative measures. Most commonly the nerve is moved several inches to a new location in front of the elbow to relieve the stretching the nerve encounters in its normal position.

Practical tips for the player
- Proper form and technique may help to prevent this injury. An

extreme Western forehand in combination with a fully extended arm when hitting the forehand should be avoided.

- Use a light racquet with a large grip, or build up the grip with over-wrap.
- Avoid leaning on the elbow, which can irritate the ulnar nerve.
- Assessment for proper serving mechanics is important prior to return to competition.

ULNAR AND HUMERAL STRESS FRACTURE

Description. Stress (fatigue) fractures occur when body breakdown exceeds the body's ability to heal. This may occur as a result of repeated loading over a long period of time or a recent change in training type or intensity over a shorter period of time. Repeated stresses on the bones can result in tiny, almost invisible breaks in the bone structure called micro-fractures. Normally, the body has time to heal the micro-fractures before they start to cause problems. However, overtraining can aggravate the micro-fractures. Also, not allowing time to fully recover from training does not allow the body to heal these micro-fractures. This causes them to become larger, because overtraining applies more stress to the bones before already existing micro-fractures are able to heal. They may continue to increase in size, causing continued pain and eventually preventing the player from participating fully or at all, and eventually requiring treatment, including surgery, a cast, or other immobilization. Stress fractures are most frequently seen in the lower extremities, but in tennis players they may also occur in the upper extremities. In principal, all bones of the upper extremity can be affected, but stress fractures of the ulna and humerus are most common. An ulnar stress fracture is usually located in the middle third of the forearm, often in the nondominant arm of someone who plays with a two-handed backhand. A humeral stress fracture is generally located in the lower third of the upper arm.

Symptoms. In case of an ulnar stress fracture, there will be gradually increasing pain in the right forearm when playing tennis. With a humeral stress fracture, the pain will be located in the upper arm, just above the elbow. The worst pain is usually with initial impact of the ball against the racquet, with lessening of the pain during the follow through. Pain tends to gradually worsen over time, and may finally also occur with activities of daily living. Radiographs tend to be normal, although sometimes a fracture line or callus formation may be seen. A bone scan or MRI will confirm the diagnosis.

Treatment. Stress fractures generally require only a temporary cessation of aggravating activity for bone repair. The duration of the rest period depends on the severity of the injury and usually varies from three to six weeks.

Practical tips for the player
- It is important to avoid nonsteroidal anti-inflammatory medications during bone healing, because this may delay healing. Cooling with ice may help with the pain.

TRACTION APOPHYSITIS OF THE SHOULDER

Description. Traction-apophysitis of the shoulder is an overuse injury of the growth plate at the upper arm (apophysis), usually involving either the greater or the lesser tuberosity of the shoulder and can be compared to Osgood Schlatter of the knee. The repetitive pulling of the rotator cuff tendons, particularly the supraspinatus at the greater tuberosity or the subscapularis muscle at the lesser tuberosity may lead to inflammation, micro-fractures, pain and fragmentation of the apohysis.

Symptoms. Rotating the arm inward against resistance or bringing the arm away from the body against resistance may be painful. The player may note weakness of the shoulder associated with pain, especially with overhead activities, such as serving. The pain may awaken the player at night. Diagnosis can be made using ultrasound, showing thickening of the cartilage and fragmentation of the apophysis.

Treatment. Full recovery is important, because thickening of the apophysis may lead to rotator cuff problems, such as impingement. Rest and activity modification are the mainstay of treatment. Then gradually stretching and strengthening exercises should be instituted prior beginning practice or play.

> *Practical tips for the player*
> - When returning to play, start with just ground strokes. Gradually add in high volleys, and then eventually overheads and serves.

LITTLE LEAGUER'S SHOULDER
(STRESS FRACTURE OF THE PROXIMAL HUMERAL EPIPHYSIS)

Description. Little Leaguer's shoulder is a stress fracture of the growth plate (epiphysis) of the upper arm (humerus), with widening and sometimes slipping of the epiphysis (ephysioloysis). The main cause is the shear and distraction caused by rotational forces around the shoulder during the serving motion. It may also result from a fall on the shoulder.

Symptoms. There is pain in the upper arm and shoulder during play. Usually, the pain is worst when serving, but later the pain may also appear on groundstrokes. Eventually, there may even be pain at rest and pain that awakens the player at night. X-rays will be helpful in establishing the diagnoses, whereby standard and axillary images should be made. If there is still doubt, an MRI should be made.

Treatment. Treatment consists of rest from tennis, anti-inflammatory and pain medications, and activity modification. Once the shoulder feels better, a program of stretching and strengthening exercises of the shoulder should be instituted prior to beginning practice or play. It may take several weeks to months to return to play with this problem.

> *Practical tips for the player*
> - When returning to play, start with just ground strokes. Gradually add in high volleys, and then eventually overheads and serves.

SHOULDER INSTABILITY

Description. Instability is a term used to describe an abnormal looseness of the shoulder joint. It may result from a traumatic dislocation or subluxation. However, instability may also develop gradually due to repetitive stretching of the stabilizing structures. In tennis players, this most commonly occurs as a result of the overhead serving motion. This stretches the capsule and ligaments in the front of the shoulder, resulting in anterior instability. Those individuals who genetically have a lot of flexibility about their joints may develop multidirectional instability of the shoulder in which the shoulder becomes abnormally loose anteriorly (forward), posteriorly (backward) and inferiorly (below). Due to the importance of the muscular stabilizers, those with weakness of the muscles about the shoulder, especially the rotator cuff and scapular (shoulder blade) stabilizers, are at risk for developing shoulder instability (Figure 7.12). Weakness most commonly results from poor conditioning and/or overuse of the shoulder muscles.

Figure 7.12

The function of the rotator cuff muscles is humeral head stabilization.

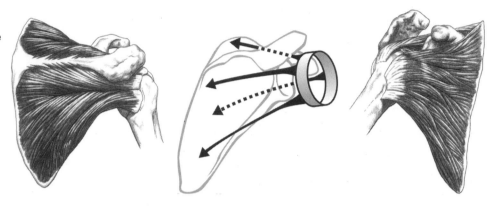

Symptoms. Tennis players with shoulder instability can have a variety of complaints, depending on the degree of instability, the direction of instability, and their activities. The most common complaints include a feeling of the shoulder "slipping," pain in the front or the back of the shoulder with the shoulder in certain positions (especially the backscratch and follow through positions during the serve) and an inability to generate normal velocity on the serve (dead arm). Because the abnormal movement of the ball within the socket can also cause problems with the rotator cuff, the athlete may present with symptoms of impingement, rotator cuff tendinopathy, or partial tearing. Diagnosis of instability can be difficult. If it is unclear based upon the athlete's complaints and examination, an MRI, with or without injection of fluid into the shoulder joint, may help to identify the problem.

Treatment. Initial treatment for shoulder instability is aimed at strengthening the stabilizing muscles of the shoulder, primarily the rotator cuff and scapular stabilizers. Activity modification to avoid provocative positions may be helpful. If symptoms persist despite a satisfactory rehabilitation program, surgery may be recommended. Surgery involves tightening the stretched out ligaments and capsule and/or repairing torn stabilizing tissues such as the ligaments or labrum. This can be done either arthroscopically or with an open procedure. Following surgery, the shoulder is immobilized for a period of time to allow adequate healing of the repaired structures, following which an exercise program is begun to regain range of motion and strength about the shoulder. Gradual return to tennis is initiated once there is satisfactory recovery motion and strength.

Practical tips for the player

- Rehabilitation exercises include strengthening of the scapular stabilizers and internal and external rotators. See Figures 28.2, 28.3, 28.4, 28.6, 28.7, and 28.8.

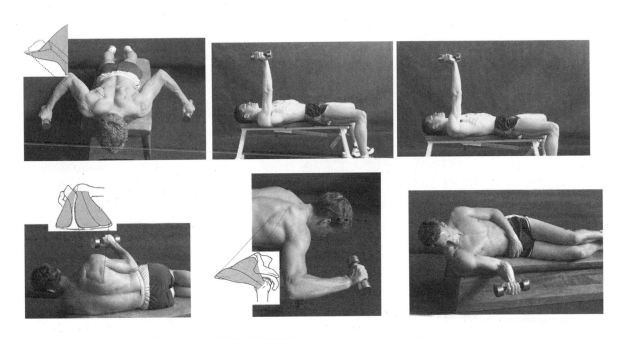

DISLOCATION OF THE SHOULDER

Description. The shoulder has more motion than any other large joint in the body and resembles a golf ball sitting on a tee. The stability of the joint relies primarily on the soft tissues, including the labrum, capsule, ligaments, and surrounding muscles. A dislocation occurs when the ball (humeral head) at the top of the upper arm bone (humerus) is displaced from its normal position in the center of the socket (glenoid), and the joint surfaces no longer touch each other. A less severe injury results in a subluxation, in which there is less displacement and the joint surfaces remain in partial contact.

The incidence of shoulder dislocation is about 32 cases per 100,000 persons per year, and occurs more often in males than females (2 to 3 : 1). The most common type of dislocation is anterior (over 90%), where the humeral head dislocates in front and below the glenoid. A posterior shoulder dislocation, where the humeral head goes out behind the glenoid, is much less common than an anterior dislocation. In multidirectional instability, the humeral head may go in front of (anterior), below (inferior) and/or behind (posterior) the glenoid. This type of instability tends to occur more often in loose-jointed ("double jointed") people.

Shoulder dislocations most commonly occur as a result of trauma, particularly a direct blow to the shoulder or backward force on an extended arm or elbow. When the shoulder dislocates, the capsule and ligaments are stretched or torn, and often the labrum is pulled off the glenoid. A tear of the rotator cuff can also result from shoulder dislocations, most commonly in those over the age of 40.

Following the first dislocation, the potential for repeated shoulder dislocations depends primarily on the severity of the trauma and tissue damage associated with the first location, the type of activities the person elects to return to following the initial dislocation, and the age of the person at the time of the first dislocation. Younger age at the time of the first dislocation has a higher risk or recurrent dislocations: if under 20 years old at first dislocation, there is a 60 to 70% risk of another dislocation of the same shoulder.

Symptoms. Those who sustain a shoulder dislocation complain of severe pain in the shoulder at the time of injury. There may be tenderness, deformity, and swelling when there is a dislocation. With an anterior dislocation, there will be fullness in the front of the armpit and loss of the normal rounded contour of the deltoid muscle. With a posterior dislocation, there will be fullness in the back of the shoulder. Those with either type of dislocation will complain of loss of shoulder function and severe pain when attempting to move the shoulder or arm. There may be tingling, numbness, or paralysis in the upper arm and deltoid muscle from injury to the nerves of the shoulder. An X-ray will show the humeral head located outside the socket when a dislocation has occurred. In the case of a subluxation, the head spontaneously returns to its normal position at the time of injury and therefore X-rays appear normal. An MRI may be performed to determine the extent of injury to the rotator cuff and labrum.

Treatment. Following a dislocation, the arm should be held as still as possible and medical attention immediately sought. The shoulder is manipulated back into its normal position by appropriate medical personnel. As this may be very painful, it is often accomplished using some form of sedation or anesthesia in a hospital setting. This is followed by immobilization in a sling or similar device. Immobilization may be recommended for a few days to several weeks, depending on the severity of the injury and the preference of the treating physician. Once immobilization is discontinued, progressive range of motion and strengthening exercises are initiated. Surgery is usually reserved for those who have dislocated the shoulder more than once despite appropriate rehabilitation. However, some sports medicine specialists recommend surgical repair for a first time dislocation, especially in competitive overhead athletes. The surgery involves repairing the damaged labrum, ligaments, or capsule. This can be done arthroscopically or through a standard incision.

In cases where the instability is not caused by acute injury, rehabilitation has a high likelihood of success. Most recurrent dislocations are caused by repeated injury, though with increasing incidence of dislocations, less force is necessary to cause a dislocation. Risks of this problem include damage to nearby nerves causing temporary or permanent weakness, paralysis, and numbness, as well as fracture or joint cartilage injury due to the dislocation or reduction of the dislocation. Rotator cuff tear may occur if the age of the player at the time of the first dislocation is after age 40. There is also the risk of an unstable or arthritic shoulder following repeated injury, or if there is associated fracture.

Practical tips for the player
- If the shoulder is unstable, you can undertake any desired activity, as long as you can see your hands in front of you while keeping your head straight.
- Rehabilitation exercises include strengthening of the scapular stabi-

lizers and internal and external rotators. See Figures 28.2, 28.3, 28.4, 28.6, 28.7, and 28.8 for instructions. Refer to Chapter 6 for additional exercises for the shoulder.

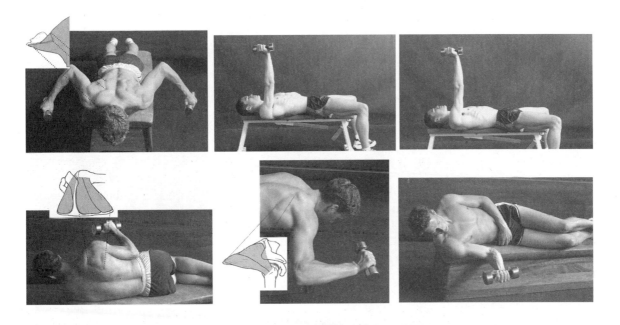

PINCHING OF ROTATOR CUFF TENDONS (IMPINGEMENT SYNDROME)

Description. Impingement syndrome is a common shoulder condition involving pinching of the rotator cuff and subacromial bursa between the ball (head) of the humerus (upper arm bone) and the subacromial arch (acromial bone and coraco-acromial ligament) above. It is characterized by pain in the shoulder and/or upper arm, aggravated with the arm in the overhead position. The rotator cuff is a series of four muscles that surround the humeral head. They assist in movement of the shoulder and help keep the humeral head within the shoulder socket. The subacromial bursa is a very thin sack that lies on top of the cuff. The space between humeral head and subacromial arch gets smaller when the arm is moved, particularly into the overhead position (Figures 7.13 and 7.14). If there is abnormal movement of the ball within the socket due to weakness of the rotator cuff or shoulder blade muscles, instability, or tightness of the capsule or muscles around the shoulder, this space may become too small to accommodate the rotator cuff and overlying bursa. This results in pinching of the rotator cuff and bursa when the arm is moved overhead. This pinching can inflame the bursa causing painful bursitis. It can also damage the underlying rotator cuff tendons causing tendinitis. Prolonged impingement over a period of months or years can eventually result in a tear of the rotator cuff and/or development of a bone spur on the undersurface of the acromion.

Symptoms. Symptoms include pain around the shoulder, often at the outer portion of the upper arm. The pain is worse with overhead activities such as serving, hitting high topspin forehands or hitting overhead smashes. There may be an aching pain after play. The pain may make it difficult to sleep, especially when lying on the affected shoulder. Sometimes there is loss of strength, usually due to pain, though in later stages a rotator cuff tear may develop which may also be responsible for shoulder weakness. There may be limited mobility of the shoulder, especially when reaching

Figure 7.13

When hitting low balls, there is sufficient space below the sub-acromial arch

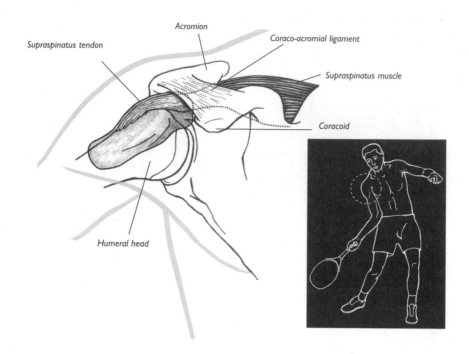

Figure 7.14

When hitting hight balls, the supraspinatus gets pinched between the humeral head and the acromion.

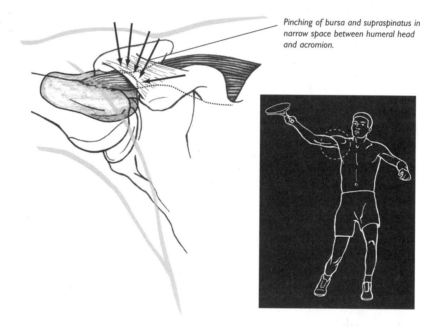

Pinching of bursa and supraspinatus in narrow space between humeral head and acromion.

behind (back pocket, bra) or across the body, or a catching or grinding sensation. Occasionally, the athlete will also note pain in the front of the shoulder, that is worse with bending the elbow or lifting due to involvement of the biceps tendon in the impingement process. The diagnosis of impingement syndrome can often be made based upon a careful examination. X-rays may demonstrate a spur on the undersurface of the acromion or irregularity of the humeral head at the greater tuberosity where the rotator cuff tendons attach. An injection of local a local anesthetic in the subacromial space which relieves the pain associated with the overhead position confirms the diagnosis. Oftentimes, an MRI is performed to see if there is an associated rotator cuff tear.

Treatment. The first step in treating impingement syndrome is reducing pain and inflammation with rest, ice, and anti-inflammatory medicines. Gentle stretching and strengthening exercises are added gradually. Strengthening exercises should focus primarily on the scapular stabilizers and rotator cuff muscles.

If there is no improvement, the doctor may recommend an injection of cortisone to the area around the tendon, within the subacromial space. Play should be avoided for several days following the injection. Although the injection may alleviate the pain, it will not cure the underlying impingement problem. The exercises are the most important part of the overall treatment program. While steroid injections are a commonly used part of treatment for impingement problem, they must be used with caution, especially in competitive tennis players, because they may weaken the tendon and can lead to tendon rupture.

If there is persistent pain despite an intensive rehabilitation program, the doctor may recommend either arthroscopic or open surgery to relieve pressure on the rotator cuff tendons and remove the inflamed bursa. If the impingement syndrome is caused by the looseness of the shoulder, surgery may include tightening of the shoulder capsule and ligaments.

Practical tips for the player

- Temporarily avoid overheads and serves, as well as high ground strokes and high volleys, if you have symptoms of impingement syndrome.
- Maintain shoulder muscle flexibility by stretching the posterior rotator cuff and posterior capsule. See Figure 5.13 for instructions.
- Strengthen the scapular stabilizers and the rotator cuff. Good exercises are extensions, scapular retraction, serratus anterior punch, external rotation, and dumbbell rowing. See Figures 28.1, 28.2, 28.3, 28.4, 28.6, 28.7, and 28.8 for instructions. Refer to Chapter 6 for additional exercises for the shoulder.

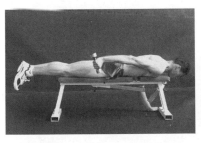
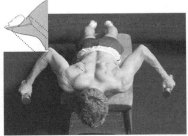

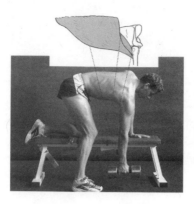

ROTATOR CUFF TEAR

Description. The rotator cuff is a series of four muscles and their tendons that surround the ball of the shoulder (humeral head) and help guide motion and provide stability to the shoulder. A rotator cuff tear is a tear in one or more of the tendons of the rotator cuff muscles (Figure 7.15). These tears may be classified as partial-thickness tears or full-thickness tears. A partial thickness rotator cuff tear is the term used when the tendon is not torn completely through its full thickness. A full-thickness rotator cuff tear is the term used when the tendon extends through the entire thickness of one or more of the tendons. Rotator cuff tears are a common problem for people over the age of 30 to 40 years, especially those engaged in overhead sports such as tennis, although they can occur in younger athletes as well.

A rotator cuff tear may occur suddenly or develop gradually. Sudden rotator cuff tears usually occur as a result of falling or while lifting heavy objects. A rotator cuff tear may develop gradually due to degeneration of the tendon due to muscle imbalance around the shoulder, shoulder instability, or repetitive overuse of the rotator cuff, or internal impingement. Internal impingement is a problem where there is a partial thickness tear of the posterior rotator cuff due to pinching of this area between the upper posterior glenoid (socket) with its overlying labrum (cartilage rim) and the humerus (upper arm) itself. Other risk factors for rotator cuff tear include a previous injury to the rotator cuff and repeated cortisone injections.

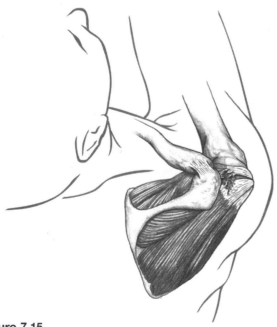

Figure 7.15

A partial rotator cuff tear.

Symptoms. Tennis players with rotator cuff tears usually complain of pain in the front or side of the shoulder, which may radiate down the upper arm. The pain is generally worse when reaching overhead or lifting. With internal impingement, the pain is more in the back of the shoulder. There may be aching when not using the arm, especially at night when sleeping on the affected side. There may be weakness when attempting to lift the arm. With small cuff tears, strength may be maintained surprisingly well, although the patient may notice diminished endurance and arm fatigue in the overhead position. With a large rotator cuff tear, the player may be unable to completely raise the arm overhead. There may be catching and grating or cracking sounds when the arm is moved and limited mobility of the shoulder, especially reaching behind (back pocket, bra) or across the body. X-rays can be helpful in evaluating a player with a suspected rotator cuff tear, however, ultrasound, arthrography (dye injection rays) or MRI are needed to visualize the tear in order to confirm the diagnosis.

Treatment. Once a rotaor cuff tear is diagnosed, treatment should be individualized depending upon a variety of factors including the player's age, skill level, size of the tear, extent of the tear (full or partial thickness), which shoulder is affected (dominant or nondominant) and the player's desire to continue to play tennis. For older players with small or partial thickness tears, a trial of conservative treatment may be indicated, including a period of rest from tennis and physical therapy to reduce pain and improve strength and motion. Anti-inflammatory medications may be helpful in reducing the pain and inflammation associated with rotator cuff tears. Cortisone injections should be used with caution in players with rotator cuff tears as this can weaken the tendon.

For larger tears and tears in high level players, surgery for the torn rotator cuff is usually necessary. Partial thickness tears may be "shaved" arthroscopically in order to promote healing. Full thickness tears generally require repair which may be done either by arthroscopic or open methods. If impingement syndrome or instability is also present, this may need to be addressed surgically at the time of the rotator cuff repair. Return to full activity generally requires three to six months, but may be as long as twelve months, depending on the severity of the tear.

Some very large tears that have been present for a long time may not be amenable to standard surgical repair, in which case treatment options may include a more complex reconstructive procedure, a limited surgical procedure to "clean up" the torn tendon(s), or nonoperative treatment. In these cases, the goal is to reduce pain and improve function, with the ability to return to competitive tennis unlikely if the dominant shoulder is affected.

Practical tips for the player
- Take any shoulder injury seriously. If the shoulder hurts, stop playing and rest the shoulder. If the complaints are minor, it may be sufficient to adapt the training program and temporarily leave out overhead strokes, high volleys and high topspin forehands.
- Start hitting from "low to high" when resuming activity after an injury. Start with neutral strokes with a bit of lift. Slowly increase the distance by starting at the service line or three quarters of the court, gradually progressing towards the baseline. Follow this with gradual incorporation of volleys, topspin forehands, overheads, and serves.
- Practice the service for short periods of time only in the early stages of recovery. The same goes for high topspin forehands, high volleys, and overheads. The intensity should be built up gradually.
- Stretch the posterior shoulder and triceps. See Figures 5.13 and 5.14 for instructions.

- Strengthen the shoulder blade stabilizers and external rotators. Recommended exercises are extensions, serratus anterior punch, scapular retraction, push-ups against the wall, external rotation, and dumbbell rows. See Figures 28.1-28.7, and 28.31-28.32 for instructions.

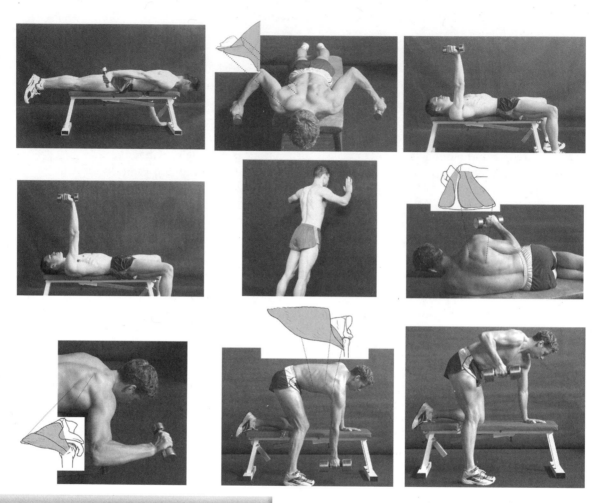

SLAP LESIONS

Description. The socket of the shoulder (glenoid) has a cartilage rim, called the labrum, that lines the periphery, deepening the socket. The labrum serves as the attachment site of the shoulder capsule, ligaments and the long head of the biceps tendon to the glenoid. The labrum is important in shoulder stability. The upper cartilage rim (superior labrum) is where the biceps tendon usually attaches. A tear of the labrum in this area is called a SLAP (Superior Labrum Anterior to Posterior) lesion.

SLAP lesions are classified from I to IV (Figure 7.16). A type I tear or degeneration is fraying of the superior labrum. In a type II tear the labrum and biceps tendon are detached from the superior glenoid. A type III is a bucket handle tear of the superior labrum. A type IV is a bucket handle tear of the superior labrum with lateral extension into the biceps tendon. Serving and overheads place tension on the biceps tendon and superior labrum, which may result in injury to this area. A SLAP lesion may also occur as a result of a fall onto the outstretched arm, a shoulder dislocation or subluxation, a traction injury to the arm, a sudden force applied to the biceps while contracted, or direct blow to the shoulder with the arm in a throwing position.

Symptoms. Athletes with a SLAP lesion may complain of pain in the shoulder that is worse with overhead activities, like serving, and especially with follow through (after ball contact.). Usually, there is little or no pain at rest. Occasionally, there is intermittent catching, clicking or snapping of the shoulder, often associated with pain. There may also be weakness when reaching overhead and loss of velocity and power when trying to serve. The shoulder may feel unstable, slipping in and out of place. There may be pain and weakness in the front of the shoulder with forceful elbow bending, lifting or rotation of the forearm, such as with using a screwdriver. SLAP lesions may be difficult to diagnose on examination alone. An MRI, with or without injection of a fluid into the shoulder joint, can usually confirm the diagnosis, although arthroscopic surgery is sometimes necessary to definitely diagnose a SLAP lesion.

Treatment. Treatment consists of activity modification and strengthening for the scapular stabilizers and rotator cuff muscles. Surgery is recommended if symptoms persist despite nonoperative treatment. Surgery is performed arthroscopically to remove pieces of the labrum or reattach the labrum back to the glenoid, depending upon the type of SLAP tear present. Reattachment may be performed with tacks and/or sutures (thread). If reattachment is undertaken, a period of immobilization is usually recom-

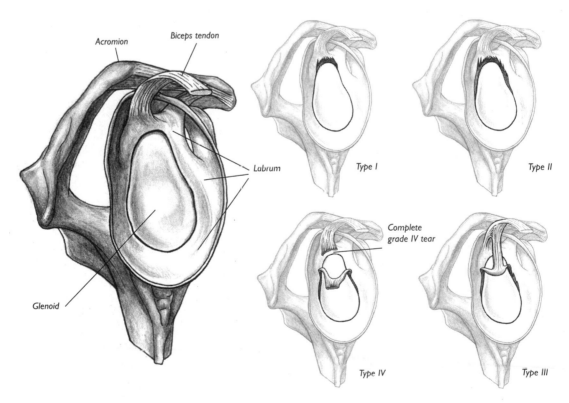

Figure 7.16
SLAP lesions are classified from I to IV. A type I tear or degeneration is confined to the superior labrum. In a type II tear the labrum and biceps tendon are detached from the superior glenoid. A type III is a bucket handle tear of the superior labrum. A type IV is a bucket handle tear of the superior labrum with lateral extension into the biceps tendon.

mended after surgery to allow the labrum to heal, following which physical therapy to regain shoulder range of motion and strength is initiated.

Practical tips for the player

- Increase the strength and endurance of the rotator cuff and scapular stabilizers as well as the biceps and triceps muscles. Good exercises are extensions, scapular retraction, push-ups against the wall, external rotation, biceps cursl, triceps kick bcks, and dumb bell rows. See Figures 28.1, 28.2, 28.5, 28.6, 28.7, 28.31, 28.32, and 28.21-28.23 for instructions.

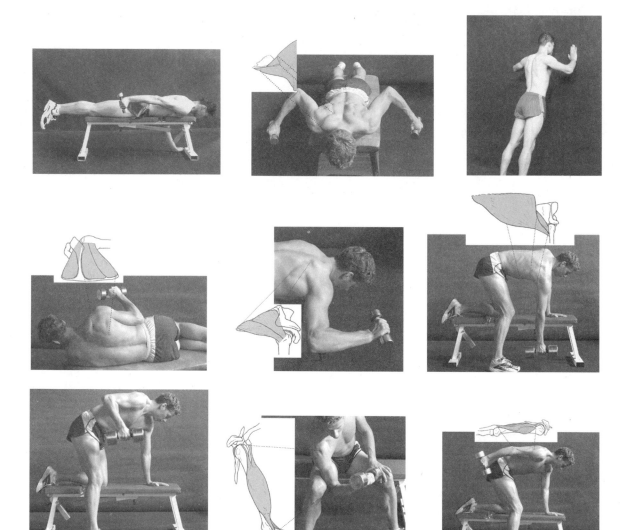

- Stretch the muscles at the back of the shoulder. See Figure 5.13 for instructions.

SNAPPING SCAPULA

Description. This is a condition characterized by pain in the region of the shoulder blade or base of the neck. Oftentimes a "snapping" or "grating" of the shoulder blade (scapula) can be heard or felt by the athlete during movements of the arm. The snapping may be painless. However, when painful, it can interfere with normal shoulder function. The snapping is usually caused by rubbing of the bony prominences of the scapula against the chest wall (ribs). Bursae, thin sacs which provide a gliding surface, are present between the scapula and chest wall to help reduce friction. These bursae may become inflamed (bursitis) and thickened by the constant rubbing of the scapula on the ribs. Bony and soft tissue alterations of the scapula (due to normal variants, benign or malignant tumors, or fractures), or weakness of one or more of the muscles which control scapula movement, may cause the shoulder blade to snap or grate. This problem may be accentuated by repetitive overhead motions, such as serving and overheads.

Symptoms. Players with this condition complain of snapping, grating and/or popping of the scapula at the back of the shoulder, with or without associated discomfort. Sometimes the scapula will feel like it is jumping out of place. There may be a bump seen or felt on the scapula. The affected scapula may be prominent, causing pain when sitting in a high back chair. Injection of a local anesthetic into the area where the snapping and pain are located should provide immediate relief of pain, confirming the diagnosis. A CT-scan or MRI is often necessary to identify prominences of the scapula or ribs, which may be responsible for the snapping.

Treatment. A period of rest and anti-inflammatory medications to reduce any inflammation of the bursae is generally recommended. A careful program of stretching and strengthening exercises of the rotaor cuff muscles and scapular stabilizing muscles may alter the movement of the scapula on the chest wall and reduce symptoms. An injection of cortisone into the inflamed bursa may be recommended. Surgery to remove the bursa, bony prominences or soft tissue masses may be recommended if conservative treatment is unsuccessful.

Practical tips for the player
- Strengthen the scapular stabilizers. Recommended exercises are extensions, scapular retraction, and dumbbell rows. See Figures 28.1, 28.2, 28.31, 28.32 for instructions.

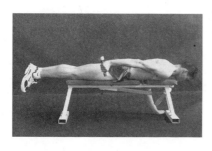

SEPARATED SHOULDER (ACROMIOCLAVICULAR JOINT SEPARATION)

Description. A separated shoulder or acromioclavicular joint separation is a sprain (partial or complete tear) of the ligaments on the top of the shoulder where the collarbone (clavicle) attaches to the roof of the shoulder (acromion). This injury most commonly occurs as a result of a direct blow to the shoulder, such as a fall onto the shoulder, and less commonly due to a fall on an outstretched hand or onto the elbow. In tennis, these situations may occur when diving for a ball, or losing balance and falling during play.

Symptoms. Players who sustain this injury complain of pain on top of the shoulder, at the acromioclavicular joint. There may be some swelling and a small or large bump may be present, depending on the severity of the injury. There is generally loss of strength due to pain when attempting overhead activities (such as with serving or overheads) or reaching across the body (such as preparing to hit a backhand if the injury involves the dominant shoulder). Radiographs that include both joints to assess symmetry or radiographs taken with weights suspended from each wrist will provide the diagnosis.

Treatment. Initial treatment at the time of injury consists of application of ice to the area. A sling or figure of eight brace may be used to rest the arm for comfort. The symptoms of a separated shoulder usually subside with time. Depending on the severity of the injury, this may take a few days or several weeks. Generally, nonoperative treatment is recommended and is successful for most sprains of the acromioclavicular joint, with full return to activity and no loss of strength. Surgical treatment is usually reserved for those with severe sprains, especially if it involves the dominant arm in an overhead athlete such as a tennis player. Surgery involves repair and/or reconstruction of the torn ligaments around the acromio-clavicular joint. A screw or pin may be used to hold the proper position of the joint while healing takes place. Return to sport following a separated shoulder varies with which arm is injured (dominant versus nondominant), use of a one-handed or two-handed backhand (if nondominant arm) and severity of injury. Injury to the acromio-clavicular joint can result in development of arthritis involving the joint years later.

Figure 7.17

Pendulum exercises.

Practical tips for the player

• Perform pendulum exercises to prevent shoulder stiffness (Figure 7.17). Lean over a table with the normal arm allowing the injured arm to hang straight down. Move in a counter-clockwise and clockwise position and then in a flexion and extension motion.

• If the injury involves the dominant shoulder, avoid overheads, serves and backhands early in the recovery period. If it involves the nondominant shoulder there may be pain on the toss and the follow through of the two-handed backhand, and these should be avoided

early in the recovery period.
- A key point is that playing with a separated shoulder rarely leads to further injury, so pain should be the guide.

CLAVICULAR OSTEOLYSIS

Description. Clavicular osteolysis is an overuse injury to the acromioclavicular (AC) joint at the end of the collarbone (clavicle) at the roof of the shoulder (acromion). The end of the collarbone resorbs as part of a slow dissolving process. The cause is unclear, but may be a reaction to stress or stress fracture of the end of the collarbone. This is in response to repeated trauma, such as serving, but may also be due to a traumatic event, such as falling on the shoulder. The clavicle moves at the AC joint with reaching overhead and reaching across the body. Thus, tennis players are susceptible to this problem due to the repeated overhead swinging of the racket during serving and the cross body actions required for preparation during a backhand and the follow through with the forehand.

Symptoms. There is a diffuse discomfort or ache, tenderness and swelling on the top of the shoulder. The pain is worsened with reaching across the body. The symptoms usually start slowly and insidiously following tennis, and progress to affect strokes or workouts with weights. Occasionally the pain may become constant.

Treatment. Initial treatment consists of anti-inflammatory medications and ice to relieve pain, and discontinuing activities that cause the symptoms, such as tennis and weight-lifting. Cortisone injections of the AC joint may be attempted to reduce the pain and inflammation. If symptoms persist despite conservative treatment, surgery to remove the end of the collarbone is indicated. Surgery is very successful in resolving the pain, with full return to activity and no weakness.

Practical tips for the player
- During strength training, push ups and bench press may provoke the pain. These exercises should be temporarily avoided.
- Big wind-ups/preparation for the backhand and crossing the body completely for the forehand follow through may irritate the AC joint. It may be helpful to shorten your swing and follow through.

AC ARTHRITIS

Description. Acromio-clavicular (AC) arthritis is degenerative arthritis of the AC joint: the joint where the roof of the shoulder (acromion) meets the end of the collarbone (clavicle). With degenerative arthritis, the cartilage of the joint wears out as a result of overuse or trauma (e.g. a fall on the shoulder). The AC joint moves with any shoulder motion, especially with reaching overhead (serving, overheads) and reaching across the body (backhands, follow through with the forehand).

Symptoms. There is a diffuse discomfort or ache, tenderness and swelling at the AC joint (top of the shoulder). The pain is worsened with reaching across the body. The symptoms usually start slowly and insidiously following tennis, and progress to cause pain during backhand wind up and forehand follow through. There often is pain when laying on the affected shoulder. The pain may become constant. Pain is alleviated by avoiding the activities which make it hurt, such as weight lifting and tennis play.

Treatment. Initial treatment consists of anti-inflammatory medications and ice to relieve pain, and discontinuing activities that cause the symptoms (including tennis play or the strokes that cause the pain). Cortisone injections of the AC joint may be attempted to reduce the pain and inflammation. If symptoms persist despite conservative treatment, surgery to remove the end of the collarbone is indicated. After surgery, full return to activity will be possible.

Practical tips for the player
- During strength training, push ups and bench press may provoke the pain and should be avoided.
- Big wind-ups/preparation for the backhand and crossing the body completely for the forehand follow through may irritate the AC joint. It may be helpful to shorten your swing and follow through.

BICEPS TENDINOPATHY (TENDINITIS)

Description. Biceps tendinopathy (tendinitis) causes pain at the front of the shoulder and upper arm due to strain and degeneration of the upper biceps tendon, which may be accompanied by inflammation of the tendon sheath (tenosynovitis). The biceps tendon is one of the anchor points of the biceps muscle, which functions in bending the elbow, rotating the forearm, and accelerating and decelerating the arm. It also helps stabilize the shoulder. Biceps tendinopathy often occurs as a result of overuse, often due to a sudden increase in amount or intensity of activity. Tenosynovitis becomes more likely with repeated injury to the biceps muscle-tendon unit, though it may also be the result of a direct blow or injury to the shoulder. It may also be seen in association with impingement syndrome, rotator cuff injury, or other shoulder problems. Serving, hitting overheads or hitting high topspin forehands particularly stress the biceps tendon (Figure 7.18).

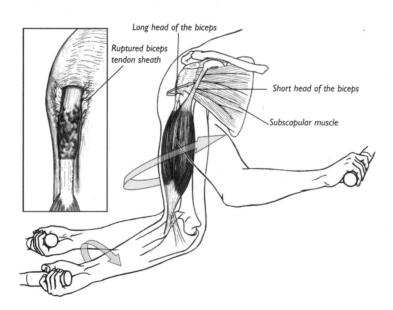

Long head of the biceps

Ruptured biceps tendon sheath

Short head of the biceps

Subscapular muscle

Figure 7.18
Biceps tendinopathy may be caused by the repetitive stress of hitting high topspin forehands. Rupture of the transverse humeral ligament may occur, resulting in biceps tendon subluxation.

Symptoms. Players with biceps tendinopathy or tenosynovitis generally complain of pain over the front of the shoulder. Lifting, hitting balls and the overhead position may be painful. There may be crepitation when the tendon or shoulder is moved or touched. X-rays are not helpful in diagnosing in this condition, however, an MRI, if performed, may show fluid within or around the tendon.

Treatment. Initial treatment consists of rest, anti-inflammatory medications and cooling with ice. A cortisone injection may be given into the sheath around the tendon to help reduce inflammation. Exercises to strengthen the biceps may be initiated once pain has subsided. If symptoms do not improve with nonoperative measures, arthroscopic surgery may be considered to remove the inflamed tendon lining and any unhealthy tendon that is present. In cases where the tendon is severely degenerated, detachment of the degenerated tendon from the shoulder socket (glenoid) and reattachment into the upper part of the arm bone may be required.

Practical tips for the player

- Strengthen the muscles of the elbow, shoulder and shoulder blade. Recommended exercises are extensions, scapular retraction, serratus anterior punch, external rotation, biceps curls, triceps kick-backs, and dumbbell rows. See Figures 28.1-28.4, 28.6-28.7, 28.21-28.23, and 28.31-28.32 for instructions.

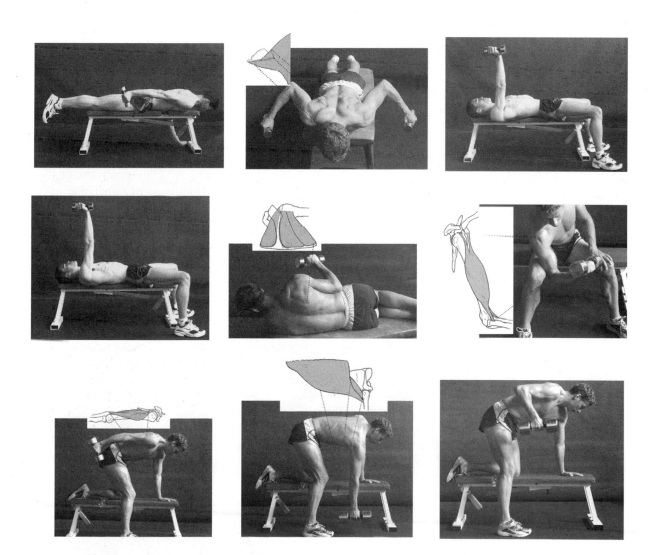

- Stretch the biceps as follows. Sit or stand up straight and turn the palm of the hand toward the floor. Extend the elbow and shoulder behind you until you feel a stretch.
- When returning to practice, gradually build up overheads and serves.

BICEPS TENDON RUPTURE AT THE SHOULDER

Description. A proximal brachial biceps tendon rupture is a result of rupturing the tendon at the shoulder. These ruptures are more common in patients who are over 50 years old. They involve the long head of the tendon occur more frequently than of the short-head or the distal tendon. Long-head tendon ruptures are often associated with impingement, rotator cuff tendinopathy and rotator cuff tears. Repetitive strenuous activity often leads to ruptures of the long head tendon.

Symptoms. At the time of injury, there is immediate pain at the front of the shoulder joint and occasionally mid upper arm. A snap or pop may also occur. Bruising and swelling involving the upper arm and elbow may develop over 24-48 hours. There will be tenderness at the front of the shoulder, and usually an obvious bulging of the biceps if the elbow is bent against resistance (Popeye sign). If the diagnosis is in doubt, ultrasound or MRI can be performed to identify the ruptured tendon.

Treatment. Initial treatment at the time of injury consists of rest from the offending activity and cooling with ice. After the discomfort from the initial injury subsides over a period of days or weeks, players usually do not notice any significant loss of arm or shoulder function following a biceps tendon rupture at the shoulder. This is because the short-head biceps tendon attachment remains intact. A slight bulge in the arm, and some twitching of the retracted muscle are usually the most significant symptoms. For this reason, surgical repair of the proximal biceps tendon is usually only considered in the younger player. Range of motion and rotator cuff and scapular stabilizing exercises may be beneficial in preventing stiffness and maintaining strength following long-head biceps rupture.

Practical tips for the player.
- Recommended exercises are pendulum exercises, extensions, scapular retraction, external rotation, and dumb bell rows. See Figures 7.17, 28.1-28.2, 28.6-28.7, and 28.31-28.32 for instructions.

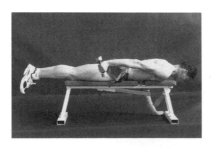
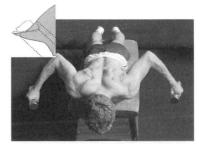
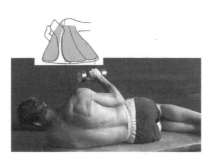

BICEPS TENDON SUBLUXATION

Description. The biceps muscle is attached to the bone via tendons - two at the shoulder and one in the elbow (Figure 7.18). The long head of the biceps (the one on the left in the figure) has a tendon that runs in a groove at the front of the shoulder before entering the shoulder joint. The groove is bordered on three sides by bone and covered by a ligament (transverse humeral ligament). The tendon should remain in the groove during motion of the shoulder and arm. If it moves in and out of the groove, this is biceps tendon subluxation. This rarely occurs without other shoulder problems, most often with a partial or complete tear of the subscapularis tendon (one of the rotator cuff muscles). A biceps tendon injury usually occurs with a quick, forceful pressure or jerking with the forearm. It may occur during tennis, as a result of the repetitive stress during serving and hitting topspin forehands, leading to degenerative injury to the rotator cuff.

Symptoms. Players with biceps tendon subluxation generally complain of pain and popping, catching or clicking in the front of the shoulder. There may be tenderness and mild swelling over the front of the shoulder. The player may also note crepitation (a crackling sound) when the shoulder is moved. When the arm is raised from the side and rotated in and out the tendon may be felt slipping in and out of the groove, resulting in pain and clunking in the area. This abnormal movement be well visualized using ultrasound or X-rays following injection of dye into the tendon sheath. MRI may show fluid around the inflamed tendon or the tendon lying outside the groove. MRI is also helpful in identifying any associated tears of the rotator cuff tendons.

Treatment. Conservative treatment consists of resting the arm to prevent rotation and tendon subluxation. Persistent subluxation may result in tendon rupture and surgical treatment is often necessary. It consists of repair of any rotator cuff tear that may be present along with attachment of the biceps tendon into the groove (tenodesis). This should be followed by range of motion and strengthening exercises.

> *Practical tips for the player*
> * Perform pendulum exercises to prevent shoulder stiffness and improve range of motion. See Figure 7.17 for instructions.

WASTING OF THE MUSCLES AT THE BACK OF THE SHOULDER (SUPRASCAPULAR NEUROPATHY)

Description. This uncommon nerve condition in the shoulder involves dysfunction of the suprascapular nerve. It usually results from stretching of the nerve due to repetitive forceful movements such as serving and hitting overheads and forehands. It can also result from compression of the nerve at the back of the shoulder, by the ligaments under which the nerve passes, or by a cyst originating from the shoulder joint.

The suprascapular nerve passes in a groove in the shoulder blade (scapula), under a ligament, and then under the supraspinatus muscle (which it supplies). It then runs under another ligament before it supplies the infraspinatus muscle (Figure 7.19). The nerve may be injured before it supplies the supraspinatus muscle (and thus causing weakness of both the supraspinatus and infraspinatus) or after it supplies the supraspinatus (causing weakness and wasting of only the infraspinatus, Figure 7.20).

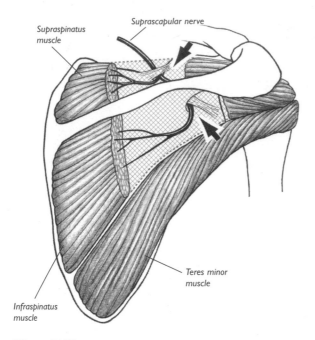

Figure 7.19
Suprascapular nerve entrapment.

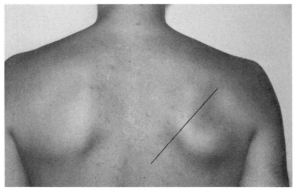

Figure 7.20
Wasting of the infraspinatus muscle of the right shoulder.

These muscles, which are part of the rotator cuff, are important in stabilizing the shoulder and in raising and rotating the shoulder and arm.

Symptoms. Players with this condition may complain of pain and discomfort (burning or dull ache) in the back of the shoulder, and heaviness or fatigue of the shoulder and arm. The pain may be made worse by playing or activities which involve moving the arm across the front of the body (e.g. bringing the hand on the affected side across to touch the unaffected shoulder). There may be weakness with raising the arm overhead (serving) and/or rotating the shoulder outward (one-handed backhand). When the condition becomes more advanced, there will be atrophy (shrinkage) of the supraspinatus and / or infraspinatus muscles in the back of the shoulder when compared visually to the unaffected shoulder.

The diagnosis of a suspected suprascapular nerve problem is confirmed by electrical nerve studies. This can determine the severity of the nerve damage and can be used to monitor recovery. An MRI scan is often recommended to determine whether there is a compressive cyst present.

Treatment. Initial treatment of suprascapular nerve injury is directed primarily at activity modification and rehabilitation (strengthening and flexibility) of the supraspinatus, infraspinatus, and scapular stabilizers. During the rehabilitation phase, movements such as bringing the arm across the front of the body or overhead, which may create tension on the suprascapular nerve, should be avoided. Spinal adjustments will help in improving homeostasis to the area. Improvement may occur in one to two months, although it may take six months or longer for full return of function.

If conservative treatment is not successful, or if a compressive cyst is identified on MRI, surgery may be considered. Surgery may involve freeing the pinched nerve by cutting the ligament which is compressing the nerve. If a cyst is seen on MRI and is thought to be compressing the nerve, the cyst can be removed through an incision in the back of the shoulder or an arthroscopic procedure can be used to empty the cyst and repair associated labral damage inside the shoulder joint which may be present. Surgery may result in significant pain relief, however, atrophy and weakness of the muscles may or may not improve. Interestingly, several successful professional tennis players have significant longstanding muscle atrophy as a result of suprascapular nerve injury, yet they are still able to play at a very high level.

Practical tips for the player

- Stretch the posterior shoulder muscles.
- Routine exercises to strengthen the rotator cuff and scapula stabilizing muscles may be helpful in preventing this problem. Recommended exercises are extensions, scapular retraction, serratus anterior punch, push-ups against the wall, external rotation, and dumbbell rows. See Figures 28.1-28.7, and 28.31-28.32 for instructions.

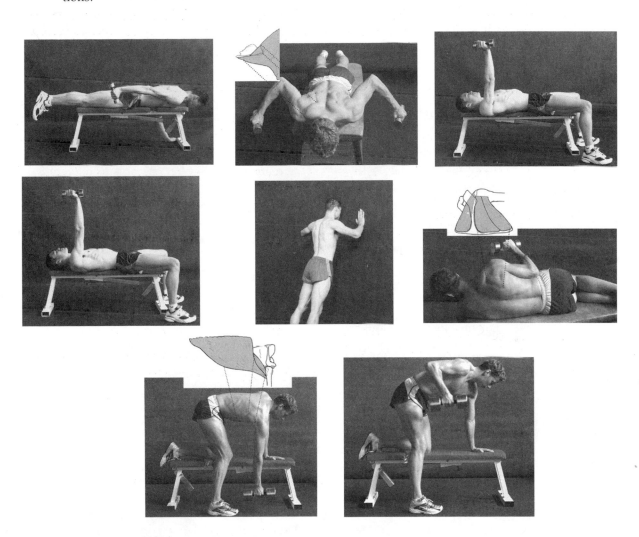

SCAPULAR WINGING
(SERRATUS ANTERIOR PALSY, LONG THORACIC NERVE INJURY)

Description. This is an uncommon nerve condition in the shoulder causing pain and weakness in the shoulder. It involves injury to the long thoracic nerve in the back of the shoulder near the shoulder blade. The long thoracic nerve runs from the neck along the back of the chest wall to supply the serratus anterior muscle. This muscle anchors the shoulder blade to the chest wall. The nerve can be stretched due to a fall on the shoulder, carrying heavy objects (backpack) over the shoulder or with repetitive forceful movements such as the serve in tennis. The nerve may also be damaged as a result of a viral illness. Injury to this nerve results in weakness of the serratus anterior muscle, a main stabilizer of the scapula (shoulder blade). Injury to this nerve causes the scapula to pull away from the chest wall with attempted shoulder movement (winging). Since the scapula is the base from which the shoulder functions, winging causes the shoulder to work off a weak base, making shoulder function weak as well.

Symptoms. Symptoms are pain and discomfort (burning or dull ache) that is poorly localized, often in the back of the shoulder and/or shoulder blade, as well as a heaviness or fatigue of the arm. There is loss of power of the shoulder with daily activities and tennis. There may be difficulty raising the arm above shoulder level and thus inability to serve or hit overheads. The winging becomes more obvious when the athlete tries to perform a push-up. Electrical nerve studies are recommended in order to confirm injury of the long thoracic nerve as the cause of the scapular winging.

Treatment. Activity modification to avoid any aggravating movements (serve) is necessary to allow the nerve to heal. Exercises to maintain shoulder motion and strengthen the rotator cuff and functioning scapular stabilizing muscles is important. This injury usually is accompanied by complete recovery of nerve function, although this may take as long as 18 months or more, depending on the severity of the injury. However, there is the risk of permanent weakness of the shoulder, particularly lifting power and overhead activities, as well as of persistent pain in the shoulder. Stiffness of the shoulder can develop. This injury may result in significant disability and inability to play or practice tennis.

Rarely is surgery indicated for this condition. However, if nonoperative treatment is not successful in restoring satisfactory function due to persistent muscle weakness, surgery may be necessary to replace the lost function of the serratus anterior muscle with a different functioning muscle (muscle transfer). This surgery, considered a salvage operation, is intended to restore function for daily activities and is not likely to allow a tennis player to return to competitive tennis.

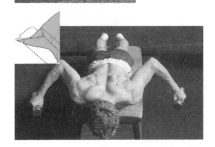

Practical tips for the player
- Performing shoulder range of motion exercises while waiting for nerve recovery is very important for preventing shoulder stiffness. Strengthing the scapular stabilizers is also important. Recommended exercises are pendulum exercises, scapular retraction, and serratus anterior punch. See Figures 7.17, and 28.2-28.4 for instructions.

THORACIC OUTLET SYNDROME

Description. The thoracic outlet is the space between the thorax (rib cage) and the clavicle (collar bone) through which the main blood vessels and nerves pass from the neck and thorax into the arm. The nerves and blood vessels leave the neck between the two scalene muscles, anterior and middle scalenes. Thoracic outlet syndrome may be characterized by pain, weakness, numbness, tingling, swelling, discoloration or coolness of the affected, shoulder or hand from compression of these nerves, and less commonly the arteries and veins. In tennis players, pressure on these structures is usually caused by the repetitive overhead motion of the serve. An extra rib in the lower neck (cervical rib), over-developed neck muscles, and/or drooping of the shoulder (tennis shoulder), may contribute to this problem. Other causes include abnormal positioning of the arm or neck for a prolonged period, such as can occur while undergoing surgery, or while sleeping, especially with a firm pillow under the neck. Rarely, a tumor that has spread to the head and neck from another part of the body may cause pressure on the nerve/blood vessel bundle.

Symptoms. Athletes with thoracic outlet syndrome usually complain of pain, numbness, and tingling in the neck, shoulders, arms, and/or hands, as well as weakness of the affected arm and hand. If the blood vessels are involved, there may be coldness, swelling and a blue discoloration involving the hand or arm. Symptoms may be aggravated by the repetitive serving motion.

Diagnosis of this condition can be difficult due to the myriad of symptoms which may be present. When compression involves the nerves, electrical nerve testing may be helpful. Arteriography or venography, involving injection of dye into the involved artery or vein, may be necessary when compression of the blood vessels is suspected.

Treatment. Thoracic outlet syndrome responds favorably in most patients to physical therapy, activity modification and a change in sleeping habits. Exercises are aimed at promoting proper shoulder muscle function and improving any posture abnormalities. Surgery to relieve pressure on the nerves and blood vessels may be indicated, particularly if symptoms persist despite activity modification and proper exercises. Surgery usually involves removal of an extra rib or releasing tight muscles or other soft tissue bands at the base of the neck responsible for the compression.

Vascular symptoms such as coldness, swelling, and blueness of the arm or hand signifies an urgent problem which requires immediate treatment (see for more details Chapter 13: "effort-thrombosis" and "axillary-subclavian artery compression").

Practical tips for the player
- Stretch the back of the neck. Sit in a sturdy chair. Turn the head away from the side to be stretched and look down until a slight stretch is felt. Reach down with the hand on the tight side and hold onto the chair. With the other hand pull the head forward, gently. Hold the stretch for twenty seconds and then slowly release it. Wait for ten seconds and repeat the stretch three times.
- Stretch the side of the neck. Sit in a sturdy chair. Hold the underside with the arm of the side to be stretched. Pull the head back making a double chin. Bend the head away from the tight side and turn the head toward the tight side. It will not go very far. Lean away from the arm holding onto the chair and reach with the opposite arm to the top of the head and gently pull to increase the stretch.
- Stretch the chest. Sit in a sturdy backed chair with the hands clasped

behind the back of the head. Bring the elbows back as far as possible while inhaling a slow, deep breath. While exhaling slowly bring the elbows together letting the head bend forward slightly.

- Avoid carrying an heavy bag or backpack over the affected shoulder.
- Improve posture by pulling the chin and abdomen in while sitting or standing. Sit in a firm chair and force the buttocks to touch the chair's back.
- Sleep on a firm mattress to avoid back and neck problems. Choose a soft low, pillow or get a cervical pillow that gives the neck proper support.
- When returning to play, avoid overhead activity initially.

SUMMARY

In this chapter, an overview of common injuries of the shoulder, elbow, wrist and hand in tennis is presented. Specifically, the mechanism of injury, symptoms, causes, treatment, prevention and practical tips for the player are described. The practical tips are relevant both for the prevention and treatment of an injury, and include stretching and strengthening exercises, equipment advice, technical tips, and suggestions for taping and bracing.

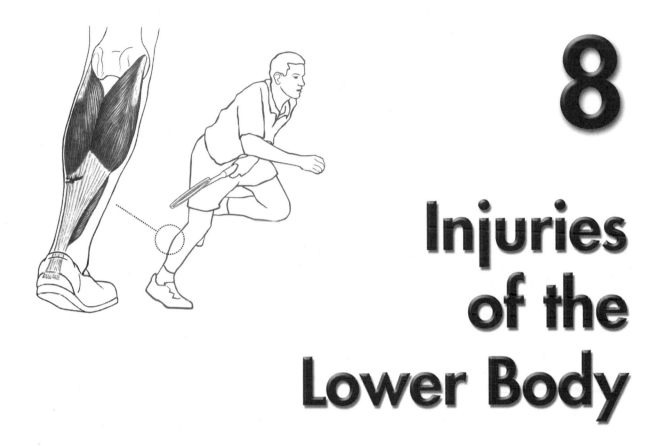

8
Injuries of the Lower Body

In this chapter common injuries of the lower extremity in tennis players are described, including injuries to the hip, thigh, knee, leg, foot and ankle. Most studies show a fairly even distribution of injuries to the upper and lower limb in tennis players. However, unlike the upper extremity, acute injuries tend to predominate over chronic injuries in the lower extremity. This is due to the sudden stops and starts, lunges, jumps and pivoting maneuvers required in tennis play. Ankle sprains and muscle strains occur most frequently. Some of the most common chronic lower extremity injuries are shin splints, anterior knee pain, and tendinopathy of the Achilles tendon.

MUSCLE STRAINS

Description. Muscle strains, also called partial muscle tears or muscle pulls, commonly occur in the muscles of the thigh and lower leg. The thigh has three sets of strong muscles—the hamstring muscles in the back, the quadriceps muscles in the front, and the adductor muscles on the inside. The lower leg has two strong muscle groups in the back—the gastrocnemius on the surface and the soleus beneath. In additon, there are several smaller muscle groups at the front and sides of the lower leg.

The hamstring, quadriceps and gastrocnemius muscle sets are particularly at risk for muscle strains because they cross two joints—the hamstrings and quadriceps cross both the hip and knee joints, and the gastrocnemius crosses the knee and ankle joints.

Muscles attach to bone through their tendons. Tendon is tough, noncontractile fibrous connective tissue. The junction between the muscle and the tendon is where the muscle is most susceptible to injury. Muscle tears usually result from a muscle being stretched beyond its limit, or, a muscle forcefully contracting against a fixed resistance. An example is stumbling forward and catching the foot on the ground as the quadriceps muscle forcefully contracts to prevent falling, causing tearing of the muscle fibers, most commonly in the junctional area.

Symptoms. Muscle strains can be classified based upon their severity. A grade 1 strain is a "slight pull" without obvious tearing (it is microscopic tearing). There is mild pain, which may prevent the player from continuing to play. There is usually no significant loss of strength. A grade 2 strain results in tearing of some of the fibers within the substance of the muscle. There is significant pain, which usually causes the player to stop playing. There may be difficulty bearing full weight on the affected leg and there is decreased strength. Swelling and bruising may develop within 24-48 hours following the injury. A grade 3 strain is a tear of all the fibers of the muscle. There is marked pain with difficulty or inability to bear weight on the leg. Swelling and bruising develop within 24-48 hours. There is significant loss of strength and a gap in the muscle can often be felt at the site of injury. Grade 1 and grade 2 strains are most common. Muscle strains may take days to weeks to heal, depending on the severity of the injury. Ultrasound or MRI may be helpful, especially in high level players, in determining the severity of the injury and estimating the time until return to competition. In most cases, rest and rehabilitation will promote muscle healing and return to tennis. In some cases of grade 3 strains, surgery may be necessary to prevent chronic pain and weakness.

Treatment. Initial treatment consists of RICE: rest from the offending activity (stop playing); cooling with ice for ten to fifteen minutes; a compression bandage to minimize bleeding and swelling; and elevation of the leg. Crutches may be necessary, especially in grade 2 and 3 injuries, and should be used until walking is relatively comfortable. In the days following injury, electrical stimulation may be used to reduce pain and swelling. Massage may be helpful in alleviating muscle spasm, however, massage directly over the injury site should be avoided in the acute phase, to minimize the risk of myositis ossificans (bone formation within the injured muscle). As pain and swelling improve, the muscle rehabilitation process can gradually be started. This consists of gentle stretching exercises of the affected muscles to gradually regain range of motion and progressive muscle strengthening.

Practical tips for the player (all muscle strains)
- When returning to play, make sure to perform a complete warm up before and cool down after play of ten to fifteen minutes each. Include stretching exercises for all leg muscles.
- Taping, elastic bandage or neoprene (wet suit material) sleeve may be used to protect and warm the muscles when returning to play.
- Adapt clothing to the weather conditions. Particularly at the start of the season or if there is cold temperatures or a biting wind, it may be wise to keep your tracksuit or running tights on during the warm up. Well-warmed muscles and tendons are better able to withstand forces that cause muscle strains than cold muscles.

TENNIS LEG (CALF MUSCLE STRAIN)

Description. A "tennis leg" is an incomplete rupture of the inner part (medial head) of the superficial calf muscle (gastrocnemius muscle). It is a common tennis injury in players in the 35 to 50 age group. The injury affects the junction between muscle and tendon (Figure 8.1). It is caused most commonly by a sudden forceful pushing off of the foot such as with jumping, landing, serving, lunging or a sudden sprint to the ball, when the muscle is stretched beyond its limit.

Symptoms. At the instant of injury, the player often feels like he has been being kicked or hit in the calf, sometimes accompanied by an audible pop. Pain, tenderness, swelling, warmth and/or redness develops over the calf and occasionally this is accompanied by muscle spasms of the calf. There is pain and weakness with pushing down with the front of the foot, such as when trying to stand on tiptoe or walking, as well as pain with stretching the calf. Bruising in the calf, ankle, heel and occasionally foot may develop 24 or more hours following the injury as a result of bleeding from the torn muscle fibers.

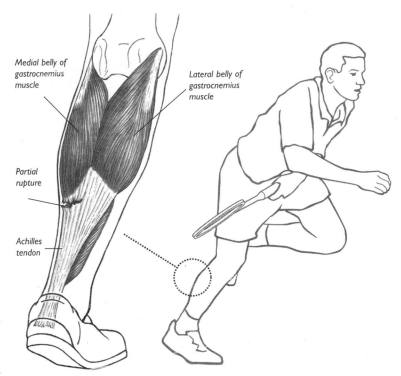

Medial belly of gastrocnemius muscle

Lateral belly of gastrocnemius muscle

Partial rupture

Achilles tendon

Figure 8.1

A tennis leg is a muscle strain of the inner part of the superficial calf muscle (gastrocnemius).

Treatment. See general section on muscle strains.

Practical tips for the player

- Perform daily stretching exercises for the calf muscles. There are two stretching exercises, one for the gastrocnemius (superficial calf muscle), and one for the soleus (deep calf muscle). See Figures 5.3 and 5.4 for instructions.

- Wear properly fitting tennis shoes with good shock absorption, side-to-side stability, proper traction on the playing surface, and optimal comfort.

- Stretch and massage your calf muscles if they feel stiff and tense.
- Maintain strong calf muscles, with adequate rest in your training program. Good exercises are swimming, cycling, balance exercises on one leg, calf raises, hopping on one foot, walking, stair climbing, and slow jogging. See Figures 28.65 (calf raise) and 28.66 (hopping on one foot) for instructions.

- Aqua jogging or running and jumping in shallow water is also recommended.

STRAIN OF THE ANTERIOR THIGH (QUADRICEPS MUSCLES)

Description. A strain of the quadriceps muscles is characterized by pain in the front of the thigh, usually as a result of injury to the rectus femoris muscle (Figure 8.2). This injury may arise from a sudden contraction of the quadriceps muscles, such as during sprinting, serving, or jumping, or a sudden increase in amount or intensity of activity, such as a long match. If serving is the cause of the injury, the affected limb is usually the leg opposite to the serving arm, due to the repetitive concentric (push off) and eccentric (landing) muscle actions that are required of this leg during the service motion.

Figure 8.2

A strain of the quadriceps muscles usually arises from a sudden contraction of these muscles.

Symptoms. There is sharp pain at the time of injury, followed by tenderness, and possibly swelling and warmth over the affected area at the front of the thigh. The pain is usually worse with activity. The player may note muscle spasm in the thigh, as well as pain and/or weakness with running, jumping, serving, or straightening the knee against resistance. If the injury is more severe, bruising may develop in the thigh 24-48 hours following the injury. There may be a palpable indentation in the body of the muscle or a visible area of muscle bulging with complete rupture. It may also be painful to fully bend the knee after this injury.

Treatment. See general section on muscle strains.

Practical tips for the player

- Perform daily stretching exercises for the quadriceps muscles. See Figure 5.5. for instructions.
- Strong leg muscles may help to reduce injury risk. Preventative strengthening exercises for the quadriceps muscles, such as half squats, step-ups, and lunges should be included in the training program. See Figures 28.61 to 28.64 for instructions.

  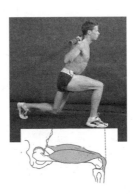

STRAIN OF THE POSTERIOR THIGH (HAMSTRING MUSCLES)

Description. A hamstring strain is the most common injury of the thigh (Figure 8.3). Symptoms are pain, tenderness, swelling, warmth and/or redness over the hamstring muscles at the back of the thigh. The pain is worse during and after strenuous activity. The player notes muscle spasms in the back of the thigh over the area of the strain.

Symptoms. Symptoms are pain and/or weakness during running, jumping, or bending the knee against resistance. With acute severe strains, the player may note bruising in the thigh within 48 hours following the injury. Occasionally there will be loss of fullness of the muscle or muscle bulging with complete rupture. A hamstring strain may occur from overuse, or from a sudden eccentric contraction of the muscle, as occurs during sprinting, sliding, and lunging. Other factors that increase the risk of hamstring strains in athletes include tight or shortened hamstrings, hamstring muscle weakness relative to the quadriceps muscles, and previous injury of the thigh, knee, or pelvis.

Treatment. See general section on muscle strains.

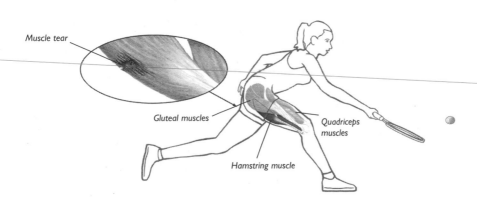

Figure 8.3
A strain of the hamstring muscles.

Muscle tear

Gluteal muscles

Quadriceps muscles

Hamstring muscle

Practical tips for the player

- Sprinting exercises carry high risk of hamstring overload and strains. Give time for adequate rest and recovery following sprint training.
- Perform daily stretching exercises for the hamstring muscles. See Figure 5.6 for instructions.
- Strong leg muscles may help to reduce injury risk. Preventative strengthening exercises for the hamstring and hip muscles, such as good mornings, half squats, step ups, and lunges, should be included in the training program (See Figures 28.52 and 28.61-28.64 for instructions).

STRAIN OF THE INNER THIGH (ADDUCTOR MUSCLES)

Description. An adductor muscle strain is a partial tear of the inner thigh muscles (Figure 8.4). The injury occurs at the junction between the muscle and tendon or at the tendon attachment into the pelvic bone. Adductor muscle strains are encountered frequently in tennis, because the sport requires strong eccentric contraction of the adductor musculature during rapid acceleration, side to side movements and sudden stops and changes of direction. When playing on grass or clay, the main cause is unstable footing, which often leads to slipping and over extension of the groin muscles (split). On hard courts and many indoor surfaces, however, good traction can also lead to injury when one attempts to recover from the lateral movements (e.g., in running for a wide ball). Risk factors include periods of prolonged overuse, a sudden increase in amount or intensity of activity, and insufficient adductor muscle strength.

Symptoms. A sudden sharp pain may be felt in the groin area or inner thigh. There may be tightening of the groin muscles that may not be present until the day after competition. There is tenderness on palpation of the adductor tendons or the insertion on the pubic bone, and groin pain during adduction against resistance. There may be bruising or swelling, although this might not occur until a couple of days after the initial injury. With a severe injury, a lump or gap may be felt in the adductor muscles.

Treatment. See general section on muscle strains.

Practical tips for the player

- Strengthening exercises for the abductor (outer hip) and adductor (groin) muscles have been shown to be an effective method of reducing the incidence of adductor strains.

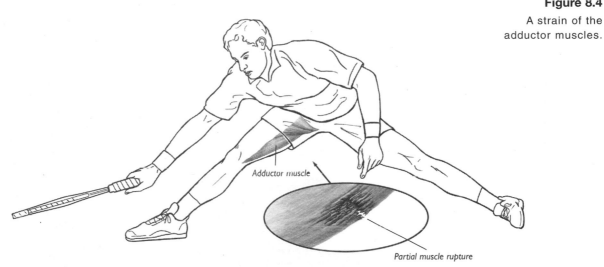

Figure 8.4
A strain of the
adductor muscles.

Adductor muscle

Partial muscle rupture

- Recommended exercises for the adductor muscles include ball
  squeezes with bent and with straight legs (Figure 8.5-8.6), straight
  leg raises (Figure 28.58), adduction against elastic resistance (28.60),
  side lunges, slide skating, and using a seated adduction machine.

Figure 8.5 and 8.6
Ball squeeze

Sit down with your knees
straight and place a ball
between your knees. Once the
ball is in place, gradually
squeeze the knees together.
This activates the adductor muscles that have been strained.
Hold the squeeze for about six
seconds, then relax a few seconds. Repeat this sequence of
"squeeze and relax" six times
and then rest for a minute.
Perform four sets of six repetitions. Repeat the exercise with
your knees bent.

- Recommended exercises for the abductor muscles of the hip include sideward leg raises (Figure 28.56 and 28.57), abduction against elastic resistance (Figure 28.59), and the seated abduction machine.

- When returning to play, make sure to perform a complete warm up before and cool down after play of ten to fifteen minutes each. Include stretching exercises for the adductor muscles (Figure 5.7 and 5.8).

STRESS FRACTURES

Stress fractures are breaks which occur in bones that undergo repeated loading, but are not sufficiently strong to withstand these forces. These fractures may occur in normal bone subject to excessive loads (fatigue fractures) or in abnormally weakened bone (insufficiency fractures). Athletes most frequently experience fatigue fractures although, insufficiency fractures are common, particularly in female athletes with osteoporosis (see female athlete triad). A stress fracture develops as repeated stresses on the bone result in a tiny, almost invisible, break in the bone structure called a micro-fracture. At this stage, an adequate period of rest normally allows the body to heal the micro-fracture. However, continued training or playing can cause these fractures to become larger and more symptomatic, eventually requiring treatment such as immobilization, casting or surgery.

Although a stress fracture can develop in any bone, the tibia (shin bone) is most commonly affected in athletes, followed by the metatarsals (forefoot). Other less common sites of stress fractures in the lower extremities include the neck of the femur (upper part of the thigh bone), the fibula (lower leg bone adjacent to the tibia), the talus (ankle bone) and the navicula (midfoot bone). Stress fractures usually occur after a sudden increase in the intensity or duration of training and competition. Other risk factors include metabolic disorders, obesity, malalignment, inadequate footwear, hormonal problems (amenorrhea), and nutritional deficiencies and eating disorders (anorexia and/or bulimia).

Since stress fractures initially are very tiny breaks, routine X-rays may not identify the problem. If there is suspicion of a stress fracture with normal X-rays, a bone scan, CT scan or MRI may be necessary to confirm the diagnosis.

STRESS FRACTURE OF THE FOREFOOT (METATARSALS)

Description. This fracture can occur anywhere within any of the five metatarsals, though it most commonly affects the lower third of the second metatarsal or the upper part of the fifth metatarsal.

Symptoms. Tennis players encountered with this problem usually complain of a vague, diffuse pain in the forefoot area. There is tenderness directly over the area of the stress fracture and there may be mild swelling in the foot. The pain is typically aggravated by weight-bearing activities such as walking, running, and playing tennis.

Treatment. If a metatarsal stress fracture is detected in its early stages, a period of rest from any running is initiated. The use of crutches and some form of immobilization or support (orthotics, a stiff-soled shoe, splinting, bandaging, casting, or bracing) may be recommended in order to protect the bone while it heals. Healing usually progresses uneventfully over a period of several weeks to three months. Stress fractures of the metatarsal that do not heal properly despite appropriate nonoperative treatment require surgical treatment with screws and/or plates in order to promote healing.

One particularly troublesome metatarsal stress fracture occurs at the base of the fifth metatarsal. This fracture generally requires immobilization and avoidance of any weight bearing activities and may take several months to fully heal. In some cases, particularly in competitive athletes, surgical treatment of the fracture may be recommended as the primary form of treatment in order to return the athlete back to competition as quickly as possible.

Hormonal, nutritional, alignment and metabolic abnormalities need to be identified and treated appropriately to help healing and prevent recurrence.

STRESS FRACTURE OF THE LOWER LEG (TIBIA AND FIBULA)

Description. A stress fracture of the lower leg can be located in the shin bone (tibia) or the smaller leg bone (fibula).

Symptoms. Players with lower leg stress fractures usually complain of vague, diffuse pain or aching in the leg and/or calf. There is tenderness of the bone at the site of the fracture. Mild localized swelling may be present as well. The pain is usually aggravated by weight-bearing activities such as walking, running, and playing tennis.

Treatment. Crutches may be needed in the early phase if there is pain during weight-bearing. Immobilization by splinting, casting or bracing is usually recommended to protect the bones while they heal. Stress fractures that are located in the fibula or high or low in the tibia tend to heal well in four to eight weeks. Stress fractures that involve the front part of the middle third of the tibia may take a longer time to heal, and must be treated with special attention. Bone stimulators, which provide electrical currents or sound waves to the bone may be used to promote bone healing. Hormonal, nutritional, alignment and metabolic abnormalities should be identified and treated appropriately to help healing and prevent recurrence.

Practical tips for the player for all stress fractures

- Wear appropriately sized and fitted shoes. Regularly change tennis shoes, and change running shoes after 300-500 miles of running.
- Gradually increase activity and training, usually no more than ten percent per week. This is particularly important for footwork exercises, running, and skipping.
- Use cushioned arch supports for flat feet.
- Strengthen the foot and ankle, to avoid sudden rolling of the ankle. It may also be helpful to protect the ankle with supportive devices, such as tape, braces, or high top athletic shoes.
- Writing the alphabet in the air or folding a towel by grasping it with the toes strengthens the foot muscles (see Figure 28.69 for instructions).
- Keeping you balance while standing on one leg strengthens the ankle muscles (see Figure 8.17 for instructions).

BUMP ON THE FOOT (BUNION)

Description. When the base of the big toe extends beyond the normal contours of the foot, the bump that results is called a bunion. This occurs when the big toe bends towards the next toe, sometimes overlapping it (hallux valgus). Bunions occur more often in women than in men. The condition may be genetic (born with or predisposed, with others in the family having it), but more often it results from forcing the foot into a tight shoe with high heels and a pointed toe.

Symptoms. The bunion is often subjected to constant rubbing, which may result in thickening of the skin or bursitis, with redness, tenderness and swelling. Sometimes a player may complain of foot pain and stiffness.

Treatment. In case of bursitis, take a couple of days rest and anti-inflammatory medications and apply ice (not directly on the skin; 15-30 minutes every few hours) to help reduce inflammation and pain. Sometimes the doctor may refer the player for surgical consideration. This involves removing the overgrown tissue (bunion) and correct the position of the first toe by realigning the bones. This is usually performed as an outpatient operation (go home the same day).

Practical tips for the player

- Wear a tennis shoe with a wide toe box.
- Apply a pad with the center cut out to reduce pressure on the bunion.
- Wear appropriate footwear not only on but also off the court (no narrow shoes with high heels).

- Wear a brace or small pad at night between the big toe and second toe to prevent overlap;
- Use orthotics (Figure 8.7) to correct excessive pronation (inward turning of the feet).

Figure 8.7
Orthotics lend support to the arch of the foot.

TURF TOE

Description. Turf toe is a hyperextension sprain of the joint at the base of the big toe (metatarsophalangeal joint), with stretching or tearing of the capsule and ligaments (Figure 8.8). The injury is most likely to occur on higher friction hard court surfaces, than on grass or clay. During a sudden stop, the foot may slide forward in the shoe, causing forced upward bending of the big toe. Players with pronated feet or other foot malalignments that increase the load on the inner side of the foot are at increased risk for this injury.

Symptoms. At the time of injury, there will be pain localized to the area at the base of the great toe. Running and especially push-off will be painful. There is tenderness primarily on the underside (sole) of the joint. Movement of the great toe, especially extension (lifting the toe up) is painful. Swelling generally develops over several hours following injury. X-rays, which may be taken to determine whether a fracture is present, will be normal in this soft tissue injury.

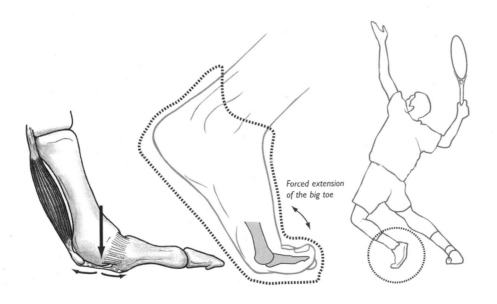

Forced extension
of the big toe

Figure 8.8
A turf toe is due to forced or repetitive (hyper-)extension of the big toe.

Treatment. Initial treatment consists of RICE: rest from the offending activity; cooling with ice for ten to fifteen minutes; a compression bandage to reduce the swelling; and elevation of the foot. The doctor may refer the player for X-rays to check for a fracture. Treatment may include modalities (electrotherapy, iontophoresis, hot and cold baths) and range of motion exercises by a physical therapist and/or athletic trainer. The physician may recommend a stiff soled shoe or orthotic during recovery from this injury and/or to help prevent recurrences. Surgical treatment may be advised when symptoms are recurrent and persistent symptoms, related to bipartite sesamoids. Recovery can take three to four weeks, depending on how bad the sprain is. There is an increased risk of developing hallux limitus (limited motion of the big toe due to arthritis), hallux rigidus (stiff big toe) or hallux valgus (big toe pointing inwards).

Practical tips for the player

- Wear wide-toed, stiff soled, well-padded shoes that fit well to reduce bending of the injured big toe.
- Use a single wing plantar metatarsal pad.
- Taping of the great toe usually is helpful and may allow for earlier return to sports.

STIFF BIG TOE (HALLUX RIGIDUS)

Description. Hallux rigidus is a chronic painful loss of motion of the joint at the base of the big toe (metatarsophalangeal joint). This condition can be caused by a single injury to the joint or from the repetitive impact associated with activities such as playing tennis over a period of years. The damage eventually results in arthritis of the joint, with development of an associated bone spur(s). The bone spur which commonly forms on top of the joint at the head of the metatarsal, limits extension (bending upward) of the toe, and this mechanical block along with the associated arthritis, results in pain (Figure 8.9).

Symptoms. Pain at the base of the great toe is present with activity, especially serving and pushing off. There is often tenderness on the top of the joint. There may also be mild redness, swelling and warmth. Depending on the severity of the condition, it may cause the athlete to limp. The player may compensate for the pain by trying to put less weight on the painful area, thus shifting more load to other areas of the foot. This can result in the development of pain or stiffness in other areas of the foot. Athletes with a previous history of injury to the big toe, a long first toe, flat feet, or those who wear tight shoes with narrow toe box are at increased risk for developing hallux rigidus.

X-rays of the metatarsophalangeal joint of the big toe will show the characteristic bone spur formation. When the condition is

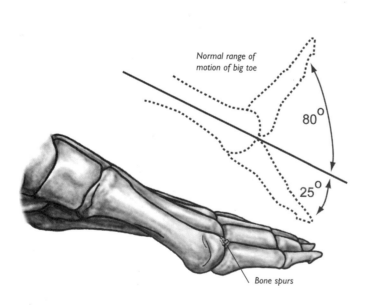

Normal range of motion of big toe

80°

25°

Bone spurs

Figure 8.9

A hallux rigidus is characterized by loss of motion of the big toe.

more advanced, narrowing of the joint space between the metatarsal head and the proximal phalanx will also be seen.

Treatment. An arch support (orthotic) and/or stiff soled shoes may help reduce pressure on the big toe and reduce the symptoms. Mobilizations are generally not recommended, because they may lead to increased pain and symptoms. The doctor may recommend a short trial of casting or bracing of the foot or give a cortisone injection into the arthritic joint to reduce the pain and inflammation. Surgery may be necessary if the symptoms interfere with playing tennis or day to day activities and do not respond to nonoperative measures. Surgical options include removing the bony spur(s) along with a portion of the metatarsal head in order to allow the toe to extend more, or fusion of the joint which totally eliminates all motion in the joint.

> *Practical tips for the player:*
> - Wear stiff soled shoes with a wide toe area to help reduce bending of the big toe and to reduce pressure to the top of the first toe.
> - Tape the big toe to reduce motion.
> - Temporarily avoid serving, as this is often associated with rising up on the toes and causing the toe pain.
> - Donut pads may help reduce pressure on the top of the big toe.
> - If there is swelling of the soft tissues around the toe, cool the painful area for ten to fifteen minutes using a melting ice cube or a polystyrene cup filled with ice.
> - Massage of the plantar fascia may also help to reduce symptoms.

MORTON'S NEUROMA (INTERDIGITAL NEURITIS)

Description. This is a nerve disorder in the foot that causes pain and abnormal feeling between the two toes that are involved. It results from pinching of the interdigital nerve near the base of the toes which causes swelling and damage of the nerve. It most frequently involves the space between the third and fourth toes or the space between the second and third toes. However, any interspace may be affected and the condition can involve more than one interspace (Figure 8.10).

Symptoms. Tennis players with this problem complain mainly of pain primarily over the ball of the foot in the area of the affected toes. They may describe feeling like they are stepping on a marble or pea. There may be painful clicking as the swollen nerve moves during activity. The pain is worse with playing tennis, running and prolonged walking. The pain may be aggravated by wearing tight shoes or shoes with a large heel and lessened by removing shoes. There may be tingling, numbness or an electric shock type sensation involving the affected toes.

X-rays will be normal, however, MRI may demonstrate the swollen interdigital nerve. The diagnosis can be confirmed by the alleviation of the pain when the area of the nerve is injected with a local anesthetic.

Treatment. Rest from offending activities and proper shoe wear helps to reduce the symptoms. A metatarsal bar or arch support (orthotic) with metatarsal bar will reduce pressure on the nerve and may lessen

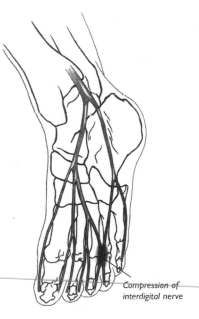

Compression of interdigital nerve

Figure 8.10
Morton's neuroma involves pinching of a thickened nerve between bones of the midfoot.

the symptoms. One or more cortisone injections into the area around the nerve may be given to reduce swelling and inflammation of the nerve. If conservative treatment is not successful, surgery may be necessary. The surgical procedure involves cutting out the swollen section of the nerve. This will relieve the pain associated with this condition. It will, however, also result in permanent numbness of a portion of the involved toes, though this is generally well tolerated.

Practical tips for the player

- Wear soft shoes with low heels that have a wide toe box.
- Place a metatarsal pad on the heel-side of the metatarsal heads to alleviate the pain or try custom-made orthotics.
- Stretch the tissues beneath the toes by placing your big toe (bent upward) against the wall and slowly increasing the stretch by lifting your heel (Figure 8.11).
- Strengthen the foot muscles by picking up a towel with your toes (Figure 28.69).

Figure 8.11
Plantar fascia stretch. Place your big toe (bent upward) against the wall and slowly increase the stretch by lifting your heel.

- Temporarily perform cross training with less impact of the forefoot (cycling, swimming).

TARSAL TUNNEL SYNDROME

Description. Tarsal tunnel syndrome is compression of the tibial nerve as it courses through the tarsal tunnel on the inner side of the ankle, just behind the anklebone (Figure 8.12).

The tarsal tunnel at the ankle is similar to the carpal tunnel of the wrist. It is a space which contains an artery and vein, tendons, and the posterior tibial nerve. The ligament that forms the roof of the tunnel prevents these structures from popping out of position during walking or running. The symptoms of tarsal tunnel syndrome occur when there is excessive pressure on the posterior tibial nerve. Common causes include a fracture or dislocation of the ankle or heel bone, an eversion or forced plantar flexion injury to the ankle, tendinopathy, edema (soft tissue swelling), varicose veins, and ganglion cysts. It may also be caused by excessive pronation (flat feet) or other malalignments of the foot and ankle, which increase pressure within the tarsal canal or place tension on the posterior tibial nerve.

Symptoms. Symptoms include pain, tingling and/or numbness involving the inner aspect of the ankle, heel, arch and/or bottom of the foot. The pain usually increases with activity and may be aggravated by standing in one place for a prolonged period of time. The player may also occasionally sense a feeling of ankle giving way. Pressing on the nerve in the tarsal tunnel will often produce pain or electrical sensations radiating into the foot.

X-rays will be normal unless a bony deformity from a previous fracture is present. MRI may show fluid in the tarsal tunnel or compressive masses such as a ganglion cyst when present. Electrical studies may demonstrate abnormalities of the nerve and/or the muscles supplied by the nerve.

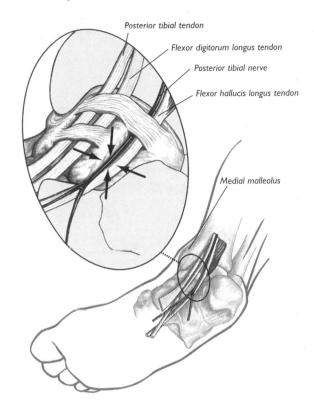

Posterior tibial tendon
Flexor digitorum longus tendon
Posterior tibial nerve
Flexor hallucis longus tendon
Medial malleolus

Figure 8.12
Tarsal tunnel syndrome is a compression injury of the tibial nerve.

Treatment. Conservative treatment for tarsal tunnel syndrome includes the use of arch supports to restore the natural arch of the foot, and ankle supports and wider shoes to avoid unnecessary pressure on the nerve. A period of immobilization in a cast or brace may be recommended. If there is inflammation and swelling of the nerve or structures around the nerve, nonsteroidal inflammatory drugs may be prescribed or a cortisone injection into the tarsal tunnel may be recommended. If conservative treatment is not successful, and particularly if a cyst or tumor-like mass is pressing on the nerve, surgery may be required to free the pinched nerve.

Practical tips for the player
- Wear proper shoes.
- Use arch supports if you have flat or pronated feet.
- Use taping, protective strapping, bracing and/or high top tennis shoes to prevent ankle sprains and nerve stretching injury.

PLANTAR FASCIITIS

Description. The plantar fascia is the strong tissue under the foot that connects the toes to the heel. In conjunction with the muscles and bones, it forms the arch of the foot. Plantar fasciitis is an overuse injury affecting the plantar fascia at the point where it attaches to the heel (Figure 8.13). Degenerative changes of the plantar fascia occur at this attachment site, as a result of repetitive microruptures. A heel spur may be seen on X-ray in the area of the plantar fascia attachment, but it is important to note that the spur is not the cause of the pain. Plantar fasciitis is more common among serve and

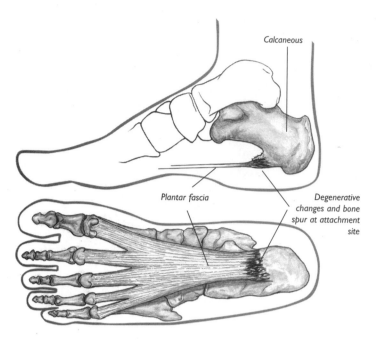

Calcaneous

Plantar fascia

Degenerative changes and bone spur at attachment site

Figure 8.13

Plantar fasciitis with a heel spur.

volley players who perform a lot of jumping and sprinting, resulting in repeated stretching of the plantar fascia. Other risk factors include playing on hard courts, being overweight, and foot abnormalities (e.g. flat feet, cavus feet, overpronated feet).

Symptoms. There is sharp pain on the bottom of the heel, which may radiate to the inner side of the heel. The pain is usually worse when first getting up in the morning, after prolonged sitting and while playing tennis or running. There may be some aching pain after exercises or at night.

Treatment. Initial treatment consists of activity modification (avoidance of running and playing tennis), ice massage, massage of the foot and calf muscles, gentle stretching exercises for the muscles of the lower extremity (especially the calf muscles, Achilles tendon, and plantar fascia), and mobilization of the ankle. Orthotics should be prescribed for those with abnormally high or low arches. Weight reduction is encouraged in overweight players. Night-splinting, with the ankle and toes extended and the plantar fascia maximally stretched, has been shown to be effective. Nonsteroidal anti-inflammatory medications and a corticosteroid injection into the area of the plantar fascia attachment may help reduce the pain. Repeated injections, however, should be used with caution as this may damage the heel pad and result in loss of its normal cushioning effect. Shock wave therapy has been used with some success in plantar fasciitis. If symptoms persist despite a six to twelve month course of nonoperative treatment, surgery may be indicated. Release of the degenerative fibers of the plantar fascia at its attachment (plantar fasciotomy) is performed either arthroscopically or through an open procedure. This is often combined with release of a small nerve in the heel which may also be causing pain.

Practical tips for the player
- Wear well-cushioned shoes with sturdy soles and a firm heel counter.
- Cool the painful area by massaging the painful spot, using a melting ice cube or a polystyrene cup filled with ice. Continue this for ten to fifteen minutes and repeat several times a day.
- Use orthotics if you have flat feet, high arches, or pronate excessively.
- Massage the soles of your feet by rolling the feet over a can or bottle. This will help to relax the fascia and the muscles.
- Temporarily, a shock absorbing heel lift can be used. If used, do so on both feet. The advantage of a heel lift is that there is less tension on

the plantar fascia because the calf muscles are more relaxed.

- Stretch the calf muscles and plantar fascia regularly (see Figures 5.3, 5.4, and 8.11 for instructions), and strengthen the foot muscles (Figure 28.69).

HEEL PAIN IN YOUNG PLAYERS (CALCANEAL APOPHYSITIS, SEVER'S DISEASE)

Description. The most common cause of heel pain in young tennis players is calcaneal apophysitis (Sever's disease). This is an overuse injury to the growth plate of the heel bone (calcaneus), in the area of the heel cord (Achilles tendon) attachment. It typically occurs in the 8 to 13-year-old age group. It involves both heels in about 60% of the cases. Contributing factors include poor footwear, foot malalignment (e.g., flat feet or high arches), tight calf muscles during the adolescent growth spurt, weak ankle muscles, and repetitive microtrauma. The prognosis is favorable, with 95% of the young players responding to conservative treatment measures within three months.

Symptoms. There is pain at the back of the heel that tends to increase with activity, particularly running and jumping. Pain is typically present at the onset of activities and continues to increase with prolonged activity. Walking on one's toes relieves the pain. There is tenderness over the back of the heel.

Treatment. Cooling with ice may help relieve the pain. A cushioned heel support or heel lift provides shock absorption and relieves the tension of a tight Achilles tendon. Orthotics with arch supports may be helpful in those with excessive pronation (inward turning of the foot and ankle). Activity modification, including limiting or eliminating running and jumping for several weeks, may be necessary in order to allow healing.

Practical tips for the player

- Stretch the calf muscles regularly. See Figures 5.3 and 5.4 for instructions.
- Poorly constructed footwear can be a major contributing factor towards heel pain, so make sure to wear proper shoes. Important aspects to check are whether the shoe fits snugly in the heel area, whether the heel base is wide enough, and whether there is adequate heel wedging of 12 to 15 mm vertical height. In addition, the shoe sole should have enough flexibility to allow bending of the toes,

thus decreasing the strain on the heel cord.

- Perform running exercises on grass or sand instead of on the hard pavement of the street, or replace the running temporarily by biking or swimming.
- Avoid exercises that put an excessive load on the heel, such as skipping. Limit the amount of running and sprinting.

TENDINOPATHY OF THE ACHILLES TENDON (ACHILLES TENDINITIS)

Description. Achilles tendinopathy is a painful overuse injury of the Achilles tendon. In some cases, it may only involve inflammation of the lining of the tendon (paratenon). However, more commonly, it is a degenerative process, which occurs following a partial tear or repetitive microtearing of the tendon, due to the tendon's inherently poor healing response (Figure 8.14). Predisposing factors to Achilles tendinopathy are increasing age, excessive weight, lateral instability of the ankle, poor footwear, previous injury, sudden increases in amount or intensity of activity, and changing court surface, such as switching from clay courts to hard courts. Excessive movement of the hindfoot (ankle and heel), especially a lateral heel strike with excessive compensatory pronation, is thought to cause a "whipping action" on the tendon, predisposing to injury (Figure 8.15).

Symptoms. Pain in the Achilles tendon area may, initially, only be present after exercise. At later stages, pain may occur during exercise and even interfere with the activ-

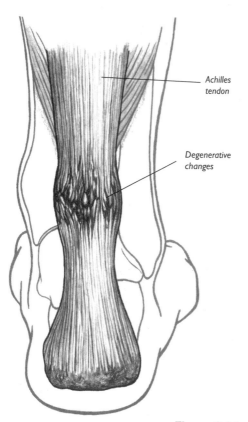

Achilles tendon

Degenerative changes

Figure 8.14

Tendinopathy of the Achilles tendon is a degenerative process.

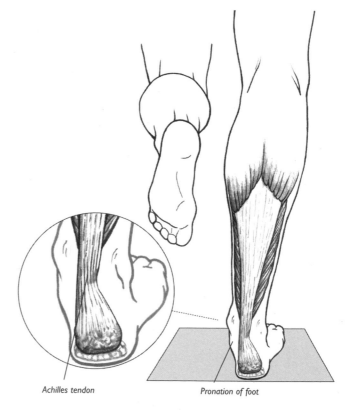

Achilles tendon

Pronation of foot

Figure 8.15

Orthotics can help to prevent the excessive stress on the Achilles tendon in players with over pronation.

ities of daily living. The pain is generally worse in the morning and after (or during) play. There may be a crackling sensation felt during movement of the ankle. The tendon is tender to touch. Mild swelling may be present and a localized thickening or "knot" may be felt within the tendon. An MRI or ultrasound scan may be used to confirm the diagnosis and evaluate the extent and nature of the lesions.

Treatment. Initial treatment consists of activity modification and cooling with ice. Massage of the calf muscles is helpful to ease the tension on the Achilles tendon, followed by gentle stretching exercises. Eccentric strengthening of the gastrocnemius-soleus complex should be initiated once the pain has improved. Calf raises have been shown to be very effective for both prevention and conservative treatment of Achilles tendinopathy. An arch support and/or heel lift may be helpful. Corticosteroid injections should be avoided, as they weaken tendon tissue and increase the risk of Achilles tendon rupture. Shock wave therapy may be considered in those cases in which calcium deposits are present within the tendon. In those cases which do not respond to above measures, surgery may be recommended to remove the inflamed tendon lining and/or degenerated tendon tissue.

Practical tips for the player

- Gradually increase the frequency or duration of workouts. Also, in the case of new shoes or a different playing surface, additional time should be allowed to ensure proper body adjustment to the new environment. Sudden changes in the training program have been shown to increase the chances of acquiring Achilles tendon problems.
- Perform running exercises on grass or sand, and try to avoid hard surfaces such as the pavement of the street.
- Badly constructed footwear can be a major contributing factor towards Achilles tendinopathy. Stability around the ankle is essential, so be sure to check whether the shoe fits snugly in the heel area, whether the heel base is wide enough, and if there is adequate heel wedging of 12 to 15 mm vertical height. In addition, the shoe sole should have enough flexibility to allow bending of the toes, thus decreasing the strain on the tendon.

- Try using a sorbothane heel lift. This will provide additional shock absorption as well as artificial Achilles tendon elongation, thus reducing the stress on the muscle/tendon unit.
- Perform daily calf raises. See Figure 28.65 for instructions. Perform the exercise both with a bent and a straight knee.
- Alternative exercises are biking, aqua jogging, or low-impact steps.
- Stretch the calf muscles on a regular basis to ensure that the tendon will be lengthened slightly. Shorter tendons tend to be subjected to large amounts of strain during exercise. See Figures 5.3 and 5.4 for instructions.

- Massage after a strenuous workout will help relax the calf and reduce the amount of tension exerted on the Achilles tendon.

ACHILLES TENDON RUPTURE

Description. Rupture of the Achilles tendon most commonly occurs in healthy, active individuals who are aged 30-50 years. Although most players who rupture their Achilles tendon have no previous history of pain in the Achilles area, some report intermittent soreness prior to rupture. Achilles tendon ruptures are located within the tendon, approximately 1-2 inches (2.5-5 cm) above its attachment to the heel bone. Most ruptures occur from a combination of a forceful stretch of the tendon with a contraction of the calf muscles (eccentric contraction). This occurs when the foot is bent upward (dorsiflexed) while there is a forward motion of the lower leg (tibia) over the foot, such as when the player tries to return a drop shot, or pushes off to play serve and volley. Oral corticosteroids, cortisone injections in the Achilles area and certain antibiotics (fluoroquinolones) may weaken the tendon and increase the risk of Achilles tendon rupture.

Symptoms. The player who sustains this injury usually feels or hears a "pop" or rip in the back of the heel at the time of injury. It is quite common for the player to feel as if someone has kicked him or something has hit him in the back of the leg at the instant of injury. There is generally little warning prior to the rupture.

There is some pain at the time of injury but, most often, it is not severe. The injured player will not be able to lift up onto his toes, although he may be able to point his toes while not bearing weight on the foot. There is tenderness in the Achilles area with swelling developing over several hours. Bruising usually becomes evident at the Achilles tendon and heel within 24-48 hours. There is a loss of the continuity of the substance of the tendon, with indentation of the area to firm pressure by an examining finger, at the site of the rupture. Squeezing the calf muscles in the midcalf region will not cause the foot to point downward like the unaffected side due to loss of continuity of the muscle/tendon unit.

This injury can initially be mistaken for a simple ankle sprain. However, with careful examination, the nature and extent of the injury can usually be determined. X-rays may show some abnormality of the soft tissue shadow of the tendon. When necessary, MRI or ultrasound can be used to confirm the diagnosis.

Treatment. Initial treatment consists of not walking on the affected leg, icing the area, applying a compressive elastic bandage, and elevating the injured leg. While surgical or nonsurgical treatment may be considered for Achilles tendon rupture, surgical repair is generally preferred for tennis players with complete ruptures. While it is possible to treat a ruptured tendon without surgery in a cast or boot immobilizer for eight to twelve weeks, this is not ideal since the maximum strength of the muscle and tendon rarely returns. Also, the risk of re-rupture is higher with nonsurgical than with surgical repair. After either surgical or nonsurgical treatment, rehabilitation to regain flexibility and muscle strength must be instituted to allow safe and effective return to sports, which usually requires four to nine months.

Practical tips for the player
- Strengthening exercises include calf raises (Figure 28.65), biking,

aqua jogging, walking, and low impact steps.

• A heel lift may be used for six months to one year.
• Protective strapping, taping, or an adhesive bandage may be recommended when first returning on court.

ANKLE SPRAIN

Description. The ankle is stabilized by three sets of ligaments—the lateral ligament complex on the outer side, the deltoid ligament on the inner side, and the syndesmosis between the tibia and fibula bones. An ankle sprain, defined as stretching or tearing of ligaments around the ankle, is the most common acute injury in tennis, accounting for 20-25% of all injuries. In approximately 90% of the cases, the relatively weak lateral ankle ligaments are affected (Figure 8.16). An injury of the much stronger ligament on the inner side of the ankle is far less common (5-10% of cases). Injury to the syndesmosis can occur in isolation or in conjunction with these other ligament injuries.

Figure 8.16

The ankle sprain is the most common injury in tennis.

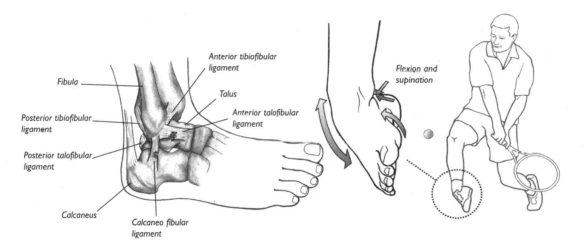

Ankle sprains most commonly occur when the player tries to stop abruptly, change directions quickly, or lands on the foot in an unbalanced position, such as can happen to the lead foot in the serve. Those with a previous ankle sprain are more susceptible to recurrent ankle sprains.

Sprains are classified into three grades of severity. In a first degree sprain, the ligament is stretched without tearing. In a second degree sprain, the ligament is stretched and partially torn. In a third degree sprain, the ligament is completely torn.

Symptoms. A player who sustains an ankle sprain has immediate pain at the time of injury. The player may note a pop or tearing sensation at the time of injury. In the case of a very mild sprain, the player may be able to continue playing. More often, there will be inability to continue playing, limping, or, in severe sprains, inability to bear weight. Mild to moderate swelling, depending on the severity of the injury, will develop within minutes to hours over the area of the injured ligaments.

Both second and third degree sprains will result in some bruising developing around the ankle, heel, or foot over 24-48 hours due to bleeding from the torn ligament(s).

Following an ankle injury, X-rays may be necessary to make sure there is not a fracture present. Special X-rays called "stress X-rays" may also be taken to determine the severity of the ligament injury and the resulting amount of instability (looseness) of the joint. Ultrasound or MRI can also be helpful in assessing the degree of ligament damage.

Treatment. Nonoperative treatment is indicated for the vast majority of ankle sprains. Initial treatment consists of ice (15 to 30 minutes every few hours) to relieve the pain and, along with a compressive elastic bandage and elevation, reduce swelling. Nonsteroidal anti-inflammatory medications may be prescribed to aid in the reduction of pain and swelling. Crutches should be used until it is comfortable to walk without them. As walking progresses, attention should be directed to the use a normal gait (i.e., from heel to toe). The healing ligaments should be protected by using a walking cast, walking boot, tape, brace, or high top shoes, and/or by putting a heel wedge in the shoe, depending on the severity of the injury. Range of motion exercises are generally started as soon as possible as they help to reduce swelling and promote ligament healing. Gradually, proprioceptive training and muscle strengthening exercises are added. These activities are important in allowing return to play and reducing the risk of spraining the ankle again in the future. Gentle jogging, starts, turns, and finally, sprints and jumping exercises are initiated as tolerated. When these activities are possible without pain or swelling of the ankle, a gradual return to play is allowed. This treatment program will result in successful healing and return to sports in a very high percentage of players. Some players with second or third degree sprains of the lateral ligaments treated in this manner may develop chronic instability (looseness) of the ankle, which may eventually require surgical repair to correct.

In most cases, a first degree sprain usually allows return to play within one to two weeks. A second degree sprain usually requires two weeks to two months before healing allows the player to return. A third degree sprain typically requires two to four months to heal before return to play is possible. Syndesmosis ("high ankle") sprains may take three to six months until pushing off the foot is no longer painful. Physical therapy is an important adjunct to treatment of ankle sprains, accelerating ligament healing and return to play, and reducing the risk of recurrent sprains.

Surgical treatment of an acute third degree sprain of the lateral ligaments is considered by some in elite level players. Generally, however, the results with operative and nonoperative treatment are the same, with less risk of complications in those treated nonoperatively. Surgery is recommended for all third degree sprains of the syndesmosis.

Persistent symptoms in the ankle despite an appropriate period of treatment following an ankle sprain are most commonly due to instability, occult bone or cartilage damage or development of scar tissue around the ankle. Stress X-rays, bone scintigraphy, CT, MRI, and ankle arthroscopy are valuable investigational tools which may be used to determine the cause of the ongoing symptoms.

Practical tips for the player
- To prevent an ankle injury, keep the court clear of balls that are not currently in play.

- Proprioceptive training is very important, both during the treatment phase and to prevent a recurrence after the injury has healed. A useful exercise is standing on the injured leg, closing the eyes and trying to keep balance (Figure 8.17). This exercise can be made harder by bending forward and sideward, standing on a wobble board or trampoline, or by bouncing a tennis ball (Figure 8.18).

- Strengthen the ankle muscles by walking on your heels, walking on your toes, and walking on the inside of your feet, pressing the big toe firmly into the ground. Using elastic tubing, you can make them even stronger. See Figure 28.67 for instructions.

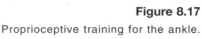

Figure 8.17
Proprioceptive training for the ankle.

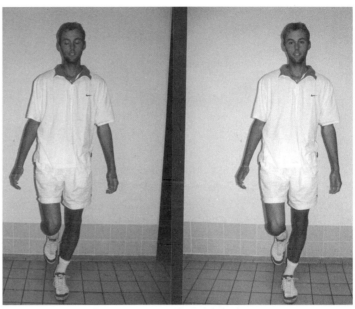

Figure 8.18
Advanced proprioceptive training: hitting volleys while standing on a wobble board!

- Taping, protective strapping, bracing, and/or high top tennis shoes with a wide and solid heel counter may help prevent injury, especially if one has been injured before. Wearing appropriate shoes with taping or bracing is more effective than either one alone.

CHRONIC ANKLE INSTABILITY

Description. Chronic ankle instability refers to an ankle which "gives way" frequently resulting in repeated ankle sprains. The most common cause of chronic ankle instability is a combination of incomplete ligament healing and inadequate rehabilitation following a severe ankle sprain. The torn ligaments heal in an elongated fashion, which results in abnormal laxity (looseness) of the ankle. When this "looseness" is combined with loss of supporting muscle strength, coordination, and proprioception, all of which occur following a serious ankle sprain, the joint becomes functionally unstable.

This condition almost always involves the lateral ligament complex on the outer side of the ankle. As a result, when the ankle gives out, the foot rolls inward (inversion).

Symptoms. A player with chronic ankle instability will complain of the ankle giving way easily when changing directions quickly on court or even off the court, when walking on uneven ground such as the beach or other unpaved surfaces. The episodes of giving way are often painful and may be associated with swelling, depending upon their severity. Each episode can potentially result in damage to the cartilage surface of the ankle bones and/or the formation of more scar tissue. Therefore, repeated episodes of instability may make persistent pain in the ankle a more prominent complaint.

In a chronically unstable ankle, X-rays may show bone spurs and other signs of damage to the joint due to the recurrent ankle sprains. Stress X-rays are helpful in confirming the diagnosis and determining the severity of ankle laxity that is present. CT and MRI scanning may be useful in detecting associated damage to the joint surfaces.

Treatment. Most players regain full functional stability and ability to return to full activity with a comprehensive rehabilitation program consisting of strengthening of the muscles around the ankle and retraining of balance skills. A heel wedge, high top shoes, and/or taping or bracing of the ankle are recommended. If symptoms of instability persist despite proper rehabilitation, surgery to correct the abnormal ankle laxity may be necessary. Most commonly, the surgery involves repairing the ligaments to "tighten" the ankle. In some cases, reconstructing the ligaments using a nearby tendon may be necessary. Following surgery, the ankle is immobilized in a cast or boot immobilizer to allow healing, following which a progressive ankle rehabilitation program is initiated.

Practical tips for the player
- It is of critical importance to rehabilitate completely after the initial injury.
- Taping, protective strapping, bracing, and/or high top tennis shoes with a wide and solid heel counter may help prevent chronic, recurrent ankle sprains. Using appropriate shoes with taping or bracing is more effective than either one alone.
- Proprioceptive exercises should be performed daily. See Figures 8.17 and 8.18 for instructions.

ANTERIOR ANKLE IMPINGEMENT

Description. Anterior ankle impingement is a painful pinching of the two ankle bones (talus and tibia) and/or the soft tissue at the front of the ankle when the foot is brought

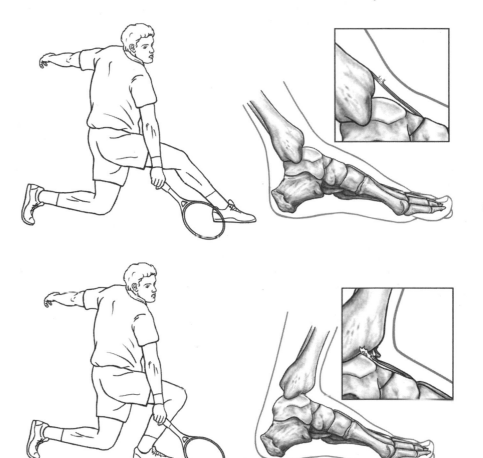

Figure 8.19
Overstretching of the anterior capsule at the front of the ankle.

Figure 8.20
Pinching of the soft tissues and bones at the front of the ankle during maximal dorsal flexion.

into an upward position (dorsiflexion). This condition is commonly seen in sports that require running, jumping, and repeated changes of direction such as tennis. The cause is most likely related to repeated impact of the tibia on the neck of the talus resulting in buildup of scar tissue and the development of bone spurs in this area (Figure 8.19 and 8.20).

Symptoms. Players with anterior ankle impingement will complain of pain in the front of the ankle with running or jumping. The pain may result in an inability to run, cut, or jump at full speed or lunge for the ball. There may be some swelling at the front of the ankle. The pain can be reproduced by pushing the foot upward into dorsiflexion. There may be some loss of range of motion due to development of bone spurs which can block full dorsiflexion of the ankle. X-rays will commonly show bone spurs at the front of the lower end of the tibia and over the neck of the talus.

Treatment. Initial treatment consists of rest from offending activity, ice, nonsteroidal anti-inflammatory drugs (NSAIDs), and taping or bracing. The purpose of the protective tape or brace is to prevent ankle hyperextension. Orthotics (arch supports) are recommended if there is malalignment of the foot. A steroid injection into the affected area may give relief by reducing soft tissue inflammation. Surrgery may be required to remove the bone spurs or chronic scar tissue and generally provides excellent results. The procedure most commonly is performed arthroscopically. Physical therapy following surgery focuses on regaining range of motion, ankle strengthening, proprioceptive training, and sports specific rehabilitation.

Practical tips for the player

- Wear three-quarter top shoes.
- Stretch the calf muscles to improve range of motion. See Figures 5.3 and 5.4 for instructions.
- Perform proprioceptive training. See Figures 8.17 and 8.18 for instructions.
- Use of a half-inch (one centimeter) high heel lift may be helpful.
- Avoid lacing shoes in a crossing pattern to provide some relief of direct pressure.

POSTERIOR ANKLE IMPINGEMENT

Description. This problem is due to pinching of the bones and soft tissues in the back of the ankle. This may be associated with a fracture in the back of the ankle bone (talus) or an extra bone behind the ankle (os trigonum). The injury is usually due to repeated forced plantar flexion, such as when sliding on clay courts, or standing on the tips of the toes repeatedly. Wearing shoes with inadequate support to prevent forced flexion of the ankle and poor court conditions may increase the risk for this injury.

Symptoms. Symptoms are pain with forced plantar flexion, pain when standing on tiptoes or wearing shoes with high heels, and/or pain with flexing of the big toe. There usually is tenderness in the back of the ankle and occasionally on the outside of the ankle. There may be pain in the lead foot when sliding on clay courts, running, jumping, or walking down stairs or hills, or squatting while standing on the toes. There may be some mild swelling and occasionally bruising in the back of the ankle or heel (with fracture).

Treatment. Physiotherapy consists of traction mobilization to improve mobility of the lower (subtalar) ankle joint. The ankle may be immobilized with a brace or walking boot to allow the inflammation to settle down. If symptoms continue to persist, an injection of cortisone and anesthetics or surgical intervention (removal of the bone that causes the pinching) may be required.

Practical tips for the player

- Taping, protective strapping, bracing, and/or high top shoes may help prevent injury. High top shoes with taping or bracing is more effective than either one alone.
- Use proper outsoles for the court surface.

TENDINOPATHY AND RUPTURE OF THE POSTERIOR TIBIAL TENDON

Description. Posterior tibial tendinopathy is an overuse injury of the posterior tibial tendon. This tendon runs on the inner side of the ankle behind the ankle bone (medial malleolus) and attaches to the navicular bone on the inner side of the midfoot. The injury usually results from repetitive stress on and progressive degeneration of the tendon that occurs with activity. Tennis players are at increased risk of this problem due to the sudden repetitive pushing off of the foot (jumping and quick starts) that is important in the sport. Individuals who are overweight and/or have malalignment of the foot and ankle are more susceptible to posterior tibial tendon problems, due the increased load on the tendon.

If the condition is allowed to progress, function of the tendon is further impaired resulting in progressive flattening of the arch. Eventually, rupture of the tendon may occur.

Symptoms. Players who have posterior tibial tendinopathy usually complain of pain over the inner aspect of the ankle. The pain is worse with pushing off or standing on the ball of the foot. There may be significant pain when playing, steadily worsening during the course of play. Swelling may be present over the course of the tendon. There may be burning, shooting, tingling, and/or stabbing pain when the posterior tibial nerve inside the tarsal tunnel becomes irritated as well (see tarsal tunnel syndrome). In more advanced stages, the player will note progressive loss of the normal arch of the foot. X-rays will not show the degenerated tendon but will show flattening of the arch of the foot if present. An MRI is an excellent tool for evaluating the extent of the tendon problem including swelling, degeneration, and rupture.

Treatment. Initial treatment consists of rest from sports and cooling with ice. An arch support and heel lift or custom orthotic help to reduce stress on the tendon. Nonsteroidal anti-inflammatory medications may help reduce pain and swelling. Physiotherapy may include mobilization of the ankle, followed by progressive strengthening exercises once pain and swelling have subsided. In some cases, a cast or walking boot may be recommended to allow the inflammation to settle down. In early stages of this condition, if it does not respond to the above measures, surgery to remove the inflamed tendon lining or degenerated tendon tissue may be recommended. In more advanced cases, including tendon rupture, reconstructive procedures including tendon transfers and bone realignments or bone fusion may be necessary in order to provide pain relief.

> ### *Practical tips for the player*
> - Use a running shoe with a medial heel wedge to prevent overpronation during running.
> - Arch supports (orthotics), taping, protective strapping, or an adhesive bandage are recommended before practice or competition.
> - Proprioceptive exercises should be performed. See Figures 8.17 and 8.18 for instructions.
> - Stretch the calf muscles. See Figures 5.3 and 5.4 for instructions.

TENDINOPATHY AND RUPTURE OF THE PERONEAL TENDONS

Description. Peroneal tendinopathy is an overuse injury or partial tear of one or both peroneal tendons. The peroneal tendons are the attachments of the muscles of the outer leg to the (1) outer foot (peroneus brevis) and (2) bottom of the inner foot (peroneus longus). The tendons are important in standing on the toes or pushing off phase of running or jumping and turning the foot outward.

These injuries are caused by mechanical wear of the tendon in its groove behind the outer ankle resulting in degeneration and gradual wear. However, it may also occur from a sudden strain when spraining the ankle. Its frequent occurrence among tennis players is due to the pivoting and rapid change in direction needed in play. It may also occur during exercise on uneven terrain or surfaces.

Symptoms. Players who have peroneal tendinopathy usually complain of pain over the outer aspect of the ankle, the outer part of the midfoot, or the bottom of the arch. The pain is worse with pushing off or standing on the ball of the foot. There may be significant pain when playing, steadily worsening during the course of play. Swelling may be present over the course of the tendon.

X-rays will not show the degenerated tendon. Ultrasound or MRI are excellent tools for evaluating the extent of the tendon problem including swelling, degeneration, and rupture.

Treatment. Initial treatment consists of rest from sports and cooling with ice. An arch support and heel lift or custom orthotic help to reduce stress on the tendon. Nonsteroidal anti-inflammatory medications may help reduce pain and swelling. Physiotherapy may include mobilization of the ankle followed by progressive strengthening exercises once pain and swelling have subsided. In early stages of this condition, if it does not respond to the above measures, surgery to remove the inflamed tendon lining or degenerated tendon tissue may be recommended. In more advanced cases, including tendon rupture, reconstructive procedures including tendon transfers and bone realignments or bone fusion may be necessary in order to provide pain relief.

Practical tips for the player

- Wear the tennis shoe with an outsole appropriate for the court surface.
- Protect the ankle with supportive devices, such as wrapped elastic bandages, tape, braces or high top athletic shoes.
- Perform proprioceptive training. See Figures 8.17 and 8.18 for instructions.
- Strengthen the peroneal muscles with eversion against resistance. See Figure 28.67 for instructions.
- Assure your rehabilitation is complete after ankle injury before returning to practice or competition.

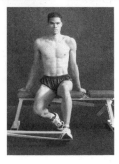

PERONEAL TENDON SUBLUXATION

Description. Peroneal tendon subluxation and dislocation are injuries to the ankle where one or both of the peroneal tendon(s) are displaced from their normal position behind the outer ankle (Figure 8.21). The peroneal tendons are the attachments of the muscles of the outer leg to the (1) outer foot (peroneus brevis) and (2) bottom of the inner foot (peroneus longus). The tendons are important in standing on the toes, the pushing off phase of running or jumping, and turning the foot outward. The tendons slide in a groove behind the outer anklebone (lateral malleolus) and are maintained in their normal position by ligament like tissue (retinaculum). A subluxation occurs when the tendon slides back and forth from its normal position in the groove. A dislocation of the tendon(s) happens when the tendon(s) is completely out of its groove. The peroneus brevis usually is the only tendon to come out of the groove.

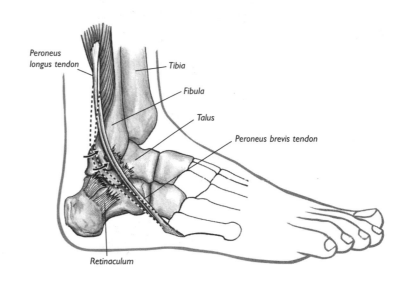

Figure 8.21

Subluxation of the peroneal tendon

These injuries, which really are a spectrum of one injury, are due to a sudden, forceful flexion of an (most often outwardly turned) ankle that the peroneal muscles try to resist. This results in the retinaculum tearing or stripping off from the bone allowing the tendon(s) to slide out of their position within the groove. This may occur by itself or in association with a severe ankle sprain. Less commonly, it may be a congenital (born with) abnormality, such as a shallow or malformed groove for the tendons. Its frequent occurrence among tennis players is due to the pivoting and rapid change in direction needed in play. It may also occur during exercise on uneven terrain or surfaces.

Symptoms. Athletes who sustain this injury note a pop or snap at the time of injury. There is pain, swelling, tenderness, and bruising at the injury site, behind the outer ankle, which initially is worsened by standing or walking. There may also be pain and weakness when trying to push the foot toward the injured side. Often, there is no problem walking forward after a few days to weeks, but persistent problems are noted when trying to cut or pivot on the injured leg, moving toward the side of injury. There may be a crackling sound when the tendon is moved or touched.

Treatment. Acute injuries may be treated operatively or conservatively. Nonoperative treatment involves casting the leg, foot, and ankle while not walking on the foot for up to six weeks. Operative treatment consists of early surgery to repair the retinaculum to bone. Chronic injuries are usually treated by surgery to hold the tendons within their groove. The leg and ankle are then immobilized in a cast or brace to allow healing. Rarely, rupture of the tendon(s) from recurrent subluxation or dislocation may occur.

Practical tips for the player

- Wear the tennis shoe with an outsole appropriate for the court surface.

- Protect the ankle with supportive devices, such as wrapped elastic bandages, tape, braces, or high top athletic shoes.
- Perform proprioceptive training. See Figures 8.17 and 8.18 for instructions.
- Assure your rehabilitation is complete after ankle injury before returning to practice or competition.

CHRONIC EXERTIONAL COMPARTMENT SYNDROME

Description. Chronic exertional compartment syndrome is characterized by increased pressure within one of the muscle compartments of the lower leg caused by exercise. The leg is divided into four main compartments separated by thick ligament like tissue called fascia. Within these compartments muscles, nerves, arteries, and veins are located. Muscle size may increase up to twenty percent during exercise due to increase in blood flow to the muscles. This can result in an excessive increase in pressure within a compartment which may compromise local microcirculation and lead to injury of the muscles and nerves within that compartment. The muscles at the front of the lower leg (anterior compartment) are most frequently involved; however, exertional compartment syndrome can occur within any of the four muscle compartments. Athletes with this syndrome may have thicker and stiffer fascia, or larger muscles from exercise/training. Although runners are most frequently affected by this problem, tennis players are also susceptible during periods of conditioning that includes endurance training. They are not likely to experience symptoms during on-court practice and matches due to the stop and start nature of tennis.

Symptoms. Athletes with chronic exertional compartment syndrome complain of leg pain during exercise, primarily running, that typically begins after exercising for a specified amount of time or running the same distance, and improves after stopping exercise (though pain may persist for hours or days). Frequently, the player will note a feeling of fullness, firmness, pressure, or ache in the leg, though occasionally the pain may be sharp. The player may note numbness, tingling, or burning in the leg, foot, and/or ankle, as well as weakness of the muscles of the foot and ankle.

Diagnosis can be confirmed by doing dynamic compartment pressure measurements. In this test, pressure within a compartment is monitored before, during, and after exercise with a needle placed into the compartment attached to a pressure measuring device.

Treatment. Activity modification including a change in the conditioning program helps to control the symptoms. Typically, biking or swimming can be substituted for running for endurance training. Cooling with ice (ten to fifteen minutes every couple of hours, especially after exercise) may be helpful to relieve pain. If symptoms persist and interfere with the player's ability to compete at their desired level, and the diagnosis has been confirmed with compartment pressure monitoring, surgery is necessary to alleviate the problem. Surgery involves cutting the fascia to relieve pressure on the structures within the compartment. Following a brief recovery period, a gradual return to full practice is initiated. Left untreated, athletes with this problem usually have ongoing symptoms that impair performance.

Practical tips for the player
- An important initial step in the treatment is to modify the activity, which initially caused the problem to occur.
- Perform stretching exercises for the calf muscles. See Figures 5.3 and 5.4 for instructions.
- In case of flat feet, orthotics can be useful to relieve the pressure in a compartment.

SHIN SPLINTS (MEDIAL TIBIAL STRESS SYNDROME)

Description. Shin splints (medial tibial stress syndrome) is a very common overuse injury. It is due to repetitive stress on the muscles at their attachment to the lower end of the tibia (shinbone). The pain is a result of the deep calf muscles (soleus, posterior tibial, and flexor digitorum profundus) pulling hard on the backside of the lower tibia, resulting in either periostitis (inflammation of the outer layer of the bone) or microfractures. Risk factors include weakness or imbalance of the muscles of the leg and calf and excessive pronation. Though most common in endurance runners, it is seen frequently in tennis due to the repetitive loading and running, particularly on hard court surfaces.

Symptoms. The player complains of pain in the lower half of the shinbone (tibia), which is aggravated by activity. Initially, the pain typically occurs after exercise. However, as the condition worsens, pain may be present in the beginning of exercise and even with activities of daily living such as walking. With continued exercise and left untreated, pain becomes constant and may linger even after cessation of the offending activity. There is tenderness to touch along the inner aspect of the lower half of the tibia.

In many cases, X-rays of the tibia will be normal. In more chronic and severe cases, X-rays may show thickening of the tibia along the attachment of the muscles. A bone scan or MRI are useful in determining the extent of the injury and differentiating periostitis from a stress fracture.

Treatment. Activity modification is the mainstay of treatment for this condition. Decreasing impact activity (running) and substituting biking or swimming for aerobic conditioning will help control symptoms and usually allow healing to occur. Ice should be applied to the tender area immediately after exercise. Nonsteroidal anti-inflammatory medication may be helpful in reducing symptoms of periostitis. Electrotherapeutic modalities can be used. Massage of the deep calf muscles, including the tibialis posterior tendon, can be very useful. Care should be taken to remain clear of the tender tibial border. Arch supports should be prescribed, both to absorb shock and to correct faulty foot mechanics, such as overpronation. This will help to prevent excessive strain on the muscles that run from the shinbone to the foot. Also, stretching and strengthening of the muscles around the ankle along with proprioceptive training are recommended.

Practical tips for the player
- Perform preseason conditioning and build up the training gradually.

The main cause of shin splints is over-ambitious training. Tennis players are particularly prone to starting too fast early in the season or after return from injury. Do not suddenly increase both intensity and duration of the training at the same time, and increase training no more than ten percent per week. Take one or two days off each week from all impact activities (running, jumping, etc) and substitute biking or swimming.

- Avoid hard courts. The problem is that the shocks from hard courts place extra demands on the lower leg. The solution—if there is no alternative to playing on hard courts—is to do the running training on more forgiving surfaces such as clay, sand, composite track, and grass.
- Choose shoes carefully. Choose shoes that absorb shock, control heel motion, and provide the degree of cushioning that is needed. For feet that are pronated (i.e., they tend to cave in toward the inside), there are many (running) shoes on the market which can help control this problem.

- Stretch the superficial and deep calf muscles. See Figures 5.3 and 5.4 for instructions.
- Strengthening exercises for the foot, calf and hips should be performed. Recommended exercises include towel pick ups, calf raises, and sideward leg raises. See Figures 28.69, 28.65, and 28.56 for instructions.

- Taping the ankle may be useful.
- When recovering from shin splints, use this progression to returning to tennis: water running, cycling, stair master, treadmill, and then tennis.

MENISCUS TEAR

Description. The meniscus is a C-shaped piece of fibrocartilage situated on top of the shinbone (tibia) at the peripheral aspect of the knee joint. Each knee has two menisci, an inner (medial) and an outer (lateral) meniscus. The menisci function as adapters between the rounded femur and flat tibia, helping to distribute the forces between the two bones over a greater area (rather than point to point). They also help supply nutrition to the cartilage that lines the bones and to stabilize the knee joint. Meniscus tears are very common, occurring in up to one-third of all sports injuries. The inner meniscus is injured more often than the outer meniscus. In tennis, a meniscus tear usually results from a twisting injury, or cutting maneuver (rapidly changing direction while running) (Figures 8.22 and 8.23). This is more likely to occur on a hard court surface than clay or grass due to friction between the court and the shoe.

The majority of the meniscus has no blood supply. For that reason, when damaged, the meniscus is usually unable to experience a normal healing process. The meniscus is frequently torn in conjunction with knee ligament injuries. Those with an unstable (loose) knee due to previous knee ligament injury, especially a torn anterior cruciate ligament, are at increased risk for meniscus tears. In addition, with age, the meniscus gradually loses strength and is more prone to tearing.

Symptoms. Symptoms of a torn meniscus may come on acutely at the time of injury or develop gradually. They include pain with activity, especially pivoting or squatting. The pain is usually fairly localized with tenderness over the area of the torn meniscus. There is often some swelling of the affected the knee, usually starting one to two days after the injury, and varying in degree depending upon activity. There may be locking or catching of the knee joint, or an inability to fully straighten the knee. Some players may experience giving way or buckling of the knee. X-rays of the knee will not show a torn meniscus but are often helpful in evaluating the knee for other possible causes of the pain. An MRI is the best test to confirm the diagnosis of a torn meniscus.

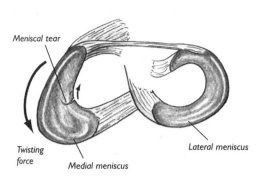

Figure 8.22
Meniscus tears most frequently occur during twisting, pivoting or cutting. Shown is a tear of the inner (medial) meniscus.

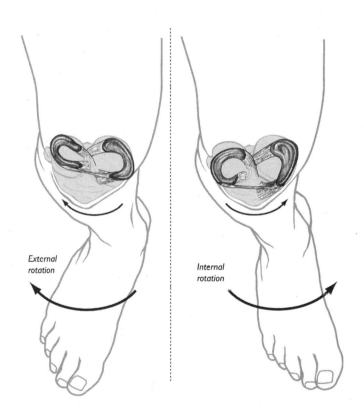

Figure 8.23
The menisci deform during rotation of the knee.

Treatment. The symptoms from a torn meniscus may subside without surgery if the tear is small, especially if it is located at or near the periphery of the meniscus. However, in most cases surgery is necessary to treat a torn meniscus. Left untreated, a torn meniscus that remains symptomatic, producing pain, catching, locking, or swelling, may ultimately cause damage to the cartilage surfaces of the tibia and femur.

Surgery for a torn meniscus is performed arthroscopically. In most cases, the torn fragment of meniscus is removed, leaving as much of the healthy portion of the meniscus as possible (partial meniscectomy). In those instances where the tear is located in the outer one-third of the meniscus and the meniscus is not severely damaged, it is preferable to repair the meniscus rather than remove the torn piece, preserving the function of the meniscus. If a significant portion of the meniscus is removed, that area of the knee is likely to become arthritic in later years. Rehabilitation is necessary after meniscal surgery to regain range of motion and strength. Following partial meniscectomy, rapid rehabilitation is possible. However, if the meniscus is repaired, rehabilitation will proceed more slowly in order to protect the knee and allow healing of the meniscus.

Practical tips for the player

- Wear the appropriate shoes for the surface being played upon.
- Avoid exercises that include full bending of the knee while pivoting (e.g., "frog jumps").
- Apply ice on the knee for 20 to 30 minutes three to four times a day until swelling has disappeared.
- Gradually rebuild the strength and coordination of the quadriceps muscles. Recommended exercises are static quadriceps strengthening, straight leg raises, double and single squats and balance exercises. See Figures 6.7, 6.8, 28.61, 28.62, 8.17, and 8.18, for instructions.

MENISCAL CYST

Description. A meniscal cyst is a sac of fluid which originates from a tear within the inner or outer meniscus of the knee. The meniscal tear causes joint irritation and fluid production. The fluid can push out the joint capsule adjacent to the meniscus, resulting in formation of the cyst. Meniscal cysts may occur with degenerative tears associated with aging or following an acute tear of the meniscus resulting from an injury. Tennis players are at risk when the tennis shoe grips the court solidly and the player suddenly changes direction, twisting the knee, resulting in a tear of the meniscus. Meniscal cysts more commonly originate from the lateral (outer) meniscus than the medial (inner) meniscus.

Symptoms. A player with a meniscal cyst generally notices a firm bump located over the joint line of the knee, most commonly on the outer side. The bump, usually not tender to touch, may be more apparent when the knee is straight and may get smaller or disappear when the knee is bent. There may be pain, especially with pivoting and squatting movements. There may also be swelling within the knee joint itself.

X-rays will not show a meniscal cyst but may demonstrate arthritic changes associated with a degenerative meniscal tear. Ultrasound may be used to confirm the presence of a cyst; however, MRI is the best test to visualize the cyst and any associated meniscal tear.

Treatment. Activity modification and nonsteroidal anti-inflammatory medications may reduce pain and associated swelling within the knee. The fluid within the cyst can be removed by sucking it out with a needle and syringe (aspiration). This may be accompanied by injection of a corticosteroid into the cyst. However, nonoperative treatment for meniscal cysts usually results in recurring symptoms. Definitive treatment for meniscal cysts usually requires surgery to address the underlying meniscal tear. Arthroscopy to remove the meniscus tear is the procedure of choice. The cyst may be removed arthroscopically at that time or by aspirating the fluid. It is usually not necessary to make a separate incision over the cyst to take it out as treating the underlying meniscus tear will allow the cyst to decompress (shrink) and disappear without other treatment.

Practical tips for the player
- Wear the appropriate shoes for the surface being played upon.
- Avoid exercises that include full bending of the knee, while pivoting (e.g., "frog jumps").
- After surgery, the same exercises can be performed as described under the meniscus tear.

MEDIAL COLLATERAL LIGAMENT SPRAIN

Description. The medial collateral ligament is a strong band of tissue that attaches the thighbone (femur) to the shinbone (tibia) on the inner side of the knee (Figure 8.24), providing stability primarily for side-to-side movement. It prevents the knee from buckling inward. A medial collateral ligament sprain is a stretch or tear of the medial collateral ligament. In contact sports such as soccer, American football and ice hockey, this injury usually is the result of a direct blow to the outer side of the knee. However, in tennis, non-contact twisting injuries, such as with pivoting and cutting, are the major cause of medial collateral ligament sprains. These sprains, like most other sprains, are graded on a scale from 1 to 3 depending on their severity. Grade 1 is a stretch injury to the ligament with no significant tearing. Grade 2 is a partial tear of the ligament, while grade 3 is a complete tear of the ligament. Other knee structures may be injured at the time of medial collateral ligament injury, including the cruciate ligaments, the menisci and the articular cartilage. When combined with damage to other structures, treatment should address all components of the injury. Sprains of the medial collateral ligament usually heal well, though they often heal in a slightly lengthened position, resulting in some residual looseness of the ligament.

Figure 8.24

The medial collateral ligament prevents the knee from buckling inwards.

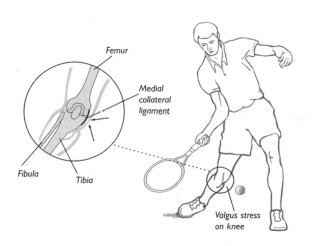

Femur

Medial collateral ligament

Fibula

Tibia

Valgus stress on knee

Symptoms. At the time of injury, there is immediate pain on the inner side of the knee. The injured player may have heard or felt a pop or snap at the time of injury. Most often, the player will not be able to continue playing. With more severe sprains, there may be difficulty bearing weight on the leg. Mild sprains may result in very mild swelling or puffiness over the inner side of the knee, developing within the first 24 hours. Grade 2 and 3 injuries, especially if combined with injuries to other structures in the knee, will cause more obvious swelling and possibly bruising around the knee. Significant stiffness with difficulty fully bending and straightening the knee commonly is present following medial collateral ligament sprains. The player may feel like the knee is unstable or loose, buckling to the inside when full weight is placed on the injured leg.

X-rays of the knee will be normal in the case of a medial collateral ligament sprain. The extent of the injury to the ligament can usually be determined by physical examination alone. However, MRI, in addition to visualizing the injured medial collateral ligament, may be useful in assessing whether there has also been damage to the cruciate ligaments or menisci.

Treatment. After an acute injury, initial treatment consists of RICE: rest, cooling with ice for ten to fifteen minutes every three to four hours for two to three days, a compression bandage to reduce swelling, and elevation of the leg (pillow under the knee). Definitive treatment for an isolated medial collateral ligament sprain is nonoperative as the ligament usually heals well with appropriate care. Use of crutches until walking becomes comfortable is helpful. A brace is often recommended to provide comfort and protect the injured ligament during the healing process. Range of motion exercises are initiated as early as possible as this movement helps to promote ligament healing. Strengthening, proprioceptive and sport-specific exercises are gradually added until return to tennis is allowed. Surgical treatment of medial collateral ligament injuries is generally considered for injuries that do not heal well over two to three months and grade 3 sprains associated with other ligamentous injuries to the knee.

Practical tips for the player
- Wearing the proper shoes for tennis surface may help reduce the risk of injury to the medial collateral injury.
- A functional brace and strengthening and coordination exercises for the leg muscles may be effective in preventing injury, especially re-injury. Recommended exercises are static quadriceps, straight leg raises, the double and single leg squat, and coordination exercises. See Figures 6.7, 6.8, 28.61, 28.62, 8.17, and 8.18 for instructions.

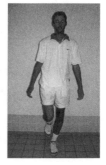

- Finally, include functional exercises such as lunges, side steps, two-foot ankle hops, starts, stops, and one-foot ankle hops. See Figures 28.64 and 28.66 for instructions.

ANTERIOR CRUCIATE LIGAMENT INJURY

Description. The anterior cruciate ligament is located in the center of the knee joint and runs from the back of the thighbone (femur) to the front of the shinbone (tibia) (Figure 8.25). It restrains excessive forward movement of the shinbone in relation to the thighbone and provides rotational stability to the knee.

An anterior cruciate ligament injury may result from a non-contact injury such as landing awkwardly or cutting or pivoting while the foot remains firmly planted, or from a direct blow to the knee in contact sports. Injuries of the anterior cruciate ligament are common in sports. Sports such as soccer, American football and basketball have the highest incidence of anterior cruciate ligament tears. Fortunately, the risk is significantly lower in tennis due to the non-contact nature of the sport and the type of movement involved. Women are more likely to suffer an anterior cruciate ligament tear than men, in part due to their different anatomy and muscle function. Injuries to the anterior cruciate ligament include stretching, partial tearing and complete tearing. There may be concurrent injury to the menisci, collateral ligaments, posterior cruciate ligament or articular cartilage.

Symptoms. At the time of injury the player often hears or feels a pop within the knee, followed immediately by pain of varying degree. The player is typically unable to continue playing due to pain and/or the knee feeling loose and unstable. Swelling of the knee is usually apparent within hours of the injury. The player

Figure 8.25

The four main ligaments of the knee: the anterior cruciate ligament, the posterior cruciate ligament, the mediale collateral ligament, and the lateral collateral ligament.

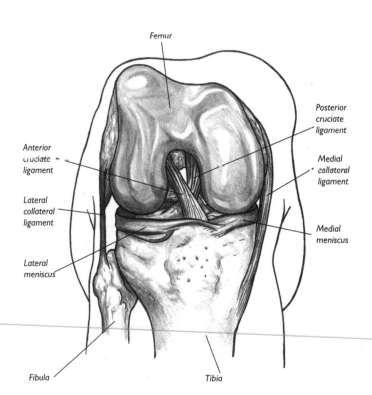

may be unable to fully straighten or bend the injured knee. A player with a torn anterior cruciate ligament that attempts to return to tennis without appropriate treatment is likely to experience episodes of giving way or buckling of the knee, particularly when trying to pivot or cut (rapidly change direction).

X-rays of a knee with an acute tear of the anterior cruciate ligament are most often normal, although they may show a specific chip fracture which is associated with anterior cruciate ligament tears. An MRI will confirm the diagnosis of an anterior cruciate ligament tear and also identify associated meniscal or articular cartilage damage.

Treatment. After an acute injury, initial treatment consists of RICE: rest, cooling with ice for ten to fifteen minutes every three to four hours for two to three days, a compression bandage to reduce swelling of the knee, and elevation of the leg (pillow under the knee). Using crutches until walking is comfortable is often recommended. Regaining knee range of motion and muscle control is the primary focus of treatment in the days following injury. Blood may be drained from the knee with a needle and syringe by the treating physician in order to relieve pain and facilitate exercises. A knee brace may be recommended, especially if other ligaments are injured along with the anterior cruciate ligament.

The anterior cruciate ligament does not heal by itself, but most people can perform normal daily activities after an appropriate rehabilitation program. If instability continues even after leg strength and knee motion have been regained, surgery (reconstruction of the anterior cruciate ligament) is usually recommended, because recurrent giving way and swelling may result in delayed injury to meniscal cartilage and an increased risk of late osteoarthritis of the knee. Surgery is usually required for those who want to return to participating in tennis as well. A new anterior cruciate ligament may be reconstructed by using a piece of the patellar tendon, or by using part of the hamstring muscles. It may take six to nine months to return to unrestricted play. Sometimes an arthroscopy is necessary in case of persistent extension loss (inability to fully extend the knee).

Practical tips for the player
- Biking at low resistance and high frequency, swimming, and aqua jogging are all good alternatives to running during the healing period.
- Stabilizing and strengthening exercises for the knee, with emphasis on the hamstring and quadriceps muscles, should be performed, such as coordination exercises, hamstring curls and good mornings. See Figures 8.17, 8.18, 8.26 and 28.52 for instructions.
- If you have access to a fitness center, include the leg press and stair master.

Figure 8.26
Leg curls can be performed with elastic tubing or with a leg curl machine. The exercise with elastic tubing is as follows. Lie down on your stomach and tie the elastic tubing to your ankle. Straighten your leg. Now bend your leg against the resistance of the elastic tubing.

- You are ready to return to play when functional exercises, such as skips, side steps, starts, stops, turns, and ankle hops can be performed without problems. See Figure 28.66 for instructions.

ANTERIOR KNEE PAIN (PAIN IN THE FRONT OF THE KNEE)

The most common causes for anterior knee pain in tennis players are the patellofemoral pain syndrome, jumper's knee (patellar tendinosis), Osgood Schlatter disease and Sinding-Larsen-Johansson syndrome (children and adolescents).

PATELLOFEMORAL PAIN SYNDROME

Description. Patellofemoral pain syndrome is characterized by pain around the front of the knee emanating from the articulation between the kneecap (patella) and the end of the thigh bone (femur), that is aggravated by activities such as squatting, running, prolonged sitting and climbing and descending stairs. The kneecap has a wedge shape and slides on extension and flexion of the knee in a groove formed by the femoral condyles. The pain is caused by abnormal contact between the undersurface of the kneecap with the femoral groove.

This excessive pressure may be due to poor tracking of the patella within the groove of the femur, as a result of a malalignment within the lower extremity. When malalignment is the cause, the patella usually tracks too far to the outer side of the groove (lateral tracking), concentrating pressure on the outer part of the kneecap. Common malalignments include inward rotation of the thighbone, knock knees, outwards rotation of the shin bone, and increased pronation (inwards rotation) of the foot. When these anatomical conditions are all present in one person, it is termed the "miserable malalignment syndrome" (Figure 8.27).

Other causes of increased patellofemoral pressure include muscular imbalances around the knee. These dynamic factors include:
- Weakness of the quadriceps muscles (especially the vastus medialis oblique).

- Weakness of the hip abductors (leading to excessive lateral tilt in the single stance phase of the gait).
- Weakness of the hip external rotators (leading to compensatory foot pronation).
- A tight lateral retinaculum and tight iliotibial band (pulling the patella laterally).
- Tightness of the quadriceps (increasing patellofemoral pressure during knee flexion).
- Tight hamstring, gastrocnemius and soleus muscles (increasing posterior force on the joint).

Figure 8.27

The miserable malalignment syndrome.

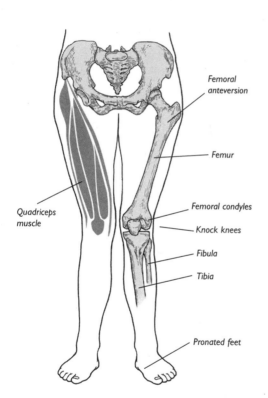

Patellofemoral pain syndrome may also occur following traumatic damage to the smooth cartilage surface of the kneecap (Figure 8.28). This is most commonly the result of a fall onto the front of the knee, a dashboard injury to the knee in a car accident or a dislocation of the patella due to a twisting injury.

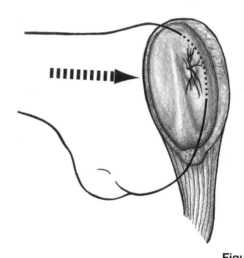

Figure 8.28

The names chondromalacia patella and patellar chondropathy are used when there is proven cartilage damage.

Symptoms. Player with patellofemoral pain syndrome complain of diffuse knee pain, around the front of the knee behind or around the kneecap. The pain is worse with sitting for long periods of time, arising from a sitting position, going up or down stairs or hills, running, kneeling, squatting, and/or wearing shoes with high heels. During tennis, serving with a deep knee bend, pushing off after having hit a wide ball, and deep bending for low volleys may be painful (Figure 8.29). The pain may be described as achy, though, at times it may be sharp. A player may note occasional feeling of the knee giving way due to reflex inhibition of the quadriceps secondary to pain, and sometimes catching of the knee. Usually there is minimal or no knee swelling. There may be a grinding heard or felt when the knee is flexed and extended. X-rays of the knee often demonstrate abnormal tracking of the patella when present.

Figure 8.29
Deep bending of the knee for low volleys may provoke anterior knee pain.

Treatment. When symptoms are mild, the player may continue to compete while undergoing treatment. In more severe cases, rest from tennis and running for a period of time may be necessary. Appropriate stretching and strengthening exercises will usually correct the problem. These generally include the following: strengthening the quadriceps muscles, especially the medial quadriceps (vastus medialis oblique); strengthening the hip muscles (abductors and rotators); and stretching the tight lateral structures (iliotibial tract), the quadriceps and hamstring muscles, the external rotators, and the calves. Emphasis should be placed on isometric and closed chain isotonic strengthening. Rehabilitation should be aimed at improving the maltracking when present.

Intermittent application of ice, particularly after exercise and at the end of the day, can help reduce pain. Electrical stimulation can be useful. Corticosteroid injections into the knee should be avoided as they seldom are beneficial for this condition and may be damaging to the normal hyaline cartilage. Proper footwear and custom orthotics may be recommended. A lightweight knee brace or patella taping, designed to improve patella tracking, may be helpful in selected individuals.

Occasionally surgery may be necessary, but indications are narrow. Surgery should only be considered after failure of prolonged conservative treatment and when anatomical disorders are present. Surgical release of tight lateral structures may be performed. Occasionally, additional realignment procedures may be necessary. When there is articular damage, arthroscopic debridement of the area may be helpful.

Practical tips for the player
- A period of relative rest is often helpful. This means avoiding activities that provoke the pain, and continuing activities that can be done without pain, such a cycling, swimming, and stairmaster. In tennis, most problems occur with low volleys, left-right drills, stooping for a drop shot, and serving with a lot of knee action, so these exercises should initially be avoided. Also, avoid explosive knee action, such as lunging, sprinting, and jumping.
- Choose Har-tru or clay court surfaces, because peak force on the knee is lower.
- Intermittent application of ice, particularly after exercise and at the end of the day, can help reduce pain and swelling.
- Strengthen the quadriceps muscles and hip abductor muscles and perform proprioceptive training. Recommended exercises include

static quadriceps strengthening, straight leg raise, double leg squat, step ups, sideward leg raise and coordination exercises. See Figures 6.7, 6.8, 28.56, 28.61, 28.63, 8.17, and 8.18 for instructions.

- Regularly stretch the hamstrings, quadriceps, soleus, gastrocnemius, and iliotibial band. See Figures 5.3, 5.4, 5.5, 5.6 and 5.9 for instructions.

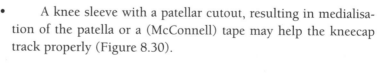

Figure 8.30

Knee brace with patella cut-out.

- A knee sleeve with a patellar cutout, resulting in medialisation of the patella or a (McConnell) tape may help the kneecap track properly (Figure 8.30).

JUMPER'S KNEE (PATELLAR TENDONITIS)

Description. Jumper's knee, also called patellar tendinosis or patellar tendonitis, is an overuse injury resulting in a small area of degeneration of the patellar tendon at the point at which it attaches to the lower end of the kneecap (Figure 8.31). It is due to the high loads on the patellar tendon in running and jumping sports. It is a common affliction among tennis players, because of the explosive quadriceps contractions that are required for jumping (serves and overheads) and the sudden starts, stops and changes of direction. Insufficient flexibility of the hamstrings and quadriceps muscles and malalignment (wide hips, bow legs, knock-knees or flat feet) may contribute to undue stress on the patellar tendon and the development of jumper's knee.

Symptoms. Symptoms of jumper's knee include pain, tenderness and occasionally mild swelling at the lower end of the kneecap at the attachment of the patellar tendon. There may be pain when bending the knee completely, such as during squatting, kneeling or lunging, and during forceful straightening of the knee, such as during jumping, running, sprinting, returning after having hit a wide ball, or serving. Ultrasonography or MRI can be useful in the evaluation of jumper's knee, demonstrating abnormal appearance of the tendon due to degeneration of the tendon fibers.

Treatment. Initial treatment consists of rest from the offending activity (stop playing or avoid exercises that require explosive knee action or deep bending of the knee) and cooling with ice after exercise for ten to fifteen minutes. A patellar tendon strap or patellar tendon taping may reduce pain during tennis. Massage of the quadriceps muscles, iliotibial band, adductors, hamstrings and calf muscles, mobilization of the patella and patellar tendon, and electrotherapy may be helpful. A rehabilitation program, aimed at improving the coordination and strength of the leg muscles should follow this. Stretching of the quadriceps, hamstrings and calf muscles is also helpful. Steroid injection should be avoided, as injections into the tendon will increase the risk for patellar tendon rupture.

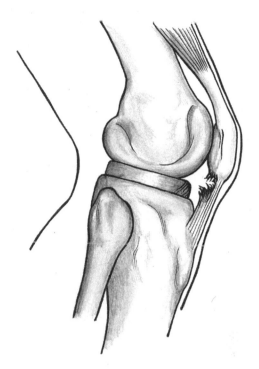

Figure 8.31
Jumper's knee.

If symptoms persist despite an adequate period of rest and appropriate treatment, surgery may be recommended. The surgical procedure may be done open or arthroscopiclly and involves removal of the degenerated tendon tissue and stimulation of healing by multiple small incisions in the tendon.

Practical tips for the player
- Biking with low resistance, swimming, aqua jogging, or using the stair master are all good alternatives to running during the healing period.
- Use a patellar tendon strap or patellar tendon taping during play. Both the strap and tape reduce loading of the tendon at its insertion.
- Wear custom-made arch supports if you have flat feet or overpronated feet.
- Include stretching exercises for the quadriceps and hamstring muscles during the warm up and cool down period. See Figures 5.5 and 5.6 for instructions.
- Use tennis shoes with the correct outsoles for different playing surfaces to avoid unnecessary strain on the knee while twisting and turning. It may be helpful to wear shoes with a moderately worn outsole on hard courts with high friction textured surfaces.

Figure 8.32
Eccentric quadriceps strengthening. Stand on the affected leg, and bend the knee. Place the unaffected leg next to the affected leg, and shift your weight to the unaffected leg. Now straighten the legs again. Repeat this sequence. Perform three series of ten to fifteen repetitions. Make the exercise harder by standing on an inclined platform, toes pointing downwards.

- Strengthen the quadriceps muscles. Recommended exercises include double and single leg squat and eccentric quadriceps squats. See Figures 28.61, 28.62 and 8.32 for instructions.

- Perform sprint training only after a thorough warm up. Build up slowly by first doing some acceleration drills, slowly increasing speed from 50% to 100% maximum speed. Allow one or two days of rest after intensive sprint training.

- Jumping and plyometric exercises may contribute to the development of jumper's knee. Therefore, it is important to build up these exercises slowly (in the course of weeks to months, not days!), to give the tendon time to adapt (become stronger and larger) to the increased load.

OSGOOD SCHLATTER DISEASE

Description. Osgood Schlatter disease is an overuse injury of the knee that commonly occurs in junior players. The affliction is seen during adolescence, particularly in ten to fifteen-year-old boys and eight to thirteen-year-old girls. It is seen more often in boys than in girls. The powerful quadriceps group of muscles converges to form the patellar tendon, which attaches to the lower leg at a vulnerable growth area (apophysis) called the tibial tubercle (Figure 8.33). Continuous pulling of the patellar tendon on the developing tibial tubercle leads to localized pain, tenderness and swelling over the tubercle. Both knees may be affected in some individuals. Occasionally, a player will have symptoms in adulthood due to fragmentation of the tubercle resulting in persistent irritation of the patellar tendon.

Symptoms. Young players with Osgood Schlatter disease complain of pain at the tibial tubercle with running and jumping. Activities such as cycling, stair climbing, deep knee bends and kneeling may also be painful. During tennis, low volleys and serving may particularly provoke pain. Swelling often develops over the tibial tubercle, and the area can become exquisitely tender to touch.

Ultrasound or MRI are more valuable than radiography for demonstrating the features of Osgood Schlatter disease, but are generally unnecessary.

Figure 0.00
Osgood Schlatter disease of the knee.

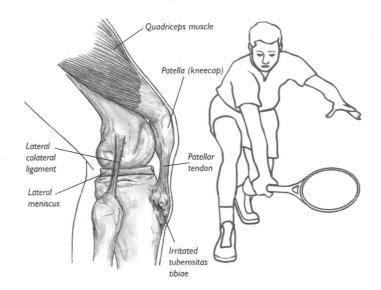

Treatment. The primary treatment for Osgood Schlatter disease is activity modification. Reducing the intensity and frequency of training and play is usually all that is necessary to promote healing and allow symptoms to subside. Playing with mild discomfort is allowed, however, if symptoms include limping, all running and jumping activities, including tennis, should be avoided.

Applying ice to the painful area for ten to fifteen minutes after exercise and several times a day will help to reduce pain and swelling. If hamstring tightness is present, stretching exercises should be initiated. Quadriceps stretching exercises must be done carefully to avoid aggravating the condition. Occasionally, if the knee is very painful, a short period of immobilization using a removable knee splint or cast may be recommended. However, prolonged immobilization should be avoided since it will result in atrophy (loss of muscle mass) of the muscles around the knee.

Fortunately, Osgood Schlatter disease is generally a self-limited condition. The injury responds well to activity modification. Ultimately, when the growth area of the tibial tubercle fuses near the end of adolescence, symptoms will resolve.

Occasionally symptoms persist after an athlete has reached skeletal maturity due to the development of bony fragments from the tubercle embedded within the patellar tendon. In these cases, if symptoms warrant, treatment consists of surgical excision of the loose fragments.

Practical tips for the player

- Use tennis shoes when playing tennis, and running shoes during physical conditioning. Make sure the shoes have adequate shock absorption and sideways stability. If any malalignments (valgus or bow knees, flat or cavus feet) have been noticed, these should be corrected with inlays in firm shoes with sturdy soles.
- Perform as much of the training as possible on clay or sandy surfaces that allow gliding and avoid playing on hard courts. Because of the longer braking phase, the peak load on the knee (and tibial tubercle growth plate) is lower on a clay court than on a hard court.
- Regular stretching of the muscles at the front and back of the thigh (quadriceps and hamstrings) decreases the tension of the muscles and the pulling forces on the patellar tendon, and thus tibial tubercle. Stretching should not hurt, so do not stretch too much in the acute

phase of the injury. See Figures 5.5 and 5.6 for stretching instructions.

- Perform co-ordination exercises. See Figures 8.17 for instructions.
- Use a patellar tendon strap or brace during play (Figure 8.32). This ensures that the load on the insertion point of the patellar tendon at the tibial tubercle is spread out over a larger area, decreasing the point pressure.
- Use a bike with gears. Use the lowest gear, which results in low resistance and a high pedal frequency. This is easiest on the knees. Try to avoid cycling uphill or against the wind.
- Avoid prolonged sitting in the same position or with the knees pulled up.
- Ensure a gradual build-up of the training load, so your body has time to adapt to the extra load.

SINDING-LARSEN-JOHANSSON SYNDROME

This is similar to Osgood Schlatter disease, except that it affects the lower pole of the patella instead of the tibial tuberosity and is much less common. The same treatment principles apply.

HOFFA'S DISEASE (INFRAPATELLAR FAT PAD SYNDROME)

Description. Hoffa's disease occurs when there is a painful pinching of the fatty tissue below the kneecap between the end of the femur and the tibia, resulting in traumatic and inflammatory changes in the infrapatellar fat pad (Figure 8.34). The fat pad protects the patellar tendon from scarring or getting stuck on the tibia below the knee. Hoffa's disease usually results from a direct injury to the knee, forced hyperextension of the knee, or repeated injury to the fat pad during activities that require maximal bending or straightening of the knee. The sudden stops and starts of tennis and occasional squatting may result in fat pad inflammation and entrapment.

Symptoms. There is pain below the patella, worsened by playing tennis or completely straightening the knee. There may be swelling of the knee and/or tenderness and swelling on either side of the patellar tendon. The diagnosis is usually made by clinical examination. MRI can be used if the diagnosis is unclear.

Treatment. Initial treatment consists of activity modification and cooling with ice. Occasionally, an injection of cortisone may be recommended to reduce the inflamed tissue that is repeatedly getting pinched. In some isolated cases surgery may be advised. This is usually done arthroscopically to remove the inflamed tissues or chronic scar tissue.

Practical tips for the player

- Stretch the hamstrings and quadriceps muscles before and after practice or competition. See Figures 5.5 and 5.6 for instructions.

- It may be helpful to temporarily wear a knee brace, knee tape or heel lift in your tennis shoes to prevent the knee from fully extending.

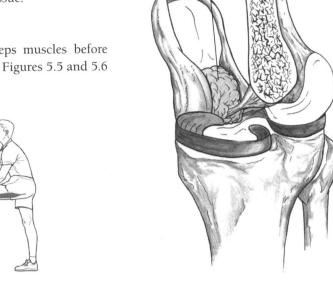

Infrapatellar fat pad

Figure 8.34
Hoffa's disease is an inflamation of the infrapatellar fat pad.

PES ANSERINUS SYNDROME

Description. The pes anserinus is the tendon insertion of three thigh muscles (sartorius, gracilis, and semitendinosus) just below the knee, to the inner front of the lower leg. The term "pes anserinus" literally means 'goose foot,' describing the webbed foot like structure. The three muscles are primary flexors of the knee and also protect the knee against rotation and inwards bending (valgus). Underlying the conjoined tendon, there is a bursa: a closed, fluid-filled sac that functions as a gliding surface to reduce friction between the tendon and bone. When the bursa becomes inflamed, this is known as bursitis. The pes anserinus syndrome may be a bursitis and/or a tendinopathy. Tennis players are susceptible to this injury due to the necessary side-to-side movements, pivoting, cutting, jumping and deceleration during tennis. Players who drag their legs excessively when hitting forehands are at increased risk, because the increased valgus stress may lead to repetitive strains of the pes anserinus. In children, there may be a bony bump (exostosis) on the lower leg that causes the symptoms, due to the continuous friction of the tendons gliding over this bump.

Symptoms. There may be pain, tenderness, swelling, warmth and/or redness over the pes anserinus bursa and tendon on the front inner leg just 2-3 inches (4-6 cm) below the knee. The pain generally increases with activity, such as playing tennis or running. Bending the knee against resistance or valgus stress may provoke the pain. There may be crepitation when the painful area is moved or touched. Generally, X-ray is not indicated. However, young patients, in rare cases, may have an exostosis in the metaphyseal area, which can be shown on X-ray. Ultrasound or MRI can show a swollen bursa and/or degenerative changes of the tendon.

Treatment. Initial treatment consists of activity modification, cooling with ice, NSAIDs, and massage of the adductor and hamstring muscles. Proprioceptive training for the knee and strengthening exercises for the upper leg muscles should be initiated. The doctor may recommend an injection of cortisone into the bursa. Surgery may be necessary if the symptoms do not respond to nonoperative measures. Surgical procedures include removing the inflamed bursa, or, if there is an exostosis present, excision of both the bursa and the exostosis.

Practical tips for the player
- Use arch supports if you have flat or pronated feet.
- A knee sleeve or bandage may help keep the tendon warm during activity and reduce symptoms.
- Place a small cushion between the thighs at night.
- Stretch the hamstring and adductor muscles. See Figures 5.6 to 5.8 for instructions.

- Strengthen the hamstring muscles by performing good mornings and squats. See Figures 28.52, and 28.61-28.62 for instructions.
- Strengthen the adductor muscles by performing ball squeezes, adduction against resistance, and hip adduction. See Figures 8.4, 8.5, 28.58, and 28.60 for instructions.

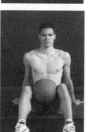

ILIOTIBIAL BAND FRICTION SYNDROME

Description. Iliotibial band friction syndrome, also called runner's knee, is an overuse injury caused by repetitive friction of the iliotibial band across the lateral femoral epicondyle (Figure 8.35). The iliotibial band is the tendon attachment of the hip muscles into the lower leg just below the knee. Anything that causes the leg to bend inward, stretching the iliotibial band, such as bowlegs, overpronation, workouts on downhill or banked surfaces, or a tight iliotibial band may cause this problem. Ramping up the training too quickly can also cause this injury. Occasionally, direct trauma to the outer knee may cause the bursa under the iliotibial band to get inflamed. Insufficient strength of the gluteus medius muscle may add to the problem, because it leads to excessive lateral tilt in the single stance phase of the gait.

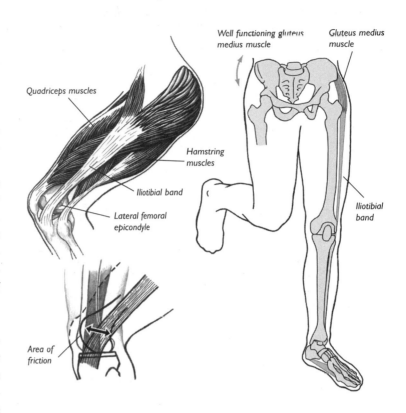

Symptoms. There may be pain, tenderness, swelling, and warmth over the iliotibial band at the outer knee (above the joint). The pain may radiate to the outer thigh or lower leg. The pain is usually experienced during running or cycling, and less often while playing tennis. The pain usually comes up after running a mile or two, forcing the athlete to stop. The pain is worsened running down hills, on banked tracks or running next to the curb on the street. The pain is felt most when the foot of the affected leg

Figure 8.35

Iliotibial band syndrome is an overuse injury caused by repetitive friction of the iliotibial band across the lateral femoral epicondyle. Strengthening the gluteus medius muscle may help prevent this injury.

hits the ground. There may be a crackling sound when the painful area is moved or touched. Imaging is typically not necessary, but if diagnosis is unclear, ultrasonograpy or MRI should be considered. Radiographic findings are usually unremarkable. Ultrasonography is useful in evaluating cystic masses and fluid. It can also reveal the dynamic motion of the iliotibial band, thus allowing visualization of the impingement. MR can reveal reactive signal in the periosteum, bursal fluid and thickening of the iliotibial band.

Treatment. Initial treatment consists of activity modification and cooling with ice. Stretching the tight iliotibial band before and after practice or competition is important, as is correction of any existing malalignment (flat or cavus feet). A heel lift may also help reduce symptoms. Core stability exercises are recommended if there are any imbalances present. The doctor may recommend a cortisone injection into the bursa. Surgery, consisting of transsection of the posterior half of the iliotibial band where it passes over the lateral epicondyle of the femur or removal of the underlying bursa, may occasionally be necessary if the symptoms do not respond to conservative treatment.

Practical tips for the player

- Stretch the iliotibial band before and after exercise. See Figure 5.9 for instructions.
- Strengthen the gluteus medius muscle with the leg raise. See Figure 28.55 for instructions.
- If you have a tight iliotibial band, cavus feet, or flat feet, have a wedge inserted in your shoes to reduce friction to the bursa or use a heel lift.

POPLITEUS TENDINOPATHY (POPLITEUS TENDINITIS)

Description. Popliteus tendinopathy (popliteus tendon tenosynovitis, popliteus tendinitis) is a strain or overuse injury of the popliteus muscle and tendon at the posterolateral (back and outer) part of the knee (Figure 8.36). The popliteus muscle stabilizes the posterolateral corner of the knee and prevent forward translation of the upper leg, especially during downhill running (see arrows in Figure 8.36). Also, the popliteus muscle will "unlock" the knee during initial flexion from an extended position. Overuse or fatigue of the quadriceps muscles is felt to contribute to an overuse of the popliteus muscle. If the fatigued quadriceps cannot adequately resist forward displacement of the upper leg, undue stress may occur on the relatively small popliteus. In tennis players, the pivoting, cutting and rotating of the leg during play may contribute to causing a popliteus tendon injury.

Symptoms. Typically, popliteus tendinopathy has a gradual onset of symptoms. The pain usually recurs after running a particular, reproducible distance or amount of playing. There is pain and tenderness at the posterolateral corner of the knee. The pain is felt when standing on the leg with the knee bent 15-30 degrees or just as the foot of

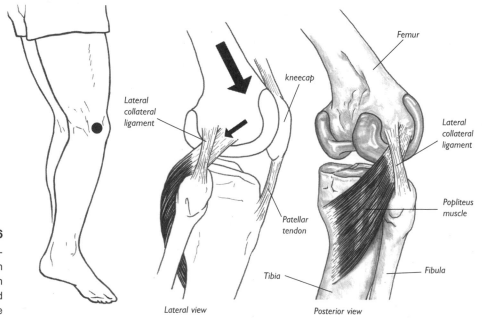

Figure 8.36

The popliteus tendon slows down the knee when going downhill and helps turn the knee inwards.

Lateral view

Posterior view

Lateral collateral ligament

kneecap

Patellar tendon

Femur

Lateral collateral ligament

Popliteus muscle

Tibia

Fibula

the affected leg lifts off the ground during walking and running. Ultrasound can be used to distinguish tendinopathy from a meniscal cyst or synovial hemangioma. MRI can be used to rule out damage of the cartilage of the lateral compartment or a lateral meniscal tear.

Treatment. Initial treatment consists of activity modification and cooling with ice. Friction massage of a tight popliteus muscle may be helpful, in addition to massage of the hamstrings and calf muscles. Strengthening exercises for the quadriceps muscles should be initiated. An injection of cortisone to the inflamed area around the tendon may be recommended for persistent cases, followed by restriction of activities for one to two weeks. Surgery to remove the inflamed tendon lining or degenerated tendon tissue is rarely necessary.

Practical tips for the player
- Bicycling is a good alternative to running during the healing period.
- Modify your running exercises, e.g. by reducing your running mileage, running uphill, shortening your stride length, and changing the side of the road or track you run on.
- A knee sleeve or bandage will help keep the tendon warm during activity and may reduce symptoms.
- Stretch the popliteus muscle by fully extending the knee.
- Shoe inserts are recommended if you have flat feet, especially a triangular varus wedge placed in front of the heel.
- Strengthen the quadriceps muscles with squats and eccentric squats on an inclined board. See Figures 28.61, 28.62, and 8.32 for instructions.

OSTEITIS PUBIS

Description. Osteitis pubis is an inflammation of the pubic symphysis and surrounding muscle insertions. It is most likely caused by repetitive micro-trauma or shearing force to the pubic symphysis. The pelvis is a ring, and any change in anatomy or applied forces to one area will be compensated throughout the ring. This is why a leg length discrepancy or sacro-iliac dysfunction can greatly change the shear forces across the pubic symphysis. In tennis, a common cause may be a combination of abdominal hyperextension and thigh hyperabduction with the pivot point being the pubic symphysis during serving and stroking the ball. Acute episodes of osteitis pubis can develop as a consequence of forced hip abduction, such as when sliding into the ball.

Symptoms. Pain can be located in the groin, hip, perineum, testis or lower abdomen. Pain may be sharp, stabbing or burning. Pain can be elicited when pushing the legs inwards against resistance and increases with running, sliding, twisting, or pushing off to change direction. Radiographs often are negative early in the disease but as the disease progresses, widening of the symphysis, sclerosis and osteolysis may be seen. Bone scan (Tc 99m) or single-photon emission computerized tomography (SPECT) scans often are positive early in the disease. MRI is useful to distinguish between muscle, tendon, periosteal, or bony disruption. Many times, inflammation of the fibrocartilaginous disk, bone edema, and sclerosis at the pubic margins can be appreciated.

Treatment. Initial treatment consists of activity modification and ice massage of the painful area (if tolerated). Electrical stimulation and nonsteroidal anti-inflammatory medications may help reduce pain. Treatment may include manipulation of the sacro-iliac joint, massage of the adductor muscles and restoration of flexibility and strength around the pelvis. Leg-length discrepancies should be corrected. A corticosteroid injection may help to speed up recovery, but this step is controversial.

Practical tips for the player
- Massage of tight adductor muscles may reduce symptoms.
- Stretch the adductor and iliopsoas muscles. See Figures 5.7, 5.8 and 5.11 for instructions.

- Strengthen the leg, hip and groin muscles. Recommended exercises are ball squeezes, adduction against resistance, squats, leg press, and stair climbing. See Figures 8.4, 8.5, 28.60, 28.61, and 28.62 for instructions.

- Any leg length discrepancy or malalignment should be corrected with orthotics or heel lifts.
- Perform core stabilization exercises. Recommended exercises include supine core stabilization, bridging and the plank. See Figures 6.10, 6.11, 28.47, 28.48, and 28.53 for instructions.

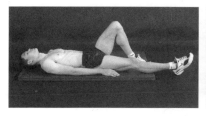

- Thermally protective compression shorts may be useful when initially returning to play.

BURSITIS OF THE HIP

Description. A bursa is a closed, fluid-filled sac that functions as a gliding surface to reduce friction between tissues of the body. There are two major bursae of the hip: the trochanteric bursa is located on the outer (lateral) side of the hip, and the ischial bursa is located in the upper buttock area. When a bursa becomes inflamed, this is known as bursitis. In tennis players, the cause of bursitis of the hip is most commonly noninfectious, due to trauma (fall on the hip) or strain. Occasionally, bacteria cause it. There may also be an underlying disease, such as gout or rheumatoid arthritis.

Symptoms. Trochanteric bursitis causes tenderness and dull or burning pain on the outer side of the hip. The pain increases when lying on this side, long walking or stair climbing. Pain of ischial bursitis is located in the buttocks and increases while sitting on hard surfaces or climbing up hill. An X-ray will show any bony abnormalities or spurs, calcium deposits or other problems within the joint that contribute to the bursitis. Real time ultrasound may be useful in confirming the diagnosis. Bone scans and MRI may be needed if a possible fracture, tumor or tissue death (osteonecrosis) of the femoral head need to be ruled out.

Treatment. Noninfectious bursitis is treated with rest, ice compresses, and nonsteroidal anti-inflammatory medications, followed by gentle stretching and strengthening exercises. If this is not effective, it can be treated with a corticosteroid injection into the swollen bursa. Infectious bursitis should be treated with antibiotics. If there is an underlying disease, this should be treated as well.

Practical tips for the player
- Wear a shoe lift if you have a leg length discrepancy.
- Stretch the muscles of the outer hip. See Figure 5.10 for instructions.
- Strengthen the hip abductors by performing leg raises and hip abduction. See Figures 28.55, 28.56, and 28.57 for instructions.

TENDINOPATHY OF THE OUTER HIP MUSCLES

Description. Tendinopathy of the outer hip muscles is characterized by pain at the outer hip caused by strain and/or overuse of the hip abductors and gluteal muscles and their tendon attachments to the femur. These outer hip muscles attach the pelvis to the outer hip and stabilize the hip during walking, running and jumping. At the beginning of the grass court season, players are often affected due to the increased bending and lunging for low balls, resulting in sudden overuse of the hip abductors. Other risk factors are: weak hip muscles, resulting in increased tilting of the pelvis; training on a banked surface, such as next to the curb when running on the street; leg length inequality; and alignment problems, such as a wide hip and knock knees.

Symptoms. There is pain and tenderness over the outer hip, which increases when moving the hip. The athlete may walk or run with a limp. There may be weakness of the hip, especially spreading the legs/hips against resistance. History and physical examination are the keys to diagnosis. X-rays and MRI may be used to rule out other pathology of the hip.

Treatment. Initial treatment consists of activity modification and cooling the painful area with ice. Deep friction massage of the hips and buttocks will help to relax the tight muscles. Stretching and strengthening of the outer hip muscles should be initiated.

Practical tips for the player

- Stretch the outer hip muscles. See Figure 5.10 for instructions.
- Strengthen the gluteus muscles and hip abductors with the leg raise and the hip abduction. See Figures 28.55, 28.56 and 28.57 for instructions.

- Wear a shoe lift if there is a leg length inequality.

PIRIFORMIS SYNDROME

Description. This is a rare nerve condition in the hip causing pain and occasionally loss of feeling in the buttocks and back of the thigh. It involves compression of the sciatic nerve at the hip by the piriformis muscle. The piriformis muscle travels from the pelvis to the outer hip and rotates the hip, allowing the thigh, foot and knee to point outward. The sciatic nerve usually passes the hip between this muscle and other muscles of the hip (Figure 8.37). Spasm or hypertrophy of the piriformis muscle as a result of strain or overuse may put pressure on the nerve. Occasionally (15-20% of the time) the nerve travels directly through the muscle, which causes pressure on the nerve.

Symptoms. There is a chronic nagging ache or pain in the buttock or posterior thigh, with maximal pain usually pinpointed in the upper part of the buttock. Occasionally, the pain radiates down the posterolateral aspect of the leg to the ankle, accompanied by tingling or numbness. The pain is worse at night while lying down, when sitting for a prolonged period or when getting up from a sitting position. Passive stretching of the legs or forced internal rotation of a straight hip increases the pain. Hitting backhands or bending down to hit low volleys tend to provoke symptoms. As compression of the sciatic nerve may occur anywhere else along its length, it is important to rule out more common causes of sciatica, such as lumbar disease. The diagnosis of piriformis syndrome generally remains one of exclusion.

Treatment. Initial treatment consists of rest from the offending activity (stop playing, running or bicycling for a while). If sitting aggravates the pain, stand up or change positions to raise the painful area from the seat. Stretching of the hip muscles should not be done until the acute pain is gone. Core stability exercises should be initiated. Deep friction massage of the buttocks and posterior thigh may be helpful to relax the tight muscles. Injections with cortisone and an anesthetic, to the area where the nerve is being pinched, may be attempted to help reduce the nerve inflammation and pinching. Surgery may occasionally be necessary to free the pinched nerve by cutting the muscle or tendon where the nerve is being pinched is conservative treatment is unsuccessful.

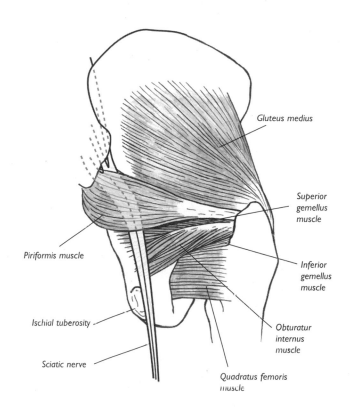

Figure 8.37
Piriformis syndrome involves compression of the sciatic nerve at the hip by the piriformis muscle.

Gluteus medius

Superior gemellus muscle

Inferior gemellus muscle

Piriformis muscle

Ischial tuberosity

Sciatic nerve

Obturatur internus muscle

Quadratus femoris muscle

Practical tips for the player
- Stretch the piriformis muscle (Figures 8.38a and 8.38b).

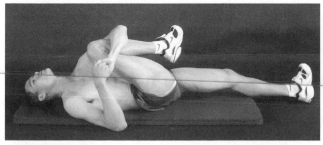

Figure 8.38a, b
Lie down on your back with the affected knee bent. Pull the knee into the chest and across the midline. The stretch can be increased by grabbing the knee of the affected leg with one hand and the ankle with the other hand (Figure 38b). Now slowly pull the leg towards you. You can fine-tune the tension in the buttock by either pulling more on the knee or on the ankle.

- Any leg length discrepancies should be corrected with shoe inserts.
- Take the time to adjust when switching from clay to grass.
- Strengthen the abductor muscles of the hip. Recommended exercises include the hip abduction and the leg raise. See Figures 28.55-28.57 and and 28.59 for instructions.

HIP LABRAL TEARS

Description. The labrum of the hip is a fibrocartilaginous structure attached to an osseous rim of acetabulum (socket of the hip). This cartilage rim can become torn, though the exact mechanism, which causes this, is unclear. It is being observed with increasing frequency in tennis players. It is thought to be associated with pivoting, and the use of open stance strokes where the hip is extended and externally rotated. Degenerative tears of the labrum can be seen in addition to traumatic tears.

Symptoms. Many labral tears do not cause symptoms. Patients with symptomatic labral tears will often complain of deep pain that is localized in the anterior groin. However, symptoms can also be referred to the outer hip or in the buttocks. Initially, patients experience discreet episodes of sharp pain exacerbated by pivoting or twisting. Over time, symptoms may progress to the point where patients have pain that is dull, positional, or activity-related. Eventually, the pain becomes continuous in most patients. In addition to pain, most patients also complain of catching, popping, or locking within the joint. Labral tears are difficult to detect on physical examination. The diagnosis can be confirmed with contrast-enhanced magnetic resonance imaging.

Treatment. Initial treatment is activity modification, whereby a trial of limited weight bearing with crutches may be beneficial for documented acute injury to the labrum. Physical therapy should be aimed at improving flexibility and strength around the hip. If conservative therapy fails, surgical removal of the torn labrum may be recommended, and has been found to be successful in alleviation of symptoms related to a torn labrum. Return to sports may be expected at two to twelve weeks following surgery.

Practical tips for the player
- Stretch the muscles around the hip area, including the adductor muscles, the gluteals, piriformis and iliopsoas muscle. See Figures 5.7, 5.8, 5.10, 5.11 and 8.37a-b for instructions.

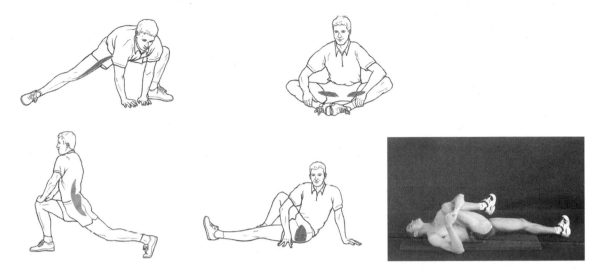

- Perform core stability exercises and strengthen the hip abductors and hip adductors. Recommended exercises include gym ball balancing, bridging, good mornings, hip adduction and hip abduction. See Figures 28,46, 28.47, 28.48, 28.52, 28.54, 28.59, and 28.60 for instructions.

SUMMARY

In this chapter, an overview of common injuries of the lower body in tennis players is presented. For each injury, the causal mechanism, symptoms, treatment, prevention and practical tips for the player are described. Important factors in the prevention and treatment of lower extremity injuries include the court surface, shoe selection, orthotics, stretching and strengthening exercises, taping and bracing, and a well-balanced training program.

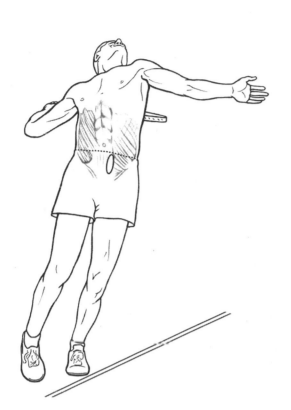

9

Injuries of the Trunk and Spine

The trunk muscles are a vital link in the body's kinetic chain. Without good trunk rotation, flexion, and extension, tennis strokes will lack power and control and may place the upper extremity at a higher risk for injury. The motions required in tennis, such as spine flexion, extension and rotation, make injuries of the trunk and spine the most prevalent problems in the tennis player. Further, trunk muscles, including the back extensors, abdominal muscles, and rotators, transfer force, placing extensive stress on the spine. In this chapter, the symptoms and causes of the various types of back, thoracic and abdominal injuries in tennis players will be described, as well as treatment options and preventative strategies, including core stability exercises.

LOW BACK PAIN (NONSPECIFIC)

Description. Low back pain is very common among tennis players. Although intense tennis practice is generally held to be a risk factor for low back pain, the prevalence of low back pain in tennis players is similar to that of the general population. Eighty to ninety percent of all players may experience low back pain at some time in their life. Low back pain may have various causes, such as postural abnormalities, muscle dysfunction (imbalances, shortening, or weakening of muscle), overuse, instability, and articular dysfunction in the lower back. In tennis, the combined rotation and extension of the back during the serve may cause problems. Prolonged standing, sitting, or running may also provoke pain. In 95% of the cases of low back pain no specific physical abnormalities are found by additional diagnostic investigations that may explain the pain. This is called "nonspecific" low back pain. This includes muscle strains and back sprains. In contrast, specific low back pain is caused by a structural abnormality, such as a herniated disc, fracture, or tumor.

Symptoms. Common symptoms are a sudden, sharp, persistent or dull pain in the lower back, sometimes on one side only, that worsens with movement. The pain may radiate to the hips, buttocks, or back of the thigh. Often, muscle spasms in the back may develop.

Treatment. Rest, medications, and ice are recommended to relieve pain and muscle spasm. Bed rest beyond two days is not recommended, as this can have detrimental effects on bone, connective tissue, muscle, and the cardiovascular system. Manual therapy may be prescribed, as this has been shown to be effective. Massage, local heat, and electrical impulses (TENS) that reduce swelling and pain may be applied. As pain and spasm subside, exercises to improve strength and flexibility (core stability exercises) are started. The prognosis of nonspecific low back pain is usually good, with 50% of the patients recovering within one week, and 95% within three months. However, an estimated 60% of the patients may have a (milder) recurrence within one year.

Practical tips for the player
- Make sure to start every training with a good warm up and stretching exercises, including the lower back. See Figure 5.12 for instructions.
- If your lower back feels stiff, you may try automassage. Roll over a tennis ball, while lying on your back.
- Mobilizing the lower back may also be helpful. Two useful exercises are as follows:
    1. Lie on your back with legs straight. Try to alternately lengthen the legs from the hips, by straightening them as much as you can.
    2. Lie on your back with bent knees and keep your feet flat on the ground. Let your knees touch the floor on each side of your body, by alternately tilting them to the left and right.
- Use proper mechanics when lifting. Bend the knees to pick things off the ground (as opposed to bending at the waist) and hold the weight close to the body to reduce the leverage.
- Lie flat on the back on a firm mattress with a pillow under the knees in bed at night, and use good posture when sitting.
- Try to limit long driving, prolonged sitting, and excessive lifting.
- After the pain has subsided, it is important to incorporate core stability exercsies in the daily training program. Recommended exercises progressing from easy to difficult are supine core stabilization, spinal extensions, bridging and balancing exercises on the gym ball. See figures 6.10, 28.43, 28.44, and 28.47 for instructions.

- Performing yoga or pilates can be helpful to treat low back pain because they include many stretching and strengthening exercises for the lower back and abdominal area.
- Recommended conditioning activities include, walking, bicycling ,and water therapy.
- If you have to stand for long periods of time (e.g., as a tennis coach), you can relief some stress on your back by placing one leg on a raised object, such as a bench.
- After a bout of acute low back pain, play should be built up gradually. Slowly incorporate serving, especially serves with a lot of back extension (kick serves).

FACET SYNDROME

Description. The facet joint bridges the vertebrae behind the vertebral foramina. The facets are the direct joint connections between adjacent vertebrae. Facet syndrome is due to the cartilage wear of the facet joint, usually from overuse. This overloading occurs as a result of repetitive hyperextension (arching) of the back, excessive hyperextension with rotation of the back, or just rotation of the back (Figure 9.1). This repetitive or excessive force causes injury to the cartilage surfaces of the facet, often associated with injury to the disc of the spine. Degeneration of the discs may lead to loss of disc height, resulting in a relative increase in facet load found in compression and extension maneuvers. Tennis is a sport in which the participant is at particular risk, due to the serve and current open stance game.

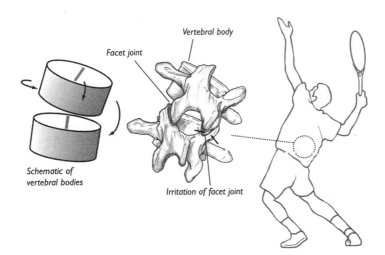

Vertebral body

Facet joint

Schematic of
vertebral bodies

Irritation of facet joint

Figure 9.1
Repetitive hyperextension of the back during serving may lead to overload of the cartilage of the facet joints.

Symptoms. Athletes with this problem usually complain of a chronic dull ache in the lower back, which worsens with sidebending, twisting, hyperextension, and rotation, such as with serving. The pain may radiate to the buttocks, hip, and posterior thigh, but usually not below the knee. The player may also occasionally complain of stiffness of the lower back. The pain is usually worse in the morning, aggravated by hyperextension, and relieved by repeated motion. The syndrome may occur after an acute injury (extension and rotation of the spine) or may be chronic in nature. Radiographic findings cannot confirm the diagnosis, but can help rule it out. Facet syndrome is most often a clinical diagnosis.

Treatment. Initial treatment consists of rest from activities that cause the pain (avoid rotation or hyperextension) and nonsteroidal anti-inflammatory medications (NSAID's). Ice (ten to fifteen minutes a few times a day to the low back) can be used in the initial 72 hours after an injury to reduce inflammation and numb the pain. One potential problem with ice is that temporarily it may tighten the musculature even more. The player may be referred to a physical therapist or manual therapist for treatment, which may include local heat, traction, manipulation, electrical stimulation, TENS, and stretching and strengthening exercises. Occasionally the facet joint is injected with corticosteroids, which may be followed by deadening the nerves of the joint (denervation) using radiofrequency ablation. A potential long term consequence of the cartilage degeneration of the facet joints is the development of spinal stenosis. Spinal stenosis is a narrowing of the canal for the spinal cord. In this scenario, the narrow canal is due to the bone spurs that result from the chronic degeneration of the facet joints. This may require surgery to relieve pressure on the nerves.

Practical tips for the player

- Initially avoid extension of the back (no overheads and serves). For ground strokes, start with half court (service line to service line), half swing and gradually work up to full swing and full distance.
- Perform stretching exercises for the hamstrings, hip flexors, hip external rotators, and lower back. See Figures 5.6, 5.10, 5.11, and 5.12 for instructions.

- Strengthening exercises should include core stability exercises, emphasizing flexion and neutral postures. The following exercises, progressing from easy to difficult, are recommended: supine core stabilization, pelvic tilts, spinal extensions and bridging. See Figures 6.10, 28.43, 28.47, 9.2, and 9.3 for instructions.

Figures 9.2 and 9.3

Pelvic tilt maneuvers can help reduce the degree of lumbar lordosis and reduce compression of the facet joints. These maneuvers should be performed with bent knees standing, straight leg standing, and sitting.

HERNIATED DISC (RUPTURED OR SLIPPED DISC)

Description. A herniated disc occurs when there is a sudden or gradual break in the supportive ligaments surrounding a spinal disc. The disc is made of a tough outer layer called the "annulus fibrosus" and a gel-like center called the "nucleus pulposus" and functions as a cushion between the bony vertebra (bony spinal column). The jelly like contents of the disc may protrude through a crack in the outer layer and may push on the spinal cord or nerves coming from the spinal cord, thereby causing symptoms. This may occur in the neck, mid-back, or lower back. A ruptured disc is caused by sudden injury or numerous microtraumas, such as from constant lifting or repeated back flexion, extension and rotation, such as with serving a tennis ball. Risk of developing a herniated disc include a family history of low back pain or disc disorders, poor mechanics of playing or lifting, and poor posture. Pre-existing back problems, such as spondylolisthesis, or previous back surgery (especially fusion) also put the player at risk for this problem.

Symptoms. There is pain in the back that usually affects one side, is worse with movement, and may be worsened by sneezing, coughing, or straining. Frequently there will be painful spasms of the muscles in the back. Most disc herniations occur in the bottom two discs of the lumbar spine, at and just below the waist. A herniated lumbar disc can press on the nerves in the spine and may cause pain, numbness, tingling, or weakness of the leg and/or foot. Symptoms down the back of the leg are often termed "sciatica." This can affect about one to two percent of all people, usually between the ages of 30 and 50. If the problem is chronic, there may be atrophy of the affected muscles. Less frequently, there is loss of bowel (stool) or bladder (urine) function. Since the soft spinal tissues can not be seen on X-ray, MRI is generally used to confirm the diagnosis and determine the level and extent of the lesions(s). (Myelo-)CT and myelography are used less often.

Treatment. Initial treatment usually consists of a short period of (bed) rest, ice (ten to twenty minutes every few hours), anti-inflammatory medications and analgesic drugs to relieve pain, inflammation, and muscle spasm. Prolonged bed rest should not be prescribed, as this is felt to do more harm than good. This should be followed by physical therapy (TENS, hot and cold packs, massage, gentle mobilization) and exercises. Manipulation should generally be avoided in most cases of herniated disc. Traction may provide limited pain relief for some patients. Occasionally, a lumbar corset (soft, flexible back brace) or neck collar at the start of treatment may be recommended to relieve the back pain. A trial of oral steroids or epidural (the space around the lining of the spinal cord) steroid injections to reduce the inflammation around the herniated disc and inflamed nerve may be attempted. This problem is usually curable with appropriate conservative treatment within six weeks (80% resolve within six weeks). Surgery is usually recommended for relief of leg pain (greater than 90% success). Surgery is less effective in relieving back pain. The most common procedure is called a "discectomy" or "partial discectomy," in which part of the herniated disc is removed. Surgery is urgently needed in patients with loss of bowel or bladder function.

Practical tips for the player
- A period of relative rest is often helpful. This means avoiding activities that provoke pain (running, tennis), and continuing activities that can be done without pain, such a swimming, aqua-jogging and cycling.

- Use proper mechanics when lifting. Bend the knees to pick things up off the ground (as opposed to bending at the waist) and hold the weight close to the body to reduce the leverage.
- Lie flat on the back on a firm mattress with a pillow under the knees in bed at night and use good posture when sitting.
- Avoid long driving, prolonged sitting, excessive lifting, and bending forward for the first four weeks.
- Incorporate core stability exercises in the daily training program. The following exercises, progressing from easy to difficult, are recommended: supine core stabilization, spinal extensions, bridging and balancing exercises on a gym ball. See Figures 6.10, 28.43, 28.44, and 28.47 for instructions.

- Strengthen the abdominal muscles. See Figures 9.8, 28.35, and 28.36 for instructions.

- When returning to play, avoid overheads and serves initially. For ground strokes, start with half court (service line to service line), half swing and gradually work up to full swing and full distance. Avoid any activity that requires twisting of the body under uncontrollable conditions. Gradually incorporate serves and overheads.

SPONDYLOLYSIS AND SPONDYLOLISTHESIS (VERTEBRAE FRACTURE AND SLIPPAGE)

Description. Spondylolysis is a stress or fatigue fracture of the arches of the vertebrae (bones of the spine), not involving the main load bearing part (the body of the vertebrae). It usually affects either the fourth or the fifth lumbar vertebra in the lower back. Spondylolysis is found in six percent of the general population, but there is a higher incidence in tennis players, especially in adolescent players. The cause is the cumulative stress of repeated hyperextension and rotation, as occurs during serving (Figure 9.4). The repetitive bending stress causes injury that exceeds the bone's ability to heal, leading to a stress fracture (Figure 9.5). In approximately half the athletes with spondylolysis, there is concomitant spondylolisthesis, defined by forward slipping of a

Figure 9.4
Repetitive hyperexten-
sion of the back dur-
ing serving may lead
to a stress fracture,
particularly in young
players.

Figure 9.5
Spondylolysis is a stress fracture at the back
of the vertebra. If there is forward slipping of
the vertebra, this is called spondylolisthesis.

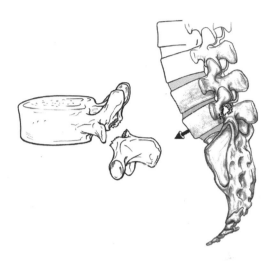

vertebra in relation to the one below it. The younger player with a stress fracture of the
pars is at greater risk of the vertebral body slipping forwards. The risk of slippage is
very small in individuals over the age of twenty-five years

Symptoms. Symptoms are a chronic dull ache in the low back, most frequently after
physical exertion. The player may have tightness of the hamstring muscles, stiffness of
the lower back, and may walk with a bent-knee, flexed-hip gait. Neurologic symptoms
(radiating pain in the leg, numbness, tingling, loss of strength) are uncommon in
young players, unless a high-grade slip is present. Sometimes a step-off can be felt, with
prominence of the spinous process of the fifth lumber vertebra.

Patients with suspected spondylolysis should be evaluated initially with plain radiography. If plain radiographs are negative or inconclusive, further imaging may be warranted. In children, a bone scan is probably best done first, followed by a CT scan in
the area of the hot spot on the bone scan. This limits the field of study, thus reducing
radiation and allowing thin slice evaluation. In adults, MRI, CT, and single-photon
emission computed tomography (SPECT) bone scintigraphy are generally used to further evaluate these patients. Spondylolisthesis can be diagnosed with plain lumbar X-
rays.

Treatment. Rest and bracing can help decrease symptoms and may permit healing of
the fracture in acute cases. Activity restriction (i.e., temporary discontinuation of tennis), and a back muscle program should be prescribed in chronic cases. A semi-rigid
back brace that decreases lumbar lordosis may be recommended. Physical therapy to
stretch the lumbo-dorsal fascia and strengthen the abdominal musculature may help
decrease hyperextension stress.

Patients with persistent pain despite appropriate conservative treatment, neurological
symptoms, and skeletally mature patients with a slip greater than 50% may be considered for surgical stabilization (fusion of two or more vertebral bodies).

Practical tips for the player
- Use proper serving techniques and limit use of the kick serve.
- Try using a cloth corset or lumbar heat retainer.
- Daily stretch the lower back and hamstring muscles. See Figures 5.6 and 5.12 for instructions.
- Incorporate core stability exercises in the daily training program. See Figures 6.10, and 28.43 to 28.50 for recommended exercises and instructions.

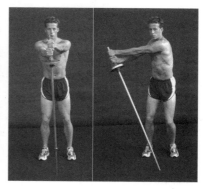

- When returning to play, gradually incorporate serving and overheads.
- Children should have good trunk control before they are taught the kick serve.

RIB STRESS FRACTURES

Description. Rib stress fractures, like any stress fracture, are overuse injuries, secondary to excessive stress on the ribs (see also Chapter 7). Rib stress fractures occur most commonly at the first rib or ribs four through nine and are associated with periods of intensive training. The cause of rib stress fractures is the repetitive contraction of muscles, which acts in opposing directions on the ribs. The fourth to sixth ribs are most commonly involved. In these ribs, muscle action of the serratus anterior (shoulder blade stabilizing muscle) and external oblique muscles (abdominal muscles) can cause stress fractures from repetitive, opposing bending forces.

Symptoms. Patients with first rib stress fractures typically report a gradual onset of scapular, shoulder, or clavicular pain that is aggravated by overhead activity, deep inspiration, and coughing. Less commonly, patients are seen with acute pain when a stress fracture progresses to a complete fracture. Physical findings are usually limited to local tenderness at the first rib.

The diagnosis of middle rib stress fractures is often confused with intercostal muscle strains, leading to a delay in diagnosis. Point tenderness over the lateral ribs may help differentiate the disorders. To confirm the diagnosis, a bone scan is recommended, because a scan is much more sensitive than plain film. More than 80% of stress fractures will not be evident on initial radiographs, while the sensitivity of bone scan for the diagnosis of stress fracture approaches 100%.

Treatment. Most first rib stress fractures heal uneventfully after a four-week period of relative rest. In cases when an acute fracture develops, there is a risk of delayed union with healing often requiring six to twelve months of activity restriction. Middle rib stress fractures respond favorably to activity modification, with complete healing seen within four to six weeks. No known cases of delayed union or nonunion have been reported for middle rib stress fractures. The rehabilitation program should include endurance exercises for the scapular stabilizers, as well as a review of possible training errors or faulty body mechanics. Menstrual, nutritional, and metabolic abnormalities need to be identified and treated appropriately to help healing and prevent recurrence.

Practical tips for the player
- Gradually increase activity and training, usually no more than ten percent per week. This is particularly important for serving and overheads.
- Strengthen the scapular stabilizers. Recommended exercises include extension, scapular retraction, supine pinches, dumbbell row, and rolling the ball on the wall. See Figures 28.1-28.4, 28.31-28.32 and 6.9 for instructions.

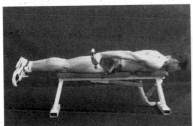

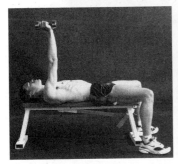

ABDOMINAL MUSCLE STRAINS

Description. An abdominal muscle strain is a partial muscle tear or muscle pull of one of the abdominal muscles. Usually, the nondominant rectus abdominis is affected, but the oblique muscles (external and internal) may also be injured (Figure 9.6). Abdominal muscular injuries are common in tennis players at all levels of competition. The tennis serve is commonly involved in the injury mechanism. During the cocking phase, the lumbar spine is in hyperextension, in order to increase distance for racquet speed. When the player's axial skeleton is completely extended, the abdominal muscles are maximally stretched, storing elastic energy. On movement reversal, these abdominal muscles contract powerfully, using this stored elastic energy (eccentric-concentric contraction). This is a high-risk moment for an abdominal muscle strain. When the

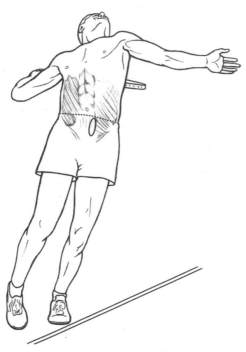

Figure 9.6

An abdominal strain is usually located on the non-dominant side of the abdomen.

ball is hit behind the body, such as with a kick service, the back is arched even more, resulting in more abdominal muscles stretch, increasing the risk for an abdominal muscle strain. The open stance forehand has also been implicated in these injuries, because of the powerful trunk rotation.

Symptoms. Symptoms are a sudden stabbing pain upon forceful use of the muscles (such as with serving or doing situps), indicating a (partial) rupture has occurred. There is tenderness over the affected area. Pain can be elicited if the player lies flat and tries to perform a sit up or lift his leg against resistance.

Treatment. Initial treatment consists of rest from the offending activity and cooling with ice for ten to fifteen minutes every few hours. In the days following injury, electrical stimulation may be used to reduce pain and swelling. Massage may be helpful in alleviating muscle spasm, however, massage directly over the injury site should be avoided in the acute phase, to minimize the risk of myositis ossificans (bone formation within the injured muscle). As pain and swelling improve, the muscle rehabilitation process can gradually be started. This consists of gentle stretching exercises of the abdominal muscles to reduce scarring in a shortened position and progressive muscle strengthening.

Practical tips for the player

- It may be possible to continue playing tennis, but avoid serves and overhead smashes initially.
- Strengthen the abdominal muscles. Recommended exercises include static contraction of straight and oblique abdominal muscles, straight and oblique crunches, side raises, the pelvic raise, leg lifts, and eccentric muscle strengthening with a medicine ball. These exercises progress from easy to difficult. See Figures 9.7, 9.8, 28.35-28.42 for instructions.

Figure 9.7

Static contraction of the oblique abdominal muscles. Stand in front of a door post, left hand against the post. Slowly press with your left hand against the post until you feel tension in your abdominal muscles. Keep your upper body straight and look straight ahead.

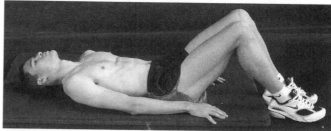

Figure 9.8

Static contraction of the straight abdominal muscles. Lie down on your back with your knees bent and feet flat on the floor. Contract your abdominal muscles. Hold for five seconds and relax. Perform three series of ten to twenty repetitions.

- Stretch the abdominal muscles. Lie down on your stomach with your hands in the push up position. Slowly press yourself up, so your upper body leaves the floor, while your hips and legs remain in contact with the floor. Keep your buttocks and lower back relaxed. Hold for fifteen to twenty seconds, and return to starting position.
- When you are able to perform the abdominal strengthening exercises without pain, you can increase the intensity of play and introduce high forehands, high backhands, easy serves and overheads. Then progress to first serves and serves with more kick. Slowly increase the number and speed of the serves, followed by practices matches. If you are able to play practice matches for two weeks without pain, you can start playing competitive tennis again.

WHIPLASH (CERVICAL STRAIN AND SPRAIN)

Description. Cervical strain is the result of stretch injury to the muscles, ligaments and tendons of the cervical spine, which may also result in irritation of the nerves from this area. Such injury can occur acutely, as in a motor vehicle accident, or over time. In tennis, it may occur due to repetitive or excessive turning of the head during serving and when hitting backhands. Players with arthritis of the spine are at increased risk.

Symptoms. There is pain or stiffness of the neck, either immediately following or up to 24 hours after playing tennis. There may be limited range of motion. The player may suffer from dizziness, headache, and even nausea and vomiting when the pain is severe. Muscles spasms with soreness and stiffness in the neck and occasionally swelling in the neck may be found. X-rays and MRI may be useful in establishing the diagnosis.

Treatment. Initial treatment consists of rest and pain medications to decrease muscle spasm. Heat therapy and massage may help to reduce symptoms. If symptoms are severe, a soft, padded, fabric or hard, plastic cervical collar may be recommended until the pain subsides. If nerve roots are injured, temporary numbness and weakness may occur in the arms. A cervical traction apparatus may be recommended in this scenario of neurologic symptoms. This can be hung over a doorway. Narrowing of the canal (stenosis) that may be due to aging or congenital (born with) may require surgery to reduce pressure on the spinal cord.

Practical tips for the player

- Stretch the muscles on the side of the neck by bending the head towards one shoulder. Repeat on the other side. Stretch the muscles in the back of the neck by bending the head forwards and looking down. Avoid extension of the neck, since this may cause dizziness.
- Strengthen the neck and shoulder muscles. Good exercises are upright rowing and shoulder shrugs. See Figures 28.9, 28.10 and 28.11 for instructions.

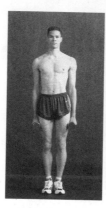

- Use proper serving technique, including a good toss. Try to toss the ball consistently in front and slightly to the left of the body. If the ball toss is too far behind the body, let the ball drop and toss again.
- Improve your posture by pulling the chin and abdomen in while sitting or standing. Sit in a firm chair and force the buttocks to touch the chair's back.
- After a hard workout, a hot shower and/or massage will help to relieve the tightness of the neck and shoulder muscles.
- Sleep without a pillow, instead using a small towel rolled to two inches in diameter, or use a cervical pillow or soft cervical collar.
- When returning to play, gradually build up overheads and serves.

SUMMARY

Injuries to the trunk commonly occur in tennis, as forces to hit the ball are transmitted through the trunk. This is compounded by the flexion, hyperextension and rotational mechanics involved with serving and open stance forehands, placing further stress to the lower back and abdominal muscles. These common injuries include low back strain and sprains as well as herniated discs and articular cartilage degeneration of the facets. Further, abdominal muscle strains are quite common. Often these injuries will resolve with the appropriate conservative management and may be prevented with appropriate conditioning and strengthening, particularly the core stabilizers.

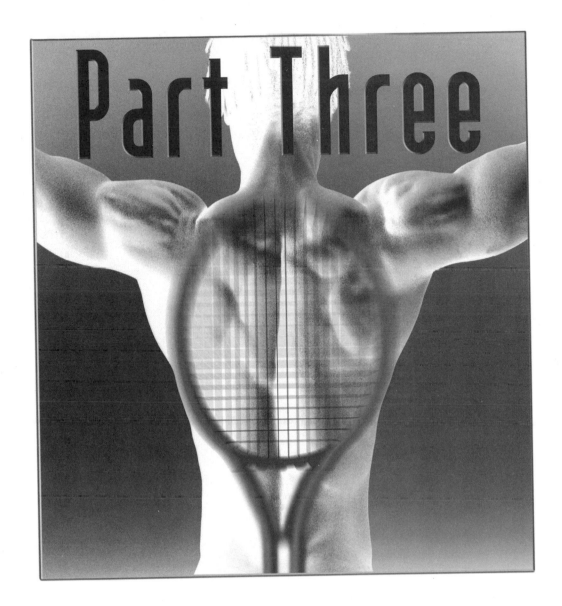

Part Three

Medical Issues

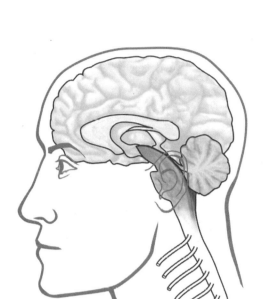

10

The Brain and Nervous System

Although there are many conditions of the brain and nervous system, not all are relevant to tennis. In this chapter we will discuss four types of headaches that are very common in tennis players: tension headache, migraine, exercise induced headache and cervicogenic headache. In addition, tinnitus (ringing of one's ear) will be discussed.

TENSION HEADACHE

Description. This is the most ordinary type of headache. The pain is localized on both sides of the head and not accompanied by nausea or vomiting. Stress, anxiety, poor posture, sudden strain or lack of sleep can all be the cause of tension-headache, possibly resulting in contraction of facial muscles.

Symptoms. A dull or pressure-like pain in the scalp, temples, or back of the head characterizes tension headache. The pain is localized on both sides of the head and is not accompanied by nausea or vomiting.

Treatment. This type of headache generally responds well to over-the-counter analgesic painkillers and rest. A massage, alternating hot and cold showers or relaxation training may also be effective.

MIGRAINE

Description. Migraine is a severe type of headache that is often preceded or accompanied by neurological symptoms. It is caused by the release of serotonins in the bloodstream from its storage sites in the body, causing constriction of the vessels of the brain, followed by vasodilatation. Three percent of the male and seven percent of the female population are affected.

Symptoms. Migraine is characterized by periodic headaches that are typically localized on one side of the head. In ten to fifteen percent of cases it is preceded by neurological symptoms such as loss of vision, flashing lights, confusion, problems with speech or coordination, and tingling, pins, needles and numbness on the affected side. The pain is usually severe and throbbing and may last from a few hours to several days. Nausea, vomiting and/or diarrhea generally accompany this. There may be increased sensitivity to light, sounds, and/or smells. The attacks occur at intervals ranging from days to several months.

Treatment. During a migraine, people often like to sleep or rest in a dark, quiet room. Medications that act directly to correct the serotonin imbalance (such as sumatriptan) may be prescribed by the doctor. There are also mediations available that constrict the blood vessels (containing ergotamine). However, these are prescribed less often because of their addictive potential. Simple painkillers such as paracetamol or ibuprofen combined with caffeine or antihistamine can also be very effective. All these medications are more effective if taken early in the attack.

If the attacks are very frequent, the doctor may prescribe a preventative medication which will need to be taken every day, such as propranolol, pizotifen, or flunarazine.

Practical tips for the player
- Precipitating factors that have been identified are stress, premenstrual changes, alcohol consumption, lack of sleep, certain foods (e.g., citrus fruit, chocolate, cheese, alcohol, caffeine) or hunger. Try to find out what triggers the migraine in order to gain more control over the situation.

EXERCISE INDUCED HEADACHE

Description. Exercise induced headache, also known as effort migraine, is similar to a regular migraine. Exercise induced headache is characterized by a severe, intense, incapacitating headache, often accompanied by other symptoms. It may be precipitated by all-out physical effort in various sports, including tennis or tennis training, where weight training or explosive anaerobic bursts may occur. Like migraines, exercise induced headache is also thought to be caused by constriction, then dilation and inflammation of blood vessels that go to the scalp and brain. Vision disturbances occur when blood vessels narrow; the headache begins when they widen again.

These headaches are associated with minor head trauma within a week prior, changes in altitude, increase in blood pressure, infection and withdrawal from certain drugs. It may also be worsened by tension and stress, use of oral contraceptives and other prescription and nonprescription drugs, excess alcohol consumption, consumption of certain foods, such as chocolate, refined sugars, spices, cheese, herbs (ginseng), fatigue and smoking. These usually resolve in minutes to hours with appropriate treatment including rest from participation.

Symptoms. Like classic migraines, the nature of attacks varies between persons and from time to time in the same person. Initially, there is inability to see clearly, followed by seeing bright spots and zigzag patterns without any headache. Visual disturbances may last several minutes or several hours, but they disappear once the headache begins. The headache is often described as a dull, boring pain in the temple that spreads to the entire side of the head. The pain becomes intense and throbbing and sometimes may affect both temples at the same time. The affected player may have nausea and vomiting. Symptoms may have an onset minutes, hours, days or weeks after the activity or develop suddenly.

Treatment. Initial treatment consists of stopping the activity and rest during attacks. Lying down in a quiet, dark room and relaxing (if possible) are helpful. Reading during an attack should be avoided. A cold cloth or ice pack should be applied to the forehead, or the face splashed with cold water. Pain relievers, such as aspirin or acetaminophen or nonsteroidal anti-inflammatory medications may also help. Antihistamines may be prescribed to expand the blood vessels, though, alternatively, vasoconstrictors may be prescribed to narrow blood vessels during attacks. Anti-emetics may be recommended for nausea and vomiting, while beta-adrenergic blocking drugs, such as propanolol, may be prescribed to prevent attacks, especially if attacks are very frequent or severe and effect normal function. These medications have side effects, and may not help everyone with this problem.

Practical tips for the player
- Taking one aspirin a day may prevent migraine attacks.
- The drug propanolol prevents attacks in some persons, but it may have a negative effect on athletic performance and have unwanted side effects, including depression and impotence.
- Relaxation techniques and anticipation training have been shown to be helpful in preventing these headaches.
- Precipitating factors that have been identified are stress, premenstrual changes, alcohol consumption, smoking, lack of sleep, certain foods (e.g., citrus fruit, chocolate, cheese, alcohol, caffeine) or hunger. Try to find out what triggers the migraine in order to gain more control over the situation.

CERVICOGENIC HEADACHE

Description. Cervicogenic headache is a mechanically provoked, unilateral headache which appears to arise in the neck. Chronic tension, inflammation, degeneration or functional blocking of the cervical vertebrae may be the cause of the symptoms. In tennis, the pain may be provoked while extending the neck during serving, worsening as a result of increased muscle tension.

Symptoms. The pain is usually localized in the back of the head on one side, and can last hours or days, with varying intensity. The headache can be provoked or aggravated by rotation or flexion of the head, sneezing, coughing or straining, and by pressure on the nervous roots of the second cervical nerve.

Treatment. Gentle mobilization techniques of the cervical column may be used. Analgesics may also be effective.

Practical tips for the player
- Try a massage of the neck and shoulders.
- Apply heat packs.

RINGING IN THE EAR (TINNITUS)

Description. Tinnitus or ringing in the ear is the condition of noises "in the ears" and/or "in the head" with no external source. It is hypothesized that most often tinnitus results from the perception of abnormal activity, e.g., activity which cannot be induced by any combination of external sounds. It occurs in a surprisingly high proportion (35%) of the general population, and in 85% of patients with ear problems. High noise levels (air travel), salicylates (painkillers such as aspirin) and quinine (an anti-malaria drug) have tinnitus-inducing properties.

Symptoms. Tinnitus noises are described variously as ringing, whistling, buzzing and humming. The noises may be heard in one ear, both ears or in the middle of the head or it may be difficult to pinpoint its exact location. The noise may be low, medium or high-pitched. There may be a single noise or two or more components. The noise may be continuous or it may come and go.

Treatment. Unfortunately, the prospects are rather pessimistic. A full examination of the ear, nose, and throat and a hearing test should be performed, and if possible, the underlying problem should be treated.

SUMMARY

In this chapter, we present four types of headache, tension headache, migraine, exercise-induced headache, and cervicogenic headache. In addition, ringing in the ear is discussed. Tension headache and cervicogenic headache generally respond well to relaxation techniques and over-the-counter medications analgesic painkillers. Migraine and exercise-induced headache may require prescription medications and avoidance of precipitating factors. With ringing in the ear, any underlying problem should be identified and treated.

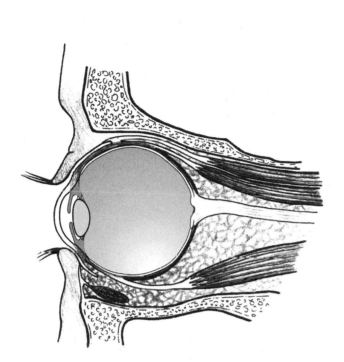

11

The Eye

Optimal vision is of great importance to tennis players, because the ball may travel with a speed of over 120 mph per hour (200 km per hour). When the ball impacts the eye, serious eye injury may result. The risk is highest when playing serve and volley or doubles. The ball can ricochet from the player's or partner's racket, or be smashed from an opposing player's racquet into the eye from a position close to the net. Players may also suffer from minor eye irritation due to foreign bodies, such as clay particles or sand. All eye injuries, even those that appear to be minor, require thorough examination and all serious eye injuries should be referred to an ophthalmologist (eye doctor).

INJURIES OF THE EYELID

Description. These can result from contact with the racquet head or the tennis ball and may result in heavy bruising or laceration of the eyelid.

Symptoms. Symptoms include swelling, discoloration, laceration and/or bleeding of the eyelid. When there is severe swelling, eyesight may be temporarily limited.

Treatment. When there is swelling, a cold compress can be applied for the first three to five days. However, beware of freezing of the very thin skin. Also, do not apply any pressure to the eye. When there is laceration of the eyelid, the player should see an eye-surgeon for primary repair of the wound. Apply a sterile bandage or plastic cap without pressure onto the eye.

EYE SCRATCHES (CORNEAL EROSION)

Description. Corneal erosion can result from scratches to the eye caused by clay, twigs, (hairs of) the ball, the racquet, or other foreign bodies.

Symptoms. The player complains of pain, sensitivity to light, a foreign body sensation, a rough feeling when blinking, tearing, squeezing of the eye, and blurred vision if the central cornea is involved.

Treatment. The doctor should inspect the eye, which involves simple outward turning of the lower lid and double turning of the upper lid to find any foreign bodies. When a light is shone into the eye, the otherwise smooth corneal surface reveals a sharply circumscribed dull area, which stains green with 2% fluorescein. Treatment consists of antibiotic eye ointment and padding of the eye in order to prevent friction from movement of the lids.

RED EYE (CONJUNCTIVITIS)

Description. A red eye is the result of inflammation of the conjunctiva ("conjunctivitis"), the clear membrane that covers the white part of the eye and lines the inner surface of the eyelids. The inflammation can have many causes, such as an irritant (e.g. clay, sand, fly, or smoke), an infection (viral or bacterial) or an allergic reaction (e.g. hay fever).

Symptoms. Symptoms may include pain, tearing, secretion and itching of the eye. There may be swelling of the eyelids and sensitivity to bright light.

Figure 11.1
Flushing the eye.

Treatment. If the conjunctivitis is caused by a foreign body, this foreign body should be removed. If applicable, first remove a contact lens. Then flush the eye with a small amount of clean water, to remove the foreign body. A way to do this is to use an eyecup or small juice glass. Fill the glass completely, put the open eye in the water and move the eye to several positions (Figure 11.1). The doctor may prescribe antiviral eye-medication and treatment as described under corneal erosion if there is also damage of the corneal surface.

If there is a bacterial or viral infection, antibiotic ointments or drops may be prescribed. Although viral infections typically do not require antibiotics, this will prevent additional or superimposed bacterial infection. Allergies can be treated by removal of the allergen and/or oral anti-allergy medication or eye drops.

Practical tips for the player
- Infectious conjunctivitis is contagious and can spread from one eye to the other by touching the eyes. Wash hands often with warm water and soap, especially after touching your eyes. Do not share eye drops, tissues, eye makeup, washcloths, towels or pillowcases with other people.

BLOOD IN THE EYE (HYPHEMA)

Description. Blood in the eye can be seen when there is bleeding in the front chamber of the eye. In tennis, this is usually caused by blunt trauma, such as when the ball or racquet (particularly one's partner's racquet) hits the eye.

Symptoms. Symptoms are blurred vision and pooling of blood in the anterior chamber. There may be increased eye pressure. There may be pain, sensitivity to light and tearing following the trauma.

Treatment. Immediate evaluation by an eye physician is of paramount importance. When there is significant hyphema, rest should be observed and strenuous activity avoided to allow the blood to reabsorb. This may take days to weeks. A doctor should monitor the pressure within the eye. If there is increased pressure, eye drops may be prescribed to control it. Aspirin and ibuprofen should be avoided to prevent resumption of bleeding. Acetaminophen may be used to manage pain.

EYELID INFLAMMATION (BLEPHARITIS)

Description. Inflammation of the eyelid margin (blepharitis) frequently occurs in people with oily skin, dandruff or dry eyes.

Symptoms. Common symptoms are irritation, itching and red eyes.

Treatment. There is no specific cure, but it can be controlled through eyelid hygiene. Apply warm compresses over the closed eyelids for five minutes. This will help soften the crusts and loosen the oily debris. Then use Q-tips or cotton balls, dipped in a 50:50 mixture of warm water and baby shampoo to cleanse the lids. Then gently rinse the eyelids with warm water. At bedtime, a topical antibiotic ointment may be applied in resistant cases.

THE COMMON STYE

Description. A hordeolum, commonly referred to as a stye, is an acute infection with abscess formation of either the oil glands of the eyelid (meibomian glands, internal hordeolum) or of the sweat and sebaceous glands around the hair follicles (external hordeolum). The most common cause is saphylococcus aureus bacterium.

Symptoms. A stye appears as a red tender nodule near or at the eyelid margin. When the eyelid is turned up, it is more yellowish.

Treatment. Usually the episode is self-limited and resolves within five to seven days with drainage of the abscess. Use warm (not too hot!) compresses to focus the inflammation at one site, e.g. four to five times a day for five minutes. The doctor may prescribe antibiotic drops or ointment if there is significant inflammation of the lid margin (Figure 11.2).

Practical tips for the player
- For prevention, use proper eyelid hygiene. Do not apply make-up behind the eye-lashes, in order not to clog the opening of the gland. Thorough cleaning of any make-up at night is essential.

Figure 11.2

Inflammation of the lid margin of the left eye.

BUMP ON THE EYELID: INFLAMMATION OF OIL GLAND (CHALAZION)

Description. A chalazion is a chronic inflammation of an oil gland (meibomian gland). It may evolve from an internal stye or may occur when the fatty secretions plugs the opening of the gland leading to engorgement and eventual rupture of the gland.

Symptoms. A chalazion appears as a swollen mass at the margin or higher in the lid. It may be a quiet lump or there may be significant inflammation with swelling of the eyelid.

Treatment. Chalazia may resolve spontaneously if the duct of the gland opens. Unfortunately, this does not happen very often. Apply warm compresses four to five times per day for ten to fifteen minutes per session to soften the plug of the material. The doctor may prescribe antibiotics if there is still significant inflammation of the eyelid. If the lump is quiet and the antibiotics and warm compress routine have failed, surgical incision is the next step. A small incision is made on the inside of the lid to drain the chalazion, and antibiotic eye drops are used for one week following this procedure.

> *Practical tip for the player.*
> • Do not manually squeeze the chalazion, as this may precipitate acute eyelid inflammation.

DRY EYES

Description. Dry eyes occur when there is reduced tear production or excessive tear evaporation. This may occur as a result of disease, aging, medication, or environmental factors (dry air, air conditioner)

Symptoms. The usual symptoms are redness, a foreign body sensation, burning or stinging, sensitivity to light, a discharge, difficulty wearing contact lenses and excess tearing.

Treatment. For those cases caused by medication or environmental factors, try to switch medication or modify the surroundings. Wrap around glasses may be used to reduce the drying effect of the wind when playing outside. Scheduling breaks while reading or using the computer may decrease the dryness associated with such activities. Tear supplements may be used, such as artificial tears every two hours or a lubricating ointment at night.

THICKENINGS ON THE WHITE OF THE EYE (PINGUECULA AND PTERYGIUM)

Description. Pingueculae and pterygia are common in adults, and particularly in tennis players, and their incidence increases with age. Pingueculae are slow-growing, small, raised, thickenings of the white lining of the eye. They may be yellow, gray, white, or colorless. They are almost always to one side of the iris, usually on the side closest to the nose. A pinguecula may develop into a pterygium. Pterygia are thickenings of the white lining of the eye, that may have blood vessels associated with them. They often have a triangular-shaped appearance. The pterygia may also grow over the cornea and may therefore affect vision.

The cause or causes of these disorders are unknown, but they are more frequent in people who have prolonged exposure to sunny and windy climates and conditions, such as may occur with outdoor tennis. It is thought these growths are the result of ultraviolet or infrared light and irritation. It is also believed that prolonged exposure to these risk factors (that is, ultraviolet light) increases the chances of occurrence.

Symptoms. Although some people with pingueculae and pterygia constantly feel like they have a foreign body in their eye, most have no symptoms. Because the lids can no longer spread the tears over a smooth area, dry areas may result. Because a pterygium can stretch and distort the cornea, some people acquire astigmatism or decreased vision from a pterygium.

Treatment. Most pingueculae and pterygia grow slowly and almost never cause significant damage, so the prognosis is excellent. Usually, no treatment is needed. Artificial tear eye drops can be used to relieve the sensation of a foreign body in the eye and to protect against dryness. Surgery to remove the pinguecula or pterygium is advisable when the effect on the cornea causes visual defects or when the thickening is causing excessive and recurrent discomfort or inflammation. Healing from this type of surgery, although usually painless, takes many weeks, and there is a high rate of recurrence (as high as 50-60% in some regions).

Practical tips for the player
- While there is nothing that has been clearly shown to prevent these disorders, or to prevent a pinguecula from progressing to a pterygium, these are associated with wind and sun irritation. Thus, protecting the eyes from sunlight, dust, and other environmental irritants is recommended. Ultraviolet and wind exposure can be reduced by use of protective sunglasses.

CATARACTS

Description. A cataract is a cloudiness or opacity in the normally transparent crystalline lens of the eye. This cloudiness can cause a decrease in vision and may lead to eventual blindness. There are many potential causes of cataracts, including excessive ultraviolet light exposure, increasing the risk of this disorder in tennis players.

Symptoms. There are several common symptoms of cataracts, including gradual, painless onset of blurry, filmy, or fuzzy vision, poor central vision, frequent changes in eyeglass prescription, changes in color vision, increased glare from lights, especially oncoming headlights when driving at night, 'second sight' improvement in near vision (no longer needing reading glasses), but a decrease in distance vision, poor vision in sunlight, and the presence of a milky whiteness in the pupil as the cataract progresses.

Treatment. For cataracts that cause no symptoms or only minor visual changes, no treatment may be necessary. Monitoring and assessment of the cataract is often needed. Increased strength in prescription eyeglasses or contact lenses may be helpful. This may be all that is required if the cataract does not reduce the patient's quality of life. If quality of life is affected, then cataract surgery to replace the opacified lens may be necessary.

Practical tips for the player
- Preventive measures emphasize protecting the eyes from UV radiation by wearing glasses with a special coating to protect against UV rays (specifically, UV-A and UV-B). Dark lenses alone are not sufficient.
- Antioxidants may also provide some protection by reducing free radicals that can damage lens proteins. A healthy diet rich in sources of antioxidants, including citrus fruits, sweet potatoes, carrots, green leafy vegetables, and/or vitamin supplements may be helpful.
- When taking certain medications, such as steroids, more frequent eye exams may be necessary.

RETINAL DETACHMENT

Description. A direct blow to the eye can cause a (peripheral) retinal tear and later (days to weeks) a retinal detachment. A retinal detachment occurs when the retina is lifted or pulled from its normal position. Retinal detachments may also occur spontaneously, most commonly in nearsighted people, those over fifty, and those with a family history of retinal detachments.

Symptoms. Symptoms include light flashes, wavy or watery vision, veil or curtain obstructing vision, floaters and visual field loss.

Treatment. Because it can cause devastating damage to the vision if left untreated, retinal detachment is considered a medical emergency that requires immediate medical attention. A retinal tear can sometimes be treated with laser coagulation, but a retinal detachment often needs surgical correction and repair.

FRACTURE OF THE EYE-SOCKET

Description. A fracture of the eye-socket (orbital fracture) may result from a blow from the racquet against the bone around the eye or result from trauma caused by the tennis ball. The energy of the ball causes increased pressure in the eye and may lead to fracture of the paper-thin floor of the eye-socket. This type of fracture is called a blow-out fracture (Figure 11.3).

Symptoms. Characteristic symptoms of the blow-out fracture include double vision, a sunken eye and restricted eye movement.

Treatment. When a blow-out or orbital bone fracture has occurred, the player should be referred to an eye doctor. Prophylactic antibiotics should be prescribed to decrease the incidence of infection as a result of communication between the eye-socket and the nose. Surgery is sometimes necessary to resolve double vision caused by entrapment of the muscles that guide the movements of the eye and/or to correct a sunken eye due to wasting of the contents of the eye-socket.

Practical tips for the player to protect the eye from injuries

- Experience offers no protection against eye trauma: most eye injuries occur at the highest level of play.
- Regular glasses do not protect the eye. Regular glasses may in fact increase injury to the eye either by shattering, or if they are shatterproof, by rotating out of the frame and lacerating the eye.

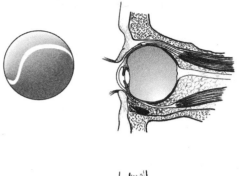

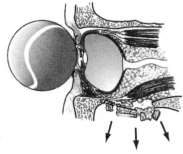

Figure 11.3

When the ball hits the eye, serious
eye injury can occur.

Figure 11.4

Polycarbonate lenses in a sturdy
frame may help prevent eye injuries.

- Contact lenses offer no protection either. Hard lenses can
  be worn, but they offer no protection and can shatter on impact. Soft
  lenses are reasonably safe.
- Optimal eye guards are wrap-around polycarbonate lenses with eye
  guard rims that are posterior to the orbital rim, anti-fog coated, and
  have secure stabilization to the back of the head (Figure 11.4).
- Glasses should have UV-A and UV-B protection.
- Some new sunglasses have color tinting to help visualize the tennis
  ball better.
- Players with only one functional eye, severe myopia, Marfan's syndrome, and previous retinal detachment are strongly advised to wear
  protection

VISION DISORDERS

Description. There are four common vision disorders: near-sightedness, far-sightedness, astigmatism, and presbyopia. A nearsighted eye is either too long or the cornea
and lens are too strong, so that the image focuses in front of the retina rather than on
the retina. A far-sighted eye is too short, or the cornea and lens are too weak, so that
the image focuses behind the retina rather than on the retina. With astigmatism, the
rays of light that are 90 degrees from each other do not focus at the same place in the
eye. Presbyopia occurs with aging. The aging process reduces the ability of the lens to
change shape from distant to near. So after 40, it becomes increasingly difficult to see
objects close by.

Symptoms. A near-sighted person can see very well when objects are nearby, but has
trouble looking at objects that are far away. A far-sighted person has exactly the opposite: he can see objects on a distance very well, but has trouble focusing when they are

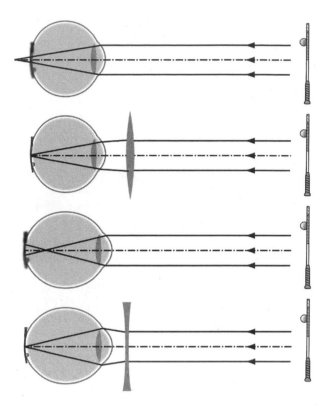

Figure 11.5

Correction of eyesight with spherical glasses:

a. Myopia, with the focal point of the optical system in front of the retinea (short-sightedness).

b. Correction with a concave lens.

c. Hyperopia, with the focal point of the optical system behind the retina.

d. Correction with a convex lens.

nearby. With astigmatism, all objects are a bit blurred. With presbyopia, the person has trouble focusing objects that are nearby, thus being somewhat similar to someone who is farsighted.

Treatment. Refraction disorders can be corrected with glasses or contact lenses (Figure 11.5). A negative glass is used for near-sightedness, a positive glass for far-sightedness, a cylinder glass for astigmatism, and reading glasses or a bifocal lens for presbyopia. The problem with glasses is that part of the peripheral visual field is lost. Contact lenses sometimes lead to allergic reactions, infections and painful eyes, especially when playing indoors or if the player suffers from hay fever. Therefore, correction of a refraction disorder by laser therapy has gained in popularity over the years, and has recently been propagated by some of the top players. There are some risks involved in eyes with high myopia, such as under- or overcorrecting; a glare, which makes it difficult to drive at night; or a haze due to central clouding of the cornea. Therefore, a careful and individualized approach is warranted.

VISUAL TRAINING

Sports optometrists have extended their traditional role in routine visual screening, testing, and lens prescriptions for tennis players to the administration of various forms of visual training designed to improve tennis performance. Most visual training programs currently used are generalized programs adapted from pre-existing programs used in clinical ophthalmology/orthoptics to improve the vision of children, particularly those experiencing reading difficulties. They include repetitive eye exercises to try to improve basic visual function (such as acuity, eye tracking and depth perception) and, through this, tennis performance. The purpose of generalized visual training programs is to improve basic visual functions, however, these are not typically the limiting factors to expert performance.

Practical tip for the athlete and coach
- Players and coaches may use general visual training programs that can be included in the program of young players (up to age 12). They do not appear to provide improvements in either basic visual function or motor performance in tennis in older age groups.

SUMMARY

Irritation or damage of the cornea and conjunctiva are the most common eye injuries in tennis. More serious injury may occur when a ball strikes the eye. Protection of the eyes with eye guards is strongly recommended to players with previous eye injuries or one functional eye only. Correction of refraction deformities is particularly important to tennis players; operative correction with laser therapy is gaining in popularity. There is no sound scientific evidence that visual training is helpful to players beyond early childhood.

12

Skin Disorders

Every movement and every stroke puts considerable pressure on the hands and feet. On hard courts in the summer, players battle with high friction between the court and the shoe and with very high court surface temperatures. On clay, greater distances are covered during a match and players often slide to hit the ball. Many friction related and traumatic skin problems of hands, feet and nails may therefore be encountered on court. Also, sun related disorders and insect stings are important matters to consider.

BLISTERS

Description. A blister is a fluid filled vesicle. It is the result of prolonged friction, causing fluid to accumulate between the layers of the skin.

Symptoms. First a "hot spot" develops. With continued friction, a blister will come up. Blisters are usually only painful if pressure is put on them or if they are infected.

Treatment. If a "hot spot" has developed, cover the affected area with an adhesive bandage. If a blister has developed, follow the next five steps:

- Clean and sterilize the blister area. Puncture and decompress the blister with a sterile needle, and express all the underlying fluid. The blister should be punctured at several points along the base, directing the needle horizontally in order to avoid bleeding. It is best not to remove the layer of skin over the blister, until new skin has formed. In general puncturing blisters should be avoided because it increases the risk of inflammation. If the player wants to continue playing, however, chances are that the blisters will rupture, and then it is better to remove the fluid before play.

209

- Place horseshoe shaped felt around the blister and/or a skin care pad directly onto the blister (Figure 12.1). The padding should cover the area around the blister, and the skin protection pad should be applied directly onto the blister.
- Cover the foam and the skin protection pad with a dressing retention sheet, making sure it holds the foam securely in place (Figure 12.2).
- Next, apply a layer of elastic adhesive bandage (Figure 12.3).
- Finish by applying talcum powder to prevent the area from sticking to the sock.

Practical tips for the player
- Preventive measures are to wear clean, well fitting socks and shoes.
- Try 100% acrylic socks or hi-bulk orlon, because they wick moisture away from the skin, which helps prevent blistering.
- If a particular finger/hand or toe/foot area is prone to increased racquet or shoe contact, it should be covered with adhesive tape, even in the absence of a blister. This barrier between the skin and the irritant prevents friction and thus blistering.

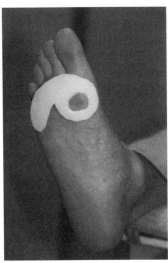

Figure 12.1
The area around the blister is covered with adhesive foam.

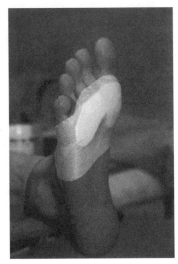

Figure 12.2
A dressing retention sheet is applied to prevent friction and movement.

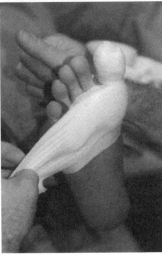

Figure 12.3
A layer of elastic adhesive bandage is applied.

CALLUS

Description. Callus is a diffuse thickening of the skin over bony protrusions, where there is increased pressure and repeated friction. It is a protective response of the skin.

Symptoms. Callus does not hurt, but thick calluses may crack and result in painful fissures. It usually forms under the central part of the heel and under the second and third metatarsal heads. In athletes who continually press down along the medial (inner) side of the foot (pronated feet), callus can also occur beneath the first metatarsal head. Callus formation is also common on the thumb and fingers of the playing hand.

Treatment. Reduce painful callus in size by rubbing with pumice stone, sandstone, a callus file or sandpaper, after soaking the thickened area in warm water.

Practical tips for the player
- Apply cushioned pads to reduce pain and pressure.
- Try a metatarsal bar within the shoe to relieve pressure on calluses on the ball of the foot or adjacent toe/foot joints.

CORNS (CLAVI)

Description. A corn is a conical thickening of the skin with the apex pointing inwards (Figure 12.4). They form in response to persistent, excessive pressure or friction. Corns are usually 3 to 10 mm in diameter and have a hard center.

Symptoms. Corns are usually hard and circular, with a polished or translucent centre, like a kernel of corn. As corns become inflamed, there is pain and sometimes swelling and redness.

Treatment. After peeling the upper layers of a corn once or twice a day with a pumice stone or other abrasive, apply a nonprescription 5%-10% salicylic ointment and cover the area with a bandage. Soak the area with warm water before rubbing, which may help to soften it. A foot specialist doctor may carefully debride (pare down) the corn and any deep seated core it may have.

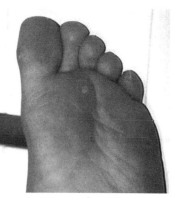

Figure 12.4
A corn on the foot.

Practical tips for the player
- Wear well fitting shoes. Avoid shoes which are too tight or too loose. Try shoes with an extra depth toe box (the part of the shoe over the toes)
- Apply a corn pad to reduce pressure on irritated areas.
- Do not apply socks or stockings tightly around the toes.

TENNIS TOE (BLACK TOE)

Description. A tennis toe, also known as black toe or subungual hematoma, is bleeding under the toenail due to separation of the nail from the toe. It occurs as a result of the frequent starts and stops in tennis, leading to repeated pressure of the shoe against the toenail. The risk is increased when the shoes are too tight or when the toenails are too long. The big toe or second toe, whichever is longer, is usually affected.

Symptoms. Pain may be experienced due to the increased pressure under the toe, but is not always present. The nail may turn blue or, in cases of repetitive trauma, black.

Treatment. Tennis toe usually heals by itself in one to two weeks. Infrequently, if pain is severe and acute, a doctor may relieve pressure by drilling a hole in the nail with a heated needle or paper clip, enabling the blood to escape.

Practical tips for the player
- Wear properly fitting shoes and socks. If there are any areas of pressure, have a shoe repair person modify the shoe by pushing out these areas. Use ointment to soften leather shoes. Ensure tight lacing and retying of shoes.

- Trim the toe nails short.
- Try wearing two pairs of socks, first sock inside out, then place Vaseline on the toe over the first sock, and the second pair over the first, right side in.

INGROWN TOENAIL

Description. An ingrown toenail is a condition in which the sharp edge of a toenail grows into the fleshy side of a toe, usually the big toe, and is the result of poor nail cutting (round instead of straight), pressure from shoes, or the sudden stops and pivoting in tennis that causes the toe to jam into the shoe. The edge of the toe becomes inflamed and often infected.

Symptoms. There is often acute pain with tenderness on gentle palpation, redness, swelling, warmth, and occasionally pus.

Treatment. If there is inflammation, soak the toe (or whole foot) for 20 minutes, twice a day, in a gallon of warm water. This may be done with the addition of two tablespoons of salts or a mild detergent. Lift the toenail, as it softens with soaks, and place cotton under the lifted edges. This will help decompress the pressure on the inflamed fleshy tissue, allowing healing.

A doctor may prescribe antibiotic therapy. Antibiotics usually start to provide relief within 48 hours. Symptoms usually resolve within one week after starting antibiotics.

For acute severe cases, for cases that do not respond to antibiotics, and/or chronic, recurrent cases, surgery is usually recommended. The operation to remove the outer edge of the toenail can be performed in the doctor's office.

Practical tips for the player
- Cut the toenails straight across and never cut them down at the edges.
- Avoid shoes with tight toe boxes.

EXCESSIVE SWEATING

Description. Excessive sweating in the palms of the hands can be a problem for tennis players, particularly on hot, humid days. The racquet grip becomes slippery and the player starts to lose grip.

Treatment. Local treatment may consist of application of an aluminum chloride solution. Another option is to use electric currents through the skin in order to disrupt the function of the sweat glands; this is known as iontophorosis. However, this has to be repeated quite often in order to get the desired results.

Practical tips for the player
- Dry the hands with sawdust or magnesium-oxide before serving.

INSECT STINGS

Description. Insect stings, such as ant, bee and wasp stings are common, painful, but rarely deadly. Each year, 10% of the population are stung by bees and wasps.

Symptoms. Insect things lead to local reactions, such as pain, swelling, redness, and itching. Rarely, an anaphylactic reaction may occur, leading to major systemic reactions such as upper airway obstruction, severe spasm of the bronchi, blue hands and face and a marked fall in blood pressure with loss of consciousness (anaphylactic shock).

Treatment. Remnants of insect parts, such as the sting, should be removed as quickly as possible. The sting continues to inject venom, and the faster the removal, the lower the dose of venom received. Suction devices are available that are thought to keep envenomation to the minimum. Cold compressions should be applied to reduce the local swelling, pain, and itching. A doctor may prescribe medication (oral antihistamines) to decrease the swelling and itching that may accompany stings.

If the patient has previously had an allergic reaction to an insect sting, it is important to see an allergist. There is a 60% chance of having a similar or worse reaction if stung again. If an anaphylactic reaction occurs, that is an emergency situation and medical treatment (intramuscular epinephrine) should be given as quickly as possible. Players known to be at risk for anaphylactic shock should either carry an emergency epinephrine syringe in their bag (Figure 12.5), or undergo venom immunotherapy in order to prevent life-threatening reactions.

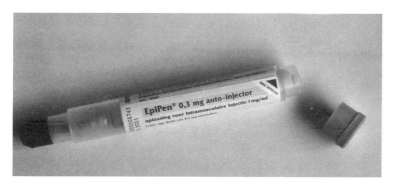

Figure 12.5
The Epi-Pen auto injector.

Practical tips for the player
- Never swat or flail at a flying insect. If need be, gently brush it aside or patiently wait for it to leave.
- Do not drink from open beverage cans. Stinging insects, attracted by the sweet beverage, will crawl inside a can.
- When bringing food on court, try to keep it covered at all times. Stinging insects are fond of the same foods as you are.
- Avoid wearing sweet-smelling perfumes, hairsprays, colognes, and deodorants.
- Avoid wearing brightly colored clothing with flowery patterns. Bees may mistake you for a flower.

TICK BITES AND LYME DISEASE

Description. Lyme disease is caused by an organism, a spirochete (Borrelia burgdorferi), that is transmitted by a certain type of tick, that has been able to suck blood for more than 24 hours.

Symptoms. A characteristic red rash usually appears at the site of the tick bite, followed by flu-like symptoms. The bite may also go entirely unnoticed. Days to weeks later, fatigue, headache, swollen lymph nodes, muscle and joint pain, and skin lesions may develop. Weeks or months later, facial paralysis, joint inflammation, neurological symptoms and heart palpitations may occur.

Treatment. Ticks should immediately be removed by pulling carefully and steadily. The tick should not be yanked or crushed. If available, use a tweezer. Removal within 24 hours protects against the development of Lyme disease. If one may been bitten by an infected tick, the doctor may do blood tests to look for antibodies to the organism (± 50% false negative). Preventive antibiotic treatment with erythromycin or doxycycline to prevent Lyme disease after a known tick bite may be warranted.

Practical tips for the player
- When retrieving a ball that has been hit into wooded or grassy areas, put on your track suit and tuck pant legs into socks and shirt into pants, so that ticks cannot crawl under clothing. When back on court, check for ticks.
- Wear light-colored clothing so that ticks can be spotted more easily.
- When playing in an area with lost of surrounding woods and brushes, spray insect repellent containing DEET on clothes and on exposed skin other than the face, or treat clothes (especially pants, socks, and shoes) with permethrin, which kills ticks on contact.
- After being outdoors, remove clothing and wash and dry it at a high temperature.

MASSAGE RASH (FOLLICULITIS)

Description. Folliculitis is a superficial or deep bacterial infection of the hair follicles. It may occur when hair follicles are damaged by friction from clothing, massage, blockage of the follicle or shaving. In most cases, the damaged follicles are infected with the bacteria staphylococcus.

Symptoms. Symptoms are a rash (reddened area of skin), pimples or pustules around a hair follicle, and itching skin. Rarely, this is accompanied by a low grade fever, generalized malaise and headache.

Treatment. Shaving the area should be avoided. Wash the area with antibacterial soaps. Hot moist compresses may promote drainage of extensive folliculitis. The doctor may prescribe topical or oral antibiotics or antifungal medications if the rash is very extensive.

Practical tips for the player
- Avoid reinfection from contaminated clothing and washcloths. Wash and dry your clothing at high temperatures.
- Minimize friction from clothing
- Ask the massage therapist to apply massage oil more generously in the future.

ATHLETE'S FOOT (TINEA PEDIS)

Description. Athlete's foot is an infection of the skin or nails, caused by a fungus. Fungal skin infections are very common among tennis players, because the fungi thrive in the warm, moist and dark conditions of tennis shoes. These infections are mildly contagious and may spread to other areas (crotch, armpit, nails). Common means of transmission include contact in public showers and swimming areas, shared towels, or contaminated bath mats.

Symptoms. Symptoms of athlete's foot are irritation and itching between the toes, usually the fourth and fifth, accompanied by moist, soft, gray-white or red scales and dead skin between the toes. Uncommonly, there are small blisters on the feet, caused by a hypersensitivity to the fungus. When fungal nail infection begins to take hold, it can cause the nail to change color, often to a yellow/green or darker color. The nail may thicken and become flaky.

Treatment. After cleaning the area, an antifungal cream or powder should be applied twice a day for two to six weeks. The treatment should not be interrupted until all the skin lesions have resolved. If the nails are infected, prolonged therapy (3-9 months) with oral medications may be recommended (Figure 12.6).

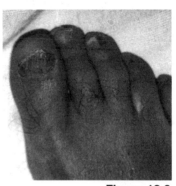

Figure 12.6
A fungal infection of the toenails.

> *Practical tips for the player*
> * Wash your feet daily and dry thoroughly.
> * Change socks daily and after play.
> * Do not share towels but bring your own.
> * Use foot powders.
> * Use sandals in public showers and dressing rooms.

COLD SORES (FEVER BLISTERS)

Description. Cold sores, also known as fever blisters, are caused by the herpes simplex type 1 virus. They usually appear on the lips, and occasionally on the gums, nose, cheeks, or fingers. The infection is transmitted by contact with another person's active infection, by touching or kissing. Eating utensils, drinking bottles, towels and razors are other common sources. The virus reverts to a latent form within the nerve cells, but emerges again as an active infection on or near the original site. Recurrences are generally milder than the initial infection and are triggered by menstruation, sun exposure, stress or any illness accompanied by fever.

Symptoms. Herpes simplex begins as a group of small red bumps that blisters. Blisters are single or clustered, small, and fluid filled on a raised, red, painful area of the skin. The blisters form, break and ooze. The blisters begin to dry up after a few days and form a yellow crust. The crust then falls off and the redness slowly goes away. Preceding the attack, itching or heightened sensitivity may be felt at the site. Symptoms usually last for seven to ten days.

Treatment. As soon as the onset of a cold sore is felt, antiviral medication should be started, as early application may prevent a recurrence. The area should be washed twice a day with a mild soap. Antivirals are available in both pill and ointment forms. Using a medication may shorten the duration of cold sores, but it will not prevent recurrences.

Some authorities recommend using L-Lysine, an amino acid, found in the vitamin section at the drugstore to prevent and/or treat fever blisters.

Practical tips for the player

- Do not share your drinking can or towel with others, to prevent an initial infection.
- When you have oral herpes you can spread the disease to others. If you have a herpes infection you should alert anyone with whom you are going to have close contact. Avoid kissing and skin contact with people while blisters are present, to prevent spreading the virus. Also, avoid sharing food or drink with others. The virus can spread as long as there are moist secretions from the blisters.
- Wash your hands carefully before touching another person when you have a cold sore.
- Be careful about touching other parts of your body. Your eyes and genital area are particularly susceptible to spread of the virus.
- Use sunblock on your lips and face before prolonged exposure to the sun — during both the winter and the summer — to help prevent recurrence of cold sores.

WARTS (VERRUCAE)

Description. Warts are noncancerous outgrowths of the skin caused by a viral infection (human papilloma virus) in the top layer of the skin. They range in size from 1 to 2 mm to large tumors (Figure 12.7).

Symptoms. Warts are usually skin colored and feel rough to the touch, but they can also be dark, flat and smooth. The appearance of a wart depends on where it is growing. On the hands, they present as circumscribed, firm, cauliflower shaped raised areas, which are irregular and rough. Plantar warts (on the bottom of the foot) tend to grow inward because of weight bearing; and they can then become painful. They can be distinguished from calluses by gentle paring with a scalpel, which will reveal soft, granular, elongated mounts of skin and small black dots.

Figure 12.7

A wart on the hand.

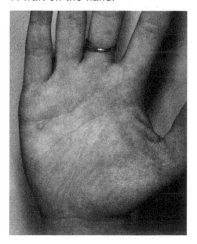

Treatment. In children, warts can disappear without treatment over a period of several months to years. However, warts that are bothersome, painful, or rapidly multiplying should be treated. Warts in adults often do not disappear as easily or as quickly as they do in children.

Warts can be treated by applying salicylic acid gel, solution or plaster. There is usually little discomfort but it can take many weeks of treatment to obtain favorable results. The doctor may use caustic acids, cryotherapy, electrosurgery (burning), laser therapy or start immunotherapy with diphencyprone. Excision and radiotherapy should be avoided.

Practical tips for the player

- Treat new warts quickly as they come up, so they have little time to spread.
- Postpone therapy when preparing for important tournaments, since treatment may lead to painful blisters.

SUN RELATED DISORDERS

During the outdoor season, tennis players are regularly exposed to the sun (Figure 12.8). Problems can occur if players are not educated about the hazards of sunshine and ultraviolet radiation. This is especially applicable to junior players who may be required to play outdoors for up to 1000 hours per year from their early teens. This prolonged exposure can produce acute reactions in the outer layer of the skin (sunburn) and more serious long-term damage to the deeper layer of the skin.

SUNBURN

Description. Sunburn is induced by ultraviolet B light. Players most likely to develop sunburn are those with fair skin, who tan minimally. A tan has a protective effect against UVB exposure.

Symptoms. The symptoms of sunburn include redness, heat, swelling, and blisters.

Treatment. Apply cool compresses of tap water, to relieve the pain and heat if sunburn has occurred.

Figure 12.8
Tennis players are regularly exposed to the sun.

Practical tips for the player
- Apply a sunscreen with a skin protection factor of 15, if prolonged exposure is anticipated.
- Sun screen products that do not have an oil base will minimize any decrease in the evaporation of sweat from the skin surface. Sun blocking agents such as zinc-oxide or titanium dioxide provide good protection for vulnerable areas such as the nose, lips or helix of the ear (Figure 12.9).

SKIN CANCER

Description. Skin cancer is a disease in which cancer (malignant) cells are found in the outer layers of the skin. Important risk factors for developing skin cancer are sunburn and UV light exposure. Both the total amount of sun received over the years, and overexposure resulting in sunburn can cause skin cancer. Other risk factors for skin cancer include heredity (a history of skin cancer in the family), a fair skin, environmental factors (e.g. thin ozone layer, such as in Australia and New Zealand), multiple nevi or atypical moles, repeated exposure to x-rays and scars from disease and burns.

Symptoms. Skin cancer can occur anywhere on the body, but it is most common in places that have been exposed to more sunlight, such as the face, neck, hands, and arms. There are several types of cancer that start in the skin.

Basal cell cancer and squamous cell cancer. These are the most common types of cancer and can be varied in appearance. The most common sign of skin cancer is a change on the skin, such as a growth or a sore that will not heal. Sometime there may be a small

Figure 12.9

Sun-blocking agents provide good protection for vulnerable areas such as the nose, lips or helix of the ear.

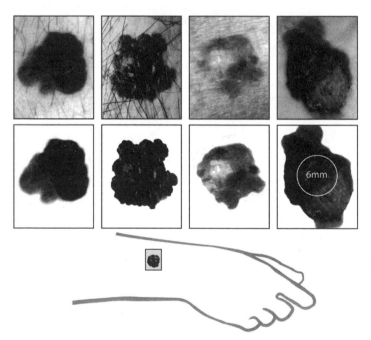

Figure 12.10

The ABCDs of melanoma

Asymmetry—one half does not match the other half.

Border irregularity—the edges are raged, notched, or blurred.

Color—the pigmentation is not uniform. Shades of tan, brown and black are present. Dashes of red, white and blue add to the mottled appearance.

Diameter—greater than six millimeters (about the size of a pencil eraser). Any growth of a mole should be of concern.

lump. This lump can be smooth, shiny and waxy looking, or it can be red or reddish brown. Skin cancer may also appear as a flat red spot that is rough or scaly.

Melanoma. Melanoma is a disease of the skin in which cancer cells are found in the cells that color the skin (melanocytes). To determine whether a mole is innocent or malignant, look for a change in size, shape and color. The features of a mole are the A,B,C, and D's of detection (Figure 12.10).

Asymmetry. Normally, moles will grow in a symmetrical, even fashion. When one area is growing faster than another this leads to irregular, uneven outgrowths producing an asymmetrical appearance. Thus, when one half does not match the other half, this should raise suspicion.

Border irregularity. The outward edge of a normal mole is well defined. When the edges become irregular, notched, or hazy, this is an indication that there is localized growth.

Color. Moles normally have a very uniform color or pigment. When the color starts to vary with the appearance of black or dark brown areas and dashes of red, white and or gray areas within the mole it is time to get a medical evaluation.

Diameter. Most moles achieve a stable size over time. Moles that are greater than six millimeters (about the size of a pencil eraser) should be evaluated. Any growth of a mole should be of concern.

Treatment. Surgery is the most important treatment for all skin cancers and in many cases all that is needed is removal of the suspect lump. Radiotherapy and chemotherapy can also be used.

Practical tips for the player

- Slip, Slop, Slap: when you are out in the sun slip on a shirt, slop on sunscreen, and slap on a hat. Lavishly apply a sunscreen with a sun protection factor (SPF) of at least 15 and reapply it every two hours according to the directions on the label. Use sunscreens that are effective in both the UVB and the UVA range. Reapply sunscreen as needed after swimming, sweating, or towel drying. Use sunscreen even on cloudy days.
- Avoid the sun during the middle of the day, especially between 10 a.m. and 4 p.m., when the sun is strongest.
- Check the UV index number and prepare accordingly.
- Us periodic self-examination to catch skin cancers in the early stage. Get familiar with your skin and your own pattern of moles, freckles and beauty marks. Be alert to changes in number, size, and shape and color of pigmented areas. Visit a doctor if any changes are noticed, or if there is any scaling, oozing, bleeding, itching, tenderness or pain.

SUMMARY

In this chapter, the most common skin disorders in tennis players are discussed. Blisters, corns, and clavi are a result of the constant rubbing and friction of the skin against irritants and may impair performance. The different options for prevention and treatment of these disorders are presented. Insect stings can be painful and annoying, and in susceptible individuals life-threatening as a result of anaphylactic shock. These individuals should carry an emergency epinephrine syringe in their bag. Cold sores, folliculitis, warts and athlete's foot can be contagious; careful hygiene should be observed and treatment installed. Tennis players and coaches should limit sun exposure in order to reduce the potentially harmful short-term and long-term effects.

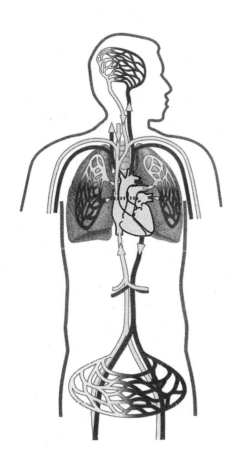

13

The Heart and Blood Vessels

Tennis places medium to high demands on the cardiovascular system (circulatory system of heart, arteries, and veins), and these demands are higher during singles than doubles. This may lead to a training effect of the heart, but may also carry certain risks for the player with cardiovascular disease. In this chapter several symptoms, signs and conditions of the heart will be discussed, including the athlete's heart, palpitations (irregular, forceful heartbeats), fainting, heart attack and sudden cardiac death.

ATHLETE'S HEART

Description. "Athlete's heart" is the term used to describe the adaptations of the heart associated with long-term athletic training. It is a normal, healthy adaptation of the heart. In the past, tennis was generally considered a technical and tactical type of sport with relatively low cardiovascular demands. However, modern tennis has evolved into a sport with high physical demands, reflected by powerful strokes, fast rallies and extended hours of play. It is therefore not surprising that most professional tennis players develop an athlete's heart. For example, German Davis Cup and Fed Cup players were shown to have a 20-30% increase in heart volume and left ventricular mass compared to sedentary controls.

Symptoms. The athlete's heart is characterized by a low resting heart rate, a soft murmur of the heart, a variety of changes on the electrocardiogram, and an increased weight of the heart. The heart rate at rest is often lower than 50 beats per minute.

Treatment. In contrast to the heart that is enlarged due to cardiac diseases such as high blood pressure, valve disease, or disease of the heart muscle itself, the athlete's heart is not associated with an increased risk of cardiovascular disease or sudden cardiac death. Therefore, no treatment is required.

PREMATURE HEARTBEAT

Description. A premature heartbeat is a small variation in an otherwise normal heartbeat. Most people experience an occasional skipped or extra heartbeat. An innocent premature contraction, which is not felt, suppresses the normally following next beat of the heart, resulting in a compensatory pause, after which the heart picks up its normal rhythm again. Because there is a compensatory pause, the heart has more time to fill, resulting in a more forceful beat after the pause, and this is the one felt. This is experienced as the heart "skipping" a beat. In most cases, premature beats are benign and may occur without obvious cause. Seldom, they are associated with electrolyte abnormalities in the blood or with a local reduction in blood supply to the heart.

Symptoms. It may feel like the heart has stopped or skipped a beat.

Treatment. Premature heartbeats do not often require treatment. It may be treated if symptoms are severe or very disturbing. Moderation in triggering factors such as alcohol, chocolate, tobacco, certain spices, stress, or caffeine-containing foods and beverages may reduce the risk of these extra heartbeats in some people. Exercise often helps people who lead a sedentary lifestyle. An underlying cause, if discovered, may require treatment.

RACING HEARTBEAT (TACHYCARDIA)

Description. An increased heart rate during exercise, after a large meal, or when frightened or nervous, is normal. However, sometimes the heart may suddenly start racing without apparent reason. This may be caused by an electrical circuit within the upper (atrial) or lower (ventricular) chambers. Such attacks may last several minutes or more than a day, with the heart rate between 140 and 240 beats per minute.

Symptoms. Common symptoms are lightheadedness, discomfort and anxiety. There may be chest pain or fainting.

Treatment. For all types of rhythm disturbances, except for the occasional extra beat, a physician should be consulted, particularly when accompanied by severe discomfort, chest pain, shortness of breath, light headedness or fainting. The diagnosis is generally made using 24-hour electrocardiography (Holter) monitoring and/or stress testing. Echocardiography, angiography or electrophysiological testing may be used as well. Most forms of tachycardia can be managed by treating the underlying cause, or by anti-arrhythmic medications, cardioversion (changing an irregular heart rhythm into a regular one by giving an electric shock), radiofrequency ablation (disconnecting an abnormal circuit within the heart), or an implantable cardioverter defibrillator (device that uses electric shock to normalize heart rhythm).

Practical tips for the player
- If it has been assessed that the origin of the tachycardia is in the atria (paroxysmal atrial tachycardia) self-help treatments may be effective, such as holding the breath, straining while sitting with the upper body bent forward, or gentle application of pressure to the arteries in the neck (sinus carotis massage).
- Patients experiencing increased heart rates and who use tobacco,

alcohol, caffeine, spices or adrenaline like drugs should discontinue these substances in order to try to reduce or eliminate these episodes.

FAINTING SPELLS (SYNCOPE)

Description. A fainting spell is a sudden, temporary loss of consciousness. Seventy-five per cent of all fainting episodes result from a vasovagal reaction, an involuntary reflex resulting in dilatation of the veins in the legs, low blood pressure and a slow heart beat, causing blood to pool in the legs and not be pumped to the brain. It may be preceded by light-headedness, dizziness, profuse sweating, and nausea, although it may occur without warning. The fainting spell may be aborted by quickly sitting down and putting one's head between the knees or by lying down. A vasovagal response may occur after prolonged standing or exertion. Such events typically occur with ball boys or ball girls, who have to stand still in the sun after sudden bursts of activity. Also, vigorous tennis in hot, humid weather may lead to syncope due to fluid losses caused by excessive sweating. It may also be precipitated by a painful or fearful stimulus.

Symptoms. The victim falls down and loses consciousness. There may be a few limb jerks, but no seizures, tongue biting or incontinence. Revival occurs automatically once the victim has lain supine for a few seconds to minutes.

Treatment. Let the player lie supine for five to ten minutes and elevate his feet. Protect his airway, record vital signs (breathing, pulse, color) and be ready to proceed with resuscitation if the episode turns out to be more than a simple fainting spell. Once the person has recovered, let him or her rest, cool down in the shade and have something to drink.

Although a vasovagal collapse is usually benign, not all loss of consciousness is due to a vasovagal response. If there is no obvious cause for the fainting, or if the fainting occurs during exercise, an extensive examination is necessary with a complete history, physical examination and careful diagnostic tests to reveal potentially serious underlying conditions.

INFLAMMATION OF THE HEART MUSCLE (MYOCARDITIS)

Description. Inflammation of the heart muscle usually occurs as a complication during or after various infectious diseases (rheumatic fever, coxsackie virus, influenza) or exposure to certain chemicals or drugs. The typical time interval between the onset of the viral illness and cardiac involvement is two weeks. The average age of patients with myocarditis is 42 years. Electrocardiography and heart muscle tissue examination (biopsy) can be helpful in setting the diagnosis. In most cases, the inflammation clears and the patient recovers to good health. Vigorous exercise may lead to serious health risks if the heart muscle is inflamed, such as fatal arrhythmia's leading to sudden cardiac death, and should be avoided.

Symptoms. Symptoms can vary greatly and may include a nonspecific illness characterized by fatigue, fever, mild chest discomfort, or fulminant congestive heart failure with shortness of breath, palpitations, and serious chest pain. However, the majority of cases of myocarditis are subclinical and the patient rarely seeks medical attention during acute illness.

Treatment. Patients with mild symptoms and no signs of cardiac failure or rhythm disturbances may be treated on an outpatient basis with bed rest. If there are signs of cardiac failure and rhythm disturbances, the patient should be hospitalized and receive heart failure medications.

Nonsteroidal anti-inflammatory drugs (NSAIDs) are contraindicated in the early course of disease because of inhibition of prostaglandin production (important in muscle contractions, blood vessel constriction and dilatation), worsened heart cell function, and increased cell death of heart muscle.

Practical tips for the player
* Abstain from tennis when suffering from a viral infection with a temperature of over 100.4∞F (38 °C). Upon returning to play after a viral illness, ensure the intensity of the initial workouts is not too high. Build up gradually. Allocate enough rest time between drill series and check your pulse regularly to monitor recovery.

ATHEROSCLEROSIS (HARDENING AND NARROWING OF ARTERIES)

Description. Atherosclerosis is the gradual build-up of fatty deposits (atheroma) in the arteries, leading to hardening and narrowing of these arteries. The fatty build-up or plaque can break open and lead to the formation of a blood clot that seals the break. The cycle of fatty build-up, plaque rupture, and blood clot formation causes the arteries to narrow, reducing blood flow. This is a process that can take many years.

Certain conditions (called risk factors) increase the chance of developing atherosclerosis. These include: elevated levels of LDL cholesterol (the "bad" cholesterol) in the blood; family history of early coronary heart disease, including a heart attack or sudden death before age 55 of father or brother, or mother or sister before age 65; cigarette smoking; diabetes mellitus; high blood pressure; low levels of HDL (the "good" cholesterol) in the blood; and a sedentary lifestyle.

Symptoms. Atherosclerosis usually does not cause symptoms until it severely narrows or totally blocks an artery. Atherosclerosis can affect the arteries of the brain, heart, kidneys, arms and legs. If the arteries to the brain are affected, a stroke or transient ischemic attack ("mini-stroke") can occur. If there is significant narrowing of the coronary arteries that supply blood to the heart, this may lead to chest pain or a heart attack. If there is narrowing of the vessels that deliver blood to the legs, there may be pain in the calves and feet during exercise, which resolves shortly after the activity is stopped. If the arteries to the kidneys are affected, this may lead to hypertension.

Treatment. The goals of treatment are to reduce the symptoms and prevent the complications of atherosclerosis. Treatment may include lifestyle changes, medications, and special procedures and surgery.

Medications may include cholesterol lowering medication, anti-hypertensive medication, anticoagulants and aspirin.

Special procedures and surgery may include angioplasty (dilating blocked or narrowed blood vessels), stent placement (a spiral to keep the artery open), coronary artery bypass surgery (heart surgery), carotid artery surgery, and bypass surgery of the legs.

Practical tips for the player
- Eat a healthy diet. This means the diet should be lower in salt, total fat, saturated fat and cholesterol, and higher in fruits, vegetables, and low fat dairy products.
- Stop smoking cigarettes or tobacco.
- Exercise regularly. In other words: start playing more tennis!
- Lose weight, if you are overweight.

HIGH BLOOD PRESSURE

Description. High blood pressure or hypertension is diagnosed when blood pressure is consistently 160/90 mmHg (millimeters of mercury) or higher. Specific diseases or health problems, such as narrowing of the aorta, narrowing of the renal artery, or adrenal gland problems, are identified in less than 5% of cases. If no specific cause can be identified, the high blood pressure is categorized as essential hypertension.

Symptoms. High blood pressure is generally without symptoms, but may lead to long-term complications, as a result of accelerated atherosclerosis such as stroke, kidney failure, myocardial infarction and peripheral artery disease.

Treatment. Encourage healthy life-style changes, such as weight loss when overweight, becoming a non-smoker when a smoker, and regular exercise. Medications may be prescribed, such as A II blockers, calcium channel blockers, beta-adrenergic blockers, diuretics, and angiotensin converting enzyme (ACE) inhibitors.

Practical tips for the player
- Tennis is generally considered beneficial to people with mild to moderate hypertension. A game of tennis leads to a temporary increase in systolic blood pressure (blood pressure in arteries during contraction of the heart) and a mild decrease in diastolic blood pressure (blood pressure during relaxation of the heart). Tennis has been shown to have a mild lowering effect on systolic and diastolic blood pressure in the long run, comparable to aerobic exercise such as running.

HEART ATTACK

Description. A heart attack occurs when a blood clot in one or more coronary arteries suddenly cuts off most or all blood supply to a part of the heart (Figure 13.1). Heart muscle cells in the affected region do not receive enough oxygen carrying blood and begin to die. The higher up in the coronary artery the blockage occurs, and the more time that passes without treatment to restore blood flow, the greater the damage to the heart.

Symptoms. Symptoms are intense, prolonged chest pain, typically described as a feeling of heavy pressure, tightness, squeezing, or aching. The pain is located behind the breastbone and can radiate to the left arm, back, neck or jaw. Other symptoms include shortness of breath, nausea, vomiting, profuse sweating and sometimes a feeling of impending doom.

Treatment. A heart attack is a medical emergency that needs immediate medical attention. Treatment is aimed at opening the blocked artery to restore blood flow as fast

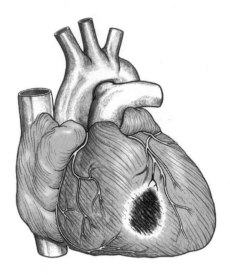

Figure 13.1

A myocardial infarction

as possible to prevent or limit damage to the heart muscle and/or to prevent and treat complications, such as rhythm disturbances. The main treatments are thrombolytic ("clot busting") therapy, other medications, and special procedures, such as angioplasty (dilating blocked or narrowed vessels) and coronary artery bypass surgery (heart surgery). To be most effective, these treatments must be given as soon as possible – preferably within one hour of the start of heart attack symptoms in order to limit the damage to the heart.

Practical tips for the player

• Patients who have recovered from a heart attack require careful screening in order to assess the risks and potential benefits of sport. Regular exercise is advised for patients who have healed well and have rehabilitated from an acute episode, are asymptomatic, in good muscular form and in stable condition. Exercise is contraindicated when symptoms or signs of clinical instability or abnormal results of laboratory investigations are found.

• Start playing doubles before playing singles, since the average heart rate obtained during doubles play is lower than during singles play.

• There should be a gradual and progressive increase in the duration and intensity of play.

• Unrestricted play is allowed after a couple of months if there are no complications.

• As a general rule, maximal heart rate during play should not exceed 90% of the maximum heart rate obtained during an exercise test.

SUDDEN EXERCISE RELATED CARDIAC DEATH

Description. Sudden exercise related cardiac death is cardiac death during or within one hour of exercise. Sudden exercise related cardiac death in the young age group (under 35) is primarily due to structural cardiac disease that is congenital in nature. Examples are hypertrophic cardiomyopathy (thickened heart muscle due to disease), right ventricular dysplasia (abnormality in size and shape of the right heart chamber), long QT syndrome (slow "recharging" of the heart after each contraction), and Wolff-Parkinson-White syndrome (extra conduction pathway between the atria and ventricles, leading to short-circuiting and attacks of very rapid heart beats). The most prevalent diagnosis in athletes over 35 who die suddenly is atherosclerotic heart disease.

Preparticipation screening. Although it is not possible to prevent all exercise related cardiac death, it is possible to identify those at increased risk. Screening for risk factors is recommended for all competitive tennis players over age 35. Risk factors include personal and family history of coronary artery disease, smoking history, high cholesterol levels, inactivity, high blood pressure, diabetes and obesity. Routine exercise testing in asymptomatic players is not warranted, however. This leads to the recommendations in Table 13.1.

Table 13.1

SCREENING RECOMMENDATIONS	
Players < 35 years (asymptomatic)	**Recommendation**
Recreational	No screening
Competitive (general)	No screening
Highly talented junior < 10 hours/week	Yearly history and physical examination. If indicated, further evaluation.
Highly talented juniors 10+ hours/week	Yearly history, physical examination, and exercise testing. If indicated, further evaluation.
Professional players	Yearly history, physical examination, and exercise testing. Echocardiogram once when becoming member of the team.
Players > 35 years	
Recreational	Questionnaire. If risk factors or symptomatic, further evaluation.
Competitive	Questionnaire. If risk factors or symptomatic, further evaluation.
Veteran Circuit	Yearly history, physical examination and exercise testing.

UPPER EXTREMITY VASCULAR INJURIES

Arm and hand complaints in tennis players are very common. Most of these are caused by injuries to the musculoskeletal system, but in some cases they are caused by injuries to the arteries or veins. The following types are discussed below: hand ischemia from repetitive blunt trauma, thoracic outlet compression resulting in venous thrombosis, and thoracic outlet compression resulting in axillary artery compression and thrombosis.

COLD FINGER (DIGITAL ISCHEMIA)

Description. Ischemia (inadequate local blood supply) of the finger may result from blocking of the ulnar artery at the level of the hamate bone at the wrist. This may be caused by repeated blunt trauma of the butt of the racquet to the wrist and base of the hand, leading to blood clotting and blocking of the arteries (see "hamate fractures"). A cold finger may also occur as a result of bulging of the arteries in the axilla or caused by blood clots arising in a higher location (see "axillary-subclavian vein compression"). Uncommonly, a cold finger may also result from compression of the artery to the index finger by gripping the racquet, though surrounding blood vessels usually prevent this complication.

Symptoms. The usual symptoms are cold intolerance of the finger, coolness, numbness, and blue or white discoloration of the skin.

Treatment. In acute cases, dissolving the blood clot with intravenous medication should be tried. When there is a predisposing cause, such as bulging of the ulnar artery, arterial reconstruction is recommended. Sometimes daily aspirin will be sufficient. Should the trouble be caused by a problem at a higher level (e.g. bulging of the artery in the axilla), this should be addressed.

Practical tips for the player
- Wrap adequate cushioning material around the grip. A cushioned grip tape can increase racket damping by up to 100% and may reduce the grip reaction force by 20%.

BLOOD CLOT IN THE ARM (EFFORT THROMBOSIS OF THE UPPER EXTREMITY)

Description. The term "effort thrombosis" of the axillary-subclavian vein is used when there is thrombosis (formation of a stationary blood clot in a vessel) related to heavy arm exertion. This is caused by strain on the axillary-subclavian vein during the wind up of the service (hyperabduction and external rotation of the arm). The axillary-subclavian vein is located under the arm, and extends across the shoulder, under the clavicle, into the lower neck. The repetitive compression during the wind up of the service action may lead to microtrauma of the veins, leading to local coagulation and thrombosis of the vessel. A mechanical compression ("thoracic outlet syndrome") of the vein by adjoining bone, ligament, and muscle structures can intensify the effects.

Symptoms. The player will describe aching pain, swelling, and a bluish discoloration of the entire arm. These features may occur abruptly or gradually. Additional symptoms include weakness, heaviness or tingling of the arm. The veins of the hand, forearm and chest may be distended and clearly visible.

Treatment. Rest and elevation of the affected arm may give some relief. The player should be referred to a vascular surgeon. Therapeutic options include anticoagulation (prevention of blood clotting) for relief of symptoms and for prevention of pulmonary embolism; thrombolysis with intravenous medications; percutaneous angioplasty; and surgery.

Practical tips for the player
- After treatment, there should be a gradual return to activities of daily living. Determining whether a player can return to play must be evaluated on an individual basis as there is a high risk of recurrence.

AXILLARY-SUBCLAVIAN ARTERY COMPRESSION

Description. Compression of the subclavian or axillary arteries occur during the wind up phase of the serve, when the arm is behind the back. This compression may be accentuated by hypertrophy of the muscles, instability of the shoulder, and bony anomalies such as cervical ribs. Actual arterial thrombosis is unusual, but the compression may lead to spasm and aneurysms (a bulging, weakened section of the artery that could rupture). Early detection can prevent the negative consequences of arterial thrombosis.

Symptoms. Symptoms include early fatigue of the upper extremity, hand ischemia, pale fingers, coolness of the hand and upper extremity, and numbness of the hand and fingers. Entrapment of branch arteries, including the suprascapular, subscapular, or posterior humeral circumflex arteries, may lead to muscle wasting.

Treatment. The player should be referred to a vascular surgeon, who may advise conservative or surgical treatment. Conservative treatment consists of thrombolytic therapy (medications that dissolve blood clots). Surgical treatment may consist of surgical reconstruction or decompression.

Practical tips for the player
- Stretch the posterior capsule of the affected shoulder by laying on your side with your shoulder blade resting against the table or bed. Cross the arm of your affected shoulder in front of you, so that your elbow is in front of you face. Grab the elbow with the other hand and pull, stretching the back of your shoulder (Figure 5.13).

SUMMARY

"Athlete's heart" is the term used to describe the adaptations of the heart associated with long-term athletic training, and is a physiological (healthy) adaptation that may develop in tennis players. A vasovagal reaction is usually benign, and may occur in ball boys and girls when they have to stand still in the sun for a long time. Playing tennis generally has a positive effect on mild hypertension; however, moderate and severe hypertension should be treated before resuming play. Tennis should be avoided by players during viral infections and high fever, to reduce the risk of exercise induced acute arrhythmias and sudden cardiac death. Arm and hand complaints in tennis players are occasionally caused by injuries to the arteries or veins. Hand ischemia from repetitive blunt trauma, and thoracic outlet compression resulting in venous thrombosis or axillary artery compression require further assessment and treatment. Tennis can be resumed by players after a myocardial infarction if they are rehabilitated, asymptomatic, in good muscular form, and after approval by their cardiologist or physician. A thorough clinical assessment, including exercise testing, is recommended for players with cardiovascular risk factors and/or premonitory symptoms. A chart flow for cardiac assessment in different age groups and competitive categories is presented.

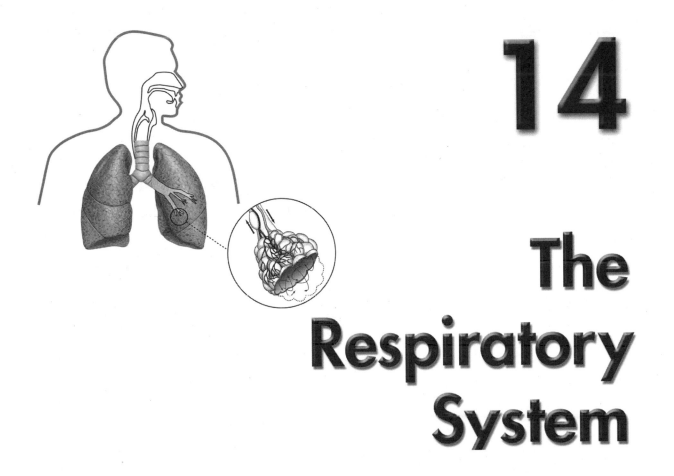

The Respiratory System

14

Well functioning lungs and airways are important for a tennis player. Diseases of the airways may inhibit breathing and negatively influence footwork and strokes and should be treated. However, a troubled breathing pattern does not always indicate disease. It may also be mentally induced by high stress levels during play and may be reduced by mental training and breathing techniques (see Chapter 5). The most common respiratory diseases in tennis players are discussed in this chapter.

HAY FEVER (ALLERGIC RHINITIS)

Description. Hay fever is the name given to pollen allergy. Actually, 'hay fever' is a misnomer, because neither is hay the usual cause, nor does it result in fever. Allergic rhinitis is a better name. It is a seasonal or long-lasting allergy that leads to inflammation of the mucous membrane in the nose (rhinitis), impairing proper nasal function. For some people, such symptoms appear during a pollen season. This is evident on the professional tennis circuit, where players with allergies tend to have problems during the spring grass court tournaments (Nottingham, Halle, 's Hertogenbosch, Queens, Newport and Wimbledon). For others, the symptoms are manifested primarily in the winter when their home is closed to ventilation and house dust mites and molds are common.

Symptoms. Symptoms are a stuffed or runny nose; frequent sneezing; itchy eyes, nose, roof of mouth, or throat; and coughing.

Treatment. The most effective method for controlling hay fever is to avoid the allergens. Adapt the tournament schedule to the pollen season and try to avoid grass court tournaments or tournaments close to blooming fields and trees in the spring or ragweed in the autumn.

Saline (salt water) nose drops are often helpful in relieving nasal symptoms. Medications that may be used to treat hay fever symptoms include antihistamines, nasal sprays with cromolyn, or short-term use of topical steroids. Also, over-the-counter nasal sprays and drops can be tried, such as xylometazoline, that reduce congestion by narrowing of the blood vessels of the mucosa. However, these drugs should not be used for more than one week, because long-term use causes development of rebound nasal congestion.

Consider immunotherapy if the nasal symptoms are significant and cannot be controlled by environmental measures or acceptable drug therapy. This consists of a series immunizing injections, which desensitize the system to allergens. Pollen, mould, dust and/or dander allergies are good candidates for such treatment.

Practical tips for the player
- You can make your own nose drops by mixing 1 cup of water, 1/2 teaspoon salt, and a pinch of baking soda. Inhale a handful of this solution at a time. Discard the home-made solution after twenty-four hours because it contains no preservative.

SINUSITIS

Description. Sinus infection is one of the most frequent chronic conditions in athletes. A sinus is an air-filled cavity within the bones of the face skull. Most commonly, the sinus in the upper jaw is affected. Infection and allergies are the usual causes with approximately 50% of infections being due to flu and pneumonia bacteriae. Specific factors that may predispose tennis players to this condition include traumatic injury of the eardrums and sinuses due to the sudden changes in air pressure when travelling by airplane.

Symptoms. Symptoms of acute sinusitis include facial pain, headache, toothache, pain when tapping on the sinus, post-nasal drip (dripping in the back of the throat), cough, runny nose, nasal obstruction, a fever and nose bleeds.
Symptoms of chronic sinusitis may be more subtle and include vague facial pain, post-nasal drip, cough, nasal obstruction, dental pain, malaise, mouth odor and nasal discharge for at least three weeks. X-rays or other technologies may be used to diagnosis chronic sinusitis.

Treatment. Start with nasal steam inhalation and/or saline nasal spray. A brief course of local decongestants can be tried. Next, intranasal corticosteroids can be applied, followed by systemic therapy, including anti-inflammatory agents, antibiotics or antihistamines (in case of nasal allergy). In persistent cases, surgery may be needed to release the obstruction and stimulate mucus flow through sinus drainage.

Practical tips for the player
- Make sure to carry a decongestant with you when you have to fly, in case you develop an infection and congestion of the airways. Two to three drops in each nose, minutes before ascent or descent will prevent injury to the sinuses.

VIRAL UPPER RESPIRATORY TRACT INFECTION

Description. Acute illnesses of the airways can be caused by over 200 different viral strains, but most often the rhino-, corona-, or entero-viruses are responsible. Most colds primarily affect the nose and throat, although the same viruses can cause bronchitis and laryngitis. More serious bacterial infections of the throat, ears, and lungs can follow a viral cold.

Colds are spread by direct contact with infected secretions (shaking hands, kissing) or indirect inhalation of the virus in the air. Contrary to common belief, exposure to cold temperatures, damp environments, or draughts do not seem to enhance vulnerability. However, either a single bout of exhausting exercise or persistent over-training or stress can increase the susceptibility to and severity of upper respiratory and other viral infections. This is because strenuous exercise has a depressant effect on the immune system that can persist for a week or more. Resistance to bacterial infections is apparently unaltered.

Symptoms. Symptoms of a viral upper respiratory tract infection can range from a runny nose, sneezing and congestion to sore throat, hoarseness and a nonproductive cough. Players often feel weak and occasionally have sore muscles, despite little or low-grade fever. Infections may greatly affect performance. Exercise during the early acute phase of some infections may worsen or prolong the illness. Therefore, if signs and symptoms indicate that viral infection is impending, the player should reduce volume and intensity of heavy training for one to two days. A cold usually lasts three to four days but can persist up to 10 to 14 days.

Treatment. Nonprescription cold remedies, decongestants, cough syrups, cough drops and gargling with warm salty water may be tried for symptom relief. Training should be reduced; bed rest may be indicated. The doctor may prescribe antibiotics to fight a bacterial infection on top of the viral infection. Antibiotics are generally not useful in the early stages of a viral infection.

Practical tips for the player
- Refrain from practice and take more rest when a viral infection is impending.
- Abstain from heavy practice or matches with a temperature of over 38°C (100.4 F). This is because a virus infection can produce symptoms of the common cold but may also invade heart muscle and produce inflammation. This is a potentially serious disease with an increased risk of acute arrhythmia's and sudden death during exercise.

EXERCISE INDUCED ASTHMA

Description. Exercise induced asthma (exercise induced bronchospasm) is characterized by a variable degree of narrowing of the airways (bronchi), minutes after strenuous exercise. It is quite common in young players, with a 10-15% incidence in adolescent athletes. Groups at high risk are those with asthma (70-80%) and allergic rhinitis (40%).

Figure 14.2

Lung function measurement.

Symptoms. Classic symptoms are wheezing, chest tightness and/or shortness of breath during exercise, with a cough in the post-exercise period. Maximal airflow obstruction typically occurs 5 to 15 minutes after cessation of exercise, with spontaneous remission within 20 to 60 minutes. There is usually a period with symptom free exercise two to four hours after the episode of bronchospasm. Some athletes have a secondary delayed phase obstructive period four to ten hours after initial bronchospasm, typically manifested as nighttime coughing.

The strongest trigger for an attack is cold, dry air. Rapid breathing during exercise tends to cool and dry the bronchial tubes, resulting in hyper-irritable bronchial systems. Therefore, tennis players are generally less hindered in their sport by exercise induced asthma than athletes participating in strenuous winter sports, such as cross-country skiing (50%). Exercise induced bronchospasm can be diagnosed by demonstrating a decrease in pulmonary function (forced expiratory volume at 1 second or peak expiratory flow rate) after exercise (Figure 14.2). This can be done by using an exercise challenge test, consisting of 6 to 8 minutes of strenuous treadmill running and spirometric measurements at 3 minute intervals for at least 15 minutes after exercise (Figure 14.3).

Treatment. Nasal obstructions should be treated. Congestion in the upper airways may decrease nasal filtration, heating, and humidification, resulting in exercise induced bronchospasm.

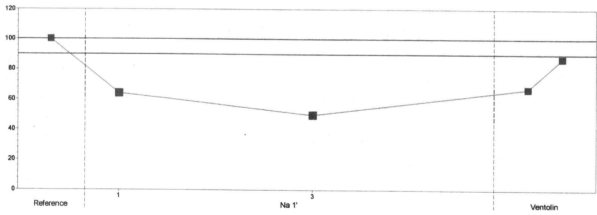

Figure 14.3

In exercise induced asthma a significant decrease in pulmonary function can occur during strenuous exercise. The x-axis displays the time; the y-axis the lung function in percentage of normal.

The doctor may prescribe a selective beta-2 agonist such as salbutamol. These should be used 5-10 minutes pre-exercise. If wheezing begins later in the exercise session, the dose can be repeated. Other medications may also be prescribed. These include montelukast, cromoglycate, and/or inhaled steroids. Regular medication helps diminish lung hyperactivity, reducing the risks of asthmatic attacks.

Practical tips for the player
• Warm up thoroughly, because a gradual, lengthy warm up prior to

more strenuous exercise has been shown to make the airways more resistant to irritants and to decrease the incidence of bronchospasms.

- Achieve and maintain a high fitness level to reduce the frequency and intensity of the attacks. A good way to build up stamina is by interval training, as this type of training has been shown to provoke fewer attacks.
- Try breathing through the nose or wearing a scarf when having to exercise in cold, dry environments.
- Avoid tobacco smoke and other obvious forms of air pollution. If you have a tendency to exercise induced asthma, you may wish to avoid practicing or competing in the afternoon and early evening, because smog is usually worse at these times.

RESPECT THE ANTI-DOPING PROGRAM

Drugs that are commonly used to treat disorders of the respiratory tract may contain substances that are on the prohibited list. Examples are corticosteroids and beta-2 agonists. Topical corticosteroids and beta-2 agonists require medical notification; oral steroids are only allowed if medical exemption has been applied for and granted.

SUMMARY

Hay fever can be very annoying for tennis players and medications may be necessary to help control it. Chronic sinusitis may be the cause of an unexplained drop in performance and is a common affliction in traveling athletes. A viral infection of the upper respiratory tract is the most common affliction in tennis players. Top athletes are particularly vulnerable, because heavy exercise has a depressant effect on the immune system. Taking enough rest will speed up the healing process. Exercise induced asthma and tennis usually go well together, because the interval type nature of the game usually provokes fewer attacks than continuous exercise. Regular medication helps diminish lung hyper-reactivity, but competitive players should respect the current doping regulations!

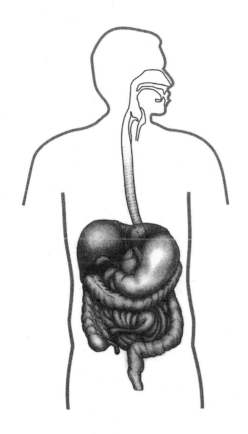

15

The Digestive System

Tennis players may suffer from the same ailments and diseases of the gastrointestinal tract as the general population. Tennis players usually do not have the increased frequency of gastrointestinal problems that endurance athletes, such as cyclists, runners and triathletes, may have. Due to the intermittent nature of the game, tennis players generally do not need to rely on liquid foods during match play. Most players are able to eat solid foods (bananas, sandwiches, crackers) during the changeovers in a match (Figure 15.1). However, players on tour may have an increased risk of diseases of the alimentary track as a result of their frequent travelling. In this chapter the most common gastrointestinal disorders in tennis players will be discussed.

Figure 15.1

Bananas are popular among players during a match.

STOMACH FLU (VIRAL GASTROENTERITIS)

Description. Viral gastroenteritis is an infection of the stomach and small and large intestines caused by a variety of viruses, including the rotavirus and norwalk virus, that results in vomiting or diarrhea. It is often called the 'stomach flu', although it is not caused by the influenza viruses. The virus is commonly transmitted through food that is contaminated by those who prepare or handle food who also have viral gastroenteritis. The risk of transmitting these diseases is increased if those that handle or prepare the food do not wash their hands regularly after using the toilet. Other sources of viral gastroenteritis include eating raw or undercooked shellfish harvested from contaminated waters. Drinking water can be contaminated by sewage and can also be a source of spread of these viruses.

Symptoms. The main symptoms are watery diarrhea and vomiting. The patient may also have a headache, fever, abdominal cramps ('stomach ache'), nausea, and muscle pains. In general, the symptoms begin 4 to 48 hours following exposure to the contaminated food or water and may last for 1 to 10 days, depending on which virus has caused the illness.

Treatment. Treatment consists of rest, clear fluids, and easy-to-digest foods (soup, rice, crackers). Although the course of gastro-enteritis is normally self-limited, fluid replacement during the illness is essential, otherwise the affected individual may become dehydrated, resulting in other medical complications. Antidiarrheal medications are generally not given, as they may prolong the infectious process. Return to play is allowed as soon as the physical symptoms, such as diarrhea, have resolved and the player is well-hydrated again, as assessed by restoration of bodyweight.

Practical tips for the player
- If you are ill, drink plenty of clear fluids, especially those containing electrolytes (oral re-hydration salts), along with caffeine-free soft drinks, fruit juices, and bouillon.
- Viral gastroenteritis is contagious, so do not share food, water, eating utensils, towels, or flannels with others.
- To prevent infection, always wash your hands after visiting the toilet and before cooking and eating meals.

FOOD POISONING

Description. Food poisoning is an infection, caused by the ingestion of food that is contaminated by bacteria, most commonly the campylobacter, salmonella and shigella bacteria. After eating the contaminated food, the bacteria multiply in the stomach and bowels and some may produce toxins. Dairy products and meats are frequently contaminated, often through the hands of a food handler. Outbreaks may occur during warm weather, when the bacterium multiplies rapidly in foods outside the refrigerator.

Symptoms. Symptoms include vomiting, diarrhea, nausea and abdominal cramps one or two hours after the food is ingested. Discomfort usually subsides after a few hours.

Treatment. The best treatment is to let food poisoning run its course. In most cases, once the body is emptied of the bad food, the food poisoning is over. Replace lost fluids with small but frequent sips of liquids, such as apple juice, broth, bouillon or oral re-hydration salts. Avoid anti-motility drugs, because they may prolong or worsen the illness. A doctor should be consulted if the patient is very ill (frequent diarrhea, fever, dehydration, bloody stools). The doctor may prescribe antibiotics and give intravenous fluids.

Practical tips for the player
- Wash all fruits and vegetables well before eating.
- Wash your hands before, during and after food preparation and after

every trip to the toilet. Use soap and warm water and wash for twenty seconds.

- Keep hot foods hot and cold foods cold. If food is allowed to remain at room temperature for two hours or longer, bacteria can multiply and cause food poisoning.
- Refrigerate all leftovers soon after meals.
- Separate raw foods from cooked foods.
- Thoroughly cook meat, poultry, and eggs. It has been estimated that 70-90% of chickens are infected with the campylobacter bacterium.

TRAVELER'S DIARRHEA

Description. Traveler's diarrhea is—as the name indicates—a diarrhea associated with travelling. It goes by different names, depending on where you succumb, such as Montezuma's Revenge (Mexico) and Delhi Belly (India)! Athletes going to Latin America, Africa, the Middle East and Asia are at highest risk of traveler's diarrhea. Approximately one-third of these travelers will get diarrhea. The disease is acquired through ingestion of food or water that is contaminated with bacteria or viruses. Escherichia coli (e-coli) accounts for approximately 50% of the cases, but salmonella, shigella, giardia lambia and rotavirus can also cause the illness. Particularly risky foods include raw vegetables, raw meat, and raw seafood. Tap water, ice, non-pasteurized milk and dairy products, as well as unpeeled fruit are also associated with an increased risk.

Symptoms. Symptoms usually start during the first week of a stay and may last 48 to 72 hours, including diarrhea, abdominal cramps, bloating, urgency, fever, nausea and malaise. Athletic performance may not be regained for a week or more.

Treatment. The most important treatment for diarrhea is to replace the fluids, including salts and sugars, that the body loses through watery bowel movements, and to take some rest. These fluids should be replaced by drinking clear fluids for 24 to 48 hours (purified water either boiled or bottled, broth, caffeine-free drinks). All solid food should be stopped for the first 24 to 48 hours. When the person starts feeling better, gradually small amounts of bland, easily-digested food (bananas, salted crackers, carrots, rice) can be introduced. Anti-motility drugs, such as loperamide, may be used if rapid relief of symptoms is desired after one or two unformed stools, accompanied by cramps, nausea or malaise, and in the absence of fever or bloody stools. The dosage is four mg initially followed by two mg after each unformed stool. Anti-microbial therapy may be used if is important to shorten the course of the disease or to decrease the severity. Consideration can be given to a short course of ciprofloxacin (250 mg twice daily for five days). However, ciprofloxacin should be used with caution in players with a history of tendinopathy, because it has been associated with a slightly increased risk of tendon ruptures. Dairy products aggravate diarrhea in some people and should be avoided. Under certain circumstances prophylactic anti-microbial agents should be considered. A physician should be consulted if the patient has a high fever, is severely dehydrated or has bloody stools.

Practical tips for the player
- Avoid tap water, iced beverages, food from street vendors, fresh leafy greens and fruit that cannot be peeled before eating.
- Hot tea or coffee, boiled water, soup, bread, butter, bottled carbonat-

ed beverages, fruit that requires peeling, and food that is well-cooked and immediately consumed are safe;
*   Fluid and electrolyte balance can be maintained by potable fruit juices, caffeine-free soft drinks, oral rehydration salts, and salty crackers.

HEARTBURN

Description. Heartburn is a deeply placed burning pain that is generally felt in the chest just behind the breastbone. The burning sensation is felt when the acidic stomach juices come in contact with and irritate the lining of the esophagus, the tube-like structure that connects the mouth to the stomach. This is a common complaint among athletes. The increased incidence of upper gastrointestinal symptoms during exercise may be caused by the delay in emptying gastric contents from the stomach. Increased stomach content may increase the athlete's susceptibility to gastroesophageal reflux as well as the likelihood of nausea and vomiting.

Symptoms. The main symptom is a burning chest pain that begins at the breastbone and moves up toward the throat. There may be a feeling that food or liquid is coming back into the mouth or throat. There may be an acid or bitter taste at the back of the throat. The pain behind the breastbone usually gets worse when the subject is lying down or bending over.

Treatment. Many heartburn sufferers significantly reduce their risk of getting heartburn by avoiding the foods and behavior that affect them most (see below). If lifestyle adjustments are not enough, medications may be used. Treatment of choice are drugs such as omeprazole or pantoprazole. These medications are powerful inhibitors of stomach acid production, leaving enough acid for normal digestion of food. Starting dose is 40 mg per day, which is gradually lowered to 20 mg per day. Eventually, it is used on demand only.

Practical tips for the player
*   Consume a small pre-exercise meal that is high in carbohydrate and low in fat, since fatty foods tend to delay gastric emptying and promote reflux.
*   Avoid foods such as citrus fruits, chocolate, peppermint, spearmint, tomatoes or tomato-based products, raw onions, garlic, black pepper, vinegar and fatty or spicy foods.
*   Avoid beverages such as coffee, citrus juices, and caffeinated, carbonated or alcoholic beverages.
*   Replace solid foods during a match, such as bananas, oranges or sandwiches by sports drinks, if eating the former causes problems.
*   Let your evening meal digest well before going to bed. Night-time symptoms can be reduced by raising the head of the bed on blocks by six inches. Some people are helped by sleeping on their left side.
*   Avoid tight belts and underclothes as they increase pressure on the stomach.
*   Avoid aspirin and other anti-inflammatory medications (NSAIDs) e.g. ibuprofen, or use them only in conjunction with medication that protects the lining of the stomach.

STITCH

Description. Many athletes complain of a sharp, stabbing pain in the left or the right upper quadrant of the abdomen during strenuous exercise. This is commonly referred to as a "stitch". The exact cause is unknown, but it may be due to muscle spasm of the diaphragm, trapping of gas in the hepatic or splenic flexure of the colon, or tugging of the ligaments of the bouncing stomach, liver, or spleen on the diaphragm.

Symptoms. A sharp, stabbing pain just below the rib cage on the right or left side during exercise. The pain usually disappears when slowing down or stoping exercising. Most players do not experience this pain during tennis, only during running. Symptoms usually disappear when the athlete slows.

Treatment. Slow down the pace or stop exercising. Another option is to press the fingers deeply into the painful spot, then purse the lips tightly and blow out as forcefully as possible. Bending over while tightening the stomach muscles a few times also helps to relieve the pain. A combination of all three, contracting the stomach muscles, leaning forward slightly and pushing the hand against the site of the pain, may make it possible to continue running if this is wished. In breathing out, the expiration of air should be resisted with pursed lips.

Practical tips for the player
- Avoid a solid meal prior to exercise. Wait one to two hours after eating before you work out and try to limit the fat content of the meal.
- Drink frequent, small amounts of an isotonic sports drink during exercise.
- To stop side stitches before they start, it may help to breathe fully and deeply by pushing your abdomen out with each inhalation during your workout. Strong abdominal muscles are supposed to provide a supportive "internal girdle" so there is less bouncing and pulling on the diaphragm.

IRRITABLE BOWEL SYNDROME

Description. Irritable bowel syndrome is a problem with the intestines. Other names that are often used for this disorder are as spastic colon, mucous colitis, spastic colitis, nervous stomach, or irritable colon. The intestines squeeze too hard or not hard enough, causing food to move too quickly or too slowly through the intestines. It is one of the most common gastrointestinal disorders. Anxiety or stress may induce attacks of this syndrome. Travelling may also be an aggravating factor, especially for constipation.

Symptoms. Irritable bowel syndrome can cause lower abdominal pain, cramping, bloating, gas, rumbling, diarrhea and constipation. The abdominal pain and cramping may go away after completing a bowel movement

Treatment. The best way to treat irritable bowel syndrome is to eat a healthy diet, increase the fibers, drink at least two liters of fluid a day, avoid the foods that seem to make it worse and find ways to handle stress.

Fiber reduces symptoms—especially of constipation—because it makes the stool soft, bulky, and easier to pass. The doctor may prescribe hydrophyllic colloids to increase bulk in the intestines. Pain and diarrhea may be relieved by an anticholinergic drug such as mebeverine.

Practical tips for the player

- High-fiber foods include bran, bread, cereal, beans, fruit, and vegetables. Psyllium is a natural vegetable fiber that you can buy at the store and add to your food (some brand names include Fiberall, Metamucil, Perdiem). Increase the fiber in your diet slowly.
- Heating pads and hot baths can be comforting.
- Try eating six small meals a day rather than three larger ones.
- If gas is a problem for you, you might want to avoid foods that tend to make gas worse. These include beans, cabbage and some fruits.
- Foods that may make symptoms worse include foods high in fat or caffeine, because they can cause your intestines to contract.

SUMMARY

Tennis players may suffer from certain gastrointestinal problems, which can be quite invalidating, painful and annoying. Most of these problems can be prevented or solved by high hygienic standards to avoid contamination of the food with bacteria, plenty of fluids, and small, frequent, carbohydrate rich and lowfat meals. Occasionally, additional individual dietary adaptations may be required. In severe cases medication, such as antibiotics, anti-motility drugs or drugs that inhibit stomach acid production may be required for a limited period of time.

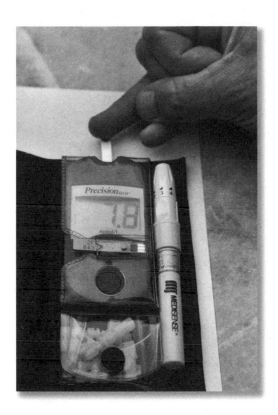

16

Other Medical Conditions

In this chapter the following common medical conditions will be discussed: diabetes mellitus, infectious mononucleosis, and anemia.

DIABETES MELLITUS

Description. Diabetes mellitus is a life-long disease characterized by high glucose levels of the blood, due to deficiency or diminished effectiveness of insulin. These high glucose levels may damage many of the body's systems, in particular the blood vessels and nerves. There are two major types of diabetes mellitus. In diabetes mellitus type 1, most common in those aged below 30, the body fails to produce the hormone insulin. In diabetes mellitus type 2, occurring mainly in the middle-aged and elderly, there is a depressed sensitivity to insulin at the cellular level.

Symptoms. In type 1 diabetes, the classic symptoms are excessive secretion of urine, thirst, weight loss and tiredness. These symptoms may be less marked in type 2 diabetes. In some cases it is possible that no early symptoms appear and the disease is only diagnosed several years after its onset, when complications are already present. The diagnosis of diabetes is made upon results of blood tests demonstrating high glucose levels. Long-term complications of diabetes include heart disease, kidney failure, gradual loss of vision, loss of feeling in the legs, and damage to the vessels of the limbs, which may cause foot problems. A full examination is therefore advisable before starting on any exercise program, paying particular attention to the heart and vessels, the feet and the eyes. For those over 35 years of age or those with 15 years of diabetes, an exercise ECG should be considered, as diabetics are vulnerable to `silent ischaemia' (insufficient oxygen delivery to the heart, without any accompanying chest pain).

Treatment. Patients with diabetes mellitus type 1 must receive insulin. Insulin can only be administered by injections. Diet and/or tablets are usually sufficient to cope with diabetes mellitus type 2 (90% of diabetics), but eventually nearly half of this population may require insulin injections. Exercise has a beneficial effect on diabetes mellitus type 2, because it increases insulin sensitivity and low blood glucose levels rarely occur. In diabetes mellitus type 1, exercise does not improve the control of the glucose levels (it does not diminish the incidence of high and low glucose levels), but does have long-term positive changes associated with regular exercise (e.g. reduction of cardiovascular risk factors, better physical condition, improved sense of well-being etc). An adjustment of insulin dosage is important in reducing the risk of low glucose levels during or after exercise (see Table 16.1).

Table 16.1 Prevention of hypoglycemia

Duration & type of exercise	Glucose level	Extra carbohydrates
30 minutes or less	Below 5 mmol per liter	10-15 gram
Light exercise	Above 5 mmol per liter	No extra carbohydrates
30-60 minutes	Below 5 mmol per liter	30-45 gram
Moderate exercise	Between 5 and 10 mmol per liter	15 gram
	Between 10 and 16 mmolper liter	No extra carbohydrates
1 hour or more	Below 5 mmol per liter	45 gram per hour
Moderate exercise	Between 5 and 10 mmol per liter	30-45 gram per hour
	Between 10 and 16 mmol per liter	15 gram per hour

At the first indication of a low blood glucose level (sweating, nervousness, tremor), the athlete should ingest carbohydrate in solid or liquid form. A semiconscious or unconscious diabetic patient requires intravenous glucose administration. Athletes should be alerted to the possibility of low blood glucose levels several hours after completion of exercise. A player should abstain from exercise when glucose levels are really high, and there is insulin deficiency at the beginning of exercise. The glucose can not be utilized, leading to increasingly higher levels, and the burning of fat in the absence of glucose will lead to the production of acetone, recognizable by the foul smell.

Practical tips for the player with diabetes mellitus type 1
- Monitor blood glucose level before, during and after exercise to learn your own response pattern (Figure 16.1).
- Adjust carbohydrate intake and insulin dosages according to how much you are going to exercise (approximately 15-30 g of carbohydrates per half hour of exercise) (Table 16.1).
- Use short-acting insulin before every meal, supplemented with long-acting insulin to cover the basal need for insulin. The dose has to be adjusted, depending on the duration and intensity of exercise.
- If exercise lasts more than 45-60 minutes, the insulin dose may be reduced.
- The greatest risk of dangerously low blood glucose levels occurs dur-

ing sleep, six to fourteen hours after strenuous exercise. This can be avoided by adjusting the insulin dose and extra caloric intake after strenuous exercise.

- Abstain from exercise if the blood glucose level is above 16 mmol per liter, because a further rise may be expected.
- Be sure to carry written certification of diabetes if you compete at high levels. Although the doping rules prohibit on-court injections, diabetics with medical certification are allowed to use a device off-court to check blood glucose and administer subcutaneous injections of insulin if necessary.

Practical tips for the player with diabetes mellitus type 2
- In general, no adjustments in medication for exercise are necessary, unless insulin is used.
- It is advised that you carry some glucose with you.

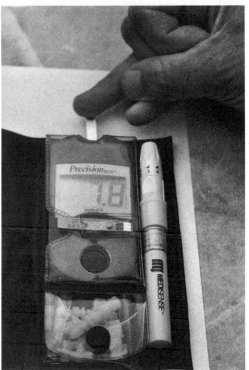

Figure 16.1
Monitoring of blood glucose level.

GLANDULAR FEVER

Description. Glandular fever (infectious mononucleosis) occurs as a result of infection with the Epstein-Barr virus. The incidence is highest in the 15-30 age group. Infectious saliva is the cause of the spreading (which is why it is known as `kissing disease'). The incubation period varies with age: from seven to fourteen days in children and adolescents to as long as 30-50 days in adults.

Symptoms. Symptoms include fatigue, fever, sore throat, headache and nausea. Clinical examination may reveal a throat infection, swollen lymph nodes and enlargement of the spleen. The illness lasts between five to fifteen days, but it may take several months before the fatigue and weakness entirely disappear.

Treatment. Take rest from tennis until all acute symptoms have disappeared. A low-fat diet should be followed if the liver is involved (hepatitis). Resumption of training may be allowed as soon as blood tests show improved liver function.

Practical tips for the player
- Training should be resumed gradually, first increasing duration and then intensity, with adequate periods of rest. Regularly monitor heart rate to determine intensity of play.

ANEMIA

Description. Anemia is defined as a subnormal number or mass of red blood cells or hemoglobin (oxygen-carrying protein) in the blood, causing the tissues of the body to be deprived of the oxygen-rich blood. As a result, exercise capacity decreases and performance may decline. There are several kinds of anemia, but the most common type is iron-deficiency anemia. It is found more often in females than males. Iron is necessary for the formation of hemoglobin and myoglobin, the oxygen carriers in red blood cells and muscles, respectively. The principal cause of iron-deficiency anemia is blood loss during menses. Other causes include insufficient consumption of iron-containing foods, poor iron absorption in the intestines, and transpiration during exercise (iron bound to transferrin). Less commonly, anemia may have other causes, such as folate deficiency, B12 deficiency or be secondary to chronic diseases.

Symptoms. The symptoms of anemia tend to appear so gradually that they often go unnoticed, but their severity increases as the condition progresses. The player may feel tired and less tolerant of exercise. The skin, gums, nail beds and eyelid linings may be pale. Eventually, anemia may become so grave that the heartbeat seems more rapid and noticeable.

Treatment. Iron-deficiency anemia can be treated by control of bleeding and restoration of adequate iron supplies by an iron-rich diet and/or iron supplements.

Practical tips for the player
- Include iron-rich foods in your diet, such as red lean meat, fish, poultry, eggs, legumes (peas and beans), potatoes, and rice.
- Drink citrus juice with breakfast, because vitamin C enhances iron absorption.
- Avoid coffee or tea with meals, because these products decrease iron absorption.
- Eat a source of animal protein with vegetable proteins to increase iron absorption from the vegetables.
- Vegetarians should include iron-rich food such as dried fruits (apricons, prunes, dates), beans, peas, tofu, kale, spinach, collard greens, and black strap molasses to their meals.

SUMMARY

In this chapter diabetes mellitus, glandular fever and iron-deficiency anemia are discussed. Diabetes is characterized by high blood glucose levels and requires the use of diet and/or medications to control blood glucose levels. Exercise, such as tennis, is generally recommended, but may require adjustment of insulin dosage and extra carbohydrates to avoid the risk of blood glucose levels that are too low or too high. A pre-participation medical evaluation is recommended in those with long-standing diabetes. Glandular fever is a common viral infection in the 15 to 30 age group and should be suspected in players with unexplained fatigue. Treatment consists of rest and gradual resumption of training. Iron- deficiency anemia, the most common type of anemia, occurs more often in females than in males, due to blood less during menses and/or an inadequate diet. Treatment consists of control of bleeding and restoration of iron supplies by an iron-rich diet and/or iron supplements.

Part Four

Special Issues

17

Heat Stress

Playing tennis in high humidity and heat can be quite demanding on the body, and usually puts the player at greater risk for heat illness. The combination of body heat production during play and environmental conditions, such as temperature, humidity, radiation from the sun, and clothing, may lead to an excessive rise in body temperature and extensive fluid and electrolyte losses. On court temperatures may rise to over 50° C (122° F)! Although an increase in body temperature is common during exercise, and is even sought after (warming up), very high body temperatures usually lead to a diminishing tennis performance and may be detrimental to the player's health.

HEAT PRODUCTION

Exercise produces heat, and the harder the exercise, the more heat is produced. Also, the body may gain heat from or lose heat to the environment, depending on whether the ambient temperature is higher or lower than the skin temperature. This heat exchange between the body surface and the environment occurs in several ways.

• Conduction. Heat flows from hot objects to cooler objects, when there is direct contact between an object and the skin, such as when you hold an ice cube against your cheek when you are warm, or a hot cup of coffee in your hands when you are cold.
• Convection: Hot air surrounding the body is transmitted away while cooler air rushes in to take its place. This process is increased when air moves around the body, such as a refreshing cool breeze on a hot sunny day. This is why tennis players should wear loose clothing on hot days.
• Radiation: Heat can be gained from direct radiation from the sun or a hot court surface. Radiant energy is directly absorbed and does not need an intervening medium to transmit that energy.

Photo: Henk Koster

Figure 17.1

When playing tennis in the heat, water helps to cool the player.

• Evaporation: Heat exchange takes place through evaporation when the sweat from the skin or clothing is converted to gas, thereby extracting heat from the body (Figure 17.1).

Sweating is the most important mechanism for cooling the body when the temperature is over 35° C (95° F), because at these high temperatures, convection and radiation result in heat gain instead of heat loss of the body. Evaporation is restricted if the humidity is high, or if the player is wearing tight clothing that restricts airflow. Tight clothing allows the air close to the skin to become saturated with water vapor and will therefore restrict the evaporation of water from the skin surface. Dry, windy conditions are ideal for evaporation. Thus, heat stress is highest when a player is playing a long, tough match, when temperature and humidity are high, when the sun shines brightly, and there is no breeze.

This "heat stress" is expressed by the Wet Bulb Globe Temperature (WBGT). WBGT consists of ordinary air temperature (dry bulb thermometer), temperature as affected by wind and humidity (wet bulb thermometer) and temperature as affected by radiant heat from the sun (black bulb thermometer). The three temperatures are then combined into a heat index using the following formula that weighs the three temperatures:

0.7 x wet bulb temperature + 0.2 x black bulb temperature + 0.1 x dry bulb temperature.

This temperature is then compared to risk range guidelines such as the following Sports Medicine Australia guide:

WGBT	Risk
< 18	Low
18-22	Moderate
23-28	High
> 28	Extreme

FLUID LOSS

Because evaporation is the most important means of cooling the body in the heat, a high temperature may lead to large sweat losses and dehydration. Dehydration may in turn lead to a reduced performance, an increase in body temperature, and an increased risk of heat illness. Therefore, maintaining optimal hydration is a key issue for tennis players. Most tennis players probably do not realize how much fluid they lose through sweating during play. One to two liters per hour is typical for most adult players, and for some it may be even higher—almost three liters per hour have been recorded during tournament match for male professional tennis players. Sweat rate increases when the player is well-trained, well-acclimatized, well-hydrated, and exercises vigorously. Furthermore, males usually have higher sweat rates than females of comparable age, and young adults typically have higher sweat rates than either children or elderly people. Prolonged tennis matches in extreme conditions may thus increase the daily fluid requirement from about 2.5 liter to up to 12-15 liters! This can only be tolerated if these sweat losses are sufficiently replaced.

SALT LOSS

Besides an extraordinary water loss, extensive sweating can also lead to a large electrolyte (salt) deficit. A well-trained, acclimatized body adapts to the heat through an earlier onset of sweating, an increase in sweat rate, and a decreased electrolyte content of the sweat. This is a protective mechanism of the body, because evaporative capacity is increased, while electrolytes are conserved. However, considerable electrolytes may still be lost, particularly sodium and chloride, present in normal table salt. The sodium content in sweat may decrease from 90 mmol per liter in an untrained, unacclimatized male to 35 mmol per liter or less in a trained, acclimatized male. The untrained, unacclimatized female has a sodium sodium sweat concentration of 105 mmol per liter, while the trained, acclimatized female athlete has a concentration of 60 mmol of sodium in her sweat. In practical matters, if one assumes the mean sodium concentration is 50 mmol per liter for a given player, this still represents a loss of almost 15 gram of salt with five liters of sweat. Because the average daily salt intake is approximately eight grams in males, and six grams in females, the salt balance in players exercising in the heat may be precarious and possibly dangerous! They may develop a sizeable sodium deficit over the course of several matches. This involves an increased risk of fluid loss, intra- and extra-cellular electrolyte imbalance and heat cramps.

Contrary to common belief, potassium or magnesium deficits are not likely to occur. With an average potassium concentration of 4 mmol per liter in sweat, a sweat loss of five liters represents a daily potassium loss of only 0.8 gram. This is easily covered by the average daily intake of potassium, which is 3.2 grams in males and 2.4 grams in females. The same calculations can be made for magnesium: the concentrations in sweat are (less than) 0.2 mmol per liter, representing a loss of (less than) 24 mg in 5 liters of sweat. This is amply covered by an average daily intake of 320 mg in females and 380 mg in males, even when magnesium losses in sweat as well as urine are taken into account.

THE RISKS OF PLAYING IN THE HEAT

The rise in body temperature along with fluid and electrolyte losses may lead to any of four recognizable heat disorders: heat cramps, heat syncope, heat exhaustion, and heat stroke.

Heat cramps. Heat cramps are painful, involuntary spasms of skeletal muscle, most commonly of the calf and thigh muscles (Figure 17.2). They may occur suddenly and can be temporarily debilitating. The exact cause of muscle cramps is not known, but suggested causes include the loss of fluids and resulting electrolyte imbalance (in particular low sodium level). It is thought that the loss of fluid volume between the muscle cells causes mechanical deformation of nerve endings and leads to increased neurotransmitter concentrations. This in turn may lead to hyperexcitable motor nerve ter-

Figure 17.2
Heat cramps can be temporarily debilitating.

minals, causing them to discharge spontaneously. Treatment of cramps consists of gentle stretching of the affected muscle and oral fluids containing glucose and salt.

Heat syncope. Heat syncope or collapse is a fainting episode that usually occurs immediately after cessation of activity or after standing motionless for a long period of time. It is thought to be due to a sudden drop in blood pressure caused by pooling of blood in the legs in the absence of muscular contraction to pump the blood back to the heart and brains. This affliction is frequently seen in ball boys and girls, linesmen, and spectators, but it may also occur when a player suddenly stops after intensive exercise or when beginning a program in environmental conditions (including weather and altitude) the player is not acclimatized to. Treatment consists of elevating the patient's feet and legs and having him drink mixtures that contain both sugar and salt.

Heat exhaustion. When the core temperature rises and dehydration ensues, heat exhaustion may develop. This is characterized by extreme weakness, exhaustion, dizziness, headache and profuse sweating or clammy skin, and is usually due to depletion of circulatory fluid volume. There may be a mild reduction in blood pressure and elevation of heart rate. This is caused by a strain on the circulation from the competing demands of the skin and intestines. Treatment consists of cooling the body, oral fluids, and cessation of play.

Heat stroke. Heat stroke, or hyperthermia, is a true medical emergency, characterized by a hot, dry skin, rapid pulse, low blood pressure and a high body temperature. The rectal temperature is usually 41 degrees C (106 degrees F) or higher. The athlete exhibits impaired consciousness and may display irrational behavior due to disturbances of the central nervous system. High body temperatures can lead to irreversible damage of the internal organs and even death. The body should be cooled as quickly as possible, and the players should be rehydrated with oral or intravenous fluids. Immediate transfer to a hospital should be arranged.

Players who are at increased risk for heat injury include the obese, the unfit, juniors, seniors, and those that are not acclimatized to the heat. The presence of a fever or diarrhea (dehydration!) also increases the risk.

Table 17.1

Type of drink	Carbohydrate (gram/liter)	Energy (Kcal/liter)	Osmotic value (mOsm/kg)
Sports drinks (isotonic)			
AA-drink	68	290	330
Aquarius	63	268	400
Born	48	204	300
Extran citron	75	300	332
Gatorade	60	250	378
Isostar	70	300	281
Sportline	80	330	300
Energy drinks (hypertonic)			
AA high energy	165	660	nd*
Dextro energy fruit	140	540	956
Extran orange	145	600	959
Perform energy drink	165	700	397
Juices and soft drinks			
Apple juice	104	440	695
Orange juice	94	400	662
Coca cola	105	440	650
Sprite	110	425	591
Power drinks			
Dynamite	125	531	885
Red bull	113	470	628

Source: "Insider", scientific newsletter of the Isostar Sport Foundation
(with special thanks to Ir. E. Kovacs, University Maastricht, for additional information)
*nd = not determined

SPORTS DRINKS

Replacing the large sweat losses that occur during tennis in the heat is essential. However, it may not be possible to entirely replace them during play, due to the limited rate of emptying of the stomach (0.1 up to 1.2 liters per hour). The stomach's emptying rate depends on the composition and volume of rehydration drinks. Drinking more will empty the stomach faster, but the presence of large volumes may cause discomfort during play. The best way to stimulate fluid delivery is by repeated drinking, so players should be encouraged to drink at every changeover. Waiting until the player is thirsty is not good, because at that point fluid loss has already become quite large. Plain water will leave the stomach faster than dilute glucose solutions, because the stomach empties more slowly when the drink is more concentrated. However, when the drink is more concentrated, more carbohydrates will be delivered, and this can sometimes be important, such as when the player is hypoglycemic (having low glucose levels) at the end of a long match. Sweat rates below two liters per hour are generally manageable.

Drink temperature has no significant effect on the rate of gastric emptying. In general, chilled drinks taste better and will therefore be consumed in greater volumes. Light carbonation has no effect on gastric emptying. A greater degree of carbonation, as used in many soft drinks, may increase gastric emptying by raising the intragastric pressure.

Absorption of carbohydrate, water, or electrolytes does not occur in the stomach, but in the small intestines. Here, the absorption rate depends on the concentration of the drink. Small amounts of carbohydrates and electrolytes will actually speed up water absorption (in contrast to the stomach where high concentration slows stomach emptying) provided the drink is hypotonic or isotonic. Hypotonic means the concentration is less than that of blood (300 mOsm per liter); isotonic means the concentration is the same as that of blood (Table 17.1). Most sports drinks are either hypotonic or isotonic. Very concentrated glucose solutions (hypertonic) will have an opposite effect. Instead of leading to water absorption, fluid will be drawn out of the cells of the small intestine into the lumen of the gut, which will worsen any pre-existing dehydration.

DRINKING DURING A MATCH

What, then, is the best drink for replacing the fluids, carbohydrates, and electrolytes lost during a match (Figure 17.3)? The choice of drink depends on whether the primary concern is to replace fluid (water), fuel (carbohydrates), or electrolytes (salt). The main determinants are the duration and intensity of the exercise combined with the environmental temperature and whether the player has had adequate fluid replacement since the last match, training session, or even the prematch warmup.

Figure 17.3

Tennis players need to drink during match play.

In most situations hypotonic drinks should be advised, with an optimum carbohydrate concentration in the range of 2-8%, because they are absorbed more rapidly and cause less gastrointestinal problems than isotonic or hypertonic drinks. The more dilute the drink, the faster it will pass from the stomach to the intestines. In addition, the drink should contain sodium, as this improves taste, maintains the drive to drink, speeds up the absorption of glucose and water in the small intestine, and helps maintain the extracellular volume. Excessive drinking of plain water in situations of high sweating may lead to low sodium concentrations (hyponatremia). The optimum sodium concentration is between 20 and 40 mmol per liter. There is no need to add other components, such as potassium, magnesium, other minerals, or vitamins to drinks intended to promote or maintain hydration status.

DRINKING AFTER A MATCH

Rapid rehydration and restoration of sweat electrolyte losses are crucial after practice and matches where significant sweat losses have occurred, and when the time for the next match or training session is limited. When speed of recovery is important, a dilute glucose solution with added sodium chloride is the most effective in promoting rapid recovery. Complete restoration of volume losses requires the total amount of fluid ingested in the recovery phase to exceed the total sweat loss. A way to monitor this is to have the player check his or her body weight before and after the training session or match. The volume of fluid ingested should be at least 150% of the volume of sweat loss. Another means of monitoring a player's hydration status is to check the color of the urine, which should be light yellow. It is important to replenish the weight loss within 24 hours, to prevent a cumulative loss during the next practice or match. However, consuming sports drinks within the first 30 minutes after the conclusion of practice or play greatly enhances the carbohydrate replenishment as well as the fluids, and is recommended.

Practical tips for the player

- Schedule practice time for short periods in the morning and late afternoon or early evening, which are the cooler times of the day. Take rest periods in the shade.
- Wear light-colored, loose fitting clothing, such as breathable cotton, which helps sweat evaporate more easily than heavier, more tightly woven fabric.
- Wear a white hat to protect the face, skull and neck. Some players wear a cap backwards on their head.
- During match play, use cover shelter (such as an umbrella) to protect from direct sun during changeovers and wet your face with water or use an ice towel and/or fans if available.
- Before play, drink 18-20 oz (500-600 ml) of fluid two to three hours prior, then again another 8-10 oz (200-300 ml) ten to twenty minutes before exercise. Your urine should be clear before a match.
- During play, drink 200-300 ml (8-10 oz) every ten to twenty minutes (during changeovers). Start drinking during the warmup and do not wait untill you feel thirsty.
- When first trying sports drinks, do so in practice and training to assess taste and gastrointestinal response, and to find the one you prefer. It is possible to "train" drinking during practice; the body adapts to it and fluid uptake during high intensity exercise will gradually increase.
- You can make your own sport drink by mixing 3 gram (0.5 teaspoon) salt and 60-80 gram (15-20 cubes) sugar in one liter of water.
- Use salt tablets only when drinking water at the same time. By sweating, more water is lost than salt. Using salt tablets without replenishing water will only aggravate any existing problem. Other possibilities are salting food to the taste at mealtimes, choosing food items with high levels of inherent salt (e.g. tomato juice, salted pretzels, canned vegetable or soups) and by using sports drinks.
- Take the time to acclimatize. When traveling to a country with a warmer climate, incorporate four days to a week of progressively longer workouts in the heat to induce acclimatization. Once acclimated to the heat, the body begins to sweat sooner and more profusely at lower body temperature. Also, blood vessels on the skin's surface will dilate sooner to keep the body cooled down.
- If you have heat cramps, stretch the muscle, and take rehydration drinks with glucose and electrolytes.

- If you feel light-headed and think you might faint, lower your head or lay down on your back with your feet up. Generally, it would be best to stop playing and to sit down in a cool area and have a rehydration drink with glucose and electrolytes.
- If you feel really weak, hot, and sick, place ice packs in your neck, groin, and/or armpit, and have someone call a doctor.

SUMMARY

Increased body temperature and dehydration may lead to heat illness (that sometimes can be life threatening) and inhibit performance by decreasing muscle strength, aerobic power and muscle endurance. Heat illness and dehydration are largely preventable. Evaporative heat loss is the main way to cool the body during tennis in the heat and may result in extensive fluid and electrolyte losses. Prolonged tennis matches in extreme conditions may induce daily fluid losses of up to 12-15 liters, and salt losses of more than 10-15 gram. These fluid and electrolyte losses should be replaced by rehydration drinks to prevent loss of performance and heat illness. Four recognizable heat disorders may be observed: heat cramps, heat syncope, heat exhaustion and heat stroke, and these are preventable. In most situations hypotonic drinks should be advised, with an optimum carbohydrate concentration in the range of 2-8%, and an optimum sodium concentration of between 20 and 40 mmol per liter. Dilute glucose electrolyte tonic drinks are absorbed more rapidly and cause less gastrointestinal problems than highly concentrated drinks. The key is to drink early and often and to not wait until feeling thirsty.

18 Nutrition and Supplements

Optimal nutrition is essential to enhance tennis performance and ensure adequate recovery. Therefore, appropriate selection of food and fluids, timing of intake, and supplement choices are important to every player. What, then, is the ideal diet that will give you the winning edge? In contrast to what many players believe, there is no single magic food source or supplement that will lead a player to the top. And, certainly, there are no magic bullets available that will make up for deficiencies in training or athletic potential. An inadequate diet, however, may inhibit performance in otherwise well-trained athletes. Thus, a player can pave the way to displaying his or her full potential by ensuring that his diet is varied and balanced, and that all essential nutrients are sufficiently present. Consuming adequate food and fluid before, during, and after exercise can help maintain blood glucose levels during exercise, maximize tennis performance, and improve recovery time and quality. Let us take a look at the various nutritional components of an optimal diet.

CARBOHYDRATES

There are two types of carbohydrates—sugars and starches. Sugars are simple carbohydrates. They are called simple because the body digests them quickly and easily. Simple carbohydrates are usually sweet tasting, such as cookies, candy, soda, and other sugary foods. Some foods from nature—like many sorts of fruits—are sources of simple carbohydrates. Starchy carbohydrates are referred to as complex carbohydrates. These carbohydrates take longer to be digested than simple carbohydrates do. Complex carbohydrates are found in foods like bread, noodles, and rice, and in many kinds of vegetables. It is generally recommended that complex carbohydrates be consumed, because they have high fiber and vitamin contents and give a sustained energy release over a long period of time. However, liquid carbohydrate sources and foods containing simple carbohydrates may be used when it is necessary to raise the glucose level quickly during a workout or match. For example, bananas can take up to four hours to be fully digested, whereas isotonic drinks will supply the body with carbohydrates within a couple of minutes.

Carbohydrates are an important fuel during tennis match play. Male players use approximately 200 grams of carbohydrates, whereas female players utilize approximately 130 grams of carbohydrates during two hours of strenuous tennis match play. Approximately 300 grams of carbohydrates are stored in the body (liver and muscle) in the form of glycogen. The storage capacity can be increased by maintaining a carbohydrate-rich diet (Figure 18.1 and 18.2). Muscle glycogen may become a performance limiting factor during tennis, especially during long matches. This is because the amount stored is limited, and it is utilized rapidly during intense exercise. Fatigue occurs when it is depleted to low levels in the active muscles. Therefore, carbohydrates consumed immediately before or during play may enhance performance. After exercise, depleted glycogen reserves need to be restored to ensure full recovery. If the next match or workout is scheduled for the same day, consumption of carbohydrates immediately after exercise is recommended, because glycogen resynthesis progresses most efficiently and effectively during the first two hours after exercise.

Figure 18.1

Unhealthy choices: these products are high in fats, empty sugars, or contain alcohol, and should be saved for occasional treats.

Figure 18.2

Healthy choices: low in fat, high in carbohydrates, vitamins, minerals, and fibers.

PROTEIN

Protein consists of polymers of amino acids. Protein is essential in the diet of a tennis player for growth, tissue repair, and an optimal tennis performance. After a workout, protein fulfills a major function in the strengthening and restoration of the muscles. What amount of protein is necessary for optimal health and tennis performance? The Recommended Daily Allowance (RDA) for the general population is 0.8 g/kg body weight daily. Recommendations for tennis players are slightly higher, about 1.0-1.2 g/kg body weight daily, provided energy intake is adequate. The average Western diet contains sufficient amounts of protein, generally exceeding 1.2 g/kg body weight. Protein is used as an energy source when the glycogen stores are depleted and exercise is continued at a high intensity level. An adequate carbohydrate intake will reduce protein turnover and is generally more important than additional protein intake to maintain an optimal performance.

After exercise, adding protein and amino acids to a carbohydrate recovery supplement enhances glycogen synthesis, promotes muscle protein synthesis and slows post exercise muscle protein degradation. To this purpose, a glass of milk with fruit or cookies is at least as effective as a fancy sports drink! Players are advised to obtain necessary amino acids through consumption of natural, high quality protein foods, such as milk, meat, chicken, fish, eggs, bread, cereal, grains, nuts, soy products, beans, peas, and dairy products. Vegetarian players should pay special attention to including high quality protein (protein with high biological value) in their diet. For a balanced diet, supplemental dietary protein, protein powders, and amino acids (the building blocks of protein) are generally unnecessary. Vegetarian athletes who play a lot are advised to contact a nutritionist for a food analysis.

FAT

There are two main types of fats: saturated (normally found in animal fats, except fish), and (mono or poly) unsaturated fats (normally found in vegetable fats, oil, and fat fish). Fats are high in calories. They contain nine calories per gram, while carbohydrates and protein contain only four calories per gram. Fats are an important source of energy during athletic activity of long duration and low intensity, such as slow, long distance running. However, fats do not provide the level of energy derived from carbohydrates, and are thus not the main source of energy during a game of tennis. It was demonstrated by Ferrauti and Weber (2001) that during two hours of strenuous match play, only 25 grams of fats were burned, compared to 200 grams (males) and 125 grams (females) of carbohydrates.

From both health and performance perspectives, no more than 30% of calorie intake should come from fats, preferably polyunsaturated fats. Because the average Western diet consists of 35-40% fat, players are generally advised to reduce the fat contents of their meals, particularly the saturated fats. There appears to be no health or performance benefit to reducing energy intake from fat below 15%, compared with 20% to 25% of energy from fat. Fat is important, as it provides energy, but also for fat soluble vitamins (E, A, and D) and essential fatty acids.

Practical tips for the player on nutrition
Taking all the information above into account, here are some key points
for the foods consumed before, during, and after a match.

Pre-exercise meal
- The pre-exercise meal should be low in fat and fiber to facilitate gastric emptying, moderate in protein, and high in carbohydrate to maintain blood glucose and maximize glycogen stores. Players should take their main meal two to three hours before play, which may be followed by lighter snacks, such as cookies, fruit or a high energy bar (without chocolate).
- The closer in proximity to the event, the smaller the meal.

- In some players carbohydrate consumption 45 to 60 minutes before the event may lead to so-called rebound hypoglycemia and early fatigue. Players who are sensitive to this phenomenon should be careful not to consume simple carbohydrates immediately before play.
- Popular choices among tennis players are bread, rice, pasta, potatoes, pancakes, muesli, cereals, toast with jam, and fruit (Figure 18.3).
- Young players are advised to bring a packed lunch to tournaments, rich in complex carbohydrates, such as wheat bread with lean meat, low fat cheese or vegetables, fresh fruit, low fat yogurt, and cereals (packed separately).

During the match

- During a match, the most effective immediate carbohydrate replenishment are hypotonic and isotonic drinks (Figure 18.4).
- Easily digestible biscuits, sandwiches, fruits, or high energy bars (without chocolate) can also be consumed during long matches.
- Bananas are very popular among players. They are good sources for complex carbohydrates, but it should be kept in mind that it takes some time before they exert their effect! A banana does help a player prepare for the next match. Yellow and brown bananas are absorbed faster and better than green bananas, that are not as ripe.

Post-match eating

- If players are scheduled for a second match the same day or early the next morning, they should start eating and drinking as soon as they have finished their match (or even during the match), to ensure that they are "refueled" in time.
- If recovery time is less than eight hours, it is recommended to consume one gram of carbohydrates per kilogram bodyweight and repeat this every two hours.
- A glass of milk is an ideal post-match "sports drink."
- Breakfast cereals, fruits, and milk shakes with skimmed milk, low fat yogurt, and bananas are good, anytime snacks (e.g., late at night).

Figure 18.3

Eating pastas is popular among tennis players.

Figure 18.4

Drinks containing carbohydrates will quickly raise glucose level.

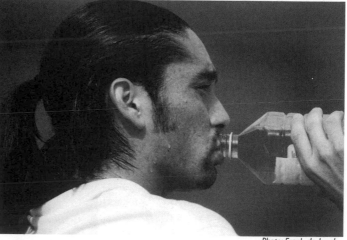

Photo: Frank de Jongh

- Foods with a high fat content such as butter, mayonnaise, and high fat dairy products should be limited, and preferably be replaced with low fat margarine or oil, and low fat dairy products. Lean ham, poultry, beef, and fish are preferred over fatty meats such as sausages and bacon.

- Players should only occasionally eat confectionery products, such as chocolate bars, toffees, ice creams etc., because of their high fat content. Cakes, potato chips, pies, and fried snacks should also be saved for special treats.

- A low carbohydrate (Atkins) diet is meant to help you lose weight, not boost your performance. This type of diet is not recommended in-season to competitive tennis players.

VITAMINS

Vitamins are essential compounds, required in tiny amounts, which trigger biochemical reactions in the body. "Essential" means that the human body is either unable to synthesize vitamins or unable to produce the amount to meet the needs of the body. Many players and coaches are convinced that vitamin supplementation will improve performance and enhance recovery. Though lack of sufficient vitamins will impair athletic performance, vitamin supplementation to a player who maintains a well-balanced diet has not been shown to improve performance and is generally not necessary. Theoretically, the athlete may have an increased vitamin requirement induced by increased loss of vitamins in sweat, urine and feces, increased turnover, as well as an enhanced energy metabolism. However, because food intake is higher as well, this will compensate for any extra loss.

Correcting a deficiency, however, does restore performance to normal levels. Certain risk groups for vitamin deficiencies can be identified, and include vegetarians, players with eating disorders, those who are on a weight reducing or low fat diet, and those eating very one-sided diets. If nutritional analysis has shown that vitamin intake is too low, attention to food choices is very important, and temporarily low dose vitamin supplementation can take place. Nutritional analysis before starting supplementation is important, because too many vitamins (megadoses) can also have a counter effect and may lead to a reduction in performance.

MINERALS

Minerals are categorized as macrominerals or microminerals (trace minerals). Macrominerals are minerals that are required by the body in relatively large quantities, generally more than 100 mg per day, and include phosphorus, calcium, sodium, chloride, potassium, and magnesium. Microminerals, or trace minerals, are required by the body in very small quantities, generally less than 20 mg per day. Fourteen trace minerals have been identified to be essential for body function: iron, copper, selenium, zinc, chromium, iodine, fluorine, manganese, molybdenum, nickel, silicon, vanadium, arsenic, and cobalt.

Mineral status can be assessed directly from samples of body tissues or body fluids, or indirectly from analysis of the diet. However, what is measured is not always an accurate representation of what is present in the body, due to intra- and extracellular mineral shifts during and after exercise. Therefore, routine evaluation of mineral status in serum, blood, or hair is not recommended; each mineral requires a special assessment technique and should only be performed if indicated. Magnesium, zinc, chromium, vanadium, and chromium are minerals that are regularly taken by tennis players. However, there is no increased risk for deficiencies of these minerals in tennis players, and these minerals have not been shown to enhance performance. There are, however, only three minerals that need extra attention in tennis players: iron (see Chapter 16), sodium (see Chapter 17) and calcium (see Chapter 23).

ANTIOXIDANTS

Strenuous exercise can produce an increase in free radicals as by-products of metabolism. Free radicals are chemical species containing unpaired electrons that make them highly reactive with other cellular components. Reactions of free radicals with cellular structures, particularly cell membranes, may result in damage. The body has several defense mechanisms to deal with the generation of free radicals. Exercise and training augment the body's antioxidant defense mechanisms. Antioxidants comprise a broad range of nutrients that can detoxify potentially damaging free radicals, in addition to the body's own defense mechanism. Antioxidants include vitamins and vitamin precursors (alpha tocoferol, ascorbic acid, betacarotene), minerals (copper, selenium, manganese, zinc, iron), and metabolic intermediates (coenzyme Q10). It has been suggested these antioxidants have a performance enhancing effect, but this has not been supported by scientific evidence. There is no consensus whether athletes obtain adequate amounts of antioxidants from their diet, or that they should also take antioxidant supplements. Megadoses of antioxidants can be harmful.

CREATINE

Creatine is an amino acid derivative naturally found in skeletal muscle, cardiac muscle, brain, testes and other organs. Creatine is obtained by the consumption of meat and fish (1-2 grams daily) and is synthesized by the liver, pancreas and kidneys (1-2 grams per day). Creatine supplementation has been shown to have a performance enhancing effect on repetitive cycle sprints of 6-30 seconds duration and repeated maximal effort strength exercise, provided the recovery periods are of 20 seconds to 5 minutes duration. Creatine supplementation does not enhance submaximal or endurance performance. At the present moment there is no evidence that creatine has a performance enhancing effect on tennis players. It may have a marginally positive effect in combination with strength training. Known side effects are weight gain (1-2 kg), an increased risk of muscle cramps, and intestinal problems.

MISCELLANEOUS PRODUCTS

Other products that may be used by athletes are ginseng, carnitine, bee pollen, glutamine, wheat germ oil, spirulina, royal jelly, yohimbe, and HMB (hydroxy methyl butazoline). None of these products has been shown to enhance tennis performance. Furthermore, the use of these products carries a certain risk, because the production process of nutritional supplements is not as strictly controlled as the production of pharmaceutical products. Thus, they may contain products that are not shown on the label, or they may be contaminated with substances that are banned by the tennis antidoping program.

Practical tips for the player
* Maintain nutritionally sound food habits by eating balanced and var-

ied meals, containing nutrients from the four food groups. The four food groups are: (1) meats, poultry, fish, beans and peas, eggs, and nuts; (2) dairy products, such as milk, cheese, and yogurt; (3) grains; and (4) fruits and vegetables. It is better to select and consume foods with high nutrient density (e.g. whole wheat bread, potatoes, grains, dairy products, meat, and vegetables) rather than to rely on supplements.

- If you have concerns regarding an adequate nutrient intake, it is recommended to contact a nutritionist to analyze your diet and check your nutrient intake.

- Be careful when using dietary supplements. Supplements that provide essential nutrients may be of help where food intake or food choices are restricted, but this approach to achieving adequate nutrient intake is normally only a short term option. The use of supplements does not compensate for poor food choices and an inadequate diet. When contemplating the use of supplements and sports foods consider their efficacy, their cost, the risk to health and performance, and the potential for a positive doping test.

- Do not use any supplements that have unclear description of its contents, are bought through the internet, or do not show their brand name. They may contain prohibited substances and lead to a positive doping test.

- Creatine supplementation does not appear to be very effective in tennis players.

SUMMARY

Carbohydrate is the most important fuel when playing tennis. Players are advised to consume a healthy low fat diet with 5-7 gram of carbohydrates per kg and no more than 25% to 30% fat, preferably polyunsaturated fats. Extra carbohydrates should be consumed prior to or during play on heavy training or competition days, preferably complex carbohydrates (starches). Protein is important for the strengthening and restoration of muscles after a workout and players are recommended to consume about 1.2 g/kg body weight daily. The average Western diet generally contains adequate amounts of protein and additional supplementation is not necessary. Vitamin, mineral, and antioxidant supplementation to a player on a well-balanced diet has not been shown to improve performance and is generally unnecessary. If vitamin and mineral intake is inadequate, it is more important to change nutritional habits toward nutrient rich foods than to take supplements. Creatine has not been shown to enhance tennis performance. No single other food supplement (e.g. ginseng, spirulina, bee pollen etc) has been shown to improve tennis performance, but may carry the risk of impurities, which may result in a positive doping test. These supplements should therefore be avoided by competitive players who may undergo anti-doping testing.

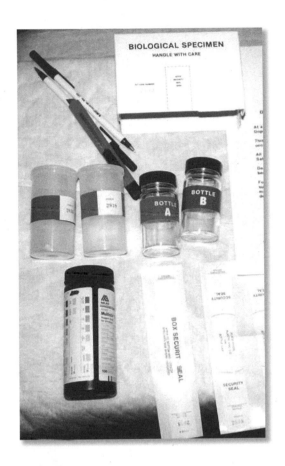

19

Doping and Drug Testing

Tennis players at all levels, both professional and amateur, may be subjected to drug testing. Those competing at tournaments sanctioned by the ITF, ATP and WTA Tour are bound by the Tennis-Anti-Doping Program. This comprehensive and internationally recognized program is a cooperative effort of the ITF, the ATP, and the WTA Tour. The goals of the Tennis Anti-Doping Program are to maintain the integrity of tennis and protect the health and rights of all tennis players. Players may also be subjected to testing by their own national association and/or government and by other national associations and/or governments when they are situated in their territories. These doping regulations and testing procedures may differ slightly from country to country.

In this chapter the Tennis Anti-Doping Program is presented, including the testing procedures, the list of prohibited substances, and the sanctions. Because doping regulations are subject to change, please refer to the website of the ITF, ATP, WTA Tour, or your national organization for the most recent rules and regulations.

WHAT IS DOPING?

Doping occurs when a prohibited substance is found to be present within a player's body or when a player uses a doping method. Doping is forbidden and constitutes a doping offense under the Tennis Anti-Doping Program. It is also regarded a doping offense when a player admits having used a prohibited substance or doping method or if a player fails or refuses to submit to a doping test, or fails or refuses to comply with any provision of the Tennis Anti-Doping Program.

THE LIST OF PROHIBITED SUBSTANCES AND METHODS

Players are tested for the WADA (World Anti-Doping Agency) list of prohibited substances (including EPO) and methods in accordance with the WADA code.

The complete list of banned substances and methods can be found at various websites including those of the ITF, ATP, WTA Tour, WADA, and IOC.

WHAT IS THE WADA?

WADA stands for World Anti-Doping Agency. The WADA was established in 1999 with the aim to promote and coordinate at an international level the fight against doping, as well as to ensure harmonization and equity in anti-doping questions. One of the goals is to create a new more universal anti-doping code, which will be applied by every international federation and every nation-state.

WHO CAN BE TESTED?

Any player who commits to enter or participate in any ATP, ITF, or WTA Tour sanctioned tournament or recognized event or has an ATP or WTA Tour ranking, is subject to testing under the Tennis Anti-Doping Program. Recognized events include, but are not limited to, Grand Slam tournaments, Davis Cup ties, Fed Cup ties, the Olympic Tennis Event, the Paralympic Tennis Event, WTA Tour tournaments, Challenger series tournaments, Futures and Satellite Series Circuit tournaments, ITF junior and veteran tournaments, and wheelchair tournaments. At national level, every member of the national federation may be subjected to testing.

WHEN CAN A TEST OCCUR?

Testing includes both in-competition and out-of-competition testing. In-competition testing occurs at events throughout the year. All players who are in the main draw of a tournament or event where testing is conducted may be subject to on-site testing. Out-of-competition testing may be carried out at any time. Players will be selected at random and shall submit to a doping test at any time and at any place when requested. A designated administrator will contact a player selected for out-of-competition testing.

WHO ADMINISTERS THE TESTING?

A team of independent professionals administers the Tennis Anti-Doping Program. This team consists of the following: (a) the anti-doping program administrator who is responsible for the overall operation and administration of the program; (b) the medical liaison, a qualified medical doctor, who receives all test results and confidentially receives player signature forms; (c) an anti-doping review board which is an outside group of experts with medical, technical and legal knowledge of anti-doping procedures. In addition to providing general assistance to the program on doping issues, the review board reviews all player therapeutic use exemption requests and all laboratory positive test results.

THE THERAPEUTIC USE EXEMPTION

A player's physician may send a request to the Tennis Anti-Doping Program administrator to receive permission to use, for valid medical reasons, a prohibited substance or doping method. This exemption request must be reviewed and approved by the therapeutic use exemption committee. An therapeutic use exemption request must provide all relevant information concerning the history and medical records of the condition or illness to be supplied by the player's treating physician. As with other medical information, the player's medical exemption request is processed with complete confidentiality.

PLAYER NOTIFICATION OF TESTING

After a match, a player will be contacted by either a supervisor or other tennis official, someone that the player will recognize and know, and informed that he/she has been selected for anti-doping testing. An escort will then accompany a player until arriving at the reception area where the testing is performed.

THE TESTING PROCEDURE

The testing may be performed by analysis of blood or urine. The player goes to a processing room where the anti-doping program administrator and other testing personnel will administer the test. A coach, parent, or other representative may accompany the player. The player will be asked to choose a sealed collection kit. For urine analysis, the player will be asked to provide the specimen under direct observation. The sample is then separated into "A" and "B" specimens. For blood analysis, blood shall be taken from a superficial vein. In some, but not all cases, the sample may also be separated into "A" and "B" specimens. Specimens shall be sealed in specially designed collection bottles and identified by a control identification number, not by the player's name. The player will sign a form with the address and phone number where he/she can be contacted. A copy of the form will be provided to the player as a record that he/she completed the test. The specimens will be sent to a WADA accredited laboratory. The anti-doping program administrator, if appropriate, will receive the results and will review them with the medical liaison and the review board.

TEST RESULTS AND REPORTING

Most organization do not notify the player if the test is negative. "A" sample test results, which are confirmed to be positive, will be confidentially reviewed by the anti-doping program administrator, medical liaison, and therapeutic use exemption committee. If the therapeutic use exemption committee determines the"A" specimen is positive, the "B" specimen must be tested. The medical liaison will contact the player to advise him/her of the decision. The player or a representative will have an opportunity to be present at the analysis of the "B" specimen.

PENALTIES

Under the Tennis Anti-Doping Program, sanctions for a doping offence are two years ineligibility at the first offence, and lifetime ineligibility at the second offence.

However, the prohibited list may identify substances that are particularly susceptible for unintentional anti-doping rules violations, because of their general availability in medicinal products (specified substances). Where a player can establish that the use of such a specified substance was not intended to enhance sports performance, the sanction may vary from a warning to one year ineligibility at the first offence, two years ineligibility at the second offense, and lifetime ineligibility at the third offence.

A player who fails or refuses to appear for required testing may be subject to a suspension from participation in or association with any ATP, ITF, or WTA Tour sanctioned tournament or event, varying from a period of three months to two years.

ANNOUNCEMENT OF SUSPENSIONS

All suspensions will be announced by the tennis organization (ATP, ITF, or WTA Tour). If a player is suspended, then he will loose all ranking points earned at the event where the player tested positive. Moreover, the player will forfeit and return to the tennis organization all prize money earned at the event, including all subsequent tournaments in which he/she competes, up until the final determination and announcement of a suspension by the tennis organization. A player suspended will not be eligible for ranking protection.

NUTRITIONAL SUPPLEMENTS

The ingestion of nutritional supplements pose a special risk because they may contain or they may be contaminated with substances that are specifically banned by the Tennis Anti-Doping Program. Unlike prescription medications, in which the purity of the product can be guaranteed by governmental regulatory authorities, the purity of supplements is at best uncertain. The labels of dietary supplement products do not always contain a full list of all ingredients. Also, manufacturing processes may be uneven, and even minute traces of contamination of dietary supplement have been shown to result in a positive doping test. A study published by the IOC in 2002 demonstrated that almost fifteen percent of 634 supplements it tested contained prohibited substances! Because anti-doping rules make the presence of a prohibited substance in the athlete's urine a doping offense regardless of how the substance got there, any player who takes a dietary supplement does so at his own risk.

Practical tips for the player
- Be careful with nutritional supplements. The risk of testing positive in a doping test must be borne by the consumer who uses supplements. In some countries, such as The Netherlands, there is a "white list" of safe nutritional supplements for athletes available. The supplements on this list have been tested and shown to be free of contaminations or impurities.
- Make sure to tell your doctor(s) and/or dentist that you are an athlete, subject to anti-doping testing.
- You may apply for a therapeutic use exemption to take, for valid medical reasons, a prohibited substance or doping method. Generally it takes up to three days to receive a response. Approval must be granted before you can take the medicine, except in an emergency situation, and except for substances that require medical notification only (e.g., local corticosteroids, beta 2 agonists).

SUMMARY

The Tennis Anti-Doping program is a joint program of the ITF, ATP and WTA Tour, in accordance with the WADA Code. Players may be subjected to urine and blood testing. Players may request a therapeutic use exemption to receive permission to take, for valid medical reasons, a prohibited substance or doping method. Sanctions for doping offences may be severe, and vary from a warning to life-long disqualification from tennis. Nutritional supplements have more and more been identified as potential sources of a positive test, and should only be taken if there is a guarantee that they are free of contaminations.

Important notice: Doping regulations are liable to change. Refer to the website of the ITF, ATP, WTA Tour, WADA, IOC, or your national organization for the most recent rules and regulations.

20

Overtraining and Burnout

Highly competitive tennis players run the risk of developing the overtraining syndrome or burnout. Overtraining and burnout may be caused by heavy training along with inadequate recovery time, with an increased risk if additional psychosocial and/or physical stressors are present. Although exact incidence rates of the overtraining syndrome in tennis are not known, numbers for individual sports range between 10% and 64%. In this chapter, the causes and symptoms of both disorders will be discussed, followed by recommendations regarding prevention.

OVERTRAINING

Description. The overtraining syndrome is the name given to the collection of emotional, behavioral, and physical symptoms due to overtraining that persist for weeks to months. Overtraining syndrome, also called staleness, is caused by an imbalance between training and recovery. It may occur after a prolonged period of high volume or high intensity training with insufficient recovery and usually requires several weeks or months of rest or greatly reduced training for complete recovery. Contributing factors to the development of overtraining are inappropriate training, sudden increments in training, infectious disease, caloric deficiency, and emotional stress (Figures 20.1, 20.2, 20.3, and 20.4). It should be distinguished from the fatigue and performance decrements of short term overtraining or overreaching, from which the player recovers after a few days of rest.

Symptoms. The overtraining syndrome is characterized by a decrease in performance, accompanied by disturbances in mood state, such as moodiness, irritability, depression, and loss of competitive desire. Other possible symptoms are inability to maintain training loads, persistent fatigue, muscle soreness, and disturbed sleep.

Figures 20.1-20.4
Emotional Stress

Figures 20.1

The tears after winning.

Figures 20.2

Frustration

Figures 20.3 and 20.4

More frustration.

Figures 20.4

Anger.

Treatment. The treatment for the overtraining syndrome is rest. The longer the overtraining has occurred, the more rest is required. If the overtraining has only occurred for a short period of time (e.g., a month) then interrupting training for a week may be sufficient rest. After this, training can gradually be resumed, whereby both the intensity and volume of the training are increased over the course of several weeks. In more severe cases, the training program may have to be interrupted for weeks, and it may take months to recover. It is important that the stressors that contributed to the overtraining be identified and corrected. Otherwise, the overtraining syndrome is likely to recur. An alternate form of exercise can be substituted to help prevent the exercise withdrawal syndrome.

BURNOUT

Description. Burnout can be defined as physical, emotional, and mental exhaustion, resulting in psychological, physical, and emotional withdrawal from tennis. It is caused by the player experiencing stress over an extended period of time, resulting in reduced motivation and interest in the activity. In short, there is a feeling of being worn out, tired of the sport, and not ever wanting to see a racquet again! Burnout is like the "end of the line" of overtraining and excessive stress. There is no specific factor that causes burnout. It is caused by the reciprocal interaction of the physical and mental stressors to which the player is exposed and the way he perceives these stressors and copes with them. Causal factors that have been identified in burnout in tennis players are a sole focus on tennis, with little opportunity to develop identities outside of the sport arena (e.g., a social life, music); little control over the decision-making relative to the sport; parental pressure; inconsistent coaching practices; excessive time demands; the stress of continuous media attention; and the stress of international travel. A personality characteristic that has been associated with burnout in tennis players is perfectionism.

Symptoms. Burnout symptoms include short attention span, body aches, insomnia, irritability, impatience, alienation, emotional and physical exhaustion, and lack of motivation to get out of bed in the morning to play.

Prevention and Treatment. Prevention is far more important than treatment. If the player has burned out and, as a consequence, has dropped out of tennis, she/he has already lost the motivation and it may be too late. In this aspect burned out players differ from overtrained players, who still have a very high motivational drive. Prevention aims to remove the causal factors and to strengthen the player's coping skills. Important preventative measures are: to let the player develop an identity outside of the sport arena (e.g,. a social life, music); to let the player have input into his training program and career development; to teach parents to be parents instead of coaches and give parental support instead of parental pressure; to educate the coaches; to limit the time on court or away to tournaments; to limit media attention; and to teach the player social and mental skills (Figure 20.5).

Figures 20.5
Ideally, tennis parents give parental support instead of parental pressure.

The Player Development Program of the WTA Tour focuses on the issues described above and allows players to develop the necessary coping skills and physical maturity to enjoy a healthy and successful career as a professional tennis player. The program includes media training, coach registration, player orientation, parent orientation, a mentor program, career development, athlete assistance, annual physicals, and an age eligibility rule.

Practical tips for the player

- Regulate the amount of training and periodize the schedule. Have rest days and plan regular short breaks and holidays during the course of the year. A break from the usual routine and stressors of tennis life can be very healthy and rejuvenating.
- Reduce training intensity and duration before tournaments and matches.
- Use recovery techniques, such as massage, stretching, relaxation techniques, hot and cold showers, and spas.
- Practice mental skills, such as imagery, relaxation, and positive self-talk.
- Eat well. A balanced diet with adequate carbohydrate, protein, and fluid intake will speed up recovery.
- Decrease training volume and intensity during a viral illness.
- "More" does not always mean "better." Most players who experience a string of losses respond to increasing their training load. However, if the cause of the decreased performance is overtraining, this will only augment the problem. Some extra rest would then be a far better solution.
- Keep a training diary, which includes training details, matches, well-being ratings, morning heart rate, incidence of illness, injury and menstruation, and causes of stress and unhappiness. This will help detect any changes and make it possible to seek medical help earlier.

Practical tips for the coach

- Be aware of the existence of overtraining, and the players at risk. Players with a high motivational drive tend to overtrain themselves and need to be protected.
- Periodize the training, with sufficient recovery time between training sessions. Alternate hard days of training with easy ones, and tough training sessions with easy ones. Best results are obtained when training is very consciously "paced."
- Set up a training plan. Many of the best coaches keep a kind of training log book for each player in which both plans and accomplishments are detailed. There are at least two benefits from such a practice: first, the player can feel that he participates in the development of his own training schedule, and second, he knows what to expect in any given day or week.
- Set up a competition plan. Good coaches often put together a 3-month or 6-month tournament plan for each player. Such a plan can be developed best in consultation with the player. There are at least two benefits: first, training can be carried out with specific competition targets; and secondly, the perils of too much competition can be

avoided. The short-term goals should be appropriate and realistic. They should be negotiated, and the player should contribute towards the decisions that are made.

- Encourage the player to take time off. Tennis training should never be a 7-days-a-week business. A good training plan will include hard days, easier days, and days with no tennis at all, so that the player does not become totally preoccupied with tennis. Moreover, no season should be too long and there should be clear breaks between seasons.

- Pay attention to nontennis activities. One of the most common causes of burnout is the pressure which a player experiences from parents, school, and peers. The best coaches not only understand that nontennis pressures exist, but are also flexible in responding and adjusting to them.

- Take injuries and pain seriously. There is no quicker way to develop chronic injuries than to force a player to play with pain. If you feel the player is using injuries as an excuse, discuss this with the player. It could be a sign that he is unable to cope with the stress in a healthier and more constructive way.

- Avoid boredom by varying the training routine. Keep it fun and challenging.

- Invest time and effort to learn to teach mental skills.

- Be flexible. Rules may be broken, and plans can be modified. The best coaches are continually on the lookout for the effects of off-court pressures such as parents, school, and peers (as noted above), but also from travel to tournaments, unfamiliar playing conditions, and even high temperatures.

SUMMARY

Overtraining and burnout are the result of an imbalance between training and recovery, with burnout being the final outcome of chronic stress. Prevention strategies focus on reducing the stresses both on and off court and teaching the players skills to deal more efficiently with these stresses. The WTA Tour has incorporated these preventative strategies into a comprehensive player development program, with the aim of preventing burnout and promoting a healthy and successful professional career.

21 The Travelling Player

Elite tennis players, including juniors, veterans and wheelchair players, travel around the globe. But not only world class players, but also those competing at national or regional level may travel a lot to play interclub competition and tournaments. Thus, travelling forms an important aspect for competitive tennis players. In this chapter medical conditions associated with travelling are discussed.

JET LAG

Description. The feelings of disorientation encountered as a result of crossing time zones are known as jet lag. Flying eastwards, and therefore resetting the "body clock" forward, is often more difficult than flying westwards and adding hours to the day. This is because the body clock adjusts more easily to a phase delay (going to bed and getting up later) than a phase advance (going to bed and waking up earlier). Also, the longer the flight, and the more time zones one crosses, the longer the jet lag symptoms will last and the worse they will be. Flying north or south does not produce jet lag.

Symptoms. Symptoms include fatigue and general tiredness, irritability, sleeping difficulties, loss of concentration, loss of motivation, general malaise, and headache. These effects are temporary and disappear during the course of a few days, when the internal clock is attuned to the new local environment.

Treatment. Jet lag will disappear by itself with time. As a general rule, for each hour of time difference approximately 12 hours to one day of "adaptation time" are needed. Thus, a trip to another country with an 8-hour time-difference requires a departure a minimum of four days in advance to ensure that the player is at least partially recovered from the jet lag the day of his first match. Melatonin has been shown to be effective for the treatment of jet lag. Daily doses of melatonin between 0.5 and 5mg are similarly effective, except that people fall asleep faster and sleep better after 5mg than 0.5mg. The melatonin should be taken close to the target bedtime at the destination (10 p.m. to midnight). The benefit is greater the more time zones are crossed, and less for westward flights. The timing of the melatonin dose is important. If it is taken at the wrong time, early in the day, it is liable to cause sleepiness and delay adaptation to local time.

Practical tips for the player

- Start to reset the individual biological clock one or two days in advance of departure by going to bed earlier and getting up earlier prior to flying west (e.g., when flying from Europe to the US), and by going to bed later and getting up later when flying east (e.g., from Europe to Asia). However, adjusting the sleep-wake cycle prior to travelling is just of marginal benefit, and an adjustment of more than two hours is not recommended.
- Try to plan the arrival time. When flying west, try to schedule arrival roughly around bedtime, and start with a good night of sleep. The best option when flying east is to sleep on the plane and planning to arrive in the morning. This way, the body systems can adapt immediately to the new time schedule.
- Set the watch to the local time of destination when stepping into the plane. This way, one starts thinking in terms of the new time zone, and use the travelling hours to start the adjustment process.
- Get some extra sleep in the plane. Close the window shade or use an eye shade or blanket to shut out the light. Use ear plugs and a neck pillow for more comfort and better sleep.
- Drink plenty of fluids. When travelling by air, the atmosphere inside the plane is very dry, ranging from 6 to 15% humidity. Drink extra fluids during the flight to avoid dehydration, but try to be moderate with beverages containing alcohol or caffeine. They increase dehydration and may disrupt sleep.
- Avoid eating heavy, fatty, and salty meals before and during the flight. A light meal is easier to digest, and will permit better sleep. It has been suggested that carbohydrate rich meals stimulate the indolamine system, thereby inducing sleep, whereas meals rich in proteins stimulate the adrenaline system and wake one up. However, there is no scientific evidence to back up these claims. Timing is more important than the contents of the meals.
- During the flight, and especially on lengthy flights, move the toes, ankles and knees from time to time while seated, and get up frequently to stretch and walk the aisles. This periodic exercise will help to improve blood circulation and avoid stiffness of the body. It may reduce the risk of the so-called "economy class" syndrome, a deep venous thrombosis caused by sitting (too) still for a (too) long period of time.
- Use the natural signals that govern the internal clock (light, activity, food) to help the body come in synch with the local time. Avoiding light in the morning and actively seeking stimulation (light, social activity, exercise) is useful after westward flights; performing moderate exercise in the morning and closing the curtains at night will help to recover faster after an eastward flight. Avoid prolonged napping

and eat meals at the appropriate time to help the body adjust as quickly as possible.

- Be moderate with sleeping pills because of possible side-effects and risk of hangovers. Occasionally, they can be helpful to induce sleep in the plane or the first or second night after arrival (especially after flying east).

VACCINATIONS

Description. A vaccine consists of a preparation of micro-organisms or their antigenic components which can induce protective immunity against a bacterium or virus, but which does not itself cause disease. Vaccinations form an important part of a sound preparation before leaving on a journey. They are an easy and highly effective way to keep tennis players healthy when travelling. Many vaccines offer protection rates higher than 95% after a single dose (e.g., hepatitis A, yellow fever), and even higher after a repeat dose.

The most common vaccinations are discussed below. However, vaccination requirements may vary, so be sure to always check the latest available information.

Tetanus, diphteria, and poliomyelitis are routine immunizations in most countries. Updating tetanus and diphtheria is recommended for players travelling to developing countries; polio is still indicated for Asia and Africa.

Hepatitis A vaccine should be used to prevent infection for travelers to countries where hepatitis A viral infection is a risk, and includes all developing countries.

Hepatitis B, if possible in combination with A, is recommended for persons travelling for more than 30 days, travelers less than 35 years of age, and for people showing special risk behavior (e.g., high risk sports, unprotected sexual intercourse).

Typhoid fever and cholera are recommended for countries with poor hygiene.

Yellow fever is compulsory for travelers to tropical Africa and Amazonian forest.

Cholera vaccination is virtually never indicated.

Annual vaccination against *influenza* may be recommended, because of the increased incidence of viral infection during periods of intense training and competition.

Practical tips for the player
- Schedule the appointment for the vaccinations ahead of time.
- Keep track of the vaccinations received on a card or in a booklet, and take this card or booklet along when travelling.

MALARIA

Description. Malaria is caused by a infection of red blood cells by a protozoum (P). There are four types: P falciparum, P vivax, P ovale, or P malariae. Malaria requires standing water nearby. It is transmitted by bites from infected mosquitoes, mainly at dusk and during the night. Malaria is resurgent in most tropical countries and the risk to travelers is increasing.

Symptoms. Malaria is usually characterized by fever (which may be swinging), increased heartbeat, rigors, and sweating. Anemia, enlargement of the liver, involvement of the brain, renal failure, and shock may occur.

Treatment and prevention. Malaria cannot be prevented by vaccination, thus in areas where malaria is common, appropriate preventive measures (tablets and protection against insect bites) should be taken. Insecticide treated nets, air conditioning, electric fans, mosquito coils, protective clothing, and topical insect repellents are all beneficial in reducing the risk. The choice of the drug depends on the countries which are to be visited and possible drug sensitivity of the traveler (e.g., chloroquine, doxycycline, mefloquine (Lariam), or a combination of atovaquone and proguanil (Malarone).

Practical tips for the player
- Just before dusk clothing should be worn that covers the arms and legs.
- A mosquito repellent should be applied on other exposed parts. Suitable repellents are those that have a high N,N-diethyl-meta-toluamide (DEET) content (more than 15%), which is the active agent. Repellents containing more than 30% DEET are not recommended.
- If wearing very thin clothing, lightly spray the clothing with repellent, because mosquitoes may bite through thin clothing.

SEXUALLY TRANSMITTED DISEASES

Description. Sexually transmitted diseases are diseases that are spread by sexual contact. This includes diseases such as gonorrhea, genital herpes, hepatitis B, pelvic inflammatory disease, chlamydia, syphilis, AIDS, etc. They affect men and women of all backgrounds and economic levels and are most prevalent among teenagers and young adults. Nearly two-thirds of all sexually transmitted diseases occur in people younger than 25 years of age.

Symptoms. Usually sexually transmitted diseases cause no symptoms. This is especially true in women. Even when a sexually transmitted diseases causes no symptoms, a person who is infected may be able to pass the disease on to a sex partner (e.g., genital herpes, HIV). Symptoms may include fever, pain on urination, and urethral discharge.

Treatment. When diagnosed and treated early, many sexually transmitted diseases can be treated effectively by drugs. Some infections have become resistant to the drugs used to treat them and now require different types of antibiotics. Some can not be cured and can be terminal (e.g., HIV, chronic hepatitis).

Practical tips for the player
- Prevention of sexually transmitted diseases involves practicing safe sex, and the avoidance of contaminated needles and contaminated blood products.
- Include sterile needles in your travel bag when travelling to a country where the hygienic standards in some areas may be low.
- Having sex in a monogamous (faithful) relationship is safe if both of you are uninfected; you both have sex only with your partner; and

neither one of you gets exposed to disease through drug use or other activities. In all other situations, condoms should be used.
- When treating a bleeding wound, use gloves.

THE TRAVEL KIT

A player should be adequately prepared to handle minor and major medical issues when away from home. A minor injury, such as a blister, can become a major issue or even a cause for withdrawal, if not treated properly. At major tournaments, sports physicians, physiotherapists, and athletic trainers may be available, but in the satellite circuit, ITF futures, and the junior, veteran, wheelchair, and local tournaments, medical staff may be scarce or lacking.

The contents of the travel kit will vary depending on the destination and the local facilities available. It is advisable to be as self-sufficient as possible when travelling. Thus, the first step the player should take when in travel preparation is to obtain information regarding the destination. This may include climate, altitude, level of pollution, accommodation, food, water, vaccination requirements, and available medical support. For example, in Western Europe, antibiotics or sterile needles need not be part of the medical kit, whereas it may be advised to include those when travelling to countries where it may be difficult and time-consuming to obtain medication or when the hygienic standards are not very high.

The following is recommended:

Instruments
Thermometer
Scissors
Sterile blister puncture needles
Spare glasses or lenses, for those who use them
(Sterile needles)

Wound dressings and tape
Steri-strips (for treatment of a deep cut)
Antiseptic solution (betadine) (to clean a wound or blister)
Band-aid plastic strips (to control bleeding of minor cuts and
    wounds)
Dressing retention sheets (to cover large wounds or abrasions)
Sports tape (to prevent blisters in areas of friction; to prevent sprains
    and strains)
Compressive bandage (to apply compression to a major ankle sprain
    or muscle strain)
Skin care pad (to treat blisters and burns)

Medication
Oral analgesics (paracetamol, NSAIDs) (to control pain)
Antidiarrheals (for symptomatic treatment of diarrhea)
Antihistamines (for the treatment of allergies)
Short-acting sleeping tablets (jet lag, intercontinental flights)
Anti-nausea (to treat motion sickness)
Throat lozenges (for treatment of a sore throat)

Miscellaneous
Sunscreen
Safety pins
Tampons (women)
Spare shoelaces
Plastic bags (for ice)
Sterile gloves (when treating bleeding wounds)
Medical passport (if using medication)
Vaccination card
List of banned substances

SUMMARY

In this chapter we discuss the preparations a player or coach should take before he travels to a tournament, and the medical problems that are associated with travelling. Before departure, the traveler should make sure he has received all the vaccinations that are needed for the countries he is travelling too. Malaria is an increasing risk to travelers, and appropriate preventive measures (tablets and protection against insect bites) should be taken. Nearly two-thirds of all sexually transmitted diseases (including HIV, genital herpes, chlamydia, gonorrhea, etc.) occur in people younger than 25 years of age. Prevention involves practicing safe sex and the avoidance of contaminated needles and contaminated blood products. The traveler should be as self-sufficient as possible by bringing a well-filled medical travel kit. The possible contents of this medical travel kit are presented.

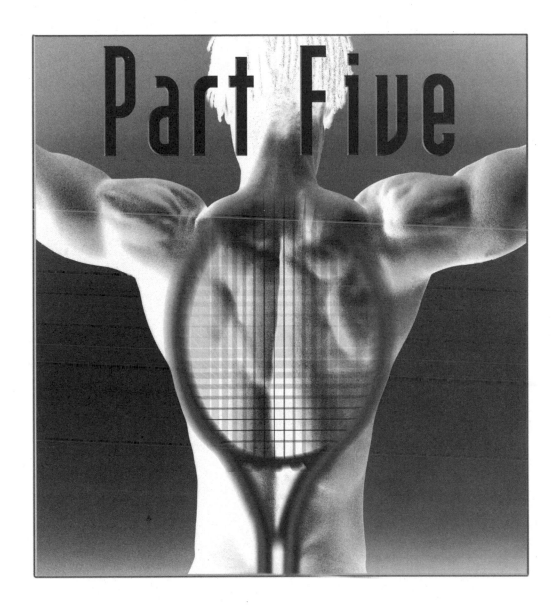

Part Five

Special Tennis Groups

22

Junior Players

Increasing numbers of children are becoming involved in competitive tennis at an earlier age and with higher levels of intensity. They start participating when they are as young as four of five years of age, with some proceeding to year-round practice, competition, and conditioning. The International Tennis Federation organizes tournaments and competitions for juniors ranging from 12 to 18 years of age, and many countries organize national championships for the 10s and under. The main difference between junior players and adults is their ongoing development: the growth and maturation of bones, muscles, tendons, and ligaments. Are young players therefore more vulnerable to injury than older players? This chapter takes a look at the process of growth, maturation, and motor performance of junior tennis players and their injury profile.

GROWTH AND MATURATION

Childhood is a period of relatively steady progress in growth and maturation and rapid progress in motor development. With the onset of puberty, differences between boys and girls start to increase. The main events of puberty are the growth spurt and sexual maturation, which change the child into an adult capable of reproduction. Most girls commence puberty between nine and thirteen years, whereas boys have a later puberty, mostly starting between eleven and fourteen years (Figures 22.1). Menarche occurs at a mean age of 13.2 years and is closely related with skeletal maturity.

The growth spurt occurs on average two years earlier in girls than in boys, and thus girls may have a temporary size advantage over boys around the age of twelve and thirteen. Girls grow fastest between the ages of ten and twelve (8-10 cm, or 3-4 inches per year), whereas boys grow fastest between the ages of twelve and sixteen (10-12 cm, or 4-4.5 inches per year). The mean difference in stature between an adult male and an adult female is about 13 cm (5 inches). Regular, intense physical activity has no effect on statural growth.

Figure 22.1

Players of the Dutch National Teams in 2002. The players are lined up according to calendar age. The youngest (on the far left) was 12, the oldest (far right) was 18 years of age. Note the wide variety in body build and size.

Age and maturation may have a distinct effect on tennis performance in juniors. Among boys playing tennis competitively in the 14s and under and 16s and under age categories, players born in the first half of the year have an advantage over those born in the second half of the year. This is because older boys are taller, heavier, and stronger than younger boys. This same effect can be found in boys of advanced maturity compared to boys of the same age who are delayed in maturity status. Among girls, there is no such obvious effect.

PHYSICAL CAPACITIES

How does the development of the various physical capacities in juniors and, more specifically, in junior tennis players progress, and at what age should physical training be started?

AEROBIC POWER

Aerobic power is similar in school age boys and girls until about age twelve. Peak VO_2 (peak oxygen consumption) increases linearly from the age of eight through the age of sixteen in boys, whereas it increases until about the age of thirteen and then remains at a plateau in girls. In elite junior tennis players, however, peak VO_2 continues to increase in both boys and girls up to adulthood, reflecting the effect of training (Table 22.1). The relative peak VO_2 (oxygen consumption per kg bodyweight) remains relatively stable. Peak VO_2 of male players is consistently higher than that of female players. This difference is mostly the result of the lower absolute and relative amount of lean tissue, and partly a result of the greater accumulation of body fat in females. Fat percentage in elite male and female tennis players is usually slightly lower than fat percentage of schoolchildren of the same age (12% vs. 15% in boys, 22% vs. 25% in girls, Figure 22.2). Running speed continues to improve from age twelve to age eighteen in both male and female players.

Up to approximately age fourteen, boys and girls can perform conditioning exercises together. After age fourteen, the training groups should be split up, or tasks should be individualized due to physiological differences in strength, power, and growth.

ANAEROBIC PERFORMANCE

Anaerobic energy production is important for young tennis players, because tennis involves many bursts of energy. However, the anaerobic lactic system is less developed

Table 22.1 Exercise test results of Dutch elite tennis players

Girls

Age, yrs	N	Height cm	SD	Weight kg	SD	Fat %	SD	Km	SD	Abs VO$_2$ max L·kg⁻¹	SD	Rel VO$_2$ max ml·kg⁻¹·min⁻¹	SD
12	14	155.6	9.2	44.3	9.0	19.2	3.2	14.6	1.4	2.6	0.4	55.5	5.2
13	23	165.2	6.5	49.9	6.7	19.0	2.3	15.6	0.9	2.8	0.3	55.7	5.2
14	28	167.4	6.0	56.0	6.4	22.0	3.9	15.6	1.2	3.1	0.4	55.1	5.1
15	23	172.2	4.4	60.6	4.5	22.1	3.2	16.0	1.1	3.3	0.3	54.5	4.9
16	43	170.5	5.8	60.8	6.8	22.3	3.5	15.8	1.1	3.3	0.4	54.3	5.1
17	22	173.9	6.5	64.7	6.5	22.7	3.0	16.3	1.3	3.5	0.3	53.9	4.8
18	20	174.2	5.9	65.8	5.7	23.2	4.1	16.3	1.1	3.6	0.4	54.3	3.7
19-21	24	174.9	6.7	67.6	5.5	23.3	3.4	16.1	1.5	3.6	0.4	54.2	4.2

Boys

Age, yrs	N	Height cm	SD	Weight kg	SD	Fat %	SD	Km	SD	VO$_2$ max L·kg⁻¹	SD	Rel VO$_2$ max ml·kg⁻¹·min⁻¹	SD
12	14	157.8	6.6	42.3	4.6	13.6	3.2	15.0	1.6	2.6	0.3	61.3	3.3
13	23	167.5	10.4	53.4	10.2	13.0	3.3	16.1	1.7	3.3	0.9	61.8	5.5
14	22	175.6	7.4	60.6	8.9	11.8	2.9	17.2	0.9	3.9	0.5	63.6	4.8
15	23	178.7	6.5	65.8	9.7	10.3	3.7	17.7	1.3	4.2	0.7	64.2	4.3
16	33	183.3	5.8	71.0	7.4	11.0	2.2	18.3	1.2	4.5	0.5	63.0	5.4
17	34	184.1	6.5	73.8	7.6	11.1	2.0	18.6	1.2	4.6	0.5	62.7	5.1
18	12	185.0	6.0	73.8	7.2	10.2	2.6	19.0	1.1	4.6	0.4	62.9	4.3
19-21	20	186.6	5.4	75.1	6.0	10.3	2.1	19.4	1.4	4.8	0.4	64.1	4.2

N= number of players tested, SD = standard deviation; KM= maximal running speed on the treadmill in kilometers per hour; Abs VO$_2$ max is maximum oxygen consumption in liters per minute; Rel VO$_2$ max is maximum oxygen consumption in milliliters per kilogram bodyweight per minute.

in children compared to adults. Children are not able to attain and sustain as high blood and muscle lactate concentrations during high-intensity exercises as adults, even relative to body size. This should be taken into consideration when young tennis players have to perform high intensity exercise (beyond their anaerobic threshold). Thus, the duration of high intensity (anaerobic) exercise should be shorter in children than in adults, and the rest periods between high intensity exercises should be longer than in adults.

STRENGTH

In childhood, there is a consistent, though small, gender difference in strength, favoring boys. Strength increases linearly with age until thirteen to fourteen years of age in boys, when there is an adolescent strength spurt. In girls, strength improves linearly with age through about sixteen to seventeen years, with no adolescent strength spurt. The marked acceleration of strength development during male adolescence magnifies the difference between boys and girls, favoring boys. As a result, after puberty boys perform better than girls in motor tasks that involve strength, such as sprinting, jumping and throwing.

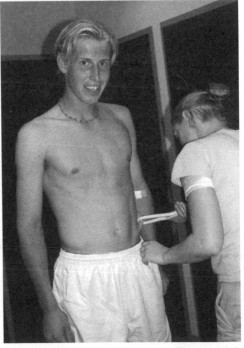

Figure 22.2

Determination of fat percentage.

There is no consensus at what age tennis players should commence strength training. Potential benefits from strength training include enhanced tennis performance and possibly a reduction in injury risk. Potential risks include injuries and deleterious effects on the musculoskeletal system. Historically, resistance training for the development of strength was not recommended for prepubertal children. It was thought that injury risk was too high, and that insufficient quantities of male hormones precluded strength improvement. However, it has been shown that a closely supervised, primarily concentric strength training program in prepubertal children may lead to significant increases in strength and to small increases in body mass, with a low injury risk (Figure 22.3). An expert strength trainer should supervise any strength training program.

Figure 22.3

A closely supervised, primarily concentric strength training program in prepubertal children may lead to significant increases in strength and to small increases in body mass, with a low injury risk.

CO-ORDINATION

Most fundamental motor skills ordinarily develop by age six or seven, although the mature patterns of some skills do not develop until later. Middle childhood (age six to adolescence) is an important time period for the acquisition of co-ordination and complex technical skills. As fundamental movement patterns are refined through practice, performance quality improves, and the fundamental patterns are integrated into more complex movement sequences. Children who start playing tennis around this age and experience a wide variety of games and sports will have a distinct advantage over children who do not have these experiences until a much later age (Figure 22.4, 22.5, and 22.6). For example, timing accuracy improves mainly between the ages of seven and ten years and tennis practice accelerates the development of timing accuracy. Contrary to popular belief, children do not go through a period of awkwardness during growth spurt. Furthermore, males and females perform equally well on most fine motor tasks.

FLEXIBILITY

Inflexibility has been associated with muscle-tendon injury, particularly muscle strains. Girls are more flexible than boys at all ages, and gender differences are greatest during the adolescent growth spurt and sexual maturation (Figure 22.7). The sit and reach

Figure 22.4

Children that experience a wide variety of games and sports at a young age will have a distinct advantage over kids that do not have these experiences until a much later age. Shown here is catching.

Figure 22.5

Kicking.

Figure 22.6

Throwing.

test, thought to be indicative of hamstring tightness, has received most attention. However, decreased flexibility in the sit and reach test during puberty has two causes. Firstly, the longitudinal growth of bones advances more rapidly than that of the surrounding muscle-tendon units. This change becomes exaggerated during the adolescent growth spurt. Secondly, rapid growth of the lower extremities occurs in the early part of the adolescent growth spurt, whereas the growth in trunk length occurs later. It is important to put emphasis on the flexibility component of the training program, but the above mentioned aspect should be kept in mind.

Stretching should be done gently. Also, stretching should be avoided after intense training programs with a lot of eccentric exercises or when the player is very sore.

Figure 22.7

Girls are more flexible than boys at all ages.

HEAT STRESS

Children are at an increased risk during tennis in the heat. Young players have a lessened ability to dissipate heat and are more susceptible to heat injury. This could make young athletes competing in the heat prone to a chronic state of dehydration with a less than optimal plasma volume. Thus, young players should carefully observe the guidelines for extreme heat conditions and it should be taken into consideration that even more conservative measures may be applied if players of a young age are not taken into account by stated guidelines.

EPIDEMIOLOGY OF INJURIES

Injury rate in juniors varies, depending on the level and intensity of play and the injury definition. Elite players and those that practice more often have a higher injury rate than recreational players that only play once or twice a week. In elite juniors, injury rate is approximately 0.5 to 1.0 injury per player per year. In juniors, approximately twice as many injuries of the lower extremity are recorded, compared to either the upper extremity or to the trunk. Those other injuries are equally distributed between the trunk and upper extremity injuries. There is an equal likelihood between the sexes of sustaining an acute (60-70%) or overuse injury (30-40%). Moreover, there is little difference between male and female players in the anatomical location of the injury.

Although juniors can sustain many of the same injuries as adults, there are several injuries that are typical for children, most notably, injuries of the growth plate (see Chapters 7, 8, and 9).

SUMMARY

Growth and maturation have a great influence on performance in young tennis players. Before puberty, sex differences in height, weight, and motor skills are small. After puberty, boys are significantly stronger, faster, taller, and heavier than girls, and they have better endurance. Because of the great effect of puberty on motor performance, in the 13 to 16 year age group, older and/or early mature boys have an advantage over boys that are younger or late in maturity. There are no sex differences in co-ordination. Injury rate in elite juniors is approximately 0.5-1.0 injury per player per year. Typical injuries in junior tennis players are injuries that affect the growth plates.

23

Veteran Players

Tennis can be played both recreationally and competitively throughout one's lifetime. More than 60 percent of the members of the Royal Netherlands Lawn Tennis Association (author Pluim's association) are over 35 years of age, and almost 30 percent are older than 50. The International Tennis Federation organizes tournaments and championships for veterans, starting at the age of 35 and going up to 80 years and older (women up to 70 years and older). The senior divisions are subdivided into age groups that increase in 5-years increments until the age of 80 (men) or 70 (women) years. In this chapter the major injuries and health issues of these players in the senior divisions will be discussed.

USE IT OR LOSE IT!

Aging changes the human body, rendering elderly people more at risk to overloading of the muscles, bones, and cardiovascular system. Connective tissue becomes stiffer as one ages, which makes muscles and tendons more prone to injury. Aerobic capacity decreases by about 10% per decade after the age of 25 years. There is a decrease in muscle mass and strength, as well as in bone mass. There is an increased incidence of high blood pressure and atherosclerosis (narrowing of the arteries). However, inactivity is as much a cause for these changes as aging is. Over half of the decline can be attributed to inactivity. Tennis may help reduce or prevent a number of these negative changes associated with aging. Because tennis is an aerobic activity, it has cardiovascular benefits and reduces risk factors associated with disease states such as diabetes and heart disease (e.g,. high blood pressure, obesity, high cholesterol levels). Furthermore, tennis helps offset loss in muscle mass and strength, reduces the risk of osteoporosis, and has a number of psychological benefits (e.g., preservation of cognitive function, alleviation of symptoms of depression). Thus, playing tennis regularly contributes to a healthier, independent lifestyle, improving the functional capacity and quality of life of elderly people.

Figure 23.1

Veteran players often prefer doubles over singles.

AEROBIC CAPACITY

Tennis is an attractive sport for many people and playing tennis regularly will help develop or preserve cardiovascular fitness. Aerobic capacity decreases 5% to 15% per decade after the age of 25 years. However, maintaining high levels of exercise training results in a diminished rate of loss of aerobic capacity with age in older adults. Tennis players have been shown to be more fit than the average population. In a study by Friedman et al. middle-aged tennis players (30-55 years) were shown to have above average maximal oxygen uptake compared to normally active populations of the same age and sex (50.2 vs. 40 ml per kg per minute in males and 44 vs. 35.4 ml per kg per minute in females). The cardiovascular demands of playing doubles are lower than of playing singles, while still offering the benefits of pleasurable social interaction and the tactical and technical challenges of tennis. Therefore, many veteran players prefer playing doubles over singles (Figure 23.1).

Practical tips for the player
- Play a minimum of two times a week singles or three times a week doubles for optimal health benefit.
- Playing singles is more demanding than playing doubles, but doubles play is still beneficial.

STRENGTH TRAINING

Aging is accompanied by a loss of muscle mass and strength, particularly after the age of 60. The decline is more marked in the fast than in the slow twitch muscle fibers. This reduction in muscle size and strength is not solely the effect of aging, but also because older people use their muscles less and less intensely. The strength loss of a 60-year old need not be more than 10 to 20% of his maximum strength. Regular practice enables the older tennis player to train both the endurance and strength of his muscles, and maintain more fast twitch muscles.

The good news is that tennis players tend to be stronger and have leg muscles that are more resistant to fatigue than their sedentary counterparts. Strength training is still not very familiar to many tennis players, certainly not to older tennis players, but players can benefit significantly from it. A stronger, well-developed muscle is better able to withstand load, and will thus help prevent injuries. Strength training will improve the quality of the tendon tissue attached to the muscle and it will have a beneficial effect on performance.

Practical tips for the player
- Single set programs of up to fifteen repetitions performed twice a week are recommended.
- If you have more time, training can be built up to two to three sets per exercise. Each workout session should consist of 8-10 different exercises that train the major muscle groups.
- Go slowly and progress gradually.

COORDINATION

Postural stability declines with aging, and is associated with an increased risk of falling. This is related to changes in coordination, eyesight, the vestibular system, the somatosensory system (proprioception), reaction time, and muscle strength. Exercises that focus on coordination, balance, reaction time, and strength have been shown to improve postural stability. Tennis is a perfect example of a sport that incorporates all these aspects. Reaction time is needed to react quickly to the ball; balance and coordination are necessary to return wide shots; and leg strength is necessary to prepare quickly for the next shot. Playing tennis for as little as one hour a week will already reduce the risk of wrist and hip fractures.

Practical tips for the player

- An excellent exercise to improve coordination and balance is to stand on one leg, with arms spread to keep your balance. Shut your eyes and try to maintain your balance. Now open your eyes and bounce a tennis ball against a wall or on the floor and catch it again without losing your balance. Try to vary the point of the bounce as much as possible. A variation on this exercise is to stand on one leg and try to juggle with one, two, three, or even more balls.

FLEXIBILITY

Flexibility is a general terms which encompasses the range of motion of joints. Flexibility declines with age, which may affect mobility. This may be due to changes in bone (arthrosis), muscle (loss of strength), and connective tissue (increase in crystalline content of the collagen fibers and an increase in the diameter of the fibers). Although not all loss in flexibility can be regained, a flexibility program may lead to significant improvements of range of motion.

Practical tips for the player

- Stretching exercises should be incorporated into the regular training program (see Chapter 5).

CARDIOVASCULAR RISKS

The main concern with the elderly is the possibility that exercise may precipitate an acute episode of insufficient blood supply to the heart muscle, resulting in a heart attack or sudden cardiac death. In the older age groups, there is an increased risk of underlying cardiovascular disease. The prevalence of atherosclerotic heart disease in asymptomatic men in the 30-39 age group is 1.9% (women 0.3%), rising to 12.3 % in those aged 60-69 (women 7.5%). Most epidemiological studies have shown that the risk of a heart attack or sudden cardiac death may indeed be increased during and immediately after exercise. However, regular exercise decreases the risk of sudden cardiac death in the long term. Therefore, tennis players should generally be encouraged to continue playing into old age.

However, it would be preferable to be able to identify those with underlying cardiovascular diseases, so that necessary precautions can be taken. Exercise testing is often recommended for those in the over-40 age group wishing to continue to play competitive tennis. Routine exercise testing in asymptomatic players is not warranted, however. A thorough clinical assessment, including exercise testing, is only recommended for players with multiple cardiovascular risk factors, premonitory symptoms, those with proven ischemic heart disease, or those who wish to play competitively on the veteran circuit (see Chapter 13 for more detailed recommendations). ·

Practical tips for the player
- Players who experience chest pain, faintness, irregular heartbeat, disproportional shortness of breath, or disproportional fatigue, should consult a physician.
- Players who are just starting out and are obese, diabetic, who smoke, have high blood pressure, a serious health problem, or a close relative who had a heart attack or died suddenly before age 55 (males) or 65 (females), should consult their physician before starting exercise. An exercise tolerance test may be recommended.

HEAT STRESS

Elderly players are at increased risk during tennis in the heat. In older players, there is a delayed onset in sweating, a blunted sweating response, a reduction in skin blood flow, and a blunted thirst drive. This could make elderly athletes competing in the heat prone to a chronic state of hypohydration with a less than optimal plasma volume.

Practical tips for the player
- Observe the guidelines for extreme heat conditions (see Chapter 17).

OSTEOPOROSIS

Description. Osteoporosis is defined as a decrease in bone mass and strength, which leads to more fragile bones and an increased risk of fractures, particularly the spine (vertebral bodies), hip (proximal femur), and wrist (distal radius). Bone mass decreases slowly after the age of 30, in women more than in men, and more quickly in women following the onset of menopause. Loss of bone mass occurs as a result of aging, low hormone levels, inactivity, insufficient calcium intake, and increased calcium loss, and it may lead to osteoporosis. A regularly maintained exercise program reduces the rate of bone mass loss accompanying age, particularly after the menopause. Mean bone density has been shown to be significantly higher in tennis players compared to sedentary controls. Thus, playing tennis regularly may help to reduce the loss of bone mass.

Symptoms. Osteoporosis is often called the "silent disease" because bone loss occurs without symptoms. People may not know that they have osteoporosis until their bones become so weak that a sudden strain, bump or fall causes a fracture or a vertebra to collapse. The most typical sites of fractures related to osteoporosis are the hip, spine, wrist, and ribs, although the disease can affect any bone in the body. Collapsed vertebrae may be initially felt or seen in the form of severe back pain, loss of height, or spinal deformities such as kyphosis (stooped posture).

Treatment. Maximal bone density will help prevent osteoporosis and can be obtained by adequate intake of calcium (1,200 mg per day) and vitamin D. Post-menopausal women need more calcium to stay in calcium balance, as much as 1,500 mg per day. Medications used for the treatment of osteoporosis include bisphosphonates, calcitonin, estrogens, parathyroid hormone and raloxifene.

Practical tips for the player

- Courts with softer surfaces, such as clay and grass, are preferred over hard courts, to reduce the risk of stress fractures.
- The best sources of calcium are milk and dairy products (cheese, yogurt), calcium fortified drinks and bars (Figure 23.2). Each dairy serving contains approximately 300 mg of calcium. Other calcium rich products are canned fish (especially if eaten with bones), some vegetables (including broccoli, spinach and collard greens), tofu, and some calcium enriched grain products.

Figure 23.2

Milk is the ideal sports drink.

EPIDEMIOLOGY OF INJURIES

Epidemiological studies demonstrate that injury risk increases with age. The incidence of acute tennis injuries in players, treated in accident and emergency departments in the Netherlands, increased from 16 injuries per 1,000 participants aged 25-34-years old up to 481 per 1,000 participants per year in the 75-years and older group. In this study, chronic injuries were not reported, so the incidence of all injuries may be even higher. Most types of injuries that appear in younger players can be found in veterans, but with a higher frequency. More typical for veteran tennis players as compared with younger players are rotator cuff tears, Achilles tendon ruptures, and tennis leg (see Chapters 7 and 8). Also, veteran tennis players are more likely than younger players to undergo total joint replacement of the knee or hip.

TOTAL JOINT REPLACEMENT

Description. A joint replacement is the procedure whereby an arthritic or damaged joint is removed and replaced with an artificial joint called a prosthesis made of metal and/or plastic or ceramics. Hip and knee replacements are the most common, but joint replacement can be performed on other joints, including the ankle, foot, shoulder, elbow and fingers. A joint replacement gives excellent results in a high proportion of cases, with relief of pain and a reasonable range of movement.

Figure 23.3

A hip replacement.

Treatment. In an arthritic knee the damaged ends of the bones and cartilage are replaced with metal and plastic surfaces that are shaped to restore knee movement and function. In partial knee replacement, also called "unicompartmental knee replacement," only the bone and cartilage in the most damaged area of the knee are removed, and these surfaces are replaced. In an arthritic hip, the damaged ball (the upper end of the femur) is replaced by a metal or ceramic ball attached to a metal stem fitted into the femur, and a metal, metal and plastic, or ceramic socket is implanted into the pelvis, replacing the damaged socket (Figure 23.3).

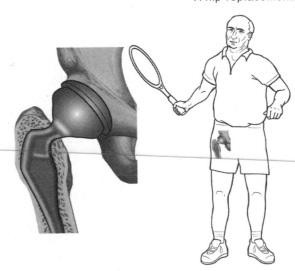

Return to playing tennis. Is it possible to play tennis again after joint replacement? It is important that patients remain active after their operation for general health and also for the quality of their bones and muscle. Increased bone quality will improve prosthesis fixation and decrease the incidence of early loosening. However, since wear of the prosthesis is the major cause of prosthetic loosening and failure, reduction in wear is one of the main factors in improving the long-term results after joint replacement. Wear is, in part, dependent on the frequency and magnitude of load on the prosthesis. Much work is being done to improve the long-term results after joint replacement. However, at present, high-intensity singles tennis is generally not recommended following joint replacement. Most implanted joints last an average of fifteen to twenty years before symptoms of implant failure occur, but the replaced joint can fail earlier. It is believed that patients who participate in high-impact sports after arthroplasty have a higher incidence of early loosening and failure and are more likely to need revision surgery than less active patients.

The 1999 consensus recommendations of the Hip Society are as follows:
- After a total hip arthroplasty, doubles tennis is allowed. Singles tennis is not recommended.
- After total knee arthroplasty, tennis is only allowed when the subject has previous experience with the sport.

The effects of either total hip or total knee arthroplasty on tennis itself are very positive. Studies suggest that tennis players are able to perform at better levels in every element of their game after either total hip or total knee arthroplasty when compared with their preoperative symptomatic states. They may, in some cases, return to their level of play prior to the development of their arthritic symptoms. In one study, only 4% of the hips needed revision after eight years, while none needed a knee revision. But since most harmful aspects of sports participation are usually not noticed until ten years postoperatively, prospective studies with a longer follow up are necessary to determine whether tennis has an adverse effect on either hip or knee arthroplasty.

SUMMARY

Regular playing of tennis prevents and reduces functional declines associated with aging. It helps to maintain and improve cardiovascular fitness, reduces risk factors associated with disease states (diabetes, heart disease, etc.), helps to offset loss in muscle mass and strength, and reduces the risk of osteoporosis. Playing tennis regularly cuts the risk of cardiovascular disease in half. During tennis in the heat, senior players should follow the guidelines for hot weather conditions. Senior players can benefit from the incorporation of strength training and aerobic training in their regular training program. Injury risk increases with age. More typical for the older player as compared to the younger player are the tennis leg, Achilles tendon rupture, rotator cuff tears, and total hip and knee replacements.

24

Women's Issues

Men and women differ in body size and shape, in body organs, and in susceptibility to certain injuries and disorders. In this chapter, differences in anthropometrics and in injury pattern between male and female tennis players will be discussed, followed by typical female issues, including the female athlete's triad, pregnancy and stress incontinence.

BODY SIZE

On average, adult females are 22 pounds (10 kg) lighter and about 4 inches (10-12 cm) shorter than males. Because females have a higher fat percentage than males (20-25% vs. 10-15%), the difference in weight is mainly found in a smaller muscle mass (approximately 51 pounds (23 kg) vs. 77 pounds (35 kg)). The main differences are found in the upper body, where overall strength of females is about half that of men, as contrasted to approximately two-thirds of male strength in the lower body. Because of this difference in height and strength, males are able to run faster, hit the ball harder and serve faster than females. The fastest serve in the men's professional circuit is approximately 153 mph (246 km per hour), compared to 127 mph (204 km per hour) in the women's circuit. With the serve dominating more in men's tennis than in women's tennis, this results in more serve and volley players among the men than among the women and more breaks of service in women's tennis than in the men's game.

INJURY PATTERNS

Injury rates in male and female tennis players are fairly similar, but there are some minor gender differences in the injury pattern. Female players have a higher rate of hip and lower-leg injuries, while male athletes report a higher rate of thigh and trunk injuries. Young girls have a higher prevalence of back, shoulder, and bilateral wrist pain, compared to young boys, possibly related to their higher laxity. The fact that males are more often serve and volley players than females may account for the higher incidence of trunk and acute thigh injuries (hamstring and quadriceps strains) in males. Women run a higher relative risk of an anterior cruciate ligament rupture and anterior knee pain, which may be related to their different build (wider hips, inward turning of knees and hips). Woman may have higher rates of stress fractures if they have low bone mineral density. Women, due to footwear design, are also more likely to have foot and toe problems such as bunions, hammertoes, and hallux valgus.

Practical tips for the player

- Strengthening the upper extremity and emphasizing core and scapular stability will help to reduce the risk of shoulder, back, and wrist injuries.
- Choose footwear appropriate to the foot type, both on and off the court, to avoid foot problems.

THE FEMALE ATHLETE TRIAD

Description. The term "female athlete triad" describes the complex interplay of eating disorders, menstrual dysfunction, and premature osteoporosis seen in the female athlete. Alone or in combination, female athlete triad disorders can decrease physical performance and cause disease among female tennis players.

EATING DISORDERS

Figure 24.1

Female tennis players are often judged according to their appearance.

Description. The two main eating disorders are anorexia nervosa and bulimia. Anorexia nervosa is diagnosed when there is a refusal to maintain a minimal normal bodyweight, an intense fear of gaining weight, a disturbed body image, and absence of menstrual cycles. Bulimia nervosa is diagnosed when there are recurrent episodes of binge eating, followed by inappropriate compensatory behaviors such as self-induced vomiting, misuse of medications such as laxatives and diuretics, fasting, or excessive exercise. Eating disorders mainly affect young females and generally start during puberty. In the US, anorexia affects 0.5-1.0% of all females, and bulimia 1-4%. The prevalence of eating disorders among female tennis players is thought to be slightly higher. Women account for 90-95% of patients with eating disorders. Factors involved in the development of eating disorders in athletes are the belief that leanness improves performance ("loose weight to get faster"); the personality traits of being perfectionist, overachieving, competitive, compulsive, and people pleasing; and the values of society in which women are judged for their appearance (Figure 24.1). In a study among tennis players, the typical player believed her body was larger than the best looking, healthiest, or ideal figure. Both players and coaches felt that the ideal female figure was thinner than the healthiest one, with their "ideal" woman having a thin, ectomorphic body—not a muscular, mesomorphic body.

Table 24.1

DSM IIIR criteria for anorexia nervosa and bulimia nervosa

Anorexia nervosa
- Refusal to maintain bodyweight over a minimal normal weight for age and height (e.g., weight loss leading to bodyweight 15% below that expected).
- Intense fear of weight gain or becoming fat, even though underweight.
- A disturbance in the way in which one's shape and weight is experienced.
- In females, amenorrhea for at least three consecutive cycles.

Bulimia nervosa
- Recurrent episodes of binge eating (i.e., rapid consumption of a large amount of food in a discrete period of time).
- A feeling of lack of control over eating behavior during the eating binges.
- Self-induced vomiting, use of laxatives or diuretics, strict dieting or fasting, or vigorous exercises in order to prevent a weight gain.
- Persistent overconcern with body shape and weight.
- Two binge episodes a week for at least three months.

Symptoms. Symptoms of anorexia nervosa include severe weight loss (more than 15% below ideal body weight) by self-starvation, an intense fear of gaining weight, and the absence of menstrual cycles. Obsessive preoccupation with food, strict monitoring of food intake, a disturbed body image, and excessive exercise are other common symptoms (Table 24.1).

Symptoms of bulimia nervosa include episodes of binge eating that occur, on average, at least twice a week for three months. The individual has a sense of lack of control over eating behavior, and body shape and weight are a main influence on self-evaluation. Menstrual dysfunction is common in players with bulimia nervosa, with fewer than 10% having normal menses. The risks associated with both types of eating disorders are nutritional deficiencies, decreased bone density, infertility, decreased immune function, electrolyte disturbances, low blood pressure, slow or irregular heart beat, gastrointestinal problems, and psychiatric problems.

Treatment. The biggest challenge in treating anorexia nervosa is having the patient recognize that their eating behavior is itself a problem, not a solution to other problems. This means that most individuals enter treatment when their condition is fairly advanced. The purpose of treatment is first to restore normal body weight and eating habits, and then attempt to resolve psychological issues. Hospitalization may be indicated in some cases (usually when body weight falls below 30% of expected weight). Supportive care by health care providers, structured behavioral therapy, psychotherapy, and anti-depressant drug therapy are some of the methods that are used for treatment. In bulimia, treatment focuses on breaking the binge-purge cycles and may consist of behavior modification techniques, as well as individual, group, or family counseling. Anti-depressant drugs may be used in cases that coincide with depression.

Practical tips for the player
- Understand that it is normal for females to have a higher fat percentage than males (20-25% in females versus 10-15% in males).

- Also, be aware that muscle mass is a performance determining factor in tennis, whereas fat percentage is not.
- If you feel you might have an eating disorder, share it with someone, instead of trying to solve it on your own. People can only help you if you allow them to help you.

Practical tips for the coach

- Look for the alarm signals in players, such as recurrent or obsessive dieting, extreme thinness, stress fractures, and loss of menstruation. Let a player know her problem has been noticed and that she can express her fear, in order to break down her isolation.
- Educate players about sound nutritional habits and the risks of eating disorders.
- Model healthy prematch, match, and postmatch eating and hydration behavior.
- Stress the health risks and the negative effects on performance of being underweight and losing muscle mass.
- Involve significant others, such as parents, in this educational process.
- Put less emphasis on weight, and do not make any comments on appearance and weight. Do not weigh the player, and do not determine his or her fat percentage on a regular basis.
- Have a referral system in place for any players with nutritional or medical concerns.

MENSTRUAL DYSFUNCTION

Description. Common menstrual cycle alterations in athletes include a reduced number of menstrual periods (three to six per year) or the absence of menstrual periods. The prevalence of menstrual cycle alterations is considerably higher in athletes (12% to 66%, depending on the study) than in sedentary controls (2% to 5%). This may be a symptom of an underlying problem and medical evaluation within three months of its occurrence is advised. Factors that seem to play a role are hormonal changes with intensive training, nutrition (low caloric diets, low fat and protein content), body composition changes (weight loss, low percentage of body fat), changes in the 24-hour rhythm due to intercontinental flights, psychological stress, and reproductive immaturity. However, other causes, such as tumors, cysts, or altered levels of hormones, should be evaluated and excluded. There are risks to active women from menstrual changes. Menstrual dysfunction, especially loss of menstruation, results in low estrogen levels and leads to low bone mineral density and risk for stress fractures.

Symptoms. Oligomenorrhea is characterized by a reduced number of menstrual periods per year (three to six per year in stead of ten to twelve). Amenorrhea is characterized by the total absence of menstrual periods.

Treatment. The doctor may advice the player to reduce the level of exercise by 10-20% and increase the caloric intake by 250-400 calories a day for at least two to three months. The doctor may also consider hormone replacement therapy. This can be given in the form of the oral contraceptive pill or as combined estrogen/progesterone therapy.

Practical tips for the player
- See a physician if the menstrual cycle dysfunction lasts more than three months.

OSTEOPOROSIS

Description. Osteoporosis is defined as a decline in bone mass and strength that leads to a weakening of bone and an increased risk of fractures, particularly of the bones in the back (vertebral bodies), thigh (femur), and wrist (distal radius). Bone mass decreases slowly after the age of 30, in women more than in men. Loss of bone mass occurs as a result of aging, low hormone levels, insufficient calcium intake, increased calcium loss, and inactivity, and may lead to osteoporosis. There is a lower bone mass among women with menstrual cycle changes compared with control women with a normal menstrual cycle. This is because the decreased hormone levels associated with the interruption of the menstrual cycle cause increased bone loss, despite the positive effect of physical activity on bone density. This may lead to an increased risk of stress fractures in exercising women with menstrual cycle changes. Also, at the time of menopause there is a sudden increase in the rate of bone loss, because levels of the female sex hormone estrogen fall rapidly at this time. A regularly maintained exercise program may reduce the rate of bone mass loss accompanying age, particularly after the menopause. In tennis players, bone gain has been shown in the playing arm, hips, and vertebral column.

Symptoms. Osteoporosis is often called the "silent disease" because bone loss occurs without symptoms. People may not know that they have osteoporosis until their bones become so weak that a sudden strain, bump, or fall causes a fracture or a vertebra to collapse. The most typical sites of fractures related to osteoporosis are the hip, spine, wrist, and ribs, although the disease can affect any bone in the body. Collapsed vertebrae may initially be felt or seen in the form of severe back pain, loss of height, or spinal deformities such as a stooped posture.

Treatment. Maximal bone density will help prevent osteoporosis and can be obtained by adequate intake of calcium (1,200 mg per day) and vitamin D. Post-menopausal women and women with menstrual cycle changes need more calcium to stay in calcium balance, as much as 1,500 mg per day. In addition, playing tennis regularly will help to strengthen the bones.

Drugs used for the treatment of osteoporosis include bisphosphonates, calcitonin, estrogens, parathyroid hormone, and raloxifene.

Practical tips for the player
- The best sources of calcium are milk and dairy products (cheese, yogurt), calcium fortified drinks, and bars. Each dairy serving contains approximately 300 mg of calcium.
- Other calcium rich products are canned fish (especially if eaten with bones), some vegetables (including broccoli, spinach, and collard greens), tofu, and some calcium enriched grain products.

PREGNANCY

Almost half of all women exercise during pregnancy, and 20% keep exercising beyond the sixth month. In general, continuing to exercise has a positive influence on both the

Figure 24.2

Continuing to exercise generally has a positive influence on both mother and child.

mother and the child (Figure 24.2). A moderate amount of exercise during pregnancy has been shown to lead to improved placental growth. However, it is important to maintain core body temperature below 38°C when exercising in the heat. Also, an adequate diet should be followed, to avoid drops in glucose levels and caloric deficiencies of the embryo.

Usually, it is not advisable for a woman to start playing tennis during pregnancy or perform exercise she was not already accustomed to prior to the pregnancy. Also, women with medical conditions should consult their physician regarding suitability and level of exercise. However, healthy, well-trained women with an uncomplicated pregnancy can safely continue to exercise at high levels without compromising fetal growth and development or complicating the course of pregnancy and labor. Maternal benefits include improved cardiovascular fitness and well-being, limited fat gain, quick recovery, and easier and less complicated labor.

Practical tips for the player

- It will generally cause no problems to continue to play in similar amounts and intensity prior to pregnancy for the first two trimesters.
- Eliminate the risk of blunt trauma to the abdomen by a tennis ball in the later stages of pregnancy by either avoiding net play or by agreeing with your opponent(s) that overheads will not be aimed at your body.
- Avoid exercise lying on your back after the first trimester.
- Stop exercising when fatigued, stressed, or very uncomfortable.
- Perform core stability exercises (see Chapter 6) or wear an abdominal support strap if you have low back pain (Figure 24.3).
- After giving birth, exercise routines should be resumed gradually. Many of the physiologic and morphologic changes of pregnancy persist four to six weeks postpartum.

Figure 24.3

Core stability exercises are important for the prevention of low back pain.

STRESS URINARY INCONTINENCE

Description. Stress urinary incontinence is the involuntary loss of urine during exercise, coughing, or sneezing. Women are twice as likely to be affected as men, and the prevalence increases with age and after childbirth. It has been reported that one out of every four female tennis players is affected. Most often in active women the cause is due to increased intra-abdominal pressure that exceeds the sphincter around the urethra. Strenuous exercise is more likely to unmask the condition in otherwise asymptomatic women, but there is no evidence that strenuous exercise can cause the stress incontinence. Also, there are no long-term consequences to athletic stress incontinence.

Symptoms. Leaking of urine during exercise, coughing, or sneezing.

Treatment. Well-functioning pelvic floor muscles can help to prevent or cure urinary stress incontinence. An active exercise program for the pelvic floor and abdominal muscles is therefore recommended in those situations. Other treatment options include changing fluid intake and voiding pattern (drink less and urinate more frequently), drug therapy, and surgery.

Practical tips for the player
- The following exercise will help to strengthen the muscles of the pelvic floor. Lay supine, with the knees bent and the feet on the floor. Begin by contracting the muscles of the pelvic floor, as one would to prevent a bowel movement or stop urine flow. Do this 20 to 30 times and hold for one second. Repeat the exercise several times a day. Gradually progress to 30 times, holding for four seconds.
- Voluntarily contract the pelvic floor muscles before and during coughing.
- Exercise the abdominal muscles using the lying core stabilization and the crunch (Figures 6.10 and 28.35).
- Decrease your fluid intake if you drink an excessive amount of fluids during the day. Do not decrease your fluid intake if you drink normal amounts of fluids.

SUMMARY

Some minor gender differences exist in the injury pattern between male and female tennis players, such as a higher rate of hip and lower-leg injuries in female players compared to male players. Also, young girls have a higher prevalence of back pain, shoulder pain, and bilateral wrist pain, compared to young boys. The female athlete triad is a serious affliction, consisting of a complex interplay of eating disorders, menstrual dysfunction, and premature osteoporosis. Female athlete triad disorders can decrease physical performance and cause increased morbidity and mortality among athletes, and should be diagnosed and treated. Pregnancy leads to considerable changes which influence performance. However, continuing to play tennis generally has a positive effect on both the mother and the child, as long as various precautionary measures are taken into consideration. The prevalence of stress urinary incontinence, which has been reported to effect one out of four female tennis players, can be reduced by following an active exercise program for the pelvic floor muscles.

25

Wheelchair Tennis Players

Over the past two decades, wheelchair tennis has been one of the fastest growing and most exciting international disability sports. On January 1, 1998, the International Wheelchair Tennis Federation was fully integrated into the International Tennis Federation (ITF), making it the first disability sport to achieve such a union at an international level. The game of wheelchair tennis follows the same rules as able-bodied tennis (as endorsed by the ITF), except that the wheelchair tennis player is allowed two bounces of the ball. Mixed competition with able-bodied players is possible, which has helped boost the popularity of wheelchair tennis—now played in more than 70 countries.

WHY PLAY WHEELCHAIR TENNIS?

Participation in wheelchair tennis builds confidence, promotes a healthy lifestyle, and promotes the quality —and possibly the quantity—of life. Regular physical activity leads to improved strength, coordination, and endurance. Sports participation by wheelchair users has been found to be associated with fewer physician visits per year, fewer rehospitalizations, fewer pressure wounds, and fewer medical complications over time. It may break the "disability mindset" in those who are physically disabled, which has been described as low self-esteem and low expectation. Sport can provide a vehicle through which equality, inclusion, and accessibility can be promoted.

WHO CAN PLAY WHEELCHAIR TENNIS?

The sport provides eligibility criteria to determine who is entitled to compete in sanctioned ITF wheelchair tennis tournaments and the Paralympic Games. To be eligible, a player must have a medically diagnosed permanent mobility-related physical disability. This permanent physical disability must result in a substantial or total loss of function in one or more lower extremities. If, as a result of these functional limitations, the player is unable to play competitive able-bodied tennis (that is, having the mobility to cover the court with adequate speed), then the player is eligible to play competitive wheelchair tennis in sanctioned ITF wheelchair tennis tournaments. There is also a quad division with separate eligibility criteria.

EQUIPMENT

In addition to tennis racquet, strings and ball, a well-maneuverable chair is essential for a wheelchair tennis player. The use of strapping may be considered, and clothing should be carefully selected.

WHEELCHAIR

The majority of players use a special chair for sporting activities, although it is possible for players to start out in their day chair (Figure 25.1). Tennis chairs are lighter with the center of gravity located more to the back of the chair. The angle or "camber" of the wheels is increased to allow the chair to turn more quickly. Players are increasingly playing with no "bucket" (angle of the seat) or even reverse bucket seat to achieve a higher sitting position. The higher sitting position allows more freedom to hit the ball. Strapping then becomes more important. Beginner players may be more comfortable with some "bucket" where the seat slopes back but with good strapping they should be all right with a "flat" seat. Many players use an anti-tip bar and a small wheel behind the chair to set their chairs in such a way that the chair is more tippy. Chair design evolved over time from a four-wheel tennis chair, to a three-wheeler, then some players added the anti tip to the three-wheeler, and today many of the top players are now in a five-wheel tennis chair.

Figure 25.1

The chair used in wheelchair tennis. Note the short wheelbase, the increased camber angle of the wheels, and the extra back wheel, providing extra stability. The player has strapped her legs.

STRAPPING

Wheelchair players aim to create a union between themselves and their wheelchairs so that their body and chair work in harmony (Figure 25.1). Strapping helps to achieve this union. To improve security and balance players may choose to strap themselves in their wheelchair. Players use a variety of strapping, including velcro straps, weight belts, normal belts, elastic bands, or bungee cords. Straps can be used around the feet (to secure them to the footrests), knees, thighs (to secure them to the wheelchair), or midsection. The choice of strapping depends on the player's needs and muscle function.

Practical tips for the player

*   Check joint areas and skin, especially in areas of limited or no sensation, to ensure that chair set up and/or strapping do not cause sores or injury.

CLOTHING

Tennis clothing should be made of light absorbent material.

Practical tips for the player

*   Avoid smooth finishes to prevent gliding on the seat.
*   Beware of wide pockets, or zip them closed to avoid the thumb being caught when pushing.
*   Use clothing guards.

RACQUET

Generally, the same recommendations can be made for the racquet of the wheelchair tennis player as for the able-bodied player (see Chapter 3). Since one has to push the chair holding a racquet, it is wise to start with a grip in the smaller range (Figure 25.2). Not only is it easier to thicken the handle by wrapping an extra grip around it than to make it thinner by replacing the factory grip by a thinner one, but grips get easily used and need to be replaced often. This can be done quite easily by adding a (relatively cheap) grip. Sticky ones are the best to have a better grip on the rim of the wheelchair.

Figure 25.2
The player holds the racquet in his hand while pushing the chair.

CONDITIONING

Amputees or those having had poliomyelitis or severe arthrosis are able to reach the same aerobic power in relation to body mass as observed in nonhandicapped persons. However, cardiovascular capacity in spinal-cord injured wheelchair players is compromised and the dimensions of the heart generally do not exceed those of untrained nonhandicapped persons, although they are larger than those of untrained spinal cord-injured persons. This is due to the lack of sympathetic narrowing of the vessels and the lack of muscle pump function below the level of the lesion, leading to inadequate distribution of the blood and a lower stroke volume in spinal cord injured persons. Furthermore, wheelchair athletes with low thoracic lesions have a better capacity for adaptation to exercise than those with a high thoracic lesion, because of the loss of sympathetic innervation of the heart, resulting in a maximum cardiac frequency of around 130 beats per minute.

Practical tips for the player
- Develop a sound aerobic fitness base and maintain this throughout the playing season. This can be accomplished by distance rolling two to three times per week during 20-30 minutes.
- Once you have acquired a good aerobic basis, supplement this by interval programs aimed at enhancing the immediate anaerobic energy system. Start with interval drills involving short work periods (less than 15 seconds) and longer recovery periods (45-60 seconds). As aerobic capacity improves, recovery period can be shortened.
- Before every workout or match, a good warm-up should include lots of starts, turns, and sprints in the same way as for able-bodied tennis. It is important to keep the racquet in the playing hand, as during a match.

Practical tips for the coach
- The coach should take the lesion of the player into account and set realistic goals for each player.
- Mobility training should be the basis of every workout. At least as much time as one spends on technique should be spent on practicing to get the chair in the right position with stops and turns, both forward and backward.

INJURIES

Wheelchair tennis players may suffer from the same type of injuries as able-bodied tennis players, but the upper extremities are affected far more often than the lower extremities. Moreover, wheelchair tennis players have a higher number of strains to the thorax and spine. Soft tissue injuries are the most commonly reported injuries, of which the majority is secondary to overuse. Carpal tunnel syndrome, tennis elbow, shoulder pain, and injuries to the trunk are discussed below (see Chapters 8 and 9).

WRIST PAIN

Carpal tunnel syndrome is a common disorder among wheelchair users (Figure 25.3). It may be due to the repetitive flexion and extension of the wrist to propel the wheelchair, the extreme hand and wrist postures required for this pushing (hyperflexion), forceful gripping of the racquet, and repetitious racquet swinging motions associated with tennis.

Practical tips for the player
- Avoid extreme wrist positions and frequently vary the position of the wrist.
- Change the wheel's contact point from the carpal tunnel to a broader area of several fingers.

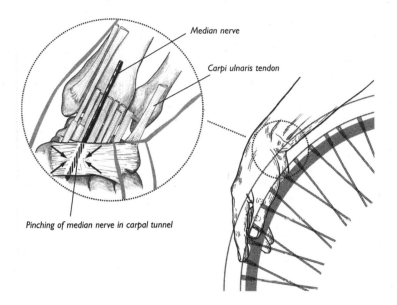

Median nerve

Carpi ulnaris tendon

Pinching of median nerve in carpal tunnel

Figure 25.3
Carpal tunnel syndrome.

- Assure the racquet grip is the right size. Use a larger grip or place overwrap to increase the grip size.
- When awakening at night with pain in the hand, hang the hand over the side of the bed and rub, shake or wiggle it.
- It may be helpful to wear a wrist brace that keeps the hand/wrist straight when not playing.

ELBOW PAIN

Tennis elbow is a common affliction among wheelchair players. There are several reasons for this: the backhand is often hit late and behind the body, which requires a lot of wrist action; the nondominant arm can not be used to support the racquet as in able-bodied tennis; the racquet is held too tight; and frequently the wrong technique for pushing the chair is used (Figure 25.4).

Practical tips for the player
- In order to push the chair correctly, the racquet should be held in the dominant hand with four fingers, leaving the thumb free. This leaves the pad of the hand free, which gives a nice contact point with the push rim or the wheel.
- The forearm on the racquet side can also be used as an additional contact point with the wheel.
- In matches, take every opportunity to rest the forearm by placing the racquet between the knees between points.

Figure 25.4
The use of a lot of wrist action increases the risk of tennis elbow.

Figure 25.5

With the topspin serve the racquet finishes at the same side of the body as the serving arm.

SHOULDER PAIN

There is a high incidence of shoulder injuries in wheelchair users, caused by the repetitious propulsive demands made on the shoulders of these athletes. However, prevalence is lower in wheelchair athletes compared to nonathletes. Two strokes in wheelchair tennis that are most likely to contribute to the development of shoulder injuries are the topspin serve, finishing at the same side of the body as the serving arm (Figure 25.5), and the semi western forehand grip used on the backhand side, using the same side of the racquet to achieve a topspin backhand. This stroke lifts the elbow up and over the knees for the shot.

Prevention of shoulder pain in wheelchair tennis players may be accomplished through a strengthening program of the scapular stabilizers and rotator cuff muscles below the level of the shoulders.

Practical tips for the player

- Perform all strengthening and stretching exercises that are described in Chapter 7 for the rotator cuff and the shoulder blade stabilizers, with special emphasis on external and internal rotation.
- Add the following exercise, which specifically addresses the shoulder adductors. Use surgical tubing or the inner tube of a bicycle to perform the exercise. Attach one side of the tubing at a doorknob, table or other stable object, and hold the other side of the tubing in the hand. Start with the arm shoulder high, elbow bent 90 degrees, and slowly pull the arm down towards the side.

Figure 25.6

Strong stomach muscles and good body rotation increase the power of the strokes.

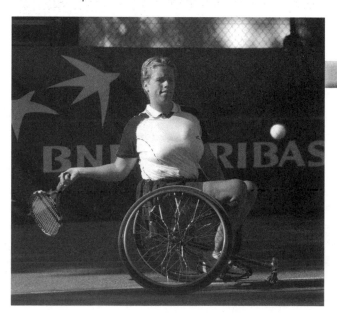

TRUNK

Strong abdominal muscles help to remain balanced and perform good trunk rotation (Figure 25.6). In players with tetraplegia, abdominal muscle strength may be markedly reduced or absent, due to loss of innervation and atrophy, and they may need an abdominal belt to fix the trunk towards the chair.

Eccentric contraction of the abdominal muscles during serving may lead to an contralateral abdominal muscle strain (see Chapter 9). Frequent trunk rotation has been associated with low back pain. Wheelchair tennis, with its many rotatory movements and long sitting positions, may thus be quite demanding on the back. Strengthening exercises of the abdominal and back muscles may help to reduce the incidence of abdominal muscle strain and low back pain.

Practical tips for the player
- If abdominal muscle control is poor, use an abdominal muscle belt.
- Otherwise, exercise the stomach muscles daily by performing straight and diagonal crunches. Electrical stimulation may markedly increase the effect of the exercises.
- Another good exercise is holding a medicine ball in several directions. Try finding a balance that is suitable. This exercise works both the stomach and the back muscles.
- Try to give the back some relief by stretching out and leaning as far back as possible or by lifting out of the chair by extending the arms.

AILMENTS

There are a number of specific problems wheelchair tennis players may encounter, including pressure sores, bladder infection, wheel burns, autonomic dysreflexia, heat stress, and seizure disorders.

BLADDER INFECTION

Athletes with neurological disorders such as spinal cord injury, spina bifida, or multiple sclerosis are at increased risk of bladder infections, because the bladder does not always empty properly or completely. Bladder infections are more common in women than in men, because a woman's urethra is close to both her vagina and anus, which often harbor bacteria, and is shorter than a male's urethra. A bladder infection may develop when bacteria invade the bladder. Those who use indwelling catheters or intermittent catherization (women and men) frequently have bacteria in the urine, introduced to the bladder via the catheter. Symptoms are discomfort on urination and frequent urination. Treatment consists of antibiotics and urine acidification. Many athletes take medication for preventative purposes in addition to antibiotic treatment for active infections.

Practical tips for the player
- Drink copious amounts of fluids to regularly flush out the bladder.
- Drinking cranberry juice may be helpful, because it contains certain substances that make it harder for the bacteria to attach to the wall of the bladder.
- Practice sterile techniques in order to avoid contamination during handling and use of catheters, connecting tubes, and bags.
- Wash the genital and anal areas daily with mild soap and water.
- Before having sex, be sure to observe careful hygiene in hands and genital areas.
- After intercourse, empty the bladder immediately to flush bacteria out of the urethra.
- Refrain from competition and training for at least eight hours after the initiation of antibiotic treatment, and for at least 24 hours after a having recovered from a fever.

SEIZURES

Although not often observed in competition, 15% of athletes with cerebral palsy and some competitors with head injuries, spina bifida, and spinal cord injury have a history of seizure disorders. Seizures may range in severity from a mild, temporary loss of awareness to violent, prolonged shaking and clenching of the head, trunk, and extremities. Seizures usually do not occur during competition because the metabolic state associated with exercise tends to stabilize the membrane of nerve cells. The most likely time for a seizure is during travel and other times of stress, dehydration, and temperature extremes. Seizure activity should be suspected following fainting or loss of consciousness for which there is no other explanation.

Practical tips for the player
- Make sure to take the prescribed medication when travelling and take enough rest.
- Drink sufficient fluids on hot, humid days.

Practical tips for the coach
- If a seizure occurs, keep athletes from hurting themselves during the seizure.
- Wait until the seizure stops before intervening.
- Protect the head and keep it in proper alignment.
- Do not put foreign objects into the mouth.
- Keep the airway open using a jaw thrust (Figure 25.7).
- Encourage the player to rest after the seizure. Hospitalization is usually necessary only if the seizure activity is new or different from that experienced previously.

HEAT STRESS

Athletes with a spinal cord injury are more susceptible to heat illness than able-bodied athletes. They have limited autonomic control for heat dissipation (e.g., sweat gland secretion, redistribution of cardiac output, and widening of the vessels of the skin), depending on the level and completeness of the spinal cord lesion. Secondly, medications (e.g., oxybutinin and phenoxybenzamine used for bladder control) may impair sweating and thermoregulation. Finally, in paraplegics with a lesion above the T6 level, heart function may be impaired. They are not able to fully compensate for a decrease in stroke volume (due to the redistribution of blood and loss of circulating volume) by increasing the heart rate as a result of a disturbed nervous innervation of the heart. This results in a significantly decreased cardiac output and a larger increase in core temperature during tennis in the heat. Therefore, special attention should be given to measures to prevent heat illness in wheelchair athletes under hot and humid weather conditions, especially in players with high spinal lesions.

Practical tips for the player
- Adhere to the guidelines for playing in the heat, as described in Chapter 17.
- Keep some ice cubes in your hat.
- Perform precooling by using a lightweight cooling device before play and during change-overs.
- Use a water spray during change-overs.

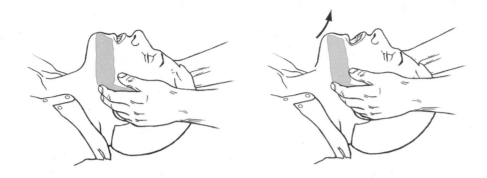

Figure 25.7
A jaw thrust.

AUTONOMIC DYSREFLEXIA

Autonomic dysreflexia occurs in more than 80% of athletes with paraplegia because of a high level lesion (above T6). The athlete presents with a rise in blood pressure, fast heart beat (or a compensatory low heart beat), pounding headache, stuffed nose, anxiety, and profuse sweating resulting from a generalized hyperactivity of the sympathetic nervous system. Many sensory stimuli can trigger an event, including bowel or bladder distention, urinary tract infection, sunburn, heat or cold thermal stress, and pressure sores.

Practical tips for the player
- The best treatment for most events is to cease the activity and remove the sensori stimuli that triggered the event.
- The doctor may prescribe beta-adrenergic blockers.

WHEEL BURNS

Wheel burns are burns caused by the friction between the wheels of the chair and the hands. The area is best cleaned with running water or iodine and should be covered with fleecy web or sterile dressing.

Practical tips for the player
- Temporarily, a glove can be worn on the nonplaying hand. Regular play will decrease the risk of wheel burns, because callus is formed.
- Protect areas that are likely to be affected with tape.

PRESSURE AREAS

Athletes with spinal cord injury, spina bifida, multiple sclerosis, and other neurological disorders often lack the normal protection that pressure, temperature, and pain sensation provide. This increases the risk of skin damage and pressure sores, especially in areas overlying bony prominences, such as the buttocks and hips. Decubitus ulcers can develop quickly, sometimes after only a few hours in a different chair. In individuals with normal sensation, a reflex causes the body to shift position to relieve any such area of increasing pressure. People who lack this sensation lose this protective reflex and are unaware of developing tissue ischemia. Wheelchair tennis players are particularly prone to skin problems, because tremendous sheer forces at the skin-wheelchair interface are created.

Practical tips for the player

- Check equipment for sharp surfaces and use cushions in all transfers.
- Frequently inspect insensitive skin for signs of friction or pressure. Any reddened, hardened, or raised area should be a cause for concern. All pressure should be relieved from sitting, clothes, or equipment until the redness or hardness resolves and normal skin color returns.
- Keep the skin dry and clean. Wear dry clothing that does not trap moisture between the skin and fabric.
- Use proper cushioning and frequent movement for pressure relief and weight shifting.
- Always evaluate a new chair for potential areas of excess pressure, especially where the hips contact the side walls or frame.
- Avoid footwear that is too tight or allows the feet to be compressed against the chair.
- Do not participate in training or competition with an open pressure sore and lie down as much as possible on the side or stomach to prevent additional pressure damage.

SUMMARY

Wheelchair tennis is a growing sport, with many mental and physical health benefits to the players. However, wheelchair tennis players may also suffer from a variety of overuse injuries to the upper extremity and trunk, and various other physical problems. In this chapter, the most common overuse injuries in wheelchair tennis players are discussed, including tennis elbow, carpal tunnel syndrome, shoulder impingement, low back pain and abdominal muscle strain. Furthermore, afflictions that may be encountered in wheelchair tennis players are presented, including pressure sores, bladder infection, heat stress, autonomic dysreflexia, and seizure disorders.

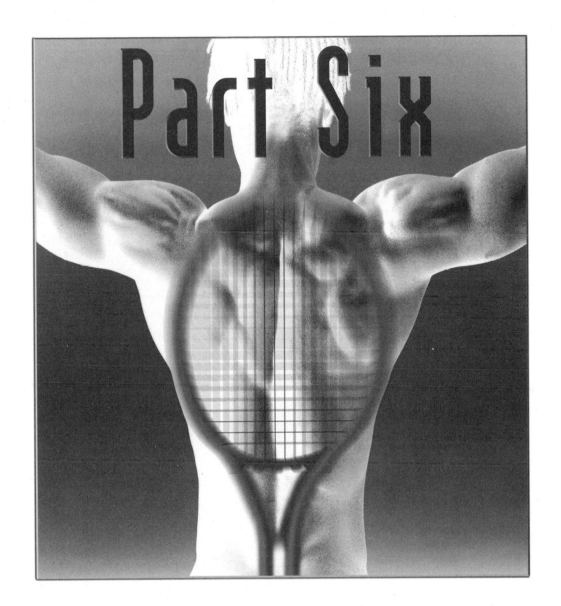

Part Six

Managing and Delivering
Tennis Medicine Programs

Chapter 26: The Sports Physician

Chapter 27: The Athletic Trainer

Chapter 28: Strength Training for Tennis

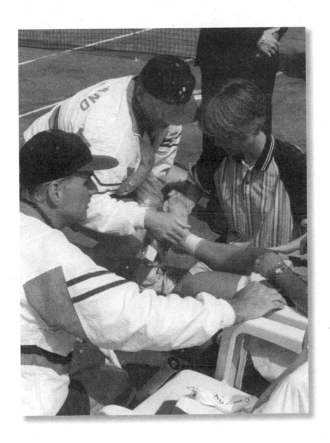

26 The Sports Physician

A tennis player may come in contact with three different types of "tennis doctor": the tournament physician, the team physician/federation doctor, and the physician in the sports medicine clinic.

THE TOURNAMENT PHYSICIAN

A tournament physician is responsible for player medical services and the supervision of the medical team during a tournament. Presence of a tournament physician during all hours of play is mandatory for qualifying and main draw matches at Grand Slams, the Olympic Games, main draw Davis Cup and Fed Cup matches, ATP international series, and all WTA Tier 1-V tour events. At smaller events, such as Challenger tournaments, Satellite tournaments, and the ITF futures, the rules require a doctor to be "on call." Rules of national federations regarding national championships and other events vary. The tournament physician is generally assisted by one or more sports physiotherapists, certified athletic trainers, and/or masseurs, depending on the size and needs of the event. A well-prepared tournament physician will have a list and good contact with available consulting specialists and access to a facility for performing diagnostic studies (e.g., X-rays, diagnostic ultrasound, MRIs, and bone scans). Further, the tournament physician is aware of the the address, phone numbers, and business hours of the closest pharmicies for prescription medications. Most often, the background of the tournament physician is primary care sports medicine or orthopedic surgery.

THE ROLE OF THE TOURNAMENT PHYSICIAN

The tournament physician must function as a generalist physician to detect and treat a variety of illnesses and injuries and provide or coordinate the care of players during the event. The tournament physician should have a working knowledge of tennis-specific injuries and medical conditions encountered in sports. It is recommended that he is trained and certified in cardiopulmonary resuscitation. The tournament physician must learn from the sports medicine staff which players have a serious illness or have special medical needs to enable the physician to be prepared to manage any emergencies with any of the players.

Court-side assessment, triage, and managing of routine injuries on court is generally not the task of the physician in tennis, but of the certified athletic trainer or sports physiotherapist. The certified athletic trainer or sports physiotherapist may call the tournament physician for assistance in the evaluation and/or treatment.

The tournament physician is responsible for developing and implementing an organizational plan for the sports medical team to handle medical emergencies, including the safe and expeditious evacuation of an injured player. This also includes contact with the closest hospital emergency room before the tournament begins. An emergency plan for all emergencies, including fire, bomb warnings, and catastrophic illnesses of the public is the responsibility of the tournament director in co-operation with security personnel and/or the tournament physician. The tournament physician may be requested to have certain medications, including special medications for players with certain medical illnesses or needs, crutches, and intravenous fluids available at the site.

It is recommended that the tournament physician write a report at the end of the week, summarizing the main issues and including recommendations to the tournament director for the next year.

MEDICAL RULES

There are several of the rules of the ITF, ATP, WTA Tour, and/or national federations that pertain to medical conditions—the Medical Time-out Rule, the Extreme Weather Conditions Rule (of the WTA Tour), and the Tennis Anti-Doping Program (see Chapter 19). The physician should have working knowledge of the medical rules in tennis that are applicable to the event. It is recommended that the tournament physician checks the current status of the rules prior to an event by consulting the relevant rulebook or an official.

The Medical Time-out Rule. Most rule books contain a paragraph regarding conditions for which a player may request a medical time-out. Generally, if a player sustains a medical condition during the match or warm-up or believes that medical diagnosis and treatment are required for a medical condition, he may request through the chair umpire to see the certified athletic trainer or sports physiotherapist. The certified athletic trainer or sports physiotherapist may call the tournament physician for assistance in the evaluation and/or treatment. The certified athletic trainer, sports physiotherapist, or doctor may authorize a one-time three minute medical time-out to treat the injured or ill player for that condition.

The time-out begins after the completion of the evaluation and diagnosis of the medical condition by the certified athletic trainer, sports physiotherapist, or tournament doctor. The physician must be present or, at least, consulted for the on-court dispensing of medications, including over the counter drugs. Players may not receive treatment for the following: general player fatigue; any condition requiring injections, intravenous infusions or oxygen on court; or any medical condition that cannot be treated appropriately during a match.

Extreme Weather Condition Rule. To protect their players from heat illness, the WTA Tour and ITF have a rule that pertains to play during extreme heat. The extreme weather condition rule comes into play when the heat, as measured by a heat stress monitor, meets or exceeds a heat stress index of 28 degrees Celsius/82 degrees Fahrenheit (see also Chapter 17). If it is so determined, a ten minute break will be allowed between the second and third sets. There may also be a delay in the starting time of the matches scheduled for play that day.

THE TEAM PHYSICIAN/FEDERATION DOCTOR

Team physicians are not as common in tennis, an individual sport, as they are in team sports such as soccer, football, and basketball etc. Unique team situations for tennis are the Davis Cup and Fed Cup Teams, and most teams have a physician accompanying them. Physicians occasionally travel with players to other events, such as the Olympic Games, the European Championships, or Grand Slam Tournaments. Physicians may also work for national federations ("federation doctors"), tennis schools, leagues, and clubs. These physicians are also referred to when the term "team physician" is used.

THE ROLE OF THE TEAM PHYSICIAN

The team physician detects and treats illnesses and injuries, and provides or coordinates the continuing and comprehensive care of players prior to and during athletic participation, as well as during periods of disability and healing. The team physician should have a working knowledge of musculoskeletal injuries, in particular tennis-specific injuries, and medical conditions encountered in sports. It is recommended that he is trained in cardiopulmonary resuscitation. He should have knowledge of doping rules, therapeutic use exemptions (TUEs), and banned substances. The team physician must know the medical histories of each of the members of the team, including the players, coaches and staff. It is imperative to know which players have a serious illness or have special medical needs, to allow the physician to be prepared to manage any emergencies with any of the players. The team physician provides for medical management of injury and illness and coordinates rehabilitation and safe return to participation. In order to do this, he must work closely with other health care providers, including medical specialists, athletic trainers, and allied health professionals. He will generally provide for appropriate education and counseling regarding nutrition, strength and conditioning, ergogenic aids, substance abuse, and other medical conditions that could affect the athlete. The team physician will coordinate the pre-participation medical evaluations.

Court-side assessment, triage, and managing injuries on court is generally not the task of the team physician, but of the certified athletic trainer or sports physiotherapist. They may call the team physician for assistance in the evaluation and/or treatment.

PRE-PARTICIPATION PHYSICAL EXAMINATION

The main goal of the pre-participation physical examination is to assess overall health of the player, detect imbalances and deficiencies that may increase the risk of injury, detect conditions that may disqualify the player from participating, and assess tennis-specific fitness. Ideally, the pre-participation physical examination should be performed on a one-on-one basis with special attention to vulnerable areas. Once weak areas have been detected, a program should be developed so the player can correct these deficiencies either on his own, or with the help of a physical therapist, certified athletic trainer, or his coach.

EDUCATION AND COUNSELING

The team physician is in a unique position in that he sees players on a regular basis, even when they are not injured. He is therefore in the ideal position to educate players, parents, and coaches about aspects such as nutrition and supplements, strengthening exercises and conditioning, injury prevention, anti-doping and other important issues.

PREPARING FOR TRAVEL

The team physician is usually responsible for organizing medical coverage for teams when they travel to compete. Whenever possible, the team physician should make a pre-competition visit to the venue. This allows for appraisal of the competition site and facilities (including water and food), housing, local first aid stations, and hospitals. Critical analysis of the triage techniques (ambulances) and accessibility of international airports is vital.

Pre-competition visits to foreign sites also allows assessment of danger zones. These include street food vendors selling unwashed products, local pharmacies with poorly labeled remedies (e.g., for colds and flu) and, of course, dangerous havens for after-hour activities.

The team physician should have significant input into selecting the medical team. The pre-departure meeting and seminars are invaluable to clarify certain roles and responsibilities. In the heat of competition, roles and responsibilities must be clear and precise.

The team physician is ultimately responsible for supplies and equipment that will accompany the team. Banned medications should be kept to a minimum and, unless vital for an emergency, should not be part of the travelling pharmacy. The team physician must counsel the athlete, staff, and complement of spectators regarding the perils of travel, particularly the risks of the location to be visited, when appropriate, and provide written material related to minimizing jet lag and traveler's diarrhea. The team physician may accompany an athlete for drug testing and must thus be fully aware of the rules and regulations, the rights of the athlete, and the importance of confidentiality.

THE MEDICAL BAG

The team physician should have a medical bag. The organization of the bag is important to ensure easy access for the physician as well as anyone sent by the physician to retrieve an item for him. The bag should be arranged with different compartments, so the contents will fit in an organized manner (Figure 26.1). A midsize bag is usually best. It will offer enough room to store all the required items and is still manageable when carrying it through airports or at tournament sites. The equipment and medications are essentially the same as those used by a tournament physician. It may be slightly adapted, depending on local conditions of the country the team is going to visit.

MEDICATIONS

This list of medications below will allow a physician to readily treat the majority of medical conditions and ailments. The list does include medications for emergency situations (heart attack, asthma, anaphylactic shock). The tournament physician should establish a pharmacy contact near the tournament site, including address, phone number, and hours open for business, which will be used for prescription medications.

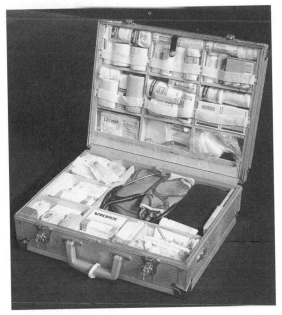

Figure 26.1
The medical bag.

Oral

- **Nonsteroidal anti-inflammatory drugs:** for treatment of pain and inflammation associated with musculoskeletal conditions. Both a standard NSAID (e.g., diclofenac, naproxen) and a Cox-2 selective NSAID (e.g., rofecoxib) for players with history of gastro-intestinal problems are recommended.
- **Muscle relaxants:** for treatment of musculoskeletal pain and stiffness associated with muscle spasm.
- **Analgesics:** for treatment of mild to moderate pain (e.g., paracetamol, aspirin).
- **Antibiotics:** for treatment of common infections including middle ear infection, sinusitis, tonsillitis, bronchitis/pneumonia, cellulitis and urethritis (e.g., amoxycilline, azithromycine, erythromycine, flucoxacilline, doxycycline).
- **Antihistamines:** for treatment of symptoms due to environmental allergies and allergic reactions (e.g., loratadine).
- **Anti-dyspeptics (antacids):** for treatment of upset stomach (e.g., hydrotalciet, magnesiumoxide).
- **Anti-diarrheals:** for treatment of diarrhea (e.g., loperamide).
- **Anti-emetics:** for treatment of nausea and vomiting (e.g., metoclopramide,); for treatment of motion sickness (e.g., cyclizine, meclozine).
- **Cough suppressants:** for symptomatic treatment of cough (e.g., codeine phosphate).
- **Decongestant/expectorant:** for symptomatic treatment of upper respiratory infections (e.g., acetylcysteine).
- **Migraine preparation:** for treatment of migraine headache (e.g., ergotamine).
- **Secretion inhibitors:** For treatment of and gastroesophageal reflux and gastric ulcers (e.g., ranitidine, omeprazol.
- **Sleeping tablets:** for treatment of jet lag or for use on long intercontinental flights (e.g., temazepam).

Nasal/inhaler

- **Bronchodilator:** for treatment of bronchoconstriction secondary to intrinsic asthma, exercise-induced asthma, infection or allergy (e.g., salbutamol).

- **Nasal decongestant spray:** For acute symptomatic relief of nasal congestion (e.g., oxymetazoline, livocab).
- **Nitrolingual spray:** for treatment of angina pectoris.

Topical
- **Antibiotic ointment:** for treatment and prevention of superficial skin infections.
- **Antiviral cream:** for treatment of cold sores (e.g., acyclovir, penciclovir)
- **Corticosteroid cream:** for treatment of noninfectious skin rashes.
- **Antifungal cream:** for treatment of fungal infections of the skin (e.g., miconazole).
- **Eye drops** (neutral): for irritated eyes (e.g., visine).
- **Antibiotic eye drops or creams:** for treatment of superficial eye infections.
- **Eardrops:** for earache.

Injectable
- **Adrenaline:** for treatment of anaphylactic shock or life-threatening coronary syndromes.
- **Atropine:** for treatment of brady-arrhythmias.
- **Corticosteroid:** for soft tissue and intra-articular injection in inflammatory conditions; for anaphylactic shock.
- **Anesthetic:** for use with or without corticosteroid for soft tissue and intra-articular injections.
- **Bronchodilator:** for severe asthma (e.g., terbutaline).
- **Diclofenac:** for colic pain (kidney stone).
- **Intravenous fluids:** for treatment of severe dehydration or when oral hydration is not possible.
- **Diuretics:** For treatment of asthma cardiale.
- **Glucose and/or glucagen:** for severe hypoglycemia in diabetics.

RESPECT THE TENNIS ANTI-DOPING PROGRAM

For substances that are on the list of banned substances (e.g., corticosteroids, adrenaline, bronchodilators, and diuretics), the tournament physician must request a therapeutic use exemption. In case of a medical emergency (e.g., severe asthma attack, anaphylactic shock), the medical exemption request may be applied for afterwards.

SPORTS MEDICINE CENTER PHYSICIAN

A tennis player may encounter a sports physician when he seeks consultation and treatment in a sports medicine center. A sports medicine center is staffed by healthcare professionals who specialize in the treatment of sports injuries and other orthopedic complaints, generally including primary care specialists, sports physicians, orthopedic surgeons, and physical therapists. Most sports medicine centers work closely with other health care providers, such as nutritionists, sport psychologists, manual therapists, chiropractors, physiologists, and podiatrists.

The main focus of a sports medicine center is injury treatment and rehabilitation. Some centers may have specialized in a certain area, such as the elbow, the shoulder, or the knee.

In addition to the management of musculo-skeletal problems, pre-participation physicals, exercise testing, body fat determinations, strength testing, and nutritional analysis and advice may also be provided. Players with medical problems, such as asthma or diabetes, may receive customized exercise programs. In some centers, arthroscopic and surgical repair of injuries is also possible.

SUMMARY

In this chapter the three possible types of "tennis doctor" are presented: the tournament physician, the team physician/federation doctor, and the physician in a sports medicine center.

A tournament physician is responsible for player medical services and supervision of the medical team during a tournament. The team physician/federation doctor provides and coordinates continuous and comprehensive medical care to players prior and during participation in tournaments. This includes pre-participation physical examinations, preparing for travel, and on-site medical care. The physician working in a sports medicine center provides sports medical services such as injury treatment and rehabilitation, pre-participation physical examinations and exercise testing to all players seeking his consultation.

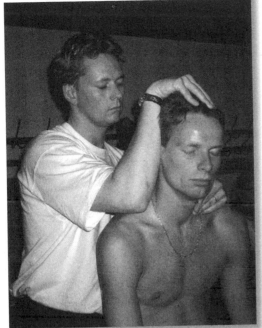

27

The Athletic Trainer and Physiotherapist

Caring for athletes, no matter the sport, involves a team approach. In tennis, this includes the tournament physician and the certified athletic trainer or sports physiotherapist. The tournament physician may have consultants in a variety of specialties, but it is the certified athletic trainer or sports physiotherapist (health care provider) that the players most depend on.

WHY A CERTIFIED ATHLETIC TRAINER OR SPORTS PHYSIOTHERAPIST IS NECESSARY

As part of the medical team caring for tennis players, certified athletic trainers and sports physiotherapists are particularly important and can be very helpful. These health care providers have classroom and practical knowledge and skills that allow them to care for athletes, with the goal of optimizing performance, prevention of injuries and rapid return to play. The goal of the trainer and physiotherapist is to provide the highest level of health care for athletes, particularly the prevention, evaluation, management, and rehabilitation of injuries. There are many reasons for this, including the differences between medicine and sports medicine. First of all, the injuries in athletes are not always treated like those of injured non-athletes. Return to professional sports considerations are affected by significantly different forces than return to activities of daily living or recreational sports considerations. Trainers and physiotherapists are individuals with both formal academic and on-the-field (on-the-court) educational experience where understanding the athlete, their needs, and return to play issues are paramount in their knowledge base.

While Certified Athletic Training, Physiotherapy and Sports Physiotherapy educational programs emphasize all sports and dealing with athletes in all sports, tennis has its own specific type of athlete and activity that leads to specific injury patterns, rates and demands. The certified athletic trainers and sports physiotherapists who are specialized in management of tennis players understand these tennis specific issues, are able to develop preventive training and conditioning programs that target the individual needs and focus reha-

325

bilitation efforts for each player and will enable safe return to play. Being attuned to the athlete, the health care provider should be able to recognize early signs of sports-induced injuries, as well as when a player is compensating for an injury. They will follow and guide a player along each stage of the rehabilitation process to ensure the player completes an effective, efficient, safe and appropriate rehabilitation and recovery program.

EDUCATION OF THE CERTIFIED ATHLETIC TRAINER

To become a certified athletic trainer, an individual must have a minimum of a Bachelors degree and undergo at least four years of Certified Athletic Training. The academic educational program includes medical sciences and specific education in the care and rehabilitation of athletes. The curriculum includes study of: kinesiology, anatomy, (exercise) physiology, biomechanics, assessment and evaluation of injury and illness, care and prevention of injury and illness in athletes, therapeutic exercise, therapeutic modalities, nutrition, psychology, pharmacology, pathology, health care administration and first aid and emergency care. Hands-on supervised athlete care during practice and competition of contact and non-contact sports is also an integral and very important part of the curriculum that provides the student with vital practical learning experiences. This applied learning occurs in a variety of settings including scholastic sports, sports medicine clinics, rehabilitation clinics and hospitals. The certified athletic trainer must then pass a three-part certification examination that includes a written theoretical exam, a practical clinical exam and written clinical exam. Certified athletic trainers are also required to receive continuing education to keep up to date on the latest knowledge in sports medicine and maintain their certification.

EDUCATION OF SPORTS PHYSIOTHERAPISTS

The qualification of certified athletic trainer exists in the United States, Japan and a few other countries only. However, in Europe and the rest of the world, there are physiotherapists with additional post-graduate qualifications in sports physiotherapy. To become a qualified physiotherapist, an individual must complete a Bachelors or Masters degree in Physiotherapy at University. The academic program entails the study of basic medical sciences and specific physiotherapeutic sciences and skills. It includes: anatomy (both lectures and practical including cadaver dissection and applied spinal and peripheral anatomy); human physiology; physiology of disease states; exercise physiology; psychology; pathology; pharmacology; kinesiology; biomechanics; first aid and emergency care; manual therapies including joint mobilization and manipulation techniques and soft tissue mobilization techniques; therapeutic exercise to improve flexibility, strength and core stability; measurement and fitting of splints and orthotic devices; and the study of electro-physical treatment modalities. All physiotherapy students receive practical hands-on supervised tuition that includes clinical placements in hospitals, community health venues and private clinics that includes sports environments. The practical component covers orthopedics, cardiology, neurology, musculoskeletal therapy, sports and spinal therapy, pediatrics, geriatrics and obstetrics and gynecology. Post-graduate qualified sports physiotherapists complete additional academic and practical university based training specializing in the care and management of athletic injuries and conditions. Physiotherapists and sports physiotherapists are also required to receive continuing education to keep up to date on the latest knowledge in sports medicine and maintain their license.

THE ROLE OF THE TRAINER OR PHYSIOTHERAPIST

The trainer or physiotherapist understands the needs of the athletic population and provides the tennis players with health care services that include:

- Preventive care, for example the annual athlete physicals of the WTA Tour and the player education "Physically Speaking" topics of the WTA Tour.
- Evaluation of musculoskeletal injury.
- Appropriate treatment of musculoskeletal injury.
- Identify weakness and muscular imbalances that can predispose an athlete to injury.
- Therapeutic exercise prescription and programs.
- Appropriate and complete rehabilitation programs following injury or surgery.
- Triage to physicians.
- Liaison between the physician and player.
- Liaison between player and her support team, including coach and parents.
- Assistance with recommendations for specialist medical consultants.
- Player health advocate.
- Player confidante.
- Provision of information on tennis medicine, health care and nutritional issues, including hydration, heat related illnesses, skin and eye care.
- Emergency procedures.
- On-court assessment and treatment of injuries.

The trainer or physiotherapist is the health care provider available at all times and whose main goal is to protect and enhance the players' health interests.

THE TRAINERS AND PHYSIOTHERAPISTS ON THE PROFESSIONAL TOURS

While athletes participate in tournament in different cities, and see different tournament physicians at each site, the ATP Tour and WTA Tour hire internationally trained and based certified athletic trainers and sports physiotherapists who travel to all the professional level tennis tournaments, set up a clinic at each venue and provide the professional players health care. This allows for continuity of care for the athletes throughout the year and builds trust and rapport between the athletes and the health care personnel.

Additionally, the ATP Tour and WTA Tour trainers and physiotherapists are well versed in the procedures and policies of the respective professional tours and help guide players and physicians accordingly. This includes understanding the Medical Time-out Rules, the Extreme Weather Conditions Rule (of the WTA Tour) and the Tennis Anti-Doping Program, to name a few. The health care provider also must maintain the player's professional medical records and maintain player confidentiality. It is the relationship between the trainer and physiotherapist and player that is the cornerstone of a successful sports medicine program.

TRAINERS AND PHYSIOTHERAPISTS AT LOCAL TOURNAMENTS

For non-professional tournaments, national and international ITF junior tournaments as well as the ITF professional level Challenger, Satellite and Women's Circuit tournaments, the tournament director or the relevant entry authority or regional governing tennis association or federation, may arrange for certified athletic trainers, physiotherapists or sports physiotherapists to provide care at sporting events. They serve to provide health care including taping, evaluation of injuries and treatment of minor injuries and triage of more significant injuries and illness.

TRAINER OR PHYSIOTHERAPIST RESPONSIBILITIES— PRE-TOURNAMENT

The trainer or physiotherapist usually meets or speaks with the tournament director prior to the tournament to ensure that there are proper training room / medical facilities. The health care provider is in charge of the training room and thus must assure that the training room is of adequate size, good lighting, appropriate climate, clean, well organized, has running water and electricity, has sufficient privacy and accessibility to the courts. Further, there need to be treatment tables (at least two), and ample counter and storage space. They must also make sure that an area for physician-player consultation and examination is available which allows for confidentiality.

The trainer or physiotherapist also meets or speaks with the tournament physician before the tournament. Things to be discussed include the emergency plan, evacuation plan, ongoing player injuries and concerns, special needs or illnesses of players (including identification of those with anaphylactic and drug allergies), provision of medical equipment and supplies, list of physician consultants, hospital and pharmacy locations and phone numbers, physician schedule for the tournament and contact numbers.

The health care provider travels to each tournament with all the items necessary for evaluation and basic care and management of the health care needs of players. This includes medical supplies and equipment, for example, Tennis Anti-doping Program approved medications and creams, taping supplies, tools for managing blisters and calluses, massage supplies, an on-court kit for use during the Medical Time-Out Rule and electrotherapy modalities if applicable.

TRAINERS AND PHYSIOTHERAPISTS RESPONSIBILITIES— DURING THE TOURNAMENT

The trainer or physiotherapist must be available on site at least one hour (usually more than one hour) before play until the end of play each day for both qualifying and main draw matches at all professional tournaments.

The trainer or physiotherapist is usually the person who assesses the weather conditions, including measurement of the heat stress index. If conditions exceed the published threshold for heat stress, then the health care provider notifies the tournament director and chair umpire who then implement the Extreme Weather Condition Rule.

The trainer or physiotherapist is the first person to evaluate the injured player on the court or in the training room. If on the court, this is done at the request of the player through the chair umpire. The health care provider evaluates the player and may request a three-minute treatment time to treat the injured or ill player. The health care provider may call the tournament physician for assistance in the evaluation and/or treatment. This time of the first evaluation is critical, often known as the "golden period" before muscle spasms and swelling occur. Since the swelling is minimal and muscle guarding of the injured area is almost non-existent, the trainer or physiotherapist can obtain the most accurate post-injury clinical examination. From this evaluation, triage and treatment may begin. It is during this "on-the-field/court" evaluation of an injury that the trainer or physiotherapist must make several decisions including proper course of emergency treatment, and determine advise the player on the treatment options that will allow safe continuation of match play.

The trainer or physiotherapist can provide treatments that may include the application of modalities, including ice, heat, and massage. Sports physiotherapists or physiotherapists can use of electrotherapy modalities such as ultrasound and interferential and can apply certain manual therapy techniques, like joint mobilization or manipulation. (certified athletic trainers are not licensed to provide these treatments; they may apply electrotherapy modalities only under the supervision of a physiotherapist). The trainer or physiotherapist can tape or splint injuries, which may enable the injured athlete to return to play. The trainer or physiotherapist can also initiate any emergency procedures necessary, including basic cardiopulmonary resuscitation.

Having a good relationship with the player, the trainer or physiotherapist can be instrumental in serving as a liaison between the player and the tournament physician, by reassuring the athlete, remembering what discussions and recommendations took place and clarifying any issues. Occasionally the player may not feel comfortable discussing issues with a tournament physician since they have just met the physician. A player may feel more comfortable discussing these issues with the health care provider with whom they already have established rapport. In these situations it is important for the trainer and physiotherapist to inform the physician and assist the player to feel comfortable with and have confidence in the physician, his or her diagnosis and treatment ideas. The trainer and physiotherapist and physician must be able to communicate to make sure they arrive at a satisfactory treatment and care plan for an injured athlete. The physician and trainer or physiotherapist must present this in a "united front" to make the athlete comfortable with the medical advice and the plan of treatment.

TRAINERS AND PHYSIOTHERAPISTS RESPONSIBILITIES— POST-TOURNAMENT

The trainer's or physiotherapist's job does not end once the finals are completed. As the tournament ends, the trainer or physiotherapist must communicate with the current tournament physician and with the trainer or physiotherapist and the tournament physician for the next tournament(s) about injured players and players' treatment plans. They can also help arrange for follow-up with physicians in other cities after the tournament.

The trainer or physiotherapist also evaluates the facilities and physician at the tournament to help recommend possible improvements in the health care team and milieu for the next year, as their goal is to continually provide the best care for players.

SUMMARY

The main task of the trainer and physiotherapist is to provide high-level level medical care for athletes, particularly the prevention, evaluation, management, and rehabilitation of injuries. To become a certified athletic trainer, an individual must have a minimum of a Bachelors degree and undergo at least four years of Certified Athletic Training. To become a qualified physiotherapist, an individual must complete a Bachelors or Masters degree in Physiotherapy at university. The trainer or physiotherapist has different tasks before, during, and after a tournament. His responsibility before a tournament are to communicate with the tournament physician and tournament director and assure that proper facilities and a good medical infrastructure are set up. He will also need to bring all the necessary medical supplies and equipment to the tournament. During the tournament, the trainer or physiotherapist is the first person to evaluate the player both on court and in the training room; he is the coordinating person for the prevention, evaluation, management and rehabilitation of all player's injuries and ailments. After the tournament, he has to communicate with the medical team of the next tournament about injured players and players' treatment plans, and help arrange follow-up, if necessary. Rules that are relevant to the daily work of the trainer and physiotherapist include the Medical Time-out Rule, the Extreme Weather Conditions Rule (of the WTA Tour) and the Tennis Anti-Doping Program.

Strength Training for Tennis

28

In this chapter a general strengthening program for tennis players is presented. Strength training has been shown to be effective for injury prevention and for improved tennis performance. Muscle weakness patterns and imbalances have been identified in tennis players that need to be addressed. This includes weakness of the external rotators of the shoulders, related to shoulder injury; weakness of the abdominal, hip, and trunk muscles ("core stability"), related to low back pain; and weakness of the thigh muscles (m. vastus medialis), related to anterior knee pain. For a strengthening program to address the needs of the individual tennis player, an appropriate evaluation in terms of fitness and injury history, must be obtained (a preparticipation evaluation, see Chapter 5). Muscle strength should be evaluated, deficiencies should be noted, and special emphasis should be placed on exercises to correct these deficiencies.

INTENSITY, DURATION, AND FREQUENCY

Beginners should generally start with 12-20 repetitions, with loads of 40-60% of the 1 repetition maximum (RM). The 1 RM value is equal to the maximal amount of weight the subject can lift successfully for one repetition. For intermediate and advanced training, a wider load range may be used, depending on the primary goal of the training. A high-intensity (90% 1 RM), low-repetition (1 to 6) exercise program with long rest periods (2-3 minutes) emphasizes strength gains, whereas a low-intensity (<60% 1 RM) high repetition (20 or more) exercise program with short rest periods (<90 seconds) leads primarily to muscle endurance gains. A moderate intensity exercise program (70-80% 1 RM) with 2 to 3 series of 8-12 repetitions per exercise would lead to both gains in strength and endurance. For tennis, a nonlinear periodization program seems most suitable, including light, moderate, and heavy resistance. Such a program permits variation of both intensity and volume, which is practical with match play and practice being year round. Also, this model is specific for the sport of tennis, with both strength and endurance demands. The recommended training frequency is 2 to 3 times per week. A 2-10% increase in workload can be applied when the player can perform the current workload for one to two repetitions over the desired number.

331

VELOCITY

A lower contraction velocity is generally used when working with higher weights, to recruit as many muscle fibers as possible. A higher contraction velocity is used in plyometrics, in exercises with many repetitions, and when the velocity of a movement needs to be increased (e.g., jumping power). Heavier weights are used for strengthening exercises close to the optimal length. Lower weights are used when training a larger range of motion (e.g., the rotator cuff).

EQUIPMENT

Many types of equipment are available to provide strength gains in conditioning programs, including own body weight, rubber tubing, free weights, and isotonic or isokinetic machines. The choice of equipment generally depends on familiarity with the equipment and availability. Exercises using body weight require no equipment and can thus always be used. Rubber tubing and elastic bands provide dynamic resistance exercises. They are popular among tennis players because they weigh little and are not so bulky, so they can easily be packed into suitcases. Disadvantage is that as the tubing or band stretches during the exercise, the resistance increases, causing more resistance to the muscle as it reaches a weaker point in the motion. Free weights include cuff weights, barbells, and dumbbells. These are easy to use at home. A variety of machines can be used for isotonic exercises. Advantages are the safety and ease of use; disadvantages are that the exercise is fixed and that one has to visit a fitness center. A pulley weight is a form of a free-weight system, and is often used for rotator cuff exercises. Isokinetic machines are generally used for rehabilitation and testing only.

BASIC EXERCISE PROGRAM

In the following exercise program, all the important muscle groups are worked, with special emphasis on the rotator cuff and shoulder blade stabilizers and core stability. The exercise program includes both concentric and eccentric muscle actions, and single- and multiple-joint exercises. With concentric exercise, the muscle shortens during contraction. In eccentric exercise, the muscle lengthens during contraction—for example, when a weight is slowly lowered against the force of gravity. The build up of the program is such that large muscle groups are exercised before small muscle groups, multiple-joint exercises are performed before single-joint exercises, and higher intensity exercises are performed before lower intensity exercises.

SHOULDERS

Figure 28.1

Shoulder extension

Lie prone on a table, arms straight at the side. Lift one arm towards the ceiling, and return to starting position.

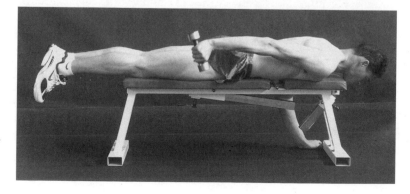

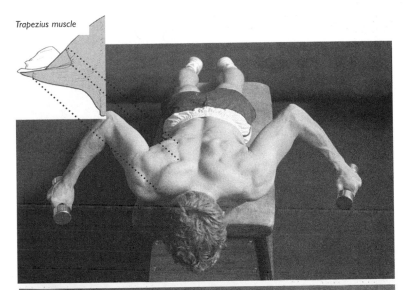

Trapezius muscle

Figure 28.2

Scapular retraction

Lie prone on a table, arms out to the side, elbows bent to 90 degrees and palms facing the floor. Lift the arms towards the ceiling, pinching the shoulder blades together.

Figure 28.3 and 28.4

Serratus anterior punch

Lie supine on a bench, and maintain the shoulder at 90 degrees flexion with the elbow fully extended and a weight in the hand. Protract the scapula to its end range by pushing the weight up.

For players with low back pain, it is recommended to place the feet on a bench or chair.

Figure 28.5

Push-ups against the wall

This is a good starting exercise for players who are not able to perform a regular push-up. Face a wall on one-meter distance, the feet approximately shoulder width apart, and the knees slightly bent. Perform push-ups against the wall. Alternate the position of the hands—close together, far apart, one high and one low, both high, both low, etc.

Figure 28.6 and 28.7

External rotation

Lie on one side on a bench or table with the elbow bent 90 degrees. Hold a small weight in the hand. Rotate the hand and forearm slowly 90 degrees outwards, holding the elbow against the side, and return to starting position.

The exercise can be made harder and more specific for tennis by lying prone and holding the arm at a 90-degree angle.

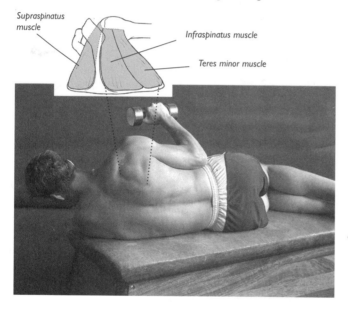

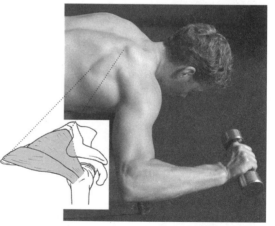

Figure 28.8

Internal rotation

Lie on one side on a bench or table with the elbow bent 90 degrees. Hold a small weight in the lower hand. Rotate the hand and forearm slowly 90 degrees inward, holding the elbow against the side, and return to starting position.

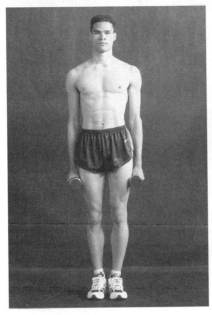

Figure 28.9 and 28.10

Shoulder shrugs

Using a barbell and pronated grip, stand holding the weight at shoulder width with arms extended and the weight resting below the waist. Lift the shoulders up, then return to starting position.

Figure 28.11

Upright rowing

This is an excellent upper body exercise, because it develops so many muscles at the same time. Using a pronated grip, grasp a barbell with the weight at waist level. Pull the weight to the upper part of the chest, then return to starting position.

Figure 28.12 and 28.13

Push-up and push-up plus

Players with wrist problems should perform the push-up on their knuckles or use a bar. From the full push-up position, the player aims to round the shoulders more.

Figure 28.14 and 28.15

Power drops

This exercise is like a plyometric bench press, using a medicine ball instead of a barbell. Lie on your back, legs bent and lower back flat down. Partner stands above your head and drops a ball (2-5 lbs, 1-3 kg). Catch the ball with straight arms and then quickly let the ball drop to your chest, flexing your arms, and then immediately throw the ball back, powerfully extending your arms.

Figure 28.16

Catch and throw backhands

Stand with your feet shoulder-width apart, with a stable base and good posture. Your partner stands to your right and throws a small ball (2 lbs, 1kg) to your hand. You catch it, then quickly take the ball back across your body, rotating your arm inward, and then immediately throw the ball back, powerfully rotating your arm out. Repeat for the left side.

Figure 28.17 and 28.18

Rotator cuff circles

Start in the push-up position, but make sure to keep the hands close together. Perform the push-up plus and now move the shoulders in small circles.

ARMS

Figure 28.19 and 28.20

Parallel bar dips

Support yourself between two benches or chairs on fully extended elbows. Lower slowly by bending the elbows until the chest is almost even with the bars. Then push up until the starting position. In order to protect the front of the shoulder, do not go too low. Players with lax anterior capsules and weak rotator cuff should be particularly careful.

Figure 28.21

Biceps curls

While seated, grasp the dumbbells using a supine grip (palms up). Rest the elbow against the inside of the knee. Begin with the arm extended and bend the arm until the weight approaches the shoulders. Return to starting position.

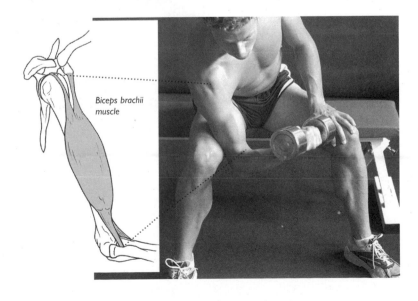

Biceps brachii muscle

Triceps muscle

Figure 28.22 and 28.23

Triceps kick back

There are many ways to train the triceps. The kick back puts less pressure on the cartilage of the elbow joint than triceps extensions with the arm straight up in the air. Also, both arms can be trained separately. Bend forward and hold a weight in one hand, elbow bent, and upper arm parallel to the floor. Now slowly extend the elbow, keeping the upper arm parallel to the floor.

ELBOW, WRIST AND HAND

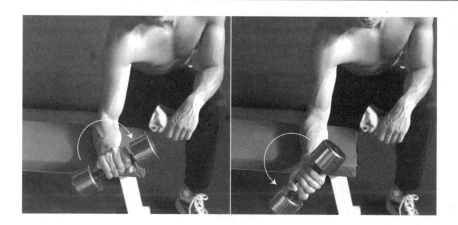

Figure 28.24 and 28.25

Forearm pronation and supination

The pronator and supinator muscles of the forearm are strengthened by holding a weight with the elbow flexed 90 degrees and rotating the hand clockwise and counterclockwise.

Figure 28.26 and 28.27

Wrist curls

To strengthen the wrist flexors, turn the palm of the hand towards the ceiling and rest the forearm with the elbow slightly bent on the knees or a bench. Hold the weight in the hand and curl upwards, and return to starting position.

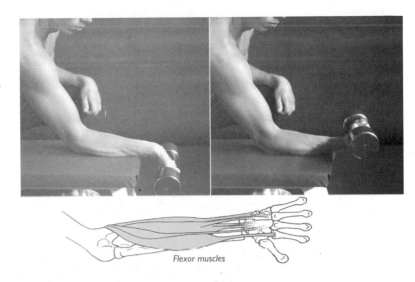

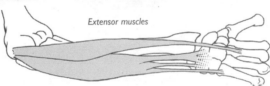

Flexor muscles

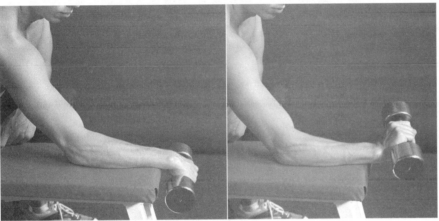

Extensor muscles

Figure 28.28 and 28.29

Wrist extensions

To strengthen the wrist extensors, turn the palm of the hand towards the floor and rest the forearm with the elbow slightly bent on the knees. Curl the hand towards the ceiling, weight in the hand, and return to starting position.

Figure 28.30

Grip strength

Squeeze a tennis ball or silly putty. This is a general exercise, which strengthens all muscles in the hand and wrist. For optimum results, use a ball which is a bit dead or which has lost some of its pressure.

UPPER BACK

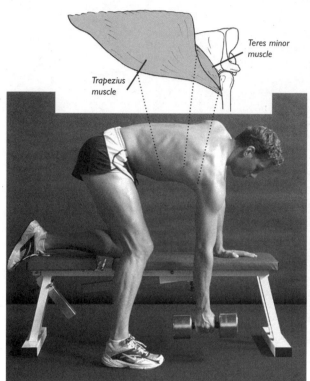

Teres minor muscle

Trapezius muscle

Figure 28.31 and 28.32

Dumbbell row

Place the hand and knee of the same side on a bench or chair, while holding a weight in the other hand. Lift the arm with the weight straight up to shoulder level and return to starting position.

Figure 28.33

Lat pull down

Lat pulls require the use of a lat machine. To work the latissimus more, use a wider grip; to work the biceps more, use a narrower grip. From a seated or kneeling position, grasp the board of the lat machine with the arms fully extended. Pull the weight down until it reaches the chest, then return to starting position.

Figure 28.34

Bend over fly

Sit down and bend forward, torso almost parallel to the ground. Hold the dumbbells down, palms facing each other. Raise the dumbbells up to the side with the elbows slightly bent, until the forearms are in a position parallel to the floor. Return to starting position.

ABDOMINALS

Figure 28.35

The crunch

Lie supine with the knees bent and the feet flat on the floor or crossed in the air, arms across the chest. Lift the shoulders up a few inches towards the ceiling, while keeping the lower back on the floor. To make the exercise easier, the arms can be brought down to the sides.

Figure 28.36

The curl up with twist

Rotate the trunk during the execution of the exercise, for example by pulling the left shoulder towards the right leg.

Figure 28.37

Pelvic raise

This works on the lower part of the abdomen. Start by lying on your back. Maintain the hip at 90 degrees flexion throughout the movement. Hold the arms by the sides for stability. Try lifting the buttocks from the bench, while keeping the legs relatively inactive.

Figure 28.38

Leg lifts

Strong abdominal muscles are needed to lift the legs straight up, without tilting the pelvis, while lying supine. The exercise can be made harder by keeping the feet in the air, while the hands reach for the shoes. After having touched the shoes, slowly return to starting position.

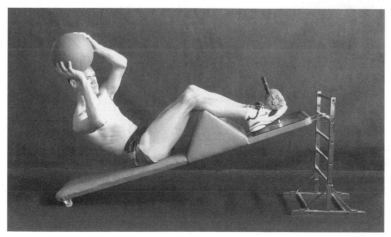

Figure 28.39

Medicine ball throwing on an inclined plane

Hold a medicine ball with two hands above your head. Throw the ball to your partner and catch the ball again above your head. Throw the ball back in one movement. Start with a light weight (1-2 lbs, 0.5-1 kg) and slowly increase the weight in the course of a few weeks.

Figure 28.40, 28.41, and 28.42

Side raises

Lie down on one side and find support on one elbow. Straighten the body by bringing the pelvis up; only the ankle and forearm may touch the floor. The exercise can be made harder by leaning on the hand instead of the forearm and by lowering and raising the hips.

BACK AND TRUNK

Figure 28.43

Spinal extensions

Balance on one hand and the opposite knee. Reach to the front with the free arm and extend the free leg to the rear. Hold for ten to thirty seconds. The exercise can be made more difficult by balancing on the arm and leg of the same side, by using a balance board, or by attaching weights to the legs and arms.

Figure 28.44 and 28.45

Gym ball balance

Sit upright on a gym ball. Raise one leg and the opposite arm and return to your starting position. Repeat with the opposite leg and arm. You can make the exercise harder by closing your eyes, extending you leg, or holding a weight in your hand and passing it from one hand to the other in a wide circle behind your back.

Figure 28.46

Gym ball balance

Lay on your stomach over a ball, with your hands and toes touching the floor. Raise one leg and return to starting position. Repeat with other leg. Do not arch your back. The exercise can be made harder by raising one arm and the opposite leg simultaneously and return to starting position. Repeat with opposite extremities.

Figure 28.47 and 28.48

Bridge

This is a tough exercise, since one needs to have both strong stomach muscles and strong back muscles to be able to perform it. Lie down on your back, with one leg bent. Push the hips up while leaning on the shoulders and on one leg; straighten the other leg. Try to bring the body in a straight line and hold this position. The exercise can be made harder by leaning on the forearms instead of the shoulders.

Figure 28.49 and 28.50

Trunk rotation

Hold a barbell vertical in front of you, one end on the ground. Quickly rotate the trunk left and right, each time stabilizing the barbell when returning to starting position.

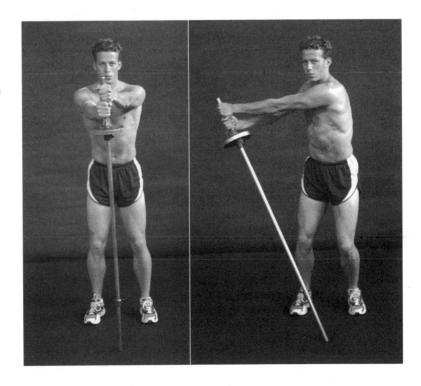

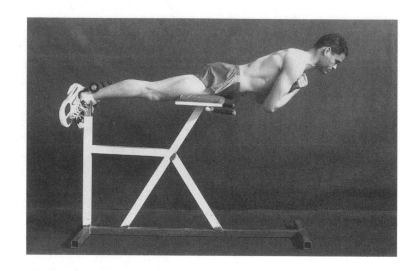

Figure 28.51

Back extensions

Lie face down on a back extension bench with the upper body extending over the edge. Lower the upper body and then lift the torso until it is again aligned with the legs. Do not extend any further back with this exercise, because that can put excessive pressure on the spinal discs.

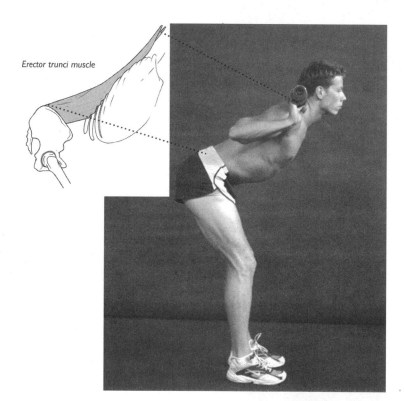

Erector trunci muscle

Figure 28.52

Good mornings

Standing, place a barbell on the shoulders and flex the knees slightly. Bend at the hip while keeping the head up as much as possible, then return to the starting position. Do this exercise slowly and smoothly, and add weight very gradually. In general, do more repetitions (10-20) and use less weight than normally during other weight training exercises. Players with (a history of) low back pain should use this exercise cautiously due to the loading of the lumbar spine.

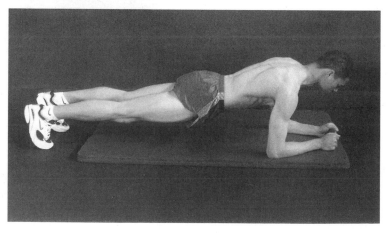

Figure 28.53

The plank

Lie on your front resting on your forearms. Go up on your toes forming one straight line from your feet to your head.

Figure 28.54

Bridging on a gym ball

Instead of performing the bridge on the floor, well-trained players can perform the bridge on an unstable surface such as a gym ball. Rest your back on a bench and place your feet on a gym ball. Once you have found your balance, try lifting one foot.

Figure 28.55

Leg raises

Use a bench, chair or stair. The height should be about 8-12 inches (20-30 cm). Put one foot on the bench, and keep the other foot on the ground. The thigh of the raised leg should be about perpendicular to the floor. Now lift the raised foot, while keeping your balance.

Gluteus medius muscle

HIPS AND GROIN

Figure 28.56 and 28.57

Hip abduction

Lie on one side, and slowly lift the upper leg to the side. Hold for three seconds, and return to starting position. The exercise can be made harder by leaning on the forearm and ankles instead of the side or by attaching a weight to the ankle.

Figure 28.58

Hip adduction

Lie on one side, and slowly lift the lower leg straight off the floor. Hold for three seconds and return to starting position. The exercise can be made more difficult by attaching a weight to the ankle.

Figure 28.59 and 28.60

Hip abduction and adduction

Stand straight with your legs shoulder width apart. Tie the elastic tubing to your leg and to a stationary object. Move your leg outward against the resistance of the elastic tubing. For adduction, move your leg inward, across your body, against the resistance of the elastic tubing.

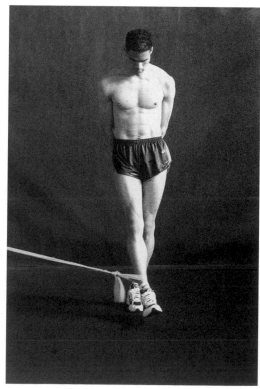

THIGH AND KNEE

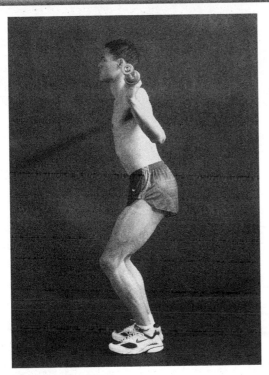 

Figure 28.61 and 28.62

Double and single leg squat

Stand with the feet shoulder-width apart. Lean slightly forward and lower the body until the knees are at a 90 degree angle. Hold for 5-10 seconds, then straighten the leg again, without locking the knees. The exercise can be made more challenging by standing on one leg or holding and extra weight. Bending the knees further than 90 degrees is not recommended because of the increased pressure on the kneecap.

Figure 28.63

Step ups

Use a bench, a stair, or the first row of some bleachers. The height of the first step should be 4-6 inches (10-15 cm) at the beginning. This height can be increased as strength improves. Step up with the leg being exercised. Follow with the other leg. Then step down with the first leg and follow with the other leg. The exercises can be performed both forwards and sideways.

Figure 28.64

Lunge

Stand upright, arms at the sides. Step forward with one leg, and slowly bend the front knee until it is in the same vertical plane as the foot. Now straighten the front leg slightly, then bend it again, while the hips move forward and down. Continue to rock backwards and forwards for 15 to 30 seconds. Repeat with the other leg. Repeat this sequence 2 to 3 times. The exercise can be made more difficult by carrying dumbbells or by stepping all the way back.

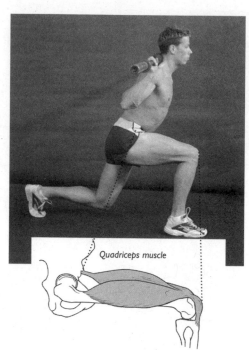

Quadriceps muscle

LOWER LEG, ANKLE, AND FOOT

Figure 28.65 and 28.66

Calf raises

Stand in an upright position and slowly rise to the toes. Hold this position for a couple of seconds and then return to the original position. The drill can be made harder by closing the eyes, carrying an additional load, or varying the speed and number of repetitions. A variation of this exercise is hopping around on one foot in a fixed pattern.

Figure 28.67

Resisted eversion

Sit on a chair or bench. Tie one end of an elastic band or rubber tubing to one leg of the chair and tie the other end around the ball of the foot, just below the toes. The tubing should be on the medial of the leg. Slowly turn the sole of the foot outwards, pulling against the tubing.

Figure 28.68

Toe raise

Stand in an upright position. Lift the toes and the front of the foot off the floor. Keep the heels in contact with the floor. This exercise can be made more difficult by leaning back against a wall or stationary object.

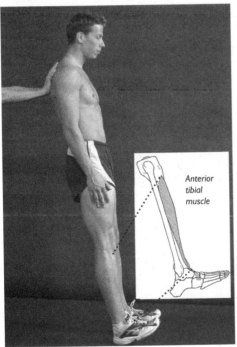

Figure 28.69

Towel pick up

Sit on a chair or bench. Put a towel on the ground and place a weight on it. Using the toes, pull the towel toward you.

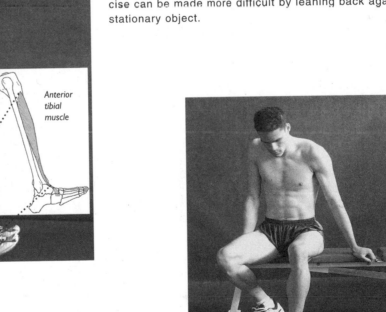

References

ADDITIONAL READING

Brody, H.1987. *Tennis Science for Tennis Players*. Philadelphia: University of Pennsylvania Press.

Brody, H., R. Cross, C. Lindsey. 2002. *The Physics and Technology of Tennis*. Racquet Tech Publishing.

Cousteau, J-P. 1999. *Médecine du tennis*. Paris: Masson.

Crespo, M., B.M. Pluim, and M. Reid (eds). 2001. *Tennis Medicine for Tennis Coaches*. London: International Tennis Federation.

Elliott, B., M. Reid, and M. Crespo. 2003. *Biomechanics of Advanced Tennis*. London: ITF.

Ferrauti, A. 1999. *Der Energiestoffwechsel im Tennis*. Sankt Augustin: Academia Verlag.

Haake, S.J. and A.O. Coe (eds). 2000. *Tennis Science and Technology*. Oxford: Blackwell Science.

Krahl, H., H-G. Pieper, W.B. Kibler, and P.A.F.H. Renstr m (eds). 1995. *Tennis. Sports Medicine and Science*. D sseldorf· Walter Rau Verlag.

K sswetter, W., J. Zacher, and S. Sell. 1989. *Tennis und Sportmedizin*. Stuttgart: Georg Thieme Verlag.

Lehman, R.C. (ed). 1995. *Clinics in Sports Medicine: Racquet Sports*. Philadelphia: W.B. Saunders Company.

Lees, A, I. Maynard, M. Hughes, and T. Reilly (eds). 1997. *Science and Racket Sports II*. Cambridge: E & FN Spon.

Maquirriain, J (ed). 2002. *Medicina deportiva aplicada al tenis*. Buenos Aires: Gr fica Integral.

Miller, S (ed). 2003. *Tennis Science & Technology*. Oxford: Blackwell Science.

Renstr m, P.A.F.H (ed). 2002. *Tennis*. Oxford: Blackwell Science.

Reilly, T., M. Hughes, and A. Lees (eds). 1995. *Science and Racket Sports*. Cambridge: E & FN Spon.

Weber, K. 1987. *Der Tennissport aus internistisch-sportmedizinischer Sicht*. Sankt Augustin: Verlag Hans Richarz.

REFERENCES

Chapter 1. The Biomechanics of Tennis

Andersson, E.A., H. Grundstrom, and A. Thorstensson. 2002. Diverging intramuscular activity patterns in back and abdominal muscles during trunk rotation. *Spine* 27: E152-E160.

Bahamonde, R.E. 2000. Changes in angular momentum during the tennis serve. *Journal of Sport Sciences* 18: 579-592.

Blackwell, J.R. and K.J. Cole. 1994. Wrist kinematics differ in expert and novice tennis players performing the backhand stroke: implications for tennis elbow. *Journal of Biomechanics* 27: 509-516.

Chow, J.W., L.G. Carlton, W-S. Chae, J-H. Shim, Y-T. Lim, and A.F. Kuenster. 1999. Movement characteristics of the tennis volley. *Medicine and Science in Sports and Exercise* 31: 855-863.

Chow, J.W., L.G. Carlton, Y-T. Lim, J-H. Shim, W-S Chae, and A.F. Kuenster. 1999. Muscle activation during the tennis volley. *Medicine and Science in Sports and Exercise* 31: 846-854.

Cohen, D.B., M.A. Mont, K.R. Campbell, B.N. Vogelstein, and J.W. Loewy. 1994. Upper extremity physical factors affecting tennis serve velocity. *The American Journal of Sports Medicine* 22: 746-750.

Elliott, B. and M. Christmass. 1995. A comparison of the high and low backspin backhand drives in tennis using different grips. *Journal of Sports Sciences* 13: 141-151.

Elliott, B.C., R.N. Marshall, and G.J. Noffal. 1995. Contributions of upper limb segment rotations during the power serve in tennis. *Journal of Applied Biomechanics* 1: 433-442.

Elliott, B., K. Tokahashi, and G. Noffal. 1997. The influence of grip position on upper limb contributions to racket head velocity in a tennis forehand. *Journal of Applied Biomechanics* 13: 182-196.

Groppel, J.L. 1986. The biomechanics of tennis: an overview. *International Journal of Sport Biomechanics* 2: 141-155.

Kibler, W.B. 1994. Clinical biomechanics of the elbow in tennis: implications for evaluation and diagnosis. *Medicine and Science in Sports and Exercise* 26: 1203-1206.

Knudson, D. and J. Blackwell. 2000. Trunk muscle activation in open stance and square stance tennis forehands. *International Journal of Sports Medicine* 21: 321-324.

Marshall, R.N. and B.C. Elliott. 2000. Long-axis rotation: the missing link in proximal-to-distal segmental sequencing. *Journal of Sports Sciences* 18: 247-254.

Plagenhoef, S.C. 1966. Methods for obtaining kinetic data to analyze human motions. *Research Quarterly* 37: 103-112.

Riek, S., A.E. Chapman, and T. Milner. 1999. A simulation of muscle force and internal kinematics of extensor carpi radialis brevis during backhand tennis stroke: implications for injury. *Clinical Biomechanics* 14: 477-483.

Chapter 2. Physiological Demands of the Game

Bergeron, M.F., C.M. Maresh, W.J. Kraemer, A. Abraham, B. Conroy, and C. Gabaree. 1991. Tennis: A physiological profile during match play. *International Journal of Sports Medicine* 12: 474-479.

Christmass, M.A., S.E. Richmond, N.T. Cable, P.G. Arthur, and P.E. Hartmann. 1998. Exercise intensity and metabolic response in singles tennis. *Journal of Sport Sciences* 16: 739-747.

Delecluse, C. 1997. Influence of strength training on sprint running performance. Current findings and implications for training. *Sports Medicine* 24(3): 147-156.

Elliott, B., B. Dawson, and F. Pyke. 1985. The energetics of singles tennis. *Journal of Human Movement Studies* 11: 11-20.

Ferrauti, A., B.M. Pluim, and K. Weber. 2001. Effect of recovery duration on running speed and stroke quality during intermittent training drills in elite tennis players. *Journal of Sport Sciences* 19: 235-242.

Ferrauti, A., M.F. Bergeron, B.M. Pluim, and K. Weber. 2001. Physiological responses in tennis and running with similar oxygen uptake. *European Journal of Applied Physiology* 85: 27-33.

Groppel, J.L., and E.P. Roetert. 1992. Applied physiology of tennis. *Sports Medicine* 14: 260-268.

Keul, J., W. Stockhausen, R. Pokan, M. Huonker, and A. Berg. 1991. Metabolische und kardiozirkulatorische Adaptation sowie Leistungsverhalten professioneller Tennisspieler. *Deutsche medizinische Wochenschrifte* 16: 761-767.

Kraemer, W.J., N.T. Triplett, A.C. Fry, L.P. Koziris, J.E. Bauer, J.M. Lynch, T. McConnell, R.U. Newton, S.E. Gordon, R.C. Nelson, and H.G. Knuttgen. 1995. An in-depth sports medicine profile of women college tennis players. *Journal of Sport Rehabilitation* 4: 79-98.

Kraemer, W.J. J.F. Patton, S.E. Gordon, et al. 1995. Compatibility of high intensity strength and endurance training on hormonal and skeletal muscle adaptations. *Journal of Applied Physiology* 78:976-989.

Lees, A. 2003. Science and the major racket sports: a review. *Journal of Sports Sciences* 21(9): 707-732.

Morgans, L.F., D.L. Jordan, D.A. Baeyens, and J.A. Franciosa. 1987. Heart rate responses during singles and doubles tennis competition. *Physician and Sportsmedicine* 5: 67-74.

O Donoghue, P. and B. Ingram. 2001. A notational analysis of elite tennis strategy. *Journal of Sport Sciences* 19: 107-115.

Seliger, V., M. Ejem, M. Pauer, and V. Safarik. 1973. Energy metabolism in tennis. *Internationale Zeitschrift für angewandte Physiologie* 31: 333-340.

Smekal, G., R. Pokan, S.P. van Duvillard, R. Baron, H. Tschan, and N. Bachl. 2000. Comparison of laboratory and on-court endurance testing in tennis. *International Journal of Sports Medicine* 21: 242-249.

Weber K. *Der Tennissport aus internistisch-sportmedizinischer Sicht. Schriften der Deutschen Sporthochschule Köln.* Verlag Hans Richarz, Sankt Augustin, 1987.

Weber, K. 1991. Das Beanspruchungsprofil im Tennissport aus leistungsphysiologischer Sicht. In: *Tennis und Sportmedizin*, K sswetter, W., J. Zacher and S. Sell, eds. Stuttgart: Thieme.

McArdle, W.D., F.I. Katch, and V.L. Katch. 1996. *Exercise Physiology* (4th edition). Baltimore: William & Wilkins.

Chapter 3. Tennis Racquets, Strings, and Balls

Adelsberg, S. 1986. The tennis stroke: an EMG analysis of selected muscles with rackets and increasing grip size. *American Journal of Sports Medicine* 14: 139-142.

Baker, J. and B. Wilson. 1978. The effect of tennis racket stiffness and string tension on ball velocity after impact. *Research Quarterly of Exercise and Sport* 3: 255-259.

Brody, H. 1988. *Tennis Science for Tennis Players.* Philadelphia: University of Pennsylvania Press.

Brody, H. 1989. Vibration damping of tennis rackets. *The International Journal of Sport Biomechanics* 5: 451-456.

Caffi, M. and F. Casolo. 1995. Ball dynamic characteristics: a fundamental factor in racket dynamic optimization. In *Science and Racket Sports*, edited by T. Reilly, M. Hughes, and A. Lees. London: E&FN Spon.

Elliott, B.C., B.A. Blanksby, and R. Ellis. 1980. Vibration and rebound velocity characteristics of conventional and oversized tennis rackets. *Research Quarterly of Exercise and Sport* 51: 608-615.

Elliott, B. 1982. The influence of tennis racket flexibility and string tension on rebound velocity following a dynamic impact. *Research Quarterly of Exercise and Sport* 53: 277-281.

Groppel, J.L., I. Shin, J.A. Thomas, and G.J. Welk. 1987. The effects of string type and tension on impact in midsized and oversized tennis racquets. *The International Journal of Sport Biomechanics* 3: 40-46.

Gruchow, H.W., and D. Pelletier. 1979. An epidemiologic study of tennis elbow. *The American Journal of Sports Medicine* 7: 234-238.

Hennig, E.M., D. Rosenbaum, and T.L. Milani. 1992. Transfer of tennis racket vibrations onto the human forearm. *Medicine and Science in Sports and Exercise* 24: 1134-1140.

Knudson, D.V. 1991. Factors affecting force loading on the hand in the tennis forehand. *The Journal of Sports Medicine and Physical Fitness* 31: 527-531.

Pluim, B.M. 2000. Racket, strings and balls in relation to tennis elbow. In *Tennis Science and Technology*, edited by S.J. Haake and A.O. Coe. Oxford: Blackwell Science.

Stone, D.A., M. Voght, and M.R. Safran. 1999. Comparison of incidence of tennis elbow in first generation and graphite composite racquets. *Sportsmedicine and Science in Tennis* 4: 3.

Tomosue, R., K. Sugiyama, and K. Yamamoto. 1995. The effectiveness of damping material in reducing impact shock in the tennis forehand drive. In *Science and Racket Sports*, edited by T. Reilly, M. Hughes, and A. Lees. London: E&FN Spon.

Wilson, J.F. and J.S. Davis. 1995. Tennis racket shock mitigation experiments. *Journal of Biomechanic Engineering* 117: 479-484.

Chapter 4. Tennis Shoes and Playing Surfaces

Andr asson, G., and L. Peterson. 1986. Effects of shoe and surface characteristics on lower limb injuries in sports. *International Journal of Sport Biomechanics* 2: 202-209.

Bastholt, P. 2000. Professional tennis (ATP Tour) and number of medical treatments in relation to type of surface. *Medicine and Science in Tennis* 5: 9.

Cox, A.L. 2000. Investigation into the sports characteristics of short and medium pile synthetic turfs and textile tennis court surfaces. In *Tennis Science and Technology* edited by S.J. Haake and A.O. Coe. Oxford: Blackwell Science.

Dixon, S.J., A.C. Collop, and M.E. Batt. 2000. Impact-absorbing characteristics of tennis playing surfaces. In *Tennis Science and Technology* edited by S.J. Haake and A.O. Coe. Oxford: Blackwell Science.

Luethi, S.M., E.C. Frederick, M.R. Hawes, and B.M. Nigg. 1986. Influence of shoe construction on lower extremity kinematics and load during lateral movements in tennis. *International Journal of Sport Biomechanics* 2: 166-174.

Nigg, B.M., E.C. Frederick, M.R. Hawes, and S.M. Luethi. 1986. Factors influencing short-term pain and injuries in tennis. *International Journal of Sport Biomechanics* 2: 156-165.

Nigg, B.M., and B. Segesser. 1988. The influence of playing surfaces on the load on the locomotor system and on football and tennis injuries. *Sports Medicine* 5: 375-385.

Nigg, B.M., and M.R. Yeadon. 1987. Biomechanical aspects of playing surfaces. *Journal of Sports Sciences* 5: 117-145.

Reinschmidt, C. and B.M. Nigg. 2000. Current issues in the design of running and court shoes. *Sportverletzung und Sportschaden* 14: 71-81.

Segesser, B. and W. Pf ringer, eds. 1987. *Der Schuh im Sport. Beitrage zur Sportmedizin*, Band 31. Gerlangen: Perimed Fachbuch-Verlaggesellschaft.

Van Gheluwe, B., and E. Deporte. 1992. Friction measurement in tennis on the field and in the laboratory. *International Journal of Sport Biomechanics* 8: 48-61.

Chapter 5. Injury Prevention

Chandler, T.J., W.B. Kibler, T.L. Uhl, B. Wooten, A. Kiser, and E. Stone. 1990. Flexibility comparisons of junior elite tennis players to other athletes. *The American Journal of Sports Medicine* 18: 134-136.

Chard, M.D. and S.M. Lachmann. 1987. Racquet sports-patterns of injury presenting to a sports injury clinic. *British Journal of Sports Medicine* 21: 150-153.

Ekstrand, J., J. Gillquist, and S-O. Liljedahl. 1983. Prevention of soccer injuries. *The American Journal of Sports Medicine* 11: 116-120.

Ellenbecker, T. and E.P. Roetert. 2003. Age specific isokinetic glenohumeral internal and external rotation strength in elite junior tennis players. *Journal of Science and Medicine in Sport* 6(1): 63-70.

Farrell SJ, A.D. Ross, and K.V. Sehgal. 1999. Eastern movement therapies. *Physical Medical Rehabilitation Clinics of North America* 10: 617-629.

Fleck, S.J. and J.E. Falkel. 1986. Value of resistance training for the reduction of sports injuries. *Sports Medicine* 3: 61-68.

Fredericson, M., J.J. White, J.M. Macmahon, and T.P. Andriacchi. 2002. Qualitative analysis of the relative effectiveness of 3 iliotibial band stretches. *Archives of Physical Medicine and Rehabilitation* 83: 589-592.

Handoll, H.H., B.H. Rowe, K.M. Quinn, and R. de Bie. 2001. Interventions for preventing ankle ligament injuries. *Cochrane Database Systematic Review* 3: CD000018.

Hartig, D.E. and J.M. Henderson. 1999. Increasing hamstring flexibility decreases lower extremity overuse injuries in military basic trainees. *American Journal of Sports Medicine* 27: 173-176.

Hemmings, B., M. Smith, J. Graydon, R. Dyson. 2000. Effects of massage on physiological restoration, perceived recovery, and repeated sports performance. *British Journal of Sports Medicine* 34: 109-114.

Herbert, R.D. and M. Gabriel. 2002. Effects of stretching before and after exercising on muscle soreness and risk of injury: systematic review. *British Medical Journal* 325: 468-473.

Hilyer, J.C., K.C. Brown, A.T. Sirles, and L. Peoples. 1990. A flexibility intervention to reduce the incidence and severity of joint injuries among municipal firefighters. *Journal of Occupational Medicine* 32: 631-637.

Kibler, W.B., and T.J. Chandler. 2003. Range of motion in junior tennis players participating in an injury risk modification program. *Journal of Science and Medicine in Sport* 6(1): 51-62.

Kibler, W.B., T.J. Chandler, T. Uhl, and R.E. Maddux. 1989. A musculoskeletal approach to the preparticipation physical examination. *The American Journal of Sports Medicine* 17: 525-531.

Knapik, J.J., C.L. Bauman, B.H. Jones, J.McA. Harris, and L. Vaughan. 1991. Preseason strength and flexibility imbalances associated with athletic injuries in female collegiate athletes. *The American Journal of Sports Medicine* 19: 76-81.

Letsel Informatie Systeem 1998-2001. *Ongevallen tijdens racketsporten.* Amsterdam: Consument en Veiligheid, 2003.

Monedero, J. and B. Donne. 2000. Effect of recovery interventions on lactate removal and subsequent performance. *International Journal of Sports Medicine* 21: 593-597.

Nelson, A.G. and J. Kokkonen. 2001. Acute ballistic muscle stretching inhibits maximal strength performance. *Research Quarterly for Exercise and Sport* 72: 415-419.

Parkkari, J., U.M. Kujala, and P. Kannus. 2001. Is it possible to prevent sports injuries? Review of controlled clinical trials and recommendations for future work. *Sports Medicine* 31:985-995.

Rodenburg, J.B., D. Steenbeek, P. Schiereck, and P.R. Bär. Warm-up, stretching and massage diminish harmful effects of eccentric exercise. *International Journal of Sports Medicine* 15: 414-419.

Safran, M.R., W.E. Garrett, A.V. Seaber, R.R. Glisson, and B.M. Ribbeck. 1988. The role of warm-up in muscular injury prevention. *The American Journal of Sports Medicine* 16: 123-129.

Safran, M.R., A.V. Seaber, and W.B. Garrett. 1989. Warm-up and muscular injury prevention. *Sports Medicine* 8: 239-249.

Shellock, F.G. and W.E. Prentice. 1985. Warming-up and stretching for improved physical performance and prevention of sports-related injuries. *Sports Medicine* 2: 267-278.

Schmikli, S.L., M. J. P. de Wit and F. J. G. Backx. 2001. *Sportblessures driemaal geteld.* Arnhem: NOC*NSF Breedtesport.

Schur, P.E. 2001. Effectiveness of stretching to reduce injury. *British Journal of Sports Medicine* 35: 138.

Shrier I. 1999. Stretching before exercise does not reduce the risk of local muscle injury: a critical review of the clinical and basic science literature. *Clinical Journal of Sport Medicine* 9: 221-227.

Silva, R.T., R. Takahashi, B. Berra, M. Cohen, and M.H. Matsumoto. 2003. Medical assistance at the Brazilian juniors tennis circuit--a one-year prospective study. *Journal of Science and Medicine in Sport* 6(1): 14-18.

Steinbrück, K. 1999. Epidemiologie vor Sportverletzungen-25-Jahres-Analyse einer sportorthop disch-traumatologisches Ambulanz. *Sportverletzungen und Sportschaden* 13, 38-51.

Taimela, S., U.M. Kujala, and K. Osterman. 1990. Intrinsic risk factors and athletic injuries. *Sports Medicine* 9: 205-215.

Viitasalo, J.T., K. Niemela, R. Kaappola, T. Korjus, M. Levola, H.V. Mononen, H.K. Rusko, and T.E. Takala. 1995. Warm underwater water-jet massage improves recovery from intense physical exercise. *European Journal of Applied Physiology and Occupational Physiology* 71: 431-438.

Winge, S., U. Jørgensen, A. Lassen Nielsen. 1989. Epidemiology of Danish Championship Tennis. *International Journal of Sports Medicine* 10: 368-371.

Chapter 6: General Rehabilitation Principles

Almekinders, I.C. 1999. Anti-inflammatory treatment of muscular injuries in sport. An update of recent studies. *Sports Medicine* 28:383-388.

Almekinders, L.C., A.J. Baynes, and L.W. Bracey. 1995. An in vitro investigation into the effects of repetitive motion and nonsteroidal antiinflammatory medication on human tendon fibroblasts. *American Journal of Sports Medicine* 23: 119-123.

Beiner, J.M. and P. Jokl. 2001. Muscle contusion injuries: current treatment options. *Journal of the American Academy of Orthopedic Surgery* 9: 227-237.

MacAuley, D.C. 2001. Ice therapy: how good is the evidence? *International Journal of Sports Medicine* 22: 379-384.

Hoffman, M.D. 1997. Principles of musculoskeletal sports injury rehabilitation. *Wisconsin Medical Journal* 96(12): 38-48.

Houglum, P. 2001. *Therapeutic Exercise for Athletic Injuries.* Champaign: Human Kinetics.

Kapetanos, G. 1982. The effect of local corticosteroids on the healing and biomechanical properties of the partially injured tendon. *Clinical Orthopedics* 163: 170-179.

Kibler, W.B. 1997. Diagnosis, treatment and rehabilitation principles in complete tendon ruptures in sports. *Scandinavian Journal of Medicine and Science in Sports* 7: 119-129.

Maffulli, N., Wong, J., and L.C. Almekinders. 2003. Types and epidemiology of tendinopathy. *Clinics in Sports Medicine* 22(4): 675-692.

Sailer, S.M. and S.B. Lewis. 1995. Rehabilitation and splinting of common upper extremity injuries in athletes. *Clinics in Sports Medicine* 14(2): 411-446.

Swenson, C., L. Sward, and J. Karlsson. 1996. Cryotherapy in sports medicine. *Scandinavian Journal of Medicine and Science in Sports* 6: 193-200.

Chapter 7: Injuries of the Upper Body

Altcheck, D.W. and M. Levinson. 2000. The painful shoulder in the throwing athlete. *Orthopedic Clinics of North America* 31(2): 241-245.

Assendelft, W., S. Green, R. Buchbinder, P. Struijs, and N. Smidt. 2003. Tennis elbow. *British Medical Journal* 327(7410): 329.

Berg, E.E. and J.V. Ciullo. 1998. A clinical test for superior glenoid labral or 'SLAP' lesions. *Clinical Journal of Sport Medicine* 8: 121-123.

Budoff, J.E., R.P. Nirschl, O.A. Ilahi, and D.M. Rodin 2003. Internal impingement in the etiology of rotator cuff tendinosis revisited. *Arthroscopy* 19(8): 810-814.

Burkhart, S.S., C.D. Morgan, and W.B. Kibler. 2000. Shoulder injuries in overhead athletes. The dead arm revisited. *Clinics in Sports Medicine* 19: 125-158.

Corso, G. 1995. Impingement relief test: an adjunctive procedure to traditional assessment of shoulder impingement syndrome. *Journal of Orthopaedic and Sports Physical Therapy* 22: 183-192.

Eakin, C.L., K.J. Faber, R.J. Hawkins, and W.D. Hovis. 1999. Biceps tendon disorders in athletes. *Journal of the American Academy of Orthopedic Surgery* 7: 300-310.

Fragnire, B., M. Landry, and O. Siegrist. 2001. Stress fracture of the ulna in a professional tennis player using a double-handed backhand stroke. *Knee Surgery, Sports Traumatology and Arthroscopy* 9: 239-241.

Guha, A.R. and H. Marynissen. 2002. Stress fracture of the hook of the hamate. *British Journal of Sports Medicine* 36, 224-225.

Hersh, C.H. 1996. Pitfalls in athletic hand injuries. *Operative Techniques in Sports Medicine* 4: 268-274.

Ho, P.C., J. Griffiths, W.N. Lo, C.H. Yen, and L.K. Hung. 2001. Current treatment of ganglion of the wrist. *Hand Surgery* 6: 49-58.

Ingber, R.S. 2000. Shoulder impingement in tennis/racquetball players treated with subscapularis myofascial treatments. *Archives of Physical Medicine and Rehabilitation* 81: 679-682.

Jee, W.H., T.R. McCauley, L.D. Katz, J.M. Matheny, P.A. Ruwe, and J.P. Daigneault. 2001. Superior labral anterior posterior (SLAP) lesions of the glenoid labrum: reliability and accuracy of MR arthrography for diagnosis. *Radiology* 218: 127-132.

Levine, W.N., W.D. Prickett, M. Prymka, and K. Yamaguchi. 2001. Treatment of the athlete with multidirectional shoulder instability. *Orthopedic Clinics of North America* 32: 475-484.

Kamkar, A., J.J. Irrgang, and S.L. Whitney. 1993. Nonoperative management of secondary shoulder impingement syndrome. *Journal of Orthopaedic and Sports Physical Therapy* 17: 212-224.

Klingele, K.E., M.S. Kocher. 2002. Little league elbow: valgus overload injury in the paediatric athlete. *Sports Medicine* 32(15): 1005-1015.

Liu, S.H. and E. Boynton. 1993. Posterior superior impingement of the rotator cuff on the glenoid rim as a cause of shoulder pain in the overhead athlete. *The Journal of Arthroscopic and Related Surgery* 9: 697-699.

De Maeseneer, M., F. Van Roy, L. Lenchik, M. Shahabpour, J. Jacobson, K.N. Ryu, F. Handelberg, and M. Osteaux. 2000. CT and MR arthrography of the normal and pathologic anterosuperior labrum and labral-bicipital complex. *Radiographics* 20: S67-S81.

Melikyan, E.Y., E. Shahin, J. Miles, and L..C. Bainbridge. 2003. Extracorporeal shock-wave treatment for tennis elbow. A randomised double-blind study. *Journal of Bone and Joint Surgery Br* 85(6): 852-825.

Nirschl, R.P. and E.S. Ashman. 2003. Elbow tendinopathy: tennis elbow. *Clinics in Sports Medicine* 22(4): 813-836.

Nishikawa, S., S. Toh, H. Miura, K. Arai, and T. Irie. 2001. Arthroscopic diagnosis and treatment of dorsal wrist ganglion. *Journal of Hand Surgery Br* 26: 547-549.

Noel, B. and D. Hayoz. 2000. A tennis player with hand claudication. *Vasa* 29: 151-153.

Ong, B.C., J.K. Sekiya, and M.W. Rodosky. 2002. Shoulder injuries in the athlete. *Current Opinion in Rheumatology* 14: 150-159.

Parker, R.D., M.S. Berkowitz, M.A. Brahms, and W.R. Bohl. 1986. Hook of the hamate fractures in athletes. *The American Journal of Sports Medicine* 14: 517-523.

Paxinos, A, J. Walton, A. Tzannes, M. Callanan, K. Hayes, and G.A. Murrell. 2001. Advances in the management of traumatic anterior and atraumatic multidirectional shoulder instability. *Sports Medicine* 31: 819-828.

Postacchini, F., S. Gumina, and G. Cinotti. 2000. Anterior shoulder dislocation in adolescents. *Journal of Shoulder and Elbow Surgery* 9: 470-474.

Press, J.M. and S.L. Wiesner. 1990. Prevention: conditioning and orthotics. *Hand Clinics* 6: 383-392.

Ramsey, M.L. 1999. Distal biceps tendon injuries: diagnosis and management. *Journal of the American Academy of Orthopedic Surgery* 7: 199-207.

Rettig, A.C. 1994. Wrist problems in the tennis player. *Medicine and Science in Sports and Exercise* 26: 1207-1212.

Romeo, A.A., D.D Rotenberg, and B.R. Bach Jr. 1999. Suprascapular neuropathy. *Journal of the American Academy of Orthopedic Surgeons* 7: 358-367.

Safran, M.R. 1995. Elbow injuries in athletes. A review. *Clinical Orthopedics* 310: 257-277.

Shih, J.T., S.T. Hung, H.M. Lee, and C.M. Tan. 2002. Dorsal ganglion of the wrist: results of treatment by arthroscopic resection. *Hand Surgery* 7: 1-5.

Sonnery-Cottet, B., B. Edwards, E. Noel, and G. Walch. 2002. Results of arthroscopic treatment of posterosuperior glenoid impingement in tennis players. *The American Journal of Sports Medicine* 30: 227-232

Struijs, P.A., P.J. Damen, E.W. Bakker L., Blankevoort, W.J. Assendelft, and C.N. van Dijk. 2003. Manipulation of the wrist for management of lateral epicondylitis: a randomized pilot study. *Physical Therapy* 83(7): 608-616.

Tsur, A. and S. Gillson. 2000. Brachial tendon injuries in young female high-level tennis players. *Croatian Medical Journal* 41: 184-185.

Zaslav, K.R. 2001. Internal rotation resistance strength test: a new diagnostic test to differentiate intra-articular pathology from outlet (Neer) impingement syndrome. *Journal of Shoulder and Elbow Surgery* 10: 23-27.

Chapter 8. Injuries of the Lower Body

Allum, R.L. 2001. The anterior cruciate ligament--current concepts. *Knee* 8: 1-3.

Baker, M.M. and M.S. Juhn. 2000. Patellofemoral pain syndrome in the female athlete. *Clinics in Sports Medicine* 19: 315-329.

Barry, L.D., A.N. Barry, and Y. Chen. 2002. A retrospective study of standing gastrocnemius-soleus stretching versus night splinting in the treatment of plantar fasciitis. *Journal of Foot and Ankle Surgery* 41: 221-227.

Bennett, J.E., M.F. Reinking, B. Pluemer, A. Pentel, M. Seaton, and C. Killian. 2001. Factors contributing to the development of medical tibial stress syndrome in high school runners. *Journal of Orthopedics and Sports Physical Therapy* 31: 504-510.

Beynnon, B.D., L. Good, and M.A. Risberg. 2002. The effect of bracing on proprioception of knees with anterior cruciate ligament injury. *Journal of Orthopaedics and Sports Physical Therapy* 32: 11-15.

Bhandari, M., G.H. Guyatt, F. Siddiqui, F. Morrow, J. Busse, R.K. Leighton, S. Sprague, and E.H. Schemitsch. 2002. Treatment of acute Achilles tendon ruptures: a systematic overview and metaanalysis. *Clinical Orthopedics* 400: 190-200

Blackman, P.G., L.R. Simmons, and K.M. Crossley. 1998. Treatment of chronic exertional compartment syndrome with massage: a pilot study. *Clinical Journal of Sports Medicine* 8: 14-17.

Brandsson, S., E. Faxen, J. Kartus, B.I. Eriksson, and J. Karlsson. 2001. Is a knee brace advantageous after anterior cruciate ligament surgery? A prospective, randomised study with a two-year follow-up. *Scandinavian Journal of Medicine and Science in Sports* 1: 110-114.

Buchbinder, R., R. Ptasznik, J. Gordon, J. Buchanan, V. Prabaharan, and A. Forbes. 2002. Ultrasound-guided extracorporeal shock wave therapy for plantar fasciitis: a randomized controlled trial. *Journal of the American Medical Association* 288: 1364-1372.

Buschmann, W.R., M.H. Jahss, F. Kummer, P. Desai, R.O. Gee, and J.L. Ricci. 1995. Histology and histomorphometric analysis of the normal and atrophic heel fat pad. *Foot and Ankle International* 16: 254-258.

Campbell, S.E., T.G. Sanders, and W.B. Morrison. 2001. MR imaging of meniscal cysts: incidence, location, and clinical significance. *American Journal of Roentgenology* 177: 409-413.

Conti, S.F. 1994. Posterior tibial tendon problems in athletes. *Orthopedic Clinics of North America* 25: 109-121.

Croisier, J.L., B. Forthomme, M.H. Namurois, M. Vanderthommen, and J.M. Crielaard. 2002. Hamstring muscle strain recurrence and strength performance disorders. *American Journal of Sports Medicine* 30: 199-203.

Crossley, K., S.M. Cowan, K.L. Bennell, and J. McConnell. 2000. Patellar taping: is clinical success supported by scientific evidence? *Manual Therapy* 5: 142-150.

Daghino, W., M. Pasquali, and C. Faletti. 1997. Superficial peroneal nerve entrapment in a young athlete: the diagnostic contribution of magnetic resonance imaging. *Journal of Foot and Ankle Surgery* 36: 170-172.

Drogset, J.O., I. Rossvoll, and T. Grontvedt. 1999. Surgical treatment of iliotibial band friction syndrome. A retrospective study of 45 patients. *Scandinavian Journal of Medicine and Science in Sports* 9: 296-298.

Faletti, C., N. De Stefano, G. Giudice, and M. Larciprete. 1998. Knee impingement syndromes. *European Journal of Radiology* 27: S60-S69.

Fink, C., C. Hoser, W. Hackl, R.A. Navarro, and K.P. Benedetto. 2001. Long-term outcome of operative or nonoperative treatment of anterior cruciate ligament rupture-is sports activity a determining variable? *International Journal of Sports Medicine* 22: 304-309.

Fishman, L.M., G.W. Dombi, C. Michaelsen, S. Ringel, J. Rozbruch, B. Rosner, and C. Weber. 2002. Piriformis syndrome: diagnosis, treatment, and outcome: a 10 year study. *Archives of Physical Medicine and Rehabilitation* 83: 295-301.

Foster, M.R. 2002. Piriformis syndrome. *Orthopedics* 25: 821-825.

Francis, A., R.D. Thomas, and A. McGregor. 2001. Anterior cruciate ligament rupture: reconstruction surgery and rehabilitation. A nation-wide survey of current practice. *Knee* 8: 13-18.

Fredberg, U. and L. Bolvig. 1999. Jumper's knee. Review of the literature. *Scandinavian Journal of Medicine and Science in Sports* 9: 66-73.

Fredericson, M, J.J. White, J.M. Macmahon, and T.P. Andriacchi. 2002. Quantitative analysis of the relative effectiveness of 3 iliotibial band stretches. *Archives of Physical Medicine and Rehabilitation* 83: 589-592.

Fredericson, M., C.L. Cookingham, A.M. Chaudhari, B.C. Dowdell, N. Oestreicher, and S.A. Sahrmann. 2000. Hip abductor weakness in distance runners with iliotibial band syndrome. *Clinical Journal of Sports Medicine* 10: 169-175.

Fu, F.H., C.H. Bennett, C.B. Ma, J. Menetry, and C. Lattermann. 2000. Current trends in anterior cruciate ligament reconstruction. Part II. Operative procedures and clinical correlations. *American Journal of Sports Medicine* 28: 124-130.

Greis, P.E., M.C. Holmstrom, D.D. Bardana, and R.T. Burks. 2002. Meniscal injury: II. Management. *Journal of the American Academy of Orthopedic Surgery* 10(3): 177-187.

Handoll, H.H., B.H. Rowe, K.M. Quinn, and R. de Bie. 2001. Interventions for preventing ankle ligament injuries. *Cochrane Database Systematic Review* 3: CD000018.

Hartig, D.E. and J.M. Henderson. 1999. Increasing hamstring flexibility decreases lower extremity overuse injuries in military basic trainees. *The American Journal of Sports Medicine* 27: 173-176.

Hersh, B.L. and N.S. Heath. 2002. Achilles tendon rupture as a result of oral steroid therapy. *Journal of the American Podiatric Medical Association* 92: 355-358.

Holmes, S.W. and W.G. Clancy. 1998. Clinical classification of patellofemoral pain and dysfunction. *The Journal of Orthopaedic and Sports Physical Therapy* 28: 299-306.

Indrekvam, K. and E. Sudmann. 2002 Piriformis muscle syndrome in 19 patients treated by tenotomy: a 1- to 16-year follow-up study. *International Orthopedics* 26: 101-103.

Iwamoto, J. and T. Takeda. 2003. Stress fractures in athletes: review of 196 cases. *Journal of Orthopedic Science* 8(3): 273-278.

Kerkhoffs, G.M., H.H. Handoll, R. De Bie, R.H. Rowe, and P.A. Struijs. 2002. Surgical versus conservative treatment for acute injuries of the lateral ligament complex of the ankle in adults (Cochrane Review). *Cochrane Database Systematic Review* 3: CD000380.

Kinoshita, M., R. Okuda, J. Morikawa, T. Jotoku, and M. Abe. 2001. The dorsiflexion-eversion test for diagnosis of tarsal tunnel syndrome. *Journal of Bone and Joint Surgery Am* 83: 1835-1839.

Kirk, K.L., T. Kuklo, and W. Klemme. 2000. Iliotibial band friction syndrome. *Orthopedics* 23: 1209-1214.

Kvist, M. 1994 Achilles tendon injuries in athletes. *Sports Medicine* 18: 173-201.

Labib, S.A., J.S. Gould, F.A. Rodriguez-del-Rio, and S. Lyman. 2002. Heel pain triad (HPT): the combination of plantar fasciitis, posterior tibial tendon dysfunction and tarsal tunnel syndrome. *Foot and Ankle International* 23: 212-220.

Van der Linden, P.D., M.C. Sturkenboom, R.M. Herings, H.G. Leufkens, and B.H. Stricker. 2002. Fluoroquinolones and risk of Achilles tendon disorders: case-control study. *British Medical Journal* 324: 1306-1307.

Maffuli, N. and D. Kader. 2002. Tendinopathy of tendo Achillis. *The Journal of Bone and Joint Surgery* 84-Br: 1-8.

Mazzone, M.F. and T. McCue. 2002. Common conditions of the Achilles tendon. *American Family Physician* 65: 1805-1810.

McCrory, P. and S. Bell 1999. Nerve entrapment syndromes as a cause of pain in the hip, groin and buttock. *Sports Medicine* 27(4): 261-274.

Miller, C.A. and J.A. Bosco 3rd. 2001-2002. Lateral ankle and subtalar instability. *Bulletin of the Hospital of Joint Diseases* 60(3-4): 143-149.

Mizuta, H., E. Nakamura, Y. Otsuka, S. Kudo, and K. Takagi. 2001. Osteochondritis dissecans of the lateral femoral condyle following total resection of the discoid lateral meniscus. *Arthroscopy* 17: 608-612.

Moller, E., M. Forssblad, L. Hansson, P. Wange, and L. Weidenhielm. 2000. Bracing versus nonbracing in rehabilitation after anterior cruciate ligament reconstruction: a randomized prospective study with 2-year follow-up. *Knee Surgery and Sports Traumatology and Arthroscopy* 9(2): 102-108.

Moller, M., K. Lind, T. Movin, and J. Karlsson. 2002. Calf muscle function after Achilles tendon rupture. A prospective, randomised study comparing surgical and non-surgical treatment. *Scandinavian Journal of Medicine and Science in Sports* 12: 9-16.

Neptune, R.R., I.C. Wright, and A.J. van den Bogert AJ. 2000. The influence of orthotic devices and vastus medialis strength and timing on patellofemoral loads during running. *Clinical Biomechanics* 15: 611-618.

Nicholas, S.J. and T.F. Tyler. 2002. Adductor muscle strains in sport. *Sports Medicine* 32: 339-344.

Nuccion, S.L., D.M. Hunter, and J. Difiori. 2001. Dislocation of the posterior tibial tendon without disruption of the flexor retinaculum. A case report and review of the literature. *American Journal of Sports Medicine* 29: 656-659.

Nunley, J.A. 2001. Fractures of the base of the fifth metatarsal: the Jones fracture. *Orthopedic Clinics of North America* 32: 171-180.

Olson, W.R. and L. Rechkemmer. 1993. Popliteus tendinitis. *Journal of the American Podiatric Medical Association* 83: 537-540.

Paterson, R.S. and J.N. Brown. 2001. The posteromedial impingement lesion of the ankle. A series of six cases. *The American Journal of Sports Medicine* 29: 550-557.

Perugia, D., A. Basile, C. Massoni, S. Gumina, F. Rossi, and A. Ferretti. 2002. Conservative treatment of subtalar dislocations. *International Orthopedics* 26: 56-60.

Pisani, G. 1996. Chronic laxity of the subtalar joint. *Orthopedics* 19: 431-437.

Porter, D.A., D.E. Baxter, T.O. Clanton, and T.E. Klootwyk. 1998. Posterior tibial tendon tears in young competitive athletes: two case reports. *Foot and Ankle International* 19: 627-630.

Puranen, J. and S. Orava. 1991. The hamstring syndrome-a new gluteal sciatica. *Annals of Chirurgical Gynaecology* 80: 212-214.

Quinn, T.J., J.A. Jacobson, J.G. Craig, and M.T. van Holsbeeck. 2000. Sonography of Morton's neuromas. *American Journal of Roentgenology* 174: 1723-1728.

Reade, B.M., D.C. Longo, and M.C. Keller. 2001. Tarsal tunnel syndrome. *Clinical Podiatric Medicine and Surgery* 18: 395-408.

Rodrigue, T. and R.W. Hardy. 2001. Diagnosis and treatment of piriformis syndrome. *Neurosurgical Clinics of North America* 12: 311-319.

Rowdon, G.A., J.K. Richardson, P. Hoffmann, M. Zaffer, and E. Barill. 2001. Chronic anterior compartment syndrome and deep peroneal nerve function. *Clinical Journal of Sport Medicine* 11: 229-233.

Segawa, H., G. Omori, and Y. Koga. 2001. Long-term results of non-operative treatment of anterior cruciate ligament injury. *Knee* 8: 5-11.

Slimmon, D., K. Bennell, P. Brukner, K. Crossley, and S.N. Bell. 2002. Long-term outcome of fasciotomy with partial fasciectomy for chronic exertional compartment syndrome of the lower leg. *American Journal of Sports Medicine* 30: 581-588.

Thacker, S.B., J. Gilchrist, D. F. Stroup, and C.D. Kimsey. 2002. The prevention of shin splints in sports: a systematic review of the literature. *Medicine and Science in Sports and Exercise* 34: 32-40.

Tol, J.L., C.P. Verheyen, and C.N. van Dijk. 2001. Arthroscopic treatment of anterior impingement in the ankle. *Journal of Bone and Joint Surgery Br* 83: 9-13.

Toth, A.P. and F.A. Cordasco. 2001. Anterior cruciate ligament injuries in the female athlete. *Journal of Gender Specific Medicine* 4(4): 25-34.

Touliopolous, S. and E.B. Hershman. 1999. Lower leg pain. Diagnosis and treatment of compartment syndromes and other pain syndromes of the leg. *Sports Medicine* 27: 193-204.

Umans, H. 2002. Ankle impingement syndromes. *Seminars in Musculoskeletal Radiology* 6: 133-140.

Verrall, G.M., J.P. Slavotinek, P.G. Barnes, G.T. Fon, and A.J. Spriggins. 2001. Clinical risk factors for hamstring muscle strain injury: a prospective study with correlation of injury by magnetic resonance imaging. *British Journal of Sports Medicine* 35: 435-439.

Waldecker. U. 2001. Plantar fat pad atrophy: a cause of metatarsalgia? *Journal of Foot and Ankle Surgery* 40: 21-27.

Weinfeld, S.B. and M.S. Myerson. 1996. Interdigital Neuritis: Diagnosis and Treatment. *Journal of the American Academy of Orthopedic Surgeons* 4: 328-335.

Wind, W.M. and B.J. Rohrbacher. 2001. Peroneus longus and brevis rupture in a collegiate athlete. *Foot and Ankle International* 22: 140-143.

Witvrouw, E., J. Bellemans, R. Lysens, L. Danneels, and D. Cambier D. 2001. Intrinsic risk factors for the development of patellar tendinitis in an athletic population. A two-year prospective study. *American Journal of Sports Medicine* 29: 190-195.

Yinger, K., B.R. Mandelbaum, and L.C. Almekinders. 2002. Achilles rupture in the athlete. Current science and treatment. *Clinical Podiatric Med Surgery* 19: 231-250.

Zwipp H, Rammelt S, Grass R. 2002. Ligamentous injuries about the ankle and subtalar joints. *Clinical Podiatric Med Surgery* 19: 195-229.

Chapter 9. Injuries of the Trunk and Spine

Arokoski, J.P., T. Valta, O. Airaksinen, and M. Kankaanpaa. 2001. Back and abdominal muscle function during stabilization exercises. *Archives of Physical Medicine and Rehabilitation* 82: 1089-1098.

Hides, J.A., G.A. Jull, and C.A. Richardson. 2001. Long-term effects of specific stabilizing exercises for first-episode low back pain. *Spine* 26: E243-E248.

Hubley-Kozey, C.L. and M.J. Vezina. 2002. Muscle activation during exercises to improve trunk stability in men with low back pain. *Archives of Physical Medicine and Rehabilitation* 83: 1100-1108.

Moseley, G.L., P.W. Hodges, and S.C. Gandevia. 2002. Deep and superficial fibers of the lumbar multifidus muscles are differentially active during voluntary arm movements. *Spine* 27: E29-E36.

Nadler, S.F., G.A. Malanga, L.A. Bartoli, J.H. Feinberg, M. Prybicien, and M. Deprince. 2002. Hip muscle imbalance and low back pain in athletes: influence of core strengthening. *Medicine and Science in Sports and Exercise* 34: 9-16.

Norris, C.M. 1993. Abdominal muscle training in sport. *British Journal of Sports Medicine* 27: 19-27.

Richardson, C.A., C.J. Snijders, J.A. Hides, L. Damen, M.S. Pas, and J. Storm. 2002. The relation between the transversus abdominis muscles, sacroiliac joint mechanics, and low back pain. *Spine* 27: 399-405.

Roetert, E.P., Th.J. McCormick, S.W. Brown, and T.S. Ellenbecker. 1996. *Isokinetics and Exercise Science* 6: 15-20.

Saraux, A., Y. Guillodo, V. Devauchelle, J. Allain, C. Guedes, and P. Le Goff. 1999. Are tennis players at increased risk for low back pain and sciatica? *Revue du Rhumatisme* 66: 143-145.

J.T. Stinson. 1993. Spondylolysis and spondylolisthesis in the athlete. *Clinics in Sports Medicine* 12: 517-528.

Chapter 10. The Brain and Nervous System

Turner J. 2003. Exercise-related headache. *Current Sports Medicine Reports* 2(1): 15-17.

Imperato, J., Burstein, J., and J.A. Edlow 2003. Benign exertional headache. *Annals of Emergency Medicine* 41(1): 98-103.

Sjaastad, O. and L.S. Bakketeig 2002. Exertional headache. I. Vaga study of headache epidemiology. *Cephalalgia* 22(10): 784-790.

Schoenen, J. and P.S. Sandor. 2004. Headache with focal neurological signs or symptoms: a complicated differential diagnosis. *Lancet Neurology* 3(4): 237-245.

Bigal, M.E., R.B. Lipton, and A.V. Krymchantowski. 2004. The medical management of migraine. *American Journal of Therapy* 11(2): 130-140.

Waddell, A. and R. Canter. 2004. Tinnitus. *American Family Physician* 69(3): 591-592.

Chapter 11. The Eye

Abernethy, B. and J.M. Wood. 2001. Do generalized visual training programmes for sport really work? An experimental investigation. *Journal of Sports Sciences* 19: 203-222.

Easterbrook, M. 1988. Ocular injuries in racquet sports. *International Ophthalmology Clinics* 28: 228-237.

Farber, A.S. 1991. Preventing eye injuries. What to tell patients. *Postgraduate Medicine* 89: 121-128.

Gregory, P.T.S. 1986. Sussex Eye Hospital sports injuries. *British Journal of Opthalmology* 70: 748-750.

Lederman, C. and M. Miller. 1999. Hordeola and chalazia. *Pediatrics in Review* 20: 283-284.

Olson, M.D. 1991. The common stye. *Journal of School Health* 61: 95-97.

Pardhan, S., P. Shacklock, and J. Weatherill. 1995. Sport-related eye trauma: a survey of the presentation of eye injuries to a casualty clinic and the use of protective eye-wear. *Eye* 9: S50-S53.

Prince, P. and L. Laurencelle. 1988. Protection of the eyes in racket sports. *Canadian Journal of Sport Sciences* 13: 149-156.

Raskin, E.M., M.G. Speaker, and P.R. Laibson. 1992. Blepharitis. *Infectious Disease Clinics of North America* 6: 777-787.

Chapter 12. Skin Disorders

Adams, B.B. 2002. Dermatologic disorders of the athlete. *Sports Medicine* 32: 309-321

Dissemond, J., R. Hinrichs and K. Scharfetter-Kochanek. 1999. Die Bedeutung des Sports bei der Entstehung und Therapie dermatologischer Krankheitsbilder. *Deutsche Zeitschrift für Sportmedizin* 50: 181-186.

Bergfeld, W.F. 1984. Dermatologic problems in athletes. *Primary Care* 11: 151-160.

Bergfeld W.F. and J.S. Taylor. 1985. Trauma, sports and the skin. *American Journal of Industrial Medicine* 8: 403-413.

Eisele, S.A. 1994. Conditions of the toenails. *Orthopedic Clinics of North America* 25: 183-188.

Elgart, G.W. 1990. Ant, bee, and wasp stings. *Dermatologic Clinics* 8: 229-236.

Gupta, S., J. O Donnell, A. Kupa, R. Heddle, G. Skowronski, and P. Roberts-Thomson. 1988. Management of bee-sting anaphylaxis. *The Medical Journal of Australia* 149: 602-604.

Helzer-Julin, M. 1994. Sun, heat, and cold injuries in cyclists. *Clinics in Sports Medicine* 13: 219-234.

Klein A.W. and D.C. Rish. 1992. Conspectus. Sports related skin problems. *Dermatology* 18: 2-4.

Visscher, P.K., R.S. Vetter, and S. Camzine. 1996. Removing bee stings. *The Lancet* 348: 301-302.

Chapter 13. The Cardiovascular System

Biffi, A., A. Pellicia, L. Verdile, F. Fernando, A. Spataro, S. Caselli, M. Santini, and B.J. Maron. 2002. Long-term clinical significance of frequent and complex ventricular tachyarrhythmias in trained athletes. *Journal of the American College of Cardiology* 40: 446-452.

Clasing, D. 1976. Herz- und Kreislaufbelastungen bei Tennisspielern. *Sportartzt und Sportmedizin* 5: 100-103.

Dugas, J.R. and A.J. Weiland. 2000. Vascular pathology in the throwing athlete. *Hand Clinics* 6: 477-485.

Eichner, E.R. 1988. Sudden death in racquet sports. *Clinics in Sports Medicine* 7: 245-252.

Ferrauti, A., K. Weber, and H.K. Struder. 1997. Effects of tennis training on lipid metabolism and lipoproteins in recreational players. *British Journal of Sports Medicine* 31: 322-327.

Hannon, D.W. and T.K. Knilans. 1993. Syncope in children and dolescents. *Current Problems in Pediatrics* 23: 358-384.

Houston, T.K., L.A. Meoni, D.E. Ford, F.L. Brancati, L.A. Cooper, D.M. Levine, K-Y. Liang, and M.J. Klag. 2002. Sports ability in young men and the incidence of cardiovascular disease. *American Journal of Medicine* 112: 689-695.

Jett, M., F. Landry, B. Tiemann, and G. Bl hmchen. 1991. Ambulatory blood pressure and Holter monitoring during tennis play. *Canadian Journal of Sport Sciences* 16: 40-44.

Keul, J., A. Berg, A.H. Dickhuth, M. Lehmann, and T. Fritsch. 1982. Kardiozirkulatorische und metabolische Anpassungsvorg nge bei Tennisspielern. *Herz und Kreislauf* 7: 373-381.

Keul, J., W. Stockhausen, R. Pokan, M. Huonker, and A. Berg. 1991. Metabolische und kardiozirkulatorische Adaptation sowie Leistungsverhalten professioneller Tennisspieler. *Deutsche medizinische Wochenschriften* 116: 761-767.

K nig, D., M. Huonker, A. Schmid, M. Halle, A. Berg, and J. Keul. 2001. Cardiovascular, metabolic, and hormonal parameters in professional tennis players. *Medicine and Science in Sports and Exercise* 33: 654-658.

McCarthy, W.J., J.S.T. Yao, M.F. Schafer, G. Nuber, W.R. Flinn, D. Blackburn, and J.R. Suker. 1989. Upper extremity arterial injury in athletes. *Journal of Vascular Surgery* 9: 317-327.

No l, B. and D. Hayoz. 2000. A tennis player with hand claudication. *Vasa* 29: 151-153.

Overstreet, D.S., W.H. Skinner, and T.M. Roy. 1993. Primary thrombosis in the upper extremity. *Journal of the Kentucky Medical Association* 91(2): 54-57.

Patternson, R.E. and S.F. Horowitz. 1989. Importance of epidemiology and biostatistics in deciding clinical strategies for using diagnostic tests: a simplified approach using examples from coronary artery disease. *Journal of the American College of Cardiology* 13. 1653-1665.

Pluim, B.M. 1998. The athlete s heart. PhD dissertation. Leiden, Leiden University Medical Center.

Rohrer, M.J., P.A. Cardullo, A.M. Pappas, D.A. Phillips, and H. Brownell Wheeler. 1990. Axillary artery compression and thrombosis in throwing athletes. *Journal of Vascular Surgery* 11: 761-769.

Spirito, P., A. Pellicia, M.A. Proschan, M. Granata, A. Spataro, P. Bellone, G. Caselli, A. Biffi, C. Vecchio, and B.J. Maron. 1994. Morphology of the athlete s heart assessed by echocardiography in 947 athletes representing 27 sports. *American Journal of Cardiology* 74: 802-806.

Zell, L., W. Kindermann, F. Marschall, P. Scheffler, J. Gross J, and A. Buchter. 2001. Paget-Schroetter syndrome in sports activities--case study and literature review. *Angiology* 52: 337-342

Chapter 14. The Respiratory System

Chester, A.C. 1996. Chronic sinusitis. *American Family Physician* 53: 877-887.

Jaber, R. 2002. Respiratory and allergic diseases: from upper respiratory tract infections to asthma. *Primary Care* 29: 231-261.

Katz, R.M. 1984. Rhinitis in the athlete. *Journal of Allergy and Clinical Immunology* 73: 708-711.

Langdeau, J.B and L.P. Boulet. 2001. Prevalence and mechanisms of development of asthma and airway hyperresponsiveness in athletes. *Sports Medicine* 31: 601-616.

Shephard, R.J. and P.N. Shek. 1994. Infectious diseases in athletes: New interest for an old problem. *Journal of Sports Medicine and Physical Fitness* 34: 11-22.

Storms, W.W. 2003. Review of exercise-induced asthma. *Medicine and Science in Sports and Exercise* 35(9) : 1464-1470.

Wilber, R.L., K.W. Rundell, L. Szmedra, D.M. Jenkinson, J. Im, and S.D. Drake. 2000. Incidence of exercise-induced bronchospasm in Olympic winter sport athletes. *Medicine and Science in Sports and Exercise* 32: 732-737.

Chapter 15. The Digestive System

Consensus conference. 1985. Travellers diarrhoea. *Journal of the American Medical Association* 253: 2700-2704.

Shephard, R.J. and P.N. Shek. 1994. Infectious Diseases in Athletes: New interest for an old problem. *Journal of Sports Medicine and Physical Fitness* 34: 11-22.

Peters, H.P., W.R. De Vries, G.P. Vanberge-Henegouwen, and L.M. Akkermans. 2001. Potential benefits and hazards of physical activity and exercise on the gastrointestinal tract. *Gut* 48: 435-439.

Shawdon, A. 1995. Gastro-oesophageal reflux and exercise. Important pathology to consider in the athletic population. *Sports Medicine* 20: 109-116.

Chapter 16. Other Medical Conditions

Cozad, J. 1996. Infectious mononucleosis. *Nurse Practitioner* 21(3):14-16, 23, 27-28.

Dang, C.V. 2001. Runner's anemia. *Journal of the American Medical Association* 286:714-716.

Draznin, M.B. and D.R. Patel. 1998. Diabetes mellitus and sports. *Adolescent Medicine* 9: 457-465.

Halstead, M.E. and D.T. Bernhardt. 2002. Common infections in the young athlete. *Pediatric Annals* 31: 42-48.

Ivy, J.J., T.W. Zderic, and D.L. Fogt. 1999. Prevention and treatment of non-insulin-dependent diabetes mellitus. *Exercise and Sport Science Reviews* 27: 1-35.

Ryan, A.S. 2000. Insulin resistance with aging: effects of diet and exercise. *Sports Medicine* 30:327-346.

Shaskey, D.J., and G.A. Green. 2000. Sports haematology. *Sports Medicine* 29: 27-38.

Zinker, B.A. 1999. Nutrition and exercise in individuals with diabetes. *Clinics in Sports Medicine* 18: 585-606.

Chapter 17. Heat Stress

Vergauwen, L., F. Brouns, and P. Hespel. 1997. Carbohydrate supplementation improves stroke performance in tennis. *Medicine and Science in Sports and Exercise* 30: 1289-1295.

Ferrauti, A., M.F. Bergeron, B.M. Pluim, and K. Weber. 2001. Physiological responses in tennis and running with similar oxygen uptake. *European Journal of Applied Physiology* 85: 27-33.

Bergeron, M.F. 2003. Heat cramps: fluid and electrolyte challenges during tennis in the heat. *Journal of Science and Medicine in Sport* 6(1): 19-27.

Bergeron, M.F. 1996. Heat cramps during tennis; a case report. *International Journal of Sport Nutrition* 6: 62-68.

Bergeron, M.F., L.E. Armstrong, and C.M. Maresh. 1995. Fluid and electrolyte losses during tennis in the heat. *Clinics in Sports Medicine* 14: 23-32.

Bergeron, M.F., C.M. Maresh, L.E. Armstrong, J.F. Signorile, J.W. Castellani, R.W. Kenefick, K.E. LaGasse, and D.A. Riebe. 1995. Fluid-electrolyte balance associated with tennis match play in a hot environment. *International Journal of Sport Nutrition* 5: 180-193.

Maughan, R.J., ed. 2000. *Nutrition in Sport*. London: Blackwell Science.

Mitchell, J.B., K.J. Cole, P.W. Grandjean, and R.J. Sobczak. 1992. The effect of a carbohydrate beverage on tennis performance and fluid

balance during prolonged tennis play. *Journal of Applied Sport Science Research* 6: 96-102.

Lukaski, H.C. 2000. Magnesium, zinc, and chromium nutriture and physical activity. *American Journal of Clinical Nutrition* 72: S585-S593.

Shireffs, S.M., and R.J. Maughan. 1997. Whole body sweat collection in humans: an improved method with preliminary data on electrolyte content. *Journal of Applied Physiology* 82: 336-341.

Chapter 18. Nutrition and Supplements

American College of Sports Medicine, American Dietetic Association, and Dietitians of Canada. 2000. Nutrition and athletic performance. *Medicine and Science in Sports and Exercise* 32: 2130-2145.

Barceloux, D.G. 1999. Vanadium. *Journal of Toxicology. Clinical Toxicology* 37: 265-278.

Clarkson, P.M. 1995. Micronutrients and exercise. *Journal of Sports Sciences* 13: S11-S24.

Clarkson, P.M. 1991. Minerals: Exercise performance and supplementation in athletes. *Journal of Sports Sciences* 9: 91-116.

Constantini, N.W., A. Eliakim, L. Zigel, M. Yaaron, and B. Falk. 2000. Iron status of highly active adolescents: evidence of depleted iron stores in gymnasts. *International Journal of Sport Nutrition and Exercise Metabolism* 10: 62-70.

Ferrauti, A., M.F. Bergeron, B.M. Pluim, and K. Weber. 2001. Physiological responses in tennis and running with similar oxygen uptake. *European Journal of Applied Physiology* 85: 27-33.

Finstad, E.W., I.J. Newhouse, H.C. Lukaski, and J.E. McAuliffe. 2000. The effects of magnesium supplementation on exercise performance. *Medicine and Science in Sports and Exercise* 33: 493-498.

Ivy, J.L. 2001. Dietary strategies to promote glycogen synthesis after exercise. *Canadian Journal of Applied Physiology* 26: S236-S245.

Liu, L., G. Borowksi, and L.I. Rose. 1983. Hypomagnesia in a tennis player. *Physician and Sportsmedicine* 11: 79-80.

Lukaski, H.C. Micronutrients (magnesium, zinc, and copper): are mineral supplements needed for athletes? 1995. *International Journal of Sport Nutrition* 5: S74-S83.

Micheletti, A., R. Rossi., and S. Rufini. 2001. Zinc status in athletes: Relation to diet and exercise. *Sports Medicine* 31: 577-582.

Newhouse, I.J. and E.W. Finstad. 2000. The effects of magnesium supplementation on exercise performance. *Clinical Journal of Sport Medicine* 10: 195-200.

Nieman, D.C. 1999. Nutrition, exercise, and immune system function. *Clinics in Sports Medicine* 18: 537-548.

Nutter, J. Seasonal changes in female athletes' diets. 1991. *International Journal of Sport Nutrition* 1: 395-407.

Venkatraman, J.T., J. Leddy, and D. Pendergast. 2000. Dietary fats and immune status in athletes: clinical implications. *Medicine and Science in Sports and Exercise* 32: S389-395.

Williams, M.H. 1999. Facts and fallacies of purported ergogenic amino acid supplements. *Clinics in Sports Medicine* 18: 633-649.

Chapter 19. Doping

Corrigan, B. and R. Kazlauskas. 2003. Medication use in athletes selected for doping control at the Sydney Olympics (2000). *Clinical Journal of Sport Medicine* 13(1):33-40.

Geyer, H., M.K. Parr, U. Mareck, U. Reinhart, Y. Schrader, and W. Schanzer. 2004. Analysis of non-hormonal nutritional supplements for anabolic-androgenic steroids results of an international study. *International Journal of Sports Medicine* 25(2):124-9.

ITF. 2004. Tennis anti-doping programme 2004. London: ITF.

Juhn, M. 2003. Popular sports supplements and ergogenic aids. *Sports Medicine* 33(12):921-939.

Maughan, R.J., D.S. King, and T. Lea. 2004. Dietary supplements. *Journal of Sports Sciences* 22(1):95-113.

Mendoza J. 2002. The war on drugs in sport: a perspective from the front-line. *Clinical Journal of Sports Medicine* 12(4):254-258.

Chapter 20. Overtraining and Burnout

Allison, M.T. and C. Meyer. 1988. Career problems and retirement among elite athletes. The female tennis professional. *Sociology of Sport Journal* 5: 212-222.

Gondola, J.C. and E. Wughalter. 1991. The personality characteristics of internationally ranked female tennis players as measured by the Cattell 16 PF. *Perceptual and Motor Skills* 73: 987-992.

Gould, D., S. Tuffey, E. Udry, and J. Loehr. 1996. Burnout in competitive junior tennis players: I. A quantitative psychological assessment. *The Sport Psychologist* 10: 322-340.

Gould, D., S. Tuffey, E. Udry, and J. Loehr. 1996. Burnout in competitive junior tennis players: II. Qualitative analysis. *The Sport Psychologist* 10: 341-366.

Gould, D., S. Tuffey, E. Udry, and J. Loehr. 1997. Burnout in competitive junior tennis players: III. Individual differences in the burnout experience. *The Sport Psychologist* 11: 257-276.

Gould, D., N. Damarjian, and R. Medbery. 1999. An examination of mental skills training in junior tennis coaches. *The Sport Psychologist* 13; 127-143.

Hoyle, R.H and S.S. Leff. 1997. The role of parental involvement in youth sport participation and performance. *Adolescence* 32: 233-243.

Hooper, S.L. and L. T. Mackinnon. 1995. Monitoring overtraining in athletes: recommendations. *Sports Medicine* 20: 321-327.

Kentt , G., P. Hassm n, and J.S. Raglin. 2001. *International Journal of Sports Medicine* 22: 460-465.

Kuipers, H. and H.A. Keizer. 1988. Overtraining in elite athletes. Review and directions for the future. *Sports Medicine* 6: 79-92.

Shephard, R.J. 2001. Chronic fatigue syndrome. An update. *Sports Medicine* 31: 167-194.

Urhausen, A. and W. Kindermann. 2002. Diagnosis of overtraining. What tools do we have? *Sports Medicine* 32: 95-102.

Veale, D.M.W. 1991. Psychological aspects of staleness and dependence on exercise. *International Journal of Sports Medicine* 12: S19-S22.

Chapter 21. Travelling

Atkinson, G., P. Buckley, B. Edwards, T. Reilly, and J. Waterhouse. 2001. Are there hang-over effects on physical performance when melatonin is ingested by athletes before nocturnal sleep? *International Journal of Sports Medicine* 22: 232-234.

Constantini, N., A. Ken-Dror, A. Eliakim, L. Galatzkia, A. Morag, G. Mann, B. Volach, J. Asharov, and D. Shoval. 2001. Vaccinations in sports and recommendations for immunization against flu, hepatitis A and hepatitis B. *Harefuah* 140: 1191-1195, 1228

Crowcroft, N.S., B. Walsh, K.L. Davison, and U. Gungabissoon. 2001. Guidelines for the control of hepatitis A virus infection. *Communicable Disease and Public Health* 4: 213-227

Edwards, B.J., G. Atkinson, J. Waterhouse, T. Reilly, R. Godfrey, and R. Budgett. 2000. Use of melatonin in recovery from jet-lag following an eastward flight across 10 time-zones. *Ergonomics* 43: 1501-1513.

Lagarde, D., B. Chappuis, P.F. Billaud, L. Ramont, F. Chauffard, and J. French. 2000. Evaluation of pharmacologic aids on physical performance after a transmeridian flight. *Medicine and Science in Sports and Exercise* 33: 628-634.

Reilly, T., G. Atkinson, and R. Bugett. 2001. Effect of low-dose temazepam on physiological variables and performance tests following a westerly flight across five timezones. *International Journal of Sports Medicine* 22: 166-174.

Sturchler, M.P. and R. Steffen. 2001. Vaccinations for overseas travelers-new evidence and recommendations. *Therapeutische Umschau* 58: 362-366.

Chapter 22. Juniors

Anderson, S.J. 2002. Lower extremity injuries in youth sports. *Pediatric Clinics of North America* 49: 627-641.

Baxter-Jones, A., H. Goldstein, and P. Helms. 1993. The development of aerobic power in young athletes. *Journal of Applied Physiology* 75:1160-1167.

Belechri, M., E. Petridou, S. Kedikoglou, and D. Trichopoulos. 2001. Sports Injuries European Union Group. Sports injuries among children In six European union countries. *European Journal of Epidemiology* 17: 1005-1012.

Benguigui, R. and H. Ripoll. 1998. Effects of tennis practice on the coincidence timing accuracy of adults and children. *Research Quarterly for Exercise Science and Sport* 69: 217-223.

Bylak, J. and M.R. Hutchinson. 1998. Common sports injuries in young tennis players. *Sports Medicine* 26: 119-132.

Connolly, S.A., L.P. Connolly, and D. Jaramillo. 2001. Imaging of sports injuries in children and adolescents. *Radiology Clinics of North America* 39: 773-790.

Damsgaard, R., J. Bencke, G. Matthiesen, J.H. Petersen, and J. Muller. 2000. Is prepubertal growth adversely affected by sport? *Medicine and Science in Sports and Exercise* 32: 698-703.

Davies, P.L. and J.D. Rose. 2000. Motor skills of typically developing adolescents: awkwardness or improvement? *Physical and Occupational Therapy in Pediatrics* 20: 19-42.

Faigenbaum, A.D. 2000. Strength training for children and adolescents. *Clinics in Sports Medicine* 19: 593-619.

Giacomini, C.P. 1999. Association of birthdate with success of nationally ranked junior tennis players in the United States. *Perceptual and Motor Skills* 89: 381-386.

Hutchinson, M.R., R.F. Laprade, Q.M. Burnett II, R. Moss, and J. Terpstra. 1995. Injury surveillance at the USTA boys tennis championships: a 6-yr study. *Medicine and Science in Sports and Exercise* 27: 826-830.

Kirchh bel, H., and H.J. Refior. 1991. Kinder und Jugendliche im Tennissport. In *Tennis und Sportmedizin*, K sswetter, W., J. Zacher, and S. Sell, eds. Stuttgart: Georg Thieme Verlag.

Kujala, U.M., K. Martti, and O. Heinonen. 1985. Osgood-Schlatter s disease in adolescent athletes. *The American Journal of Sports Medicine* 13: 236-489.

Loud, K.J. and L.J. Micheli. 2001. Common athletic injuries in adolescent girls. *Current Opinion in Pediatrics* 13: 317-322.

Micheli, L.J., and M. L. Ireland. 1987. Prevention and management of calcaneal apophysitis in children: an overuse syndrome. *Journal of Pediatric Orthopedics* 7: 34-38.

Omey, M.L. and L.J. Micheli. 1999. Foot and ankle problems in the young athlete. *Medicine and Science in Sports Exercise* 31: S470-S486.

Orava, S., L. Malinen, J. Karpakka, M. Kvist, J. Leppilihati, J. Rantanen, and U.M. Kujala. 2000. Results of surgical treatment of unresolved Osgood-Schlatter lesion. *Annales Chirurgiae et Gynaecologia* 89: 298-302.

Reece, L.A., P.A. Fricker, and K.F. Maguire. 1986. Injuries to elite young tennis players at the Australian Institute of Sport. *Australian Journal of Science and Medicine in Sport* 18: 11-15.

Rians, C.B., A. Weltman, B.R. Cahill, C.A. Janney, S.R. Tippett, and F.I. Katch. 1987. Strength training for prepubescent males: is it safe? *The American Journal of Sports Medicine* 15: 483-489.

Rossi, F. and S. Dragoni. 2001. The prevalence of spondylolysis and spondylolisthesis in symptomatic elite athletes: radiographic findings. *Radiography* 7: 37-42.

Sales de Gauzy, J., C. Mansat, P.H. Darodes, and J.P. Cahuzac. 1999. Natural course of osteochondritis dissecans in children. *Journal of Pediatric Orthopedics Belgica* 8: 26-28.

Stanitski, C.L. 1988. Management of sports injuries in children and adolescents. *Orthopedic Clinics of North America* 19: 689-698.

Stricker, P.R. 2002. Sports training issues for the pediatric athlete. *Pediatric Clinics of North America* 49: 793-802.

Chapter 23. Veterans

American College of Sports Medicine Position Stand. 1998. Exercise and physical activity for older adults. *Medicine and Science in Sports and Exercise* 30: 992-1008.

Barnard, R.J., R. MacAlpin, A.A. Kattus, and G.D. Buckberg. 1973. Ischemic response to sudden strenuous exercise in healthy men. *Circulation* 48: 936-942.

Bradbury, N., D. Borton, G. Spoo, and M.J. Cross. 1998. Participation in sports after total knee replacement. *The American Journal of Sports Medicine* 26: 530-535.

Fielding, R.A., N.K. LeBrasseur, A. Cuoco, J. Bean, K. Mizer, and M.A. Fiatarone Singh. 2002. High-velocity resistance training increases skeletal muscle peak power in older women. *Journal of the American Geriatric Society* 50: 655-662.

Friedman, D.B., B.W. Ramoa, and G.J. Gray. 1984. Tennis and cardiovascular fitness in middle-aged men. *Physician and Sportsmedicine* 12: 87-91.

Hakkinen, K., W.J. Kraemer, R.U. Newton and M. Alen. 2001. Changes in electromyographic activity, muscle fibre and force production characteristics during heavy resistance/power strength training in middle-aged and older men and women. *Acta Physiologica Scandinavia* 171: 51-62.

Healy, W.L., R. Iorio, and M.J. Lemos. 2001. Athletic activity after joint replacement. *The American Journal of Sports Medicine* 29: 377-388.

Jacobson, P.C., W. Beaver, S.A. Grubb, and T.N. Taft. 1984. Bone density in women: college athletes and older athletic women. *Journal of Orthopedic Research* 2: 328-332.

Kalinen, M. and A. Markku. 1995. Aging, physical activity and sports injuries. *Sports Medicine* 20: 41-52.

Kuster, M.S. 2002. Exercise recommendations after total joint replacement: a review of the current literature and proposal of scientifically based guidelines. *Sports Medicine* 32: 433-445.

Laforest, S., D.M. St. Pierre, and D. Gayton. 1990. Effects of age and regular exercises on muscle strength and endurance. *European Journal of Applied Physiology and Occupational Therapy* 60: 104-111.

Leach, R.E. 1991. The senior tennis player. *Clinics in Sports Medicine* 10: 283-290.

Mont, M.A., D.M. LaPorte, T. Mullick, C.E. Silberstein, and D.S. Hungerford. 1999. Tennis after total hip arthroplasty. *American Journal of Sports Medicine* 27: 60-64.

Sonnery-Cottet, B., T.B. Edwards, E. Noel, and G. Walch. 2002. Rotator cuff tears in middle-aged tennis players: results of surgical treatment. *The American Journal of Sports Medicine* 30: 558-564.

Therminarias, A., P. Dansou, M-F. Chirpaz-Oddou, C. Gharib, and A. Quirion. 1991. Hormonal and metabolic changes during a strenuous tennis match. Effect of ageing. *International Journal of Sports Medicine* 12: 10-16.

Therminarias, A., P. Dansou, M.F. Chirpaz-Oddou, and A. Quirion. 1990. Effects of age on heart rate response during a strenuous match of tennis. *Journal of Sports Medicine and Physical Fitness* 30: 389-396.

Vodak, P.A., W.M. Savin, W.L. Haskell, and P.D. Wood. 1980. Physiological profile of middle-aged male and female tennis players. *Medicine and Science in Sports and Exercise* 12: 159-163.

Sipila S, M. Elorinne, M. Alen, H. Suominen, and V. Kovanen. 1997. Effects of strength and endurance training on muscle fibre characteristics in elderly women. *Clinical Physiology* 17: 459-474.

Chapter 24. Women

American Psychiatric Association. Task Force on DSM-IV. 1994. Eating Disorders. In: *Diagnostic and Statistical Manual of Mental Disorders*, 4th edition. Washington, DC: American Psychiatric Association.

Baxter-Jones, A.D., P. Helms, J. Baines-Preece, and M. Preece. 1994. Menarche in intensively trained gymnasts, swimmers and tennis players. *Annals of Human Biology* 21: 407-415.

Beilock, S.L., D.L. Feltz, and J.M. Pivarnik. 2001. Training patterns of athletes during pregnancy and postpartum. *Research Quarterly for Exercise and Sport* 72: 39-46.

Bo, A.K., and J.S. Borgen. 2001. Prevalence of stress and urge urinary incontinence in elite athletes and controls. *Medicine and Science in Sports and Exercise* 33: 1797-1802.

Clapp III, J.F. 2000. Exercise during pregnancy: a clinical update. *Clinics in Sports Medicine* 19: 273-286.

Clapp III, J.F. 2000. Beginning regular exercise in early pregnancy: effect on fetoplacental growth. *American Journal of Obstetrics and Gynecology* 183: 1484-1488.

Harris, M.B. 2000. Weight concern, body image, and abnormal eating in college women tennis players and their coaches. *International Journal of Sport Nutrition and Exercise Metabolism* 10: 1-15.

Harris, M.B. and S. Foltz. 1999. Attitudes toward weight and eating in junior women tennis players, their parents, and their coaches. *Eating disorders: Journal of Research and Treatment* 7: 15-29.

Kannus, P., H. Haapasalo, M. Sankelo, H. Sievanen, M. Pasanen, A. Heinonen, P. Oja, and I. Vuori. 1995. Effect of starting age of physical activity on bone mass in the dominant arm of tennis and squash players. *Annals of Internal Medicine* 123: 27-31.

Kannus, P., H. Haapasalo, H. Sievanen, P. Oja, and I. Vuori. 1994. The site-specific effects of long-term unilateral activity on bone mineral density and content. *Bone* 15: 279-284.

Kardel, K.R. and T. Kase. 1998. Training in pregnant women: effects on fetal development and birth. *American Journal of Obstetrics and Gynecology* 178: 280-286.

Karegeanes, S.J., K. Blackburn, and Z.A. Vangelos. 2000. The association of the menstrual cycle with the laxity of the anterior cruciate ligament in adolescent female athletes. *Clinical Journal of Sports Medicine* 10: 162-168.

Kontulainen, S., P. Kannus, H. Haapasalo, H. Sievanen, M. Pasanen, A. Heinonen, P. Oja, and I. Vuori. 2001. Good maintenance of exercise-induced bone gain with decreased training of female tennis and squash players: a prospective 5-year follow-up study of young and old starters and controls. *Journal of Bone and Mineral Research* 16: 195-201.

Lanese, R.R., R.H. Strauss, D.J. Leizman, and A.M. Rotondi. 1990. Injury and disability in matched men s and women s intercollegiate sports. *American Journal of Public Health* 80: 1459-1462.

Larsen, J. 1991. Tennis injuries- incidence and pattern. *Ugeskr Laeger* 153: 3398-3399.

Loud, K.J. and L.J. Micheli. 2001. Common athletic injuries in adolescent girls. *Current Opinion in Pediatrics* 13: 317-327.

Lumbers, E.R. 2002. Exercise in pregnancy: physiological basis of exercise prescription for the pregnant woman. *The Journal of Science and Medicine in Sport* 5: 20-31.

Otis, C.L., B. Drinkwater, M. Johnson, A. Loucks, and J. Wilmore. 1997. The Female Athlete Triad. American College of Sports Medicine position stand. *Medicine and Science in Sports and Exercise* 29: i-ix

Otis, C.L. and R. Goldingay. 2000. *The athletic woman's survival guide.* Champaign(Ill): Human Kinetics

Sallis, R.E., K. Jones, S. Sunshine, S. Smith and L. Simon. 2001. Comparing sports injuries in men and women. *International Journal of Sports Medicine* 22: 420-423.

Sapsford, R.R. and P.W. Hodges. 2001. Contraction of pelvic floor muscles during abdominal maneuvers. *Archives of Physical Medicine and Rehabilitation* 82: 1081-1088.

Sapsford, R.R., P.W. Hodges, C.A. Richardson, D.H. Cooper, S.J. Markwell, and G.A. Jull. 2001. Co-activation of the abdominal and pelvic floor muscles during voluntary exercise. *Neurourology and Urodynamics* 20: 31-42.

Teitz, C.C. 1997. The female athlete: evaluation and treatment of sports-related problems. *Journal of the American Academy of Orthopaedic Surgeons* 5: 87-96.

Warren, M.P. and N. E. Perlroth. 2001. The effects of intense exercise on the female reproductive system. *Journal of Endocrinology* 170: 3-11.

Chapter 25. Wheelchair Tennis Players

Armstrong, L.E., C.M. Maresh, D. Riebe, R.W. Kenefick, J.W. Castellani, and J.M. Senk. 1995. Local cooling in wheelchair athletes during exercise-heat stress. *Medicine and Science in Sports and Exercise* 27: 211-216.

Bernard, P.L., J. Marcier, A. Varray, and C. Prefaut. 2000. Influence of lesion level on the cardioventilatory adaptations in paraplegic wheelchair athletes during muscular exercise. *Spinal Cord* 38: 16-25.

Burnham, R.S., L. May, W. Nelson, R. Steadward, and D.C. Reid. 1993. Shoulder pain in wheelchair athletes; the role of muscle imbalance. *The American Journal of Sports Medicine* 21: 238-242.

Curtis, K.A. and K. Black. 1999. Shoulder pain in female wheelchair basketball players. *Journal of Orthopedics and Sports Physical Therapy* 29: 225-231.

Dingerkus, M.L., A. Radebol, M. R ckgauer, and P. Bernett. 1994. Verletzungen und berlastungssyndrome im Rollstuhltennis. *Praktische Sport-Traumatologie und Sportmedizin* 2: 46-51.

Estenne M., C. Pinet, and A. De Troyer. 2000. Abdominal muscle strength in patients with tetraplegia. *American Journal of Respiratory and Critical Care Medicine* 161: 707-712.

Ferrara, M.S., G.R. Palutsis, S. Snouse, and R.W. Davis. 2000. A longitudinal study of injuries to athletes with disabilities. *International Journal of Sports Medicine* 21: 221-224.

Groah, S.L. and I.S. Lanig. 2000. Neuromusculoskeletal syndromes in wheelchair athlete. *Seminars in Neurology* 20: 201-208.

Hopman, M.T.E., B. Oeseburg, and R.A. Binkhorst. 1993. Cardiovascular responses in persons with paraplegia to prolonged arm exercise and thermal stress. *Medicine and Science in Sports and Exercise* 25: 577-583.

Jackson, D.L., B.C. Hynninen, D.N. Caborn, and J. McLean. 1996. Electrodiagnostic study of carpal tunnel syndrome in wheelchair basketball players. *Clinical Journal of Sports Medicine* 6: 27-31.

Lai, A.M., W.D. Stanish, and H.I. Stanish. 2000. The young athlete with physical challenges. *Clinics in Sports Medicine* 19: 793-819.

Mayer, F., D. Axmann, T. Horstmann, F. Martini, J. Fritz, and H.H. Dickhuth. 2001. Reciprocal strength ratio in shoulder abduction/adduction in sports and daily living. *Medicine and Science in Sports and Exercise* 33: 1765-1769.

Miyahara, M., G.G. Sleivert, and D.F. Gerrard. 1998. The relationship of strength and muscle balance to shoulder pain and impingement syndrome in elite quadriplegic wheelchair rugby players. *International Journal of Sports Medicine* 19: 210-214.

Shephard, R.J. 1988. Sports medicine and the wheelchair athlete. *Sports Medicine* 4: 226-247.

Chapter 26: The Sports Physician

Brown, D.W. 1998. Medical issues associated with international competition. *Clinics in Sports Medicine* 17:739-754.

Brown, D.G. 1994. Perspectives of a rheumatologist team physician. *Ballière's Clinical Rheumatology* 8: 225-230.

Buettner, C.M. 1998. The team physician s bag. *Clinics in Sports Medicine* 17: 365-373.

Herring, S.A., J.A. Bergfeld, J. Boyd, W.G. Clancy, H.R. Collins, B.C. Halpern, K. Jaffe, W.B. Kibler, E.L. Rice, and D.C. Thorson. 2000. Team physician consensus statement. *Medicine and Science in Sports and Exercise* 32: 877-878.

Herring, S.A., J.A. Bergfeld, J. Boyd, W.G. Clancy, H.R. Collins, B.C. Halpern, R. Jaffe, W.B. Kibler, E.L. Rice, and D.C. Thorson. 2001. Sideline preparedness for the team physician: consensus statement. *Medicine and Science in Sports and Exercise* 33: 846-849.

Howe, W.B. 1991. The team physician. *Primary Care* 18: 763-775.

Jaffe, L. 1994. Perspectives of an orthopaedist team physician. *Ballière's Clinical Rheumatology* 8: 221-223.

Orchard, J.W., P.A. Fricker, and P. Brukner. 1995. Sports medicine for professional teams. *Clinical Journal of Sports Medicine* 5: 1-3.

Chapter 27: The Athletic Trainer

George, F.J. 1997. The athletic trainer's perspective. *Clinics in Sports Medicine* 16(3): 361-374.

Vaughan, J.L., King, K.A., and R.R. Cottrell. 2004. Collegiate athletic trainers' confidence in helping female athletes with eating disorders. *Journal of Athletic Training* 39(1): 71-76.

Osborne, B. 2001. Principles of liability for athletic trainers: managing sport-related concussion. *Journal of Athletic Training* 36(3): 316-321.

Chapter 28: Strength Training for Tennis

Cronin, J.B., P.J. McNair, and R.N. Marshall. 2002. Is velocity-specific strength training important in improving functional performance? *Journal of Sports Medicine and Physical Fitness* 42: 267-273.

Chandler, T.J. 1995. Exercise training for tennis. *Clinics in Sports Medicine* 14: 33-46.

Jones, K, P. Bishop, G. Hunter, and G. Fleisig G. 2001. The effects of varying resistance-training loads on intermediate- and high-velocity-specific adaptations. *Journal of Strength and Conditioning Research* 15: 349-356.

Kraemer, W.J., N. Ratamess, A.C. Fry, T. Triplett-McBride, L.P. Koziris, J.A. Bauer, J.M. Lynch, and S.J. Fleck. 2000. Influence of resistance training volume and periodization on physiological and performance adaptations in collegiate women tennis players. *The American Journal of Sports Medicine* 28: 626-633.

Kraemer, W.J., K. Adams, E. Cafarelli, G.A. Dudley, C. Dooly, M.S. Feigenbaum, S.J. Fleck, B. Franklin, A.C. Fry, J.R. Hoffman, R.U. Newton, J. Potteiger, M.H. Stone, N.A. Ratamess, and T. Triplett-McBride. 2002. American College of Sports Medicine position stand. Progression models in resistance training for healthy adults. *Medicine and Science in Sports and Exercise* 34: 364-380.

Kramer, W.J., J.F. Pattton, S.E. Gordon, E.A. Harman, M.R. Deschenes, K. Reynolds, R.U. Newton, N.T. Triplett, and J.E. Dziados. 2002. Compatibility of high-intensity strength and endurance training on hormonal and skeletal muscle adaptations. *Journal of Applied Physiology* 78: 976-989.

McBride, J.M., T. Triplett-McBride, A. Davie, and R.U. Newton. 2002. The effect of heavy- vs. light-load jump squats on the development of strength, power, and speed. *Journal of Strength and Conditioning Research* 16: 75-82.

Jones, K., P. Bishop, G. Hunter, and G. Fleisig. 2001. The effects of varying resistance-training loads on intermediate- and high-velocity-specific adaptations. *Journal of Strength and Conditioning Research* 15: 349-356.

Mont, M.A., D.B. Cohen, K.R. Campbell, K. Gravare, and S.K. Mathur. 1994. Isokinetic concentric versus eccentric training of shoulder rotators with functional evaluation of performance enhancement in tennis players. *The American Journal of Sports Medicine* 22: 513-517.

Traiber, F.A., J. Lott, J. Duncan, G. Slavens, and H. Davis. 1998. Effects of Theraband and lightweight dumbbell training on shoulder rotation torque and serve performance in college tennis players. *American Journal of Sports Medicine* 26: 510-515.

Index

About the Authors

Babette M. Pluim, M.D., Ph.D.

Babette Pluim, MD., Ph.D., is sports physician and Medical Director of the Royal Netherlands Lawn Tennis Association. She is the current President of the Society for Tennis Medicine and Science (STMS). Dr. Pluim is the team physician of the Dutch Davis Cup and Fed Cup teams, and tournament doctor at the ATP and WTA tournaments in 's-Hertogenbosch, Amersfoort, and Rotterdam (the Netherlands).

Dr. Pluim is a member of the ITF Sports Medical Commission, the ITF Wheelchair Tennis Medical Commission, and the Age Eligibility Panel of the WTA Tour. She is editor-in-chief of "Medicine and Science in Tennis," the journal of the STMS, and "Geneeskunde en Sport," the scientific journal of the Netherlands Association of Sports Medicine. With Miguel Crespo and Machar Reid, she co-edited the book "Tennis Medicine for Tennis Coaches." She wrote the chapter "Medical Care of Tennis Players" for the "IOC Handbook of Sports Medicine and Science: Tennis."

Marc R. Safran, M.D.

Dr. Safran, a former junior and collegiate tennis player, is a board certified orthopaedic surgeon specializing in sports medicine and interested in biomechanics. He is a board member of the Society for Tennis Medicine and Science and chairman of the Sports Medicine Committee of the San Diego Sports Science Council. He is a fellow of the American College of Sports Medicine and the American Academy of Orthopaedic Surgery, as well as a member of the American Orthopaedic Society for Sports Medicine. He has been actively involved in tennis injury related research since 1995. Dr. Safran has been the medical director of the WTA Tournament in San Diego since 1995 and the medical consultant of the USTA Girl's 16's National Hardcourt Championships in San Diego since 1996. He has served as a neutral site physician at several Davis Cup ties since 1996.

Dr. Safran's has written several book chapters and papers on tennis injuries in addition to lecturing on the topics related to specific tennis injuries and injuries in junior tennis players. He has co-authored a book on sports medicine written for physicians and trainers – "The Spiral Manual of Sports Medicine" (Lippincott-Raven Publishers, 1998) and "Instructions for Sports Medicine Patients" (WB Saunders-Mosby, 2001) written for sports medicine patients.

without so much as recognizing each other, they confront one another as enemies.

Unconscious grief is followed by an insight into its causes, and their next meeting will provide them with an explanation of why their hatred was inevitable. But this consciousness covers only one aspect, and so it is false. Only when the world conceives of their suffering as necessary will it be reconciled to itself. Only when all one-sidedness ends will it be possible to be conscious of the whole. But the end of one-sidedness is death. As Wagner wrote to Röckel, 'We must learn to die – and to die, moreover, in the fullest sense of the word.' The third act of *Götterdämmerung* is Wagner's lesson in the right way to die.

Shortly before the end of the story, the *Ring* returns to its origins. The Rhinedaughters re-emerge from the waters to greet the light of the sun. But instead of the golden-eyed child of the world that once caught heaven's gaze, night has now cast its pall upon its depths. The spirit of God that had revealed itself as love to the human couple of Siegfried and Brünnhilde no longer finds a response in the universe. Its radiance has been swallowed up by the darkness. It is no longer the gods who rule, but matter and the strict laws that regulate its possession.

These three children of nature innocently beg the 'sun goddess' to send them the hero who will restore their stolen gold to the depths. This is not, of course, the solution itself but merely a symbolic act that illustrates the reconciliation between God and world, light and darkness. Similar feelings seem to have affected Wagner himself when he returned home by boat from a visit to his publisher on the opposite bank of the Rhine. According to the boatsman, he drew from his jacket pocket the gold ducats he had received as his fee and 'with silent emotion' threw them into the river that had just been gilded over by the setting sun.[102]

Announced by his jaunty horn call, Siegfried appears on the riverbank and with his usual lack of inhibition jokes with the naked sisters who for their own part tease him, just as they had once teased the foolish Alberich. This burlesque scene suggests that the hero has no inkling of all that has happened. If, as Wagner insisted, the consciousness of 'the most perfect human being' was 'bound up exclusively with his most immediate life and actions', then Siegfried is this man of the future, except that he himself does not know it. He acts and suffers while unconscious of his fate. As the repository of knowledge, Brünnhilde is on the other side and, her information having remained one-sided, impatiently awaits his death.

But according to Wagner, Siegfried, too, is in possession of knowledge derived not from historical experience but from his own basic nature: 'The tremendous importance that I attach to this consciousness – which can almost never be stated in words – will become clear to you,' Wagner told Röckel, 'from Siegfried's scene with the Rhinedaughters; here we learn that Siegfried is infinitely wise, for he knows the highest truth, that death is better than a life of fear.' But as Wagner explains in the same letter, fear is 'the source of all lovelessness', and so, in a final reversal, Siegfried is revealed as the representative of divine love. The apparently innocent hero turns out to be a saviour, his love more potent than death.

The water sprites are like children, begging Siegfried to give them the ring, but when – equally teasingly – he refuses to do so, the mood suddenly changes and they solemnly foretell his imminent death, much as Brünnhilde once announced his father's death. The ring is cursed, and no one who owns it can escape that curse: he will die that very day, they tell him, unless he returns it to them at once. But it is by no means compassion that motivates them, for, as Wagner told Cosima, 'it is with all the childlike cruelty of nature' that they consign him to his 'ruin'.[103] But like the Norns with whom Wagner occasionally equated them,[104] the Rhinedaughters are let down by their lack of knowledge of fate.

In Siegfried's case, they are wrong twice over: as Alberich himself had conceded, the hero is immune to the curse as he has no interest in material possessions. As he explains to these baffled prophetesses, he is not even attracted by 'the world's inheritance'. And as for 'life and limb', he adds high-spiritedly, 'lo: thus do I fling them far away from me!'

These children of nature cannot help Siegfried. The answer lies not in the unconscious nature of the beginning but only in human self-consciousness. In order for this to dawn in Brünnhilde, her lover must perish. On this point at least, the Rhinedaughters' prophecy will come true soon enough.

While working on the score of *Götterdämmerung*, Wagner spoke of the necessity of this death in terms of the history of the world. The 'deed that will redeem the world' and that is expected of Siegfried and Brünnhilde did not consist in the procreation of new life, he explained to Cosima: the 'supreme happiness that results from the union of two perfect beings' cannot be followed by the creation of an even more perfect being but only by consciousness of this union. 'As a man' Siegfried is 'concerned only with action', and so he abandons his lover in order to go off into the world as a man of action and garner experience. But wherever he thinks of himself as a man of action, he incurs suffering. Whenever he trusts his instincts, he finds himself the plaything of others. 'Siegfried does not know what wrong he has done', Wagner explained. 'He has to fall in order that Brünnhilde may rise to the heights of perception.'[105]

For Wagner, there was an unmistakable parallel both here and in *The Wibelungs* between the Franconian solar hero and the Paschal Lamb. Like Jesus, Siegfried ignores the warning of his death and in that way unconsciously takes upon himself the cross of history. It is for this reason that, on stumbling upon Hagen's hunting party, Siegfried is made to utter the biblical words 'I thirst!' According to Saint John's account of the crucifixion, 'Jesus knowing that all things were now accomplished, that the scripture might be fulfilled, saith, I thirst.' Unlike Jesus, Siegfried does not know that all things are now accomplished, but even if he had known it, he would have given it no further thought. For him, there is no more question of a life of fear and lovelessness than there had been for Christ, our Saviour.

Yet in Siegfried's case, too, the tradition had to be fulfilled. Even the God of the first creation had 'thirsted' and bent over the darkness of his own ground. Wotan had also drunk of the waters of the primordial wellspring, a drink that had likewise disagreed with him. Now we come to the third attempt to complete the work of creation. Siegfried drinks, and already there awakens in him a memory of his own life. The hero who seemed entirely bound up with the moment has in fact a past. It is no accident that it is Hagen who feeds him his cues.

Siegfried's reminiscences, with which he is to talk himself into an early grave, begin with his stepfather Mime and pass to the forging and successful deployment of his splendid sword, before lingering over the talking Woodbird in the forest. He repeats the latter's recommendations word for word, including the acquisition of the hoard and Siegfried's murder of Mime in self-defence. His memory of his maternal adviser evidently melts his heart, and Hagen reckons that the time has come to offer him an antidote and make him susceptible to sentimental reminiscences. Whether it is Hagen's magic spell or that of the Woodbird awakening within him his longing for his mother, the effect is the same: Siegfried sinks for a moment into a state of pensive sadness.

Suddenly he remembers everything that has happened to him as though for the very first time. The Woodbird had shown him the way to 'the most glorious woman', who answers to the name of Brünnhilde. Did he follow the Woodbird's advice, Hagen asks, as though cross-examining him. Of course, retorts Siegfried: fearlessly he passed through the fire and, 'as a reward', he discovered a 'wondrous woman'. He then loosened her helmet and, 'emboldened', woke her with a kiss, so that the fair Brünnhilde clasped him to her 'in her ardour'. He admits to all this so readily as to make one think that he has forgotten his oath on Hagen's spear.

This is enough. Two ravens – Wotan's birds of death – fly up to report to their master that his hapless son has just perjured himself. Hagen, contemptuously pretending that he is merely heeding their call for vengeance just as Siegfried had earlier heeded the Woodbird's advice, plunges his law-enshrining spear into Siegfried's back. A cry, a final rearing up, then sickening silence.

Hagen has nothing for which to reproach himself. The admission has been made in the presence of witnesses. He has satisfied the terms of the law, so why should he remain among fools any longer? 'Hagen turns away calmly,' reads Wagner's stage direction, 'and disappears over the cliff top, where he can be seen walking away slowly through the gathering gloom.'

His victim does not die instantly. The man who had lived only for the moment had returned to the past and remembered his history in order that he might finally appear in the present. But his present is not the bloody evening scene in the forest over which the moon now raises its pallid countenance.

His somnambulistic state is over, and he finally wakes up in the arms of his wife. His self-consciousness returns with the sound of the six harps expressive of light – the same sounds as those to which Brünnhilde had woken. Just as he had risen over the darkness of her life like the godlike sun, so the beginning of the world is now re-enacted, as glorious as on the very first day.

Once again he allows his light to fall into the night of death that holds his lover in thrall. Yearningly, he calls out her name and, as when he first awoke her, entreats her to waken and open her eyes, tenderly asking her who has locked her in sleep once again. He has finally returned to wake her and, kissing her awake, he breaks the bonds of death. And Brünnhilde does indeed awaken in his arms, and her joy begins to laugh on him once more. He knows that her eyes, wide open, will now remain open for ever. God's light has fallen into the dark ground, and night has opened its radiant eye, never again to close it. Nothing exists any longer but love.

Then he feels death reaching out for him, but the feeling is one of sweetness: the terror that draws him down feels like bliss. He sees her greeting him, and then it is all over. He 'sinks back and dies', Wagner notes. 'Motionless grief on the part of those around him.' The moon breaks through the clouds, and the cortège with Siegfried's body sets off over the cliff top, while mists rise up from the Rhine.

The music remains behind to sum up the life of the god's sacrificed son in a phenomenology of the spirit in which all his life's phenomena are interpreted as transitional stages on the road to ultimate self-consciousness. But what concerns us here is not the power of the concept, as was the case with Hegel, but the power of emotion. The spirit of God has come to the end of its period of alienation, a period that culminates on the Golgotha of the law. Its resurrection after a harrowing night of death now takes place in the music.

The passion and resurrection of the redeemer form the climax of *Götterdäm-merung*. Just as Siegfried's self-sacrificing death in the evening necessarily follows the universal morning of love, so it remains for Brünnhilde to gain an insight into the link between these two events. Like her lover before her, she has returned to the beginning, where the Rhinedaughters have explained their version of events to her. At the place where Siegfried meets his death Brünnhilde finds enlightenment.

When she returns, transformed, to the Gibichung court, she finds the world in its old state of chaos. Bitter discord has broken out between Hagen and his half-brother and half-sister over who owns the 'sacred right of booty' to the ring. When Gunther claims it for his sister, Hagen strikes him dead. Brünnhilde's voice cuts through the keening of the women's anguished cries. The senseless noise of history is silenced and the confused world sinks back into its meaningless state.

With Brünnhilde's threnody to her dead lover, Wagner provides a summation of his creation: the world that had arisen through love and been alienated from itself by greed and the law now returns to love. It lives in the union of Siegfried and Brünnhilde, a union more powerful than death. It is not just since the downfall of the hero but from the very outset that this love has sacrificed itself to itself. The lovers had first abandoned themselves to each other, and now they sacrifice themselves to the world. Wagner called this the 'ultimate sacrifice of love'.[106]

It was this 'consuming love', he later told his second wife that 'Brünnhilde glorifies'. Whereas love had initially been no more than a natural occurrence with the Rhinedaughters, it leads 'through Brünnhilde to the destruction and redemption of the world'.[107] But it is Siegfried's passion that allows Brünnhilde to attain to this self-consciousness in which the whole history of the world is subsumed: 'It was I whom the purest of men had to betray, that a woman might grow wise.'

Her threnody thus becomes a triumph over death. Just as the grief of the early Christian community had turned to the Pentecostal jubilation of enlightenment in Wagner's *Liebesmahl der Apostel*, so the despairing Brünnhilde sees the light of undying love. She now knows that Siegfried lives, for 'purer than sunlight streams the light from his eyes'. Its beams come from outside and kindle within her an all-consuming flame. As on the occasion when she first awoke, so the fire flares up again, a fire whose divine force the world of matter cannot resist. The glow of a new beginning, once kindled by Siegfried from the withered World Ash, now burns brightly in Valhalla's proud-standing stronghold, where the gods and their world of laws sit numbly awaiting their downfall.

But the fire that destroys the old world flares up in Brünnhilde's heart as the life-giving ardour of love. She feels the 'laughing fire' burning within her, feels 'bright flames' seizing hold of her heart and yearns 'to clasp him to me while held in his arms and in mightiest love to be wedded to him!' Quickly she gives the golden ring back to the Rhinedaughters, while Hagen, plunging into the floodwaters after it, finds the redemption of Ahasuerus: death.

The Gibichung stronghold and Wotan's Valhalla go up in flames. But the lovers' funeral pyre dissolves all that still divides them, melting it down in the living ardour of their embrace. Now the light that had shone in the beginning can rise at last over the crowd of onlookers standing 'in profound emotion'. This light is the sun of the new man.

Brünnhilde had preached this gospel in her original peroration: 'Not wealth, nor gold, nor godly pomp; not house, nor garth, nor lordly splendour; not troubled treaties' treacherous bonds, not smooth-tongued custom's stern decree: blessed in joy and sorrow love alone can be.'[108]

This is also how Wagner summed up the message of the *Ring* in his letter to August Röckel: only 'by living and dying in joy and sorrow' can we achieve true humanity. 'This is simply "being subsumed by the truth".' That Wagner finally decided against setting these words to music had nothing to do with any change of heart, as some commentators have claimed, but because they sought 'in a sententious sense to pre-empt the musical impact of the drama'. Their meaning, Wagner insisted, was 'already expressed in the drama, as it rings out in the music, and expressed, moreover, with the greatest clarity'.[109] Listeners who had understood the whole had no need of any 'moral'.

And so the *Ring* ends as it began. With the jubilant strains of Brünnhilde's love it harks back to the beginning, when the rising sun and the radiant depths together formed the first morning of creation. And the drama that comes full circle in the music likewise speaks but a single language. The motifs of Valhalla and the World Ash, the ring and the curse, disappear in the floodtide of sound, superseded for ever. One alone remains, striving upwards towards the sun like the billowing depths of the beginning, then sinking back again, before soaring aloft to the light in a renewed access of longing: the infinite melody of love.

'There is no ending to this music,' Wagner explained to Cosima while working on this scene, 'it is like the genesis of things, it can always start again from the beginning or switch to the opposite, but it is never really finished.' This non-existent ending is provided by the motif that Wagner himself called 'Sieglinde's theme in praise of Brünnhilde'.[110]

It had been heard for the first time when the austere goddess was transformed into a compassionate human being and placed love above her own existence. This 'most sublime of wonders' occurs in the midst of the despair that reigns in *Die Walküre* and now returns following the long period of suffering that is history. Love was Wagner's last word in the *Ring* and, as he told Cosima, he had 'reserved' this motif especially for it.

The 'choral song to the heroine'[111] that Wagner recycles at the end of the *Ring* needs no further words. In Brünnhilde's love, the world has attained to self-consciousness.

6   Grand Passion

Mathilde

Wagner's creation of a new world coincided with the great love of his life: the decade in which the poem of the *Ring* assumed its musical and dramatic form was marked by a woman who remained unattainable to him. As the embodiment of the longed-for life in which he might find himself at peace with the world, 'blessed in joy and sorrow', she became the goal of all the desires that were to prove unassuageable. Neither of his two wives had a comparable impact on his creative powers. Neither Minna nor Cosima inspired him creatively but merely provided a channel for his art, functioning as advocates of quotidian reality and its daily needs, to which they sought to open Wagner's eyes.

Mathilde Wesendonck, by contrast, offered him the eye in which, like the god of creation, he could see himself as though in a mirror. 'When I look into your eyes,' he wrote to her, 'I am lost for words; everything that I might say becomes meaningless! You see, everything then becomes so indisputably true, I am then so sure of myself, whenever these wonderful, hallowed eyes rest upon me and I grow lost in contemplation of them! Then there is no longer any object or any subject; everything then becomes a single entity, deep, immeasurable harmony! There I find peace, and in that peace the highest and most perfect life!'[1]

In the course of this decade of yearning, which began in 1852, Wagner not only succeeded in making a start on the music of the *Ring* but conceived the three dramas that round off not just the idea underpinning the tetralogy but the whole of his life's work. *Tristan und Isolde*, *Die Meistersinger von Nürnberg* and *Parzival* (later renamed *Parsifal*) all owe their origins to Mathilde Wesendonck. With its powerful undertow, Wagner's love for her, although forced to conceal itself from the world, unleashed forces that created a new world in place of resistant reality. Only in this new world did the new man, made up of 'I' and 'you', find refuge, discovering a realm and a truth infinitely superior to those that existed in the world of sordid reality.

This relationship derived its strength from the fact that it remained wholly unrealized in real life, finding its fulfilment in its lack of fulfilment and thereby offering Wagner's world of ideas a perfect surface onto which those ideas could be projected. The archetype of the disinherited hero corresponded exactly with that of the sacred sister languishing in another's bonds. Whether Wagner saw himself as Siegmund, Siegfried or Tristan, it was always his longed-for and at the same time unobtainable bride Sieglinde, Brünnhilde or Isolde who smiled on him from Mathilde's eyes. Even Walther von Stolzing could think only of her when he waxed lyrical about 'Eve in Paradise'. She was the ideal image that reflected Wagner back at himself with the utmost clarity. Later he described her as a 'blank sheet of paper' that he was 'determined to write all over'.[2]

Once their relationship was over, Wagner sought to erase everything that he had written there. The compulsive denial of his sources of inspiration and hence of the past to which he owed his whole being assumed a particularly heartless aspect in the case of Mathilde Wesendonck. No doubt, of course, it was partly out of deference to Cosima's feelings that he denied that he had ever harboured any such sentiments for the other woman. His capacity for 'denying the very thing that he had once loved' struck his friend Peter Cornelius with some force: once Cosima appeared on the scene, he wryly observed, 'it was no longer permissible to speak about Frau Wesendonck'. What had once been an ideal relationship now became taboo, her influence on Wagner's creativity dismissed as a misunderstanding.

Wagner's betrayal of his lover extends to Cosima's diaries. In 1870, for example, he looked back on their non-affair and claimed that he had 'thrown a poetic veil over it in order not to admit to its triviality'.[3] As a result, he asked Mathilde to burn his letters 'for I do not want anything to remain that might suggest it was ever a serious relationship'.[4] His request was ignored.

Such tell-tale pointers inevitably fuelled Cosima's jealousy, which Wagner repeatedly had to allay. In 1872 he even declared his former lover to be 'of unsound mind' as she had never had any inkling of 'what things were all about'.[5] Indirectly he even accused himself of a similar failing when he assured Cosima the following year that his former suggestion that he and Mathilde should marry had been no more than a whim, adding with a laugh, 'for basically and in my subconscious mind I was not being serious'.[6]

As a result of this, he drew a sharp, not to say surgically neat, dividing line between *Tristan und Isolde*, in which his blissfully desperate couples from the *Ring* assumed the features of Mathilde and himself, and the work's origins. The real catalyst, he assured Cosima, with total disregard for the truth, had been his second wife's arrival in Zurich in 1857, when she and Hans von Bülow had interrupted their honeymoon and spent four weeks in the city. 'When I think what impelled me so forcefully to sketch *Tristan*', he told her in 1872, 'just when you and Hans were paying your first visit on me in Zurich', it became clear to him that 'everything is metaphysical, and how deceptive the things of which one is conscious can be'.[7]

By the time he came to dictate his autobiography to Cosima, the drama of an impossible love had been exposed as an act of self-deception, his closeness to Mathilde of no importance for the work of art. 'Curiously,' he wrote in his memoirs, 'the period of this neighbourly rapprochement coincided with the start of my work on the poem of *Tristan und Isolde*.'[8] Mathilde was particularly moved by a 'collective private reading of the subject', but showed herself regrettably slow on the uptake, whereas the perceptive Cosima immediately agreed with the poet's commentary on his work, thereby clearly confirming her claim to being hailed as its only begetter. In 1867 Cosima assured King Ludwig II that there could be no question of any deeper liaison between a genius like Wagner and the Wesendonck woman: 'I cannot begin to describe my sense of shock', she wrote after meeting Mathilde: 'This coldness, this lack of inner sympathy with all that is beautiful.'[9]

Even if Cosima's comment was true in 1867, it had not always been so. When Wagner was first introduced to the twenty-three-year-old Mathilde Wesendonck, she was what was then termed a 'beautiful soul'. The daughter of a businessman from the Rhineland, she had married the silk importer Otto Wesendonck in 1848 when she was nineteen and 'almost straight out of college'. Their first son died in infancy in 1850, but in 1851 – the year in which the Wesendoncks settled in Zurich – she presented her husband with a daughter. Of the three sons who were subsequently born to the couple, only one survived infancy.

For the sake of her husband, who was her elder by thirteen years, Mathilde had to give up not only her maiden name, Luckemeyer, but also her baptismal name, Agnes, as Otto insisted on renaming her after his first wife Mathilde. In return he offered her a life of luxury in which she was relieved of all material cares and could pursue her fancies as much as she liked. These included playing Beethoven's piano sonatas, writing poetry and making the acquaintance of famous men.

Wagner fell into this category. He was the only real attraction that Zurich could offer in terms of the performing arts. He conducted *Der fliegende Holländer*, performed excerpts from his early operas from *Rienzi* to *Lohengrin* to mark his fortieth birthday in 1853, and read from his latest poems to a growing circle of friends. 'With a splendid, ringing, resonant voice whose modulatory smoothness allowed him to express every nuance of the language from the tenderest gentleness to the most unbridled passion,' reported the *Eidgenössische Zeitung*, 'Wagner declaimed his works of art with a degree of inspiration, emotion and dramatic life that almost gave his audience the illusion of an actual performance.'[10] As the town had nothing to offer him, he himself provided the glamour for which he longed. The local beauties turned up on his doorstep and, as Minna complained with some warmth, 'devoured him' with their eyes.

In February 1853 he declaimed the entire poem of the *Ring* before a distinguished audience at the city's leading hotel, breathing life into all its characters with his highly charged voice, investing the sets from Nibelheim to Valhalla with a vital presence and adding nuances through mime and gesture. For four evenings the lakeside hotel in Zurich seemed to be the axis around which the world turned. For the work's secret dedicatee, it was a home fixture, as Mathilde Wesendonck was temporarily staying at the Hôtel Baur au Lac with her husband and their daughter Myrrha. She had long known that the *genius loci* was writing solely for her and that his concert performances were 'laid at her feet' alone.

And the same was soon true of his music. After a long break, he had finally returned to composition, conjuring up the beginning of the world on the bed of the Rhine. But prior to this he had written a piano sonata for Mathilde, thus returning to the roots of his skills as a composer by going back beyond *Lohengrin*, *Rienzi* and his *Faust* Overture. When he finished the piece in the early summer of 1853, Mathilde was taking the waters at Bad Ems. Sorely missing her, he sent the work to her by post, appending the portentous sentence 'Wißt ihr wie das wird?' ('Do you know what will happen?').

These words are sung by the Norns. When Wagner came to set them twenty years later in Bayreuth, he underscored them with the saddest motif in the *Ring*, the so-called 'Todesklage', usually known in English as the Fate motif. Evidently, it was not just the deaths of his heroes Siegmund and Siegfried over which Wagner was grieving here. These sounds of despair also recall the sonata that he inscribed to Mathilde Wesendonck, the very first theme of which incorporates the motif first heard in the Annunciation of Death scene in *Die Walküre*, where it is associated with the fate of the hero.[11] Here Wagner's music reveals what he sought to deny in words. As if trying to deceive Cosima, he ridiculed the sonata's 'triviality' in 1877, claiming that it now struck him as 'shallow and vapid'.[12]

What did Wagner see in the woman who was still exercising his thoughts on the eve of his death? There is nothing to be said about her appearance except that it presumably gave little away. Two faded visiting cards show a tight-lipped face with no special distinguishing features. Significantly, writings on Wagner reproduce only stylized busts, drawings and paintings, including one by the composer's friend Ernst Benedikt Kietz. All of them presumably reflect the ideal that Wagner saw in her, an unworldly, 'ethereal' beauty gazing into the distance, with dreamy, almost expressionless eyes.

In addition to her pale complexion, it was her clothes that showed her off to particular advantage. According to the local soprano Emilie Heim, who was a rival for Wagner's favours, Mathilde was 'a somewhat insignificant woman, more of a mild-mannered angel, and richly dressed to boot'.[13] Another female inhabitant of Zurich who knew Mathilde personally was more spiteful in her assessment: Mathilde was a 'small, insignificant woman', a 'pitiful person with the face of a tiny rodent'.[14]

But she was Wagner's 'blank sheet of paper'. And soon this sheet contained familiar features, for Mathilde, formerly known as Agnes, resembled Wagner's lost lover Jessie in every way and hence was the archetype of the heroic sister. Like Rosalie and Jessie, Mathilde played Beethoven and may even have sung his songs. Above all, she yearned for the brotherly genius who would fly to her side and free her. For art alone could make her loveless life endurable. Like Jessie, Mathilde was married to an older man who spent his time ensuring that his classy wife enjoyed a commensurate lifestyle.

In her faraway expression, Wagner recognized their spiritual affinity. It also told him that the bushy-bearded, hypochondriac Otto was her husband but not her lover. Her heart was fettered by the bonds of marriage. In order to greet her as his 'bride and sister', Wagner called her his angel, his Elisabeth and, soon, his Sieglinde, who should really have looked like Jessie. For the present she bore the pale features of the millionaire's languishing wife.

Wagner wrote *Die Walküre* under Mathilde's watchful gaze. She offered him the dark ocean of emotion into which his poem could sink. 'What he composed in the morning', she later recalled, 'he would play on my grand piano in the afternoon, checking over what he had written. It was the hour between five and six; he called himself "the sandman".'[15] Countless dedicatory abbreviations in Wagner's sketches attest to his muse's creative contribution to his works.

The tempestuous prelude to Act One of *Die Walküre* bears the letters 'G.s.M.', 'Gesegnet sei Mathilde' ('Blessed be Mathilde'), while Siegmund's mournful retrospective of his life includes the initials 'W.d.n.w.G', believed to mean 'Wenn du nicht wärst, Geliebte' ('If it were not for you, beloved'). At the point where the sun smiles on Siegmund again, we find the letters 'I.l.d.g.', which presumably stand for 'Ich liebe dich grenzenlos' ('I love you boundlessly'). And when Sieglinde leaves her brother alone in Hunding's front room, we read 'G.w.h.d.m.verl.', for 'Geliebte, warum hast du mich verlassen?' ('Beloved, why hast thou forsaken me?').[16] When Wagner rewrote his *Faust* Overture and dedicated it to Mathilde, he added the letters 'S.l.F.' Was she really 'seine liebe Frau' ('his dear wife') in the literal sense of the term?

As with so many other issues, writers on Wagner are divided. One camp pleads in favour of a purely platonic relationship – the sort of relationship that Wagner himself appears to have decided in retrospect that it was. The other camp, meanwhile, drawing on its intimate knowledge of the hero, insists that there was a physical component to it, a claim that could equally well find endorsement in Wagner's own statements and in the rumour, which he himself retailed, that his noble Mathilde had 'come into disrepute' in elevated circles.

The first person to concern himself with this dilemma seems to have been the hapless husband, who was soon prey to the green-ey'd monster. He was in fact the only person for whom this question had any wider-reaching significance, as Minna, who was likewise exercised by the illicit relationship, was one of the most tenacious supporters of the second school of thought. 'It's often the case', she admitted to an acquaintance, 'that men have affairs, so why shouldn't I allow mine to have one?'[17] But apart from Otto and Minna, who could really be interested in what the 'sandman' was thinking when he declared that 'an angel came to me, blessed me and refreshed me'?[18] When his sister Klara wrote to him in 1858, asking for an explanation, Wagner commented sagely: 'Only a very few people will understand what is at issue here.'[19]

Wagner's letter to his sister provides a version of events that appears to be grist to the mill of the first camp. In it he admits that 'without the love of that young woman' he would not have been able to endure his marriage to Minna. For six years, Mathilde had 'sustained and comforted him' and above all given him 'the strength' to tolerate living with Minna, a claim that recalls the 'refreshment' cited a moment ago. It was Mathilde, Wagner went on, who had made the first move, 'her initial response one of diffidence, doubt, hesitation and shyness', before her love had revealed itself as 'increasingly certain and confident'. But there could never be any question of any 'union' between them, Wagner assured his sister, as they were both married, with the result that their love 'assumed that sadly melancholic character that banishes all vulgarity and baseness'.

There does, in fact, seem to have been a certain vulgarity in their relationship, for it appears from Wagner's letter to his sister that Mathilde was blackmailing her husband. After informing him about the affair, she persuaded him 'to resign himself completely', but when he insisted on his rights as a husband, she threatened to kill herself. In order 'not to lose the mother of his children', Otto saw himself obliged to support his rival. Although Otto, in Wagner's words, was 'consumed by jealousy', he had to lend the composer a helping hand, provide him with some of his 'heavenly cigars' and other valuables and even make available to him a home next to his own villa in Zurich.

Wagner and Minna moved into the little half-timbered house that his benefactor had placed at his disposal in 1857, and according to Wagner's letter to Klara, it was around this time that the love between Wagner and Mathilde was finally revealed. He had barely given her the finished libretto of *Tristan und Isolde* 'when, for the first time, her strength failed her and she told me that she now had no choice but to die'. In the linguistic idiom of the drama, the meaning of this phrase is unmistakable, but Wagner could be sure that Klara would have little inkling of what was actually involved here.

The Wagners' move to their expensively furnished summerhouse facing the elegant Villa Wesendonck, with its view of the lake and instant access to the woman Wagner worshipped, meant a number of changes for Minna, too. According to the much later reminiscences of her daughter Natalie, she was 'banished from their communal bedchamber for the first time in their twenty-two years of marriage', to be replaced by the woman who was ultimately financing this whole arrangement and who 'very often went up to see Wagner in the morning in a ravishing, elegant morning suit', often remaining 'in his room for some considerable time'.[20]

Like Jessie Laussot, Mathilde benefited from her husband's frequent absences, and as Minna did not dare to disturb the two souls communing in the upstairs room, there was no reason for the couple to make any more effort than Tristan and Isolde, for example, when King Marke is away hunting. Wagner patronizingly described Wesendonck, who made over a small fortune to him, as his 'uncle',[21] just as Tristan is the nephew of the generous Marke. But he named the little house he had been given the 'Asyl' – the 'refuge', presumably in memory of Goethe's second Roman Elegy in which the Sage of Weimar finally felt 'secure' in the south: 'You'll not discover me so soon within the refuge that Prince Amor, with his kingly care, has granted me.' Choosing his metaphor carefully, Wagner wrote to his co-refugee: 'Your caresses – they are the crown of my existence.'[22]

The two met almost every day, either in the columned villa when it was used as a concert hall, or in Wagner's *chambre séparée*, where Minna – already suffering from a weak heart – could overhear them. When they were unable to meet, Wagner would stand at the window and gaze across to the neoclassical pile that embodied not only the unattainability of his beloved but all the splendours and riches of the world. If Mathilde offered him unlimited refreshment, there was a limit to the luxury that she would allow him to share. As with Jessie Laussot, there was no question of her giving up her life of luxury entirely. As Wagner later told Emilie Heim, Mathilde 'should really have forgone her husband's millions'.[23]

Cosima, too, was struck by this inconsistency. Newly married to Wagner's disciple, Hans von Bülow, she noted in 1858 that this 'pale and sickly' woman was 'as incapable of living a simple and honest life as of breaking with her earlier commitments and abandoning herself to her love and supporting her lover'. Instead, she told Marie von Wittgenstein, she merely rescued him from his 'famous bankruptcy' and thereby 'offered her poet a glimpse of the heaven of material tranquillity and uninhibited luxury'. These, Cosima added contemptuously, were probably 'the only values in which he believes'.[24]

Wagner's reference to the 'trivial' nature of his love for Mathilde Wesendonck seems to confirm a picture of poetically transfigured adultery and blatant opportunism. But this is in fact only half the picture. While their real-life relationship operated on a level of personal intimacy, that relationship was simultaneously the object of an artistic process that acknowledged its impossibility. Its subject was not fulfilment, which was possible only when snatched surreptitiously from real life, but insatiable longing. However 'refreshing' their meetings may have been, they brought no end to their torment. Through philosophy, poetry and music they raised that torment to the level of a medium that lent it its aura of eternity.

The lovers' parting – a recurrent source of suffering in Wagner's oeuvre – now acquired a life of its own. Just as the resolution of the conflict, as the actual aim of the drama, was now marginalized, so the music no longer sought to resolve its dissonances but strove to delay them, with all their torments and yearning, a delay that strangely coincided with their experience of sex. *Tristan und Isolde* tells of the impossibility of union in love and does so over three acts. The tension, made unbearable by the constant prick of desire, longs to be resolved and at the same time pleads for the torments to be perpetuated.

'Just consider my music,' Wagner wrote to his lover, 'with its delicate, oh so delicate, mysteriously flowing humours penetrating the most subtle pores of feeling to reach the very marrow of life, where it overwhelms everything that looks like sagacity and the self-interested powers of self-preservation, sweeping aside all that belongs to the folly of personality and leaving only that wondrously sublime sigh with which we confess to our sense of powerlessness –

how shall I be a wise man when it is only in such a state of raving madness that I am entirely at home?'[25]

Mathilde, too, had made herself at home here since her first meeting with Wagner, adding five poems to his compositional outpourings, which were now flowing in rare profusion. All were dedicated to that sweet cave of desire in which she sweltered with Wagner. No doubt under his guidance, she had already taken over from its mythical depths not only Elisabeth's 'ardent prayer' but Siegfried's 'eye in eye' and the 'joys' that can be found only in anguish.

Set to music by Wagner as 'Five Dilettante Poems', these songs are known to the world of music as the Wesendonck Lieder. Just as the drama of *Tristan und Isolde* emerged from the *Ring* to complement it, so *Tristan und Isolde* spawned these melancholic songs for female voice, two of which were explicitly described by Wagner as 'studies' for the work. No other woman in Wagner's life, not even the ambitious Cosima, was ever to be shown a similar honour.

In keeping with its own claims, the end of the relationship proved painfully protracted, but it began with one of the Wesendonck Lieder. Wagner performed 'Träume' as a birthday serenade for his lover in December 1857, when he conducted a chamber orchestra with solo violin at the Wesendoncks' villa. Mathilde alone could have known that this song begins with a mute invitation from *Tristan und Isolde*: 'O sink upon us, night of love.' The overwhelming performance, which was to serve as a model for the famous 'stairwell music' at Tribschen, had a postlude when the head of the household, returning from a lengthy business trip, like King Marke returning from the forest, expressed his outrage that his rival had now taken possession of his villa. Wagner considered it advisable to spend a few weeks in Paris, where Cosima's sister provided him with a distraction.

On his return to Zurich, he found that things had changed. He now had to share Mathilde's attentions with a Neapolitan academic who was teaching her Italian. Jealousy of his rival tempted Wagner into rashly asking one of his servants, Friedrich, to take his love a message that Minna lost no time in intercepting. It contained the prelude to *Tristan und Isolde*, together with an accompanying letter that on the one hand expatiated – harmlessly enough – on Goethe's misguided conception of Faust and on the other hailed the letter's recipient as the eye in whose depths his salvation uniquely rested.

For Minna, whose eye was rendered all the more keen by her laudanum addiction, this was a written confession of guilt, although it remains unclear why she was so convinced that her husband had penned it 'after a wild night of love'. To a confidante she claimed that Wagner was referring to this when he wrote to his lover: 'And so it went on all night. By the morning I'd come to my senses and was able to pray to my angel from the very depths of my heart; and this prayer is love! Love! My soul rejoices in this love, which is the wellspring of my redemption!'[26] What exactly Minna meant by a 'wild night of love' is not clear from Wagner's letter to Mathilde, for he speaks only of his nightmares during the period in question. Did Minna perhaps think that her rival had secretly made her way to Wagner's bedroom? Or, borne on the wings of her opium dependency, had she herself crossed the forbidden threshold?

Whatever the answer, Minna showed a great sense of purpose in stirring up trouble, confronting the hated woman, threatening to inform Mathilde's ostensibly unsuspecting husband and holding out the prospect of a full-scale scandal if the liaison were to continue. Only in this light can we explain the subsequent actions of the various parties involved. Minna was packed off to Brestenberg to take the waters, the compromised Wesendoncks hurried away to Italy 'in search of pleasure', and Wagner was left to devote his energies to completing the Wesendonck Lieder and the second act of *Tristan und Isolde*.

The first page of this last-named draft includes the pessimistic note 'Still in the Asyl'. But by 17 August 1858 Wagner had fulfilled his own implied prophecy and left the Wesendoncks' summerhouse, exchanging it for a Venetian palazzo. He was bankrupt as usual and left a mountain of debts behind him in Zurich, so Wesendonck dug deeper into his pocket and provided him with the means to travel to Italy.

Eduard Devrient had already witnessed Wagner's flight from Dresden in 1849. Nine years later, his diary contains two entries on his former colleague's new start in life. One, dated 29 September 1858, repeats Wagner's own version of events, whereby 'considerations of a delicate nature' had 'driven' him from Zurich. 'So it must be true', the diarist concluded, 'that he behaved disloyally towards Wesendonck and turned his wife's head.'

In February 1859, Devrient, who was now running the Court Theatre in Karlsruhe, added a postscript, noting that it was now being rumoured in Zurich that Wagner had 'got rid of his wife in the most insulting manner, because she was too ill and too much of a nuisance. Wesendonck had then got rid of his disloyal friend who had been trying increasingly to ensnare his wife. With this degree of selfishness, everything seems to be permitted.'[27]

On the night of his departure from the Asyl, Wagner had a hallucination. He had gone to bed 'after eleven o'clock' and imagined that Mathilde had come to his bedside and one last time taken him in her arms in the presence of everyone and 'received his soul' with a kiss. He had seen this scene acted out before his eyes just before falling asleep: 'You entered through the study curtains; thus you wrapped your arm around me; thus I died, gazing upon you.'

He was roused from his 'uneasy dreams' by a 'strange rushing noise: on awakening I was sure I felt a kiss upon my brow: – a shrill sigh followed. It was so real that I started up and looked round. All was silent. I turned up the light: it was just before one, the end of the hour when ghosts are said to walk.'[28]

Two days later an announcement appeared in the local paper: 'For sale, due to departure, a large elegant mirror with a fine gilt frame, a new walnut games table with an engraved base; a large round walnut table. A walnut dining table for 14 persons, 12 walnut chairs. Walnut beds, feather mattresses, silk sofas, armchairs, carpets etc. A wine cupboard holding around 300 bottles, can be locked. Apply to Frau Wagner on the Gabler in Enge, near the home of Herr Wesendonck.'[29]

Schopenhauer

The end of Wagner's liaison with Mathilde Wesendonck also marked a new phase in that same relationship. In Venice, Wagner was no longer disturbed by jealous partners and tiresome tutors and was able to become completely absorbed by the idea of a love that had perished in real life. But the idea created its own reality in the form of letters, diary jottings and his work on the score of Act Two of *Tristan und Isolde*. Only in the draughty Palazzo Giustiniani overlooking the Grand Canal could the night of love conjured up in 'Träume' blow itself out with all the requisite thoroughness and ferocity.

For eight months Wagner worked in this Gothic building, which was as seedy as his own life but which offered him the right setting for his imaginary ecstasies and agonies. He had the walls covered in red hangings and the ill-fitting doors hidden behind curtains of the same colour. An iron bedstead was moved into his bedroom, and his Érard grand piano placed on the cold mosaic floor of the main reception room. He called it his 'Swan'. Here he spent his days and nights, his gaze shifting restlessly to and fro between his score and the waterway outside the palazzo. In the stone-floored room the 'Swan' rang out like an orchestra.

Wagner's uneventful life was interrupted only by gondola rides and by walks and conversations with Karl Ritter, but was otherwise strictly planned around his work. Symbols replaced reality. On his desk he erected a series of icons in the form of portraits of his stepfather Ludwig Geyer and his wife Minna, both of whom stared back at him with a deeply meaningful expression in their eyes. As archetypes of his subconscious they fed his creative imagination no less than his sister Mathilde, who was now elevated to the ranks of sainthood, just as Rosalie had been. 'I have no picture of her,' he noted in his diary, 'but I bear her soul within my heart.'[30]

In the meantime, Wagner had been neglecting his health, and his body responded by reminding him of its existence. He was plagued by digestive troubles of a nervous nature, for which he blamed the 'foul drinking water' of La Serenissima. A boil on his leg tormented him for weeks with an intensity reminiscent of the wound suffered by his hero Tristan. The boil was the size of a two-franc coin and so deep that it was possible 'to insert six four-groschen coins into it'. When his money ran out, he pawned his watch. 'May the kindly world forgive me this luxury,'[31] he commented sarcastically on this turn of events.

His invisible companion on his excursions through the city's labyrinth of canals was Arthur Schopenhauer. The Sage of Frankfurt had recently brought pessimism back into fashion and had proved a valuable helpmeet during the composer's love affair in Zurich, an affair whose prospects were pessimistic in the extreme. Wagner had scarcely got to know Schopenhauer's principal work, *The World as Will and Representation*, when he drew his lover into its sombre world of ideas. 'In 1852,' Mathilde wrote later, apparently advancing the date by two years, 'he introduced me to the philosophy of Arthur Schopenhauer.'[32]

If Wagner regarded his renunciation of his lover 'as a critical moment' in his inner life, he also felt that the philosopher gave him 'the courage to endure and the strength to renounce'.[33] If it had been hard for them both to abstain from sexual relations, the delights of renunciation were made more palatable in this way. Instead of sex, which Schopenhauer roundly proscribed, they dreamt of the saintliness of asceticism, at least for the foreseeable future. In his purple silk housecoat, Wagner bade farewell to the world, gratefully acknowledging the embittered misanthropist's writings as 'a gift from heaven'.[34]

One wonders whether Wagner was aware that Schopenhauer, like the icons beside his inkwell, was a voice from his past. The Leipzig advocate Wilhelm Wiesand, who had been one of the witnesses at Wagner's christening in the city's Thomaskirche in 1813, was friendly with the philosopher and in 1818 represented his interests in his dealings with the publishing house of Brockhaus that had been entrusted with the publication of *The World as Will and Representation*. The work had been written in the Ostraallee in Dresden at the very time that the little Richard Geyer was first becoming afraid of ghostly fifths.

Wagner had scarcely read this weighty tome when he was seized by a sense of missionary zeal. It was not only Mathilde who was to hear the glad tidings of how to escape from this vale of earthly sorrow; messages of jubilation were also fired off to Franz Liszt and to August Röckel, who was currently being detained at His Majesty's pleasure and who was now regaled with a detailed account of the advantages of renouncing the world. Wagner assured him that he owed the thinker a 'great revolution' in his 'rational views' and that only now did he understand his own works. The intoxication of his Zurich affair, for which there was no solution, encouraged him to proclaim that the solution to all the world's riddles was to be found in Schopenhauer. He had now 'seen the essence of the world and recognized its nullity'.[35]

The forty-one-year-old composer readily believed in the wonder that had finally opened his eyes, and so his disciples willingly followed suit, Wagner being hailed as the leading Schopenhauerian. From Nietzsche, who sought to fraternize with Wagner in the name of their common idol, to Houston Stewart Chamberlain, who declared that Wagner's discovery of Schopenhauer was 'the most important event in his whole life',[36] to Dieter Borchmeyer, who believes that Wagner's inability to make any real progress on *Siegfried* over a twelve-year period was triggered by a 'Schopenhauerian crisis',[37] there has been a consensus on this point: only thanks to the restless spirit of world renunciation did Wagner become Wagner. There would have been no Tristan, no Hans Sachs, no Parsifal without it.

Wagner, too, continued to appeal to Schopenhauer as his authority right up to the end of his life. But there remains the question whether he really meant Schopenhauer whenever he referred to the philosopher by name. Inasmuch as no other contemporary was as showered with praise as Schopenhauer, doubts seem to be in order. Why did Wagner appeal to him so often when he normally concealed the source of his ideas? What is the significance of the fact that, unlike other writers, he lauded Schopenhauer to the skies? Why, in this one particular case, did he renounce his claim to absolute originality and independence, a claim on whose altar he otherwise sacrificed every other victim?

The reason why he proclaimed his dependence from the rooftops lies in the simple fact that no such dependence existed. Wagner had not helped himself to another's ideas, as was generally the case, but had merely poured the wine of his own ideas into new bottles. It was his own thoughts that seethed beneath the Schopenhauerian label. The first person to see this was Schopenhauer himself. The latter simply did not know what to make of Wagner's art and exclaimed 'Bravo!' when one of his followers criticized Wagner, a criticism which in his view was 'fully justified'.[38] And he also sent word to Wagner that he should 'hang up his boots as a composer'.[39]

Even here, then, there was a divergency of opinion. In *The World as Will and Representation*, Wagner had discovered to his delight that Schopenhauer accorded music supremacy over the other arts: whereas the latter offered no more than a reflection of reality, the very essence of existence could be heard in music. In short, music did not represent something, but revealed the very thing that lay at the basis of everything else. To Schopenhauer's way of thinking, this meant that it did not belong to the deceptive world of 'representation' or 'ideas' but 'directly depicted the will itself'. Music as a metaphysical entity seemed to chime so astonishingly well with Wagner's own philosophy that in 1870, in his Beethoven essay, he presented himself as Schopenhauer's plenipotentiary on earth.

But Wagner's revealingly convoluted train of thought can scarcely conceal the fact that Schopenhauer intended more or less the exact opposite of the ideas trumpeted by the author of the Beethoven centennial study. For Schopenhauer, the value of music consisted precisely in the fact that it did not have to represent anything. It was music alone. It expressed nothing, but spoke directly to the listener's feelings. Inasmuch as it 'achieves its ends entirely by its own means, it needs no words or the plot of an opera'. Again: 'The words are and remain a foreign extra of subordinate value', hence Schopenhauer's entirely serious suggestion that it would be better 'to write the words to go with the music than to compose music to an existing text'.

As a result, it is neither ideas nor the dramatic plot that impose 'order and cohesion' on the music. This is achieved, rather, simply by mathematical proportions and the formal divisions created by the use of rhythm. Rhythm is the temporal equivalent of structural symmetry in space, creating the mathematically calculable blueprint for existence. In Schopenhauer's view this explains why 'even in its most terrible discords' music remains 'enjoyable'. Anyone who listens to music sits calmly in the lap of the will, untormented by distracting ideas. But this is precisely the sort of music to which Wagner had bade farewell during his days as a pupil of Weinlig.

It is not only in musical matters that these two ostensibly like-minded thinkers reveal themselves as poles apart. Of the two chapters in *The World as Will and Representation* to which Wagner paid particular attention, one dealt with the metaphysics of music. The other was headed 'The Metaphysics of Sexual Love'. What he read here was so much at odds with his previous ideas on love that it initially seems to have escaped his notice altogether. In his earlier essays, Wagner had seen in love the essence of all creativity and in the union of lovers the supreme goal of human existence, whereas Schopenhauer declared this to be a case of ludicrous self-deception. All that people generally passed off as romantic love was mere obedience to bare necessity. 'All amorousness is rooted in the sexual impulse alone . . ., however ethereally it may deport itself.'

Schopenhauer's 'metaphysics' was in fact the very opposite of that: like desire, the elevated notions that were associated with love served solely to tempt individuals into propagating the species. 'What is all the fuss about?' asked Schopenhauer, pouring out his contempt for a humanity blinded by love. 'Why all the urgency, uproar, anguish and exertion? It is merely a question of every Jack finding his Jill.' And with cynical candour, Schopenhauer invites his gentle reader to 'translate this into the language of Aristophanes'. In short, it is not individuals who are magically drawn together but genitalia. 'The true end of the whole love story, though the parties concerned are unaware of it,' writes the childless misanthrope, 'is that this particular child may be begotten.' Everything else – longing, the intoxication of love, emotional disasters and so on – is no more than 'insubstantial soap bubbles'.

Wagner, who produced many such soap bubbles, evidently failed to notice this blatant contradiction even though he claimed to have read the book four times. Schopenhauer's mortification of the will had little in common with Wagner's 'noble renunciation' in the matter of Mathilde Wesendonck, a renunciation that was ultimately not entirely serious. And the awareness of the 'nullity' of all earthly existence that drives Wagner's heroes to despair scarcely springs from Schopenhauer's cold, dissecting gaze. Rather, it derives from the ardent longing for a love that cannot be assuaged in real life. If this desire were to be no more than a figment of the imagination that could be overcome by regular sexual intercourse, then the Dutchman and the Wanderer, Tannhäuser and Tristan, would be revealed as poor fools, their endless sufferings soap bubbles of a misdirected reproductive drive.

Any affinity between Schopenhauer and German idealism, which he loathed and cursed in much the same way that Alberich curses his divine alter ego, consisted in essence in his turning it on its head. For Hegel and Schelling, it was the idea of God that expressed itself in nature and that, as such, was alienated from itself in order to achieve self-awareness in humankind, whereas for Schopenhauer self-consciousness, thought and God were illusions that nature used to delude itself. Whereas idealism sought to reconcile us to the sufferings of history by granting us an insight into them, Schopenhauer was convinced that one thing alone mattered: an insight into the sufferings that nature inflicted on itself and, as an immediate consequence of this, withdrawal from the world's deceptive goings-on and total renunciation of our instincts. Everything that came into existence deserved to perish, and the sooner, the better.

The decisive difference between Schopenhauer and idealist thinkers lay in the fact that the former, as demanded by his extreme position, had no choice but to renounce love in its entirety. Intelligent and learned though he may have seemed, his conceptual edifice rested on the wit with which he exposed creation and the whole history of humanity as a misunderstanding. For ultimately all that existed was nature, which he called 'will'. But as Wagner once succinctly summed it up, the will wanted 'nothing more than to live for ever, i.e., to nourish itself (by exterminating others) and to reproduce itself'.

In order for the will to be able to take an interest in its own activities, it had to have a clear idea of itself. And so it imagined itself, without knowing it. The 'world' that incited people's passions was a mere 'idea' or 'representation' that the will created of itself. Thus the will – Wagner went on to explain – was 'something that is perpetually at variance with itself, something that is in a state of constant discord, and the only element of this discord that we can feel is pain and suffering'.[40]

Schopenhauer regarded man's self-awareness as a delusion on the part of the will, and he saw no possibility of reconciling this contradiction. The redemption of history through love was inconceivable to him not least because love, too, was one of the delusions of the blindly driven Moloch known as will. In short, it was possible to feel only pity for the will's poor creatures. Schopenhauer had bound his own hands with this monism of the will, leaving himself with no alternative but amputation in the form of a withdrawal from all instinctive activities, a cessation of all delusive ideas and the denial of the will to live. In place of a society liberated by revolution to which the idealists looked forward, Schopenhauer dreamt of oblivion, which he euphemistically called Nirvana.

This too must have seemed familiar to Wagner. Even before being introduced to Schopenhauer's philosophy of the will, Wagner had told August Röckel that his Wanderer had 'raised himself to the tragic heights of willing his own destruction'. Decades later he was still proud of anticipating his reading of Schopenhauer in this way. 'I am convinced', he announced in Bayreuth, 'that Schopenhauer would have been annoyed that I'd discovered this before getting to know his philosophy.'[41] But in his delight at his own discovery, Wagner seems to have overlooked the fact that there was no longer anything tragic about a Wotan who was a convert to Buddhism. The composer's world drama drew its strength from the very contradiction that Schopenhauer claimed did not exist. Wotan does not suffer from the impossibility of leading a painless existence but from the impossibility of finding love.

And it was precisely this that became a secret dilemma for Wagner. Where there existed only a bovine will and its cunning supersession, there could be no question of any 'tragic heights', still less of Wagner's world drama. Strictly speaking, Schopenhauer's master key did not fit the lock of this particular conceptual edifice but granted access only to its vestibule. His depressing view of things coincided exactly with the world that is characterized in the *Ring* by the early Wotan and Alberich and in Wagner's Zurich essays by the materialism of the modern world. What Schopenhauer described was the world of laws, a world ruled from the very outset by insatiable egoism and desperate greed. Inasmuch as he did not believe in freedom, love and suchlike fripperies except to the extent that they were projections of this egoism and greed, all that was left for him was resignation and a living death – death with our eyes wide open.

But it was very much this open-eyed gaze, recognizing itself in the gaze of the beloved, that was central to the *Ring*. Only in the self-consciousness of 'I' and 'you' did the new man arise, a human being who was no Schopenhauerian exemplar of the species but a wholly unique individual. It was not the chance coupling of two anonymous bodies called Jack and Jill that was crucial to the cycle but the conscious union of two individuals who were willing to abandon all the glories of the world and even sacrifice their own lives in order to belong to each other. That their 'radiant love' can only laugh at death and suffering must have remained a total mystery to Schopenhauer.

It is at this point that Wagner's critique kicks in. If he had carried it through to its conclusion, Schopenhauer's philosophy would have been refuted, at least when judged by Wagner's criteria. In order to avoid this, he decided against sending off the letter in which he planned to put the Frankfurt thinker straight and did not even complete it, no doubt because he was afraid of the self-contradictions into which he had long since fallen. The penny finally dropped in December 1858, when Wagner was working on *Tristan und Isolde* in the Palazzo Giustiniani, suffering from a boil on his leg and dreaming of Mathilde as Isolde. In the midst of his renunciation of the world, he discovered in his beloved Schopenhauer 'worrying gaps in his system', as he puts it in *My Life*,[42] without going into any further detail. In a letter to Mathilde Wesendonck of December 1858 he even speaks of 'major findings that supplement and correct my friend Schopenhauer', but they were findings that he 'preferred to keep in his head rather than write them down'.[43]

The attempt to strike up a correspondence with the Sage of Frankfurt was prompted by a passage in 'The Metaphysics of Sexual Love' in which Schopenhauer expresses his astonishment at a familiar phenomenon: the 'common suicide of two lovers' whose union is 'thwarted by external circumstances'.

Somehow this absurd undertaking could not be squared with his philosophy of the hegemony of unbridled instincts, and so Wagner, drawing on his own experience, offered to help him out. Writing with the gold-nibbed pen given to him by Mathilde Wesendonck, he ventured the view that in 'sexual love' he had found 'a path to salvation through self-knowledge and the denial of the will – and not just the individual will'.[44]

This was a weighty objection, because for Schopenhauer the sex drive was the most concrete expression of the will, with the result that its longed-for denial seemed inconceivable without strict abstinence. But how were Jack and Jill to achieve 'self-knowledge' through that cunning trickster, sexual love? For as soon as 'the eyes of two lovers meet in longing', Schopenhauer had written in 'The Metaphysics of Sexual Love', they strive in secret to 'perpetuate the whole trouble and toil that would otherwise rapidly come to an end'. And this is ultimately what mattered to Schopenhauer.

For Wagner, sexual love meant something completely different. In the eyes of the lovers, in which, according to Schopenhauer, one animal recognized another, Wagner believed that the individual came to an understanding of himself and hence of the whole. As the 'I' recognized itself in the 'you', it lost its sense of isolation and selfishness. It merged with the other and in that way became a new being. As a result of this self-sacrifice it lost the very egoism that Schopenhauer felt was embodied in sexuality. And so Wagner regarded the suicide of lovers not as the mindless flight from reality over which the philosopher racked his brains in vain, but as the conscious fulfilment of a love which in keeping with its very nature meant the total abandonment of the self.

The death of Wagner's lovers does not take place in nature or in social reality, however, but in each other. The self-sacrifice of each of them is accepted by the love of the other. Dying leads not to oblivion but to the new man. Not only are the differences between the sexes reconciled in his consciousness, so too is nature itself. Just as love unites men and women, so it resolves the contradiction that fragments human history.

Wagner had recently interwoven these mystical insights into the second act of *Tristan und Isolde*, and now he wanted to share them with Schopenhauer, who would no doubt have replied by return of post and declared his correspondent a fool. Either the philosopher was right, and Wagner was indeed a fool, as Schopenhauer appears in any case to have believed, or Wagner was right, in which case Schopenhauer would have had to come up with some new ideas.

And so Wagner failed to complete his inflammatory letter but confided its findings to his Venice diary for Mathilde Wesendonck. Here too he refers to a 'correction' to Schopenhauer's thinking, although it amounts in effect to a wholesale refutation of it. But in that case he would have had to forgo the Schopenhauerian label that he liked for other reasons. The 'path of salvation' that sexuality offers us, he explained here, had revealed itself to him alone because there had never been an individual who was both a poet and a musician in the sense that Wagner himself understood those terms.

As in his Zurich essays, both types of art were like lovers: the poet threw himself into the dark sea of music that rose up to meet him, yearningly, like a woman, so that the contradictions of their loving union were reconciled and the living work of art was born. And this is exactly what happened in the self-consciousness of the first consummate word-tone artist, which explains why the nature of art was revealed to him at the same time as the nature of love.

In Wagner's view, creative activity was not the result of the 'intellect' breaking free from the 'will', as Schopenhauer believed, but the other way round: the intellect conceived of itself as the supreme expression of the will and hence as its 'organ of cognition'. Translated into the language of the German idealists, this means that only when the mind immerses itself in nature can nature achieve self-consciousness in man. Only when the individual conceives of himself as conscious of the whole can he recognize himself in creation and depict creation through his art.

The will, wrote Wagner, is 'something completely different from the mere will to live, namely, the will to recognize, i.e., to recognize oneself. Hence its lofty, ecstatic, inspiriting sense of satisfaction.'[45] Precisely because this self-knowledge on the part of nature leads to a new creation, Wagner argued, rebutting Schopenhauer, the artist feels 'a wonderful, enthusiastic joy and rapture in the supreme moments of the insights that are vouchsafed to his genius'.[46]

And this is exactly what happens in love. The individual outgrows himself in order to begin a new creation with his lover. The ecstasy of their union is like that of the artist's *furor* and allows the individual consciousness to reach a new level on which, according to Wagner, 'the will of the species achieves full consciousness'. This 'will of the species' differed from Schopenhauer's on one decisive point. In the philosopher's view, it concealed only one particularly sophisticated form of the egoistic and prototypical will. For Wagner, by contrast, it was synonymous with the idea of humanity. And this in turn revealed itself only to the lover and the artist.

As a loving artist himself, Wagner was able to find all other ideas encapsulated within that of a humanity embodying the divine element in nature. The stages through which the history of nature and humankind had passed in their development were repeated within the artist's consciousness. By turning to this inner world, the poet discovered ideas that revealed themselves to him 'more clearly and more certainly than any other object of cognition' and that demanded artistic expression. All 'poetic conceptions', Wagner explained to his distant beloved, were invariably 'far in advance of my experience'. The 'Flying Dutchman, Tannhäuser, Lohengrin, the Nibelungs, Wodan [sic] all existed in my head before they existed in my experience'. But the task of developing the idea and turning it into a finished work of art involved the generally grievous experience of life, with all its attendant sufferings.

This is exactly what happened with *Tristan und Isolde*. Never before, Wagner assured his correspondent, had 'an idea so clearly passed into experience'. What he discovered within him found perfect reflection in reality. What he experienced as an individual was simultaneously the self's experience of the whole. Another philosopher, whom Schopenhauer had dismissed as a 'university buffoon' and a 'purveyor of journalistic nonsense', had given the name 'world spirit' to this self-knowing whole.

This ability to objectify the situation, Wagner explained to his distant beloved, who was currently being plagued by pangs of conscience and consumed by lovelorn desire, might offer the cuckolded Otto a certain consolation. 'For if another guessed at it or knew it,' Wagner wrote in reference to Mathilde's husband, while emphatically breaking free from Schopenhauer, 'he would no longer be angry with us, and every painful experience that invades his heart from outside he must offer up with exalted, ennobled emotion as a sacrifice to the higher aims of the world spirit that creates from within itself experiences for us to suffer and which through those sufferings raises itself still higher. But who can understand this?'[47]

Presumably not Mathilde. Otto, Wagner insisted, should learn to see that in Wagner's love for Mathilde it was not just the composer alone who had scaled a new peak of experience and of self-consciousness but the whole of humanity. Given the pioneering impact of *Tristan und Isolde* as a drama, this was no exaggeration. Mathilde would have been no less astonished to discover that her beloved disciple of Schopenhauer had in this way returned to the world of idealism, a world that he had long since consigned to the rubbish bin of the history of ideas as 'the nonsense and charlatanism of Fichte, Schelling and Hegel'.[48]

In short, Wagner's philosophy of love sailed under a flag of convenience from the time of his years in Zurich, and barely anyone noticed. Only the Hegelian privy councillor Jakob Sulzer, with whom Wagner had discussed the ideas of *Opera and Drama* during his early period in Zurich, was under no illusions. 'However highly he valued Arthur Schopenhauer,' he wrote to Mathilde Wesendonck following Wagner's death, 'he never took over so much as a single comma from his cognitive philosophy.'[49] Schopenhauer abhorred the world, whereas Wagner thought he could be reconciled with it through love. Behind the profoundest resignation, there still lay his longing for his lost lover, a longing shared by Wotan. The self-consciousness that Schopenhauer despised as a deception mechanism on the part of nature became for Wagner the fons et origo of all creativity. But if all that Wagner passed off as Schopenhauer was really Wagner himself, why did he need the philosopher at all?

What attracted him to the waspish misanthropist had less to do with epistemology than with his philosopher's view of the world: the contrast between Christianity and Judaism within whose field of tension Wagner's perception of reality tended to operate was emphatically confirmed by Schopenhauer. In his first proselytizing letter to the incarcerated Röckel he had ascribed his own conversion to Schopenhauer's account of Judaism: 'The prodigious force of friend Schopenhauer's genius' helped him 'to cast out the last remnant of Jewish superstition', a superstition that consisted in affirming the 'devouring and self-propagating' monster that is the will. In this way, all Alberich's qualities could be attributed to the religion of the Old Testament, a religion that held people captive in a cave of suffering as a result of their greed and lovelessness. 'This affirmation is implemented at all costs,' Wagner complained to his imprisoned friend in 1855, 'and is nothing other than Judaism, which has again grown so powerful at the present time.'[50]

To Christianity, by contrast, the Sage of Frankfurt ascribed the redemptive power of denying existence. Just as Wagner had done in the case of his Wibelungs, so Schopenhauer traced the source of the Christian religion back to the Indian subcontinent, from where it had brought to the West 'the need for redemption from an existence that is prey to suffering and death'. And he contrasted the severity of the religion of Mosaic law with that sense of compassion in which all egoism finally finds rest.

Yet even Christianity, Schopenhauer had argued in his *Parerga and Paralipomena*, had perpetuated the basic error of Judaism, namely, that it had 'flown in the face of nature and torn humankind away from the world of animals'. For Schopenhauer, there were only suffering creatures, and the difference between man and beast consisted simply in the fact that man could grasp this. As a result of the mistaken 'Jewish view' that man was superior to all other creatures, animals were 'regarded as an object to be used by humans'. From time immemorial, animals had been flayed and exploited, but to these evils modern man had added 'the horrors of vivisection', 'the most terrible cruelty to animals' inflicted for scientific ends. 'And alas,' wrote Schopenhauer, whose lifelong companion was a poodle, 'it is the creature which from a moral point of view is the most noble of all animals that is used most often in vivisection: the dog.'

Wagner must have felt that Schopenhauer was speaking to him directly. He hated the Jews, and Schopenhauer showed him that there was a metaphysical rightness to this. And he was passionately fond of animals, especially dogs, and here too he discovered that his love concealed within it a profound wisdom. It was not Schopenhauer's philosophy that convinced him but his private views, views glorified as a philosophy, investing his personal whims with the status of a system of thought.

Not until a quarter of a century later was Wagner to elaborate these ideas, when the *Bayreuther Blätter* provided him with a suitable forum for his Schopenhauerian propaganda.

Tristan

Whereas Schopenhauer refused to acknowledge the very idea of love and made do with mistresses, Wagner thought of nothing else. Her name was Mathilde, and the fulfilment of his desires was written in the stars. 'As I have never known the true happiness of love,' he confided to Liszt in 1854, 'I intend to raise a further monument to this most beautiful of all dreams, a monument in which this love will be properly sated from start to finish: I have planned in my head a Tristan and Isolde, the simplest but most full-blooded musical conception; with the "black flag" that flutters at the end, I shall then cover myself over, in order to die.'[51]

Written at the height of his first great enthusiasm for Schopenhauer, this was a thoroughly unorthodox idea, for according to the philosopher's concept of the will, death brought no solution to the problem, being merely part of the revolving wheel of existence. To die with one's lover, as Wagner imagined it, seemed the height of absurdity to Schopenhauer, being surpassed only by Wagner's conviction that the greatest love was manifest in a double suicide. Schopenhauer saw in this no more than a sentimental gloss on a deeply prosaic situation, so that a piece that glorified this passion was bound to strike him as suspect. However much scholars may assure us that Wagner's journey took him 'from Schopenhauer via Wotan to Tristan,'[52] his tale of the love of Tristan and Isolde took him in exactly the opposite direction: the drama became the musical alternative to Schopenhauer's grimly loveless universe.

Wagner described *Tristan und Isolde* simply as an 'action'. Its subject matter seemed to be in the air, as both Schumann and his pupil Karl Ritter had tried their hands at operatic versions of it. But Wagner's drama is only superficially related to the medieval romance by Gottfried von Straßburg that had served as a model for both Schumann and Ritter, and his protagonists would be as out of place in the Tristan legend as his redemptive couple of Siegfried and Brünnhilde would be out of place in the *Nibelungenlied*.

Just as Wagner's *Tristan und Isolde* had emerged directly from *Siegfried*, so their main characters differ virtually only in their costumes. Like twins they suffer the same fate, and this is something that Wagner did not need to take from any existing source, for his heroes had already experienced this for themselves, and since getting to know Mathilde Wesendonck he too had become caught up in it. Once again he found himself confronted by the familiar situation of the disinherited hero and the sister who is torn from his heart. Once again an 'abyss' opened up wherever he turned.[53] And once again there seemed little prospect of a bloodless denouement.

Rather, the drama was resolved in new, unheard-of sounds. In keeping with the impossibility of the situation, Wagner devised a musical language impossible to justify by existing standards. Inspired by the harmonic audacities that Liszt had allowed himself when setting melancholy love poems, Wagner built up his whole music drama on a single magically mystifying chord. Out of the melodic line that leads to this chord and out of its dialectic reflection as the melodic line leads away from it again, Wagner created a kind of musical supernova by dint of constant refractions, inversions, mirror images and interlinkings.

Its light outshone everything that existed in the operatic firmament. Once heard, the 'Tristan' chord rendered its listener deaf to traditional harmonies. And the listener who plunged into this billowing sea of tone colours would find that all other music was no more than a black-and-white painting. Wagner's ocean of sound had engulfed all terra firma. The age in which the music merely accompanied the events on stage was definitively over. Now the sounds from the world's abyss determined the direction that the story took. 'In my other works the motifs serve the action,' Wagner told an astonished Cosima in 1873, 'but here one could say that the action derives from the motifs.'[54]

The very first motif, sinking down questioningly into the dark ground of the 'Tristan' chord before receiving a yearningly ascending answer, sums up the whole of the drama. Everything else – a world of joy and suffering – follows from it, for this opening motif merely states clearly what had already been hinted at in *Das Rheingold* and in the scenes describing the Wälsung twins' impassioned rediscovery of one another: this is the eternal moment of the first creation as evoked by Wagner in *Opera and Drama*.

The divine light falls into the night of nature that rises up radiantly to greet it. The male word plunges into the female abyss of music, which nestles around it in its rapture. In the beginning was love, and love was a dialogue. From this eloquent union there emerged a whole new world. Creation rose up and fell into the extremes of alienated consciousness, in order to be reconciled again at some indeterminate date in the future.

For Wagner, this indeterminate date came with his tragedy about love and death, *Tristan und Isolde*. But the first four notes, gently intoned by the cellos, give mute expression to what he called 'the bashful profession of tender attraction'.[55] In human terms, this no doubt means 'ich liebe dich'. But the answer given by the yearning ground remains dark and unfathomable. It needed a further act of creation, presented over the drama's three acts, to bring some conceptual clarity to this point.

The creation of the world in *Tristan und Isolde* begins at the onset of all existence. Just as the divine spirit approached its own ground, so Wagner, shutting himself off from all outside influences, drew solely upon his own subconscious. The ideas and relationships from which he wove his drama lay ready for collection, he had only to clothe them in physical form. 'In total confidence,' he wrote retrospectively, 'I plunged once again into the depths of inner emotional events and from this innermost centre of the world I fearlessly constructed its outward form.' As though in confirmation of the philosophy of creativity that he had once expounded to Berlioz, a world of archetypal ideas arose from this centre, developing out of itself. 'The whole of the affecting action', wrote Wagner in reference to *Tristan und Isolde*, 'appears only because the inmost soul demands it, and it emerges into the light in the form prefigured from within.'[56]

As a result, the prelude is no mere introduction but recounts the whole of the plot, although this becomes clear only when the bud has already blossomed. With the very first notes in which the space for this dialogue opens up, the original unity is shattered and consciousness is alienated from its origins. Where love had once existed, all that now holds sway is an insatiable desire for love.

Wagner himself wrote that the prelude describes the emergence of an 'insatiable longing' that grows 'through anxious sighing, hope and apprehension, plaints and desires, rapture and torment and finally to the most powerful impulse, the most violent attempt to find a breach in the dyke that might open a way for the inexhaustibly craving heart to enter the sea of love's endless delight'. Cut off from its own life-giving sea, the sense of 'homesickness' builds up in ever higher waves as though the two were already one.

'In vain!' declares Wagner. 'The swooning heart sinks back again, to pine away in yearning desire, a yearning that never reaches its goal, since each attainment of such a goal brings only renewed desire.'[57] The feeling that had motivated all Wagner's heroes from the time of the Dutchman onwards finds its consummate musical expression in the form of the infinitely circling movement that after every apparent assuagement rises up in renewed desire.

Wagner also described this as the 'unvictorious struggle against an inner fire'. But where there was fire, the light of the beginning would one day rise up again, and the struggle that lacerates the protagonists was not to be Wagner's last word on the subject.

Following the prelude, in which Bernard Shaw thought that he heard 'an astonishingly intense and faithful translation into music of the emotions which accompany the union of a pair of lovers',[58] the curtain rises on a complex, not to say embarrassing, situation. Two people, who are secretly in love with each other, find themselves on a sea voyage that will end in their definitive separation. While the woman is promised in marriage to another, the man plans to leave the country for good in order to avoid all further complications.

The situation is made worse for them both by the fact that the woman would prefer to die, rather than submit to her fate. Meanwhile, the man adds to the sense of unease as it is he who has paired his lover off with another man and who is now standing at the vessel's helm merely in order to hand her over. According to Wagner, the similarity with Siegfried cannot be overlooked inasmuch as Tristan, too, 'acts under the constraint of a delusion that makes this deed of his not free, so that it is on another's behalf that he woos the woman destined for him by primeval law'.

In short, these are no random lovers who find themselves facing each other on board ship but a man and a woman who were meant to be united in love according to the 'primeval law' of creation, just as creation was meant to be united. 'Deception' has led to their estrangement, but it was an act of deception unmotivated by Hagen's potion, with its powers of amnesia. As with Tannhäuser, amnesia stems from a mere change of scene. The unspoken love that has scarcely burgeoned is replaced in Tristan's case by the world of the law in which all that counts is power, honour and possessions, including the possession of women.

With the everyday world comes evil, working its way into Tristan's heart when he vaunts the fair Isolde. Instead of preserving her image in his 'heart's chaste night', he praises her openly. Envious of the successful hero, the Cornish king's advisers, led by Tristan's friend, demand that the hero's latest conquest become the king's wife. The hero is caught in a trap of his own devising. If he refuses to present the king with this gift, he will be exposed as a dishonourable egoist, but if he hands her over, he will betray his own feelings and at the same time violate the oaths that he has sworn to her out of gratitude.

Tristan defies his feelings. Driven by thoughts of prestige and perhaps also by an unacknowledged fear such as Siegfried had already felt in the presence of a woman, he sides with his enemies and urges King Marke to take Isolde as his wife. The act of betrayal, which in the case of Siegfried is triggered by Hagen's potion, acquires its own momentum with Tristan, a momentum that stems from self-denial and that ends only with his own downfall. The king – his uncle – resists his advisers' suggestion as he has appointed his nephew Tristan his sole heir. Only when Tristan extortionately threatens to leave the country if Marke opposes the marriage does the latter relent. Out of 'defiance', as he calls it before seeing through his jealous friend's intrigue, the hero forfeits his love and at the same time loses his inheritance and ultimately his life as well.

Exactly the same happens to Isolde. And it is to Tristan that the Irish princess owes the fact that she stands here loveless and lacking any inheritance. Tristan has killed her lover in single combat and placed her country under Cornish rule before finding himself, wounded, in the hands of his Irish enemy. He obtains Isolde's help by assuming a false identity and thanks to her magical skills recovers. But then she sees through him and raises her sword to kill him and gain revenge, only for their eyes to meet.

That is enough. The world stands still. The old 'glittering serpent' disseminates its light. A few questioning notes on the cellos descend into the queen's dark heart, and from them there arises a yearning answer, albeit one whose meaning is hard to unravel. Tristan prefers not to understand it at all. The pulse of life starts to beat once again, then begins to grow faster and soon acquires a life-threatening violence, for scarcely has the 'I' found its 'you' before both are torn apart again.

Tristan abandons his Isolde, only to return in a hideously transmogrified guise. Without needing a magic helmet, her lover confronts her as a 'miserable, low pimp' who drags her off 'to market' as a serving maid – thus the prose sketch.[59] Resistance is useless, as even her parents advise her to marry the new ruler: once again political expediency has triumphed over love, and Isolde, previously raised to the skies from the depths of her humiliation, is now thrust down into an even deeper state of degradation.

It is at this desperate juncture that the curtain opens. The self-destructive Tristan assumes a heroic façade, while Isolde, in her own words, is no more than a living 'corpse'. Two people who should love each other have now lost not only each other but themselves. Just as Tristan is carrying out another's wishes, so

Isolde can no longer command her former magic powers. Ever since she emu-
lated Brünnhilde and laid aside the armour of her virginity, she has been a vulnerable woman with human feelings. The god who woke her sold her into the
slavery of marriage with an 'ageing king', while, to add insult to injury, 'the most
glorious of men' looks set to be a constant, lowering presence in her life.

On this point, at least, Isolde is mistaken, as Tristan has 'vowed to leave as
soon as he has handed her over to the king'. He is in any case a foreigner who
had lost his parents and who came from Brittany to stay with his uncle. Perhaps
he wants to have another look at his abandoned family home at Kareol? Fate
will grant him his wishes, albeit in a way that he had not expected. First, however, his eyes will be opened to the very nature of existence. And he will not survive the infinitely painful process that leads there, for, as Wagner's prose draft
promises, 'Love has taken it upon itself to carry out the death sentence.'

As love's advocate, Isolde summons Tristan to appear in court, but she has
already pronounced sentence: 'Revenge for the act of betrayal', revenge that will
also bring 'calm to her heart in its anguish'. The death potion stands ready.
Tristan has only to do her the favour of drinking it with her. When the two of
them finally stand gazing into each other's eyes once again, the music that we
hear tells of majestic sadness, anticipating the following dialogue, in which
Isolde's barely repressed anger, repeatedly flaring up, encounters Tristan's
weak-kneed courtly reserve. But first there reigns a long and eloquent silence.

The dialogue, with which the actual drama begins, represents a challenge
even for readers experienced in the art of interpreting librettos, with the rhetor-
ical and conceptual difficulties increasing from scene to scene, reaching the ne
plus ultra of reflective intensity with the catastrophe at the end of the second
act, where all operatic conventions are left far behind. Even the apparently petty
squabble between the frustrated lovers may strike the listener as stilted and cir-
cumlocutory.

But this indigestible mass is in fact the earth's molten magma forcing its way
to the surface beneath a thin crust of convention. In its dialectic cut and thrust
are reflected the contradictions typical of human history. What we find here are
not only the rules of social behaviour that bury beneath them all natural emotions, but also categories like honour and vengeance that drive out human feelings. But what is involved above all is the art of deception, an art that seems
indispensable if power and dominion are to be exercised. And that indispens-
ability stems from the fact that human beings cannot endure the truth.

This explains why in their dialogue the lovers begin by avoiding the issue.
Only after Isolde's harsh reproaches and Tristan's legalistic response do they
approach the crux of the matter, albeit circumspectly. 'The mistress of silence

bids me be silent', Tristan sums up their eloquent speechlessness. 'If I grasp what she keeps silent, I keep silent what she won't grasp.' Like the world itself, he suggests that their conversation suffers from a lack of truthfulness. The crux of the matter has not been addressed. He sees that Isolde, too, is speaking only in order to conceal her love for him. Conversely, he implies, she will never understand that he made her queen of Cornwall only out of his love for her. Yet she understands at once and reproaches him in turn with using this as a means by which to avoid her.

She can avoid the truth no longer. In a world that lives by deception, the truth is synonymous with death. The poison is already waiting, bringing ultimate certainty to the couple. The 'atonement' that she demands from him is no more than a pretext, for the world in which guilt and atonement have any validity already lies far behind them. The only question now is whether they can live without one another. If their love is a delusion, the world stands open to them, and the vial of poison can remain sealed. But if they really love each other, there is only one way of asserting their union in the few hours left to them before they are cut off from the world, and that is to cut themselves off from the world. The death of the lovers, to which Schopenhauer reacted with no more than a bemused shaking of his head, becomes the supreme sacrament for them.

The final oath that Tristan swears to his Isolde signals his volte-face: the honour to which he had sacrificed her and the defiance that is the basis of his self-esteem he now sees as a source of very real wretchedness. At the same time, his heart, robbed of its true happiness, is filled with the dream of a vague new idea. Here is solace for his eternal grief at the loss of his love in the form of the poison that he welcomes as a draft that will bring oblivion. Without averting his eyes from Isolde, he drinks from the goblet that she snatches away from him at the very last moment: 'Betrayed here too? Half of it's mine!' In the prose draft this is even more clearly expressed: 'Laß ihn dir zutrinken' ('Let me drink it to you'), she says, using the intimate 'du' form after previously preferring the more formal 'Sie'. In the face of death, there is only 'ich' and 'du'. Isolde drinks to him, emptying the goblet of poison. The silence is audible.

Drinking one another's health has its dangers, for this is exactly how the tribulations of Siegmund and Sieglinde began. The lovers now expect to die together. But it is 'Love' who has taken it upon herself 'to carry out the sentence of death', and so something totally different happens. Isolde's servant has exchanged the bottles, and the lovers, weary of life, have drunk the aphrodisiac intended for Marke. Isolde has drunk to Tristan's health with a tonic.

Needless to say, this exchange of potions is no more than a theatrical device to express the fact that love and death are the same – not death as we usually understand it, death that puts an end to life, but the conscious death that ends a life of falsehood and self-interest, a life squandered on money, fame and honour. This is the death with which the lovers give themselves wholly to each other and merge with each other completely. Death is the wrong word for this: 'love' alone suits the situation.

Now the lovers awake for a second time. What they thought would be their death is merely the start of their resurrection in the form of a new being made up of both 'I' and 'you'. Thinking themselves dead, they are able to abandon all pretence. They catch each other at the moment of falling. Their first loving encounter had passed like a fleeting glance of doubtful credibility, but once they have survived all their sufferings it is repeated as a revelation. Creation is repeated in their eyes as they drink in each other's gaze. According to the stage directions, 'Both are seized with shuddering and gaze undaunted and with deepest emotion into each other's eyes, in which the look of defiance in the face of death soon melts into the glow of passion.'

From the silence there rises up once again the elemental motif that turns into a veritable frenzy of passion, this time with no transition. The masks fall and with them the old world. Tristan's honour, he now realizes, was merely an empty dream. And the same is true of Isolde's sense of shame, she tells him. What blinded them – so-called 'reality' – has turned out to be a spiteful trick on the part of a 'deceitful spell'. But their period of separation is now over. They embrace and, like Siegfried and the awakened valkyrie, almost crush each other to death. Even as late as 1882, Wagner was struck by the fact that 'at the end of the opening act Isolde breaks out into a violent expression of love'.[60]

Just as their jubilation reaches 'love's highest pleasure' – a moment percep-tively described by Shaw – reality, briefly forgotten, bursts upon the scene: Brangäne drags in the royal regalia and Tristan's servant announces the approach of the king, joyful anticipation of the pleasures of his bridal night already etched into his features.

'Which king?' asks Tristan. Had they not entered the realm of death? 'Where am I?' asks Isolde. 'Am I alive?' The blare of trumpets and a choral outburst leave the lovers in no doubt that the world they thought they had long since left behind them is about to re-enter their lives and blind them with its glare.

Tristan und Isolde is not about theatre but reality. A year before his death, Wagner explained that nature itself constantly seeks out love, for only in love can it find redemption and 'produce something great and redemptive'. For that reason his love drama struck him as 'the greatest of tragedies' because here nature is 'thwarted in its highest task', which is to redeem itself in man. *Tristan und Isolde*, then, is not a medieval romance with a tragic outcome but a work about the very essence of what it is to be a human being, a state that is threatened with failure. Although Wagner wrote it for the stage, he soon began to wonder whether it was 'absurd to give such a work for money'.[61]

Was the work understood at all? Wagner doubted it. It was possible to enjoy it, possible to be stirred by it and to feel sympathy with the unhappy lovers and still fail to understand what the piece was about. With *Tristan und Isolde*, nature had 'produced something great and redemptive', using Wagner as its agent. Through Wagner, it had raised itself to a new level of consciousness. As representatives of the whole of humanity, the lovers experience the impossibility of love and, in a remarkable reversal of priorities, the birth of love from that very impossibility. And not only do they experience it, they also think it through to its ultimate conclusion, putting into words something that had never previously been imagined.

In this way, the second act, which superficially looks like a garrulous love duet, became a *locus classicus* of German idealistic philosophy. In the frenzy that draws them into its sway, the lovers exchange not endearments but perceptive definitions of the dialectical relationships between day and night, joy and sorrow, loving and dying and even the 'death and immortality' that provides the title of Ludwig Feuerbach's mystical essay, a work that left its mark on Wagner's empirical philosophy of the night of love. Tristan and Isolde studied not with Schopenhauer, who despised love, but with Feuerbach, whom his predecessor contemptuously dismissed as a 'Hegelian (c'est tout dire)'. And they completed their course with distinction.

The couple's musings, in which Martin Gregor-Dellin found only 'sophisms',[62] reflect Feuerbach's thinking in a series of antitheses. 'As you love,' he wrote in his Hegelian German in 1830, 'you acknowledge and proclaim the nothingness of your mere being-for-self, of your self. You acknowledge as your true I, as your essence and life, not yourself, but the object of your love.' Death, therefore, was 'the manifestation of love', inasmuch as it leads to union with the 'beloved object', showing that 'you can exist only with and in that object'. For 'how would you be everything, how would you be love, if you were only the unity in that which is one and not also the distinction in that which is distinguished?'

As if suspecting that such thoughts are ill suited to the arid language of the lecture hall, Feuerbach appended to his essay a poem whose dithyrambic élan anticipates the dialogue in Marke's garden. The sentiments that Tristan and Isolde whisper to one another, lips pressed to lips, reflect Feuerbach's mystical approach to death, even to the extent of sharing the same linguistic formulas. 'The ground is nothingness, the nothingness is night,' he rhapsodizes in a passage that looks forward to *Tristan und Isolde*, 'this is why we burn in such fiery splendour. The darkness of nothing, the darkness of the ground, perfectly sets off colours. The power of thought and life does not expand its influence without limit all the way to the dark chamber of death, there weakly to flicker itself out, but compresses itself in you, this is why it can burn so intensely here. . . . Only in the life-force, only in the drive to death is love pressed into motion; only at the highest pinnacle of life does love's lightning strike.'

The second act of *Tristan und Isolde* consists of a single series of love's lightning strikes flaring up against a doom-laden sky that is black with storm clouds. The idea that this is a nocturnal debate about abstract trifles was refuted by Wagner himself through his music, the overwhelming drama of which, based on the principle of statement and contradiction, proves precisely the opposite: what seems to be sophistry and hair-splitting contains the principles of the birth of creation that assume such concrete form in the music that they become visible to the ear's inner eye. When Nietzsche later described *Tristan und Isolde* as the 'true opus metaphysicum of all art', this is precisely what Wagner intended.

And it is the false world that forms the threatening backdrop to the dialogue between the lovers, a dialogue that seemed to have left the world behind it once and for all. In the eyes of the world, Tristan was his king's leading vassal, while Queen Isolde was the king's leading servant. Their union was not part of the plan of the legalistic world, any violation of whose laws was regarded as a crime worthy of death. The entire night of love, in the course of which the first act of creation was to be repeated, is merely a visible enactment of this, Tristan's zealous friend Melot attempting to indict the lovers for this very offence – namely, the unity to which they lay claim. While feeling that they are imbued with the very beginning of all existence, the lovers violate the existing law.

Meanwhile they have secretly constructed a world of their own that is connected to the old one by nothing more than the fact that it remains dependent upon it. The new kingdom of 'I' and 'you' has not triumphed over the world of day but sought refuge in the seclusion of night. Only Marke's absence has made it possible for them to see one another again. Only when Isolde douses the burning torch outside the door can Tristan approach. Luckily for the lovers, a hunting party has set out by night into the forest, and Isolde is waiting impatiently for the moment when the sound of the hunting horns dies away in the distance, giving the lovers the signal on which they have agreed.

No longer able to bear the intensity of her longing, Isolde the philosopher overlooks the most obvious point. As her servant can see all too clearly, she is about to walk into a trap: the hunt is for a 'more noble head of game' than she thinks. But Isolde's thoughts are on higher things. It is 'Frau Minne', the goddess of love herself, who exercises her omnipotent sway here. What is the point of resisting? She is the 'ruler of the world's becoming', and so 'life and death' are both subject to her. 'Joy and sorrow' lie in her power. 'I became her vassal: now let me show her obedience!' Love reigns supreme, and so it cannot be wrong to heed her urgent command.

It is not wrong, but it results in death. This too seems to worry Isolde but little. After all, death is part of Love's realm in Feuerbach's dialectics. In order to persuade her servant that the torch must be doused forthwith, she offers a brief account of her philosophy of day and night. Just as the bright light of day has become inimical to their love, so night has proved their sole refuge. But within its depths, in the ground of the soul, a light has arisen that shines on them alone. 'She who laughs as the day of the soul', Isolde explains darkly, 'the goddess of love demands that night descends and that she may shine forth brightly where she drove your light into hiding.'

The *Ring* had begun with a simple opposition between light and darkness, but this has now developed into a new and more complex pair of opposites. When the world fell away from love, the sun of the beginning lost its divinity and turned into the cold light that casts its harsh beams on the world of law. The light of love, meanwhile, has been driven from the world and has withdrawn into people's hearts, in whose darkness the outlines of a new creation are dimly discernible. In the love that 'fans the flames in my breast', the divine sun rises once again – the sun that has disappeared from humankind. Compared with its pure light, it is the blackest night that now reigns on earth by day.

When the light of the torch that embodies the glare of false day is at last extinguished, the night of love can begin, a night during which Shaw got his money's worth but only at the price of misunderstanding. The love that enters the world on the first day of creation has withdrawn into the night of love. That which was concealed from the light of day is revealed only to the 'night-seeing eye' of the lovers, perhaps also to the eye of the inner ear.

What follows is the mutual recognition and merger of 'I' and 'you', 'mine' and 'yours' that are now united 'for ever and ever'. Wagner spoke of the 'outpouring of long repressed emotion',[63] an outpouring that, as he told Cosima, had first struck him when he saw Schröder-Devrient's Romeo. The 'beautiful frenzy of caresses' was best depicted by siblings, 'specially trained for it by their father'.[64] Tristan and Isolde, then, are the hapless brother and sister destroyed by the paternalistic world of the law. But now, for the first time, Wagner had discovered a unique world that no one could take away from them, the 'wondrous realm of night' to which death alone opens its door.

Objectively, too, this door stands wide open tonight. 'Oh sink upon us, night of love', the two apostrophize their alternative world, at the same time celebrating their ability to forget reality and start a new life. Once the horrors of day have finally left them behind, the true sun rises within them and the hostile day is replaced by the world that is the lovers themselves. 'If I no longer see the world', Tristan assures his lover in the prose draft, 'then I myself am the world.' According to the German idealists, finite existence ends at the moment that consciousness posits itself. As with Siegfried and Brünnhilde, so with Tristan and Isolde all that remains is 'love's holiest life'.

This has nothing in common with Schopenhauer's metaphysics of sexual love: 'Frau Minne', the goddess of sexual love, differs from Schopenhauer's 'genius of the species' on one essential point – namely, it is not the impersonal will of the species that is manifest in the lovers, driving them on to anonymous procreation, but the individual self-consciousness that recognizes itself in another non-interchangeable individual. The love of Tristan and Isolde is personal. Everything else – no matter how cunningly it disguises itself – stems from mere lust.

'But our love', Isolde asks, 'is it not called Tristan *and* Isolde?' Thanks to this 'sweet little word "and"' they become the person who comes into existence 'when the "I" is subsumed by the "you"'. Even if one of them were to die, Tristan explains, the only thing that would perish would be that which stands in the way of their boundless love, 'that which prevents Tristan from loving Isolde for ever and from living for her for ever'. But if he were to become one with her as a result of his death, she retorts perceptively, she too would be unable to remain alive any longer but must merge with him completely. 'With Isolde's own life' death would be granted to Tristan. And so they would both have to die. This step has already been taken in their hearts long before the physical death that awaits them has sealed it. 'And so we died', they sing together, 'in order that undivided, eternally one, without end, without awakening, without fear, namelessly enfolded in love, we might be given entirely to ourselves and live for love alone.'

As the prose draft succinctly puts it, there follows a moment of 'heightened ecstasy', then 'the most ardent embrace', and then a brief cry prompted by the all too predictable disaster. Against the wan morning sky, the figures of Marke and the treacherous Melot rise up like ghosts. The world of day has reported back for duty. Death, longingly entreated, reveals its cruellest mask. First it exposes Tristan, who does what he can to cover his lover with his cloak, then it cuts him to the quick with the pangs of conscience triggered by Marke's heart-rending lament, before finally transfixing him with the traitor's sword, on which he throws himself in his transcendent urge to die.

What has remained? No comfort, no excuses for Marke, only Tristan's question to Isolde as to whether she will follow him to the land where the sun of day never shines. Only now does he admit that he has been there before, for this is where he came from. 'It is the dark nocturnal land from which my mother once sent me forth,' he explains, oblivious to the world, 'when she conceived me in death and in death brought me into the light. That which was love's refuge for her when she bore me – the wondrous realm of night from which I once awoke – that is what Tristan now offers you: there he goes before you. Isolde must now tell him whether she will follow him loyally and lovingly.'

She promises to do so. She wants to follow him loyally to the place where their love will be secure for ever, wants to repair for ever to Tristan's house and home. She gives him her tearful word. And yet she does not keep it.

The woman's act of betrayal is one of the archetypal situations that keep on repeating themselves in Wagner's life and works. Just as Sieglinde recoils from loving Siegmund and just as Brünnhilde attacks Siegfried from behind, so Mathilde Wesendonck left her lover in the lurch. This, at least, is what Wagner himself felt, attributing her betrayal to her husband's filthy lucre.[65] The initial act of betrayal on the part of Wagner's mother that made it possible for his inheritance to be usurped became a bitter adjunct of every act of love that he experienced in later life. Yet this process was never as clearly identifiable in all its fathomless incomprehensibility as in Isolde's attitude to Tristan. So clear is it, indeed, that no one seems to have noticed it.

The fact that Isolde, following their common love-death, slips back into her role as queen and presumably also into Marke's marriage bed may have been all well and good when judged by the rules of the world of day. Scholars have not dwelt on this point, and audiences, too, have realized that a queen, after all, has her duties. That the rules of the world of day have been invalidated by the queen herself seems to have been forgotten, as does the indivisible unity between the lovers. And so Tristan atones for the breach of a marriage that Isolde continues to maintain as though nothing whatsoever has happened. While her lover lies mortally wounded, she keeps her distance, for all that she is well versed in the art of healing.

It is neither the wound dealt by Tristan's treacherous friend nor the pangs of conscience inflicted by his betrayed king that precipitate his third-act agony, but Isolde's act of betrayal. She has left her blood-soaked lover in the lurch. It was his servant who brought him home to his run-down ancestral castle, while she herself is nowhere to be seen. Just as the first awakening of their love was betrayed by Tristan's bridal quest, so Isolde declares its second awakening an irrelevance. And so the eye no longer finds the mirror in which it may recognize itself, and the dark ground of nature, rising up to greet the loving light, falls away again in insatiable longing. And now Schopenhauer's will has its way, consuming itself in perpetual desire for itself and helplessly falling victim to its own delusions of happiness.

Tristan finds himself back in the vicious circle of desire. Just as his wound prevents him from assuaging his longing, so his longing will not allow him to die of his wound. 'No salvation,' he laments, 'no sweet death can ever free me from longing's plight.' Even the prelude, with its dragging strains of grief rising up from the night like the weary sighs of the damned, recalls the question about longing first heard at the start of the work. On that occasion 'the most timid confession of the tenderest affection' had received a mysterious answer that rose up to meet it from the ground. It had been the voice of longing. Only now, on a bed of living death, does Tristan understand its words: 'To yearn while dying, but not to die from yearning.'

Tristan is not alone in his ruined ancestral castle, for he is invisibly surrounded by all the heroes who have ever fallen prey to hopeless despair in Wagner's works, from the lion-hearted Leubald to the itinerant Dutchman, from Tannhäuser and Lohengrin to the unknown Elis and the far-famed Wälsungs. Yet none has suffered as he does: 'You feel compassion when I suffer,' he tells his servant and hence the audience, 'but what I suffer – that you cannot suffer!'

Only he who has known the secret of the unity of 'I' and 'you' can understand what it means to be wrenched apart. Siegfried is the only character to realize this in the throes of death. But when Tristan hears the Shepherd's sad piping and recalls how 'as a child' he learnt of 'his father's death' and 'his mother's fate' and how 'the former fathered me and died, while she, dying, gave me birth', he reveals himself as Siegfried's brother, perhaps even as himself.

The exchanges about love on the part of the living are followed in the final act by the 'great symphony of pain with singing'[66] that is the dying Tristan's monologue. However much he may have desired it, death shuns him now that his vital spark proves stronger than death. His vital strength torments him as an expression of the will for which there is no release save in love. But following Isolde's betrayal its sovereign self-consciousness sinks back to the level of an idea, promising fulfilment without ever being able to offer it in practice. The celestial light of 'Frau Minne' has vanished from night's wondrous realm. As it sinks into the horrors of non-being, surviving only in the spark of yearning, so the glaring sun of day reasserts its ancient rule.

Driven by his longing from the night of non-being, Tristan is helplessly exposed to this merciless light of day. 'Night casts me over to day,' he grieves, 'so the sun's eye may feast for ever on my sufferings.' The loving sun of the world's origins has been transformed into the 'scorching ray' of endless annihilation. It was Tristan himself, the hero notes perceptively, who fuelled this murderous sun from 'father's need and mother's grief, from love's tears then and aye'. It was his own sun whose fiery furnace consumed him. As Wagner once ironically remarked, Tristan is 'like a fish left out to dry in the sun'.[67]

With Tristan's realization that the heaven of communality is closed to him and that only his self-made hell remains open, Wagner felt that he had reached the 'apex of the pyramid to which the tragic thrust of this *Tristan* towers up'.[68] And not only *Tristan*. Never again was Wagner to expose himself and his heroes to such suffering, but neither was it necessary for him to do so, as they were now all prepared for it philosophically and creatively. *Tristan*'s pyramid of suffering had been built up over the preceding works, achieving its penultimate peak in Siegfried's death, but from now on the drama of life grew calmer and the tension sank back to a rather more tolerable level.

Even in *Tristan und Isolde*, hellish torment does not have the final word. Like Senta, whose somnambulistic powers of imagination conjure up the Dutchman whom she loves, Tristan seems able to summon the distant Isolde by means of a hallucinatory vision fuelled by his longing. Although his servant has sent a messenger requesting medical assistance, something that had apparently not occurred to Isolde herself, her arrival follows too soon after Tristan's vision of her to be dismissed as mere chance. Love still works its wonders, then.

The Shepherd plays a 'merry tune' that seems a direct echo of the sense of jubilation inspired by Siegfried's love. And Kurwenal expresses his joy in a series of natural sounds. Yet in the midst of this mounting happiness, the hero finally enters his death throes. Paradoxically, death alone – the total abandonment of the self's existence – is the appropriate response to love. With the woman of his desires before his eyes, Tristan now seeks a swift quietus. To the strains of a joyfully desperate waltz, he tears the dressing from his wound and, his life's blood ebbing away, rushes to meet his beloved 'in jubilant haste', laughing, dying and reeling blindly across the stage.

Wagner admitted to repeatedly 'bursting into floods of tears while working on the score'.[69] He knew very well that in the third act he was staging something of unbearable intensity, something that would 'drive people mad': 'I can't imagine it otherwise.' And as he confessed to Mathilde Wesendonck, he was afraid that if the work was properly understood, 'it ought by rights to be banned'.[70] His fears proved unjustified.

As with Siegfried at the moment of his death, so with Tristan there follows one final recognition and a new beginning. Death has already enfolded him in her sable wings when he hears his name on Isolde's lips, and the world that seemed to have been lost is opened up to him again. He sees with his ear's inner eye, hears the light, and as the beacon of his life is snuffed out, the sun of love rises over him once again.

And it is Isolde who is the sun. Nor is it long before the forgotten secret is revealed to her, too. During their night of love she had become one with Tristan, and the world of day that had forced her to commit her act of betrayal deservedly becomes a matter of total insignificance once again. Only Tristan and Isolde still exist, and just as he breathes in her breath and sees with her eye, she too sees only his smile and the radiance of her lover who is reborn within her.

Just as he had heard her light, so she is aware of the infinite melody that he has begun to sing to her, never to end. And thus she sinks back into the beginning of all things that Wagner had first described in *Das Rheingold*. Beneath her lies the surging ocean, billowing towards her, longingly, in waves of sound, in perfumed breakers, and in the wafting fragrance of their commingled breaths. She leaps and sinks down. The world is born once again from love, while the mysteriously opaque words of the ground with which the tragedy had begun are resolved in the work's final harmonies.

There is no trace here of Schopenhauer's famous 'nothing'. Instead an act of resurrection takes place before the eyes of an audience which, moved by what it sees, follows events disbelievingly. Death has at last been overcome. The lust for life has not been extinguished but restored to the love from which it had been divorced. Wagner himself insisted that the lovers had found 'the most blissful fulfilment of ardent yearning'. It was 'that wondrous realm from which we wander furthest away whenever we strive to enter it with all the tempest's fury'. It is the realm, in short, of love, a world that opens up not to desire but to reciprocal love alone.

'Are we to call it death?' asks Wagner, Schopenhauer at the back of his mind. 'Or is it, rather, that wondrous world of night from which, so the legend tells us, tendrils of ivy and vine grew up, in intimate entwinement, over Tristan and Isolde's grave?'[71] Wagner's wondrous realm, triumphing over death and the torments of oblivion, is nothing more nor less than nature as summoned into existence and into the light of day by the love of the first God. This God, in turn, is creative love itself.

It is not ultimate oblivion, of which Schopenhauer dreamt, that puts an end to the age-old torment, but divine nature growing up ever new from the ground as though from its own grave.

The pinnacle of self-consciousness achieved by Brünnhilde at the end of *Götterdämmerung* is now embodied by Isolde, who, abruptly waking from oblivion, sacrifices her life to her lover and hence to love itself. Something that Wagner was never to know in the reality of the Wesendoncks' villa soon appeared before his gaze, and as fate would have it, it was the Wesendoncks, now reconciled to him, who were responsible.

In order to 'cheer up' the exhausted composer, they invited him to Venice in 1861, and here, within the framework of a sightseeing programme more befitting a party of tourists, they took him off to the Gallerie dell'Accademia. 'Armed with an enormous pair of opera glasses,' the bearded Otto and his artistic spouse 'indulged their enjoyment of the paintings', while their guest had difficulty concealing his 'lack of interest'.

But suddenly his attention was caught by a particular painting by Titian. It was an *Assunta*, the Assumption of the Virgin, the very subject with which Ludwig Geyer had won acclaim at the 1816 Dresden art exhibition, although Geyer's *Assumption* had been skilfully copied from the Baroque artist Luca Giordano. This image now turned up once again, a reminder of Wagner's distant past, depicting the Mother of God soaring heavenwards and accompanied by a group of winged children. At her feet are astonished disciples, while above her radiant head God the Father gives his blessing. But it is she herself, the Mother, who is the picture's focus of attention, drawing to her the gaze not only of all the other figures in the painting but of its observers, too.

Brought about by his lost lover, Wagner's encounter with this icon of the Madonna produced an unexpected response. In the features of the Virgin he recognized those of the woman standing beside him. She was pregnant once again. The year before his death, when he felt drawn back to see Titian's painting, he insisted in Cosima's presence that it represented not 'the Mother of God' but 'Isolde in the transfiguration of love'.[72]

Wagner's God-fearing wife evidently did not share this view. In April 1882 he explained to her that the sublime Assunta in her radiant colours and otherworldly transfiguration represented the only potent force in nature, the 'sex drive'. The 'glowing head of the Virgin Mary' revealed that, 'as the will enraptured and redeemed from all blind desire', she desired one thing alone, to give birth to the Saviour.[73]

It was not insipid saintliness that caused Titian's beauty to soar aloft but the joys of world-renewing sexuality. In her ardent expression, Wagner explained to Cosima on another occasion, 'the pain of a woman in childbirth is mixed with the ecstasy of love',[74] as is also clearly the case with Isolde, who speaks of 'love's highest joy' only at the moment of her death.

Wagner was inhibited by no false piety, and so he was able to see his lover in the saint, just as he had seen every lover since Rosalie as a saint. As a result the figures surrounding the Virgin were bound to strike him as deeply suspect. He was particularly worried by the disciples and by the dear Lord who gazes expectantly towards her like Marke gazing towards his heavenly bride Isolde. Inasmuch as Titian had captured her at her most intimate moment, Wagner found 'the closeness of the apostles and disciples and all these false relationships very disturbing'.[75] Even worse was the image of God in his firmament. In October 1880 Wagner returned on his own to look at his favourite painting and on his return home told Cosima of his serious 'reservations' about it 'since he is so disturbed by God the Father in it'.[76] Two years later he fleshed out these misgivings, claiming that the dear Lord resembled a 'bat'.[77]

This surprising encounter in Venice, in which the archetype of the immortal beloved appeared alongside the lover he had just lost, roused his creative powers. 'Titian's *Assumption*', he wrote in his autobiography, had 'an effect of the sublimest kind' on him, so that 'thanks to this conception I found my old creative powers reawakening within me with elemental suddenness. I decided to write *The Mastersingers*'.[78]

The decision had in fact already been taken, as Wagner had written to his publisher a week earlier, whetting Schott's appetite for a subject 'full of rapt amiability' and preemptively praising its 'clear, transparently earthy music of the most cheerful hue'.[79] But something else had been awakened in Wagner by this Venetian 'conception', which had been preceded by the real-life conception of his former lover. He saw a lover before him who did not have to pay for her ardently lovesick desire with a love-death. Her transfiguration was to take place not in heaven but in childbirth.

Her sisters Senta, Elsa and Elisabeth had died childless, but following their transformation into the consciously heroic Brünnhilde and Isolde, there now emerged a simple, natural soul. As the mother of the new human race, she was to be called Eva.

Interior Design

Wagner was always conscious of the historical dimension of his life. All that happened was immediately worked into that life, just as the latter became part of the history of the age in which he lived. And in parallel to it, he worked from the outset on an account of his life in which corrections were made to all that was incomprehensible and unwelcome. His autobiography served as a regulatory authority, accepting only what seemed suitable for posterity. All that was unsuitable was destroyed by the censor.

In spite of this, not everything in the countless volumes that have gone down in history as his 'life' is actually Wagner. No matter what he did and however much he interfered and exerted a decisive influence whenever he could, he was generally the victim of circumstances: forces vented themselves on him and compelled him to obey them, however embittered his resistance. As he was no doubt aware, his insolvency made this inevitable.

'A life like mine', he mused in a letter to his Muse Mathilde, 'is bound to deceive the observer who sees me engaged in actions and undertakings that he takes to be mine but that are basically entirely alien to me.' No one noticed the 'revulsion' that 'inspired' him in all this. 'But', he added prophetically, 'the day of enlightenment will come. . . . And the world will see certain things that it has never dreamt of.'[80]

In the matter of Wagner's means of subsistence, Mathilde's husband had for years being supporting his unfortunate rival and doing so, moreover, at his wife's insistence. Wesendonck's money had been acquired through the silk trade and so it seemed somehow appropriate that Wagner should spend it by preference on silk, which he used for his wardrobe and for furnishing his rooms. When in the autumn of 1859, Wagner finally left Switzerland after his ten-year exile in the country, his 'friend Otto' was persuaded to make a particularly generous gesture. In an attempt to ensure that the composer could genuinely go his own way, he bought the exclusive publication rights to three parts of the *Ring* for six thousand francs each, no doubt well aware that while Wagner was happy to take the money, he would continue to dispose of the rights to the cycle as and when he liked.

With his pockets well lined, Wagner set off back to Paris and in a side street just off the Champs Élysées rented a pavilion-like house with a small garden for four thousand francs a year. Having paid three years' rent in advance, he sent for the rest of his furniture from Zurich and engaged an interior designer.[81] On the strength of Wagner's own sketches, the salon was transformed into a rose-tinted dream in the style of *la dame aux camélias*.

The walls were covered in red silk, with appliqué silk roses along the frieze. The ceiling was hidden by ruched silk, which was divided into four triangles by garlands of roses, their intersection adorned by a lavish bouquet of the same flowers. The impression of entering the boudoir of a woman of dubious taste was compounded by the strong scent of roses rising up from small concealed bowls.

But the centrepiece of the room was hidden from inquisitive eyes by damask curtains. Lit by the faint glow of a lantern, the alcove walls were covered in ruched silk into which mirrors had been let. Garlands of roses wound their way up the sides of the alcove and also framed the large mirror in the ceiling, in which observers could admire themselves, full-length: for beneath it lay a double bed decorated with rose ribbons, covered in the finest silk and filled with duck down. Beside it stood a comfortable causeuse upholstered in costly brocade and likewise filled with duck down.

Within the operetta-like ambience of this secret mirrored alcove, Wagner received his visitors, an exotic creature entertaining the most eccentric representatives of Paris's intellectual life. His callers included not only his admirer Charles Baudelaire but also the illustrator Gustave Doré, the composers Charles Gounod and Camille Saint-Saëns, the journalist and lawyer Émile Ollivier and, finally, the latter's charming wife Blandine, who seems to have enjoyed the privilege of becoming better acquainted with the alcove at the rear of the room.

Minna, at all events, complained about the 'frequent visits' of Cosima's elder sister, visits from which she herself was excluded. On one point, things had changed since Wagner's days at the Asyl: he now received his lady friend on the ground floor, while his wife had to suffer and prepare morsels of food on the first floor. 'I'm no more than a housekeeper,' she grumbled, 'I've only three servants at my beck and call to complain about, although I do have access to the salon in order to show my silk dress off to people.'[82] It was to act as his housekeeper that Wagner had invited her to Paris, having previously asked her doctor, Anton Pusinelli, to advise her against sexual intercourse with her husband on the grounds of her delicate health. Wagner no longer felt any inclination to indulge in intimacies with her.

Apart from the witty dandies who basked in his reflected glory, there were also visitors of a more useful kind. Society ladies of all ages milled around the composer, who generously regaled them with excerpts from his works and whom they repaid by making available the means they had at their disposal. Above all, it was money that interested Wagner – not fun. Although he did not exactly pass the hat round at these receptions, he made no secret of the financial predicament in which he yet again found himself.

He left a particularly deep impression on Julie Schwabe, the widow of a Jewish businessman, whom Wagner described as a 'fairly grotesque woman' who regularly attended his soirées and equally regularly fell asleep. In spite of this, she opened her purse and gave him three thousand francs which, as Wagner drily commented, 'were extremely useful' to him at that moment.[83] By the time the bill of exchange was presented to him by a court bailiff five years later, Wagner was enjoying the patronage of a more prestigious benefactor.

Wagner's visitors included not only Liszt's elder daughter but also his former mistress Agnes Street-Klindworth and his friend Marie Kalergis, who was later to become Countess Muchanoff and who gave Wagner ten thousand francs to cover the deficit on his Paris concerts. Another caller was the Princess Pauline Metternich, a woman as famous for her connections as for her hideous appearance and whose influence as wife of the Austrian ambassador meant that *Tannhäuser* was finally staged in Paris by imperial command.

In a feverish dream that Wagner had in November 1860 and that he considered remarkable enough to record in his autobiography, his two female benefactors appeared to him in order to gratify his most secret desires: he remembered exactly how 'Princess Metternich and Madame Kalergis set up a complete court for me, to which I also invited the Emperor Napoleon'.[84]

Among his guests at his Wednesday receptions, when 'visitors really saw and heard only him and forgot all the others', one notable absentee was his old friend Hector Berlioz. Having once championed Wagner's artistic ideals, the French composer had become one of his most vehement critics, publicly mocking the prelude to *Tristan und Isolde* and claiming that it consisted only of 'a sort of chromatic moan', with 'dissonances whose cruelty is further accentuated by long appoggiaturas which completely replace the true harmony-note'. In short, 'If this is the new religion, I am a very long way from becoming a convert; I never have been, am not and never will be one.'[85]

Wagner thought he knew who had persuaded his former comrade-in-arms to 'stab him in the back' like this.[86] It was none other than Meyerbeer who had made it his business to poison the sweet wine of success for Wagner. From Liszt's secretary he learnt that 'Madame Berlioz has just received a valuable bracelet from Meyerbeer', a memento that persuaded Marie Recio to have a word in her husband's ear and that was apparently by no means Meyerbeer's only reaction to Wagner's 'Parisian plans'. According to *My Life*, it was thanks to 'the most monstrous bribes' that Meyerbeer turned the whole of the Paris press against him, generating 'an extraordinarily hostile atmosphere'.

If Wagner's three Paris concerts proved a poor investment, the production of *Tannhäuser* turned out to be a veritable fiasco. His failure in Paris had passed unnoticed on his first visit to the city but twenty years later it was repeated on the front pages of the gutter press. For the first time in his career, the doors of the Grand Opéra were opened to him, albeit with a work that he had long since outgrown. Yet the money put up by the state flowed not into his own coffers, where it was most urgently needed, but into those of the singers, dancers and designers. In return he shouldered the entire burden of care and ultimately suffered only shame and humiliation.

The project dragged on for six months, requiring no fewer than 164 rehearsals. Wagner moved to a more modest apartment and rewrote the opening scene of the opera in the style of *Tristan und Isolde* but refused to comply with the request of the administration that he should introduce into the second act a ballet that would represent value for money to the admirers of women's bare legs. Instead, he devised a Bacchanal that left nothing to be desired even by Parisian standards. Unfortunately, the admirers of women's bare legs preferred to dine before joining the performance for the second act, and so the orgy was over by the time they arrived at the theatre.

The performances sealed Wagner's downfall. Not until 1870 was he offered a chance for revenge, which he seized by advising Bismarck to raze the hated city to the ground.[87] The performances of March 1861 taught him that it is possible to destroy a work of art just as surely as it is possible to destroy a human being, and not only in terms of bad reviews but in real life, too. *Tannhäuser* was greeted with catcalls and boos and ultimately laughed off stage, an élitist gentlemen's club having made a point of disrupting the performances by means of witty interruptions, commenting loudly on the action and creating a racket with their hunting whistles that triggered an embittered and no less disruptive counter-demonstration by Wagner's supporters. Following the chaotic third performance Wagner withdrew the score, leaving the scene of his humiliation a month later, richer by seven hundred and fifty francs and bent on staging *Tristan und Isolde* in either Karlsruhe or Vienna.

Wagner was in no doubt as to who was responsible for *Tannhäuser*'s downfall: it was his old adversary who had bribed journalists into destroying his younger rival. For Meyerbeer, wrote Glasenapp, it had been a question of 'whether the iron grip that he maintained over the Paris stage was to remain in his hands in future or not'. Egged on by the press, a part of the audience had proceeded to vent its spleen on Wagner – the part that the composer's ardent admirer Hans von Bülow identified as 'the German [i.e., Jewish] rabble in Paris'. Indeed, Glasenapp was convinced that Meyerbeer was concerned not only to destroy Wagner but to usurp his whole position: 'By 1 April the costumes created for *Tannhäuser* were already being used at a performance of *Robert le diable*.'[88]

Pauline Metternich, who had suffered her fair share of the 'mortifying contempt' heaped on Wagner, had an alternative explanation: it was Wagner himself, she argued, who turned the Parisians against him and who at the rehearsals 'worried the musicians to death. He was simply insufferable; and if the command to perform "Tannhäuser" had not been issued directly by the Emperor, the whole thing might well have fallen through. Musicians, singers, members of the chorus, scene-shifters, even those in charge of the lighting, I believe, were nearly driven mad, and often refused to comply with the great man's whims and crotchets.' The true reasons for the débâcle presumably lay elsewhere. The dog had been kicked, but the master had been intended. Wagner was booed off stage as Pauline Metternich's protégé in a demonstration directed at Napoleon III's pro-Austrian policies.

Disaster continued to stalk Wagner. Since 1857 Eduard Devrient had encouraged him to believe that *Tristan und Isolde* would be performed at the Court Theatre in Karlsruhe, of which Devrient was now director. The grand duchess herself demanded a production, and in Ludwig Schnorr von Carolsfeld Wagner now had a suitable heroic tenor. Grand Duke Friedrich of Baden even asked the king of Saxony for a safe-conduct for the composer, but his request was unceremoniously turned down.

In the event, it was thanks to Marie Kalergis's connections that Wagner was able to obtain a partial amnesty, in the wake of which he arrived in Karlsruhe in April 1861. Here he was received by Eduard Devrient, who has left an account of the composer's positively oriental rig-out – 'a green velvet dressing gown, lined in purple satin, with Turkish trousers of the same material and a broad brown velvet beret perched askew on his head'.[89] In spite of the grand duke's patronage, there were new difficulties to deal with: Schnorr and his soprano wife Malwina had decamped to Dresden, and Devrient, whom Wagner now felt he had seen through as a false 'friend', advised him to look for suitable singers in Vienna.

In Vienna Wagner found not only suitable singers but also a suitable theatre. He also heard his own *Lohengrin* for the first time at the Court Opera and thought the voices 'surprisingly agreeable'. But although he was 'profoundly moved' by this encounter, he managed during the interval to offend the city's leading critic, Eduard Hanslick, who was also a member of the opera house's advisory board. Hanslick had been his ally since their meeting in Marienbad and now sought to renew their acquaintance, only to be brusquely brushed aside. Wagner had already seen through him as his 'most vicious enemy', and so Hanslick duly assumed that role in his life.

Plans to stage *Tristan* in Karlsruhe had foundered, not least on Devrient's opposition, and so Wagner placed all his hopes in a Viennese production, having first made himself its secret adversary. The preparations dragged on from August 1861 to the spring of 1864, repeatedly interrupted by outbreaks of illness amongst the protagonists, before finally being broken off for good. The whole enterprise seemed to be in thrall to a 'demonic fate'.[90] Wagner believed that it was Hanslick who was pulling the strings. He also thought Hanslick was Jewish.

Wagner sought to escape from these blows of fate by resuming his quest for intimacy, and even one of his standard biographers notes with some surprise that he 'spent the next two years of his life mainly indulging in a number of passing "love affairs"'.[91] By now his relations with Mathilde Wesendonck existed only in his mind, while those with Minna existed only on paper, and so he opened up lines of attack on all fronts. The roll call of beauties from these years includes representatives of every social class, all of whom rendered him service either briefly or over a longer period of time. If we include those women who may well have eluded his chroniclers' enthusiastic tally, Wagner resembles a Dutchman famously coming in to land every seven days. 'My curious situation', he admitted at this time, 'can be summed up in the idea of a restless quest for peace and quiet.'[92]

Even if we except those women who presumably granted their favours only in the form of notes of the realm, there were still enough interested parties eager to see his mirrored cabinet from the inside. Even interested members of the male sex seem to have put themselves forward: in 1863 Wagner claims to have found a note hidden among his linen headed 'Dear Sir, I love you!' Wagner thought that its author was the 'young husband of my friend Madame Kalergis-Muchanoff'.[93]

The writer who has delved most deeply into Wagner's love life, Julius Kapp, included not only Blandine Ollivier among the suspects but also Blandine's mother, the Comtesse d'Agoult. A more open relationship, on the other hand, developed between Wagner and his almost certainly underage housekeeper in Vienna, Seraphine Mauro, who was the niece of Wagner's host Josef Standhartner and who had been asked by her uncle – the personal physician to the empress – to keep an eye on his guest. She is said to have impressed the composer with her 'Italian blood' and 'well-developed bust'. Wagner took her as his lover and from then on referred to her as 'the doll'. 'In such matters,' he later admitted to his admirer Peter Cornelius, who was likewise in love with her, 'my sense of morality is incurably naïve.'[94]

From Seraphine's Venus-like embrace, Wagner felt drawn, like Tannhäuser, to an Elisabeth by the name of Mathilde Maier, a notary's daughter from Alzey.

Blue-eyed and blonde, she was accounted a 'German beauty', even if Martin Gregor-Dellin's euphemistic encomium that 'she knew how to listen' is somewhat wide of the mark: Mathilde Maier was hard of hearing. Wagner himself praised her 'beautiful silences'. Was there anything more to it? He also called her 'dearest' and 'sweetheart' and wrote to tell her that his 'delightful need' was 'already swelling and becoming too great'. In 1864, at a time when Cosima was preparing to enter Wagner's life, he invited Mathilde to live with him on a respectable basis. A photograph shows the abandoned Mathilde as Eva in *Die Meistersinger*, and this is no doubt how Wagner, too, regarded her.

In Biebrich am Main, where Wagner was working on his new opera, Mathilde/Eva encountered a dangerous rival in the form of a representative of the school of Aphrodite. Friederike Meyer was one of those women who first inspired Wagner as an actress on stage. He wrote effusively to her and she visited him at Biebrich, which he dubbed his 'Beaver's Nest' and where Mathilde's rose bushes were still in full bloom. They soon discovered common interests, and there followed what Julius Kapp describes as a 'relationship devoted to life's pleasures'. Unfortunately, the unruly Friederike was already in a relationship with the director of the Frankfurt Opera, who suddenly turned up one day when the actress was feeling unwell and took her home, where two illegitimate children were awaiting their mother's return. Barely recovered, she returned to Wagner in Biebrich, where, to quote Peter Cornelius, the locals were much exercised by 'the couple's spasmodic affair'.

In Wagner's luxurious household, silk was the order of the day, just as it had been in Paris. Here he smoked an oriental hookah and drank nothing but champagne. Visitors included not only the Misses Maier and Meyer but also Minna and, accompanied by her husband, Liszt's younger daughter Cosima. Even Frau Wesendonck sent a number of mementos at Christmas, precipitating the old 'storm of madness' in Minna. In Vienna, where Friederike's sister Luise Meyer-Dustmann was due to sing the part of Isolde, the couple's arrival triggered a veritable scandal, with the soprano sententiously declaring that Wagner had 'exploited her sister twice over',[95] possibly a reference to the fact that he had also touched her for his travelling expenses. From now on Luise did all she could to undermine *Tristan und Isolde*, a project that was in any case close to collapse.

By way of consolation, Wagner was pleased to accept a gift of one thousand florins from the Empress Sisi, a gift suggested by the ever-present Marie Kalergis. When he was in Prague, he renewed acquaintance with his adolescent love from Leipzig, Marie Löw, transferring his feelings of 'infatuation' from Marie to her fifteen-year-old daughter Lilli, whom he received in a yellow damask dressing gown beneath a black sleeveless cloak lined with pink satin. 'I only remember that Wagner embraced me stormily', she later recalled, 'and kissed me so much that I became uneasy and frightened. At home I vowed with tears that I did not want to go there any more.'[96] In 1876 Lilli Löw, by then known as Lilli Lehmann, sang one of the Rhinedaughters in Bayreuth.

There were also secret approaches to 'Mimi' von Buch, who was later to become Countess Schleinitz, and to the landowner Henriette von Bissing, who would have rescued the indigent composer in 1863 if she had not been informed that 'ultimately he loves only Frau Wesendonck'. By the time he came to rent a whole floor of a villa at Penzing overlooking the palace gardens at Schönbrunn, Wagner had already made other provisions. The apartment, which was looked after by Franz Mrázek and his wife Anna, also accommodated two young sisters: the seventeen-year-old Lisbeth Völkl, a butcher's daughter from the Josefstadt, who made herself useful serving tea but with whom Wagner had no luck, and her elder and 'more experienced' sister Marie. The latter proved a palpable hit and seems to have suited Wagner down to the ground. She may already have had some experience of the stage.

At all events, the Wagner expert Eduard Hanslick reports that the Master's eye was caught by a 'pretty little ballerina who did the honours when guests came to visit him',[97] a claim that prompted a furious rejoinder from Glasenapp, who dismissed it as 'perfidiously personal gossip' about Wagner's 'housekeeper'. In order to prove his case, Glasenapp quoted from a 'brief' but harmless note that Wagner had written to Marie, announcing his return home for 'half past seven next Wednesday evening'.[98] But lines from the same note that were suppressed by Glasenapp tell a rather different story.

In them Wagner asked his 'dear little Marie' to heat the 'pretty little closet' and 'spray it with perfume: and buy the best bottles, so that it smells really sweet'. And he followed this up with the anxious query: 'I hope the pink drawers are ready, too???'[99] These were almost certainly not his 'dearest sweetheart's' frilly underwear, but his own. For reasons known only to himself, he wore tailor-made silk underwear and elegant indoor clothing decorated with all manner of ruches, tassels and rosettes that seem more in keeping with a woman's wardrobe than a man's. He also had negligees made to his own designs, dressing gowns of a kind that Madame de Pompadour might well have worn, and even in Bayreuth he read Paris fashion magazines in order to keep abreast of the latest trends.

The ladies' drawers, undershirts and colourful Russia leather bootees may have recalled his childhood with sisters whose 'more delicate wardrobe items', as he confessed in his autobiography, cast a 'subtly exciting spell' on his imagination from a very early age. In order to be really 'happy', all he then needed was maternal affection. 'You need only take me in hand and wrap me up nice and gently,' he later confided to Cosima, 'and the gas in me will become compliant and rise freely into the air, where you'll then find me smiling and blissful.'[100] The dour Cosima must have thought that this fit of infantile eroticism was a particularly tasteless joke.

Needless to say, Wagner wore women's clothing only when he was alone, and whenever he was caught in flagrante by his wives, he always had an excuse. When Minna discovered him 'dressed to the nines in a splendid coat',[101] he dismissed it as a charade. And whenever he had clothes of a feminine cut made for him during his years in Bayreuth, he claimed that it was the bemused Cosima who had ordered them. On the one occasion when she criticized his 'passion for silk materials', the result was a 'certain amount of ill feeling'.[102]

It was, of course, only in his 'beautiful closet' that he wore the silk creations that he had designed for himself – there was invariably one such room in each of the houses he inhabited from the time of his roseate dream in Paris. When his Viennese seamstress Bertha Goldwag was asked whether she had ever seen him wearing silk suits, she emphatically denied it: 'Never. Neither I myself nor anyone else. I can tell you that for certain.' But Bertha knew at first hand the inner sanctum in which Wagner tried on these costumes, as she had furnished the entire apartment for him.

Whereas all the other rooms in his Penzing apartment were conventionally furnished, this secret cabinet was 'decorated with extravagant splendour', she reported. 'The walls were lined in silk, with relievo garlands all the way round. From the ceiling hung a wonderful lamp with a gentle beam. The whole of the floor was covered in heavy and exceptionally soft rugs in which your feet literally sank. The furnishings of this boudoir – as I should like to call this room – consisted of a small sofa, a number of armchairs and a small table.' Perhaps it was out of discretion that she omitted to mention the mirror and bed. But she was sure that 'no one was allowed to enter this room'.[103]

Thanks to Bertha Goldwag we also know that Wagner had brought with him to Penzing his favourite Swiss maidservant, Verena Weidmann. Ever since he had stayed at the Schweizerhof in Lucerne in 1859, 'Vreneli' had been assiduous in wanting to serve him whenever he asked her to do so. She followed him to Penzing in 1863, to Munich in 1864 and to Geneva at the end of 1865 – not even Cosima was allowed to accompany him to the last of these. Married to the Lucerne groom Jakob Stocker, Vreneli enjoyed Wagner's particular goodwill, so that on one occasion he even asked Mathilde Wesendonck to obtain a beautiful dress for her, 'no matter what it costs'.[104]

For her own part, Vreneli saw to all Wagner's needs. As his personal servant, she was expressly forbidden to undertake any 'menial work' but was enjoined to 'look after' Wagner and 'make life pleasant' for him. In Munich she devoted herself to the luxurious aspect of his existence. Here, in the Brienner Straße, hidden from the gaze of unauthorized observers, was another of his secret cabinets. Not inappropriately termed the 'Grail' by his friend Peter Cornelius, this holy of holies was lined with yellow satin under the guidance of the experienced Bertha, while the draperies and curtains were made of pink satin. From the ceiling shimmered white satin over which ruched ribbons of pearl-grey satin were diagonally drawn. Silk roses were worked into these garlands, which also ran along the upper edges of the walls. Here too the centre of the ceiling was ornamented by a bouquet of silk flowers shot through with little red roses. On the deep-pile Smyrna carpet beneath it stood the soft and well-sprung bed, covered in moiré silk with a floral design, which Bertha Goldwag could not remember, facing the large mirror whose frame was covered in puffed pink satin. Lit by a dim light, an image of the Madonna also hung in this room.

Each of these secret cabinets was abandoned with a speed that recalled a headlong flight, culminating in an escape that struck a positively wondrous note. By the spring of 1864 Wagner was once again on the brink of disaster. *Tristan und Isolde* had finally been abandoned and his debts had reached a level that made a spell in the debtor's prison seem unavoidable. In this 'ruinous situation' he fell back on the tried and tested method of clandestinely changing his place of residence. 'Accompanied to the station by his few loyal friends', Glasenapp summed up Wagner's position, Wagner 'travelled via Munich to Zurich'. Martin Gregor-Dellin provides an even more succinct version of events: 'He fled from Vienna on 23 March.'

Both writers fail to mention the one thing that Wagner himself refused to forgo: as Cornelius faithfully reports, he left his doll's house 'wearing women's clothes'.[105]

Cosima

By the age of fifty Wagner had manoeuvred himself into a position from which only a miracle could save him. His plans to stage *Tristan und Isolde* had come to nothing, financially he was faced with what he termed 'evident and inevitable ruin', and the many affairs he had chalked up could do nothing to replace the love he had lost. 'Truly,' he wrote to Peter Cornelius in April 1864, 'I feel that, deep down inside me, the end is near. . . . Some good and truly helpful miracle must now befall me, otherwise it will all be over!'[106]

The miracle did indeed occur – and it came in triplicate: his old adversary disappeared, the Messiah appeared, and new life was born. Meyerbeer died in Paris on 2 May 1864, and the very next day, Wagner, fleeing from his creditors, received a surprise invitation from King Ludwig II, in whose villa on Lake Starnberg he fathered his first child shortly afterwards. (For legal reasons, Wagner was obliged to play the part of the child's godfather rather than its actual father.)

The woman who performed this service came to epitomize the change in his life, for not only did she bring his daughter Isolde into the world, she also brought about a virtual rebirth in Wagner himself, a rebirth of which the composer was fully aware, even it was different from what he may have envisaged: the Bayreuth 'Master' in whose guise he was to go down in history was entirely Cosima's creation, Cosima's Wagner.

And who was Wagner's Cosima? She had first met him in Paris in 1853 as the younger of Liszt's two illegitimate daughters, tall for her age – she was then fifteen – and bashful, 'angular and with yellowish skin, a large mouth and a long nose', down which tears of confusion ran.[107] At this period, however, Wagner had eyes only for Liszt's 'adopted daughter', Marie von Wittgenstein, who was the same age as Cosima and already a blossoming society lady with only a smile of contempt for the 'storklike' Cosima.

They met again at the Asyl in Zurich in 1857, by which time Cosima was married to Hans von Bülow, the favourite pupil of both Wagner and Liszt. As yet, however, she was unable to share her husband's conviction that 'Wagner must be worshipped like a god'.[108] And whenever the composer exchanged any words with her, she again burst into tears. At this period Wagner had eyes only for Mathilde Wesendonck, while Cosima was plagued by feelings of jealousy as her husband evidently had eyes only for his god.

They met again in 1861 at Bad Reichenhall, where Cosima was completing a whey cure. On this occasion their travelling companions were Blandine and her advocate husband Émile Ollivier. Now the mother of a young daughter, Baroness von Bülow had still not managed to overcome her inhibitions, and occasionally there were outbursts of emotion and 'some minor but harmful excesses' about which Wagner gives no further details. He was so in thrall to the sisters, who in terms of age could have been his daughters and who were wholly neglected by their father, that he even planned to adopt them.

On the other hand – as Ollivier perceptively complained – this did not prevent him from commandeering a double room and leaving the ailing Cosima to make do with a sofa.[109] For at this stage Wagner had eyes only for the pretty Blandine, whose gentleness and sensuality marked her out to her advantage from the storklike Cosima. If we may believe Julius Kapp, Blandine even inspired Wagner to create the love-struck frenzy of the *Tannhäuser* Bacchanal. Cosima, meanwhile, had failed to make any progress on translating the libretto into French.

The following year they saw each other again at the Beaver's Nest in Biebrich, where Wagner had eyes only for the unruly Friederike. Even so, there was a comical rapprochement between the two of them when the Master pushed Cosima to her hotel in a wheelbarrow. Hans was not amused, not least because Cosima was three months pregnant. The child was born in March 1863 and was christened Blandine.

Cosima's sister Blandine had died the previous autumn following the birth of her son. Wagner again saw the influence of his own unlucky star in the death of the woman he loved. 'The eerie, literally demonic state that this news has induced in me is terrible,' he wrote to Blandine's brother-in-law, Hans von Bülow. 'I feel as if it was designed to strike at me personally, as if it was aimed at *me*, and me alone.'[110] The fact that Wagner's favourite sister, Rosalie, had also died in childbirth was something that Bülow could not have known.

Wagner's Cosima was not only Liszt's daughter and Bülow's wife but also Blandine's sister. In his dreams the two became merged. 'Gazing upon my sister's face,' Cosima noted in 1874, Wagner 'suddenly recognized me in it. "Only Cosima has this expression," he said as he woke up.'[111] In another dream that he described to her in 1880, he saw her at a performance of *Tannhäuser* in Paris. She had been sitting, palely, in her box and he had addressed her with the words 'Comment as-tu osé avoir le courage et le mérite de venir ici seule?' ('How did you manage to find the courage and merit to come here on your own?').[112] This memory, too, could relate only to Cosima's elder sister, who, it is clear from Wagner's Annals, had come to Paris in 1858 to attend a performance of the *Tannhäuser* Overture. At the time, Wagner told Minna, people had taken Blandine to be his wife.[113]

In this way, Cosima became her sister's natural successor in Wagner's eyes, just as Wagner assumed the role that her father had once taken. At all events, Liszt had been more of an idol than a real-life figure for her. Following the breakdown of his relationship with her mother, the Comtesse Marie d'Agoult, the children were abandoned by both their parents and lived with Liszt's mother, Anna. For years their only contact with their father was by correspondence, while Marie d'Agoult made a point of keeping her distance. Cosima later complained that as children they had 'neither father nor mother'.[114]

Both had other priorities. Liszt had pursued his career as Europe's leading pianist before forming a liaison with the wealthy Princess Carolyne Wittgenstein and her daughter Marie. Meanwhile, Marie d'Agoult was making a name for herself as a cigarillo-smoking socialite and a writer who, in Carolyne's words, was 'plagued by fits of erotic delirium'.[115] The children, conversely, felt only the disadvantages of their illegitimate origins, living in the reflected glory of their illustrious parents, their longing for love pedagogically channelled into other pursuits by a whole series of strict governesses. Both daughters were married only after their parents had consulted each other. Just as Marie d'Agoult recommended her protégé Émile Ollivier as a suitable match for Blandine, so Liszt bestowed the less attractive Cosima on his favourite pupil Hans von Bülow. In both cases love played only a subordinate role.

Based on social calculation as they were, both marriages were unhappy. The outgoing Blandine became withdrawn, and her piano, on which she had played with some skill, fell silent.[116] A similar fate befell her younger sister. If she had hoped that her marriage would bring her closer to her father – a point on which she agreed with her husband – her hopes proved sadly misplaced. For 'twelve long hours', she later recalled, she cried on the eve of her wedding, no doubt suspecting that there would be no room for her between the two men in her life. Nor was it long before her husband revealed where his true preferences lay. If one half of Bülow's heart belonged to Liszt, it was clear at least from the time of their honeymoon that the other half was in pawn to Wagner. Cosima's tears were not just the tears of embarrassment.

Both women sought to break free from their unhappiness. According to Minna Wagner, writing as the mouthpiece of marital fidelity, Blandine was a 'common, not to say vulgar person who does not enjoy a good reputation with any of the people who know her', while Cosima was a 'somewhat dissolute creature' who was responsible for the breakdown of Karl Ritter's marriage.[117] All we know for certain is that Ritter and Cosima planned a suicide pact on Lake Geneva, calling it off only at the very last minute, an incident Ritter later admitted to in conversation with the grandmaster of all love-deaths in Venice. Perhaps it was his memory of this that persuaded Wagner to think that Cosima was permanently on the edge of the abyss and 'ready to throw herself into it at any moment'.

It was after the wheelbarrow incident that Wagner's Cosima began to cast aside her inhibitions, as Wagner himself was pleased to report. And evidently it was not only these she cast aside. In 1863 – the year in which Wagner assured Mathilde Maier that 'I love you most deeply' and in which he let it be known that the other Mathilde was his 'first and only love' – the couple became guilty of adultery, with Cosima later referring to it in her diary as their 'first union'.[118]

If we are to believe Wagner's colourful account in *My Life*, it was on a winter's day in Berlin when the couple drove through the city in a 'beautiful carriage', rather in the manner of Madame Bovary. They began by 'gazing silently at each other' in the spirit of Tristan and Isolde, after which they were 'overcome by a violent longing', and 'after admitting to the truth of the matter' they finally sealed their confession 'with tears and sobs', agreeing 'to belong to each other, and each other alone'.[119]

Cosima will scarcely have deluded herself into thinking that she was the only woman in Wagner's life at this time. Mimi von Buch and Henriette von Bissing both lay claim to his attentions, while the Misses Maier and Meyer, to say nothing of the eternal Mathilde Wesendonck, continued to exercise his thoughts. And in Penzing the terpsichoreally gifted butcher's daughter heated his rose boudoir for him and presumably already had his silk drawers to hand. But at least Cosima will not have known about this last liaison: had it not been for Hanslick and Bertha Goldwag, it would no doubt have remained a secret.

Following the miracle in the Marquardt Hotel in Stuttgart, when Bavaria's cabinet secretary had arrived out of the blue with an invitation from King Ludwig, time was clearly of the essence for Wagner, who fired off no fewer than eight letters and telegrams to the Bülows, begging them to visit him in his new quarters in the king's villa on Lake Starnberg. His ninth letter, addressed to 'dear Cosima', produced the desired results, perhaps because he avoided the familiar 'Du' that had long been established between them, perhaps also because he held out the prospect of a post for Hans as 'Vorspieler' to the king on a salary of 'at least' fifteen hundred florins, or perhaps because there was 'a wonderful cowshed' behind the building 'with forty wonderful Swiss cows – just think of all that milk for the children!!!'

Cosima von Bülow turned up at the Villa Pellet on 29 June 1864 with her two daughters and their nurse. Bülow himself did not arrive until a week later, and according to the testimony of Wagner's domestic servant Anna Mrázek on the occasion of the resultant paternity case, he found himself standing outside Wagner's locked bedroom door, whereupon he repaired 'to his living room, threw himself on the ground, beat on the floor with his hands and feet like a man possessed, and cried and even screamed'.[120] Behind the door, he knew that his wife was in bed with his god. The case revolved around Isolde, whom Wagner fathered at this time. She was born on 10 April 1865, the day on which the orchestral rehearsals began for the first performance of *Tristan und Isolde*. The conductor was Hans von Bülow.

For Wagner, this was a dream come true. He had finally found a woman willing to sacrifice herself to him in a way that he expected a true sister to do.

In keeping with his wishes, she was prepared to abandon everything in order to get the man for whom she yearned. In this way she revealed a degree of courage that neither Jessie Laussot nor Mathilde Wesendonck nor Blandine Ollivier had been able to summon up. In addition there was the double satisfaction for Wagner not only of supplanting his 'vassal' Hans von Bülow but of once again trampling on the toes of Liszt, the 'friend' whom he so much envied.

Years earlier, Wagner had flirted with Liszt's favourite, Marie von Wittgenstein, who in turn had questioned 'the sort of "chains"' in which he was 'languishing' on account of Marie d'Agoult, with whom Liszt was then at daggers drawn.[121] Wagner had then entered into a liaison with Blandine, with the result that, according to Julius Kapp, Liszt's inamorata Carolyne Wittgenstein 'broke off all contact with Wagner for the duration'.[122] With the conquest of Cosima, Liszt had finally had enough. Although he had no illusions about the younger of his two daughters, whom he called a 'serpent', it was he himself who had set up the marriage that Wagner was in the process of destroying. And the husband whom Wagner had destroyed was his favourite pupil, a man he treated as a 'son'.

But Liszt had his revenge, from the euphoric beginning of this relationship to its depressingly bitter end. He was the shadow cast by the new sun. Just as Cosima temporarily took on the part of the self-sacrificing sister in the drama of Wagner's life, so Liszt embodied the archetype of the wicked father whose one aim in life was to force the two lovers apart.

However unequal they were as a couple, Cosima and Wagner had at least one thing in common: both spent their lives feeling that they were excluded from their true inheritance. But they differed in their ideas of the nature of this inheritance and the means by which they could regain it. Wagner sought the love that the world withheld from him and that could be given to him only by his mother's tender cares and by his sister's willingness to sacrifice herself to him. Through love alone he could rediscover the paradisal peace of the beginning and at the same time be subsumed within a higher form of existence made up of both 'I' and 'you'. To this he devoted all his creative powers and intellectual acumen, and if there was a force that drove him as restlessly as it drove his heroes, it was his longing for love.

Cosima's inheritance was more literal than Wagner's. Born into the world of the Citizen King, with its impassioned advocacy of aristocratic glamour and self-enrichment, she felt a natural claim to both. Whereas her mother embodied the exclusive world of the aristocracy with its liveried servants, her father was an international idol who earned money by his playing. Moreover, both her parents were wealthy, and Cosima was long exercised by the thought of how much money they would leave her.

In reality she was not allowed to eat from silver salvers and unlike her father's favourite, Marie von Wittgenstein, she could not wear silk dresses when riding in a carriage. Her early awkwardness in Wagner's company, with its ambience of champagne and ruched silks, was bound up not least with the fact that she did not feel at home here. Nor did her association with Hans von Bülow do anything to rid her of this sense of inferiority. Although he brought her the title she coveted, he did not have access to the fortune she likewise longed to own. He had to go out and earn it. As a result, Cosima's prime ambition remained to climb the social ladder, and if she spent her entire life pursuing this goal with such grim determination, it was because she felt that as the daughter of two exceptional individuals she was entitled to no less.

Wagner, too, strove for aristocratic prestige, a prestige to which his family tradition entitled him. And he also sought the wealth that others withheld from him. Yet both were merely a means to an end, the end in this case being the realization of his life's illusory dream. For Cosima, they were an end in themselves. When the twenty-five-year-old Cosima threw in her lot with the fifty-year-old composer, the points they had in common seemed plain for all to see. In Cosima, Wagner found the woman he desired, a woman in whose reflection he thought he could recognize himself, whereas for Cosima, Wagner represented everything she had hitherto had to forgo.

In Cosima's eyes, Wagner embodied the glamour of fame, including the incommensurable greatness of his art and, not least, the fortune that his scores represented if turned to financial gain. If Cosima offered her lover the gift of a family, he gave her in turn the boon of his works' performing rights. She had in any case already gained control of his life, with 'Richard Wagner' becoming an enterprise to which all else was subordinated. She represented him in the eyes of the world, asserting the highest claims and refusing to rest until she had implemented them.

It was not until later that the potential for conflict made itself felt. Historically speaking, they were from opposite sides of the barricades. As a member of Parisian society, Cosima remained impervious to the world of ideas associated with the liberation of the human race, while Wagner, for his part, could never accept her aristocratic ways and propensity for hypocrisy. As an artist, Wagner subscribed to the concept of philosophical truth, a concept that Cosima could counter only with the bombast of pretension. His need for love refused to be shackled by the laws of marriage, but her only response was marital fidelity as a categorical imperative. His oversensitivity and self-indulgence fell foul of her rigorous austerity, so that each time he kicked over the traces, she would take him in hand lest she lost sight of her actual goal: the triumph of the enterprise that bore his name.

His lack of self-discipline was punished as though it were conduct injurious to the company's interests, with her main weapon corresponding to his main weakness. More than anything, he feared the withdrawal of her love, which duly proved to be her most effective weapon. The archetype of the sister who sacrificed herself for him passed imperceptibly into that of the mother who expected exactly the same from him. The mother meted out her punishments and rewards, and the son felt only respect. Thus Wagner imagined that he had found in her the ideal woman who was familiar to him from his subconscious, and while enjoying the incalculable benefits of knowing that he was loved, he accepted as part of the bargain the disadvantage of lapsing into childlike dependency. Cosima's Wagner came into existence at the same time as Wagner's Cosima, and the two came together in him. For him, the young Cosima became the medium of an encounter with himself that he both longed for and feared.

But for all his infatuation, he could scarcely fail to notice that the real Cosima did not understand what he wanted in life. His philosophy remained as foreign to her as his works which, it is clear from her later diaries, she knew mostly from hearsay. Her 'unnatural' manner, which Romain Rolland claimed was designed to achieve a 'superficial brilliance' and which, he contemptuously added, 'occasionally encouraged her to take an interest in more serious issues and even to think',[123] was bound to remain alien to her uninhibited husband. But whereas he tolerated her airs and graces, she made no secret of the fact that she despised the friends who gathered round him. Wagner gave way, and from then on his artistic followers were banished from his residence. At the same time she airbrushed out of his early life all that did not fit in with her concept. From now on it was she who decided who and what was 'Richard Wagner'.

In pursuing this aim, Cosima lay claim to what Ferdinand Lassalle termed 'a level of education more appropriate to a French girls' boarding school',[124] with an amateur approach to music that persuaded even her admirers to think that she was 'completely unmusical'.[125] At the same time she cultivated an ostentatious piety that Ernest Newman described as 'Jesuitical'. The managing director of Wagner's publishing house saw in her 'a terribly eccentric, effusive woman and, like her papa, holier than thou'.[126] Her view of heaven was coloured by governesses and father confessors and as such was light years away from the world's perfumed ocean of music in which Isolde had so recently drowned. Wagner seems not to have noticed this.

The fact that – as they often observed – their hearts beat in unison persuaded Cosima that there was agreement between them on an intellectual level, too. 'How utterly he has only me to understand him', she wrote proudly in her diary.[127] Wagner allowed her to go on thinking this. They agreed to use the same weapons. Wagner condescended in all things, and Cosima felt herself vindicated. If he escaped from her control, she responded by imposing sanctions. Like Minna, she demanded an explanation for everything, criticizing his conduct and, to the extent that he allowed her to do so, making up his mind for him. Every approach to other women was answered with violent jealousy, in which the predominant emotion was not so much the threat to her love as fear that she might lose her most hallowed possession. At the same time, she tormented him with her love for the Other – the usurper etched in his unconscious – in the form of her father, of whom she was 'the spitting image'.[128]

Wagner, too, saw in Cosima 'Liszt's wonderful likeness'[129] and so it was not just himself whom he caught sight of in this mirror. It was Liszt who inspired his tormenting jealousy, so much so that the mere mention of his name could provoke feelings of frightening anger. And whenever Cosima went to visit her father, the old fear of loss would reassert itself. The final weeks of Wagner's life were marred by Liszt's presence in Venice – and only because Cosima wished it so. She survived her husband by almost half a century.

The international reputation that Wagner gained for himself affected the picture that Cosima painted of him and that resembled the man she could understand. In turn Wagner strove to resemble it. Cosima's arrival at the Villa Pellet on Lake Starnberg coincided with a change in him that he himself will scarcely have noticed as the features that it brought out were already present within him. It was only the other characteristics – misunderstood or misprized by Cosima – that were now lost. This diminution was triggered not by their equality, which Wagner was the first to believe in, but by Cosima's narrow-mindedness, which she self-consciously flaunted. She saw the world from a single perspective, subordinating it to the goal that she had set herself, and so a homeless individual like Wagner, abandoned to the play of caprice and the spirit, was bound to be subordinate to her precisely because of his superiority. Wagner abandoned the field without a struggle, identifying with the usurper. He had gazed into the abyss without her, whereas *with* her everything seemed to go better for him as long as she kept him alive.

Wagner himself made great play of Cosima's alleged ability to stimulate him creatively, and so the puzzling atrophy of his creative powers has never been laid at her door. None the less, it is striking that following their 'union' he produced no new works. Although he completed *Die Meistersinger* and the *Ring* and wrote *Parsifal*, all had been conceived before she arrived on the scene, and the sense of intoxication associated with the score of *Parsifal* has with some justification been attributed to another woman in his life. The same is true of his writings. They too draw on old familiar ideas that suddenly assume an element of monomania, much like their author himself. Once so rich in contradictions, Wagner ultimately seems to have suffered from voluntary self-restraint. The fact that when she copied out his writings for King Ludwig Cosima 'arbitrarily altered' them is all part of the same picture,[130] as is the observation that she helped to dictate some of his final essays.

The change that took place in Wagner led him from art to politics. Of course, he had always interpreted art in a political sense, as something bound up with humanity as a whole. His whole art was part of the process of liberation that began with German idealism. Man finds his true self-consciousness in art, something that allows him to rise even above the gods. Only in the revitalized drama of the Greeks would the Germanic nation find its transfigured likeness. And only in the love conjured up by his drama could creation achieve its true goal.

For Cosima, who believed only in one God in Heaven and one god on earth, this was scarcely conceivable. She was no more capable of understanding it than she was of sharing Wagner's enthusiasm for reconciliation. For her, politics consisted not in social upheaval but in the attainment of personal goals. She was the first person to recognize the value of Wagner's capital which, currently unexploited, was scattered to the four winds but which now had to be brought together under one roof. And long before Wagner himself, she saw the opportunity presented by the guileless King Ludwig. Above all, she realized that the enterprise needed resolute leadership: the genius was no longer to be dependent on the benevolence of men more powerful than he. He himself had to become powerful in turn.

In this way a process took place, unobserved by Wagner's admirers, that closely resembled the one instituted thirty years later by Elisabeth Förster-Nietzsche in dealing with her brother Friedrich. But unlike Nietzsche, Wagner was conscious of the metamorphosis. He had dreamt of holding court, and now his first lady-in-waiting had fallen into his lap. A master of adaptation, Wagner accepted her regime, albeit with mixed feelings. He enjoyed the fact that he was worshipped as a god within his own lifetime but hated the attendant need for self-control. For Franz Wilhelm Beidler, the son of the repudiated Isolde, it was clear that 'Wagner resented this process of removal and alienation, reacting all the more violently the more he became aware of its fatal inevitability.'[131]

And the process was inevitable because of the archetypal situation that it represented. If Cosima was supremely well suited to adopting the persona of the sister that Wagner so desired, she also dominated him as a strict mother who when necessary played off against him the alternative stereotype of the paternal rival. As with Minna, Wagner 'spoilt her and gave way to her in everything',[132] with the result that he had nothing with which to resist her reprisals.

The idyll on Lake Starnberg was scarcely over before Wagner was suffering from the anguish of desire and the cuckolded Bülow was confined to his room at the Bayerischer Hof in Munich, suffering from signs of paralysis. 'In me all heroes shall perish' is a remark that Nietzsche the psychologist later ascribed to Cosima. And so, regardless of the fact that her husband was a broken man, Cosima hurried off to join her father at the annual meeting of the Society of German Composers in Karlsruhe. It was the first of many such visits she paid to Liszt of her own accord, no doubt in part in the hope of offering Wagner a chance to brood on his deep dependency on her.

By mid-October 1864 Wagner was able to move into a seigneurial villa in Munich and furnish it, to his own designs, at Ludwig's expense. Within weeks, he had been joined in the city by the Bülows. Hans had recovered from his paralysis and was now the king's official pianist, while Cosima leapt into action as secretary to Wagner, the royal favourite. As his plenipotentiary, she simultaneously began a voluminous correspondence with the juvenile king in which she represented the interests of Wagner, Liszt and Bülow in the style of an arch-intriguer.

Her success justified her. Caught in a pincer movement between the Master and his carrier pigeon, the boy king was left powerless. In turn it dawned on the dramatist that he would henceforth be dependent on the services of his energetic female diplomat. Hitherto he had retained the prerogative of abruptly disappearing from the scene whenever he felt the need to do so, but now he was required to settle down. On the other hand, there was no longer any reason to flee. He called the royal villa his 'ship', and as soon became clear, it now rested safe and sound on dry land.

Like Bülow, Peter Cornelius was summoned to Munich in an official capacity and by his own admission 'often did not recognize the once so generous Wagner'. The composer now seemed to strike a note of artifice, to 'lack freedom' and to 'deny what he had once loved. We were no longer allowed to speak about Frau Wesendonck.' Instead – to quote Cornelius's eloquent if unfortunate image – Cosima sought 'with a certain pride to wield the slipper over Richard'. If Wagner attempted to act the fool, as he had often done in the past, 'Frau von Bülow expressed her evident disapproval of such vulgar jokes.'[133] This relationship between the punitive mother and her naughty child was to remain unchanged from that time to Wagner's death. As late as 1881 the Wagnerian

Engelbert Humperdinck noticed that the effervescent Master 'became timid and despondent before the strict gaze of the mistress of the household'.[134]

There was undoubtedly little similarity between the Cosima who had stammered in Wagner's presence in the Asyl and the mistress of the household before whom his courage failed him. When visiting Wagner on Lake Starnberg she had manoeuvred herself into a position in which she must either fail or rise above herself. With no parents to speak of, she had eked out her existence in the shadow first of a more talented sister, then of an egocentric conductor, before suddenly finding herself mediating between Europe's leading opera composer and the king of Bavaria. She came through with flying colours. Together with Wagner, Cosima, too, was reborn. From now on she stood by her husband. A conductor like Bülow had a bad hand in comparison.

But she played even with her idol Wagner whenever the balance of power demanded it. In a 'desperate attempt to salvage her marriage',[135] Liszt summoned his daughter and cuckolded son-in-law to Budapest in August 1865. Both followed the summons as though Wagner did not exist. Newly installed as an abbé, Liszt wore a black cassock to conduct his oratorio on the life of Saint Elizabeth, after which the estranged couple accompanied him on a six-week triumphal tour of Hungary. On her return, Cosima wrote to the king in Liszt's name, asking if her father could dedicate the oratorio to him 'in the deepest reverence' and, adopting the style of a press officer, praising it as 'perhaps the most beautiful work ever composed' by her father.[136] Ludwig not only accepted with delight but ordered a performance the following February under Bülow's baton.

And what was happening to Wagner in the meantime? Throughout Cosima's absence he behaved like a child snatched away from its mother's arms. She could later have read his litany of complaints in the 'Brown Book' that she gave him for this purpose. Sentiments that he had confided to his Venice Diary for Mathilde Wesendonck six years earlier now filled the pages of the 'Brown Book' with confidential uninhibitedness: the torments of his Tristanesque longing, the Dutchman's thoughts of death and Lohengrin's indictment of the faithless lover whom he transformed in the delirium of his loss into his heroine Isolde. In the mountain solitude of one of the king's hunting lodges where he had sought refuge with his manservant Franz and his dog Pohl, Wagner found himself confronted by the whole wretchedness of his existence. Cosima, who had left her three children in care in order to go off and celebrate with her father, can only have welcomed this development.

'Your letter, my love,' the abandoned composer raged on 11 September, 'again, it's sheer madness! Madness and no end to it!' In the midst of 'rapture, love and adoration', he had been visited by 'terrors and fears'. All that remained was to 'cry out and perish'. 'If it must be so, then so be it: I surrender. Perhaps this is what you need,' he added with bitter clear-sightedness. 'Your father will be pleased: he likes having you there – you like being there. Why should I be there, too?' Coldly, the mortified composer threatened her: 'And you go running away from little Isolde, for five weeks now. . . . If you go off on adventure again, I'll take charge of the child myself.'

Liszt, the wicked father, had 'never loved' him and was a 'devil'. The truth of the matter, wrote Wagner with a sideswipe at Cosima, was that 'the God-fearing' abbé was incapable of love. 'He's only interested in dominating others.' There follows a remark that probably not even Cosima will have been able to understand. As though plagued by memories of his stepfather Ludwig Geyer and his favourite sister Rosalie, he alludes to a vague suspicion that seems to have tormented him for some time.

What was it in fact that shackled Cosima to Liszt, who had after all neglected her throughout her entire life? Was there something that went beyond the bonds of fatherhood? Had he ultimately taken holy orders because he was weighed down by the burden of guilt? 'To me all this Catholic nonsense is profoundly repugnant,' wrote Wagner with wounding candour. 'Anyone who takes refuge in this no doubt has a great deal to atone for. Speaking in a dream, you once revealed it to me: it was terrible. Your father disgusts me.' This mysterious revelation ends with the phrase: 'Don't talk to me about your love!'[137]

Triggered by the nightmares of the past, Wagner's torments were not without consequence. On 27 August, while Cosima was taking her seat beside the Primate of all Hungary, Cardinal Scitovszky, at a banquet in Esztergom, Wagner began to write down the story of *Parzival*. He had conceived it in Marienbad twenty years earlier, but now it returned, fully armed, during the period of *Tristan und Isolde*. The lonely composer completed the prose draft in a four-day frenzy of creativity. He could at least rely on the vacillating figures who drew near him once again.

7 Big Time

'The springtime of our three lives in one'

The radical break that the summer of 1864 brought to Wagner's life was hailed by the composer himself as a cause for great celebration: the king of Bavaria's love for him, he concluded the following year, was 'simply inconceivable'. Ludwig was 'myself reborn as a beautiful youth'. He felt the same for Liszt's daughter, who had offered herself to him much as Sieglinde offers herself to her Wälsung brother. 'O my Cosima!' he rhapsodized in his diary. 'We shall be happier than mortals have ever been, for we three are immortal.' This love-struck threesome of composer, king and cleric's daughter certainly seemed exceptional. 'We cannot be happier. It is not possible. The springtime of our three lives in one is in full bloom.'[1]

Wagner's 'I' had found its longed-for 'you' and had done so twice over. Ludwig had entered his life as his male counterpart, while Cosima nestled up to him as his female equivalent. Reflected on both sides as though in his private cabinet, the world now corresponded to Wagner's own idea of it for the very first time in his life. The will, which according to Schopenhauer was perpetually unsatisfied, had now found what it wanted on every front. Thanks to Ludwig's Croesus-like wealth, Wagner was relieved of his material cares, the spectre of a life of debt exorcized and his own court – 'as at Versailles'[2] – brought a step closer. And thanks to Cosima, love was no longer limited to his world of dreams but was now a part of his life, and he had even been blessed with a real-life Isolde. He could not, of course, suspect that long after his death his daughter Loldi would be repudiated by her mother.

If the poet was right when he wrote that to attain one's life's supreme goal is as tragic as to fall short of it, then Wagner had two chances in life to know tragedy. And he seized them with both hands. The sufferings of privation were followed by the unhappiness of satiety. The fulfilment of his wishes, which he invested with an aura of the miraculous, brought equal satisfaction to his two partners, both of whom could have been his children. Just as he fashioned them according to his own archetypal ideals, so they had long since raised him to the status of the godlike idol of their generation. Not only was Wagner reflected in them, but they discovered their transfigured ideal in him. The events that followed were reflected as though in multiple mirrors, and in retrospect it is as hard to say who played the active part and who was the reflection as it is to decide who exploited whom and who ultimately was cheated and betrayed.

Wagner's biographers have all been convinced that his encounter with Ludwig and Cosima brought with it a decisive turn for the better, allowing him to achieve a breakthrough that was to lead to Bayreuth and to the fulfilment of his life's dream. After all, he himself saw events in this light, and Cosima – described as early as 1865 as the 'Delphic oracle' – raised it to the status of a dogma: it was *her* Wagner who was the true Wagner. Only at her side did he begin to lead a proper life. And in order to reinforce this, she appropriated his life in its entirety.

As read by his biographers, Wagner's life was written by Cosima. The texts in question are his autobiography, which he dictated to her for Ludwig's edification; the various essays that she reclaimed from his friends and arbitrarily changed when copying them out; the diaries in which, chronicling current events, she recorded his life on earth as it appeared to her in her own distorting mirror; and the articles to which, with Wagner's blessing, she lent her personal touch while he was dictating them to her. Wagner spoke, and Cosima added the emphases.

Whenever she was prevented from making an active contribution, she would interfere retroactively. This applies not only to the correspondence that she published in censored versions but also to the exchange of letters with August Röckel, Heinrich Heine, Hector Berlioz, Georg Herwegh, Gottfried Semper, Mathilde and Otto Wesendonck, Charles Baudelaire, Friedrich Nietzsche and Arthur Gobineau, all of which, by her own admission, she destroyed.[3] The same is true of her correspondence with Wagner himself, which she reduced to a pile of ashes. Everything was a part of Wagner's life, and she collected its traces with the meticulousness of an archivist. But ultimately it was she who decided what should be included. What she did not like had to go. Wagner's book of life bore her imprint, which in the course of their lives together became Wagner's. So comprehensively did she adapt her ways to match those of her idol that she blotted out everything that resisted alignment. The act of usurpation that Wagner suspected lay in his distant past was taking place all around him and would continue to do so in the future, long after he was dead.

In short, it was a business transaction that evolved between the three parties from the summer of 1864, and it was Wagner who came off the worst. True, he seemed to have achieved his two main objectives of economic independence and social advancement as a result of his summons to the Bavarian court, and even the king's request that in return he should complete the *Ring* and perform his works in Munich reflected the composer's own desires, so that to all appearances he could be entirely content. But in reality he had been duped.

Although Wagner had got everything he wanted, it was at a price, and that price was the loss of self. For a long time he was forced to play the part of the hybrid creature that Ludwig, incapable of coping with life, needed to bolster his own existence. Wagner provided the help that made it possible for the other-worldly adolescent to withdraw into his dream world with a clear conscience, with his idol even guaranteeing that this world acquired a higher reality. And inasmuch as Wagner assured his aristocratic benefactor that he too felt touched by the divinity about which Ludwig himself had legitimate doubts, the boy king could feel doubly justified by the composer. Ludwig would have gone down in Bavarian history as a failure, but thanks to his mentor he could now be a larger-than-life figure. Even his empty castles, to which he owes his worldwide fame, were merely a Wagnerian backdrop turned to cold stone.

Wagner was flattered not just to be tolerated by the king but to be idolized by him, too, and so he sought to suppress the knowledge that he was no longer allowed to be himself. In hundreds of letters he mimicked the effusive, kitsch-like tone that Ludwig chose to regard as the soulful language of the court. And in order not to forfeit the influence that Ludwig granted him through his sheer helplessness, Wagner resorted to the sort of intrigues that were associated with court antechambers and the politics of back staircases. For the sake of Ludwig, whom he called 'the German', he denied his revolutionary past, vilified his former comrades-in-arms and expressed his support for the monarchy and the divine right of kings, doctrines whose lackeys he had mocked in 1849 in the person of a courtier like August von Lüttichau. Now he was an 'aristocrat', insisting that his own manservant, Franz, addressed him as 'Your Grace'.[4]

More difficult was the denial of his own feelings. During his days on Lake Starnberg he had fallen into a regular trap from which he could no longer escape unscathed. Only by the king's grace and favour could he invite his lover to join him and at the same time placate her husband. Although Wagner and Cosima were guilty of committing adultery within the precincts of the royal villa, the cracks in the Bülows' marriage were temporarily papered over by the cuckolded Bülow's appointment as pianist to the king. At the same time, that appointment made it inevitable that Cosima and her family would move to

Munich, where they would come under Wagner's sway. But on her arrival the baroness seized the initiative and soon let both Ludwig and Wagner know that she was a force that was most certainly to be reckoned with.

The tragedy of what was in itself an ideal relationship lay in the fact that the king, who had made it possible, was not supposed to know about it. This game of hide-and-seek, which went on for years and which even as loyal a Wagnerian as Martin Gregor-Dellin described as 'the most pitiful, shameful and underhand intermezzo' of the composer's whole life, robbed Wagner of the very peace of mind that he hoped to find by his play-acting with the king. The basic lie that the relationship between Wagner and Cosima was purely platonic, while Bülow accepted responsibility for the children that issued from their liaison, had to be bolstered by countless ancillary untruths, including the character assassination of all who honoured the truth.

In the end, Ludwig, whom Wagner made to look the fool that he perhaps was, was required to issue a public declaration attesting to the immaculate conception of Wagner's soul mate. The disgrace that Wagner brought down on his Messiah was ultimately his own, as he knew very well. Later he himself spoke of his shame and embarrassment, confirming that he was at least acutely aware of the loss of identity that was the price he paid for his survival. When Nietzsche later expressed his bewilderment at the curiously contemptible life that Wagner led, he was thinking in part of the composer's tendency to betray his true self for the sake of some future advantage.

Wagner's betrayal of his 'godlike friend' and 'higher self' was first and foremost a betrayal of himself. If he was guilty of a further act of self-denial, it was for Cosima's sake. Like Ludwig, she had come to Wagner in search of help, and like the fawning king, she concealed her cry of distress behind an act of worship. As though her arrival at the Villa Pellet had brought about the violent eruption of a passion concealed all her life, she abandoned herself to Wagner as the most ardent of his admirers and gave no further thought to her deeply unhappy marriage. She stood at the edge of the abyss, where Wagner had been standing for some time and where they now clung to each other for support. But Wagner was so overwhelmed by her willingness for self-sacrifice that he failed to notice that Cosima had nothing to lose.

Conversely, she knew very well what to expect from the man to whom she was sacrificing herself. She also knew what he himself had to give up in order to be worthy of her sacrifice. The first thing he had to renounce was other women. And this meant not only their physical presence, as it had done in Minna's day, but also all memory of them. Whether it was Mathilde Wesendonck or Mathilde Maier, they all continued to provoke a violent defence reaction in Cosima for years to come, until Wagner, robbed of his true self, finally abandoned not only his relationships with other women but all memory of them, too. All his affairs, he suggested to Cosima with a smile in 1879, were 'pure fiction'.[5] He said exactly what she wanted to hear from him. And biographers have followed suit.[6]

The next thing Wagner had to renounce was his lifestyle. Rightly or wrongly, Cosima pilloried his extravagance, his mania for silks, the reason for which she presumably never guessed, and his fondness for alcohol, a fondness that grew with the years in direct proportion to her disapproval. She refused to sanction friendships that she considered beneath him socially but encouraged all who could lay claim to rank and title. The man who had once wanted to get rid of the aristocracy now paid court to the nobility, as did Cosima's father, whom he had once despised for doing just that. He was permitted to play the part of solo entertainer to baronesses, while that of the Saxon clown – a part that suited him much better – was now anathematized.

Ironically, it was not long before Cosima began to discriminate against the very person who had made her mania possible. Out of jealousy of Ludwig, who seemed to want too great a share of Wagner, she deepened the rift that had already opened up between them. Wagner had been underhand in deceiving the king, but it is clear from the subtlety of her letters that Cosima raised this deceit to the level of open calculation. Almost every one of the one hundred and twenty-seven letters she wrote to the king in a style reminiscent in part of Louis XIV and in part of an illustrated weekly pursued a single aim, which she sought to achieve with all the means at her disposal. Whether she had her eye on a valuable trinket, on her husband's advancement or on the character assassination of a soprano, she used a mixture of entrapment, flattery and open blackmail – all of them traits that writers on Wagner have refused to acknowledge.

Whereas Cosima regarded the naïve youth as worthy only of exploitation, it is not entirely out of the question that the love Wagner professed to feel for the handsome young man was genuine. His letters, in which he heaped praises on the God-sent king in a barely supportable falsetto, prompting Ludwig to respond with his stilted encomium of Wagner's own God-sent status, occasionally assume a sympathetic, almost emotional tone that could have allowed Cosima to suspect whatever she liked.

This did not, of course, extend to the belief, colported by Munich's scandal-mongers, that Wagner had gratified the king's homophiliac tendencies, something that Ludwig presumably did not expect from his god. After all, there were grooms, members of the Household Cavalry and railway stokers to perform this service. But there may have been a hint of a quality that Ludwig had found favourably mentioned in Wagner's Zurich essays and that the inhibited nine-teenth century, following the Greek Platonic model, described as 'pedagogic Eros'. Wagner himself called it 'the love that unites an older and a younger man'.

As he explained to the king, such love resembled the relationship neither between father and son nor between teacher and pupil but rested on 'total equal-ity' between the partners, deriving its special charm from the 'divinely inspiring difference in age' that resulted in the creation of a being of previously unsus-pected perfection. That, as Wagner explained in September 1865, was why his own philosophy found consummate expression in their friendship. 'The work of love between these two seemed to me to be the true "artwork of the future".'[7]

And where did this leave Cosima? Was there any place for a woman in Greek love? When Wagner confided these thoughts in the juvenile king, she had just left him, having gone off 'on adventure' with her father and husband to Hun-gary. But even if his profession of love was inspired by his annoyance at Cosima, there still remains the possibility that it was not entirely sham. Wagner certainly loved his 'boy', as he called him, even if he lied to him. He praised their rela-tionship as 'a love affair hitherto unprecedented in history',[8] for all that he ridiculed Ludwig behind his back and circulated his stilted handwritten letters among his circle of friends. He loved Ludwig as one loves the mirror that shows the observer only what is agreeable to him.

But Cosima would tolerate no other gods and refused to hear of a relation-ship with Ludwig. In the exclusivity of her liaison with Wagner, there was no room for a third party. His declarations of love for the king pierced her heart 'like a serpent's tooth'.[9] He finally let her have her way, retrospectively dismiss-ing Ludwig as 'incompetent'[10] and a 'cretin',[11] reducing their historic love to the level of a swindle and distancing himself from his own true self. The game that had given him new life was now said to be based on falsehood, with the result that that life in turn appeared in a dubious light. If Wagner betrayed the king, his act of betrayal was directed as much at his own heart as it was at the king's.

While believing himself doubly rewarded by fate, Wagner suffered a double loss of self as a result of this three-way relationship. Just as he had to deny his love of Cosima to Ludwig, so he denied his love of Ludwig to his jealous mis-tress. The man who had reinvented the essence of love in his works betrayed that love in real life and in the process betrayed himself, too. As though he was aware of this, he compared himself in his letters to Ludwig with his tragic god Wotan.

The play that was later branded a farce had begun for Wagner as a great drama on the subject of fate. When the king's emissary visited him in his hotel room in Stuttgart on 3 May 1864 and handed him the ring that was to open the gates of Paradise for Wagner, this merely mirrored the dream that he had long entertained. It was as though he had never abandoned his belief in the legendary heir apparent who would restore his stolen inheritance, and so he had continued to expect a German prince to become his fatherly protector and adopt him as his son.

This had now happened, and it mattered not a whit that the king in question was himself in need of a paternal protector. Quite the opposite, in fact, for it opened up a perspective that had previously never offered itself to Wagner. Ludwig was clearly unequal to the responsibilities of his position. The passionate otherworldliness that he sought to cultivate through his faith in Wagner could scarcely be ignored. The works of the 'godlike' composer gave his life its meaning, while the state that he was supposed to be ruling was a matter of sincere indifference. What was more natural than for Wagner to satisfy the dreamer's idealism and at the same time fill the power vacuum before anyone else could do so?

Ludwig certainly seemed willing to do whatever his god demanded of him. Indeed, Wagner was convinced that he had no choice in the matter. 'Yes! Believe me,' he wrote to Cosima, 'it's like this with him, he is under the same sort of spell as Joan of Arc.'[12] Even more, he declared soon afterwards, 'he is the only person who belongs to us: he is marked out – he has to!'[13] Above all, Ludwig had to assume the role that Wagner had conceived for the German prince of the future at the time of *The Wibelungs*. The self-conscious Ludwig, who hid himself away from his people, was to become his nation's Messiah. The man who shunned every confrontation was to 'slay the evil gnawing serpent of humanity' and reunite the fragmented empire.

Herein lay the decisive change in Wagner's fate, a change unnoticed by all observers. His dream of Germany had seemed to lie in ruins following the débâcle of 1849 but now it sprang into life once again. While the Munich faction that resented the intruder remained fixated on his dubious private life and kept a close count of the money that flowed to him from Ludwig's exchequer, Wagner himself was planning to seize power. With Ludwig at its head, Bavaria was to become a national and revolutionary model state that would place itself in turn at the head of the movement for German unity. His ultimate aim was the empire on whose abandoned throne 'Ludwig the German', as Wagner was already calling his 'boy', would take his rightful place as Barbarossa's natural successor.

This, Wagner explained, could be achieved only through his influence on the king. In 1866 he wrote openly to the political scientist Constantin Frantz, claiming that the king's love for him made it possible to implement his 'wishes' as a result of the impact his art had had on Ludwig's 'ideas'. His works had rendered the king 'lucid and wholly clairvoyant', whereas previously Ludwig had been 'incapable of properly appreciating the most everyday aspects of real life'. In short, the king was a simpleton whose eyes had been opened by Wagner and who was now ready for the decisive challenge that lay ahead.

And Wagner went on: 'That I may hope to persuade the king to embrace the grandest and most far-reaching resolves and actions because of his inspired love for me – this must fill me, in my exalted mood, with a well-nigh momentous presentiment of the spirit and manner in which I may yet be called upon to influence Germany itself.' And Wagner was 'called on' to do so because his own activities were directly bound up with his country's fate. 'My own artistic ideal stands or falls with the salvation of Germany', he concluded, clearly aware of his role; 'without Germany's greatness my art is only a dream'.[14]

Even at the outset of his friendship with the king, then, Wagner had already conceived a role for the young ruler that the latter could never play without lapsing into puppetlike dependence on him. In July 1865, August Röckel, now released from prison, was apprised of Wagner's advantageous political position: the latter was now so close to his 'heart's true desire' that the 'political agitation' that continued to 'obsess' his old comrade-in-arms would inevitably be counterproductive. Instead of creating 'premature confusion', it was important, rather, to allow the situation to mature of its own accord.

The king, wrote Wagner conspiratorially, evidently unconcerned that his letters might be read by the censor, was so devoted to him, his love so 'infatuated', that he would not only satisfy his artistic expectations but with no further prompting would then strike out in the direction that Wagner desired. The longer people were left in the dark, especially at 'foreign courts', the easier it would be to manipulate Ludwig. 'May these people continue to regard him for a while solely as a "music enthusiast" – a "friend of the future" and so on – I like the idea of his wearing a mask like Brutus's: behind it, right behind it, something most curious will quietly grow and develop.'[15] At the mere idea that he had been cast in the role of a conspirator and of Caesar's murderer, the peace-loving Ludwig would no doubt have fallen from his throne. Yet he was much taken by the notion of going down in history as Germany's saviour. 'From here let's free our German land,' his poetic muse inspired him to write to Wagner from Nuremberg in 1866, 'and evil's futile work withstand.'[16]

For a dreamer like Ludwig, such a notion was bound to have a theatrical dimension to it, an action performed against the historical backdrop of *Die Meistersinger*, whereas for his mentor it was a matter of deadly seriousness. If fate had miraculously rescued him, why should it not have a further miracle in store, one that would invest the earlier miracle with its true meaning? Wagner lost no time in laying the foundations for the national revival that would inevitably follow on from his own rebirth. First, he invited Ludwig to pay off all his debts, before obtaining a princely annuity and thereafter the use of a villa in the Brienner Straße. In turn, Ludwig commissioned the completion of the *Ring* and also decided to build a festival theatre 'so that the performance of the *Ring* shall be perfect'. Here – uniquely in the history of the theatre – only 'the god-like works of my dear and only friend shall be staged'.

It was also planned to build a new and impressive thoroughfare leading past Ludwig's residence and his 'dear' friend's villa and up to the hill overlooking the Isar, from where the monumental theatre would gaze down on an awestruck city. In order to equip it with the right artists, it was decided to begin by establishing a Wagnerian school of music that would render superfluous the existing conservatory and its tone-deaf teaching staff. 'In our – Wagner's – organization', its director, Hans von Bülow, proudly declared, 'there will be no other ideas save Wagner's.'[17] As a foretaste of the new golden age of art, Ludwig ordered model performances of Wagner's older works from *Der fliegende Holländer* to *Lohengrin*, followed by the world premières of *Tristan und Isolde* and *Die Meistersinger*. In the composer's view, these last two productions set new standards for excellence. Munich had become a Wagnerian capital, even if it had never been asked if it wanted this honour.

There has been much speculation about the cost of this exercise. According to the latest calculations, it amounted to 248,200 florins during Wagner's first two years in Munich, not including the 40,000 florins that led to the famous incident on 20 October 1865, when Cosima went to the exchequer to collect the sum in question, only to receive it not in notes but for the most part in coins of the realm, requiring her to carry it away in sacks.[18] All biographers have had difficulty with these figures and with their conversion to present-day values. But comparisons with, for example, a haircut, which cost a florin, or with the annual salary of Wagner's servants, Franz and Anna Mrázek, who earned 600 florins between them, or with the purchase price of Wagner's well-situated and well-appointed villa, which was valued at 55,000 florins, make it easy to convert the figure. According to this calculation, Ludwig paid four million euros at today's prices to subsidize his early passion for Wagner. Half of this sum went on Wagner's private household, including servants, and the rest on promoting his music.

Of what use was all this expense, however, as long as Munich shut itself off from its new saviour? In an attempt to extend his control to other areas and ensure that all were aligned, Wagner invited to the city a whole colony of party activists who in concerts, lectures and press reports were to devote themselves to the radical cause that bore his name. Apart from musicians such as Bülow and Cornelius, Wagner fell back exclusively on colleagues who had rendered sterling service to the earlier revolution of 1849. Gottfried Semper, who had once helped to build barricades, designed the festival theatre; the incendiary August Röckel was initiated into the composer's secret plans; the former revolutionary Julius Fröbel was to become editor-in-chief of a new pro-Wagnerian newspaper; and the painter Friedrich Pecht, who, like the others, was a former member of the Dresden party of overthrow, was invited to paint the Master's portrait for the king, with a bust of the king in the background. While Wagner 'revealed the most fatherly tenderness' for his patron, it struck Pecht that he 'already imagined himself as the joint ruler of the whole kingdom of Bavaria'.[19]

Wagner soon summarized these ideas in a system that seemed to him to be politically practicable. Inasmuch as the new Messiah first had to understand the writings that were to prepare the way for him, Wagner dispensed with any dialectical fine-tuning and simply stressed their common ground. And inasmuch as his new lover-cum-secretary owed her view of the world to religious zealots, it seemed only courteous to stress this particular aspect. Otherwise, it is impossible to explain the fall in standards that we find in Wagner's writings from the summer of 1864. It is as though the visionary of the artwork of the future had abdicated in favour of the Wagner of *The Wibelungs*, with the result that an idealized view of the Middle Ages is back at the top of the agenda. Ludwig felt that Wagner was addressing him personally, and immediately gave instructions for these precious ideas to be shared with his ministers. Here, in black and white, was a view of politics that Ludwig could get his head round.

The most remarkable thing about Wagner's first educational pamphlet, which was completed in mid-July 1864, is its title: 'On State and Religion.' Only a short time previously, this would have seemed an anachronism, but now it was raised to the level of a dogma. Suffering humanity, he explained, needed to be consoled by faith, and having only recently broken free from the apron strings of the Church, should clearly return to the Church's bosom without delay. As the doctrinal expression of renunciation and voluntary martyrdom, religion, accompanied by Wagner's strains of redemption, should take its rightful place in the temple of the future state.

As in the days of the Vaterlandsverein, this state was to be ruled by a 'superhuman' idealized king, while democratic rights such as the freedom of the press – rights of which Wagner had always made ample use – now fell into disfavour. Proclaimed in the tone of a preacher, his change of attitude took place with dizzying speed. The freedom, creativity and redemptive force of sexual love that had once been central to Wagner's thinking were now replaced by 'the tonic that only true religion can grant', accompanied by art as 'the most ineffable vision of the most sacred revelation'. Wagner had wanted to satisfy everyone, from the autocratic Ludwig enamoured of his exceptional status to Liszt's bigot of a daughter. The result was all too predictable.

This otherworldly music of the spheres was followed by a more sombre assessment of the situation, initially intended for the king's eyes alone. In a secret document drawn up for Ludwig in the form of a diary dated 1865, Wagner evoked the fatal danger that threatened the German spirit as a result of foreign infiltration. Germany's princes traditionally supported only art imported from abroad, so that popular culture was thrown back on its own resources. In this way, the country's rulers had not only slept through the astonishing revival of the German spirit, they had also laid the foundations for its ruin. Italian frivolousness and French affectation had entered the land at the invitation of its princely courts, driving away the purely human element of German art. Popular rebellion at this act of usurpation had been misinterpreted as revolution and nipped in the bud.

Far worse, however, than this 'Latin' danger (Wagner uses the word 'welsch', originally meaning 'Romance' and later used derogatively of the French and Italians) was the 'curious phenomenon of the intrusive infiltration into the German character of the most alien of all elements'.[20] Once again, it was the Jews whom Wagner meant. Although they represented absolutely no threat to Ludwig's government, Wagner raised them to the level of the great adversary whose influence was all the more pernicious in that it was secretly burrowing away at the state from within. Just as in nature parasites appear 'as soon as there is something to batten on' and a 'dying body' is immediately 'found by worms that completely dissect and assimilate it', so Ludwig should regard the 'emergence of the Jews' in Germany as a symptom of dissolution.

Thanks to the patronage they enjoyed in the highest places, these intruders had seized control of 'every branch of public intellectual life', including banks and newspapers. They had infiltrated popular assemblies as 'political agitators' and had finally launched their assault on the very essence of all that was German: 'The quintessential thought of the German spirit, its most heartfelt musical emotion, is presented to the nation in the garbled guise of speculative Jewish jargon; Jewish playwrights and music-makers ply the theatre with their novelties, and Jewish reviewers offer a critique of our artistic achievements.' But art serves the nation as a mirror of its true nature, and so all that it can see is 'the repellent distortion of the German spirit', with 'one of the finest dispositions of the human race perhaps killed off for ever'. Ludwig must have rubbed his eyes in disbelief.

However much Wagner may have tried to bring the youth up to be a dragon killer, Ludwig continued to stand firm, at least on this one point, refusing to accept that every evil was caused by the Jews or that those evils would be removed if the Jews 'disappeared'. Or did he seriously share his mentor's conviction that as soon as the Jew was trained in the use of arms and integrated into the militia, he would be 'turned into a genuine German'? Did the essence of the German spirit really depend on the expert handling of firearms? High-minded as ever, Ludwig passed over Wagner's crude notion in silence.

But Wagner would not give up and for the rest of his life continued in his attempts to make the king change his mind. The dreamer proved resilient. In 1881, when Wagner resisted the idea of using the conductor Hermann Levi in Bayreuth at the head of Ludwig's Court Orchestra,[21] the king left Wagner in no doubt as to his strength of feeling: 'Nothing is more repugnant, nothing less edifying than such squabbles; people after all are brothers, in spite of all denominational differences'.[22]

Put in his place in this way, Wagner flew off the handle, emphatically insisting that he considered 'the Jewish race the born enemy of pure humanity and all that is noble in man. There is no doubt that we Germans especially will be destroyed by them, and I may well be the last remaining German who, as an artist, had known how to hold his ground in the face of a Jewry that is now all-powerful'. Ludwig, too, held his ground and somewhat mischievously noted that it was 'extremely strange' that the 'Jews who are so repugnant to you, my dear friend, remain attached to you with such tenacious devotion, a devotion that must often annoy you but which nothing will deter'.[23]

Perhaps Wagner would have realized just how ridiculous his crusade was if he had not recognized himself in Cosima's mirror. But he had found a sworn ally on this very point – a point that alienated most of his friends. Cosima did not need to be converted to anti-Semitism.[24] Through her, Wagner's weak point was dignified with a status it did not deserve, and an armchair discussion was raised to the level of a religious dogma celebrated on the high altar of his art. All the points that divided them faded into insignificance beside the great danger that now revealed itself to their horrified gaze.

Although permanent strangers to one another at the very deepest level, the two were never more united than in their hatred of the people who remained alien to them. Thanks to Cosima, Wagner's childhood fear became the principal article of faith in the Bayreuth creed. While the Master suspected the existence of a Jewish conspiracy at every turn, Cosima was haunted by the fear that her idol might be murdered by a Jew. Unlike Wagner, who sought open confrontation, the diplomatically disposed Cosima preferred a clandestine struggle: as she once admitted to Nietzsche, one should not disturb a 'wasps' nest' unnecessarily.

It was not only fear that bound Wagner and Cosima together. They also conspired together, refusing to give ground to their enemies. In the autumn of 1865, for example, Wagner began to encounter increasingly violent opposition from Ludwig's ministers, who refused to accept his insidious seizure of power, and so he demanded a cabinet reshuffle. When Ludwig baulked at the idea, Cosima fired off an anonymous newspaper article in support of Wagner's demand. Outraged by the transparent intrigue, the prime minister, accompanied by members of the royal family, the archbishop of Munich and even the king's personal physician, Max von Gietl, demanded to see Ludwig, prompting the latter to apply the emergency brakes: 'My resolve is firm – R. Wagner must leave Bavaria.'

There may in fact have been a more compelling reason for the step taken by Ludwig than the opinion of his entourage, an opinion that was normally of little concern to him. Unnoticed by the world, an exchange of notes had taken place at this time, calling into question the very basis of the relationship between the three correspondents. Acting in conspiratorial collusion, Wagner and Cosima had forced their 'godlike' friend into such a tight corner that his only option was to use force to break free.

In an attempt to persuade Ludwig to dismiss his then cabinet secretary Ludwig von Pfistermeister, Wagner had written to the king at the end of November, informing him about the 'shamelessness of the most indiscreet rumours' that owed their origins to 'confidants' and that were being peddled by 'the most degenerate press'.[25] Within days he claimed to have heard that there was a 'full-scale conspiracy against the honour' of his 'royal master', whose 'freedom' was under threat. Two days later, on 29 November 1865, Cosima's anonymous article appeared in the *Neueste Nachrichten*, whereupon she summoned up all her abilities for a masterstroke of psychological warfare, an achievement so brilliant and at the same time so perfidious that it is easy to explain why later writers have preferred to ignore it.

'We now discover', she wrote to Ludwig on 1 December in a state of real agitation, 'that an unprecedentedly brazen calumny concerning the sacred person of the king is circulating among the populace.' The report was so terrible, she went on, that she and the Master had burst into tears on hearing it. It related not to Ludwig's friendship with Wagner but concerned 'simply and solely Your dear Majesty alone'. The Master had been beside himself and was now hinting 'darkly' at 'haling the wretch before the courts, but he could not express his true feelings, and everyone says after all that it is a matter of indifference to certain people whether or not they swear false oaths'.[26]

Needless to say, Ludwig knew very well what Cosima and Wagner were alluding to: it could only be the secret that until then had involved him in no danger. But the situation would change if he were to be confronted with a sworn statement and were suddenly to find himself facing his accusers in court. If this were to happen, he would be in the greatest possible danger. It was this to which Cosima's note referred – not the suggestion that the king may have been 'mentally deranged', as claimed by the editor of her correspondence with him (an accusation that would scarcely have been the subject of an oath). Rather, it was Ludwig's notorious homosexuality that was the issue.

'The most sordid rumours were circulating in the city,' Carl Maria Cornelius writes of this period, citing as proof a letter penned by his father: 'Wagner is being accused of an unspeakable vice by his enemies here,' Peter Cornelius informed his wife. 'Undoubtedly without any reason, without any grounds. But who can vouch for the fact that my own intimacy with him won't be associated with this vice as people are not afraid of dragging a far loftier friendship through the mud of such suspicions?'[27]

In terms of his own private life, of course, Wagner had no reason to fear such reproaches, but the same could not be said of the king, whose fondness for stable lads can have been no secret to the composer. Cosima no doubt knew very well what she was not supposed to know about. Having been dragged by her through the mud of certain suspicions, Ludwig asked his godlike friend for an explanation. 'I beg you,' he wrote to Wagner on 3 December in a state of panic, 'tell me the calumny that is at work against me; I entreat you, my dear friend; oh, the black and vicious world, nothing is sacred to it!'[28]

Wagner kept Ludwig waiting three days for a reply, then proceeded to add to his agony of suspense. 'You demand from me certain information about the calumny that is directed at your august person and to which I have already alluded,' he calmly wrote. He was, he continued, more than willing to believe the urgency of the king's request, as they were dealing not just with a 'calumny' but with a regular 'crime' that demanded 'the immediate and severest punishment of the miscreant'. Unfortunately, he could not provide a name, as the regrettable circumstance that the king had refused to sanction his minister's 'immediate dismissal', as demanded by Wagner, 'obliges me to withhold the information, in spite of your wishes to the contrary'.[29]

Within hours of Ludwig's receipt of this infamous letter, Wagner had received a visit from Johann Lutz, a high-ranking court official, who, acting on

Ludwig's orders, instructed the composer to leave the country forthwith. According to Lutz, Wagner exploded in a 'torrent of abuse', including in his tirade references to 'sodomites' and 'shit snufflers'.[30]

It seems that Wagner soon tired of Paradise. The Wesendoncks' Asyl that had offered him ideal working conditions and proximity to his beloved lasted only a year; and the Munich idyll that provided him with not only ideal working conditions and the woman of his dreams but also a huge private fortune ended after only fourteen months.

Wagner had been fully aware from the outset that he would have to play by the rules. 'Fortunately,' he had told a friend a few days after receiving the royal invitation, 'I have reached a period in my life in which sufferings and experiences of every kind fill me only with a longing for peace and quiet. I am certain that I shall soon dispel people's suspicions and fears. Above all, I must take care not to do anything that might appear to be an abuse of the young king's temperament: and so I accept what he offers me and demand nothing in return.'[31]

In fact, the opposite was the case. Wagner had lived dangerously, and disaster promptly struck. As though intentionally, he flouted every rule, only to find himself once again rejected and disinherited. Cornelius reported emotionally on Wagner's departure from Munich in the grey mists of dawn, when the composer had seemed 'like a ghost, with pale, confused features, his long lank hair looking quite grey'.[32] His only companions, Cornelius added, were his servant Franz and his dog Pohl.

His later biographers, too, have clung to the story of an austere bachelor's existence that unfolded in exile in a two-storey country house near Geneva. Pohl in fact died in January at almost the same time as Minna in Dresden, filling Wagner with a sense of loss directed more at his faithful dog than his long-estranged wife. As a result, the months he spent at Les Artichauts have gone down in his life as a sad little interlude dominated by the picture of an exile robbed of his dearest friends by an act of the blackest betrayal.

But there is much evidence to support the notion that Wagner survived the disaster with aplomb. Writers evidently failed to notice an entry in the Annals, according to which Wagner invited his 'Vreneli' to Geneva to help him while the time away.[33] And in order to ensure that there was no shortage of creature comforts, he peremptorily ordered his villa in the Brienner Straße to be 'stripped of its splendours' and for all its 'silk hangings, carpets and net and satin curtains' to be sent on to Geneva.[34] Here he instructed a decorator to furnish the rooms in keeping with his detailed instructions. It is said that if he liked a particular arrangement he would 'go into ecstasies and jump into the air'. And it is even reported that he sent for Bertha Goldwag from Vienna in order for her to see to his rosettes.[35]

His dream of silks and satins had again come true, with everything smelling of a perfume that rose from bunches of artificial violets. Here he worked on *Die Meistersinger* at a desk commanding a panoramic view of Mont Blanc, drank beer shipped in from Munich and stroked his Newfoundland Russ, for whom Vreneli scrimped and saved. Apart from Vreneli, who functioned as his 'principal maidservant', Wagner also had at his disposal a chambermaid and a cook, who was presumably Franz Mrázek's other half. The cost of maintaining this household was naturally borne by Ludwig, who was already being plagued by serious scruples.

Meanwhile, Cosima, too, was sitting at home and moping. Her lover seemed perfectly able to get by without her. A meekly worded telegram has survived from 20 January 1866, in which she informs him that she would really 'like to set off to see you tomorrow; heart and reason advise me to do so. May I come?' Wagner's reply, sent by return of post, was a slap in the face: 'My friend is requested not to disturb me in my resolve.'[36] Two things may have precipitated Wagner's brusque retort, which he went on later that same day to tone down, for all that its thrust remained the same. First, he was afraid – and with good reason – that Cosima, acting in Ludwig's name, would attempt to persuade him to return to the fleshpots of Egypt. And secondly, her advent would have been tantamount to a 'terrorist attack', disrupting his newfound freedom. He wanted to enjoy the independence that had previously been the most important element in his life. Cared for by Vreneli and the Mrázeks, he managed for exactly three months without Cosima and the king, surviving with nonchalant ease.

During Wagner's absence, Cosima was able to slip into his role. She had now been elevated to the status of the king's foremost correspondent, and the sealed letters passed to and fro on an almost daily basis. Steeled by asceticism and conditioned by fate to adopt a tone of sublime seriousness, she admitted to the champion of formal etiquette that she was again becoming attracted to 'the Spanish idea of kingship, which most people now regard as so alien and even repulsive'. Later she even dreamt of an auto-da-fé on the Odeonsplatz in Munich, where women's fashions from France would be burnt.[37]

She saw herself as a saintly penitent and told Ludwig that she would 'lie before the crucifix' for half a day at a time, praying for her lover's return. Then, for a change, she would kneel 'before the little image of the Resurrection' and pray that 'the chalice of life may not be too bitter for the angelic' Ludwig.[38]

Cosima was fond of including excerpts from the Master's letters in her missives to the monarch, a fondness that finally put her in a position to gain control over both of them. Neither could reach the other except through her. She had triumphed in her defeat. And in her secret victory she even wished her lover dead, writing to her royal master on 18 January 1866 that the endless peregrinations of her 'friend', traipsing around Europe, had again filled her with the 'appalling wish that once stole into my soul in terrible times – namely, that he may close his weary eyes to the light that reveals only misery to him! O God, forgive me for writing this down!' Ludwig showed the sound common sense that Cosima seems to have lacked. 'No, no,' he replied, 'however hostilely disposed the world may be to Him, our only Friend, however much pain it still has to offer Him, let us not wish Him dead.'[39]

After all, he was still needed. Liszt's daughter, vacillating between calculation and hysteria, collected her lover from his austere Genevan exile in March, accompanying him not to Munich but to nearby Lucerne, where he signed a lease for the villa at Tribschen as early as the beginning of April. Within days the annual rental of 5,000 francs had arrived from the royal exchequer. The indispensable Vreneli was summoned, followed by Cosima (again pregnant with Wagner's child), although on this occasion she did not stay for long. Ludwig, too, would have liked to renounce his solemn duties and hurry into the arms of the man whose presence he had been denied for far too long, but Wagner strenuously advised him against doing so. Instead, Ludwig allowed himself the pleasure of turning up unannounced in Tribschen to celebrate the Master's fifty-third birthday, presenting himself as 'Walther von Stolzing' and bringing with him his man of the moment, Prince Paul von Thurn und Taxis.

Wagner was trapped. His three lives in one had caught up with him again, and now he discovered for himself the 'austerity' that Cosima associated with the 'Spanish kingship'. In 1867, when Ludwig was expecting Wagner to visit him in Munich to celebrate the composer's fifty-fourth birthday, the latter turned down the invitation on the grounds that he was busy completing *Die Meistersinger*. Cosima, who was in Munich at this time, intervened and surprisingly came down on the side of the capricious king, categorically 'demanding' Wagner's acquiescence. Although she later sought to draw a veil over this episode, it is clear that, as even the editor of the composer's correspondence with the king concedes, she tried to 'coerce Wagner into travelling to Munich'.

Such was the Master's status that he felt himself 'much offended' and telegraphed back: 'Too much of the saddest misunderstanding, the most wounding self-deceit. Impossible to heed such an invitation, health unsatisfactory too.' Cosima's reply left nothing to be desired in terms of Spanish rigour. 'Suggestions unacceptable. Come here and maintain Tribschen, otherwise total breakdown. Take note of my last wish, I shan't write again.'[40] Reprimanded like some obstinate child, Wagner duly travelled to Munich. *Die Meistersinger* could wait.

Wagner likewise came off badly in the next trial of strength, a record of which has survived in spite of attempts to censor it. By 1868 Cosima was expecting Wagner's third child, even though she was still officially known as Baroness von Bülow, and so the parties concerned considered a divorce, something that was impossible as long as Cosima was Catholic. As a result, we find an entry in Wagner's Annals for October 1868 referring to her 'promise to change her denomination', a promise bound up with her announcement that she first intended to consult her God-fearing father. Wagner thus saw that his life's fate was placed in the hands of his adversary and lapsed into a state of 'confusion and extreme concern'. In order to dissuade Cosima from undertaking her pilgrimage, he summoned her half-sister Claire Charnacé to Munich.

According to the Annals, Cosima was 'beside herself' at this. Claiming that Wagner had meddled in family business that was no concern of his, she sent him a telegram, informing him that his 'wilful interference' was 'making life intolerable' for her. Her 'most painful sense of anger' found further expression barely an hour later in a second telegram: 'Claire's arrival has had the most repugnant outcome for me, your refusal to let me go to Rome the saddest result.'[41] There was no greeting. While the mortified Cosima called off her trip to Rome and Liszt broke with the adulterous couple without a word, Wagner – surprisingly – sought refuge in the past, travelling to Leipzig to see his sister Ottilie Brockhaus and Rosalie's widowed husband Oswald Marbach. It was at the home of Hermann Brockhaus that on 8 November 1868 he encountered the future in the form of a student of philosophy by the name of Friedrich Nietzsche.

Wagner's own future was sealed by his return to Tribschen the following day. Cosima herself arrived a week later, this time for good. Already the mother of four daughters, she was now pregnant with Siegfried and fully determined never again to sever the bond between herself and Wagner. It was a bond that was to last until the end of his life. Just as she had literally taken charge of his life by writing down his memoirs,[42] so she now proceeded to record all his remarks in the form of a diary that she started in 1869. All that befell the Master or passed his lips first had to flow through her pen before it reached posterity.

At the same time, Cosima began to train the man she loved for the role in which she had always seen him. Wagner finally became the person he had always wanted to be, without ever having been able to imagine what he would have to forgo if this were to come about. Yet he had no choice in the matter. He loved Cosima as an ideal sister, worshipping her to distraction, just as he feared her as a strict mother, and so he submitted to a regime that both criticized him implacably and raised him, uncritically, to the status of an idol. Whether or not he felt comfortable with this in the longer term, the role fitted him like a glove.

Even so, he often felt a tightness round his heart: breathing difficulties began to plague him, and chest pains prevented him from sleeping. 'Yesterday R. had palpitations,' Cosima noted in her diary on 9 August 1872, 'which then found expression in a dream; he dreamt he was in a carriage with me and the children and, his attention drawn to it by Loldi, he saw a donkey tied up by a pool, sinking deeper and deeper into it, until it was left there floating and dead, without R. being able to go to its aid.'[43]

It was his own fate that the vision had shown him: while part of him drove merrily along in Cosima's children's carriage, the other part, firmly 'tied up' ever since he had fathered Isolde on Cosima, sank into the morass of marriage. In the language of his subconscious, this part was a donkey.

The Mastersingers

Ever since *Rienzi*, art had been synonymous with tragedy for Wagner. Only in the death of the hero and heroine could the idea of humanity be born, only through the sacrifice of individual finity could a consciousness of the whole be achieved in the form of love. The heart-rending realization that the price of loving union was death dominated his works from the outset, and it did so, moreover, with implacable logic. The basic situation that is reduced to its most succinct formulation in *Tristan und Isolde* left its mark on even his very last work, *Parsifal*. Wagner could never break free from the bitter sufferings caused by an existence that drew no distinction between real life and the stage.

Except once. When working on *Tannhäuser* in 1845 Wagner had again experienced for himself the torment suffered by his characters, but on completing the tragedy he had happily put behind him the 'consuming' anguish of identifying with its hero. Indeed, for the first time in his life he had even been afraid that his sudden death might prevent him from completing it, so that on writing the last note he had 'felt extremely happy, as though I had escaped from some mortal danger'.

While recovering in Marienbad, where his thoughts were already turning to the Swan Knight and Parzival, he hit on an idea for a comedy. 'Just as an Athenian tragedy was followed by a comic satyr play',[44] so the wounds caused by the

oppressive 'Wartburg Song Contest' were to be healed by laughter at its paro-
distic mirror image. Before turning to *Lohengrin* and thence to increasingly
sombre subjects, he had conceived an actual comedy. Had it been realized, his
work – and no doubt also what was later to be regarded as 'German art' – would
have taken a different course.

The tragedy of *Die Meistersinger* consisted in the fact that it was prevented
from becoming the 'comic opera' that it was originally intended to be. What
might have been possible in 1845, before various attempts to foment revolution
and find love had led to disaster, was no longer on the agenda when the project
was revived in 1861. It was no longer a laughing matter. Although Wagner hoped
that audiences would 'laugh at its strangely pedantic nonsense',[45] the emphasis
had shifted since Marienbad: a satire on the drolleries of art culminating in
the carefree triumph of love and of naturally inspired singing had been overshadowed by the renunciatory seriousness of the main character, just as this
latter element was to be overshadowed only a few years later by the work's new
political message.

In the twenty-three years that elapsed between this initial idea and the work's
first performance at Ludwig's Court Theatre in 1868, *Die Meistersinger* ceased
to be a satyr play and became a German national opera. The sly humour with
which Wagner had made fun not only of artists as a profession but also of their
aristocratic antagonist now served only to embellish more serious conflicts that
conceal their tragic character behind an artistic façade. The mockery that was
supposed to be directed at both the guild and the knight was now aimed solely
at the latter's adversary in order to expose him to the cruellest contempt.

Never did Wagner the dramatist and Wagner the tract writer come closer to
each other than in the final version of the opera. The irony of 1845, which could
be used to make fun of the artist's own seriousness of purpose, is replaced by
the prototype of 'German humour' that can express itself only at the expense of
others. The Mastersingers were originally to have been the butt of Wagner's
satire but in the end they are gloriously rehabilitated. The onstage Nuremberg-
ers burst into 'booming laughter' at their adversary, laughter that was later to
wipe the smile from the face of every listener.

Wagner discovered the source of his comedy not in Gervinus's history of
German literature, as he claims in his autobiography, but during his school-
days. In 1826 his sister Luise had appeared in a dramatized version of E. T. A.
Hoffmann's tale about the Mastersingers, *Meister Martin der Küfner und
seine Gesellen* ('Master Martin the Cooper and His Apprentices'), and three
years later Wagner himself encountered the same theme in Johann Ludwig
Deinhardstein's play *Hans Sachs*, a version also familiar to him from Lortzing's

opera of 1842. Both works dealt with a competition in 'Mastersinging', a specific historical form of singing that was bound to strike Wagner the composer as an involuntary parody of true art. Deinhardstein's play additionally presented its subject matter in a form acceptable to Wagner.

In the tradition of the Mastersingers – a tradition that developed hand in hand with the artisanal guilds – music was subjected to strict rules that had more to do with craftsmanship than art and that meant that the great model of Meistergesang, Minnesang, was transformed into its exact opposite: nature was forced to give way to arbitrary rules. As in their professional lives, tests were set to assess these craftsmen's skills and public competitions were held, comparable to the shooting contests of marksmen's guilds. A strict adherence to the rules and a spirit of competition were intended to foster the sanctity of art.

But with their 'entirely comical pedantry, with its stress on the poetics of the *Tabulatur*,' to quote Wagner's account of 1851, the worthy Mastersingers created the straitjacket that was to stifle their creativity. In particular, nature, which had been revealed through Minnesang, found that its wings were clipped by the rules of artisanal craftsmen. Where love had once reigned supreme, arbitrary laws were now making themselves felt on all sides. Instead of creativity and novelty, with their tendency to trigger sudden fears, the supreme aim of art was now seen as slavish imitation. Conjured up by artificial rituals, the sublime now wore the cap and bells of absurdity.

And it was at this point that Wagner took up the subject while taking the waters in Marienbad. The legendary model of the Wartburg Song Contest now reappeared in comic guise in the Mastersingers' competition. In order to qualify for this contest, the singer has to pass a test set by a 'Marker' whose only task is to judge all entries by the same standards. Every infringement of the rules is ruthlessly criticized by this artistic equivalent of a law enforcement officer, who in the process robs the individual of his natural delight in singing. Needless to say, this was entirely at one with the picture that Wagner had formed of his critics: he did not compose in ways that corresponded to their craftsmen's canon, and so he failed their test.

In short, the subject matter of *Die Meistersinger*, which Wagner tacitly took over from Deinhardstein, not only offered him a comic variant on his drama about medieval minnesingers, it also gave him an opportunity to give his enemies a sound, if ironical, drubbing. He recalled in his autobiography that while out walking he had been struck by a certain scene as the nub of his satyr play: having just rubbished a love song by an artistically inspired singer, the pedantic critic unexpectedly suffers the very same fate when he attempts to serenade the woman on whom he has set his sights. He had listed the candidate's 'errors' with loud chalk marks on his blackboard, but now his own mistakes are registered by hammer blows as the shoemaker, well versed in the ways of singing, strikes vigorously on his cobbler's last.

The result is a piece involving fantastically distorted mirror images. Just as the love-drunk minnesingers seem to return in the earthy and eccentric craftsmen, so Tannhäuser is reborn in the romantic and otherworldly knight. As impoverished as his forerunner, he hopes to find salvation in the old imperial splendours. In his ardent love of heroism and Minnesang, whose heyday lay centuries earlier, he is unrealistically drawn to the guild of Nuremberg burghers. Allowed to sing a trial song, he thinks his judges are a 'meeting of minnesingers':[46] he has reinvented the world on the strength of heroic legends. When planning to abduct his lover, as in a tale of medieval chivalry, he even thinks that he will have to defend her against a 'Hagen who slew Siegfried'. And when he hears a noise and 'clasps his hand to his sword with a tragic gesture', his sweetheart mocks him: 'What are you planning to do? Kill the night-watchman?'

Wagner's comedy was likewise concerned exclusively with love – and love, moreover, in its non-fatal variant. The youth who, like Don Quixote, confuses reality with his dream of it does not find the essence of poetry in Nuremberg. Rather, he discovers its true origins by falling in love with the very woman who, like Elisabeth in the Wartburg Song Contest, has been offered as prize in the forthcoming singing competition. His mind made up, he presents himself as a candidate. But the Marker who slates his trial song also lays claim to her, resulting in a uniquely Wagnerian confrontation, with two fantasts facing each other: the youth who is imbued with love but who understands reality as little as he does the rules of Nuremberg's poetics must confront a confirmed bachelor who has an outstanding grasp of the rules but who knows little about love and a young woman's inclinations.

Fortunately, there is still Hans Sachs, who on the one hand is one of the involuntarily comical 'rhyme smiths' resident on the banks of the River Pegnitz, while on the other feeling an attachment to a bygone world that the entire guild regards as its ideal. In the shoemaker-poet, the 'artistically creative spirit of the people' finds its ultimate expression, a spirit that Wagner describes in *The Wibelungs* and that preserves the lost imperial tradition. In Deinhardstein's play, it is in fact Emperor Maximilian who assumes the role of the protector of art that in Wagner's work is played by Hans Sachs. After 'Konrad's head had fallen in Naples to the blows of Charles of Anjou', wrote Wagner in his history of the Hohenstaufen emperors, 'the hoard of the Nibelungs vanished into the realm of poetry and the Idea'. While the world was ruled only by power and possessions, memory of the first German kingship was kept alive in the poetry of the people, where it was associated with the hope that the messianic Hohenstaufen emperor would one day return.

As Wagner makes plain, Sachs is well aware of the rules but is also clear about their limitations. And as soon as he hears the knight singing about the old imperial majesty, he recognizes the unspoilt heroic strength that is bound to remain a mystery to his anxious colleagues, with their obsessive mania for order. Just as Wotan, as the god of the law, prepares the way for Siegfried in his role as liberator of the world, so the cobbler initiates a plan that ensures that, like Mime, the hero's adversary will be caught in a trap of his own devising.

Sachs uses one of the knight's poems as a bait, and the Marker, believing it to be by the cobbler, 'unconsciously' steals the sheet of paper on which it is written.[47] But when he tries to sing it to his own tune at the competition, the text, in Wagner's words, 'is in striking contrast to its delivery'. The tender love lyric will not be forced into the straitjacket of the Mastersinger's artificial rules for composition, and so the audience breaks into mirth. In order to prove that the song is not by Sachs, as the furious Marker maintains, the knight is given a second chance. The words remain the same, but this time they seem to pour from the young man's heart, just as they once poured from the naturally talented Siegmund's. Love itself begins to sing, the populace bursts into enthusiastic acclaim, and the knight effortlessly wins the woman for whom he longs.

Having achieved his heart's desire, the youth is offered membership of the guild of Mastersingers, but to their dismay he declines, whereupon Sachs 'calms' their displeasure. 'Half ironically, half seriously', he sings in praise of true craftsmen's poetry, praise from which the duped Marker is not excluded. Even before the lovers have walked down the aisle together, the comedy ends with all the characters making their peace. Only some years later, at the time of the revolution, did Wagner add the cobbler's rather less comical final lines: 'Though the Holy German Empire were to vanish into mist, holy German art for us would still exist.'

But whose art did Wagner mean? That of the comically pedantic rhymesters who pursue their daily round as craftsmen in order to succumb to the rules of singing when they sign off work for the evening? Or the suspiciously Wagnerian love song of the knight who rides roughshod over all arbitrary rules in his attempt to help nature itself find expression? And where does the Marker stand in all this – this embodiment of the 'masterly but narrow-minded burghers' whom Sachs explicitly defends when he notes that he himself would have fared no better with his song? Does the critic have a part to play in Holy German Art or will he too dissolve into mist?

Wagner's subsequent reinterpretation of the comedy was to begin at this very point.

For all that Titian's *Assunta* was influential in persuading Wagner to return to *Die Meistersinger*, it did not in fact trigger his decision. On his completion of *Tristan und Isolde*, he found himself facing a situation similar to the one that he had known with *Tannhäuser*. A tragedy had played itself out, and like Elisabeth, Isolde/Mathilde had sunk into the ocean of love. Now life went on as though nothing had happened. This in itself was comical enough. Moreover, with the Paris staging of *Tannhäuser*, Minnesang had once again come to life for Wagner, a type of poetry whose sinful antithesis he had brought stylistically up to date, with the result that the Venusberg now sounded like Tristan and Isolde's night of love.

Only weeks after he visited Nuremberg with Blandine Ollivier in August 1861 and rekindled his memories of the past, his *Meistersinger* project, long since forgotten, resurfaced. In the meantime he had given the prose draft to Mathilde Wesendonck, but now the project seemed the ideal antidote to the melancholy strains of *Tristan und Isolde*. The happiness of cohabitation that had been denied the unhappy couple now beckoned to the knight and his artisanal bride. And whereas the earlier couple had had to forgo the joys of parenthood, children now seemed to be a matter of course. Thus Wagner, standing alongside the pregnant Mathilde in Venice, could well have seen Titian's transfigured Madonna as a mother whose ecstatic expression proclaimed new life. Since this 'conception', as Wagner expressed himself ambiguously in his autobiography, his 'old creative powers had been reawakened with elemental suddenness'.

But *Die Meistersinger* was no longer the ironical comedy that he had planned in Marienbad. Light-footed banter gives way to ponderous seriousness, the knight who had once raised only a smile for his quixotic behaviour now finding his rightful place in the pantheon of Wagnerian heroes. Even his name, Konrad, marks him out as a man who upholds tradition, and inasmuch as he had grown up in a 'desolate castle' as the 'last living representative of his race', we may surely see in him a descendant of Konradin, the last of the Hohenstaufens.

But this completely changes the situation. The witty arrangement whereby a nostalgic nobleman, searching for a bygone age, wanders into the very place where the craftsmen's guilds have sunk to new depths gives way to a far more serious, mythic narrative about the winning back of a hoard. In Konrad, the legendary Frederick – the 'glorious Siegfried' as Wagner apostrophized him in *The Wibelungs* – returns to repossess his stolen inheritance and, almost in passing, despatches the wormlike 'canker' that gnaws at the roots of the tree of German life.

The fact that Konrad's arrival in Nuremberg is a homecoming is made clear by the knight himself in his song in praise of his lover. As soon as he sets foot in the town, he sings, he is overcome by a déjà vu experience. On his first night in Nuremberg he falls asleep 'as though in his father's house', surrounded by the scent of the elder blossom.[48] In his dream he sees his mother, who, like Siegfried's Woodbird, takes him to his beloved, who then flutters on ahead of him as a little dove with a 'twig' in its beak, guiding him to her familiar parental home.

The meaning is clear: the little dove is the stage bride, who was soon to acquire the name of Eva, the mother of all humanity. Her green twig, a tiny branch of the 'tree of Paradise', holds out the promise of children to go with his victor's garland. But for Wagner, Eva also embodied the unavailable Mathilde Wesendonck. In Venice he had written down a 'wonderfully lovely dream' for her during the wildest excesses of his work on *Tristan*, a dream in which his erotic longing finds barely concealed expression: his arrival in her garden was heralded by a pair of doves flying in close formation. Mathilde had then proceeded to catch them with a 'large and bushy laurel wreath', then 'teasingly waved them to and fro'. 'I dreamt all this,' Wagner explained in a letter of March 1859, 'except that it was infinitely more beautiful and more exquisite than can ever be put into words.'[49] But in Konrad's love song, which he wrote a good two years later, Wagner tried to do just that, allowing his hero to experience vicariously 'the most rapturously beautiful of all life's dreams', which he himself was prevented from enjoying.

Not only the knight and his leman acquired mythic associations. In Marienbad, the Marker had been no more than a grotesque embodiment of Mastersong at its most extreme, but now he becomes the lovers' adversary, thwarting all that is good and availing himself of both cunning and baseness drawn from the arsenal of evil. As he involuntarily admits, his prime objective is 'the goldsmith's rich legacy'. He is determined to 'become his heir' and 'sue for the hand of his dear little daughter'. It is the very future that is at stake, and the crafty pedant seems to have the better hand.

He succeeds above all because he pays no heed to the community's rules. In 1845 he had pocketed his rival's prize song more by mistake, but now he steals it on purpose as theft and plagiarism are part of his nature. Unfortunately, he is unable to decipher the handwriting, so that his version of it tells not of a paradisal dream of love but of the nightmare of a poor devil who, driven from his homeland, suffers only unhappiness. 'Much pain I felt without rest', he laments, much like the wretched Ahasuerus, before breaking out at the end in the prescient cry: 'Ah! I'm burning down!'

Wagner's name for this evil-minded booby, who is left suffering only contempt, was Hanslich. He comes not from late medieval Nuremberg but from the present, his name an allusion to the Viennese critic Eduard Hanslick, in whom Wagner saw an embodiment of all the perfidiousness of his pedantic profession. Wagner had just set down the initial draft of his comedy during the summer of 1845 when Hanslick, still a student and an ardent admirer of his, first entered his life. But in 1847 the critic committed the error of comparing *Tannhäuser* with Meyerbeer's *Les Huguenots*, while at the same time making no secret of his admiration for Wagner's Jewish rival.

Wagner's response – namely, that he 'found everything associated with the term Meyerbeer repulsive'[50] – left Hanslick unimpressed, with the result that Wagner thereafter branded the respected music theorist a lickspittle of his great adversary, including him under the heading of 'musical Jewry' in 1869 and in all seriousness claiming that his study *On the Beautiful in Music* had 'raised musical Jewish beauty to the level of a full-scale dogma'.[51] Hanslick's mother, it should be added, was Jewish, and for Wagner that said it all.

And so the Nuremberg town clerk – the German 'Schreiber' can mean any sort of writer – took on not only the features of the hated critic but also those of the no less hated Meyerbeer. On the one hand he attempts to use strict rules to prevent nature from manifesting itself, and on the other he steals the fruits of nature in order to pass them off as his own in a distorted and mutilated form. And this is true not only of the aesthetic field in which the comedy was originally set. Since reading Hegel and Feuerbach, Wagner had come to believe that Judaism was distinguished from the Christian faith by dint of the fact that it stifled love through laws, placed egoism above the community and selfishly enriched itself by battening on the latter's possessions. This is precisely what the Marker Veit Hanslich expresses, and Wagner, who was in no mood for joking, even placed this idea in his mouth at the end.

Anxious that the blow should strike home, Wagner used the same trick as Hans Sachs and set his libretto as a bait, announcing that on 23 November 1862 he would read his new poem at the home of his friend Josef Standhartner. Hanslick, too, was invited. Needless to say, Wagner's Viennese listeners had no inkling that one of their number – a prominent member of the Opera's advisory council, to boot – was being made to look ridiculous by the composer. Exposed as a pedant and a plagiarist, Hanslick found himself trapped and had to remain till the bitter end. As Wagner recalled in *My Life*, Hanslick became 'increasingly pale and ill-humoured', before finally taking his leave 'with an obviously piqued tone of voice' as though 'the whole libretto had been a pasquinade directed at him'.[52] Evidently he had no sense of humour either.

In the event Hanslick was spared his namesake's worst indignity, for it was only at the very last moment, by which time the Marker was called Sixtus Beckmesser and Wagner could provide him with a maxim that rhymed with his name ('Keiner besser', meaning 'None better'), that Wagner revealed his true nature. In January 1867, almost five years after the libretto was printed, Hanslick was made to pronounce his own symbolic death sentence in the final version of the garbled Prize Song.

It is clear from the resplendent C major of the opening bars of the overture that we are dealing not with a comedy but with an apotheotic vision. The powerfully strutting motif associated with the guild of Mastersingers constitutes the self-assured signal of a new world whose radiant rebirth follows on from the victory of chivalric love poetry over the pedant's bleating, with a bombastic *fortissimo* to underline the message of a new faith in which there is no longer any room for the subtleties of irony.

The audience finds itself transported, appropriately enough, to a church, where the congregation sings an emotional hymn in praise of John the Baptist, who prepared the way for our Saviour just as surely as Hans Sachs is to do for the proud knight, who is now called Walther von Stolzing. But between the lines of the pseudo-archaic chorale, with its references to baptism, self-sacrifice and salvation, we hear a silent dialogue between two lovers empathizingly illustrated by cello and viola.

By means of glances and gestures, Walther asks his intended a question that is answered unmistakably with a beatific smile. The question mark of the 'Tristan' chord is replaced by a radiant exclamation mark. In this way Wagner again depicts the very beginning of all existence, a moment that coincides with the glance of loving recognition in the other person's eye. All that the old religion sought to express with its antiquated sacraments, Wagner gives us to understand, takes place as a living reality in the affection between two individuals. In the merging of 'I' and 'you' they become a saviour for one another.

Like Senta and the Dutchman, Eva first saw her Walther in a picture, in this case that of the biblical hero David – not, she insists, the bearded king of the Jews who is emblazoned on the sign of the Mastersingers' guild but Dürer's flaxen-haired youth who slew his adversary Goliath. As soon as she sets eyes on Walther, she is lost: 'It was this that caused me such sudden torment,' she exclaims in her astonishment. The famous glance has sparked a response, something immediately noticed by the suspicious Beckmesser, just as it had been by Hunding in his forest hut: 'What does he want here? How his eyes laugh!'

The lovers have found each other very quickly, but the road to their union is strewn with thorns. For Eva – evidently having no further say in the matter – has been chosen by her father as first prize in a singing competition, forcing her lover to make some awkward concessions. Just as Tannhäuser has to face his rivals with Elisabeth's love before his eyes, so Walther has to submit to the Trial Song before he can qualify to take part in the competition itself. Adopting the tone of the minnesingers, he sings freely and frankly of the call of spring that echoes throughout the forest, awakening new life that answers him in its jubilation. But Walther's 'sweet spring song' produces only the chalk marks of the Marker, who with his ill-humoured sighs makes it plain that nature's awakening is not in the rule book.

But the Marker and his hostility to all living forms still have a place in Walther's song. As in the Grimms' fairytale of 'The Jew in the Thornbush', Beckmesser is transported into a 'quickset hedge' where, as the 'wintery foe of spring', he 'lies in wait and listens for ways of spoiling this joyful singing'. Exactly the same is true of the fairytale, where an old Jew is incapable of listening to a lark warbling without selfishly wanting to own it: 'I'd give anything to have it.' And so the hero of the story shoots down the bird from the tree. But when the old man crawls into the hedge to claim his dead booty, the hero decides to punish him for his greed and, taking out a magic violin, makes him dance in the midst of the thorns. Having further been charged with theft, the old man, his clothes in shreds, ends up on the gallows. In order to ensure that the punchline is not lost on his audience, Wagner describes winter ensconsed within the hedge as 'Grimm-bewehrt'. The past participle 'bewehrt' means 'armed with', while 'Grimm' is both the word for 'fury' and the name of the fairytale's compilers: only when 'armed' with the Grimms' narrative can listeners grasp Walther's allusion.[53]

As was only to be predicted, the knight fails the test, but he continues undaunted with his flight of poetic fancy. On the spot where the dead songbird had fallen, he now sees a sinister owl flying out of the thicket, its screeching waking a whole chorus of hoarse ravens, who are evidently the Mastersingers in metaphorical form. And it is clear from one of his stage directions that Wagner saw in the allegorical night bird a further reference to the Marker, who, he insisted, should declaim the text in an 'impassioned, screeching tone of voice'. There should be 'little question' of actual 'singing'.[54]

These sombre associations of the Wolf's Glen are underscored by the Nibelung-like 'nightly horde' of birds of prey but are then followed in Walther's Spring Song by a radiant vision of a phoenix. On a golden pair of wings it soars aloft as a reborn singer triumphing over death. By this, Walther means himself, of course: 'His heart swells with sweet anguish', he rejoices like Wieland; 'wings spring from his need, he soars upwards on his bold course, to fly through the air from the tomb of the cities'. But first he has to free his bride.

Without Master Sachs he could no more succeed in this than Siegfried could wake Brünnhilde without Wotan. Wagner was conscious of this parallel and even told Ludwig that the heroes of *Die Meistersinger* had 'turned up' to ensure that Wotan and Siegfried should 'not perish'.[55] (Wagner had temporarily suspended work on the *Ring*.) And so the shoemaker exerts his silent, godlike influence, instructing Walther in the ways of art and life and giving the evil Marker a lesson in how to criticize art before finally taking him to task.

Things are not so easy where Eva is concerned, because Sachs has lost his heart to her, just as Wotan had once done to his valkyrie: and neither can take the woman as his wife. The result is renunciation and resignation, two qualities that seem to chime with Wagner's weakness for Schopenhauer. Indeed, Wagner himself spoke of the 'lament of a man imbued with the spirit of renunciation'.[56] But the renunciation that speaks from Sachs's melancholy words is no such thing. If the girl had once fallen in love with her fatherly neighbour, there can never be any question of serious affection. And once the sparks start to fly between Walther and Eva, the decision has already been taken.

In short, Sachs's 'renunciation' has nothing to do with love, which is now a lost cause, and everything to do with marriage. Now that Walther has failed the test and is out of the running, Sachs could easily defeat Beckmesser in the song contest and thus win Eva's hand. But like Wotan he has come to recognize the superior force of love, and so he forgoes the contemptible victory that is offered him by the law and instead takes Walther's part. Sachs's merit lies in his overcoming not love but the law. As he tells his neighbour's daughter, he has no wish to share the same fate as Isolde's legal husband, King Marke. But this has less to do with renunciation than with shrewdness, as he knows very well.

Like Wotan, Sachs now proves himself a philosopher, imperceptibly interfering in the action in order to help love on its way – the very love that he himself is prevented from enjoying. On the eve of the competition, Beckmesser serenades Eva, allowing Sachs to expose him as a hypocrite who judges others by rules that he himself does not obey. After all, the Marker's arrogant presumption in attempting to obtain love by means of calculation causes the whole system to break down. By dint of his meddling, he sparks a riot that affects the entire town, showing that the middle-class idyll is a mere illusion: the apparent harmony of these petit-bourgeois burghers is transformed into an orgy of violence for no apparent reason.

The next morning, the cobbler consults his books of wisdom in order to find an explanation, an explanation that suggests he has been reading Schopenhauer's *The World as Will and Representation*: the 'Wahn' – folly or delusion – that he blames for the riot is the exact equivalent of Schopenhauer's 'will', which, in its search for gratification, causes more and more suffering. Although it can be temporarily appeased, notably by 'Nuremberg's peacefully faithful customs', the situation remains explosive because this folly is ultimately untameable, for all the laws that control it. As Sachs notes, echoing Schopenhauer, folly 'acquires new strength while it sleeps'. A volcano seethes beneath the glossy surface.

On this occasion it is Beckmesser who causes the explosion. As an elderly fop in search of a wife, he puts his egoism before nature and in doing so wakens the dormant selfishness in others. In turn this selfishness finds expression in hatred of 'others'. In Sachs's metaphorical language, a 'glow-worm' fails to find its mate (this can refer only to the thwarted love of Walther and Eva), and so the 'goblin' – as he calls Schopenhauer's 'genius of the species' – seeks revenge. An argument breaks out, leading to a mass riot that almost ends in murder and manslaughter. The Nightwatchman had earlier warned that 'no evil spirit should ensnare your souls', and following his sound beating, Sachs tells the Marker that his 'wedding haunted people'. What he does not say is that because his wedding would have been forced on the bride, it was immoral. In short, the 'evil spirit' is Beckmesser. Having recognized this, Sachs resolves to put a spoke in his wheel.

As a result, Sachs has to go beyond Schopenhauer. Resignation is not for him. Just as such resignation is merely a concession to reality, so Schopenhauer's 'pessimistic' diagnosis of existence is no more than the starting point of Sachs's active intervention. The shoemaker indulges in a spot of therapy. After all, the blind will is not creation's last word: rather, it is a question, in Sachs's words, of 'subtly guiding folly'. Then the sick would grow healthy, and evil would yield to salvation. Herein lies the shoemaker's 'more noble work'.

And it is love that provides a way out of the dilemma created by folly. For it is love that is concealed within the blind lust that turns existence into a Schopenhauerian slaughterhouse. It was the desire of the dark ground for the divine light that allowed it to be misled by selfishness. Just as Alberich's fist closed round the Rhinegold, so nature became concentrated in the gravity of lightless matter that drew everything into its sway. While this law was repeated in countless acts of individual egoism among humanity, the original force that yearned for the light and, as it did so, created new forms was revealed in love. From the night of unredeemed desire there arose the archetypal image of existence as a dreamlike vision of the divine that drew near the darkness in order to bring redemption.

Chaos is unleashed in Nuremberg, but during the night that follows Walther von Stolzing dreams a metaphysical dream. Born of his longing for the lover who has been snatched away from him, it takes the form of an image that depicts the rise of creation and the light-filled dawn of eternity. A similar vision had appeared at the start of *Das Rheingold,* and now – five years after the completion of the poem – Wagner used it to replace Walther's original Prize Song about his dream of doves, with its personal wish fulfilment of the knight's acquiring a sprig of laurel from his lover. Instead, Wagner has his hero enter a transformed world embodied in an equally transformed lover.

Walther recounts his dream to his mentor and Sachs seizes his chance: the revelation vouchsafed to the knight will prove who really deserves the bride and who does not. For in itself the dream constitutes a riddle that has to be solved, a mystery that demands to be interpreted. If the competition is about true art, then the victor will be the man who can interpret the oneiric vision of the first creation. For art, as Sachs explains, is synonymous with 'the interpretation of dreams'.

But to interpret means to find oneself in the other person. He who recognizes himself in the divine light becomes a creator himself. He who understands love's message of the world's dawn is himself a part of that love. It is no longer a question, as it was in the *Ring,* of 'he who never knew the meaning of fear' but simply of proving who is capable of experiencing love for himself. The place once occupied by Wotan is now taken by John the Baptist, who, as we know, was called 'Hans' on the Pegnitz. Sachs will 'subtly guide folly' and in that way bring light to the universal darkness.

As Sachs is quick to realize, Walther's dream has led him to the Garden of Eden – nature before the Fall – where the tree of life grows. In the midst of its radiant abundance, the knight sees a woman who hands him the choice fruit of the tree, the taste of which confers immortality. Beyond good and evil (symbolized by a different tree) he may 'drink joy from her eyes', and to the murmur of the Castalian spring he may recognize their transfigured love in the nightly dance of the stars. The spring water is a source of poetic inspiration for him, reuniting the earthly love and divine creativity that had been divided since the Fall. Although he is not aware of it, this is Walther's new gospel, and Sachs is to prove its prophet.

And its baptist, too. In the song about Paradise, Sachs recognizes a newborn child that is sprung from Walther's love of Eva and that he christens the 'Blessed Morning Dream Interpretation Tune'. In this tune the lovers 'recognize' themselves. It is no accident that they find themselves together in the cobbler's workshop. As Eva admits, it is Walther's song that has 'succeeded in interpreting and subduing her heart's sweet burden', just as the knight assures her in the same breath that her love for him has helped him 'to interpret and subdue his heart's sweet burden'. Both are united in their longing, and the child of their union comes into the world as a work of art.

This is the work that Wagner had once described as 'the artwork of the future', a work in which the masculine word plunges into the sea of feminine music. The pedantic rules of art have now given way to the resounding self-knowledge of liberated humanity, while even the torment of folly that Sachs has bewailed finally yields to love's yearning, a longing that he now sets out to assuage. While the baptist Sachs descends, as it were, into the Jordan, the world's new morning dawns and the people sing the solemn chorale that the historical Hans Sachs had once written in honour of Luther: 'Awake, the dawn is drawing near; I hear a blissful nightingale singing in the green grove.' Ever since he rose as a phoenix from the thornbush, this songbird has been Walther von Stolzing.

Love, then, has triumphed even before the competition has got under way. Now it is a question of getting rid of the adversary, the arrogant wooer who is attempting to usurp another's inheritance. It seems a mere formality to have the Marker fail to bring off Walther's song about Paradise, but Wagner was not yet finished with Beckmesser. After the Midsummer Eve riot, he presents him as a descendent of the thieving Nibelungs. Like the dwarfish Mime limping from his wounds, Beckmesser hobbles and twitches, snivellingly rubbing his back before finally stealing the poem that Sachs has written down and unthinkingly left on his desk. Beckmesser is a nightmare-like figure. The more clearly Wagner brings out the messianic features of the knight, the more satanic his antagonist becomes. The 'evil spirit' that the Nightwatchman had warned against finally gains access to the action.

Through his theft of the true work of art, Beckmesser reveals himself as Meyerbeer's kinsman. It was to be made clear to audiences that he understands nothing of such a work but always 'distorts' what is beautiful. Whereas Mime forfeited his head in his battle of wits with Wotan, Beckmesser loses his even before he has sung the first word, so incapable is he of understanding what he reads. The glad tidings of love remain lost on him. The Marker's blindness to art thus exemplies his race's hostility to the gospel preached by the 'Wach' auf' chorus.

But his singing not only distorts and disfigures art, reducing it to nonsense, it also reveals the goals that the suitor is pursuing. Just as Siegfried sees through

Mime's intentions when nature acts as his mentor, so Beckmesser's true nature is revealed to the townsfolk through his garbled delivery. When juxtaposed with the revelation of love, this nature emerges as something unnatural, something that leads inevitably to its own supersession. Irreconcilable contradictions such as 'horrid and fine' and 'won and at the same time dissolved' and his paradoxical admission that he is 'secretly afraid because things are going to get lively here' demonstrate his inner turmoil and hence his worthlessness as an individual. The blind folly that he embodies vanishes like darkness before the light. Ahasuerus is destroyed on Nuremberg's noisy Festival Meadow, in the 'thunderous unanimity of all the voices'.[57]

Whereas Walther had felt only astonishment on contemplating the 'morning radiance' ('Morgenlich leuchtend') of the first creation whose garden invited him 'to be its guest', Beckmesser can see only himself: 'Tomorrow I shine' ('Morgen ich leuchte'), he sings, already looking forward to Eva's inheritance and not even denying the uses to which this Garden of Eden may be put: 'Into the garden I invited fatted calves and swine', he sings in the initial version of this scene.[58] In the event this overemphatic reference to the sort of Jewish livestock dealers who were still exercising Wagner's thoughts in Bayreuth was replaced by a much more harmless line, 'In the garden I invited, horrid and fine'. But the very next strophe contains an unmistakable allusion to the Marker's true nature: 'If I live passably in the same space, fetch money and fruit' – in short, he seeks to harm the community and increase his own wealth.

This coexistence with Christians brought certain advantages, it is true, but the Marker's theft is immediately punished. If he trembles 'out of fear of wood and sword', as one of the earlier variants reads,[59] it is because his end is already preordained. Whereas Walther's poem had told of the tree of life responding to the lover's 'desire with its fair splendour' ('mit holdem Prangen dem Verlangen'), the anxious Beckmesser can read only: 'The aspirant fetches me from the pillory – scarcely on airy path I hang from the tree' ('Mich holt am Pranger der Verlanger – auf luft'ger Steige kaum – häng' ich am Baum'). Beckmesser is thus exposed as the Jew in the Thornbush, and in accordance with his worst nightmare, he is placed in the pillory before being strung up. His Nuremberg listeners, clearly armed with Grimm, can only agree with him, exclaiming, as they do: 'He'll soon hang from the gallows.'

The usurper storms away as 'furious' as the Grimms' Rumpelstiltskin, leaving the field clear for the Song of Songs to love. If Beckmesser had failed to understand the gospel, Walther now proves himself a master of exegesis. Once again he is borne aloft by the Holy Spirit, the wellspring of his inspiration flows freely, and over the poem that had first come to him in a dream there arises its inspired interpretation,[60] with 'the earth's loveliest image' now appearing to him in hallowed form as a divine Muse, the biblical Eve of the Garden of Eden merged with the Hellenic goddess of art from Mount Parnassus. Earthly love is again united with mental creativity, and everything seems as glorious as on the very first day of creation.

In this way Wagner has achieved the aim that all his tragic couples had failed to achieve from the time of *Rienzi*: divine love finally comes into its own, the error into which world history had sunk has achieved a state of self-consciousness, and there is no longer anything in the way of a healthy propagation of the species. True, Wagner has moved some considerable distance away from the comedy that he had once envisaged. But instead he has enabled the archetypal tragedy of his art to find fairytale expression. The final tableau that he had planned in Marienbad, with Sachs's defence of the Masters and the bridal procession taking up its position, now proved superfluous, and Wagner decided to end his opera at this point.

But now something extraordinary happened, something so exceptional that most writers on Wagner have preferred to pass over it without comment. What happened next illustrates not only the uncertainty that Wagner regularly felt on completing a work but also the influence that his lover Cosima already exercised over him, for it was at her request that he altered something that he already thought was good.

Writing to the twenty-one-year-old king of Bavaria in January 1867, the twenty-nine-year-old Cosima explained that she and Wagner had spent virtually the whole day discussing the end of the work. Whereas the composer thought that 'the drama is actually over with Walther's poem and that Sachs's great speech is irrelevant' – it was 'the poet's address to the audience' and so he was thinking of 'omitting' it – Cosima argued the opposite. 'I pulled such a pitiful face', she told Ludwig, that Wagner 'got no rest all night'. He 'wrote the strophe out, deleted what I'd indicated, and sketched the music to it in pencil'.[61] And she enclosed proof of her statement with the letter.

The change that she had coerced from Wagner had repercussions that no one could have predicted that winter in Tribschen, for the message that Wagner normally left unspoken in his works now emerged with total clarity. More seriously, what we find here is not the glad tidings that Walther had preached at the end of his Prize Song. Instead of the philosophy of universal love reconciling all contradictions, we now find a political speech on a point of principle that drives a coach and horses through that philosophy. We are no longer dealing with the union of 'I' and 'you' that will put an end to the history of human suffering but with the German Empire and its doughty representative, the burgher classes.

Prior to this, Wagner had been in correspondence with the politician Constantin Frantz, who was an advocate of German unity and who by his own admission had enjoyed reading *Opera and Drama*. Only the saintly Antigone's self-sacrifice and the ensuing destruction of the state had filled him with misgivings. For in Frantz's view the state was now the Reich, the supreme embodiment of all things German, 'a bond linking heaven and earth'. Wagner promptly inscribed the second edition of *Opera and Drama* to the nationalist thinker and even allowed Frantz to advise him on the poem of *Die Meistersinger*. 'It is important that the Empire should be seen in the background', Frantz told him with no trace of any false modesty.[62]

This advice may have played a part when Wagner changed the ending of the opera and hence altered its underlying thrust. Another reason may be sought in the patron whom Cosima assiduously allowed to look behind the scenes. The mythic role played by Walther in *Die Meistersinger* suited Ludwig down to the ground, allowing Wagner himself to assume the part of Hans Sachs. The young monarch was more than happy to see himself proclaimed on the operatic stage as Germany's next prince of peace, especially if a man of Wagner's stature played the part of his herald. When he turned up at Tribschen on the composer's birthday in 1866, he was already dressed for the part.

As for the message proclaimed by the impassioned knight, things were not quite so straightforward. After all, the sexual congress of man and wife was hardly for Ludwig, and an Eve or Eva was the last thing he wanted from Paradise, for all that Eva was the name that he gave to Sophie of Bavaria, to whom he was briefly engaged. By contrast, Sachs's powerful sermon on the Empire was bound to echo his own sentiments, hence Cosima's haste to spread the glad tidings. She was therefore all the more annoyed when at the first performance in 1868 the king invited the composer into his box but excluded the woman who had pulled the strings. She was never to forgive him this snub.

For Wagner's royal disciple, this change to the end of *Die Meistersinger* cannot have come as a surprise, for ever since the Master had entered Ludwig's life and begun to exert a formative influence on it, the political tracts that Wagner had penned for his benefit had contained ample evidence of the opera's underlying ideas on the future of the Empire. In the diary that he wrote for the king, he described how 'the German princes' had 'forgotten how to understand the German folk and its true spirit', a failing that he saw as the 'principal danger' then facing the country.[63]

Instead of natural German geniuses like Walther, these princes sponsored only foreign affectations. Above all, however, they encouraged the infiltration of 'that most alien of all elements' that is embodied in the figure of Beckmesser.

Wagner's attempts to indoctrinate the king with regard to the Jews may have proved futile, but this did not prevent him from giving them a very real presence in the person of the Marker. Above all, Wagner wrote quite openly, the German artist's 'most heartfelt musical emotion' was being 'presented to the people in the garbled guise of speculative Jewish jargon'. This is precisely what happens on the Festival Meadow, where Beckmesser's garbling of the true work of art is synonymous with its speculative misreading.

Even the positive hero Walther turns up in Wagner's homework for Ludwig. Unlike the thieving Jew, Ludwig could read in Wagner's diary jottings of 1865, the German artist would 'spend the long winter months sitting by the warming hearth fire' in his castle, recalling 'ancestral memories'.[64] This is precisely what Walther reports doing in the opera, where he remembers sitting 'at the silent hearth in wintertime' and learning the art of singing from 'an ancient book, bequeathed to me by my forebear'. As a 'German youth', Wagner wrote in *German Art and German Politics,* he was called upon 'to cast aside the constraint of rules',[65] a call that Ludwig was happy to heed, though not in the way Wagner was hoping for.

In short, Cosima's suggestion for changing the ending reflected not only the role in which Wagner had cast the king but also the whole idea of a German Empire, and as such it found a willing listener in Wagner. All that he had expressed in his political manuals from 1864 onwards was now to be placed in the mouth of the popular poet Hans Sachs and proclaimed from the lofty heights of the stage. True art, it would be made clear, was preserved not by anarchical natural geniuses like Wagner but by the mastercraftsmen who cultivated it 'in their own way' – namely, in a manner that was 'just right' and certainly preferable to that of the princes who had long withdrawn their support from it. Abandoned by the aristocracy 'in the stress of evil years', it had remained 'German and true' thanks to the Mastersingers.

In this way Wagner distanced himself from Walther's new gospel, a gospel that the guildmasters Kothner, Pogner, Volz and Nachtigall regarded as 'bold and strange', yet he had still remained on familiar ground: ever since *The Wibelungs,* the Barbarossa tradition had lived on silently among the people, just as the common people, at least from the time of *The Artwork of the Future,* had become the epitome of common need and hence the expression of the communal work of art in whose mirror they would recognize themselves once again.

But the ideas that Wagner's Sachs expresses in his final exhortation are redolent less of the age of the Hohenstaufen emperors than of contemporary Germany, with its imperial aspirations. 'Beware!' warns Sachs. 'We are threatened by evil tricks.' Listeners familiar with the poem of the *Ring* may have been reminded of Alberich's threat: 'Beware of the army of night.' But for the work's principal addressee, King Ludwig, the warning of 'false foreign majesty', 'foreign mists' and 'foreign vanities' was intended to relate unambiguously to the destruction of German culture by the French and the Jews. Hence, in turn, Wagner's fear of the Beckmesserian Babel that meant that 'soon princes will no longer understand their own people'.

Then comes the sentence about the Holy German Empire that will survive in holy German art even if the Empire were to dissolve in foreign mist. But what is the art that is meant here? The union of 'Parnassus and Paradise' that Walther had glimpsed in his vision? Or the rules and regulations of the 'German Masters' whom Sachs has just hymned? Since no one has ever asked this question, it has always been tacitly assumed that holy German art is the art that we have just seen paraded before us – namely, Wagner's *Die Meistersinger von Nürnberg*.

This is certainly how contemporaries responded to it, as an apotheosis of the German middle classes, composed by a reformed enfant terrible. A work conceived as a satyr play pillorying German solemnity became a German national opera whose 'Wach' auf' chorus was to awaken very different choruses in the course of the following century. The piece that was designed as a comedy had become a German tragedy.

The Case of Nietzsche

Die Meistersinger may have lost its way as a comedy, but a comedy was still staged – not in the theatre, but in real life. The new piece had already been put into rehearsal in Munich, before being performed to perfection in Tribschen and later in Bayreuth. A three-hander, it was called *A Lesson in Subjugation*,[66] and was about a somewhat egocentric youth who is introduced into the service of an exalted thinker by a cunning lady of the court, who manipulates servant and master in so sophisticated a manner that they both end up in her power.

The whole point of the play was that neither of them should notice what was happening, for the youth, a highly gifted variant of the Knight of La Mancha, and the thinker, who saw himself as a latterday Aeschylus, were both so preoccupied with their roles that they lost all sense of reality. In this they differed from the female intriguer, who was more than capable of distinguishing between playfulness and earnestness and who set things up in such a way that the youth thought of himself as a kind of Walther von Stolzing for whom the older man prepared the way, just like Hans Sachs. When it dawned on the would-be hero that he was in fact being trained as a servant, he stepped out of his role and in the eyes of both the Master and his lady turned into Beckmesser instead. And as such he was hounded out.

And it was with *Die Meistersinger* that the comedy began. In 1868, the year of the opera's first performance, Friedrich Nietzsche – at that date a model student in Leipzig – heard the overture and felt intoxicated by the piece, which brought a 'lasting feeling of otherworldliness' to his highly strung nature. His feeling was increased when he was introduced to the composer who, fleeing from Cosima's nagging, was staying with his brother-in-law Hermann Brockhaus in Leipzig. The twenty-four-year-old Nietzsche attracted attention with his impassioned performance on the piano of Walther's Prize Song, whereupon the fifty-five-year-old composer repaid the compliment with a one-man show featuring highlights from his new opera, 'imitating all the characters with total self-abandon. He is', Nietzsche explained to his friend Erwin Rohde, 'an incredibly lively and impassioned man, who speaks very quickly, is very witty and certainly livens up a very private party of this kind.'[67]

By the time the two men met again six months later, their roles had radically changed. Wagner had been shackled by Cosima to his Tribschen court with their four children and six servants, where, as an incommensurable thinker, he was discouraged from playing his favourite roles as a Saxon joker and vocal impersonator. Nietzsche meanwhile had harvested the fruits of his exceptional talent and settled in Basel as a precocious professor of classical philology. His problem consisted in the fact that more and more miracles of industry and productivity were expected of him, an expectation that his delicate health was simply incapable of meeting. But he hoped to solve this problem with Wagner's help.

Playing the part of the university professor with an old-fashioned top hat made of felt, he arrived at Tribschen in May 1869 and pressed his newly printed visitor's card into Vreneli's hand, bringing with him precise ideas of the role that his new friend had to play for him. Ever since his father's early death, he had been casting round for a surrogate and in Wagner he thought he had found one. Wagner had been born in the same year as Nietzsche's father. At the same time, Nietzsche urgently needed someone to talk to about his idol Schopenhauer. For it was from Schopenhauer's philosophy that he derived the pessimistic maxims that made it possible for him to tolerate his life as an academic. The son of a pastor, he had been inured to asceticism from an early age and had developed an ethos of renunciation that was transfigured by Schopenhauer's philosophy.

For Nietzsche, Wagner, too, basked in Schopenhauer's reflected glory. The redemptive function that Schopenhauer ascribed to artists seemed in Nietzsche's eyes to be embodied by the dramatist who as both genius and saint appeared to have triumphed over the world's will in his vision of art. In the delirium of recognition he raised Wagner to a level 'close to the divine', even calling him his 'Jupiter' and planning to build altars and offer sacrifices to him. Not only did he believe that he had rediscovered in Wagner the idols of his student days – 'Schopenhauer and Goethe, Aeschylus and Pindar'[68] – but as Hanslick mockingly remarked, he used almost 'the same words for his Messiah as those employed by our books of religion when discussing Jesus Christ'.

Self-deluded though Nietzsche may have been, his delusion coincided fairly closely with the picture that Wagner himself was required to provide under Cosima's manipulative guidance. He played the part of the world ruler whom Nietzsche worshipped and at the same time encouraged the latter in his belief that he would one day be accepted into the composer's intellectual Olympus as his celestial successor. In the frenzied excitement associated with his sudden elevation, this generally depressed professor found himself initiated by the lady of the house into a decisive aspect of the act of idolatrous worship that he had hitherto overlooked – namely, that of running errands for his god, while simultaneously having to maintain his distance from the object of his veneration. The more Nietzsche prostrated himself on Cosima's instructions, the more superhuman his god appeared to him. For Nietzsche as for so many others, the way to Wagner led through Cosima's antechamber.

Whereas the younger man dreamt of a 'friendship' between equals, Liszt's daughter gave him to understand that he had to treat even her with kid gloves. Correspondence with the party follower was dealt with almost entirely by her, and as in her letters to the king, she would graciously include the views and wishes of the 'Master', while making no secret of her criticism of 'the most honoured Herr Professor' and 'most worthy friend', as Wagner called him. Nietzsche's style of writing and way of thinking were both censured, his absences regarded as so many acts of betrayal. The university teacher was subjected to directives of every description.

The errands that he was asked to perform in order to prove his worth were comically disproportionate to the hopes he placed in Wagner. First he had to track down a portrait of the composer's Uncle Adolf in Leipzig and then arrange for the books in the Tribschen library to be tastefully bound. In Basel he was sent off to buy Christmas presents, including sequinned tulle, and to oversee the printing of Wagner's autobiography with the local printer Bonfantini. In Dresden he had to find a lamp that Semper had designed for the city's synagogue and in Strasbourg he was required to buy 'several pounds of caramels, a similar amount of pâté d'abricots, a box of candied fruit (not the ones in bottles with syrup, but crystallized) and a bag of glacé oranges'. And Cosima added pointedly that she would 'very much like to have these provisions by early August'.

The stiffly formal professor, short-sightedly squinting at Cosima's wish list while a shop assistant fetched the Dutch herrings or Russian caviar ordered by her, seemed to have sprung straight from the pages of a novel by Gottfried Keller. He must have been particularly embarrassed by Wagner's last order in September 1876, when he was required to arrange shipment of 'two pairs of silk under-jackets and trousers of the finest quality' from the firm of Rumpf in Basel to Venice. 'He who loves his god should decorate him,' was Nietzsche's laconic comment.

The burlesque aspect of the relationship, which writers have effusively likened to the 'friendship between Goethe and Schiller',[69] soon reached unsuspected heights. For just as the ostensible junior partner in the association was opportunistically misused as a general factotum, so his lord and master refused to conform to the picture of the Schopenhauerian saint living for his art. As Nietzsche noted to his dismay, Wagner failed to practise what he preached. When the disciple, with his Schopenhauerian love of animals, professed his belief in vegetarianism, Wagner called him an 'ass'. And Nietzsche was no less disturbed by the fact that on one essential point Wagner departed from Schopenhauer's doctrine of the will: abstinence – indispensable to anyone bent on redeeming the world – was not for him. Cosima, still married to Hans von Bülow, was again carrying her idol's child.

Wagner regularly took pleasure in making the serious-minded young professor look foolish, making snide remarks about his 'unnatural reserve', causing him to blush with shame at his crude jokes and pouring scorn on his attempts at composition, works that were more sacred to him than anything else in the world and that he played on Wagner's grand piano in ardent self-absorption. 'No, Nietzsche,' Wagner once said, tongue in cheek, 'you play too well for a professor.' The label that he attached to him was taken from one of E. T. A. Hoffmann's short stories: Anselmus, the hero of *Der goldene Topf*, stumbles through life as a bumbling dreamer before finding his true vocation as an assistant scribe in the library of the archivist Lindhorst. Just as Wagner identified with the powerful magician, so his clumsy and myopic disciple was left with the derisive nickname of Anselmus.

The Tribschen farce, which was played out at Nietzsche's expense, escaped the attention of writers on Wagner as surely as did the reciprocal projections that caused the ostensible friendship to resemble nothing so much as a comedy of disguises and mistaken identities. If Nietzsche saw in Wagner an inspirational father figure who would help him gain power, the philosopher merely filled a temporary vacancy in Wagner's life, a vacancy for which Cosima had consciously to prepare him. Candidates qualified for the position solely by dint of their unconditional willingness to sacrifice themselves to the Master. All who revealed this readiness could count on Wagner's boundless love, chiefly in the form of devoted letters. Anyone who dithered would inevitably suffer the consequences.

Among the dozens of young men who occupied this position were Theodor Apel and Karl Ritter, Hans von Bülow and Peter Cornelius, King Ludwig and Nietzsche himself. By the time Wagner settled in Bayreuth there was a veritable jostling for the position, the most prominent of the petitioners being Heinrich von Stein, Hans von Wolzogen, Carl Friedrich Glasenapp, Paul von Joukowsky and Joseph Rubinstein, the last of whom sought Wagner's help in 'redeeming' him from his Jewishness. For Wagner, Nietzsche was only one among many. Nor did the composer shy away from making comparisons. 'I've had some nice friends', he commented sarcastically to Cosima. He was thinking, she added, 'of K. Ritter, Nietzsche etc.'[70]

Comparisons certainly suggested themselves. Each of these men had come to Wagner in a spirit of self-denial and offered all they could. Whether through money, their own reputation, social support or dirty work of every description, all who were attracted by the idea of becoming friends with Wagner helped wholeheartedly, hand and foot. At the same time, none of them seemed disposed to commit himself to the loving union of man and wife that the Master's works so explicitly enjoined. While profiting from this one-sided expression of support on the part of his disciples, Wagner simultaneously sought to marry them off, repeatedly advising Karl Ritter and even King Ludwig to take a wife, advice that inevitably fell on deaf ears, given the sexual preferences of the individuals concerned. With Nietzsche, too, the plan miscarried. And Heinrich von Stein, who had awakened a desire for commitment in the professor, chose instead to form a close friendship with Paul von Joukowsky, who under Wagner's gaze carried on an affair with a youth from Naples by the name of Peppino.[71]

Wagner demanded total surrender — in the case of Peter Cornelius, he even went so far as to suggest that they lived together 'like a married couple'[72] — yet when the object of his attentions was at hand, he avoided the contact that he was fond of invoking from a distance. At the same time he seems to have been troubled when these relationships were compromised by the arrival of the opposite sex. And so he helped himself to his favourite Cornelius's 'doll' with the same ease with which he stole Cosima from under the eyes of Hans von Bülow, his 'kindred spirit' who, as Cornelius was fully aware, suffered in silence throughout the ordeal. With his other disciples, there appears to have been no one to steal.

If these relationships generally began on a note of ecstatic understanding, they invariably ended in bitter discordancy. Whereas Wagner was happy to drop ordinary backers as soon as they had served their purpose, he regarded the breakdown of his relations with his disciples as so many acts of disillusionment that subsequently led to his 'eyes being opened'. The black betrayal that poisoned his love affairs seemed in retrospect to affect his friendships, too. The other person had evidently sought only his own advantage, hence, in turn, Wagner's insistence on his right to malign them behind their backs. None of these 'apostates' escaped this fate.

While Ludwig was dismissed as a characterless 'cretin', Bülow was described as a 'gnat who is bound to be burned up in the light'.[73] Occasionally he even decried the very quality that had disposed his disciples to sacrifice themselves to him in the first place. When his friend Karl Ritter, whose homosexuality was well known to Wagner, refused to give him some money, he denounced him to Theodor Uhlig as an 'onanist! That says it all!'[74] It was not this perversion that had 'destroyed' Ritter, but a more deep-seated shortcoming.

Whenever Wagner discussed these renegades with Cosima, describing them as 'blocks of ice that melted in the sea of wretchedness', he would mention 'K. Ritter among others' and claim that 'the article on Jewishness destroyed him, just as it did poor Tausig; he had Jewish blood in his veins'.[75] Another of Wagner's self-sacrificing friends, Carl Tausig, prepared the vocal score of *Die Meistersinger* and helped to organize the first Bayreuth Festival. When the thirty-year-old pianist lay dying in 1871, Cosima expressed the conviction that 'even if he recovers, he's lost to our organization. His death strikes us as metaphysically justified.' As we might expect, it was 'the curse of Jewishness' that provided this justification.[76]

When Nietzsche turned up at Tribschen on Whit Saturday in 1869, most of the other heroes had already stepped down. Completely unsuspecting, he now had to fill their role. And he could not even console himself with the thought that his self-sacrifice might be rewarded by Wagner's love. For Baroness von Bülow kept a close watch over this. Even the 'friendship' of which Nietzsche boasted was never seriously on offer. And so he had to learn the bitter lesson of subjugation in return for kind words and jovial confidences. The fact that he pretended not to notice merely added to the farcical nature of the situation.

The relationship between Wagner and Nietzsche was not only comic in character, for it also offered an exchange of intellectual views and ultimately struck a note of tragedy. But to describe it as an 'epoch-making encounter', as certain scholars have done, is true only of the younger of the two men. For Nietzsche learnt not only a lesson in subjugation but also one in self-liberation. Later he described himself as a camel that good-humouredly accepted every burden until it was sent into the wilderness, where it became a raging lion. The 'will to power' that enabled Nietzsche to turn into 'Nietzsche' is something that he could scarcely have learnt at the University in Basel.

As for the intellectual synergy between master and pupil, there is really only indirect evidence of this, as nearly all of Nietzsche's letters fell victim to the Bayreuth auto-da-fé. In the wake of the breakdown of their relationship, both sides were at pains to strip that relationship of its deeper significance, with the later Nietzsche denying that Wagner had any philosophical influence on his early writings. Wherever the names of Wagner or Schopenhauer occurred, he insisted, they could confidently be replaced by his own. Of course, the opposite was also true. If, in his autobiography Nietzsche describes himself as 'the mouthpiece and medium of all-powerful forces', these forces were initially called Wagner and Schopenhauer.

From the time of Nietzsche's first meeting with the composer in Leipzig, Wagner and Schopenhauer seem to have become merged in his mind in the person of the dramatist: for him, Schopenhauer's spirit spoke through Wagner. But when he thought he had rediscovered Schopenhauer's 'ethical air' and 'Faustian aroma' in Wagner, he was guilty of projecting his own beliefs onto the latter. As we know, Wagner had a low opinion of Faust, and ethics, for him, were simply a question of seizing the right opportunity. But the philosophical texts that Nietzsche wrote between 1870 and 1876, from his lectures on Greek tragedy to 'Richard Wagner in Bayreuth', were in the main examples of Wagnerian exegesis.

Wagner influenced not only Nietzsche's magisterial style but also his dialectical way of thinking. Wagner's emotionalism, which created an anachronistic impression even during his days in Zurich, lent the charm of penitential sermons to the pamphlets that Nietzsche wrote during the early years of the Reich. Never before had Wagner seen his ideas so comprehensively adopted by another writer. He felt that he had been understood, even if not in the way Nietzsche had hoped. Hanslick – that most suspicious of observers – saw in the younger man 'arguably the most outstanding of Wagner's champions in terms of talent and education, and the most outrageous in his exaggerations'. The later Nietzsche admitted in his contrition that he had been 'one of the most corrupted of Wagnerians'.[77]

Cosima, on the other hand, who largely monopolized all conversations with Nietzsche, can have had little influence on his intellectual development. His elder by seven years, she constantly sought to lecture him, but from a philosophical point of view she was incapable of holding a candle to him. Strictly speaking, she understood only as much as the Master told her, and even this she judged by Christian standards. In her 'philosophical training', Nietzsche later admitted in a fictional dialogue, she was 'about two thousand years' behind him.[78]

The rudiments of her philosophy remained a lifelong mystery, revealing themselves only once in the course of one of the moments of mystic absent-mindedness that she cultivated from the time of her union with Wagner. These abnormal states, during which she sank into a 'magnetic sleep', invariably attracted the greatest attention – in Cornelius's view, this was their whole purpose. 'Frau von Bülow evidently still felt a little unsure of Wagner,' Cornelius noted in 1865, 'so that she had to think of ways of binding him to her. And so, whenever Wagner had played or read something to her, she would lapse into a state similar to that of a somnambulist, whispering prophetic words by which Wagner was powerfully attracted.'[79] She would then speak like Erda in a deep trance, and Wagner would struggle to decipher her Pythian utterances.

In one such mystic trance, she described a dreamlike vision in which she had seen the interior of the 'Grail Church' – thus Wagner's account to the king. 'That is the right altarpiece,' she had then whispered, 'and this is the true meaning of Michelangelo's *Last Judgement* in the Sistine Chapel. On one side,' she revealed, speaking as the Delphic Oracle, 'your works, each more radiant than the next: on the other side, your experiences in life, each more hideous than the last; and above in the clouds – Parzival (thus are you called among us, dear friend!) as the judge of the world. Down there, right at the bottom,' the visionary had then groaned in her dismay, 'oh, how terrible! I don't care to look! The eternal betrayal!' She had then fallen silent and 'on awakening did not have the least memory of what had happened'.[80]

Wagner assumed that this was a divine sign, but the truth of the matter is simply that in the image of the Last Judgement Cosima had repeated her own simple view of the world, with its image of sheep and goats. For her, Wagner's works were on the side of good, uncomprehending humanity on the side of evil, while above them reigned the Saviour – here called Ludwig for tactical reasons – with the hell of betrayal gaping open below him, a hell represented in the main by the race of Judas, who betrayed his Saviour. Worthy of a children's primer, this view of the world struck a very real chord with Wagner.

As expressed in *The Wibelungs* and 'Jews in Music', Wagner's view of the world, like Cosima's, revelled in black-and-white imagery, blowing the trumpet of the Last Judgement, fearing the great adversary and longing for the salvation that comes from on high. His actual philosophy, however, illustrated by his music dramas and underpinned by the theoretical writings of his Zurich years, fell by contrast on deaf ears in Cosima's case. Even worse, concepts such as revolution, freedom, consciousness and sexual love – concepts without which his entire output remains incomprehensible – struck the Second Empire *parisienne* as highly suspect. And so, bestriding her Pythian tripod, she reinterpreted the Master's works. From now on it was Cosima who decided what Wagner really meant.

Nietzsche witnessed this transformation in Tribschen, but it took almost two decades for him to see how Wagner's ideas had been turned into a cult. 'You know very well', he wrote in 1888 in a draft letter to the composer's widow, 'how well I know the influence that you exerted on Wagner – you know even better how much I despise this influence.'[81] What he was thinking of, as he made clear in a contemporary note, was 'Wagner's condescension, in the matter of taste, to the Catholic instincts of his wife, Liszt's daughter'. His psychologist's insight recognized in this 'a kind of gratitude and humility on the part of a weaker, more varied, more suffering creature' – by which he meant Wagner – 'towards one who knew how to protect and encourage – that is, to a stronger and more narrow-minded one' – in other words, Cosima.[82] When Nietzsche spoke contemptuously of Wagner's 'prostration before the Cross', he was also thinking of his prostration before the woman who prayed at the cross every day.

By the time the young professor of classical philology stumbled across Wagner, he had already dipped into *Opera and Drama* and, as Cosima proudly noted, quoted from it 'in his lectures'. Its subject matter – the metaphysical significance of art, which derives from the same dialectic process of creation as nature – was to preoccupy Nietzsche all his life. The whole idea of thinking in contradictions, which Wagner took to excessive extremes, likewise remained Nietzsche's hobby horse, although he was less attached to the idealistic synthesis of 'redemption' than to the dazzling paradox in which the 'enigmatical aspect of existence' is both revealed and concealed. While Nietzsche was finally to become lost in the world's circling labyrinth as a 'question mark crushed between two ciphers', Wagner thought that he had found in love the answer to all life's questions.

Cosima thought differently. If the pupil felt that he could gain an idea of Wagner's teachings through *Opera and Drama*, she was determined to teach him otherwise. After reading an idealistically coloured essay on Wagner by her husband's Jewish disciple Heinrich Porges, she wrote to tell Nietzsche that she had found in it 'too much talk of freedom, consciousness, infinity etc.' Her 'mind' was 'so badly attuned to such things' that it invariably caused her 'capacity for thought suddenly to falter'.[83] Inevitably she attributed this failure to what she regarded as the author's confused Jewish thinking rather than to her own intellectual shortcomings.

The extent to which she was plagued by these alien intruders is clear from a letter she wrote to Nietzsche a fortnight later. 'Friend Porges' had been staying with them at Tribschen, a visit that had been 'embarrassing to the highest degree', she complained, like one vicar's daughter writing to another. She had 'not believed', she added conspiratorially, that 'thanks to someone to whom I am entirely well disposed' she would 'relate so decisively to the article of nineteen years ago. The alien element, that's what it is!'[84] For Cosima, Wagner's essay 'Jews in Music' of 1850 was the last word on the subject. So eagerly did she look for certain distinguishing features among her contemporaries that even a biographer as loyal to Bayreuth as Newman was able to suggest that her motto was 'Cherchez le Juif'.[85]

And so the republished pamphlet 'Jews in Music' was one of the first of his writings that Wagner forwarded to his new party member in 1869 with the note 'A hint!'[86] Previously he had familiarized him with his latest attacks on the 'arts pages gossip' of the Jewish musician Ferdinand Hiller and on a volume of memoirs about Felix Mendelssohn whose author, Eduard Devrient, he compared with E. T. A. Hoffmann's venomous and fraudulent dwarf, Klein Zaches. Among the tasks that Nietzsche was set during his first year of contact with Wagner was to work through several of the composer's older essays as well as 'On State and Religion', a programmatical tract written for Ludwig and described by the philosopher as a 'profound summary' of Wagner's ideas. It was only a shame, Nietzsche concluded, that the young king 'seems to have learnt nothing from it'.[87]

Nietzsche, by contrast, learnt something. Wagner's main preoccupations were the rebirth of antiquity and his opposition to the Jews, and so when he came to write his lecture 'Socrates and Tragedy', Nietzsche worked into it barbs that reduced his audience, who were presumably expecting something edifying, to shaking their heads in astonishment: his propaganda speech in support of the Wagnerian cause culminated in the warning that the harm done by Socrates' credulous belief in reason in ancient Greece could still be felt today. 'This Socratism', claimed Nietzsche, striking a belligerent note, 'is today's Jewish press: I need say no more.'[88]

Nietzsche had wanted to break a lance for his master at Tribschen, who saw in the 'Jewish press' his principal enemy, but in the process he almost broke his own neck. Such polemics on the lips of a servant of the state seemed scandalous far beyond Basel. Hitherto untainted, Nietzsche's reputation suffered its first serious blow. In Tribschen, too, alarm bells rang: after all, the Wagners could hardly have expected that their disciple would set out quite so soon in pursuit of the dragon.

The Master immediately wrote to him, warning him 'not to break his neck', and Cosima proved herself yet again to be a schoolmistress more than capable of giving the disciple a good dressing down. 'I have a favour to ask you,' she wrote, 'one that I should like to describe as maternal – namely, that you do not stir up this mare's nest. I think you will understand me. Do not mention the Jews, especially not in passing; later, when you want to take up this terrible struggle, you may do so in God's name, but not for the present.'[89] This was the language of a quasi-religious sect, and Nietzsche, duly reprimanded, understood it as such. He destroyed the incriminatory section of his lecture and from then on avoided the word in question, with all the dangers it posed.

The fact that Cosima was only too pleased to make her own contribution to Wagner's writings – and not only as his plenipotentiary – had become clear to Nietzsche only a short time earlier, when she had asked him in the context of his lecture on the 'Greek music drama' to 'think of the return of the creator of the German music drama to Germany'.[90] And in the case of the study that was to establish Nietzsche's reputation in the Wagnerian world, her interventions were nothing if not far-reaching. *The Birth of Tragedy from the Spirit of Music*, in which Wagner's philosophy of art, as expounded in *Opera and Drama*, is merged with his philosophy of history, as set forth in *The Artwork of the Future*, to create something unprecedentedly new, was intended to end with the apotheosis of the composer.

The ending was discussed in great detail in Tribschen in April 1871, so much so, in fact, that Newman was convinced that it was here that the book's 'strange destiny' was decided. 'One sees here a very gifted man imbued with R.'s ideas in his own way,' Cosima noted in her diary.[91] And on this point she was right. Long after the breakdown of their relationship, Nietzsche continued to concede that his book had been written 'as though in a dialogue' with Wagner. At the same time, however, he regretted that he had spoilt it 'by introducing the most modern things'. What he meant by this was the belief in the German Empire, in Wagner's strength and in Bayreuth's majesty – all of them ideas before whose shrine Cosima prostrated herself.

The Wagners interfered in the next group of essays, too. Having ruined his academic career with *The Birth of Tragedy* in 1872, the young professor was now entirely dependent on 'Herr Meister' and 'Frau Meisterin', both of whom made sure that he felt that dependency. In order for him finally to be able to enter the fray in support of Wagner's ideas on cultural reform, it was decided that he would write a series of propagandist essays that were initially to have been titled 'Observations on Bayreuth's Outlook'. But Wagner's friend Theodor Uhlig had already distinguished himself with several 'Timely Observations' in 1850, and so they finally settled on the less obtrusive 'Untimely Meditations',[92] which were intended to glorify Wagner and Schopenhauer and at the same time rout their 'Socratic' enemies.

Under the heading 'To be attacked',[93] Nietzsche had drawn up a list of targets in 1872, intending to tick them off once they had been dealt with. It reads like a summary of Wagner's own private feuds from the past. On it we find the name of the popular Jewish writer Berthold Auerbach – a friend from the composer's days in Dresden – alongside that of Gustav Freytag, who had criticized him for 'Jews in Music'. 'Young Germany' and 'Leipzig, Wagner's birthplace', were both to be summarily dismissed, while two of his enemies in Munich, Wilhelm Heinrich Riehl and Moritz von Schwind, were to be dealt with individually. Another name on the list was that of Eduard Hanslick, with whom Wagner still had unfinished business, and finally there was David Friedrich Strauß, about whom Nietzsche had as little to say at this stage as he did about the others.

Wagner provided the ammunition, imparting various whispered confidences to his young disciple when they met in Strasbourg in November 1872, with the result that the first of the 'Untimely Meditations' was directed at the theologian David Friedrich Strauß.[94] Nietzsche accomplished the deed with a brash superiority suggesting that he had gained the courage to write the piece by reading 'Jews in Music'. Even the image of worms in culture's decaying cadaver resurfaces here. He disposed of Strauß in the most literal sense of the term, as the object of his attack died six months later, leaving Nietzsche to be plagued by a guilty conscience. 'I feel somewhat affected by it', he confided to a friend. But when Cosima heard about Nietzsche's weakness, she took him to task once again, adopting the tone of a governess and informing him that she 'refused to allow herself to become sentimental in matters of the mind, and it is all the same whether the person in question is ill or dying if he appears harmful'.[95] The pastor's son accepted the reprimand and even seems to have been impressed by it. Later he adopted a more sneering and cynical tone, claiming that he had 'publicly laughed Strauß's book to death', its author likewise, albeit 'unexpectedly'.[96]

Although Nietzsche soon broke free from his function as principal propagandist of the Bayreuth enterprise, he tacitly remained true to the Wagner he had discovered behind Cosima's façade. And it is Wagner's Zurich ideas on the origins and demise of art that formed the starting point for his later conceptual labyrinth. The idea of the first creation, as described by Schelling in his natural philosophy and as depicted by Wagner in his works, returns in *The Birth of Tragedy* and continues to preoccupy his thoughts right up to his hallucinatory union with the god Dionysus on the threshold of the madhouse.

The creation of the world – this was the common starting point of their respective philosophies – had not taken place at some remote point in the past but was part of the here and now. As soon as the light of the spirit illumined its dark ground in Schelling's version of events or, in Wagner's variant, as soon as the masculine word of the poet plunged into the feminine sea of music, the incomprehensible miracle took place that was achieved for Nietzsche in the union of the light god Apollo with Dionysus as the god of music: a new world came into being.

It came into being, but only to fall at once into its constituent parts. From the interplay between these antithetical parts sprang the development that would allow a universe to arise and to perish in turn. According to Nietzsche's first universal formula, it was from the spirit of music that tragedy was born, just as the drama of the *Ring* had arisen from the ringing depths of the Rhine. Thus the difference between the theatre and real life was superseded, so-called reality no more than a pale reflection of all that finds visual expression in the drama. In tragedy existence stares itself in the face. The tragedy that the spectator witnesses and suffers is synonymous with the tragedy that tears the hero apart, just as the hero enacts the rise and fall of the god. But the god is nothing more nor less than the world, as part of which spectators experience themselves before recognizing themselves in the mirror of the drama and becoming one with God and the world.

The mystical idea of an all-embracing oneness that was revealed to Wagner most clearly in sexual love, with its union of opposites, was also to exercise Nietzsche. He too discovered this love, with which all things began and in which all things were superseded. And he too saw in it a basic principle of creative existence. For him, however, it took place not between partners of the opposite sex, as Wagner imagined it, but between the same-sex gods of art, Dionysus and Apollo. In their 'mysterious marital bond', wrote the 'mystic soul' (as Nietzsche was later to see himself), they incite each other to 'new and more powerful births', finally creating 'in their coupling an equally Dionysian and Apollonian form of art – Attic tragedy'.[97] Even after the arrival of the Superman, Nietzsche's creation of the world was to manage without the female component.

Although neither Wagner nor Nietzsche ever discussed their conceptual metempsychosis, the earliest readers of *The Birth of Tragedy* were struck by its dependence on Wagner's Zurich essays. Even closer, not to say personal, was the relationship between *The Birth of Tragedy* and the commemorative essay that Wagner wrote to mark the Beethoven centenary in 1870, an essay that dealt less with the subject of the centennial celebrations than with Beethoven's role within the metaphysical framework of Wagner's thinking. Like both *Opera and Drama* and Nietzsche's 1872 study, it examined the question of the conditions that make art possible, together with its origins and decline. In short, it could equally well have been called not *Beethoven* but *The Birth of Tragedy from the Spirit of Music.*

There was even something special about the 'spirit' of this music, a spirit related in name only to its 'holy' variant. Discovered by Wagner and invoked by Nietzsche, this spirit belonged to the dark world of dreams and clairvoyance, of magnetic sleep and second sight. Just as Senta and Elsa had revealed themselves as somnambulists and just as their mythic prototype, Erda, had ascended prophetically from the depths of the earth, so Cosima had proved brilliantly successful at creating occult states into which she fell, transported by her husband's music and even by the sound of his voice. According to both Wagner and Nietzsche, it was from just such a state of hypnotic raptus that the music drama had been born in ancient Greece. Tragedy issued from an act of 'spirit seeing'.

The starting point of this idea – and it is one that takes some getting used to – may be found in Schopenhauer, who had immortalized his weakness for spiritualism in his 'Essay on Spirit Seeing', an elaborate treatise, peppered with abstruse examples, in which he attempted yet again to prove that the reality that presents itself to our senses is a mere 'idea' on the part of the brain, with the result that the brain is in a position to create its own reality, without the help of the senses. And this alternative reality does not differ in any way from the reality that is claimed as the only true one.

Schopenhauer was referring to the imaginary world of 'spirit seeing', a world that humans are able to enter thanks to a special 'dream organ'. As soon as they fall into a magnetic sleep, this hitherto unidentified psychological tool springs into action and conjures up a visionary world that exists independently of the 'outer world'. According to Schopenhauer, the 'will' observes itself here and, if it so chooses, crosses the boundaries of time and space. In this way, the clairvoyant can see the past and the future and does not even need to open his or her eyes.

Here Wagner had stumbled for the first time upon an explanation for the traumatic events of his childhood. In Schopenhauer's view, this was nothing less than the archetypal will's encounter with itself within man's consciousness. In Wagner's vision the 'will' had seen its own nature, and the result was terrifying. The fear of ghosts that the young composer had experienced and that continued to haunt him right up to the end was the actual source not only of the great world theatre that was called 'reality' but also of his own world theatre that he contrasted with this imaginary reality. If Cosima regularly sank into a trance and saw ghosts, it may also have been because she knew about Wagner's past and was familiar with certain passages in Schopenhauer's 'Essay on Spirit Seeing'.

In Wagner's *Beethoven* essay this rare discipline finds particularly prominent expression, while at the same time revealing a remarkable link between on the one hand the composer's earliest ideas on music, which date back to that other clairvoyant, E. T. A. Hoffmann, and on the other his latest ideas, which were inspired by the occultist Schopenhauer. The old world of ideas to which Wagner's very first article was devoted now celebrated an astonishing come-back with that sworn enemy of idealism, Schopenhauer, from whose 'Essay on Spirit Seeing' Wagner derived his belief that the world of ideas did not imitate reality as experienced through our senses but sprang from an inner vision of the world that revealed itself to our 'dream organ'. In its visions, the mind was conscious of itself, just as it was in Hegel's self-consciousness and in Schelling's first creation, aware of itself both as a single entity that transcended time and space and in the state of inner turmoil that triggered fear and suffering.

This vision, then, contained within it both the promise of divine love and the torment of mortal fear. From it there arose in Wagner's view the human voice, which formed the basic element of music. In its cry of fear and call of desire was revealed the perceptible nature of the world, a nature that could be understood by all who heard it. But 'to understand' meant responding to the call from the depths. Music arose through life's dialogue with itself. 'Thus the child wakes from the night of its mother's womb with a cry of longing,' Wagner wrote in his *Beethoven* essay, 'and thus it is answered by its mother's soothing caress; thus the yearning youth understands the alluring song of the woodbirds, thus speaks the lament of beasts and of the breezes', so that the anxious consciousness finally understands 'that its innermost nature is at one with the innermost nature of all that it perceives'.[98]

As soon as the language of this self-understanding begins to be heard as music, it produces from within itself a dreamlike vision that reveals its own origins to us in figurative form. In this way, the process by which art comes into being is repeated, but this time in reverse: just as music arose from the first vision, so a new vision now arises from music, a vision revealed to the ecstatic individual like a hallucination. This inner vision, rising above the music, mirrors the onstage actions of ancient Greek tragedy. The 'chorus in tragedy', wrote Wagner in 1872, 'raised spectators to a pitch of enthusiasm in which the hero, appearing on stage in his mask, created the impression on the far-seeing public of the truthfulness of a ghostly apparition'.[99]

In turn, this corresponds with Wagner's notion of the ideal audience, an audience which, far from gaping at painted backcloths, is hypnotized by the orchestra and clairvoyantly follows a 'waking dream' that is interpreted for it by art. The essence of existence is expressed in tragedy alone, a form of art that owes its birth to the interaction of ecstasy and dream. 'From the choral singing', Wagner wrote in his *Beethoven* essay, 'the drama was projected onto the stage', where the audience sees how 'the inner law, which can be understood only from the spirit of music', conditions 'the outer law, which orders the world that we see all around us'.[100] Music alone reveals what is presented to the 'dream organ' of the rapt audience, just as it puts into words only what the archetypal consciousness has glimpsed within itself.

It is at this point that *The Birth of Tragedy* begins, Nietzsche drawing Wagner's attention to the fact that 'I began to assemble these ideas at the time that your glorious commemorative essay on Beethoven was being written.'[101] Tragedy, in short, springs from the spirit that is manifest in music. Like Wagner and Schopenhauer, its young author had a weakness for spirit seeing, and if their names reminded him of the concepts of 'cross, death and grave', it was because he too had an evolved relationship with the world of shadows. Even as a child, he was gifted with second sight and could predict deaths and conjure up ghosts in his imagination. And like Wagner he suffered all his life from nightmares.[102] Sometimes he even heard ghostly voices, so that Schopenhauer's 'Essay on Spirit Seeing' must have been extremely welcome reading, for the trauma that paralyzed him was shown here to be the womb of creativity.

And it was also the womb of Greek drama. From the archetypal vision of horror there arose the cry that found musical expression in the choral singing of the satyrs and provided the basis for the ghostly apparition of the tragic hero. As a piece of theatre, this took place on stage, of course, but it was properly visible only in the 'convulsions of the Dionysian state'. Listeners who allowed themselves to be intoxicated by this music would see before them the god in human guise, a god worthy of their adoration. In this way Dionysus and Apollo united to create the supreme work of art in which the whole of existence achieved fulfilment and perfection. When Wagner read this, he thought that his own existence had finally achieved fulfilment. 'I've never read anything more beautiful than your book,' he wrote to Nietzsche in 1872, striking an unusually enthusiastic note, and Cosima added her psalmodizing gloss: 'Oh, how beautiful your book is! How beautiful and profound, how profound and bold!'[103]

But even their mutual jubilation was marred by a misunderstanding. In the study that Nietzsche regarded as a quintessential product of his own imagination, Wagner was delighted to recognize elements of himself. He was thus praising himself when he praised Nietzsche, while the latter, feeling himself raised aloft to Wagner's throne, was merely being shown his place at the feet of the tragic actor.

Far more epoch-making than the encounter between Nietzsche and Wagner was the breakdown of their relationship. Two worlds that had never really come together moved apart with a tremendous crash. Only long after the lightning flash had faded did the thunder begin to roll, its distant rumble remaining everpresent. The disciple who thought he had beheld the real Wagner cut himself off from him when the false Wagner celebrated his triumph at the first Bayreuth Festival. Thus, at least, Nietzsche depicted the affair, and there is much to be said in favour of his own particular version of events.

Writers on the subject have generally failed to see that the break between the two men took place in three stages, partly because, with the blindness of partisanship, they have misinterpreted the process and partly because the participants themselves attempted to shroud it in obscurity. What for Nietzsche was a trauma from which he was never able to free himself was for the Wagners a loss of face at the defection of their most famous propagandist to the opposing camp. It was in order to save face that both parties preferred lies to the truth, with their respective followers treating their conflicting accounts as gospel.

Comparatively speaking, Nietzsche lied less than the Wagners, a state of affairs that may also reflect the fact that he had less to lose. Strictly speaking, he had nothing else to lose, as he had already forfeited everything as a consequence of his Wagnerian allegiance: his professorship, his reputation and his health. Even his readers, who were recruited from the ranks of the Bayreuthians, turned their backs on him. At the same time, Wagner's version of events, manifestly tendentious though it is, could at least appeal to a long tradition of broken friendships that always followed the same pattern, at least in the composer's memory of them. For him, Nietzsche was merely one of a long line of traitors whose depravity of character became clear only after the event. 'Serious forebodings,' Cosima noted in her diary in 1878; 'in R.'s eyes they shed great light on Nietzsche.'[104]

Nietzsche had set off the first explosive device two years earlier, when his essay 'Richard Wagner in Bayreuth' had arrived at Wahnfried just in time for the first Bayreuth Festival, eliciting an enthusiastic 'Your book is tremendous' from Wagner. It was presumably for this reason that the pamphlet continues to be regarded as a hymnic tribute on the part of Wagner's admirer, in spite of the fact that, with the exception of a later order for underwear, it marked the abrupt end of the composer's correspondence with his disciple. Evidently Wagner had not yet read the book when he hastily thanked its author for it. Unlike his biographers, he then made up for this omission and drew the inevitable consequences. After all, Nietzsche's Wagnerian essay is neither a 'panegyric', as claimed by Peter Wapnewski,[105] nor 'virtually entirely lacking in criticism', as Dieter Borchmeyer argues.[106]

Far from it. The truth of the matter is that while larding his language with hyperbole, Nietzsche had submitted a devastating critique, and one, moreover, that was bound to affect a composer who was used to Cosima's 'idolatry' and to his worshippers' fine words. And the attack hit home, as Nietzsche's aim was accurate. He knew his enemy's weaknesses, not least because he had read the first part of Wagner's memoirs, the often down-to-earth comedy of which was in stark contrast to Cosima's grand manner. And so he praised the Wagner whom he loved, while secretly attacking the man who was now carrying on like the emperor of Bayreuth.

His attack consisted in telling the celebrated genius all that Cosima was attempting to hide from the world. After all, as no one knew better than the proofreader of *My Life*, Wagner's life had 'a great deal about it' that was comical, 'and a remarkably grotesque type of comedy at that'. And Nietzsche knew that Wagner, too, realized this. 'How the feeling and recognition that whole stretches of his life are marked by a grotesque lack of dignity must affect an artist who, more than any other, can breathe freely only in the sublime and more than sublime – that is something for the thinker to reflect on.'[107] This was bound to bring Wagner down to earth with a bump at a time when even the emperor of Germany was honouring him with a visit.

The portrait of Wagner's character that Nietzsche cheekily sketched will also have given the thinker something to reflect on. If it was true, then his airs and graces as a Bayreuth gentleman were emphatically refuted. In particular, Nietzsche stressed the 'violent, noisy' element in Wagner's character, the 'boundless, tyrannical desire' that compelled him to obtain by force all that reality withheld from him. 'Born in fact to be a dilettante', he pursued his 'dark personal will, with its insatiable desire for power and glory', and scaled the heights of true art. Unfortunately – as Nietzsche noted with reference to Wagner's secret Meyerbeer complex – he observed 'with an envious, deeply prying gaze' everything 'that smacked of success'. None of this squared with Cosima's image of her god receiving the homage of the whole world from his temple at Wahnfried.

Although Bayreuth represented 'the first circumnavigation of the world of art', Wagner's mission seemed to have been accomplished with the discovery of this new land. The old man was already old hat, Nietzsche ended his candid analysis, for Wagner was 'not the seer of a future, as he would perhaps like to appear to us, but the interpreter and transfigurer of a past'.[108] Top of the agenda, therefore, was not the coming empire, for which the Wagner community was dutifully preparing itself, but a sublime, not to say 'more than sublime', fairy-tale. It could hardly escape the Wagners' notice that this undermined the cult that achieved its first high point in 1876. Nietzsche had not only broken away, he had called the whole system into question.

The second stage in the breakdown of the relationship took place in Sorrento, where Wagner had gone to recover from Bayreuth and Nietzsche to recover from both Wagner and Bayreuth. Needless to say, he had been snubbed ever since the Wagners had read his premature obituary of the Master earlier that summer. Unable to find his feet in Bayreuth, he no longer existed in Cosima's eyes, and her diaries tell of everything but Nietzsche. Like Beckmesser at the end of *Die Meistersinger*, he had 'rushed away furiously and become lost in the crowd'. If he later claimed that he had fled in disgust from Bayreuth's vanity fair, his departure no longer excited attention. He had so disgraced himself that Bayreuth affected not to notice.

But he had found consolation. The young philosopher Paul Rée had hurried from Nietzsche's sickbed in Klingenbrunn to Basel, where the two men spent what they called the 'honeymoon' of their new friendship together. At the invitation of another of Wagner's friends, Malwida von Meysenbug, the platonic pair arrived in Sorrento at the end of October 1876 and immediately called on the Wagners. Whatever they may have expected from their visit, they walked straight into a trap.

For Cosima soon spotted whom Nietzsche had brought with him to the Hotel Vittoria. 'On closer examination', she noted, 'we discover that he must be an Israelite.'[109] According to Nietzsche's sister, Wagner immediately felt an 'insuperable aversion' to Rée and henceforth refused to tolerate his presence. Cosima confided to her friend Mimi – now Countess Marie von Schleinitz – that 'Israel has turned up in the person of a Dr Rée, apparently entirely taken in and subjugated by Nietzsche, but the truth of the matter is that he has outwitted him, the relationship between Judaea and Germania on a small scale.' It was on account of Rée, Cosima concluded, that Nietzsche had 'broken faith with Schopenhauer and Wagner', and she knew instinctively that 'evil has triumphed here'.[110]

Within twenty-four hours of meeting Rée, Wagner had sprung into action, warning his former disciple to be on his guard against Jewish influence and at the same time drawing the pastor's son's attention to the tried and tested anti-dote in the form of the sacraments of Christianity. During their last walk together, which probably took place on 2 November 1876, Wagner told Nietzsche about his next project, *Parsifal*, and about the 'enjoyment that he owed to the celebration of Holy Communion'.[111] For Nietzsche, their conversation on this 'beautiful autumn day' sealed the breakdown of their relationship, Wagner, too, being overcome by a 'valedictory mood'. They said goodbye, never to see each other again. Thus at least runs the account left by Nietzsche's sister Elisabeth. But it was not independently confirmed by Wagner, and so this final encounter was banished to the realm of fantasy. 'Nothing is right about this account,' writes Nietzsche's biographer Werner Ross, 'not even the weather.'[112]

It now seems, however, that the account is in fact accurate in every detail, including the weather. According to Cosima's diary entry (unpublished until 1976), it was as 'beautiful' as Elisabeth maintained. As for Wagner's rapt expression of his faith, Nietzsche later recalled that the composer was moved 'by "the blood of the Redeemer"' and that 'there was a moment when he confessed to me the delights that he was able to derive from Holy Communion'.[113] Wagner's surprising pleasure in ritual is repeatedly attested by Cosima's diaries, and it may even have been she who gave him a taste for it.

There is also evidence for the final walk in Sorrento, evidence furnished by the Wagner camp: the poet Michael Georg Conrad, who was later to become known for his support of Thomas Mann and Adolf Hitler, told the Wagner scholar Otto Strobel that he had been present 'when Wagner returned from his last conversation with Nietzsche in Sorrento and made it clear that the bridge between him and his former and most important disciple had been definitively torn down'.[114] From that time on, Cosima's Italian diary says nothing more about Nietzsche, whom she was never to see again.

But they heard from each other. For there now followed the third and final stage in the breakdown of the relationship, a stage so hair-raising that writers on the subject, with their love of order, have simply failed to take note of it. Thereafter the shadow of calumny lay over the relationship, with its victim – Nietzsche – determined not to give ground to his hated model.

Nietzsche himself described Wagner's treatment of him as a 'mortal insult' that he could not bring himself to speak about until after the composer's death.[115] In his letters of 1883, he circles around this trauma on no fewer than four occasions, a trauma that apparently drove him to the brink of taking his own life. But only once did he actually break his silence, even though his correspondents could surely have guessed what he meant by the expression 'mortal insult'. In *Human, All Too Human*, which appeared in the year in which the incident took place, he included a section 'On Friends', in which he drew attention to the commercial basis of such relationships. They were almost always based on the fact that 'some things are never said, indeed never even touched upon'. And he went on to ask the question 'Are there people who cannot be mortally wounded if they discover what their most intimate friends basically know about them?'

But only those people who have something to hide can be 'mortally wounded'. It was evidently Wagner's friend Malwida von Meysenbug who was the first to receive hints from Nietzsche as to the actual meaning of the term. But when she asked exactly what the 'mortal insult' consisted of, Nietzsche must have realized that she would pass his reply on to Cosima, who was one of her closest friends. Only in this light can we explain the evasiveness of his answer: 'I'll tell you!' he said, only to back-pedal. It was Wagner's 'slow retreat and crawling back to Christianity'.[116] But this was neither new nor particularly interesting to Malwida, who may well have wondered whether Nietzsche, in spite of his way with words, had perhaps used the wrong expression. For the phrase 'mortal insult' really implies something different.

If she had seen the letter that Nietzsche sent the very next day to his only real confidant, she would have had her doubts confirmed. Writing to the critical theologian Franz Overbeck, Nietzsche did not repeat this explanation of the breakdown of his relations with Wagner but said only that 'there was something between us amounting to a mortal insult, and it could have ended terribly if he'd lived any longer'.[117] If this had referred simply to Wagner's 'crawling back to Christianity', then Overbeck, critical of the established Church as he was, would have been the first to sympathize with his correspondent. But why should Nietzsche's 'terrible' reaction have been precluded by Wagner's death? As Nietzsche was to prove in due course, it was as easy to attack a dead Wagner as a living one. In short, the explanation must lie elsewhere. Might things have even ended in a duel? Overbeck was in fact used to all manner of acts of madness from his friend, and so he will hardly have been unduly troubled by what he read on this occasion.

Perhaps that is why Nietzsche proceeded to put more wood on the fire. In July he told Overbeck's wife that 'a number of examples of an unfathomable perfidiousness in the matter of revenge' had come to his attention: their perpetrator was Wagner. Although he was unwilling to say more, he risked a comparison whereby the 'glass' of his life, 'which has already survived quite a lot', had on this occasion almost shattered.[118] In 1878, following the incident in question, Nietzsche had noted: 'To blast out the basest calumnies under the hypocritical name of fellow feeling.' And 'To blot oneself out.'[119]

Only once did he lift the veil of secrecy, when writing to his assistant, Heinrich Köselitz, to whom he gave the pen name of Peter Gast, and then only 'on condition that you burn this letter straightaway'. Here he noted that during his lifetime Wagner had 'teemed with wicked ideas'. 'But what do you say to the fact that he exchanged letters on the subject (even with my doctors), in order to express his conviction that my new way of thinking is the result of unnatural excesses, with hints of pederasty.'[120] Far from burning the letter, Köselitz later published it in his correspondence with Nietzsche, omitting only the incriminating phrase 'with hints of pederasty'.

This certainly constitutes a 'mortal insult'. The mere suspicion of pederasty, as homosexuality was known at this time, was enough to destroy a middle-class life and, if proven, would lead to imprisonment, with the result that many of the men denounced in this way preferred to end their own lives. Those who denounced their fellow humans tended to use innuendo, in order not to appear in the wrong light themselves. If we may believe Nietzsche, this is precisely what happened in his own case. He was convinced that 'since 1876' Wagner had regarded him as 'his one and only enemy' and that he put into circulation a rumour that was bound to 'mortally offend' his secret adversary. In order to punish Nietzsche for his apostasy, Wagner described him as a pervert.

Nietzsche discovered this when he called on his doctor, Otto Eiser, at his surgery in Frankfurt, probably on 4 April 1878. Eiser was an ardent Bayreuthian, in which capacity he had founded the Frankfurt Wagner Society and written an article on the *Ring*. He wasted little time examining Nietzsche but showed him a letter from which he could have gathered all he needed to know about his patient's medical history. It was from Wagner. And inasmuch as Wagner himself had encouraged Eiser not to leave his patient in the dark about its contents, Eiser, evidently having taken leave of his senses, confronted the unsuspecting Nietzsche with Wagner's long-range diagnosis.

'Why Nietzsche broke with Wagner', Eiser recalled with some pride, 'is something that I alone know, for the break took place under my roof, in my surgery, when, motivated by the best of intentions, I showed that letter to Nietzsche. A furious outburst was the consequence. Nietzsche was beside himself – the words that he found for Wagner are unrepeatable.'[121]

Nietzsche was right to be furious. In violation of his oath of confidentiality, Eiser had corresponded with Wagner, and the latter had used the opportunity to circulate a dangerous calumny that Nietzsche alone knew to be true. Once such a secret was out, it spread of its own accord, thanks not least to the Bayreuth rumour mill. Hans von Wolzogen – Nietzsche's successor in the

Office of Propaganda – was party to the correspondence, with the result that Wagner's stance was soon an open secret.

What, then, had caused Nietzsche to explode? As was obvious to Wagner's erstwhile disciple, the composer's inspired, not to say virtuosic, letter was a masterpiece of hypocrisy that could most certainly be described as an 'example of unfathomable perfidiousness in the matter of revenge'. Such was his concern 'for the health of our friend N.', Wagner wrote, that he had been encouraged to draw certain comparisons with other young men whom he had watched 'being destroyed by symptoms' similar to those evinced by Nietzsche.

Although he did not mention them by name, Wagner was thinking of Theodor Apel and Karl Ritter. The former was said to have gone 'totally blind' as a result of his depraved excesses, while the latter was 'eking out a pitiful existence, his nerves completely shattered'. Not to put too fine a point on it, Wagner was in error in both cases. His old friend and benefactor Karl Ritter was living in Italy as a dramatist and writing prolifically on the theatre. He died eight years after Wagner. And as Wagner was perfectly well aware, Apel – another of his benefactors – had lost his eyesight in the wake of a riding accident in 1836, not that this prevented him from marrying and, like Ritter, continuing to write plays. When he died, much respected, in 1867, he had not seen Wagner for a quarter of a century.

In spite of this, Wagner claimed that he had seen both men destroyed by similar symptoms and discovered 'only too clearly that these symptoms were the result of onanism. Guided by these experiences, I observed N. more closely, and on the strength of his traits and characteristic habits, this fear of mine became a conviction. I do not believe that I need express myself more circumstantially on this point.'[122]

Further explanations were unnecessary, for in the nineteenth century the term 'onanism' was often used as a euphemism for homosexuality. After all, Wagner had taken exception to Nietzsche's gentler characteristics, which were similar to those of the king, just as he had objected to Nietzsche's typical habit of surrounding himself with men 'during the hours of darkness'. Nietzsche understood what he meant, and the barb struck home. News of Nietzsche's 'perversity' did the rounds in Bayreuth and from there it even reached the Nietzsche archives in Weimar. If the disciple had pointed out in his celebratory essay of 1876 that the emperor was wearing no clothes, the emperor had now got his own back in a cruel and terrible way.

Wagner had sought his revenge because he regarded Nietzsche as a traitor. According to Cosima, he had 'wormed his way' into their confidence 'like a spy'.

Having gained what he needed, he had then thrown in his lot with the Jews. For Wagner, Nietzsche's apostasy reflected an archetypal situation, so much so that in 1878 he told Cosima that his circle of friends was so small that he 'kept coming back to the same experiences'.[123] Time and again his friends turned out to be his enemies, seeking to rob him of his inheritance. 'This good-for-nothing has taken everything from me,' he complained on reading *Human, All Too Human*, 'even the weapons with which he now attacks me. How perverse, how subtle and at the same time how shallow!'[124]

The harmless Anselmus had finally become the thieving Beckmesser. Even as late as February 1883, only a few days before his death, Wagner saw Nietzsche before him with the classic attributes of the adversary: 'Everything of value' was 'borrowed' from Schopenhauer. Now he 'disliked everything' about Nietzsche. A single photograph was enough to 'show what a fop he is'. Nietzsche was 'a complete nonentity'. He had 'no ideas of his own, no blood of his own, it is all foreign blood that has been poured into him'.[125]

If Wagner insists on blood, it is because his inheritance was at stake. The future of Germany hung in the balance, the perverse Nietzsche having seized the pure Wagnerian inheritance before going over to the side of the enemy. Thus fortified, he could enter the great and decisive battle. Wagner sensed that in Nietzsche he had found his greatest enemy, and he was to be proved right both then and in death. His former disciple fought against him, using his own weapons, as though he was still alive.

And he was indeed still alive – in Nietzsche. For Nietzsche saw the battle that he fought with his dead model through the latter's eyes. 'Who, apart from Wagner, can teach us', he asked in 1888, 'that "the old god", having morally compromised himself in every way, will finally be redeemed by a freethinker and an immoralist?'

Of course, he meant himself: like Siegfried, he would cast aside Wotan, the father of the gods. 'Admire in particular this final profundity', he added coquettishly. 'Do you understand him? I – guard against understanding him.'[126]

Soon after this Nietzsche was to merge with his idol completely, informing the staff at the asylum in Jena on 27 March 1889: 'My wife Cosima Wagner brought me here.'[127]

'Qualhall'

Once Wotan had fathered Siegfried and married his goddess, he built his Valhalla and, not far away, his residence Wahnfried. From now on, Bayreuth was regarded as the one achievement that set Wagner apart from all other opera composers. Yet Bayreuth was in fact the least of his distinguishing features.

After all, the Festspielhaus in Bayreuth, even if it belonged to Wagner, was an ordinary opera house like any other, just as his dramas were staged there as ordinary operas, for all that they were not supposed to have anything in common with traditional opera-house fare. True, Wagner's theatre had certain features that set it off to its advantage from other theatres, just as the operas performed there had no difficulty maintaining their dominance over their rivals. But the one essential difference existed only in the deluded imagination of the faithful. Bayreuth's aura consisted in Wagner's aura, an aura of which the community that had summoned it into existence wanted to be a part.

Wagner did not share their delusion. According to his own later reconstruction of events, he had not dreamt of Valhalla during his post-revolutionary depression in order to realize it decades later at the same time as the *Ring*. A resplendent citadel-like theatre had been of no interest to him at that time, not least because such buildings were liable to be destroyed, whereas the work that had revealed himself to him could lay claim to eternal validity. Moreover, he had scarcely planned a family, and it was certainly not the hope of progeny that drove him into Cosima's arms. Since 1864, when Ludwig's intervention had entitled him to regard himself as a fellow royal, he had been able to afford whatever he wanted, and so he graciously allowed the unhappy Cosima to bask in his new and apparently boundless glory. But this brought her up against her own limitations. Whatever meant happiness for him was henceforth measured by the yardstick of his family. Bayreuth was not the dream come true of a man with a great vision of future humanity but – as history was to prove – a family concern run on the lines of a limited company.

The Wagner household moved from Tribschen to Bayreuth in 1872. Within that household there was a balance of power similar to the one that Cosima instantly noted between Nietzsche and Paul Rée. The younger of the two men, she wrote, pretended to be 'entirely taken in and subjugated' by the older Nietzsche in order to 'outwit' him. It may not have been wit and cunning that dictated Cosima's attitude towards the volatile Wagner, but it was certainly the shrewdness of the weaker woman who knew when to play her trump cards, including the one that always took the trick and that went by the name of Franz Liszt.

Her diaries begin in 1869, six months before the birth of Siegfried, and end in 1883 with Wagner's death. Throughout these thirteen years, the conflict between Cosima and her husband, which she exploited as a means to gain power, runs through their pages like a satanic motif. The mere mention of his father-in-law's name was often enough to cause Wagner to grow agitated and have difficulty breathing. And if he felt neglected in favour of his rival, an emotional disaster was the outcome. One such incident marked the completion of *Götterdämmerung*. When Wagner put the finishing touches to his life's work on 21 November 1874, Cosima failed to cast a glance at the final page of the finished score and to shower Wagner with the praise that he expected, handing him instead a letter from her father. 'Offended, he shows me that it is finished and then says bitterly that, when a letter arrives from my father, all thought for him – everything – is swept away.'[128] Wagner then withdrew to his room, complaining, and it was not until 3 December that Cosima continued her diary. This 'gap of more than a week', comments the Wagnerian John Deathridge, 'is in many ways more eloquent than the rest of the diaries put together.'[129]

This may be a slight exaggeration but it certainly goes to the heart of the matter. Cosima exercised power over Wagner, and he responded by relapsing into childhood patterns of behaviour. For Cosima had only briefly remained true to the type of sisterly lover who turned her back on a world of slavish marriage in order to enter the sun-drenched land of freedom with her brother. The only composition that seems to have been inspired by his love for Cosima was dedicated to this archetype. The *Siegfried Idyll* is a Song of Songs to Brünnhilde, who is destined for the hero 'from time immemorial' and who, in contradistinction to the drama, presents him with a son recalled in the work's second subject, headed 'Schlaf, Kindchen, schlafe'.

Cosima's transmogrification into a mother figure naturally brought with it a whole string of disadvantages, with the problems that Johanna Rosine had caused her son half a century earlier now seeming to repeat themselves. Even the early diary entries of 1869 speak of the two main torments – the fear of loss and jealousy – which, in all their irrationality, were to cast their pall over the final years of Wagner's life. Whereas his mother had often abandoned him as a child, the mature composer was constantly afraid that Cosima might suddenly disappear from his life. 'During the morning,' she noted on 11 July 1869, 'R. comes up to my room "in order to see whether I'm still here", he keeps thinking I'm going to run away.'[130] As a result, he often described her as 'the girl from the fairy world who will soon disappear'[131] – no doubt a reference to the fairytale character who abandons her children and visits them only on certain nights. 'He calls me Melusine.'[132]

As in Geyer's day, he was tormented by twin jealousies as head of the family, too. Not only was there the threatening ghost of the father figure in his black cassock, but five children contended for their mother's love. He repeatedly reproached Cosima for 'literally killing' herself 'with bringing up the children,

I am now all mother, and he is losing me entirely'. That same evening he remarked that 'it looked as though I was expecting to die and wished only to sacrifice myself on all sides'.[133] In one of his dreams, he even saw the thirty-one-year-old Cosima 'on her bier, surrounded by the children'.

The imaginary loss of the mother figure had its counterpart in the very real loss of his lover. Not only had he to make do without his secret rose-scented chamber, he soon had to forgo sexual relations, as Cosima – partly out of decorousness towards her children and partly out of a guilty conscience caused by her cuckolded husband – reduced their couplings to a minimum, making no secret of the fact in the pages of her diary. The apostle of sexual love was left to comment with some bitterness that she would 'dearly like to introduce that renunciation business here'.[134] On another occasion he ventured a feeble pun: 'Justice a splendid word, sex is not to be deterred.' According to Cosima, he suddenly blurted this out, laughing, at table.[135] For her part, she resisted his demands with the 'curious voluptuousness of the suffering' with which she had hoped to achieve sanctity even as a girl.

Sanctity and majesty: the nobility that was denied her by her illegitimate birth she now sought to acquire by dint of a strict regime. In this, her secret models were her distinguished father, who was a house guest of Europe's aristocracy, and his well-to-do mistress, Carolyne Sayn-Wittgenstein, who was said to be a frequent visitor to the Vatican. The bad habits that Wagner had acquired as a child in Leipzig were beaten out of him, together – if possible – with all memory of his origins.

When Wagner, a gifted vocal impersonator, 'high-spiritedly' mimicked the Saxon accent of his Dresden colleague Ferdinand Heine, Cosima was 'not amused', as she humourlessly reported, prompting Wagner to retort by making a point of principle: 'You do not care for my friend – well, that's the world that brought forth Tannhäuser and Lohengrin.' Cosima could only laugh at this, causing Wagner to become even more explicit, as faithfully minuted by Cosima: 'And it is just the same with the Nibelungs and Tristan – not a whit different.'[136] Did she understand what he meant? Namely, that his essential nature, to which he owed these works, would always remain a closed book to her?

She seems not to have understood him. When he read to her from Wilhelm Heinse's Utopian novel on the theme of free love, *Ardinghello und die glückseeligen Inseln*, pointing out to her in advance that it had had a deep influence on him and his 'artwork of the future', she interrupted his reading, claiming that the author's permissive descriptions 'annoyed and vexed' her.[137] She even took exception to a classical writer like Aristophanes: 'There is too much licentiousness, in which women can take no part.'[138] Wagner – the Knight of the Silk

Garter – must have thought that he had ended up in a ladies' seminary. Once, for reasons that she could not begin to understand, he decided on a whim to have a jacket made 'like my negligee', but, just to be on the safe side, first asked his governess 'whether it was proper'.[139]

Just as Cosima kept her master under constant control, so she trained his entourage to be fawningly obsequious. Anyone who failed to show the necessary devotion found himself excluded. When Peter Cornelius produced an entertainment for the revered composer on the occasion of his sixtieth birthday, he once again felt the 'hostile spirit' that had come between Wagner and his former friends. For Cosima, only aristocrats and saints were of any account, and she herself made every effort to appear to be a cross between the two. Inclined to asceticism, she once confessed that lobster was 'the only dish for which I really have any appetite'. And so she named it 'le cardinal des mers'.[140]

For all her abstemious ways, she dressed in a 'most elegant' manner, carried a fan and a lorgnon and could be 'utterly charming', but generally spoke in a 'blasé' tone of voice. According to Wagner's publisher, Ludwig Strecker, 'she often mentioned her father and, it seemed, spoke of him with great love'. But she 'worshipped the Master to distraction, following his every movement and hanging on his every word'.[141] As Wagner was soon to notice, his wife was Argus-eyed.

Among the unresolved contradictions in Cosima's life was her French background. She hated the country that had left such an indelible imprint on every aspect of her character and longed to see the downfall of the city whose bigotry and élitist snobbery she embodied. No less worthy of destruction in her eyes were the French fashions through whose journals she eagerly leafed. She loathed the novels of Flaubert, Zola and Victor Hugo, novels in which she herself was portrayed as a classic example of a parvenu society. The 'get rich quick' mentality that she despised among Jewish bankers was one of her own most sacred maxims.

Precisely because she affected a German lifestyle, her borrowed nationalism assumed grimly determined sectarian features. With Catholic fervour she converted to Lutheranism and in Bayreuth's provincial backwater created a private religion that her husband and an entire community were persuaded to adopt. Her god was called 'Wagner', and 'Germany' was her future kingdom. Wahnfried became her Versailles, but in reverse: only after Wagner's death did it become clear who was to assume the role of the Sun King.

The Wagners followed the unfolding of the Franco-Prussian War of 1870–1 in a state of xenophobic fervour, Wagner not only writing a poem in praise of the German army outside Paris but also composing a *Kaisermarsch* for the victorious Kaiser, into whose cannons he had once stared, and finally feeling avenged for all the humiliations he had suffered on the banks of the Seine. The Wagners encouraged each other in their Francophobia, much as they did with their anti-Semitism. The outcome was equally pitiful.

During the Prussian siege of Paris, Wagner even thought up a comedy in the style of Kotzebue, the better to show his contempt for the vanquished enemy. *A Capitulation* can take its place effortlessly alongside the farcical 'comedy' in which the prompter Barnabas Kühlewind had played a prominent role. The Kühlewind of *A Capitulation* was no less a personage than Victor Hugo, and it may have helped to raise Cosima's spirits that Wagner has the poet of *Les misérables* emerge from the Paris sewers, sweating and groaning, here suitably transformed into a prompt box.

If Nietzsche called his erstwhile idol a born actor, this was certainly true of the years that Wagner spent with Cosima. Just as he played the part of the universal genius, he could also assume the role of a writer of trivial literature from the age of Geyer. But observers noted the effort that this cost him, and the impression of ventriloquism left by *A Capitulation* embarrassed even disciples like Nietzsche. And the respectful record left by the diarist as she gleaned the words from his lips suggests that Wagner did not feel at all happy in his present role. True, he completed the *Ring* and wrote *Parsifal* under the eyes of his omnipresent wife and surrounded by his teeming court, but her diaries fail to answer the question whether he owed all this to his new life or achieved it in spite of it.

In his last substantial letter to Nietzsche, written before the latter's envenomed essay arrived in Bayreuth, Wagner revealed the man behind the mask for one last time. 'Unfortunately I've reached the point', he wrote in May 1876, 'where I can get through the morass of daily life only by means of good and bad jokes.' He would have been happy, he went on, to forgo the prestige which, as Nietzsche did not need telling, was one of Cosima's main concerns. At a banquet, one of his artists had proposed a toast to the 'tremendous increase in my reputation through the success of the festival'.[142] In his reply, Wagner had noted only that he had unfortunately found a hair in his reputation, which he was happy to cede to the restaurateur.

Wagner was not the man to accept things as they were. If he did not like something, he could not live with it. Not since he had begun working in it had the theatre given him any pleasure. At first he directed his criticism at the repertory, but he was soon attacking the institution itself: operas would exist only as long as there were opera houses to perform them. It was impossible to burn them down, and so they would have to be reorganized. In vain he drew up plans to reform the theatre, submitting a whole series of schemes, first in Dresden, then in Zurich and finally in Vienna and Munich. With a shrug of their communal shoulders, the authorities gave him to understand that there was no need for any such plans and that, as was to become clear in due course, there would never be any need for them. It seemed obvious, then, for Wagner to build a theatre of his own, a theatre in which he would no longer be subject to the whims of an intendant and the public at large. What was more obvious than Bayreuth?

But however self-evident the idea may seem now, it struck Wagner only relatively late in the day. Originally he wanted no theatre of his own. His answer to the pitiful situation of opera in his own day was not to build an alternative theatre but to have no theatre at all. The very idea disturbed him. After all, the reality that interested him could not be achieved in the theatre, where it was upstaged by artificiality. People sat in the auditorium, staring at the proscenium stage, in order to forget their own lives.

For Wagner, by contrast, art meant the end of all illusion, for it taught us to grasp reality – in other words, to understand ourselves within the universe of ideas. Art had now taken over the role that had earlier been played by philosophy. Art was where the truth of the whole was revealed. In its mirror humanity could recognize itself again. Exactly where this happened was a matter of some indifference.

For the first of his works that was intended to do justice to this demand, Wagner devised 'the boldest' of plans in Zurich in 1850. *Siegfried's Tod* was to be performed three times to a non-paying audience in an improvised wooden theatre run up 'where I am now'. The theatre would then be 'torn down' and the 'whole business would be over'.[143] Shortly afterwards he added that not only would the theatre be knocked down but his 'score would be burnt'. 'It is my one hope in life to achieve this.'[144] Later still he even thought of throwing himself on the funeral pyre – not as a token of his failure, but as a symbol of his success. As in Hegel's *Phenomenology of Spirit*, history was now complete. Over the Golgotha of the spirit there rose in radiant brightness the absolute self-consciousness of humanity.

One such incident would strip away the theatre's chrysalis-like covering and reveal itself in a radiant vision as transformed reality. No 'play' would be performed here for money. Rather, people would be confronted with the meaning of their very existence in the guise of Siegfried's death. Like a religious miracle, such an event demanded to be seen as unique. After all, Christ's crucifixion was not repeated, except in Oberammergau. Once people understood what was happening, they could dispense with a repeat performance and instead tear down the wooden theatre and burn the libretto.

Another word for this transformation of the world was 'revolution'. But it was not enough to set fire to the world and hope that a new spirit would arise from its smouldering ruins. This spirit would be found only in Wagner's Nibelung tragedy. 'With this new conception of mine,' he wrote to Uhlig in 1851, 'I am moving completely away from our present-day theatre and its public.' Once the revolution had done away with the ossified theatre and with all that was bound up with it, he planned to 'run up a theatre' on the banks of the Rhine in order to 'reveal to the men of the revolution the meaning of this revolution in its noblest sense'.[145] If the performance achieved this aim, he assured the readers of A Communication to My Friends, then 'a further series' of performances was of 'as much indifference' to him 'as it is bound to appear superfluous'.[146]

As late as 1854 Wagner was still stressing the uniqueness of this performance, after which 'house and work may be destroyed as far as I am concerned'.[147] But by the time he came to publish the poem of the Ring in 1863 he was already thinking in terms of a production line: the 'safest means' of 'saving the work from gradually being lost completely', he now believed, was if he himself 'organized revivals of the great original performances'.[148] Needless to say, this did not represent a return to the idea of repertory performances but tacitly took its cue from the religious custom of regularly reviving divine revelations in the form of cultic festivals. For Wagner, it remained a matter of indifference whether these performances were modelled on those of Greek tragedy or whether their basis was the Festival of Transubstantiation celebrated by Cosima.

The royal miracle of 1864 brought with it an end to the idea of a wooden construction. Ludwig bought the performing rights to the whole Ring and in consequence wanted to see it staged at his own convenience, together with Wagner's other operas. A suitable theatre was to leave all existing theatres far behind it, an august and proud-standing pile on the heights above the Isar, where the city and land could gaze up at it in awe. It would have been the first Richard Wagner Festival Theatre, contributing to the greater glory of its founder Ludwig, who already spoke of it as the 'magnificent building of the future'.[149] When it was later built in Bayreuth on a more limited budget – still by the grace of the fairytale monarch, albeit in a less obvious manner – all that remained of Wagner's Zurich dream was the half-timbered exterior. No one had any time now for the meaning of the revolution in its noblest sense – or in any other sense, for that matter.

But without that meaning, the whole idea of Bayreuth was meaningless – unless, that is, audiences returned, remorsefully, to the stage spectacular, to the traditional business of the theatre with its all-powerful general intendant, its cult of the diva and a public that paid through the nose. But this would have marked a return to tired operatic routine, something that Wagner could not want to see happen without calling the whole of his life into question.

In fact, if audiences returned to a state that had long been superseded, it was not in a spirit of remorse but with their heads held high. Bayreuth was a triumph of tradition. The town's festival was an onstage celebration of Wagner's victory over himself. His desire 'to dispense entirely with outward splendour and present the work to men and women with no conventional extras',[150] as he had expressed himself with some passion in Bayreuth in 1873, could not be realized. Not only for Cosima did the solemn imitation of reality become the touchstone of art. Audiences, too, wanted perfect illusion, and they got it, albeit in a creakily old-fashioned style. Wagner's theatrical revolution was bound to fail, but apart from Nietzsche, the composer himself was the only person to notice.

And he fought against the idea. Why should the perfection that he had achieved in the music not also be attainable on stage? Why did the eye of the spectator always have to see something different from that which the orchestra revealed to the ear's inner eye? Could one art form not hold another in thrall, just as the dancing sisterly Muses had done in *The Artwork of the Future*?

The reality of the theatre showed that this was not possible. The overwhelmingly eloquent power of the symphonic writing, helped to achieve precise expression by the sung text, degraded the visual spectacle to the level of something both pitiful and sobering. The acting and gestures of the artistes on stage fell hopelessly short of the eloquence of the music, so that Wagner even advised increased activity. Yet the dilemma remained: all that was acted out on stage took place in an infinitely livelier, more graphic and hence more appropriate manner in the music. For anyone with ears, the theatre of illusion could only be disillusioning.

Wagner solved the problem in a predictably brilliant way by calling on the help of Arthur Schopenhauer. According to Schopenhauer, the blatant reality of life that seemed nowhere more embarrassing than in the theatre, with its costumes and painted sets, was only apparently real, being in fact one of the illusions that the will conjured up to delude the senses. It was a mere 'Vorstellung', meaning both 'idea' in the Schopenhauerian sense and a stage presentation or performance. Unlike everyday reality, in which this fact remained obscured, audiences were conscious of it in the theatre: here everything was mere semblance. Inasmuch as reality was actually a form of theatre, audiences could rediscover the essence of reality there.

And this is exactly where the music comes in. It alone reveals this essence, which Schopenhauer called the 'will', in all its vibrant immediacy. Existence appears in all its manifold forms, being broken down into its contradictory parts and revealing a tensely suffering infinity that none the less emerges as a unity. Through musical sounds it allows man to recognize the essence of creation not outside but within himself. In that way he is able to recognize his own true nature in turn. From this ocean, which is beyond time and space and which is barely distinguishable from Schelling's account of the world's origins, a true picture of the world rises up, like the divine spark of light.

This, in turn, is revealed not to the outer but to the inner eye alone. As described by Schopenhauer in his 'Essay on Spirit Seeing', our consciousness sees itself in a dreamlike vision that reflects the very thing that is taking place in the music. In the ecstatic awareness of the ocean of sound, whole scenes are created before the ear's inner eye, scenes that could present themselves to our outward senses in only a makeshift manner.

Wagner himself had noted on the occasion of a performance of *Tannhäuser* that he could 'no longer bear these theatres in which everything is so close – it all seems so crude'.[151] Instead of real scenery, he hoped that in Bayreuth the audience would see 'a scene removed, as it were, to the unapproachable world of dreams'. At the same time, 'music, rising up eerily from the "mystic abyss"', would be heard, so that the audience, recalling the vapours ascending from beneath the seat of the Pythia, would be transported into that 'inspired state of clairvoyance in which the picture on stage merges into the truest effigy of life itself'.[152]

In order to achieve this hypnotic effect, Wagner lowered the orchestra pit and designed the auditorium in the form of an amphitheatre, darkening it to the point where it was no longer possible to see where the stage started. Audiences would thus be unable to tell where reality ended and illusion began. As a result Wagner banished everything that drew attention to the 'theatricality' of the experience, so that the senses, stirred by the invisible orchestra, could be held in thrall by the onstage vision, which seemed to hover like an apparition in the darkness of the space around it.

A phenomenon that Cosima had experienced in her exhibitionist moments of somnambulism and that Nietzsche had described as Dionysian clairvoyance in his study on Attic tragedy was by no means unknown to Wagner himself. It struck him while he was working on *Götterdämmerung* that 'such a musician, when he is composing, falls into a sort of insane, somnambulistic state'.[153] And he expected exactly the same from his audience, who would otherwise be only too painfully aware of the inner contradiction within his synthesis of the arts.

If in 1872 Wagner advised the Schopenhauerian Nietzsche to remove his spectacles when attending a performance of *Tristan und Isolde* ('You should hear nothing but the orchestra!')[154] and if in 1876 he told Malwida von Meysenbug, 'Don't look too much! Just listen!',[155] he meant precisely this: the 'unvisible theatre'. Only when the music fired the imagination was the stage transformed into a higher reality. Then the divine element would appear, the Idea, and the world would recognize itself, raptly, in its own mirror. It is not just in *Parsifal* that time becomes space and history is superseded in the self-consciousness of the whole. Yet the sight of the tenor's tonsils invariably brought the audience down to earth again with a bump.

Cosima felt the same. In 1871 she confessed to Wagner that 'to a certain extent all performances', whether of *Die Meistersinger* or *Tristan und Isolde,* 'left her cold'. When introduced to these works by the Master in person, she regularly went into ecstasies, but in a theatre auditorium she felt 'rather as though she was cut off from the work'. Whether she really felt this or whether she was merely echoing her husband, Wagner immediately sensed that she understood him. He felt exactly the same, he told her, and knew 'that we shall regard our Nibelung theatre with cold pleasure, watching and observing'. Significantly, he added that 'for ourselves we do not need it, our pleasures lie in the idea'.[156]

The entry into Valhalla took place in several stages, with Ludwig providing the rainbow bridge. The Wagners had first visited Bayreuth together in 1871 and had liked what they saw of the provincial Franconian town, with the result that they announced the first festival for 1873. Initially it was thought that they would have to manage without the king's help, and so the enterprise was to be financed by wealthy music lovers whose contributions were added to those of the newly founded Wagner Societies. Unfortunately, these 'patrons' proved less open-handed than had been hoped, so that by 1874, Wagner, who since 1872 had taken personal charge of the building work on the Festspielhaus and on his villa, Wahnfried, was faced with the threat of bankruptcy.

He approached Kaiser Wilhelm, suggesting that the *Ring* might be staged to celebrate the fifth anniversary of Prussia's defeat of France, but the suggestion came to nothing. Even so, the emperor donated 22,500 marks and even exercised his right to attend the performances, a right acquired by his purchase of twenty-five Patron's Certificates. But this in itself was insufficient to avert financial disaster, and it was again the king of Bavaria who had to sort out the mess. He had already invested 30,000 thalers in the *Ring* and now made available a further sum of 100,000 thalers by way of a loan for the theatre, in addition to a gift of 25,000 thalers for Wahnfried. Following the deficit on the first festival, he lost little time in granting a further loan of 100,000 thalers. Wagner knew very well that the realization of a dream he had never imagined would come true in this way had been made possible by funds he was really not entitled to claim. After all, one does not extort money from a cretin, and if Wagner took advantage of Ludwig's whims, this does not alter the fact that the king was a fantast who from a legal point of view was barely responsible for his actions.

With his move to Bayreuth, Wagner ceased to be a Romantic genius and became a Wilhelminian enterpreneur, albeit one who still had to play the part of a Romantic genius. Indeed, not only did he play the part, he *was* a Romantic genius, overseeing the building work on both the Festspielhaus and Wahnfried, rehearsing his singers, commissioning sets and costumes, raising money by means of concert tours and, to the same end, doing the honours in high society, while completing his 1848 revolutionary drama with Siegfried's death and transfiguration.

Caught up in marriage, oaths and contracts, Wagner thus buried his freedom fighter, a hero who meets his downfall in society. The constant torment caused by the dreams that Cosima dutifully noted down, together with what she called his 'exhaustion' and 'profound ill humour', suggests that he was burning the candle at both ends. On one occasion he played her the scene between Wotan and Fricka in which, as he explained to her, the god's 'love of life is broken'.[157]

Wotan had lost his freedom and had done so, moreover, by his own hand. In addition to the breathing difficulties and chest pains from which he suffered and which his doctors ascribed to an excessive build-up of gas in his digestive tract, he was also plagued by ulcers on his gums and limbs and a troublesome rash on his hands. 'R. much tormented by the rash on his fingers', Cosima noted, evidently incapable of seeing the connection between exhaustion and illness. The escape route that had once allowed Wagner to break free from intolerable situations was no longer open to him in Bayreuth.

Yet his past was more present than Cosima suspected and so too was a time over which she had no influence. The theatre that was built to Wagner's instructions was a recreation of the one in Riga, whose darkened, amphitheatrically rising auditorium had impressed Wagner in 1837, the very year in which Cosima was born. The *Ring*, which he was currently rehearsing, dated back to a period when she was still saying her rosary with an obdurate governess in Paris. The front of Wahnfried, likewise designed by the Master, bore a striking resemblance to the Wesendonck villa, which Cosima had seen as Hans von Bülow's new wife. The columned portico of the original was now replaced by an allegorical sgraffito on the 'artwork of the future' in which Wotan, doomed to perish, is seen between two women, while two ravens flutter round his head. As

Cosima learnt to her cost, nothing had changed about this archetypal relationship, with the sister on one side and the mother on the other.

'I'm now a pure businessman,' Wagner wrote to Nietzsche in 1875, 'in other words, I've become a theatre impresario. I feel dizzy, not just sometimes, but every day!'[158] Dizzy and dizzyingly manipulative, Wagner was absorbed by his new role, which was in fact an old one. As in his days as a Kapellmeister, he found himself fighting on every front, taking upon himself all the burdens that others were unwilling to bear, playing each of his characters with total self-abandon, clambering around the stage, dictating business letters, holding piano rehearsals for hours on end and in the evenings presiding over a salon, where his presence was expected. Spry to the point of collapsing with exhaustion, he concealed from himself and from others the fact that he had turned sixty and was suffering from a weak heart.

He had already had to tout for trade in the past, and now, escorted everywhere by Cosima, he sought to interest high society in his novel project, whether in Dresden, Leipzig, Berlin, Vienna or Hamburg, and so found himself bowing and scraping just as he had done as a court servant in Dresden, even if on this occasion there was an element of condescension to it all. He was later ashamed to admit that, as usual, he had merely been stared at like a curiosity and that not for a moment had anyone thought of parting with any funds for his project.

In spite of all this, he succeeded, and when the emperor patted him on the back and praised him with a double-edged compliment ('I never thought you'd bring it off'),[159] he seemed to have reached the very pinnacle of his existence as an artist. The crypto-aristocrat received the nation's high nobility in a temple to the arts that had been conjured out of thin air: among their number were the open-handed king of Bavaria and his equerry Count Holnstein, Prince Constantin's descendant the Grand Duke of Saxe-Weimar, the Prince of Hesse, the Dukes of Anhalt-Dessau and Schwarzburg-Sondershausen, the Countesses Dankelmann and Usedom, and finally the puffed-up Marie von Schleinitz, who had entered the Master's life many years earlier as Mimi von Buch, and her husband, the Prussian minister of the interior, who evidently felt the need to greet all and sundry with a sarcastic smile. Even the emperor of Brazil was determined not to be left out and came from tropical climes to see the blood of the Wälsungs bloom. It duly bloomed and flourished, and the distinguished congregation that had come to worship at the shrine and that included countless ordinary mortals such as Tchaikovsky, Bruckner, Saint-Saëns and the painter Adolf von Menzel lay sweating in each other's arms during these hot summer weeks. But only the press made a stink.

In his 'Retrospective Glance at the 1876 Festival', Wagner meditated on the palpable success of the event. 'It seemed', he wrote two years later, 'that no artist has ever been so honoured; for although people had witnessed such an artist being called to emperors and princes, no one could recall their ever coming to him.'[160] As John Deathridge has noted, these 'proud words' have been used by all later biographers to prove their point that Wagner was enthusiastic about Bayreuth.[161] Yet their meaning is in fact the exact opposite. After all, Wagner used the phrase 'it seemed', indicating that the situation could be seen in a different light. And only a few lines later, he adds his own view of it: if emperors and princes had come to him, it was merely 'out of a sense of amazement that the project had actually come about'. As always, people had gaped at him in astonishment but had 'given little heed to the idea that had inspired the undertaking'.

The audience's lack of understanding reflected the shortcomings of the staging. Although 'no company of artists' had ever been moved by such dedication, Wagner wondered whether this was enough. Had the result not been a theatrical undertaking like any other, rather than bringing enlightenment and understanding? Was the ponderous stage spectacle, plagued as it was by accidents, not completely compromised by the music? Had old-style opera not wormed its way into the very heart of his universal drama? Wagner thanked his loyal donors and singers and stage crew for their help in making the festival happen. But 'would anyone expect me to repeat it'?

No, this was not the revolutionary celebration of the end of history and the beginning of a human world of freedom and love. Who could have grasped the mystery of creation when distracted by the Rhinedaughters' treacherous swimming machines? How was it possible for the nine-year-old nag playing Grane to steal the show from the jubilant representatives of future humanity by ambling out from the wings? And if the audience was reduced by the sweltering heat and heady delights of the music to a state of somnambulism, Wagner himself was denied that mercy.

All the performances had remained 'botched affairs', he later complained, as he had 'staged them far too quickly, far too much and far too prematurely for our age'. He expressed the same misgivings even more clearly in his birthday letter to King Ludwig in 1879: the 'tremendous effort' expended on 'as stylish as possible a first performance of my Nibelung work' had 'in the end led simply to the birth of an ordinary child of the theatre'. Of his Valhalla on the Green Hill at Bayreuth, all that remained was an 'empty shell'.[162] In conversation with Cosima he called it 'Qualhall' – literally, his 'hall of torment'.[163]

To its creator, then, Bayreuth was an ordinary child of the theatre, and for those lacking the gift of spirit seeing it was to remain so for ever after. The enterprise, moreover, was in debt. By the end of the festival, the deficit stood at 148,000 marks, and had it not been for Ludwig's remaining steadfastly loyal to his idol, Wagner could have filed for bankruptcy. Six months after the festival was over, he hoped 'never again to hear of the *Nibelung's Ring*' and wished that 'the theatre might be burnt down'.[164]

For what would be achieved by going on? The gulf that had opened up between the music and the staging, in spite of the mystical darkness, could never be bridged. Wagner alone knew what he had aimed to achieve with the *Ring*, and so only he could judge the extent to which he had failed. His 'main feeling during the peformances' was 'never again, never again',[165] a point that he emphasized 'with some violence' two years later, when he exclaimed 'It was all wrong!' Cosima described it as an outburst of anger.[166]

Had the woman to whom he confided this sentiment really understood him? Inasmuch as his vision remained a closed book to her, his self-criticism was bound to be meaningless. And so she dismissed his opinion as though it were no more than a passing whim, before raising the 1876 production to the level of a dogma after his death. Until well into the twentieth century, a production that had filled Wagner himself with 'oppressive melancholy'[167] was regarded as emblematic of the 'Bayreuth style'. The notes taken by his fellow artists, recording his often contradictory wishes in terms of acting, gesture and diction, henceforth determined the canon of the onstage liturgy, with the theatrical Cosima functioning as its medium. The stone that the architect had rejected served as the foundation of her new faith.

She should have known better. Even during the rehearsals, Wagner had confided to her his 'increasingly profound insight into the inadequacy of the production', although she may not have realized that he was referring less to the weaknesses of the staging than to the problem of how to present the work at all. What, indeed, was there left to present if the music was able to conjure up a world entirely out of itself and if the singers had only to mime the promptings from the mystic abyss? How could the inner vision of the drama's world of ideas be reconciled with the outer world of winged helmets and bearskins? Would not any representation of the piece that failed to capture the spirit of the work's human drama sink back ineluctably to the hated level of operatic routine?

When in 1850 Wagner had been struck by the idea of performing his Nibelung drama in an open field, he had assumed that this spirit would prevail. It was not kings and ambassadors who were intended to make up his audience but the men and women of the revolution who would grasp their newfound freedom in the mirror held up before them. The spirit evoked by the tragedy of

Siegfried was the spirit that had inspired them to cast aside their yoke. Seized by the divine spark of joy, they would cease to notice the difference between 'I' and 'you' and between audience and stage. Then all that had previously been only theatre would finally be revealed as real life. Once this had been understood, there was no longer any need for the work or the stage or even for the work's author. For 'blessed in joy and sorrow, love alone can be'.

Was it this memory that left Wagner feeling so wretched? When he told Cosima about the 'inadequacy of the performance', he added an insight that had come to him in a flash and that explains his reaction in an elaborately dialectical manner: the inability to depict the drama on stage reflects the audience's inability to see its own drama on stage. The visible shortcoming on the one hand thus reveals the invisible shortcoming on the other. It was not the individual human being who could resolve this contradiction but only the ongoing course of history. Or in Wagner's words: 'The performance will lag as far behind the work as the work is from our age!'[168]

8 Retreat

The Praying Mantis

Only the final fifth of Wagner's life was marked by his symbiotic relationship with Cosima. She gained the whip hand by feigning subservience, while he submitted to the role that she allotted to him, an arrangement that attracted no further attention as it was the dominant role that she gave him, turning him into the lord of the universe. While this was the role he had long felt called upon to play, it came at a price, for he was no longer his own master, no longer the master of his own works. Although the fourteen years he spent under Cosima's control had no decisive impact on his creativity, they certainly affected the picture of him and of his works that was to be handed down to posterity.

Wagner scarcely seemed to remember that there had been a life before Cosima – it was as though she had handed him Hagen's potion, causing him to forget the past. His memories already bore the hallmark of the woman to whom he dictated them. From the outset, *My Life* was *her* life. If in this case he exercised a certain semi-conscious, semi-subliminal self-censorship that was also designed to take account of his memoir's dedicatee, the young King Ludwig of Bavaria, the other main record of his private life – Cosima's diaries – is additionally marked by the chronicler's conscious censorship.

Cosima's aim in keeping a diary was to sketch a true picture of Wagner for their son Siegfried, an aim which, in the opinion of the couple's biographers, proved eminently successful. Yet for the most part their only yardstick for the truth has been her own. Having no choice but to believe her, writers have been only too willing to do so. The fact that she was fond of revealing her great husband in all his weakness has been seen as proof of her credibility, but commentators have failed to note that this allowed her to stress her own greatness: greatness in forbearance, greatness in subservience, greatness in self-denial and greatness in self-sacrifice. Cosima was a convincing Mary Magdalene who proved her idol's superior precisely because of her pronounced inferiority.

Everything Wagner said during his fourteen years with Cosima was subjected to the censorship of her sacred office before it reached his contemporaries and hence posterity. That a great deal of material was not only suppressed but also altered and even destroyed is beyond doubt, although it is impossible, of course, to know exactly how much. She also tended to stamp the Master's thoughts with their joint hallmark, frequently writing 'we' where she should in fact have written 'he' and writing 'he' where she really meant 'I'. Wagner enjoyed holding forth in front of an audience and had turned this gift into something of a fine art, but these monologues are generally recounted as though they were dialogues between a loving husband and wife, Cosima often failing to notice her husband's ironical dismissal of her interjections. German, moreover, was a foreign language for her, and it is clear from her occasionally awkward constructions that many of his subtleties, puns and allusions were lost on her. His down-to-earth humour was as alien to her as it was to his disciple Nietzsche. What she jotted down in her notebook before transferring it to her official diary tended to reflect what she thought Wagner had intended to say, rather than what he actually meant.

Yet what he actually meant has also been preserved. The most important evidence for all that fell victim to her urge to control Wagner's life and thoughts has survived, ironically in her own hand. That part of the truth about Wagner that she sought to conceal in her diaries is none the less to be found precisely there. All that he really felt and wanted and feared, all that he longed for and that appalled him, his image of himself and the wife who has gone down in history as his alter ego: all this is to be found in his dreams. Cosima wrote them all down exactly as he recounted them, and inasmuch as she suspected no danger, she did so without editing them or commenting on them, as was her usual practice. In the four hundred or so dreams that Cosima recorded, we find a picture of the Wagner who asserted himself in the face of Cosima's censorship.

Thus, in the holy of holies of her diary, his unsuspecting wife recorded the hidden truth, a truth that she would have preferred to expunge from memory. It was not the truth concerning the will and its world, as Schopenhauer imagined it, but the truth about Wagner, a truth that Cosima would never have thought possible, not even in her wildest dreams. Wagner, by contrast, was no doubt aware that forces were at work here that were no longer under conscious control. 'When you go to bed,' he once mused, 'it is as though you are abandoning yourself to subterranean forces, to a full complement of demons that are lying in wait for you.'[1] Almost two-thirds of his dreams exposed him to that panic-stricken fear that had plagued him since childhood and that nothing could assuage. However much he may have felt that he was master of Bayreuth, his nightmares placed a serious question mark over that sense of sovereignty.

These oppressive visions were distinguished from ordinary dreams in one important respect. If their substance conjured up no more than a fleeting image that was gainsaid the instant the dreamer awoke, the fear that that image triggered proved that it was real by forcing him to wake up and face up to his sense of shock. Almost every one of his nightmares followed its own momentum in which the sense of fear increased in proportion to the threat. Once it had reached the point where Wagner could bear it no longer, he awoke from his torment, screaming or weeping like a child. The man who had reached the final phase of his life was reduced to the howls and misery of its first phase. The old man became a child whose mother had to comfort him. Yet it was generally the mother who had triggered his fear in the first place.

Wagner was fully aware, of course, that dreams are profoundly significant and cannot be dismissed out of hand. If that student of Schopenhauer Hans Sachs was right, then 'man's truest folly' is 'revealed to him in his dreams'. Although Freud was later to express this somewhat differently, the meaning remains the same: 'true folly' – or 'delusion' and, with it, those of our instinctive wishes and desires that are suppressed during the daytime – finds symbolic expression in dreams. These desires may also include the wish to break free from a false identity. The role that individuals play and that plays with the individual results in the loss of the true self, with all its wishes and desires. The more exclusively we identify with our false selves, the more the true self is forgotten. Only through the complex 'interpretation of dreams' – to quote Hans Sachs – can the lost individual find himself again.

Wagner's dreams sounded the alarm, inasmuch as they confronted him with the loss of his true self and at the same time reminded him of the need to shake off his false self. The violent wish to remove the false mask found expression in the no less violent horror at the alien forces that pursued him. The mortal fear of losing the self that he loved coincided with the wish to be rid of the other self that he feared as though it were a ghost. In one 'ghostly dream', for example, he was 'frightened by his double',[2] while in another he suffered from the idea that the phantom of night could turn up at his house in person. According to Cosima, he then forced himself to 'stay quietly in bed out of fear of meeting his double'.[3]

Not only his early torments from the Thomä House in Leipzig returned to haunt him so too did his early experiences of betrayal and unassuaged longing, of the fear of loss, homesickness and the dizzying intoxication of greatness that left its mark on the whole of his life and works. The theatre of his dreams brought all the old puppets back to life. And so the archetypes from the beginning of his life returned with the childhood that now established itself as a nocturnal alternative to the role that he was reduced to playing in Bayreuth.

Each night Wagner was reminded of the truth of the old adage that there is nothing new under the sun. Though the sets may have changed, the situations on stage remained the same. Wagner's 'truest folly' drew its strength from the eternal return of the same: the figures who appeared before his mind's eye were familiar to him from times long past, while the relationships between them formed the secret nucleus of his art. However much it may have been drowned out by the noise of his unloved life as an impresario, the law that had brought him his power maintained a tyrannical hold of his dreams, masterminding the performance of a puzzle with comic elements which, in keeping with the logic of the loss of self, was to end on a note of heartbreaking tragedy.

Although the whole fury of the later Wagner seems to have been directed at the Jews, they had only a walk-on part in his night-time theatre and seem not to have been one of his archetypes. They generally appear at the edge of the stage and often have positive features, bringing him honours and receiving his apologies. If his conscious view of the world was implacable in its extreme hostility, the night brought reconciliation. Evidently Ahasuerus was only one of the changing masks of the demon who stood up to him as his all too vivid adversary, bent on robbing him of both his legacy and his lover.

The usurper who presented himself in the guise of a negative father figure was joined by the wicked mother who tormented the dreamer with the fear of punishment and loss before betraying him to the usurper in all his vulnerable defencelessness. It is clear from Wagner's dreams that the betrayal of his love was more basic than that of the mythical Judas, and that he had suffered the loss of his rightful inheritance even before the hated nation entered his life.

Even Meyerbeer, who was otherwise the true embodiment of the curse that seemed to pursue Wagner, proved as kind and amiable as he had been in the beginning. They walked through Paris together, 'arm in arm', and when the older composer admitted with some embarrassment that he 'knew very well – it's the big nose', Wagner responded with a generous gesture, whereupon the public applauded their 'reconciliation'.[4]

The archetypes of the treacherous parents were joined by that of the kind father in whom the features of the police actuary Friedrich Wagner merged with those of the legendary ancestral ruler. The dreamer was finally allowed to approach the mythical king who, like a true father, received him with tears and embraces before handing over his legacy. Frederick the Great summoned him to his court and, in another dream, proved a true Wagnerian. Friedrich Wilhelm IV showered him with honours of every description and 'showed him boundless love',[5] reminding him in a later dream of the biblical parable of the prodigal son. The long dead monarch was 'so moved' that he could speak 'only with tears in his eyes'.[6]

Wagner's early suspicion that he had blue blood in his veins was confirmed by the dreams that he had about his mother. If on one occasion the queen of Prussia revealed herself as his mother, it emerged from another dream that 'all the princes at the Prussian court were his kinsmen'.[7] Other family members, too, appeared in a positive light. His good sister Rosalie assumed the form of a rosebush growing beside his bed. But as soon as the composer, still dreaming, showed the large flowers to his wife, they fell to the ground, all except the last one, which turned into a pineapple just as he was about to pick it and was served as a meal to Isolde, his first daughter by Cosima.

It was presumably his sisters who shone down brightly from the night sky, first as voluptuous moons, then, 'immensely large', as the Pleiades. In Leipzig, Wagner once recalled, Geyer had taken under his wing the 'seven orphaned members of the Wagner family',[8] hence his decision to use the Pleiades as his coat of arms.[9] It was with some pleasure, therefore, that he saw the symbol of his troop of sisters in a dream, only to notice a shadow 'creeping away downstairs' when he 'suddenly turned aside'. The shadow, Cosima added, was 'me!'[10]

But it was not only Wagner's real-life sisters who saw to his creature comforts; so too did his sisters in spirit. He dreamt of flaxen-haired women weeping because they were neglected; he dreamt, too, of fair-haired children whom he sired in secret, and he dreamt of Cosima delighting him with her 'beautiful golden blond hair' – it was as though Blandine were standing before him. Evidently it was again his dead lover and not Cosima – as Wagner flattered her into thinking – who had waited for him alone at the Paris *Tannhäuser*, heedless of her reputation. For in the same dream he saw his wife carrying a photograph of him as a trophy 'on the back of my hat beneath the veil':[11] unlike her self-sacrificing sister, Cosima was clearly turning her back on him. On another occasion she appeared to him wearing a 'rose-coloured sash', an object that normally reminded him of secret sensual pleasures, but which in Cosima's case left a 'pitiful' impression. 'My God!' he exclaimed forbearingly, 'she's doing it simply to please me!'[12]

For Wagner's 'sisters', Cosima had little understanding. He told Cosima of a 'troublesome dream' in which he was exposed to 'the importunities of a former female acquaintance', but his only concern, according to his wife's diary entry, was: 'My God, what will Cosima think?'[13] What Cosima does not seem to have realized is that in the exclamation 'My God!' lay clear disapproval, not of the woman's importunacy, but of the sanction that Wagner expected. The extent to which he feared this is revealed by a dream of 1881 in which he met 'all his old sweethearts', who, in keeping with the archetype, were 'all mixed up into a single person'. When his ideal sister 'pestered' him into taking her to his 'theatre', he 'would have been pleased if a policeman had misunderstood him and arrested him'.[14] This does not mean, as he gave Cosima to understand, that he would have preferred to serve a term of imprisonment rather than running the risk of being placed in the way of temptation, but that force alone could prevent him from entertaining such thoughts.

The fear of being caught out was deep-seated, as it threatened to bring with it the loss of self that he both feared and longed for. This ambivalence was to typify many of his most paradoxical dreams. Following one 'very bad night', he recalled a 'journey with his sister during which their carriage fell into a ravine'. But the frightening feeling of plunging headlong to his death was associated in Wagner's mind with the comforting consideration that Schopenhauer was 'right in his assertion that one wakes to death from life as if from a frightening dream'.[15] In other words, the abyss into which he was plummeting with his sister also brought with it redemption. Cosima can scarcely have imagined that this was expressed by the symbol of the carriage. Or did she recall the first time she had exchanged intimacies with Wagner while riding in such a carriage? They had plunged adulterously 'into the abyss', while enjoying themselves enormously.

For years this ambiguous carriage rumbled along while Wagner tossed and turned in his sleep. Once, when a certain 'old Aunt Friederike', who had 'grown much younger' and who may have been Friederike Meyer of blessed memory, turned up, Wagner sought desperately to find a carriage, while simultaneously wondering: 'What will Cosima say if I bring my old aunt?'[16] On another occasion, he hurriedly took his leave of his wife, before running to a bridge that was open only to cabs, but from all of them 'fat fellows' stared back at him and 'in despair he told himself that his journey was by no means necessary'.[17] A similar sense of despair overwhelmed him when he saw his dog run over by a carriage. Barely had he revived it with his 'caresses' when a second carriage arrived, this time full of women, whom he was on the point of sending packing when a third carriage hove into view.[18]

The ominous carriage is also found in one of Wagner's epic dreams from 1870, the sort of dream that was made up of a whole series of scenes. This time his journey took him to Constantinople, a city which he had never visited but which may have been significant for two reasons. The name recalls not only his princely ancestor, Constantin, but also Countess Nesselrode-Kalergis, later Countess Muchanoff, who was very close to Liszt and who had helped Wagner out of a tight financial spot in Paris in 1860, when she had given him ten thousand francs. 'But I was jealous of your father,' Wagner later confessed to Cosima, 'because he had sent her from Constantinople.'[19] Although this will not have been the real reason for Wagner's jealousy, the name of the city was undoubtedly associated with a certain longing that may well have been directed at the beautiful countess. In his dream, therefore, he lingered in the city and was 'so overwhelmed by the beauty of the place' that he could express his happiness only by praising it to the skies.

'Rapture' soon turned into its opposite. After he had 'lost' Minna, his dog Russ came to see him. The dog had injured its leg, but he managed to drag it to a tavern, where he found himself surrounded by ruffians. He left the inn and, after sleeping in the open air, woke to find himself in a carriage, with the dog hidden away beneath the seat. But his delight at finding Russ again was set at naught by the loss of his hat, which he could none the less see rolling along behind the carriage 'following me like a little dog'.[20] Yet the driver refused to stop. Meanwhile the carriage began to gather speed, rolling downhill towards the abyss, at which point Wagner woke up.

This incident might have opened Wagner's eyes to the discrepancy between his dreams and real life. With the start of his liaison with Cosima, the happiness for which he had yearned for so long seemed finally to smile on him, bringing him not only women's beauty but also the inheritance that was rightfully his. But he soon saw the animal side of his nature curbed, his freedom of movement trammelled, so that, for his own safety, he was forced to abandon the guest house that his monarch had provided and found himself in life's carriage once again, a vehicle that plunged inexorably towards the abyss, pursued by his loyal headgear, while his dog lay concealed at his feet.

The hat was a regular feature of his dreams and seems to refer to the protection that he longed to enjoy: in German 'Hut' means 'hat' but is also the word for 'protection' or 'safe keeping'. This emerges from the fact that he was reduced to a state of panic whenever he lost his hat. In 1882, for example, he dreamt that he tried on a hat at the home of Mathilde Maier, whom he had intended to marry immediately before Cosima arrived on the scene. At that juncture, his son Siegfried entered the room and presented him with 'a small one: here, papa'.[21] In turn, his dream about Constantinople implies that the woman who cared for him ran after him like a little dog. Whether the hat that she placed on his head suited him is called into question by another dream: once, when

Wagner was conducting in her native Paris, 'he lost his hat and, while he was looking for it, the players, to the sound of mocking laughter, brought him all manner of children's hats'.[22] These were not the last hats that he wore. Three months before his death, he saw himself wearing a 'remarkably large hat from which hung tassels that were very annoying'.[23] The God-fearing Cosima had given him a cardinal's hat.

No less frequent than these familiar standard figures were dogs. Although he treated them like members of the family and was deeply affected by their deaths, they were not among his archetypes. Rather, they stood for something else. As though under some evil spell, they represented Wagner himself – not the official Wagner of the Bayreuth Festival but the one who had, as it were, to hide beneath a bench because his doglike instincts had to be curbed. In fact it was instinct itself – the 'truest folly', in other words, the sex drive – that was condemned by Cosima to lead a dog's life. At the time of *Tristan und Isolde*, this instinct had still signified humanity's highest potential, but now it had to beg for every morsel and leap through every hoop. Whenever he referred to the deeper feelings he harboured for his four-legged friends, Wagner was thinking of himself. The sufferings that his dreams inflicted on them were his own.

Time and again Wagner's unredeemed nature forced its way back into his dreams. After one particular performance, he found himself surrounded by wild beasts 'which he had attracted'.[24] They licked his hand but at the same time bit him, preventing him from going on, something which Cosima, not understanding what was being said, interpreted as an act of homage on the part of the animal kingdom. On another occasion he found himself pursued by a beautiful greyhound that even addressed him and, 'becoming increasingly affectionate and importunate', placed its paws on his chest. Wagner thought it an 'enchanted beast', and as he tried to push it away, the animal assured him that if he were to take it in, it would never again be importunate.[25] Wagner's dog Marke likewise had the power of human speech and to its owner's astonishment sang an Italian duet with a stonemason's apprentice.

Wagner's favourite dog, at least in his dreams, was Russ, which Vreneli had given him as a love token. A black Newfoundland, it reminded him of the intermezzo in Geneva in 1866 when he had been cared for and no doubt also loved by his faithful chambermaid and had enjoyed a break from the rigours of his 'three lives in one' with Ludwig and Cosima. In one dream he was horrified to see Vreneli's gift 'run over', a sight that also expressed the severity with which Cosima dealt with Wagner's less desirable tendencies. In his grief over the animal, which lay on the ground 'like a shadow', he began to wonder 'whether it could be revived by love'. Wagner tried 'caressing' it, and it was duly restored to life.[26]

Six months later, the animal turned out to be a lion that 'suddenly ran down a slope with a labourer'.[27] Only a few days later Wagner dreamt that he had clubbed to death his dog Putz, which was 'incurably sick', before sadly calling after him: 'No one is bothering about you, you poor creature – now at least you'll find release.'[28] He then hid the dog beneath a pile of rubble that workmen had left in the garden at Wahnfried.

Described by Hans Mayer as a 'noble couple sans pareil', Wagner and Cosima lived in his dreams like dog and cat. According to one particular 'wild' dream, Cosima set a 'fierce black cat' on the doglike Wagner, and it was obvious to him that the cat was none other than Cosima herself.[29] Years later he was troubled by another 'bad dream', in which his wife countered him with catlike 'coldness', while her father stood behind her. The image, she noted in her diary, was triggered by a particular incident. While walking in the Hofgarten behind his house, Wagner had seen a cat being chased by dogs. It had then sought refuge in a tree in order to mock the pack of dogs from a safe height, 'assured of its victory'. The dreaming Wagner, so he himself believed, was 'the barking dog'.[30]

The fear that haunted him in his dreams often took possession of him during daylight hours, too. His final years brought with them an increasingly gloomy view of the world that assumed positively apocalyptic features. The man who, unnoticed by his doctors, was suffering from a fatal heart disease, sensed that the end of the world was at hand. His days began with 'chest spasms' and ended with sleeplessness and nightmares. And the world that had once lain at his feet as the radiant creation of the solar hero now revolved only around the dark nucleus of fear.

In 1881 he explained 'the birth of the universe' to Cosima: 'some central sun begins to revolve, out of desire, no, out of fear, and now this whirling that was born of fear is everywhere, with everything a matter of some indifference until we give things a moral significance'.[31] The 'whirling' that was born of fear and that Wagner associated with the restless course of the planets also expressed the feeling that his life no longer bore its centre within itself but revolved powerlessly around a foreign body.

This feeling of the loss of self, abandoning the victim to a superior force until he was finally annihilated, was one of Wagner's most faithful companions in life, familiar to him from his earliest childhood. If he had once resisted it and sought help and comfort from his fellow humans, he now realized that no provision had been made for such solace, either in his own life or in the blindly whirling chaos of the universe.

The first force that threatened to destroy him was the archetypal adversary, who now returned in his dreams, still closely associated with the woman Wagner loved and no less resolved than before to steal her from him, together with his inheritance and the life that depended upon her. Generally that adversary wore the mask of Franz Liszt. Once Wagner's bosom friend and benefactor, Liszt was now his keenest rival, contesting the favours of his lover. To add to his horror, his lover was playing into his adversary's hands. The perfidious conspiracy between Geyer and Johanna Rosine was now repeating itself, and the result was annihilating. Unsuspecting, Cosima heard only the cry of terror with which her husband awoke, allowing her to enter a new dream in her diary the following morning.

Even so, she could flatter herself that she played a leading role in most of his dreams. When her father wanted to 'kill' him and attacked him with 'an instrument of torture', she turned away 'with a cold expression in her eyes' and in keeping with her father's instructions refused to admit anyone who might come to his aid. She featured even in the dream in which a 'mighty vulture plummeted down' on a child suckled by Mathilde Wesendonck, who on this occasion appeared as a widow dressed in black, pale and sad, like Johanna Rosine after Geyer's death. On the earlier occasion Wagner's hopes of returning to his mother had been shattered, much as Cosima's attempt to 'lead him home' came to nothing when they 'lost each other in the increasingly confusing mass of streets'.[32]

Cosima's intimacies with her father, with whom she played duets in Wagner's dreams or whose playing she listened to on bended knees, an ecstatic expression on her face, were generally followed by their running away together. Wagner's desperate attempts to pursue them came to nothing because she 'ran so quickly' that her husband 'could not catch up' with her,[33] or because he was unable to light a fire in his room in order to dress. Instead he discovered a 'large dog' and asked: 'How has this got here?'[34]

Alongside the black-cassocked fiend, there was also Franz von Lenbach, apparently happy to help out as a fellow usurper. One of Germany's most famous portraitists, Lenbach set up his easel in Cosima's boudoir, triggering dangerous associations in Wagner's imagination. The fires of jealousy smouldered, for Lenbach was not the first portraitist in Wagner's life. The composer had repeatedly expressed his impulsive loathing of imitators, and now he dreamt that Cosima had left him, returning from Lenbach's studio only after midnight. Perhaps because Geyer had been a skilled tailor, she then explained, quite calmly, that she had been 'trying on dresses at Lenbach's', provoking a reaction in Wagner that makes sense only when we recall the archetypal adversary. 'Are you trying to drive me to suicide?' he exclaimed, beside himself with anger.[35]

Later that same year, the connection with Geyer became even more explicit. Once again Wagner woke up with a scream, the old trauma of betrayal having repeated itself. 'I abandoned him for some accursed painter, not one who was well known,' Cosima noted the next morning. Lenbach is ruled out because he was well known, while the epithet 'accursed' suggests that some archetypal event lay behind this episode, too.

Certainly, the painter had already proved himself capable not only of abducting women but of rewriting the past. He fled with Cosima only 'after a picture had been taken from his room and a hole made in the wallpaper'. Is this a memory of Friedrich Wagner, who had been written out of the plot and of whom no portrait is known to have survived? When Wagner, in his dream, asked the painter about the missing portrait, he had a 'feeling of very bad manners on his part', presumably like a child asking for something that it has been told not to ask for. The painter had 'nothing to say' to this. The 'most hideous thing imaginable' had then happened, Wagner concluded, at which point he woke up with a scream.

The most hideous thing imaginable is not described in any greater detail here, but what woke Wagner from his dream was evidently the headlong descent into the abyss, his ill treatment by a father's instrument of torture, the attack by a bird of prey. For years the mere appearance of Minna was enough to trigger the loss of self. She threatened him like a ghost that mocked his weaknesses, calling him to account for past injustices, refusing to recognize his marriage with Cosima and repeatedly pricking his conscience. His desperate cry 'But you're dead!'[36] initially roused him from his nightmare, but his dead wife taught him otherwise by returning that same night, 'brazen and angry', in order to haunt him all over again.

Of course, Minna was no more dead than was the archetype of the wicked mother whom she embodied. Or at least this was true until such time as she was replaced in the role by a woman more powerful than she. Only then was Minna allowed to return to playing the part of Wagner's erstwhile lover to whom he called out longingly in his dreams and whom he suddenly wanted to remarry. Embarrassingly, this plan was thwarted by the fact that, as Cosima noted, 'he was in a relationship with me'.[37] When Cosima abandoned him, as she did so often in his dreams, he addressed her as Minna, before assuring her: 'It was you after all.'[38]

It was certainly Cosima. For once Wagner's first wife had been released from her nightmarish existence, Cosima took over this ungrateful part. The hideousness now came from his present partner, as she was able to confide to her diary almost every morning. In March 1878, after a particularly 'frightening dream', he conceded for the first time: 'Minna is no longer enough when it is a question of giving me a fright – now you have to take over.'[39] When in the September of that year Wagner woke up from a bad dream, he confirmed that 'Minna no longer suffices to wake me up.'[40] When Cosima, dissatisfied with her role, complained the following January, Wagner asked her to be more understanding and accept his dreams and the routine associated with them: she should be pleased that 'if he has to be frightened into waking up', she was 'the only effective means of achieving this'.[41]

The comparison with Minna was not entirely accurate, for the Cosima of Wagner's dreams was a far more terrifying figure: she interfered in his dream world whenever she liked, and things that he kept from her during the daytime, sometimes not even admitting to himself, found unequivocally clear expression in his dreams. All the qualities he had ever ascribed to the 'wicked mother' now came together in Cosima, the woman he so volubly idolized proving to be a brilliant witch and the saint emerging as a monstrous product of hell. She had at her disposal a richly stocked arsenal of the most sophisticated mental torments, all of which ultimately produced the same result in the form of the loss of self. From his encounters with Cosima, Wagner always emerged as the loser.

By far the most frequent of Wagner's dreams revolved around Cosima's treachery. In endless variants she was forced to record in her diary that she had broken with him, gone behind his back and abandoned him; that she had left him and divorced him, running off with other men, including her father, not wanting to know him and not even wanting to hear of him ever again. Coldly and arrogantly she rejected him as a stranger who had forfeited his right to remain, ensuring that he was sent to prison while she danced a mazurka or played duets with her father. His lover left him in the lurch. And she laughed as she did so.

This had been the most painful, if not the most 'hideous', of notions since his childhood, and Cosima now proceeded to present it to him in all manner of possible variants. In order to get rid of him, she went mad, contracted the plague, drowned herself, sought death from a broken heart, had Liszt execute her as an act of penance or had herself driven away in a hearse. Whatever she did, it always proved effective, and Wagner screamed until he was blue in the face, just as he had done in the Thomä House in Leipzig.

A year before his death, he woke up with a scream from another such nightmare and told Cosima 'by way of a joke' that she 'seemed to him like Lady Anne beside Richard III'.[42] Cosima was familiar with the play as Wagner had read it to her in 1881, but she evidently preferred to pass no comment on the deeply unflattering comparison. Anne was, after all, Shakespeare's embodiment of cold-blooded betrayal committed by a woman against the man she loves. As she stands by the bier of the dead king, whom she grieves as her father-in-law just as she had earlier grieved the death of her husband, the king's son, the murderer of both men – the wicked Richard of Gloucester – appears before her with the aim of wooing her.

Anne has scarcely cursed him from the bottom of her heart when she lends an ear to his flattering advances. The scene begins on a note of grief and anger but by the end she is wearing the seducer's ring on her finger and 'with her whole heart' invites him into her empty marriage bed. It had struck Wagner as 'particularly horrible' that Anne, as willed by Nemesis, 'cannot sleep on account of her terrible dreams about her husband'.[43] This was a fate that she shared, of course, with Cosima.

If we may believe Wagner's bad dreams, his beloved spouse usurped not only his bed but his life, too. Just as she made the former unusable by returning home from an excursion with her father and filling his bed with 'nothing but watering cans and metalware', so she organized his life in such a way that he himself was no longer necessary. Was it, indeed, still his life? It was his works that first brought home to him the extent to which he had become alienated from his true self. Whenever he dreamt of performances of them, everything about them seemed wrong, and he no longer recognized himself in the reflection of the dramas on which he had worked all his life.

He and Cosima arrived too late for a performance of *Rienzi* and heard only the 'church music' from the first act.[44] At a gala performance of *Der fliegende Holländer* he discovered that a ballet had been added, written by a pupil of Liszt, a discovery that prompted him to explode: 'And you put up with that!'[45] At a performance of *Tannhäuser* he burst out screaming the words 'But that's scandalous!' because the singers spoke their parts instead of singing them. Although he hoped that at least Wolfram's 'Ode to the Evening Star' would be sung, this hope, too, proved futile, as the number was cut.[46] In *Lohengrin* the performers all forgot their parts, and in *Siegfried* the 'lights went out', whereupon Cosima was executed.[47]

Not even *Tristan und Isolde* was spared this catalogue of disasters, for the piece had been subjected to 'a complete change of words and music',[48] while *Die Meistersinger* was disfigured by being 'more spoken than sung' and by the fact that virtually the whole orchestra went home early.[49] There remained only the Bayreuth *Ring*, the failure of which was confirmed in another of Wagner's dreams by a twelve-page letter written by Cosima in which she summarized her 'reservations' and other 'objections' to the production.[50] And at a performance of *Götterdämmerung* she commented so loudly on the production that the singers made fun of her and Wagner 'wondered whether it really was Cosima'. But he recognized her by her 'rose-pink dress'.[51]

The mistress of the house could certainly manage without him. As early as 1870 he had dreamt that she had redecorated his house for him, something that struck him very favourably as she had previously been very strict with him. Everything was 'simple but practical, everything had been thought of', except that the piano was not in Wagner's room but in Cosima's, and it was clear that 'it was there that I had to work'. Then he realized that the room was a great hall: 'Here Cosima will receive her guests, I thought.' He was on the point of throwing himself at her feet in gratitude when he woke up.[52]

And he was right to wake up, for the unspoken fear that he associated with the 'hall' was soon confirmed, when he dreamt of a 'great party' that Cosima gave 'without his knowledge'.[53] To his annoyance, this same episode then repeated itself. On this occasion, there were inquisitive strangers everywhere, so that he could find 'nowhere to change out of his indoor clothes'. In his dream, Cosima kept saying to him smugly: 'But this is how you like it!'[54] These parties, which brought out Cosima's organizational skills, were soon followed by 'musical performances' that she arranged for 'no one in particular', promptly provoking Wagner's jealousy.[55]

Even more annoying was the fact that at one particular banquet Cosima sat 'on high table' next to Bülow's mother, rather than Wagner, leaving the latter no choice but to 'move down to the end of the table'.[56] But at least he was comparatively well off here, for by September 1882 there was no longer any room for him at all. Six months before he died from heart failure, he dreamt in Venice that the Villa Wahnfried had been 'completely altered' and that 'arrangements' had been made 'for a reception'. When asked who he was, he 'angrily gave his name in a loud voice'. In other words, nobody knew him any longer. And where was Cosima? Certainly not with Wagner. At the very moment that he spoke his name, he heard 'her laughing in a neighbouring room'. And with that he woke up.

At least in the world that revealed his 'truest folly' to him, the act of usurpation was complete. His works were no longer recognizable, his home was occupied by strangers, and the woman whom he loved and who had just assured him, somewhat exaggeratedly, that 'all the emotions I had previously laid before the Godhead I now offer up to him'[57] was enjoying his possessions while he had to beg to be admitted.

One particular image from his dream world sums up these bitter experiences. Three months before he died, Wagner saw himself sporting the cardinal's hat that his father-in-law should by rights have been wearing. The monstrous headgear annoyed him and so he tried to straighten the tassels a little, something it would have been better not to attempt, for a creature now appeared before him that wanted him to remain as he was – namely, as the likeness of the great Liszt. 'Thoroughly startled', he saw a 'giant grasshopper' staring back at him, motionlessly. The idol had found a praying mantis to worship it.

The World as the Wolf's Glen

Wagner's later essays do him little credit. From 1878 onwards, they appeared in the *Bayreuther Blätter*, the Bayreuth enterprise's central organ, expressing a change in his intellectual development that reflected the change in his personality. They confirmed his reputation as Germany's best-known anti-Semite, permanently blackening his image and obscuring his true achievements. In them, a writer whose Zurich essays had marked him out as a visionary in matters of art and who regarded himself as the last word in German idealism finally took his leave of philosophy. After a life dedicated to reflective thought he abandoned himself to the fears triggered in him by the adversary and to the hopes that he attached to his Redeemer. In this he was inspired and seconded by his wife. The conventicle that was profoundly alien to his nature proved to be her true form of existence, and thanks to Cosima a man who had once set out to liberate the world now became the founder of a sect.

Its articles of faith were promulgated in the pages of the *Bayreuther Blätter*, with its limited circulation of no more than 1,500 copies,[58] and were in the same relation to Wagner's true philosophy as the Bayreuth Master was to the homeless genius who had once declared love to be humanity's true god. But like its prophet, this love, born of the divine spark of joy, had suffered many privations. Its new name was 'compassion', and its new god was the Aryan Redeemer nailed to the Cross.

Although Wagner had in this way succeeded in reconciling the waspish Schopenhauer with Liszt's bigoted daughter, he could no longer appeal to the logic that had typified his earlier essays on art. Where a veritable edifice of ideas had once stood, a plushly furnished salon now invited passers-by in for a lively chat. The only requirement was faith. The miracles that would confirm that faith would follow as a matter of course.

The contradiction was so deep-seated that it cannot have escaped the attention of a man like Wagner, who had once had a virtuosic grasp of dialectics, for the universal compassion that was to bring salvation to the world did not apply to the very people who had brought disaster to it. If Wagner was racked by emotion at the thought of human and animal suffering, he was wholly implacable towards the Jews – not that this prevented him from tolerating their proximity as pianists, benefactors and conductors.

Wagner was not interested in individual cases groaning beneath the burden of Ahasuerus's curse but in Ahasuerus himself and in the idea of God's mocking murderer. As in Cosima's oneiric oracle, the world now fell into two distinct halves, with the crucified on one side and the army of crucifiers on the other. Life was a Golgotha spanning the whole of the earth. Preached to the tiniest of audiences, these sermons on the end of world at least touched on 'the idea of the global destruction of the Jews', as even the pro-Wagnerian *Wagner Handbook* concedes.[59]

But this was not their true aim, as it was to become for the Wagnerite Adolf Hitler. Nor was it a question of turning the world into a vegetarian's Paradise or of redeeming the animal kingdom by abolishing laboratory experiments on dogs. Still less was it a question of a much-touted 'moderation', this third pillar in the process of 'regeneration' that was to ennoble mankind through teetotalism and asceticism.

Wagner liked his half-bottle of champagne too much to give it up. In spite of his horror of slaughterhouses, he refused to stop eating steak. And as for Godfearing moderation, it was left to Cosima to set an example with her 'aspirations towards sainthood',[60] an attitude that Wagner mocked by singing 'We Belong to the Temperance Society'.[61] Even his promise to 'set the Christian religious holidays to music – they'll be my symphonies' was not intended to be taken entirely seriously,[62] although Cosima certainly assumed that it was, motivated as she was by the zeal of the founder of a new religion.

The true meaning of the essays of Wagner's old age lies in their attempt to reconcile the contradictions not within the world at large but within Wagner's own life. For it was these that were destroying him. The price of his union with Cosima was the loss of his own inmost nature, which subconsciously rebelled against this loss. Throughout these years he suffered not only from insomnia and depression but also from their somatic equivalents. All the illnesses that had ever plagued him returned at the end of his life.

He was troubled by rheumatism, constipation, a hernia, stomach-catarrh and boils, and he complained about haemorrhoids, flatulence and allergies. He suffered from eczema, including the dreaded erysipelas, which caused his nose and face to swell, just as it had in the past. Worst of all, however, were the heart spasms that 'rose up from his stomach' and left him wishing he were dead.

Modern medicine has suggested that he was suffering from angina pectoris that outsiders thought was a severe attack of asthma. During these attacks, Wagner turned blue and 'made violent movements with his hands as though he were literally wresting with an invisible enemy'.[63]

It appears from both Cosima's diaries and Glasenapp's biography that Wagner had recourse to 'opium drops'[64] in an attempt to ward off these life-threatening symptoms. He could not know, of course, that his constant constipation was a direct result of his intake of opium. When his doctor in Venice, Friedrich Keppler, later claimed that he 'took many powerful medicines that had been prescribed to him by various doctors whom he had consulted in the past, often taking them in large quantities and in no particular order', he was presumably referring to opium and chloral. When he 'mixed up his tablets' in November 1881 and swallowed 'five of the ones of which he should have taken only one', he fell back on what the chronicler described as his tried and tested antidote, 'more opium drops'.[65] This constant overdosing was something that his doctor could only regret but not prevent,[66] and resembled nothing so much as suicide by degrees.

Faith alone seemed to offer a means of escape from the vicious circle of self-denial that led to nightmares and ill humour, just as these found expression in turn in illnesses that could be offset only with drugs. But the question is what kind of faith? Certainly not that of Cosima and her priestly father, a faith too closely associated for Wagner's liking with the God of the Jews.

And so he created a new religion, just as he had once created a new art and a new philosophy to go with it. It was a religion that satisfied the saintly demands that Cosima placed on it, while at the same time taking account of Schopenhauer's denial of the world and a number of ideas that the later Wagner picked up from the writings of the ethnographer Joseph-Arthur Gobineau and two Christian ameliorists, Antoine Gleizès and the otherwise unidentified H. Haug. Although Wagner dismissed Haug as 'mad', he was happy to avail himself of his definition of the Jew as a 'calculating predator'.[67]

Wagner not only reinvented a faith that held out the promise of redemption to him, he also invented the godlike saviour to whom its cult was to be devoted, with only the name of the Messiah remaining common to both. Everything about the crucifixion and Communion had a Christian ring to it, yet it was no more than the phantasmagoria of an ageing magician and confirmed atheist. For Nietzsche, Wagner had 'wrapped himself up in the clouds of improbability to such an extent that paradox alone' seemed to be the only adequate way of dealing with him. The apostate disciple described him as a 'bundle of superstitions even during his own lifetime'.[68]

The paradox was intentional. Once again Wagner attempted to pull himself out of the morass by his own bootlaces, the morass in this case being his life in Bayreuth, including the appalling local weather. Although he sometimes lacked the true seriousness of the founder of a new religion and dictated arrant nonsense to his secretary, all that passed his lips was regarded as divine revelation. If Cosima and her circle of initiates believed it, then Wagner himself was happy to do so. Or at least to make them believe that he did so. His ability to switch from utter seriousness to a type of humour that was rarely appreciated by his humourless wife is certainly one of the hallmarks of his later essays, investing them with the intangible, will-o'-the-wisp-like quality that Cosima may well have regarded as proof that they emanated from some higher source.

Yet not everything was as new as subscribers to the self-righteous *Bayreuther Blätter* might have imagined. In spite of his cardinal's hat, Wagner was still the man he was, and so the later essays of an artist described by Liszt as 'incomprehensible' retained the core of his earlier philosophy, with the world still resembling the Wolf's Glen in his eyes. From the 'yawning abyss' of existence there rose up the 'hideously shaped monsters of the deep', the 'diseased litter of the self-destructive will which daylight – alas, the history of humankind – has forced on us'.[69]

But it was no longer the murder of the solar hero and the theft of the hoard that marked the start of our endless history of suffering, as they had in *The Wibelungs*. Ever since Wagner had read Schopenhauer, the will had become responsible for all this, incessantly violating itself in its blind fury with acts of murder and theft. Existence became a slaughterhouse not because an adversary had destroyed the primeval unity and betrayed God's love but because it was a slaughterhouse and graveyard from the outset. Of God's love there was no longer any trace. Existence was now its own enemy. For the Sage of Frankfurt, the time had come to put an end to it.

The old division of the world into heroes and demons no longer applied, as there was no God to create life and therefore no Satan to drag creation down into the abyss. Where there is no light, there is no darkness either. Echoing Schopenhauer, Wagner saw nothing but a perpetual twilight that would vanish only when the inner sun of enlightenment rose and the phenomenal world disappeared in a nirvana that extinguished all trace of existence.

Even so, this uniform view of the world could not manage without an antagonistic element, the gloomy Schopenhauer proving implacable in his hatred of all those who resisted his attempt to convert them. Wagner was fully conscious of the parallel with his own thinking. Humanity was no longer divided into the guardians of the hoard and its despoilers, but into those who denied the will and those who affirmed it. All who had seen through the voracious, insatiable urgings of the world's most elemental force contributed to the redemption of the whole. All who abandoned themselves to it served only to perpetuate human suffering. Just as the sheep were divided from the goats at the Last Judgement, so the saints who triumphed over the world stood apart from the pleasure-seeking fetishists of existence.

And with this Wagner found himself back at the point where he had started. He had simply relocated the Fall, transferring it from the past to the present, or rather to the metaphysical moment beyond time and space that decided which camp the individual belonged to. From time immemorial the side of good had worked away at superseding the will, their actions manifest in the achievements of art and religion and above all in the procreation or rather the breeding of a type of person who would triumph over the world. The Redeemer came into the world not as a gift from God but as the result of a heroically world-denying line of descent. Unfortunately, the world failed to receive him with open arms, just as it spurned his inventor.

In keeping with its metaphysical conditioning, the side of evil strove to subvert this miraculous stage in human evolution and at the same time to root out culture and eradicate pure humanity by destroying the Redeemer who embodied that purity. The struggle that had raged in the *Ring* between love and its antithetical principle was now fought out between the idea of the will-denying individual and that of the world-affirming, inhuman monster. Wagner's names for the antagonists whose battle decided the fate of the universe are familiar, Christ the crucified Redeemer being contrasted with his eternal tormentor in the form of the 'material demon of humanity's decline': Judas was ranged against our Saviour.

Wagner's apocalyptic scenario has been a source of considerable embarrassment for modern scholars and biographers, most of whom have refused to believe their eyes and glossed over what the composer wrote in an attempt to get round the intellectual aberrations of a man who created a whole new universe. And so writers have shut their disbelieving eyes, assuring the world, as Dieter Borchmeyer has done, that Wagner drew 'a clear line between his own individual philosophy and a movement whose racist principle, emblazoned on its banners, was the strengthening of the Aryan race'.[70] Other writers, such as Martin Gregor-Dellin, have blamed Wagner's heirs, Glasenapp and Chamberlain, for a 'construct' that later critics 'seized on'.[71]

Just as the older parishioners had abandoned themselves to the deluded belief that everything was to be taken at face value, so the new congregation has convinced itself that this was not at all what Wagner intended.

If we read the articles that Wagner published in the *Bayreuther Blätter* as part of a wider context, we shall find that they constitute an internally coherent *summa theologica* whose structure stems from the fact that their ideas gradually fell into place in the process of dictation. In no fewer than ten interrelated essays, beginning in 1878 with a reissue of 'What Is German?' and culminating in 1882 with the daring profundities of 'Religion and Art' and its various supplements, Wagner promulgated the canon of his new faith. While its founder stuck none too closely to his own doctrine, Cosima and the community that it presupposed found in it proof that their religious instincts had not led them astray.

In the beginning, it was not the divine spirit that was on the face of the deep in order to recognize itself once again in that deep, but chaos. Thanks to Schopenhauer, all that Wagner experienced each night in his nightmares now seemed to him the very essence of existence. The will, in Wagner's account of Genesis, tore itself apart in its insatiable hunger, went out of its mind through greed and fear and created nature as its own slaughterhouse. Wherever life arose, it was met by suffering, only to take its leave again amidst torments. 'This world of greed and hatred', wrote Wagner in 'Religion and Art', was 'a world of ever-dying death'.[72] From time immemorial it had created that unspeakable 'wretchedness that everywhere holds us in thrall today'.[73] Wagner no longer believed in the famous sense of progress that his contemporaries saw in history. For him, humanity and its enlightenment were merely an empty trick.

Within this boundless misery there developed a race of humans who resisted the dictates of the blind will. As though from a sea of suffering the Himalayas rose up, on whose rarefied heights Wagner's Wibelungs had once drawn breath. By a happy coincidence, his first kingship lay conspicuously close to the Indian subcontinent on which the world-denying wisdom of the Brahmans and Buddhists was later to flourish. A connection was quickly made: at some unspecified date the subcontinent's 'original inhabitants' had naturally descended into the valleys of the Indus and disseminated their 'gentle religion'. The new gospel no longer consisted in the cult of the solar hero but in eating plants. The will that butchered beasts and humans was broken. With a smile of profound contentment, these vegetarians renounced their delight in murder and lost their appetites, and from the charnel house of the world rose the fragrant lotus of nirvana.

But not everyone chose the path of renunciation. Just as in *The Wibelungs* the first nation was divided and scattered to the remotest regions of the world, some of these gentle ascetics travelled westwards, where they necessarily degenerated into 'conquerors and founders of mighty empires'.[74] Hunger taught them to eat the herds that had given them milk, and the primal will, waking like a vampire, evolved a 'boundless desire for power'[75] that Wagner's pupil, Nietzsche, was to declare the most noble of instincts.

The return of the will inevitably reactivated our predatory instincts, and history became a scene of enslavement and destruction. 'Blood and corpses' covered the earth. Wagner discovered a mythical image for this in the Greek legend of the banquet of Thyestes, the grandson of the Titan Tantalus. Thyestes seduced the wife of his brother, Atreus, and seized the latter's possessions, whereupon the cuckolded Atreus served up Thyestes' children at their unsuspecting father's table and offered him their blood to drink. This macabre banquet formed the starting point of the Atrides tradition, which was to inspire Aeschylus to write his *Oresteia* and Wagner to write his *Ring*. Rape, dispossession, infanticide – there had been nothing new under the sun since the days of the ancient Greeks.

But they not only lived like beasts of prey, they also understood this. The Greek spirit, Wagner and Nietzsche agreed, saw through the terrors and horrors of existence. True, cruelty did not lead to resignation, but the spirit could use it as the 'source of artistic insight'. While its view of goodness was still distorted, it had none the less discovered beauty, which rose above life's fathomless suffering like some sublime vision. In art it celebrated the phenomenon that helped it to transcend the ragings of the will. But it failed to find redemption. While its creations 'filled the world with a deceptive fragrance like a beautiful dream on the part of humanity, a fragrance that only those minds that were set free from the will's constraints were allowed to enjoy', the greater part of nature continued to suffer Tantalus's old torments, and the play of beauty delighted its onlookers 'without drying the poor man's tears'.[76]

The Jews now appeared as the antithesis of the Greeks. Whereas the latter had sought to break free from the world will and found release at least for a time in the contemplation of art, the inhabitants of the wilderness found no greater pleasure in life than to abandon themselves entirely to the greed of the ground, raising the desire for possessions and the pursuit of enjoyment to the point where these became their god, a god who brooked no rivals. This implacable 'maker of the Jewish world, Jehovah',[77] confirmed the chosen people in their predatory behaviour by spurning the harmless fruits of the fields and developing a taste for reeking animal sacrifices.

Inasmuch as the innermost nature of the world-destroying Jews was identical to that of the will, the demon of existence worked directly through them. Although they were almost human in their appearance, they were none the less the willing agents of chaos, and it was with some justification, therefore, that they could regard themselves as next in line for world dominion. All that stood in the way of their aspirations was eradicated. The heirs of the Himalayas' noble inhabitants degenerated through miscegenation, their possessions were expropriated and their art disfigured and debased to the point where it was no more than an object of sensual enjoyment.

As fate would have it, the Redeemer was born among this demonic nation. With Christ the forgotten spirit of the will's denial returned to the world. According to Wagner, it was not only the ancient Indian doctrine that was reborn in him, but the blood of the earth's first races, too. He could not have been Jewish, not least because the God who was his father had nothing in common with the God of the chosen race. 'That the God of our Saviour', wrote Wagner in 'Public and Popularity', 'should have been identified with the tribal god of Israel is one of the most terrible confusions in the whole history of the world.'[78] All that Jehovah set in train was rendered ineffectual by a knowledge of the true God, Christ. 'He who has recognized him', Wagner went on, 'sees the world and all its goods as vain.'

Above all, there was the question of the consumption of meat. A German translation of Antoine Gleizès's *Thalysie, ou La nouvelle existence* showed Wagner how man had developed from a state of vegetarian innocence to become a savage beast, while Gleizès's 'elucidated Christianity' also provided the composer with the decisive proof that he needed to demonstrate that Christ was a practising vegetarian and that the Last Supper represented a set of instructions on what his disciples should eat.[79]

Christ's sacrificial death now appeared in a new light. In a passage of biblical exegesis, Wagner explained that Christ 'gave his own flesh and blood as the ultimate and supreme expiation of all the sinfully shed blood and slaughtered flesh, and offered his disciples wine and bread for each day's meal: "Taste this alone in memory of me."' The Jews inevitably saw their hopes of world domination threatened by this gentle vegetarian.

Once again they revealed their predatory nature by persecuting and slaughtering the Lamb of God. Since then, however, the will that they had transfigured in the form of their cruel Jehovah had become an increasing burden for them. The huntsmen found that they were the hunted, pursued by an insatiable instinct for survival and condemned to endless flight. Assuming the name of Ahasuerus, the Wandering Jew began his journey through world history. Only death, Wagner had already predicted in 'Jews in Music', could redeem him from this curse.

As the free quotation from the Bible suggests, Wagner's Jesus of Nazareth owed less to the New Testament than to his own 1849 draft for a drama. Inspired by Feuerbach's critique of religion, Wagner had realized that the essence of the Messiah lay in his capacity for self-sacrifice. Having seen through the world as a place motivated solely by self-interest, Christ subsumed the fatal principle within himself and in doing so destroyed the hegemony of natural egoism. Under the impression left by Feuerbach's metaphysics of love, Wagner developed his thesis of the life-giving love-death suffered by his heroic couples. They too triumphed over the history of alienated humanity – not, however, by fading away into some never-never land but through the union of 'I' and 'you', a union that conquered death itself, finding in it the precondition for their total oneness.

The Jesus of Wagner's later works, by contrast, was a confirmed bachelor. There is no longer any trace of his revolutionary love of Mary Magdalene; instead, he is consumed by asceticism and voluntary suffering, performing the miracle of the 'reversal of the will' and, having transcended this basic instinct, proclaiming 'the kingdom of God',[80] a kingdom open to all who follow him. Love, once tainted by sex, is replaced by compassion at the heart of the redemptive process. For Wagner, compassion was synonymous with love based on the 'complete breaking of the individual will'.[81] It was not Feuerbach, however, who had initiated him into this mystery, but Cosima.

The mysticism associated with the Cross was only the negative aspect of revelation. Inasmuch as the 'raging' of the will expressed 'nothing more nor less than its self-denial', it followed logically from Wagner's dialectical line of reasoning that 'as a supersession of the will' this act of compassion constituted 'the negation of a negation, which according to the rules of logic we regard as an affirmation'.[82] What seems like a backward step and a return to the 1850s was merely intended to forge a link with the positive aspect of the crucifixion.

The affirmation of self-denial lay in Holy Communion. Just as Siegfried's self-sacrifice was subsumed by Brünnhilde and just as the dying Tristan was subsumed by Isolde, so Christ was consumed by his disciples in order for him to continue to live in them. Destroyed by death, his flesh and blood were resurrected by the spirit of love. They became his body, and it was his blood that throbbed in them. Instead of destroying nature by eating it in the manner of all living things, his disciples absorbed the very essence of love through Communion, and this love was then reborn in them. In this way the joy associated with the union of Wagner's loving couples returns in the Pentecostal ecstasy of the disciples inspired by the breath of love.

But Wagner wanted more than this. Encouraged by Gobineau's *Essay on the Inequality of the Human Races*, he combined the mystery of Communion with that of the noble inhabitants of the Himalayas. For the blood that flowed through Christ's veins stemmed from this ancient race and, according to Wagner, this blood had 'a peculiar capacity for conscious suffering'. In other words, the world-denying compassion that persuaded Christ to sacrifice his life was an inherited characteristic. By passing it on to his disciples at the Last Supper, he passed on the traditions of world-denial and racial purity. The only question is how? For 'blood' in the sense of genetic make-up cannot be passed on by the digestive tract but only by sexual union. Or did Wagner the atheist share Cosima's belief in transubstantiation?

Wagner was clearly aware of this dilemma and with unusual matter of factness admitted that he was operating 'at the extreme limit of a speculation hovering between physics and metaphysics'.[83] But what was he looking for here? In the first place, it was a reconciliation of opposites, for when he speaks 'rapturously' of Communion (to quote Nietzsche's malicious comment), he really means three different processes: first, there is the purely physical process of vegetarian ingestion that exonerates the individual from the sin of butchery. But to abandon the consumption of meat is tantamount to renouncing egoism and hence to evincing a willingness for self-sacrifice, with the result that to stop eating meat is coterminous with the metaphysical act of Christ's self-sacrifice. Christ's denial of the will abolishes the distinction between himself and his disciples, as his disciples in turn became one with their Saviour through the ingestion of his flesh and blood, both of which have been transformed into vegetable matter.

But there remains the third and trickiest part of the sacrament. This could be understood only by those readers who forgot their Feuerbach and Bible and turned instead to *The Wibelungs*. When the first kingship arose in the Himalayas, the hoard served as a symbol of world dominion, but this was then lost and the hoard was stolen by the Jews, at which point all the old desire for it was transferred to the Grail and to the blood of the Redeemer. This blood was generously made available to all Christians in the Eucharist, the example of their Redeemer giving them the strength to mortify their own will. Through the bread and wine they became one with Christ, but only in a figurative sense.

Only the descendants of the first king – the 'purely human' Germans – could grasp the essentially metaphysical meaning of this mystery, a meaning that paradoxically was physical in nature. The true blood of Christ, which he had given to the world, was the genotype that had been transmitted from the old inhabitants of the Himalayas to the modern Aryans. But no one knew this. In most people, the pure blood of their ancestors – as Wagner had discovered from his latest reading – had become corrupt as a result of their notorious consumption of meat and their intermarriage with less noble races.

At its deepest level – a level that the Evangelists could never have imagined – Communion signified the act of purifying degenerate blood. According to Wagner, this miracle had already taken place in Christ himself, who was from a mixed-race background. Only through the power of the compassionate spirit had his blood been restored to its original purity. This detoxification process produced the 'divine sublimate of the species', the quintessence of the 'purely human'.

This was possible because the authentic blood of the Aryans differed from that of the inferior races not by virtue of physical plasma but solely through their capacity for conscious suffering. If the blood had lost its purity by being mixed with animal fats and with blood that was impure, it could still be restored to its original state by the decision to reverse the will and by the power of compassion or, in Wagner's words, by 'an extreme effort on the part of the will that desires redemption'.

This is precisely what happened at Communion, where, through the power of the spirit, the blood regained its lost spirituality. All those who attended Wagner's celebration of the Eucharist, which he was shortly to arrange on the Festival Hill, could, if they were lucky, experience for themselves the miracle of this transformation of their Saviour's blood. It could then be perpetuated not through vegetarianism but, as with Siegmund and Sieglinde, in the flesh.

Cosima's influence on Wagner's late writings was an open secret within the Wagnerian community. As in Munich he listened to her as though to a Pythian prophetess. All that he thought up and wrote down was first read out to her, so anxious was he not to cause her any displeasure. If it failed to find favour, it was immediately altered. Her voice is clearly audible in 'Religion and Art', as well as in its three fatal supplements, 'What Use Is This Knowledge?', 'Know Yourself' and 'Heroism and Christianity', where Wagner's officialese is permeated by an affectedly pious and precocious style that qualifies the Master's thoughts, making them more precise but ultimately rendering them a disservice. The reader almost has the impression that the Mistress of Bayreuth was afraid of the severe gaze of the Abbé Liszt and that she was attempting to bring Wagner's ideas into line with the Catholic faith that she had officially abjured. If Newman stressed the Jesuitical side of Cosima's character, this aspect of her personality certainly finds eloquent expression in her husband's 'regeneration essays'.

The term that Wagner uses – 'regeneration' – is unusual in German. He must have derived it from the Latin expression for the water in baptism, water whose 'supernatural power' is described by Feuerbach when he writes that 'the lavacrum regenerationis cleanses man from the grime of original sin, driving out the innate devil and reconciling him with God'.[84] Among the principal aims of Bayreuth's programme of regeneration was the expulsion of the Jews. Here Wagner could be assured of Cosima's ardent support, but whereas he tended towards a frontal assault that had led to a regrettable sense of isolation, she preferred a diplomatically clandestine struggle.

Like Wagner's, her hatred originated within her own family. Her mother, Marie d'Agoult, was descended on her mother's side from a Frankfurt family of bankers that had cold-shouldered her illegitimate children. The Bethmanns were rumoured to be of Jewish descent, and while the rumour was almost certainly groundless, the taint of foreign extraction still clung to their daughter just as surely as it did to the woman who supplanted Cosima's mother in her father's eyes: in Cosima's estimation, Princess Carolyne was to blame for all her life's sufferings, including Liszt's betrayal of his children and even her brother's premature death. Like Marie d'Agoult, Cosima saw in her a mortal enemy who held her idolized father 'in the clutches of an evil witch'.[85] In her diary she calls the princess a 'ghastly product of Jewish Catholicism'.[86]

Thanks not least to Cosima's help in formulating his venomous thoughts, Wagner's crusade against Christ's murderers acquired a new dimension. Initially he had been a lone voice crying in the wilderness, but now there was a popular movement which, as he noted with pride, owed its origins to his essay 'Jews in Music'.[87] In short, his cries had been heard, and dramatic consequences could no longer be ruled out. For tactical reasons the Wagners distanced themselves from the loose-knit assemblage of anti-Semites, while reinforcing their rear by means of the *Bayreuther Blätter*. The popular anti-Semitic movement was building up considerable momentum, which the Wagners were determined to exploit and if possible increase. The most appropriate means to this end seemed to be a public confession on the part of the celebrated Bayreuth Master.

Wagner's confession has generally been overlooked by the most recent writers on the subject but is to be found in the first of the 'continuations' of 'Religion and Art'. It leaves the reader in no doubt that he not only shared the resentment felt by his contemporaries but was the only person to draw the logical consequences. At the very beginning of 'Know Yourself', he refers to the 'present movement against the Jews', noting that the movement seems not to be entirely clear in its aims. Inasmuch as it has never asked itself 'what has given the Jews the power that they now have among us and over us and that strikes us as so pernicious',[88] it has inevitably failed to come up with the right answer.

If the question had caused much scratching of heads, it was because the German character risked being overwhelmed, a risk that suggested that its adversaries were better prepared for the struggle for survival than the Germans. If the Jews succeeded in asserting their supremacy, it was clearly because they were the more powerful race. Wagner had already proposed a solution to this troublesome problem in 'Jews in Music': it was not the strength of the intruders that mattered but the Aryans' acquired immunodeficiency.

Among lower organisms, too, the 'death of the body' gave foreign elements the strength to devour it. 'Then', wrote Wagner in 1850, 'the flesh of this body no doubt dissolves into a swarming colony of worms.' The image struck him as so apt that he returned to it a year before his death, arguing that the Jews did not cause any harm but merely 'signified' such harm. They were not the illness, but the symptom. In the 'wound of a poor horse or some other animal', declared the animal lover, 'one immediately sees a swarm of flies'.[89]

In what did this illness consist? In existence itself, an existence that tore itself apart through the blind will. While the noble Aryans rose above this eternal round of self-deceit and self-torment, a willing agent of universal egoism emerged in the form of the Jews, who took up arms against the forces that denied the will, finally crucifying the saint of compassionate world-renunciation. As this signal began, menacingly, to inspire the world, the Jews were forced to wage their war underground.

They were able to do so because the race of heroes had grown weaker, forfeiting the advantage of its early birth by dint of mindless mixed marriages and 'eating the bodies of murdered animals'.[90] The Aryans' loss of form was exploited by the demons of egoism, who infiltrated Christianity and replaced the loving self-sacrifice of Christ with the 'terrors' of Jehovah, with whose help they managed after all to 'rule the earth', just as they had been promised.[91]

This spiritual seizure of power went hand in hand with an equally unnoticed seizure of material power, ensuring possession not only of the earth's riches in the form of the hoard but also of its metaphysical counterpart, the Grail. This insidiously slow blood transfusion led to the 'degenerative commingling of the heroic blood of the noblest races with that of former cannibals now trained to be the business leaders of society'.[92] The former 'raging beast of prey' of the wilderness now sat side by side with the city's 'calculating beast of prey' at Thyestes' fun-packed feast.[93]

With 'Know Yourself' (1881) Wagner held up his mirror to the Germans, a mirror in which he wanted them to see not only their self-inflicted weakness but also the demon who ruthlessly benefited from it. As Wagner had already made clear to King Ludwig in 1865, this meant that 'one of the finest dispositions of the human race' had 'arguably been killed for good'.[94] The hope that his lone voice crying in the wilderness would finally be understood began to bear fruit only once the anti-Semitic movement had begun to form in Germany. It was this movement to which he addressed himself and which he hoped would be the first to draw the necessary consequences.

The situation seemed abundantly clear. On the one hand there was 'humanity's original tribe' enslaved in its own country and on the other the 'living demon of decline', a demon that had decked itself out as a 'German citizen of the Mosaic faith'. Wagner left his readers in no doubt that if his contemporaries did not want the Aryan race to be definitively destroyed by the Jews, thereby bringing an end to a soteriological movement that was designed to triumph over the world and that had lasted several millennia, consequences had to be drawn. The nature of these consequences was hidden rather than revealed by the puzzling language in which they were couched and left plenty of scope for interpretative niceties. But regular subscribers to the *Bayreuther Blätter* could certainly work out for themselves what Wagner really wanted. Or what Cosima really wanted, depending on what was at stake.

In retelling the story of the Passion of the race of heroes, Wagner used the metaphor of a nightmare from which only a sudden awakening could offer any release. The Germans were 'caught up in a dream that was now worrying, now oppressive',[95] and believed that their present misery was true for all time, whereas nothing could be further from the truth: it was merely a 'brain-spun fantasm on the part of the demon of suffering humanity'. Seduced by a mixture of Jewish Christianity, democratic ideas and errors of diet, the common people refused to listen and failed to notice that they had been robbed of their most sacred inheritance. But the 'demon' in whom the avaricious will finds its most graphic expression had created this nightmare simply in order to seize control of reality.

As in *Die Meistersinger*, with its 'Wach' auf!' chorus, there follows a wake-up call: 'At last, one crowning terror', writes Wagner, drawing on his own experience, 'gives the utterly tormented wretch the strength he needs: he wakes up, and what he had previously regarded as utterly real' turns out to be no more than a 'figment' of the will, which, aided and abetted by the demon of egoism, has led man astray through the labyrinth of his ideas. It was these ideas alone that persuaded Wagner's German contemporaries to attack each other in the 'madness of their partisan struggle', much as the guilds lay into each other on Saint John's Eve in sixteenth-century Nuremberg.

But dawn now approaches, and the nightmare recedes. What remains is what Wagner describes as his 'ultimate insight', which he articulates as though it has been imparted to him by some Pythia in the reeking cleft at Delphi. 'But only when the demon who gathers around him these maniacs in the madness of their partisan struggle is no longer able to find a where or when to lurk among us,' runs Wagner's oracular pronouncement, 'only then will there no longer be any Jews.' That this was the goal was something that every anti-Semite and every Bayreuthian knew very well. But how was it to be achieved? To the traditional cures of baptism, emancipation and expulsion was now added a new one, one whose import is not instantly clear.

In fact, Wagner's mysterious message can be decoded in one of two different ways. If we read the sentence with Schopenhauer as our guide, the 'where or when' represents the perceptual forms of time and space which, as fictional constructs of the will, provide the basis for all our sufferings. If we assume that the 'demon' of Wagner's oracular pronouncement is the will, man's madness will end when he denies the will and transcends the empirical schemata of time and space and, duly enlightened, achieves nirvana. Then there will certainly be no more Jews, but reality, too, will have vanished and with it the race of heroes that are part of that reality.

Wagner did not intend this, but there was – if need be – a neat way out. And he certainly needed one. In February 1881, shortly before he published 'Know Yourself', Wagner assured the Jewish impresario Angelo Neumann that he had 'absolutely no connection with the present "anti-Semitic" movement' and that an article of his 'which is shortly to appear in the *Bayreuther Blätter* will prove this so conclusively that it will be impossible for anyone of *intelligence* to associate me with that movement'.[96] This apparent apology is regularly cited by modern writers anxious to exculpate Wagner, but it needs to be seen in context.

Wagner had sold the performing rights of the *Ring* to Neumann, who wanted to tour the whole of Europe with the work. Shortly before the production opened in Berlin, Wagner's well-known anti-Semitism led to a certain amount of ill feeling in the capital, encouraging the Jewish journalist and editor of the *Börsenkurier*, Georg Davidsohn, to intervene on the composer's behalf. Davidsohn drew Neumann's attention to the fact that 'the Berlin undertaking would be seriously endangered if it were to be widely known that Wagner had taken a personal interest in the movement's demonstrations'. Fearing that his production would come to nothing, Neumann appealed to Cosima. The rest was merely a formality. That Wagner's comment to Neumann was merely a tactical ploy is clear from Cosima's diaries, in which Wagner expresses his delight at the 'great state of ferment against Israel. R. laughs: Is our journal responsible for that?'[97]

The true interpretation of Wagner's mysterious message, which he advances in 'Know Yourself', is less subtle than this and as such more suited to the 'movement' to which he commended it. Here the demon is none other than the

Jewish agent of the world will who will continue to egg the Germans into destroying themselves until banished from time and space and in that way achieve not nirvana but his own non-existence.

Wagner describes this as his 'great solution'. If the Germans had been blind to this situation hitherto, this had changed with the emergence of organized anti-Semitism. 'Only the present movement, which is conceivable amongst us alone' – in other words, the anti-Semitic movement – 'may bring this great solution within the reach of us Germans', Wagner declares with wholly unsibylline frankness. He evidently sensed the moral repugnancy of this insight, for he concludes that 'after overcoming all false shame' the Germans should shy away from it no longer.

This leaves little scope for misunderstanding: readers who had recognized themselves in the mirror of 'Know Yourself' should draw the ultimate conclusion if they did not wish to perish: only then would there be authentic Germans again, but no longer any Jews. And Wagner advised his readers to cast aside their natural timidity at so terrible an idea as it would rouse them from the nightmare that had been artificially induced. And in this case they should not feel inhibited at attacking their fellow humans because the Jews were very real demons, present in time and space. If they were deprived of their plasticity – in other words, robbed of the 'where and when' of their present abode – nothing would remain. In making this recommendation to the anti-Semitic movement, Wagner had crossed the Rubicon, for it went far beyond anything he had previously committed to paper. In encouraging his readers to cast aside their 'false' shame, he had abandoned his earlier passivity and passed over into the camp of his active supporters.

It was Cosima who was to blame, for it was she who had ensured that Wagner himself had cast aside all shame. The insidious ending of 'Know Yourself' bears her imprint. Evidently proud of having put her hand on the wheels of history that the great Master was turning, she admitted in the pages of her diary that she had influenced the article's shameless ending. On 10 February 1881, Wagner read the new piece to his wife, who reacted by 'referring back to the first ending'. In turn this led to a discussion between the two of them over 'whether the Jews can be redeemed at all'. She does not reveal the outcome of their discussion but later the same day, feigning innocence, noted that Wagner 'maintains that I do not like his article, which sounds very funny'.[98] Clearly he did not mean to be funny, for he returned to the subject the next morning, noting ironically that 'everything one writes, all articles, are silly nonsense'. By lunchtime he was back at his desk, 'altering the ending of his article' – to Cosima's 'regret', as she insisted in her diary.

His corrections found favour, and when he read her the revised ending, it struck her as 'more in keeping with the whole than the first one, and R. himself says that he always meant to write about us' – that is, about the Germans – 'not about the Jews. And yet I have to tell him', Cosima adds with scarcely concealed pride, 'how strange it feels when he alters anything at my instigation', for 'every idea' of his seemed to her 'sacred'.

'You foolish woman', Wagner retorted, evidently happy at having satisfied her. 'As if everything were not harmonious!' Yet there had been no question of harmony that morning when he had voiced his anger. Clearly it was due to his need for accord that he rewrote the ending as Cosima wanted, ambiguously expressing the unequivocal result of her interference. 'Jews in Music' had proposed 'redemption' ('Erlösung'), whereas thanks to Cosima 'Know Yourself' now ends with a reference to the 'great solution' ('Lösung'), with the prophetic final sentence claiming that this solution 'lay more readily within the reach of the Germans than within that of any other nation'.

Wagner had turned a huge wheel. Placed in position by Cosima, it influenced a movement that at its heart was terrorist in character. How far this influence was to carry would depend in part on the rise in fortunes of his name. If his success increased, as was already predictable, his political impact would also gain in importance. But as a cult figure, honoured by the Reich and worshipped in Bayreuth, his sombre pronouncements acquired the lustre of sublime directives. The tracts of a sectarian journal that any sober assessment would dismiss as 'silly nonsense' became Holy Writ, with the Wilhelminian Empire and even the fleet-building Kaiser recognizing themselves in them.

Was this what Wagner wanted? The fact that Cosima herself worked towards this goal with the obsession more normally associated with a religious fanatic is clear from the course taken by German history. And her diaries suggest that Wagner was keen, as far as possible, to want what his wife wanted. He too had dreamt that Bayreuth would be the Grail Temple of a race of heroes, but by 1881 his faith in that dream had been shattered and the Bayreuth project struck him as being a failure. Corrected by Cosima, his essays read like the tormented outpourings of a man overtaken by his life's worst nightmare, a nightmare that forsook him only in death. Wagner saw only death and destruction ahead of him, whereas Cosima divined the future of a national and religious enterprise.

In the 'truest folly' of his dreams, Wagner was plagued only by Cosima and the archetypes of childhood. There was little trace in the latter of his lifelong hatred of the Jews, a hatred that Liszt's daughter elevated to the status of the central dogma of the Bayreuth faith. The Jews were not the adversaries who every night forced him to face up to the loss of his self. Instead, he was overcome by the sense of shame that he advised others to cast aside. Did he suspect that the Jews were just a pretext designed to prevent him from admitting to a personal trauma? And that his hatred of them was only a transmuted form of the pain he felt at having lost hold of love?

Time and again he stressed that the teeming demons of decay appeared only when living matter died, only when love itself perished. In July 1881, while he was waxing rhapsodical on the subject of regeneration, Cosima noted in her diary that her husband had had a 'somewhat restless night': 'First he dreamt that I did not love him,' she noted, 'then that the Jews are all around him, turning into worms.'[99]

Judith

Cosima's sectarian sanctuary was none the less illumined by a transfiguring ray of light. While she herself proved to be the harsh mother of regeneration, Judith Gautier emerged as the Mathilde Wesendonck of *Parsifal*. In this respect, Wagner's final music drama was in the same relation to his late essays as the young Frenchwoman was to her somewhat older compatriot: for although Cosima was less than ten years older than Judith, the two women were in reality worlds apart.

Both came from Paris and both could lay claim to famous fathers, yet the differences began even here. Preoccupied with Carolyne Sayn-Wittgenstein, Liszt left his children in the claustrophobic care of father confessors and governesses, while a proud Théophile Gautier introduced his daughters to the society of dandies and libertines, mocking morality, advocating the enjoyment of exotically subtle pleasures and giving his children the Bohemian freedom of which Cosima and Blandine could only dream. As such, Gautier was a source of inspiration to the artists of aestheticism drunk on hookahs and oriental perfumes.

It was to this 'parfait magicien ès lettres françaises' that Baudelaire dedicated his *Fleurs du mal*. Baudelaire, as we know, was one of the earliest French Wagnerians and when Gautier took his then fifteen-year-old daughter to see the 1861 production of *Tannhäuser* that Baudelaire praised so much, the circle was complete. It was a circle that did not include the sanctimonious Cosima. Only with Huysmans's Black Mass were the circles to overlap at the end of the century when the black widow was already well embarked on the road to extremism.

For a long time, writers on Wagner found it hard to accept the idea that the Master loved another woman besides Cosima, and the related question whether during his Bayreuth years he could have loved another woman besides Judith seemed to them simply inconceivable. Although he himself admitted in various ways that he loved the highly gifted poetess, writers refused to believe him, partly because she seemed too young for the mature genius – she was probably born in 1845 or 1846, though she herself claimed it was in 1850 – and partly because Cosima's diaries have nothing to say on the subject. Unless Cosima herself confirmed it, it could not be true.

Wagner's biographers squirmed with embarrassment. While Glasenapp studiously averted his eyes and Westernhagen confessed himself baffled by this 'oddly illusionistic infatuation of Wagner's old age',[100] Martin Gregor-Dellin visualized a hypothetically inhibited scene in which the 'stern, bewitching Muse gently returned his kisses with girded bosom and blessed his endeavours in respect of *Parsifal*.[101] For his part, Hans-Joachim Bauer – a biographer entirely worthy of the era of Wolfgang Wagner – opines that Judith left on the Master 'the impression of sparkling wine'.[102] No doubt it was a cheap one.

Even Willi Schuh, who edited Wagner's letters to Judith Gautier when they came into the public domain in the 1930s, was certain that there was 'no real intellectual or emotional affinity' between them.[103] Judith's letters can no longer throw any light on the subject as they fell victim to the usual auto-da-fé by Cosima, who would no doubt have liked to burn her rival with them. In fact, some of the blame must also attach to Wagner himself, such was his fear that his inquisitorially gifted wife might discover them and read them in secret. If their contents had been even half as permissive as those of his own letters to Judith, Cosima would probably have filed for a divorce or at least put the fear of God into him.

Many writers on Wagner have been unable to grasp that works about love must have been based on the physical experience of love. And if a delight in love's shared pleasures reflected the procreative pleasure felt in creating the work of art, then the lovers' anguish must resemble the pain of the mother's birth pangs. Wagner had always felt this, and his aesthetic theory said as much. The poet's words descended into his own feminine ground, from whose night the answer came back, striking a note of musical mystery. The light of his eye fell into the darkness in which another's gaze shone back at him. From their act of recognition sprang the first act of procreation, while from creation sprang the history of its self-alienation: only through a process of suffering and mortal torment would creation regain its former wholeness. This was the tale that Wagner had to spend his whole life retelling. But it was only when he rediscovered himself in another's gaze and the darkness began to resound that this 'cruelly difficult' task could hope to succeed.

Judith seemed to embody all the 'sisters' whom Wagner had ever loved. Even before she entered his life, she had revealed herself as a distant admirer. More than that, she had come to his defence in print, while he in turn had divined in her articles 'a deep and intimate understanding that truly astonishes and moves me'.[104] When she finally appeared before him, she presumably took his breath away. Later he made her a confession that expresses the whole force of this sense of rediscovery, writing that 'I can do nothing but suffer and produce a little, a man whose life is a perpetual hurricane and whose movements in the face of this world are no more than convulsions'.[105] When he wrote 'I' he meant 'you', the 'you' with which he longed to merge. For 'Hurricane' was Judith's pet name.

Judith figures repeatedly in the diaries of the Goncourt brothers, two writers who throw light on a city that Wagner, pining away with unrequited love, would have most liked to raze to the ground. These literary daguerreotypes show a woman through whom the whole age spoke, caryatid and odalisque in one and the same person, alluring and annihilating and with an insatiable curiosity for the secrets of Araby and sex. When she was only sixteen, the Goncourts were already struck by her 'langorous, deep eyes, shaded by the shadows of long eyelids'.

Already the famous brothers feared for her reputation, as the two Gautier sisters brought 'to society the freedom and boldness of manner of a woman who, at a masked ball, has her face hidden behind a mask'. Later that same year – 1862 – the Goncourts met the object of their observations at a masked ball in honour of her father's birthday, at which she wore an Italian hoop skirt, 'with serpentine graces beneath her basquine and a virginal lasciviousness'. By the following year they could already see in the movements of this 'pretty and mischievous Oriental from Paris' a 'certain tender softness', while her 'hips swayed with a rhythm that recalled a harem', suggesting nothing so much as 'the intimate sweetness of pretty little animals'.

Ten years later, by which date Wagner already belonged to her, the promise of 1862 seemed to have been kept. Judith was now 'a strange, almost frightening beauty', her complexion 'of a whiteness hardly tinged with pink'. Edmond Goncourt also noted her 'pure, almost somnolent features and her large eyes, whose animal-like lashes – harsh lashes like tiny black pins – do not soften her expression with a shadow'. According to the astonished chronicler, Judith had 'the indefinable and mysterious quality of a sphinx'.[106] Goncourt omitted to add that this sphinx was notably well endowed, as Nadar's photograph indiscreetly reveals.

What a trial this was for Cosima. But worse was to come. On a whim, Judith arrived at Tribschen in 1869 in the company of two dandies who must have struck the lady of the house as the living refutation of her own austere endeavours. Catulle Mendès, to whom Judith was briefly married, she will immediately have recognized as Jewish, and a homosexual to boot – not that this prevented him from featuring in the pages of the Goncourts' journal as a 'hot-blooded stud' who joined Maupassant in orgies with masked women from high society. The high-spirited Catulle was a passionate Wagnerian who brought with him his friend the poet Auguste Villiers de l'Isle-Adam, in whom the Goncourts noted 'the febrile gaze of a man much given to hallunications and the small head of an onanist or opium eater'. In Lucerne, where the trio spent the night, the locals thought he was King Ludwig of Bavaria.

In short, it was a double ordeal for Cosima, and it was made worse when the Master fell for their exotic visitors and especially for the sphinx. Judith was an artist who could lay claim to the privilege of a total lack of constraint, encouraging Wagner to abandon the reserve urged upon him by Cosima and to fool around, climbing trees, rowing small boats, delivering himself of whimsical speeches and, suddenly recalling the seriousness of his situation, holding forth on the 'miseries' of his life and the mysteries of his creativity.

Judith was one of the first people to be permitted, under Cosima's envious gaze, to listen to the ecstasies of Siegfried and Brünnhilde, which Wagner sang to her himself – a role that her presence made it easy for him to assume. Though she was no blonde valkyrie but owed her charms to the miscegenation that her hosts condemned, she none the less possessed the stature and temperament of a Schröder-Devrient, to say nothing of the childlike enthusiasm that reminded Wagner of Jessie and the attentiveness of Mathilde Wesendonck.

In the course of one particular steamer ride, the two exchanged a fatalistic glance, although it remains unclear whether it was Wotan's eye gazing sadly into Brünnhilde's or the ardent valkyrie fixing her gaze on her solar hero Siegfried. 'The face of the Master,' wrote Judith, 'his beaming eyes, where blended the most beautiful shades of sapphire – that was what I saw, and I said to Madam Cosima, who thought quite as I did, "Now, at last, I comprehend that happiness of paradise, so extolled by believers, the seeing of the Gods face to face!"'[107]

If Cosima shared this sentiment, she certainly had no intention of sharing her god. On that very first radiant summer's morning in 1869 when Judith first set foot in Wagner's refuge at Tribschen, she was already aware of the 'glittering serpent', reporting in her diary on her disagreement with her godlike husband. He had immediately given his all, entertaining his guests with excerpts from *Die*

Walküre and *Tristan und Isolde*, following these up the next day with Wotan's emotional farewell, while Cosima remained on her guard. 'She is very remarkable,' she commented on the wild woman who had burst into their idyllic life of privation, 'so lacking in manners that I find it downright embarrassing, yet at the same time good-natured and terribly enthusiastic.'[108] When Wagner played Wagner, Cosima started to cry.

In the company of the sphinx, the stork cut a sorry figure. That Cosima was striving to achieve sainthood within her own lifetime was all too obvious from her appearance. Judith by contrast could never get enough of it and according to at least one recent writer pursued the delights of a bisexual relationship,[109] her pleasure in her own sexuality obvious not only from her appearance but from everything she thought and did. Striving to regain his old uninhibited manner, Wagner was quickly inflamed. 'Terrible dream,' Cosima recorded on 27 July, 'R. set his head on fire by carelessly turning up a gas flame.'[110]

Wagner's new flame caused violent displeasure not only to Cosima but to the other female members of Wagner's entourage, including both Valentina Serova, who, according to Cosima's diary, 'appears to be furious with Judith', and another of Wagner's benefactors, Marie Muchanoff, who, feeling that she had been passed over, could not believe her eyes. When Alexander Serov, not wanting to be left out, showed Cosima an article by Judith, she was 'horrified. I do not think we shall be able to have much more to do with these people.'[111]

She was wrong. Wagner, it is true, managed to reassure her in his long-winded way, repeating his expressions of love as often as she wanted to hear and immortalize them in her diary, but this did not alter the fact that he had found the 'you' to go with his 'I', kindling a fire that was almost certainly to remain alight until the time of his death. When Cosima, mortified by the return of his lust for life, wrote in her diary that she had 'renounced all forms of personal joy, may God grant that my beloved and the children are made happy by my silent presence',[112] she was wrong twice over. Her 'business of renunciation' gave Wagner no pleasure, as he repeatedly made clear to her, and he much preferred the noisy presence of the 'Hurricane' to his gaunt spouse's silent presence.

But the Parisian threesome finally left, and Cosima could breathe again. The next day, Wagner announced that he had 'had a very bad night with violent chest pains'.[113] Later that afternoon he showed his wife a letter in which he told Judith's enemy Serov that 'the French people who had so disturbed him had now left'. His music, he added – and Cosima recorded this without comment in her diary – 'could now proceed as earnestly and as gloomily as his wife could wish'. Did Cosima not understand? Or did she assume it was a joke? When Wagner went on to assure her 'Oh, how happy we shall be – what is Goethe's happy old age compared with mine?' she no doubt failed once again to note the sarcasm of his remark, with its reference to Goethe's 'happiness' in Marienbad. Nine years later he pointed out the parallel to Judith. 'What inspiration I found in your arms', he lamented in one of his clandestine letters. 'But everything is tragic, everything inclines at best towards elegy!'[114]

In order to be able to remain in contact with Judith following her return to France, Wagner pursued a twofold strategy, starting by convincing Cosima of the harmlessness of their relationship, with the result that the two women were soon exchanging friendly letters, Cosima's contribution to their correspondence resembling nothing so much as an attempt to neutralize the situation by fraternizing with the enemy. Indeed, she even gave Judith little errands to run, much as she had done with Nietzsche, asking her to obtain some 'mannequins' displaying the latest fashions and prevailing on her good offices as an emissary with her father in her attempts to obtain a divorce.

'Judith is still very dear to me', she noted cursorily in September. If she had known how much her husband echoed this sentiment, she would no doubt have expressed herself somewhat differently. For as the second part of his plot to remain in contact with Judith, Wagner had started to write to her in secret. While officially writing only to Catulle Mendès, whom he informed, for example, that Cosima was 'flattering herself into hoping that she will receive another letter from Madame Mendès',[115] Wagner used go-betweens to send billets-doux to his lover. Since these messages were destroyed, there is only indirect evidence of their contents, but it includes the following postscript to a letter that Wagner sent to Munich: 'Kindly pass this note on to Madame Mendès as quickly as possible.'[116]

Even during his wedding ceremony with Cosima on 25 August 1870 his lover was present in his thoughts: the date coincided not only with Ludwig's birthday but also with Judith's. And immediately after leaving the church in Lucerne, Cosima sent a note to her 'dear friend', its contents seeming to reflect her bridegroom's mood more than her own: 'We expected you at any moment and are very worried: where are you? As soon as our wedding was solemnized, my very first thought was for you. We embrace you with all our hearts, very concerned about you. The christening is on Sunday. Cosima.' Although she had been asked to be Siegfried's godparent, Judith was unable to attend the ceremony and therefore to assume this function, whereas the equally absent King Ludwig was entered in the church registry as Siegfried's godfather, even though he had no inkling that this honour had been conferred on him.

The extent to which even the family holidays were permeated by Wagner's longing to be with Judith is clear from a letter that he sent to Mendès on 5

September 1870, the day after Siegfried's postponed christening. 'If only you had stayed with us!' he wrote, before tactlessly alluding to the Prussian victories in the advance on Paris and adding that he would dearly like to have 'imprisoned' them. 'Not as prisoners of war. But in honour, in love and above all in music. And with that we would have been married, christened and everything else!'[117] The letter went off to the very city that Wagner described as 'this kept woman of the world'.[118] Its recipient was the woman whose clothes and luxuriant chignon the strict Cosima would have most liked to see incinerated. It was on the day before her wedding that she had her vision of the latest fashions being burnt to a cinder on the Odeonsplatz in Munich.

The fire that Judith had kindled could no longer be put out. Although nominally dedicated to Cosima, the *Siegfried Idyll* of 1870 expresses the Wälsung's ecstasy that Wagner had just addressed to his oriental valkyrie. Three years later he tried to 'lure' his lover to Bayreuth by using an official letter to both Judith and her husband to express what had previously been a secret: 'We love you with a very real love.'[119] His addressee understood. Wagner's 'you' no more included Judith's husband, Catulle Mendès, than the 'we' could refer to Cosima, who was already living in fear of the Hurricane's next onslaught.

Wagner loved Cosima. But this love of his cannot be compared with the love that he felt for his generally unavailable sisters. Perhaps the word that he was so fond of using did not even apply to this close relationship with Cosima. Rather, it was the love of a child that knows itself wholly dependent on its mother, a love whose omnipotence it feels only when it is withdrawn. This unbalanced relationship would become a passion only when it was felt to be deficient, when domestic bliss was in short supply and Wagner was threatened with loss. Then the nightly Wolf's Glen would begin to stir and he would plunge once again into the abyss of his bottomless existence.

Daily life, meanwhile, was conditioned by habit and by the power Cosima was able to exercise because the husband she worshipped feared the loss of her affection and obeyed her in advance. When Nietzsche, who knew about the love between men and women only from books, claimed that his former master was 'besotted' with Cosima, he was right, in spite of everything. It was he, after all, who discovered the 'will to power'. Yet there was no question of sexual addiction in the case of the 'noble couple', only an infantile dependency based not on enjoyment but on fear and on the deceptive feeling of being a little more protected within a hostile universe.

Bayreuth was again lashed by Hurricane Judith at the time of the first festival in 1876. If Cosima regarded Judith's presence as a threat to her very existence, for Wagner it was like the dawn of a new day. It was not the organizer of the social events accompanying the festival but Judith who, in his own words, was 'the only ray of love at a time that some people found delightful but that I found so unsatisfying'.[120] 'Some people' no doubt included the mistress of Wahnfried, who was completely absorbed by her role as admired hostess, a circumstance that in turn allowed her exhausted husband to go a-wooing.

In a secret note to Judith, Wagner sighed that his wife 'sacrifices herself to the habits of her father – alas!' In Willi Schuh's 1936 edition of Wagner's surviving letters to Judith, this sentence was imaginatively but erroneously translated as 'She sacrifices herself to her father, who is used to large parties.'[121] But Liszt had already left, and Wagner was in any case not referring to the receptions at Wahnfried, which he increasingly avoided, but to Cosima's courtly manner, to her concern for etiquette and her ability to shine in elevated conversation. Wagner's own character was diametrically opposed to this, just as it was to her father's, and he had no time for either.

But he did have time for Judith. She had separated from Mendès in 1874, and if she had come to Bayreuth, it was not for the music. She sat next to Wagner at the performances, and he held her 'warm hand'. Among all the 'prevailing stiffness' of the festival, he later confided to Cosima, Judith was the only person to exude any 'natural warmth'.[122] And this was the only thing to interest him about her: warmth and love. The fact that the *Ring* revolved around this very point struck no one, least of all Cosima. Thus the creator of a world that was running out of control found refuge in a love that meant the world to him.

The letter in which Wagner complained about Cosima's condescending manner had begun with the desperate exclamation 'Love, I am sad' and ended with the question 'Did I embrace you for the last time this morning?', a question that he answered with the firm resolve to see her again as soon as he could. Wagner's biographers have never been quite certain whether he really meant this. Was it acceptable for a sixty-three-year-old married man to write to a young woman and tell her that 'instinct' had led him to her and that 'I enjoyed your embraces'?[123] Yet he told her so again and again.

'I remember your embraces as the most intoxicating thing ever to have happened to me,' he wrote to her imploringly, 'nothing has filled me with a greater feeling of pride.'[124] Martin Gregor-Dellin assures us that at most 'they exchanged glances and kisses which Wagner described in retrospect as the proudest and most rapturous he had ever known'. Apparently he 'sat at her feet' while she 'sat in her corner of the sofa, her cheeks aglow, and let him pour out his heart to her'.[125] His passion must have revived memories of Jessie and encouraged him to suggest an 'elopement'. With an unmarried thirty-year-old woman, this could only have meant abandoning Bayreuth and disappearing with her. Perhaps it was her rejection that later persuaded him to write that she had 'thrown him out' of the wretched house.

Wagner had no reason to boast of embraces that had not taken place. To have done so to his lover would simply have made him look ridiculous. Following her departure, he repeatedly walked past the house where she had stayed and where he had been 'filled with a gentle, calming and intoxicating fire'. 'I am not crying,' he wrote in another love letter, 'but in my best moments I retain so gentle and pleasurable a desire – this desire to embrace you still and never to lose your godlike love. You're mine, aren't you?'[126]

The desperate feeling of not being able to hold on to his lover was now mingled with the sense of melancholy left in him by his festival. Whenever he walked past her lodgings, he was regularly overcome by the pain at what now seemed to have been lost for ever. His lover had gone and with her 'the Nibelungs. I no longer think of them and recall nothing save that which happened down there, down there!' His meetings with Judith were 'one last gift from the gods, who did not want me to succumb to the false glory of the performances of the Nibelungs'. Wagner could live without this 'false glory', in whose rays others were happy to bask. Judith later confirmed that the *Ring* was by now 'remote from the thoughts of a man already brooding on new creations'.[127]

The new work was *Parsifal*, the prose draft for which had been written down in 1865 amidst the pangs of yearning caused by Cosima's absence on a visit to see her father. Twelve years later he began work on the score in a delirium of lovelorn excitement caused by the prospect of seeing Judith again. To show that not only he himself but also the work had changed, he altered the hero's name from its usual spelling of 'Parzival' to 'Parsifal', an ostensibly Arabian form that he had picked up from Joseph Görres and that may have forged a link with the oriental beauty, even though she herself insisted that no such 'Arabian dialect' existed. It was, he added mischievously, his own 'invention. I wanted to attribute the word to some dialect or other, because it suits me to do so.' As if suspecting the amount of scholarly effort that his followers would later expend on the word's etymology, he went on: 'I scoff at the actual meaning of the Arabian words.'[128]

The hero with the fantastical oriental name now began to acquire a musical reality all his own. 'Yes, it is a question of the music for *Parsifal*', Wagner wrote to Judith on 1 October 1877, filled with 'love' and the old familiar strains of *Tristan und Isolde*. 'I couldn't exist if I were unable to throw myself into such an undertaking.' While Cosima listened to the unfamiliar sounds whose inspiration she ascribed to her own influence on her husband, the latter continued to maintain a clandestine correspondence with the distant sphinx who was his true source of inspiration.

'Je me sens aimé, et j'aime. Enfin, je fais la musique du Parsifal,' he wrote to her in November. Necessity having proved the mother of invention, he had discovered that by writing to her he could continue their embraces. Even the sceptical Newman was struck by the fact that it was 'almost simultaneously with his commencing work on the opera that he began a new correspondence with Judith Gautier', a coincidence that Newman describes as 'one of the most curious characteristics of his complex nature'.[129]

The contents of this intimate correspondence must have seemed all the more mystifying to Newman inasmuch as they help to throw light on another aspect of Wagner's character that is generally decorously concealed, for the messages that passed to and fro between Bayreuth and Paris contained more than just vows of love and poetic effusions: Wagner wanted Judith to restore to him the Paradise that he had lost. His lover was to fulfil his dream of harem perfumes and ruched silk, a dream to which he had succumbed in the Rue Newton in Paris, as well as in Penzing and Biebrich, then, with his sights somewhat lowered, in Munich and Tribschen. And she was to fulfil that dream with a hitherto unknown degree of perfection. During the festival she had been his 'wealth and intoxicating superfluity',[130] and now he literally wanted to bathe in those feelings.

The flood of requests with which Wagner overwhelmed Judith was not unlike the sort of shopping list that a kept woman in Paris might have drawn up for her perfumier and purveyor of sexy underwear. Wagner wanted a veritable Gesamtkunstwerk of the senses, regaling the eyes with iridescent fabrics, the taste buds with bubbling champagne, the nose with heady perfumes and incense sticks, the skin with silk garments and lace negligees and his whole body with 'bath oils and so on by the dozen. For we live in a desert, abandoned by all *aménité*'.[131] He himself would ensure that the ear was gratified, a latterday Klingsor ensconced in his magic garden.

Having decided between 'Exquisité' by Rimmel and 'pure but strong Rose' as their 'correspondence perfume', they consulted each other on the perfumed sachets that Wagner wanted to place with his linen. He had been 'delighted' to discover this stunning perfume in a box of gloves. Was it Verbena or Iris? It was Iris. This would strike the right note for the sachets. 'In this way I shall be on good terms with you when I sit down at the piano and write the music for *Parsifal*.' Judith's perfume rose up towards him from his silk dressing gown.

The same was true of his bath. On mature reflection they had agreed on Milk of Iris – 'flowing in abundance' – as it was impossible to use too much of this.

The 'Milk of Iris', he noted, adopting a style reminiscent of Mijnheer Peep-
erkorn in Thomas Mann's *The Magic Mountain*, was 'excellent. But I need a lot
– half a bottle for a bath. And I take one every day. Think about it.'[132] Was he
serious or was he striking a playfully ironic note? At all events, it was not just as
a joke that he splashed around with the sponges that Judith sent him –
'immensely large' and 'with lots of holes'.

His bath tub also offered him more serious delights reminiscent, rather, of
Isolde. Only in Judith's Milk of Iris, mixed with Bengal Rose, White Rose
Powder and 'perfumed cold creams', did he gain a sense of all that Isolde had
felt at the moment of her love-death: 'Are they waves of gentle breezes? Are they
clouds of blissful perfumes? How they swell and rustle around me, shall I
breathe or shall I listen? Shall I sip or plunge beneath them?'

And that was not all. For the seething swell of the world's fragrant breath was
of a twofold benefit. Once Wagner had refreshed himself in his morning bath,
he would go upstairs to the instrument whose hideous coffin-like black he concealed beneath silk covers. Even before he had played the first notes, he was
already visited by memories of Judith. 'I have my bathtub below my "atelier"',
he confided in his supplier, after he had prevailed on her to be 'prodigal above
all in the quantity of bath salts'. For 'I like to smell the perfumes rising', perfumes that still permeated the bathroom below him.[133]

But in spite of the Milk of Iris and Ambra, it was roses that held sway as
usual. The scent of roses was everywhere – in the scented cushions, in the
powder that he rubbed into his skin and sprinkled over his clothes, and in the
sprays that impregnated his boudoir with the smell of his favourite flower.
Clothes, walls, armchair covers, all were made for the most part of pink satin
that he ordered in vast quantities from the capital of cultural decline: rosettes
singly and severally, rose patterns on yellow satin. 'I want satin,' Wagner
declared, 'it's the only type of silk that gives me any pleasure, as the light plays
around its folds so gently.'

Pink satin then, a satiety of satin. But what shade of pink? The only one
worth considering was 'my pink, very pale and delicate'. But how could Wagner
describe it when it could no longer be found among the latest samples? This
was the only pink he could live with, the others he could manage without. 'I'm
obsessed with one particular colour that can't be found any longer', he wrote.
'What people offer me is chamois or flesh-coloured', a term that conjured forth
a poetic sigh: 'Ah, if it were the colour of *your* flesh, then I'd have the pink that
I want!'[134]

It is an instructive admission. In Wagner's silken dream of folds and frills and
buds a woman's pale pink flesh returns again and again. And with the scent of

roses came the memory of her, perhaps his sacred bride and sister Rosalie who, inaccessible to him, caused his erysipelas – in German, 'Gesichtsrose' – to return while he was working on *Parsifal*. As soon as he sank into the perfume, he told his new sister, he felt as though he were 'plunging deep into your beneficent soul'. He wept on receiving her perfumes through the post. For him, there was more in her crates 'than I can tell you: they contain your soul's very fragrance'. This was not the flattery of an infatuated lover but the simple truth. The creature that he longed for lay within the perfume as a very real presence, as 'le parfum de votre âme'.[135] All these items had to be sent to Wagner's confidant, the barber Bernhard Schnappauf in the Ochsengasse. It was like something out of a play by August von Kotzebue.

Watched from all sides, Wagner ran the risk of being discovered. But he wanted the woman who could not be with him to be with him even so. Of what concern to him was his 'false glory'? For his chaise longue he wanted a 'very beautiful and exceptional cover' with a particular pattern on a pale yellow satin background: only 'roses' would satisfy him. Nothing else would do, he insisted, when she tried to suggest alternatives. The background could be white for all he cared, but as for the pattern, it should 'simply be roses'. This cover was to be called 'Judith'.[136] In this way he could lie on her, wrap himself up in her and warm himself on her. All that surrounded him was Judith, whether in the form of perfumes, liquids or flesh-coloured fabric. And no doubt also the strains of *Parsifal*.

Worthy of a *dame aux camélias*, these commissions provide a clue to Wagner's feminine nature. All that he ordered reflected a woman's tastes. Nor was it a mere accident that it did so. It was the affectation of femininity as such. An essential part of this picture are the particoloured slippers and silk underwear that he ostensibly commissioned for Cosima, to say nothing of the Japanese dressing gown that he ordered for himself and that was presumably worn next to his skin, hence his wilfully disingenuous question: 'Evidently an undergarment is necessary – let's say a sort of petticoat that can be adapted to suit this comical kind of costume? Well then, invent something, order it, arrange it.'[137]

The expensive finery delivered to Schnappauf's barber's shop was naturally intended for Wagner himself. Although Cosima's diary makes it clear that among the gifts laid out for her at the foot of the Christmas tree was a 'Japanese negligee', there is no mention here of petticoats, nor of a black velvet dress that a Paris tailor offered to send to her. We know that Wagner intercepted the message and ordered the garment himself. Cosima's lavish satin wardrobe which she wore in public served as a secret source of inspiration for him within the precincts of his own home. When the children's governess discovered several large crates at Wahnfried containing 'satin in bright colours, delicate pink, sky blue and green', the Swiss chambermaid Asra explained that they were 'for dressing gowns and trousers to go with the master's negligee'.[138] Wagner sometimes surprised even his own friends, notably one teatime, when, as Wolzogen innocently records, he appeared 'as a joke in a woman's jacket that had been discovered outside'.[139]

Was Nietzsche right, then, when he described the later Wagner as 'feminini generis' – 'of the feminine sex' – and, to use a modern expression, 'outed' him? Feminine by nature, Nietzsche must surely have known. In short, was Wagner a woman? When we see, on the one hand, Wagner the passionate lover and, on the other, the rose cabinets and silk garments with lace panties and silk stockings, to say nothing of the perfumes, powders and bath salts, the answer can only be that while he was not a woman he surrounded himself with feminine objects, enveloping himself in the essence of the fair sex. Like the skins of an onion, he was surrounded by perfume, underwear, flowing garments and the rosily ruched interiors of his various homes. He immersed himself fully in the world of femininity, yet without becoming a woman.

But this was entirely at one with his whole philosophy of art. Only when the male element entered the female element could the true work of art arise. The masculine word, the spirit and light, descended into feminine nature, plunging into the surging ocean and the ringing womb of the deep in order that, clothed in harmonies, they might return to the surface as a work of art. According to *Opera and Drama*, the artist needed more than just himself to 'summon into existence the life that is so necessary to him and that will redeem him'. 'It is the Other, all that is opposed to him and for which he yearns that urges him on' because it 'absorbs him and reflects him back at himself in a recognizable form'. Only from the union of independent opposites could the artwork of the future arise. Garlanded by roses, Wagner showed the way forward.

The master of contradiction found himself on the horns of this very dilemma, the final years of his life being determined by two women, both equally indispensable to him yet completely incompatible. Cosima was the mother of his children, but even more she was his own mother reborn in a more extreme and incomparably stricter form. Cosima had not known love in her youth, as she had been virtually repudiated by her parents, while her first husband had been tormented by unpredictable mood swings, preventing her from gaining any understanding of the affairs of the heart. As she was later to admit, he did not even know what women liked. He lived only for his art, for Wagner.

Cosima wanted to do the same, only in an even more rigorous and extreme way than Bülow. By the time she finally achieved her objective, 'love' was a form of currency assiduously traded by the two partners but unfortunately with dif-fering exchange rates. Their 'love' was uncoordinated, and when children came the incessant assurances of that love that are recorded in Cosima's diaries lost all their value. Cosima shone as an ascetic, an asceticism to which Wagner of necessity had to submit. Her ritualized references to her love were not reflected in real life but only in the illusion of a 'noble couple'.

The only reality was Judith Gautier. While downplaying her true significance in Cosima's eyes, Wagner effectively disowned his dour wife in his contacts with Judith. And no doubt he meant it. In a letter probably written in London in May 1877, he complains about the 'endless annoyances' to which he has 'been exposed since last seeing' Judith.[140] How often he had complained to Cosima in the early days of their relationship that she should have moved in with him in Zurich and certainly in Biebrich. Now the younger woman became the object of his retrospective rewriting of history when he dreamt of her picking him up in the street in Paris, taking him home and 'covering him with kisses. Ah, it is very touching! very touching!'[141]

Instead, he found himself sitting in Wahnfried, surrounded by perfumes and waiting for Schnappauf's contraband goods. According to an early remark of Siegfried's, 'Papa is always wearing pomade.' But just as beauty is merely a promise of happiness to come, so the perfume and powder offered him only the illusion of Paradise within his wilderness. Judith sent him the 'abundance' of his 'poor life', a life which, as he wistfully added, was 'pacified and sheltered' now that he 'had Cosima'.[142] Such a remark would have struck ordinary mortals as unexceptional, but it must have seemed like sheer mockery to the erotic hur-ricane that was Judith. Presumably that is what Wagner intended, for in another letter we find him writing: 'Love me and let's not wait for the Protes-tant heaven, which is bound to be terribly boring!'[143] This was certainly a side-swipe at Cosima.

Elsewhere in Wagner's letters to his lover, the mistress of Bayreuth plays an unflattering role. It was bad enough that she disliked flesh-coloured silk, which, as we have seen, was the object of her husband's desire. 'Don't say anything to Cosima about your enquiries regarding the pink satin,' he warned Judith. 'Even if you'd been successful, I'd have had to force this fabric on her.'[144] Even worse was the fact that Cosima clearly understood next to nothing about poetry, Judith's natural terrain, Wagner taking an evident delight in his wife's cack-handed attempt to translate *Parsifal* into French, an attempt that was no more successful than her earlier stab at rendering *Tannhäuser* into French verse.

'Cosima has simply sought out expressions of deathly sobriety (hence this stiffness)', he mocked. 'It strikes me that you must have suffered terribly on reading these pages, being obliged to regard it as poetry.' Such was his Schaden-freude, he even suggested that the more talented of the two women should make no secret of her horror at her rival's witless endeavours: 'Tell Cosima your honest opinion. Don't be afraid of offending her.' He knew, of course, that his wife was sensitive to a fault.

By the end of 1877 matters had started to come to a head, when Cosima evidently discovered that there had been a protracted correspondence between her husband and her rival to which she had been denied access. Wagner assured his wife 'in sacred and solemn words' that he loved her, prompting her to note in her diary: 'I should like to be silent for ever, to disappear, to know nothing, hear nothing, do nothing except serve him – him alone!' To serve was really the only solution as the other alternatives were not viable. And ideally she should adopt a form of service before which her husband was bound to capitulate.

But her next blow was directed at her rival: 'I am filled with dread when I think of the world and think that masks and grimaces can still disturb this harmony, this life of ours!'[145] That she was really thinking of the 'performances and concerts' that she goes on to mention seems doubtful, as she invariably set great store by social occasions of this kind. No, the 'masks and grimaces' must refer to the ill-bred Judith's pretty little mask, an object that she regarded as a threat to her very existence.

It was not just Judith's face that featured in Wagner's dreams. Three days prior to the above entry, Cosima had noted in her diary that Wagner had seen some 'antique busts in a hall' and that they had 'spoken'. Clearly they symbolized Wagner's former lovers, all of whom were well proportioned in comparison with the flat-chested Cosima. One of them was Wilhelmine Schröder-Devrient, he admitted, before immediately adding that 'I wouldn't like to dream that I was kissing her, for it's not good to kiss dead people in dreams.' Two days later Wagner reported a further dream to Cosima that seems like a continuation and explanation of the earlier one: both Cosima and their son Siegfried had died and Wagner was 'carrying around a relief of them both in his pocket'.[146] Where others revealed their busts, the dead Cosima clearly had nothing edifying to show.

But Cosima was still very much alive. Just as Minna had done over Jessie Laussot and Mathilde Wesendonck, she invoked all the threatening powers that Wagner ascribed to his mother figures. In January 1878 she stumbled upon her husband secretly incinerating some papers, provoking only 'surprise at my question as to whether something had been burning'[147] and persuading Wagner to agree with Judith that from now on she should write to Wahnfried directly so that Wagner would not need to hide her 'dear letters'.[148] The result was that

Judith's subsequent letters were all burnt, but this time it was Cosima who was the arsonist.

A showdown was inevitable. On 10 February we find Wagner assuring his lover that from now on Cosima would be responsible for his 'Paris errands', with a confrontation between the couple following two days later. 'The grief that I was fearing has not passed me by,' Cosima noted in her diary, 'it has come upon me from outside. May God help me! . . . Oh, sorrow, my old companion, come back and dwell within me.' Grieving suited Cosima. Wagner's thoughts turned to death. In the final clandestine letter that he wrote to Judith, he asked for her 'compassion' and told her not to torment herself for his sake. 'What is troubling me will pass soon enough.'[149]

But not as soon as he thought. Just as Minna had done, Cosima emerged victorious, with a note in her diary indicating her husband's capitulation following Siegfried's intervention as go-between: Wagner had 'taken a decision' and sent his son with it to Cosima, who had sent the boy back with a 'Yes'. With that, Wagner gave Siegfried a kiss with instructions to pass it on to Cosima.[150]

The enforced breach left its marks in her diary, too. Wagner's nights became restless. In a single night, he took not only Seidlitz powder, valerian, Carlsbad salt and castor oil but also red wine and, for good measure, opium. Cosima was also worried that he was 'drinking more cognac than usual'. That same month he made it clear to her that Minna was no longer able to frighten him at night: 'Now you have to take over.'[151]

Cosima had won a battle but not the war. Judith resurfaced at the 1882 festival, radiant, bubbling with wit and joie de vivre. She had come to hear her *Parsifal*, the melancholy music of which, as Wagner dutifully explained, had been inspired by her. She came not as a penitent, like the rest of the congregation, but in triumph, a born victor, who knew what Wagner owed her. And she was as badly behaved as on the first day Cosima met her. But now she had a place of honour in Wagner's Pantheon.

Neither Cosima's diary nor Glasenapp's authorized biography mentions the Master's demonstrative tribute to his Muse, yet there is no doubt that it took place. At the large banquet held on the eve of the first performance on 26 July, it was not Cosima or any of the rest of the swarm of female admirers but Judith who occupied the place of honour next to him. 'Beside Wagner, to his right,' one guest recalled the scene, 'sat a very pretty woman, some thirty years of age, with whom the Master appeared to be getting on like a house on fire, for he was haranguing her in a particularly lively manner and taking a great deal of interest in her.'

Judith chatted loudly 'in the most glorious French you could imagine. Her high-spiritedly pealing laughter, her fresh, lively features, framed by dark, luxuriant hair, and her eyes that sparkled with wit' struck the observer as forcefully as what she was wearing. Whereas all the other women wore evening dress and carried the obligatory fan, she attracted attention with her 'very comfortable and extremely simple linen blouse and her half workman's, half sailor's jacket, while around her neck she had tied a broad, bright red tie'. The demon incarnate of the French Revolution had infiltrated the Castle of the Grail.

Opposite her sat a hostile world, at its head the black-cassocked Abbé Liszt occasionally conversing with his daughter, who, as usual, was dressed in black satin, peering short-sightedly through her lorgnon and playing the part of the unapproachable mistress of the house. What a satanic pleasure for the Master to bring these two extremes into such sharply contrastive focus. Indeed, he was even to take them a stage further.

Put in the best of moods by Judith, he gave one of his usual improvised speeches of which he could not remember a single word afterwards. But this time he had the devil in him. Staring straight at Judith's sinful curves and at the two bigots seated opposite him, Wagner described as a black Mass a work that depicts Holy Communion and that Cosima already regarded as the centre of a future cult.

'The end of his speech', recalled the same eyewitness on the eve of the work's first performance, 'is still fresh in my memory. "Children," explained the Master, emphasizing each word, "children, tomorrow it can finally start! Tomorrow all hell will be let loose! And so all of you who are involved in the performance must see to it that you have the devil in you, and you who are present as listeners must ensure that you welcome the devil into your hearts!"'[152]

One final image from the *Parsifal* banquet: when the table was cleared, the woman in the worker's smock called over the valet, took Wagner's coat from him and helped the Master into it. 'She did this so thoroughly,' observed our eyewitness, 'that, laughing out loud, she finally lifted both him and his coat right up from the ground, like a shuttlecock.' Judith had shown them.

Parsifal

While Wagner was working away at the score of *Parsifal*, 'Judith' was always around him. The rose-embroidered satin coverlet that allowed him to sense his lover's presence seems to have conjured up the sounds that he wanted. The cover had been intended from the outset for his 'good mornings with *Parsifal*'[153] and had been spread over his piano. When Wolzogen asked him what it was for, he explained that he needed 'dreamlike colours in his surroundings'. When he was working on the Good Friday Music, his disciple noted that he kept rearranging the folds in the 'flowery meadow' of silk, 'scarcely conscious of what he was doing'.[154] Wolzogen did not omit to stress that the cover had been provided by Frau Cosima.

However likely this suggestion may be, it was presumably not true. The Master was responsible for choosing his own surroundings, including his clothes (even when those clothes hung in Cosima's wardrobe), following his own exquisite taste in everything. The 'black velvet dress' that he ordered from Paris could have turned up again as the 'Parsifal coat' in a Bayreuth fashion atelier. According to a local tailor, it was made of 'black velvet, with a huge tippet lined by twelve assistants with the softest musquash fur'. 'I am often struck at night by themes for my new work,' Wagner explained. 'Then my wife gets up with me and sits next to me while I write them down; for this, she needs to be able to wrap herself up warmly.'[155]

But in order to wear his 'Parsifal coat', Wagner needed Cosima no more than he needed her to compose. Swathed in fur and velvet, he felt himself transported to another world, and for the lovelorn longing that put him into the right frame of mind only Judith's silks and rose-scented perfumes would do. Cosima as the ostensible Muse of *Parsifal* was not the only misunderstanding that was to accrue to Wagner's last work.

Liszt's daughter was determined to see in *Parsifal* the sacrament of the true faith, a faith on whose modern manifestation she had turned her back, such was her spirit of orthodoxy. For her, *Parsifal* was a mystic service, the Festspielhaus a place of pilgrimage, and Wagner was wary of contradicting her. If his dream play was later to become established as an Oberammergau for Wagnerians, it was because Cosima, adopting her father's priestly predisposition, willed it so. What Wagner himself saw in it is something he shared with no one: it was his own tragedy in life and the solution that he hoped to find, a solution to which Cosima – as the piece itself amply demonstrates – could contribute nothing at all.

Among the various misunderstandings that Wagner himself encouraged is the idea that *Parsifal* sprang from his 'Bayreuth period', that it was written exclusively for the Festspielhaus and that it owes its setting to a visit that he and his family made to Italy in 1880. In fact the work belongs to the Romantic Zauberoper tradition, with its magical elements and spectacular stage effects, and had preoccupied Wagner ever since he had spent a summer in Marienbad in 1845, accompanying him throughout more than half his life. By the time he completed the work, that life was almost over.

Although the libretto states that it is set in Moorish Spain, the action unfolds, in fact, in the city where Richard Geyer had once attended the Kreuzschule, the city of *Das Liebesmahl der Apostel* and the memorial service for Carl Maria von Weber, the city whose bells both greeted the revolution and tolled its death knell. Not for nothing does *Parsifal* build to an apotheosis of the Dresden Amen, which, following its prominent appearance in *Das Liebesverbot* and *Tannhäuser*, serves as a central motif for the whole of Wagner's 'Bühnenweih-festspiel', or 'stage-consecration festival drama'. In the edifying harmonies of his childhood, Wagner rediscovered the holy relic of the Grail. The motif of redemption that had graced Mendelssohn's 'Reformation' Symphony had finally been rescued from hands not qualified to use it.

It was not Cosima's Bayreuth that witnessed Parsifal's birth and christening but the Dresden of Wagner's early fears and desires. There, as he admitted in his autobiography, his obsession with pink silk had been fired in the very years in which he was plagued every night by dreams of ghosts. The 'more delicate objects' from his sisters' wardrobe had 'excited and stimulated' his imagination to such an extent that merely to touch their negligees could cause his heart to beat faster with fear. The nine-year-old pupil from the Kreuzschule, who was often tormented by erysipelas, not only felt a sense of 'terror' at the theatre but, in 'liberating' contrast to it, developed a mystical boyhood piety. He had 'gazed with painful longing at the altarpiece in the Kreuzkirche and yearned to take the place of Our Saviour on the Cross'.[156]

Just as the pandemonium of the stage, the charms of his sisters and the Saviour on the Cross all return in *Parsifal*, so the idea of a religion of art that Wagner had long ago discovered in E. T. A. Hoffmann's *Serapionsbrüder* has left its clear traces on the work. Wagner was thirteen when, abandoned in Dresden by his mother and sisters, he plunged into Hoffmann's dreamily visionary worlds and discovered a philosophy that regarded art as uniquely important. The solitarily poeticizing Wagner felt that Hoffmann was speaking to him directly.

Only in music, he read here, could one find a 'presentiment of all that is highest and most sacred', something which, as in Schelling, 'kindled the spark of life in the whole of nature'. In keeping with its 'inner and essential nature', wrote Hoffmann, music was a religious cult at whose centre lay love as the 'harmonious accord of all that is spiritual in nature'. This was to remain Wagner's creed, just as the *Serapionsbrüder* was to serve as a lifelong source of inspiration. For Hoffmann, the 'divine' element in nature had found its clearest expression in Palestrina's music. In much the same way, Wagner, writing in 1870, felt that 'the innermost nature of religion' was manifest in Palestrina's music inasmuch as it created an 'image as timeless as it is independent of space'.[157]

The religion from which *Parsifal* developed had as little to do with Cosima's religion as Hoffmann's world of ghosts did with her concept of sin. Wagner hated the idea of tying people to God's apron strings by means of commandments, and his idea of the 'divine', by drawing on the Romantics' philosophy of art, could hardly have been further removed from that of the God of the Bible. 'I do not believe in God,' he insisted in 1879, while working on *Parsifal*, 'but only in the divine, which is manifest in the sinless Jesus.' By this, Wagner meant not a moral quality but the freedom of the divine element from egoism: 'I believe in the divine element that once – and once only – permeated the human element in all its naïvety and beauty, showing us the way to redemption.' This redemption, he went on, consisted in 'dying a beautiful death, to which a beautiful life leads'.[158] Such beauty could already have been found in the *Serapionsbrüder*.

In *Parsifal* Wagner raised a monument to this exceptional human being, a monument whose base had already been built in Dresden. For in the 'ghost world'[159] of the Bühnenweihfestspiel we rediscover the sufferings of the young Wagner, while the artistic relic of the Grail incorporates, by the composer's own admission, an 'image of the bleeding Saviour on the Cross'.[160] This symbol of a godless world tearing itself apart embodies Wagner's childhood terrors as surely as it does Schopenhauer's 'slaughterhouse' of the will, while at the same time pointing beyond them. For the Cross promises both liberation from the torments of existence and the redemption of a failed history of humankind.

The only question is what this redemption consists of. Wagner certainly did not believe in Cosima's heaven, for, as Carolyne Sayn-Wittgenstein immediately noted, he 'struck at the very heart of the most sacred mystery of our Christian faith'. Worse still: 'There is no trace of God in *Parsifal*.'[161] Even the love that is taught in church seems to be no more than a weak reflex of the world-creating and world-destroying archetypal process that Wagner had experienced for himself. And so it was only logical that his own life should offer him an answer: creation had been usurped by an alien force and its divine light obscured by the underworld.

The legal entitlement to the world had been seized by the rightful heir's adversary, causing the former to suffer and perish, when confronted by the loss of his world in the image of his lost lover. Redemption could come only from a love-death. By this, however, Wagner meant not happiness in some remote world beyond the grave, as misconstrued by Christianity, but happiness in a life beyond the existing world of laws. It is not metaphysical consolation that his music dramas offer but the true metaphysics of sexual love from which a new world would emerge.

To Wagner's tormented heroes, this seems like a heavenly revelation. The lost pilgrim Tannhäuser is denied salvation by Rome but learns from Wolfram von Eschenbach that true redemption is vouchsafed by Elisabeth's love-death. Wagner had already found the prototype for this encounter in Hoffmann's *Serapionsbrüder*, where Wolfframb (as he is called here) approaches the minnesinger's sickbed in order to offer him 'words of consolation'. But he does so in vain, as the latter, 'with a mortal wound in his bleeding breast', is consumed 'by the pain of inconsolable yearning' for the lover whom he has lost.

The bleeding wound – Hoffmann's symbol of love's insatiable torments – returns in *Tristan und Isolde*, whose hero lies on the minnesinger's sickbed, tormented by the same 'mad fever' that is triggered in the *Serapionsbrüder* by the 'blazing fires of love'. 'Away from her, shall I not die a more beautiful, sweeter death of longing?' Hoffmann has his hero ask, thereby giving Wagner's Tristan his cue.

Like Hoffmann's hero, the lovesick Tristan was originally to have received a visit on his sickbed, with the Grail knight Parzival appearing in 1855 in the earliest sketches for the third act. The listener was meant to hear only his 'singing from the deep', the refrain of which would be repeated by the Shepherd. Within a mere handful of notes, Parzival's brief song was to offer an answer to Tristan's desperate question as to whether 'the whole world is nothing but unassuaged yearning? How can it ever be stilled?'[162] Later, too, Wagner repeatedly returned to this idea of having 'Parzival, searching for the Grail', encounter Tristan lying 'on his deathbed, suffering the most desperate pangs of love: here death, there new life'.[163]

When the now elderly Wagner told his disciple Wolzogen about this plan, which was ultimately to remain unrealized, he explained that 'a particular melody of the wandering Parzival should rise up and strike the ear of the fatally wounded Tristan, rather like an answer, mysteriously fading away, to the latter's life-destroying question as to the "why?" of existence. From this melody', Wagner explained, 'the Bühnenweihfestspiel evolved.'[164] It is not clear what this melody was, as Glasenapp, who reports this conversation, maintains a tantalizing silence on the subject. But Mathilde Wesendonck preserved Wagner's sketch of the music accompanying Parzival's appearance at Tristan's sickbed, a sketch that he presented to her in the summer of 1858, and it is clear from this that the melody that the wandering knight was to sing to the words 'Wo find' ich dich, du heil'ger Gral?' quotes the Dresden Amen at a critical juncture.

Just as *Tristan und Isolde* came into being when Siegfried lost his way in Weber's forest murmurs, so the sketches for *Die Sieger* ('The Victors') and *Parzival* sprang from Tristan's lovesick agony. Within a matter of only a few months in 1855 and 1856, during which his love of Mathilde blossomed no less floridly than his wearisome erysipelas, Wagner engaged with three of his heroes, Tristan, Parzival and Ananda, each of whom, in his own way, was to grasp the nettle of love's insatiable yearning. While the hero of the completed *Tristan und Isolde* found solace in death and the hero of the unfinished *Sieger* achieved redemption through renunciation, the knight of the Holy Grail saw his own confrontation deferred to some indefinable date in the future, when he will none the less have to find a solution to life's problem not only for himself but for his heroic brothers.

This was already adumbrated in Wagner's 1856 sketch for *Die Sieger*, a sketch which would make sense, in Wagner's view, only when the reader had 'digested' the third act of *Tristan und Isolde*. Only when Tristan had died a living death would the reader grasp the meaning of the new life that the Buddha promised the lovers. As so often with Wagner, passion was kindled when the hero was refreshed by the heroine with water from a fountain or spring. In this case, the young Prakriti feels 'love's violent anguish' when the Buddha's favourite disciple, Ananda, gazes deep into her eyes.

But the Buddha himself opposes Prakriti's urgent entreaty that the two should marry, drawing her attention to Ananda's vow of chastity and adding that in an earlier life she was cursed for contemptuously dismissing a no less urgent entreaty by a prince who wanted to marry her. Enlightened by the Buddha, the lovers see for themselves that sexual desire is a curse, holding out the empty promise of pleasure, only to punish them with insatiable anguish. As a result, they are accepted into the Buddha's circle of followers and 'shown the way to full redemption'. Although this presupposes abstinence from the concupiscent demands of the will, the union favoured by Wagner was able to manage without such abstinence, as he was shortly to explain to Schopenhauer. Prakriti and the apple of her eye lie in each other's arms, bereft of will, allowing Ananda to greet her as his 'sister'.[165] With this, the way to the ultimate union of opposites is finally open to both of them.

This non-physical pairing under the Buddha's patronage brings redemption not only to the two Indian characters but also, as Wagner explained to Mathilde Wesendonck in 1860, belatedly to Lohengrin and Elsa. And it finds musical expression, too, for one of the 'sublime themes' that was to have been used to articulate the triumph of the lovers' mutual renunciation of love struck Wagner as too memorable to perish with his plan for *Die Sieger*, with the result that he incorporated it into the scene between Wotan and Erda in the third act of *Siegfried* 'as the so-called World Inheritance motif'. According to Glasenapp, 'this identification of the solemnly sublime theme of joyful renunciation is to be taken quite literally and was imparted to the present writer by the Master himself'.[166]

But Glasenapp appears not fully to have understood the Master, for although the rising motif accompanies Wotan's announcement that he is relinquishing his world dominion to Siegfried, the motif's momentum and thrust scarcely suggest the renunciation of a resigned god, but tend rather to indicate his world-affirming self-sacrifice in the name of love. If we follow the course taken by this motif through the third act of *Siegfried*, we shall find its triumphal character emerging with increasing clarity until it finds its most radiant expression in the jubilation of Siegfried and Brünnhilde as the two of them finally unite. The fact that the ostensible renunciation of the world by Ananda and Prakriti climaxes on the words 'Radiant love, laughing death' certainly shows the god-fearing lovers of *Die Sieger* in an altogether new light.

The 'almost steamrollering triumphalism' of the end of *Siegfried* puzzled the writer Wolfgang Osthoff, for whom the Renunciation motif 'increasingly changed its meaning' until Wagner finally used it in a wholly different sense to praise the transports of love. When Wagner set Brünnhilde's discarded final speech during the first Bayreuth Festival in 1876 and presented the setting to Ludwig II as a private gesture, he set the anarchical admission 'Blessed in joy and sorrow, love alone can be' to the triumphant motif from *Die Sieger*, leaving a bemused Wolfgang Osthoff to comment that 'it must no doubt remain an open question whether Wagner was being intentionally naïve or ironical here or whether this is simply another of those irreconcilable contradictions'.[167]

Such contradictions had ceased to exist for Wagner ever since he had presumed to set Schopenhauer straight. Sexual love and renunciation of the world were by no means incompatible, and what may strike outsiders as the death of love actually results in its rebirth, bringing with it the revelation of the very first act of creation. Any death from love, the Greek mysteries taught, always led to a beginning from love, and the death of the hero in the mother's womb allowed new life to emerge into the world three seasons later. When Wagner played the motif from *Die Sieger* to his disciple Heinrich Porges in 1876, he spoke of the 'sudden illumination by which Wotan himself is overwhelmed', adding that 'it must sound like the proclamation of a new religion'.[168]

Whatever the Buddhist framework might suggest to the contrary, *Die Sieger* is not about redemption from love but about redemption through love. For it is this that constituted Wagner's new religion. Humanity could be liberated only through more love, not less, and ever since his days in Dresden, love for Wagner had meant the same sort of willingness to sacrifice oneself as Christ himself had shown. Wagner called it 'Mitleid', literally 'fellow suffering', but it could equally well be the 'fellow joy' in which the self is dissolved in the other. That is why *Parsifal*, which picks up intellectually and spiritually where *Die Sieger* leaves off, deals not with the denial of sexual love but with its supersession in a oneness that leaves far behind it all the selfishness associated with the separation of the sexes.

In spite of its Catholic framework, which was provided by Wagner's source in Wolfram von Eschenbach's romance, *Parsifal* also deals with the supersession of Catholicism. It was Wagner's conviction that the Church had long since betrayed Christ's message of love to the egoistical God of the Jews, to whom the Saviour was related neither by blood nor by marriage. It was a 'scandal', he complained in 1878, that Catholicism 'still existed'. The following day, as Cosima dutifully noted, he even described Catholicism as a 'universal pestilence'.[169]

Not that this prevented Cosima from remarking only a few years after Wagner's death to his former friend Mimi von Buch, who following the death of Count Schleinitz was now Countess Wolkenstein: 'If I knew that my dear children were provided for and that the theatre up there could survive, I'd convert to Catholicism.'[170] But, she went on, she also felt capable of becoming an ascetic 'Brahman', as she could 'imagine the world only as being strictly separated into above and below and I see the caste system as something very sensible'.

Celebrated by his widow as a Wagnerian Eucharist, *Parsifal* had first come to the composer's attention in 1845, while he was taking the waters in Marienbad during one of his summer breaks from his post as court Kapellmeister in Dresden. Here he withdrew into the forest with a pile of courtly romances and encountered virtually all the heroes who were later to people his dream landscapes. In Wolfram's *Parzival* he also discovered the Grail and its knight Lohengrin, who was sent out in vain on a mission to the Scheldt and whose father Parzival, king of the sacred mount of Monsalvat, henceforth led a secret life of his own, turning up ten years later to pay a visit on Tristan and thereafter maintaining a permanent presence on Wagner's stage.

It was during his infatuation with Mathilde Wesendonck in Zurich that Wagner finally decided to devote a whole opera to the mysterious Grail king. On Good Friday 1857, he reported in his autobiography, he had woken up for the first time in the Asyl next to the Wesendoncks' villa and had been reminded of Wolfram's romance by the springtime mood in the garden and in his heart. 'Setting out from the idea of Good Friday' that was central, he argued, to

Parzival, he had immediately conceived a three-act drama, which he had jotted down in a cursory sketch.

Writers subsequently worked out that Wagner was being fanciful here. In 1857, Good Friday fell on 10 April, whereas he did not move into the Asyl until eighteen days later. Wagner's account was declared by Peter Wapnewski to be yet another of the composer's 'myths' about the inspiration of his works. But not even Wagner himself denied this. Cosima was keen to eradicate all memory of the Wesendonck woman and so Wagner had assured her that there was no basis to his legendary conception of the work. 'Today R. recalled the impression that inspired the Good Friday Music', she noted in her diary in April 1879. With a smile her husband declared that it was 'all as far-fetched' as his 'love affairs, for it was not a Good Friday at all, just a pleasant mood in nature that made me think: "This is how a Good Friday should be."'[171] Such an act of self-betrayal was not hard for Wagner, as he knew better than anyone how things really stood. At the same time he made it clear that his information was to be interpreted phenomenologically rather simply than in terms of the calendar.

It was the contradiction between Christ's sad death on the Cross and the riant springtime morning that was resolved in the concept of the Good Friday Music. Just as God's self-sacrifice redeemed mankind from the world of the laws, so it freed nature from winter's stranglehold. It too joined with humankind in celebrating its resurrection – and not just at Easter but at the moment when the solar hero floods the whole universe with his light. The magic of this union was something that Wagner had discovered not in Schopenhauer, as he would have us believe, but long before that in Schelling's mystical approach to nature.

Schelling had set out from the idea that God gave freely of his love and that in order to become a creator he cast his light into the darkness of his own ground where, to quote E. T. A. Hoffmann, he 'kindled the spark of life in the whole of nature'. By the same token, Wagner's epiphany in the Asyl in Zurich sprang not from his renunciation of the world but from its opposite, from the love that gives and that awakens life. When Wagner wrote to King Ludwig in 1865 and recalled the 'sunny Good Friday' that was really 'the first beautiful spring day of the year', he spelt out the link that he denied to Cosima.

Delight in nature coincided with delight in his own rebirth. For years he had longed for a house of his own and proximity to the woman he loved, and now both wishes had come true thanks to Mathilde's 'loving, tenderly emotional woman's heart'. Her gift brought to an end his nomadic existence and allowed him 'to conceive *Parzival* after a period of profoundly rapt self-absorption'.[172] That he referred explicitly to the drama's 'conception' in his correspondence with Ludwig, explaining how it then grew 'like a child in its mother's womb', underlines the erotic, generative nature of an experience that finally culminated in the 'universal birth' of his Bühnenweihfestspiel.[173]

But in order to understand this redemption on the part of 'nature', it is first necessary to have undergone the opposite experience. While working on the third act of *Tristan und Isolde*, Wagner had realized that the 'nub and chief subject' of *Parzival* was in fact King Amfortas, who was in need of release and redemption. Just as every pain is an expression of the archetypal suffering of the world's will, so it 'suddenly became terribly clear' to Wagner that the wounded guardian of the Grail was his 'third-act Tristan' reborn and 'immeasurably intensified'. But the emotion that consumed Tristan had already destroyed the lives and happiness of the Dutchman, Tannhäuser and Lohengrin, as well as their Wälsung brethren. In his new drama about the Grail, it was nothing less than Wagner's own life of suffering that was to be depicted. 'And you expect me to carry out something like that? And write the music for it into the bargain?' he wrote half jokingly to Mathilde Wesendonck. 'No thank you very much! Others can do so if they feel like it!'[174]

Six years later he himself felt like it precisely because he had suffered a relapse and was once again suffering as Tristan had done. In August 1865 he wrote out a detailed prose draft for King Ludwig, beginning: 'Anfortas, the guardian of the Grail, languishes from an incurable spear wound received in some mysterious love affair.'[175] Inspiration came to him only because it was Wagner himself who was suffering from an open wound.

His secret mistress Cosima had just left on an extended visit to Hungary to see her God-fearing father, taking her cuckolded husband with her. Left behind, Wagner, to whom 'all this Catholic nonsense' was 'profoundly repugnant', felt that the devoutly Catholic Cosima had been 'thoroughly unfaithful' to him.[176] Tormented in equal measure by longing and jealousy, he sat down to write about his own life, completing the *Parzival* draft in four days and heaving a sigh of relief at the end: 'So! That was a help in time of need!'[177]

Barely twelve years later he returned to the work, now renamed *Parsifal* in keeping with Görres's oriental etymology, and once again it was Cosima who was causing him to suffer from nightmares and to have difficulty breathing. But his thoughts of love were now directed elsewhere: for five long years, from 1877 to 1882, Wagner worked away at his own redemption, with an image of the inaccessibly remote Judith before his eyes. Then his 'day's long task' was 'done'.[178]

No other work by Wagner has invited such contradictory readings as *Parsifal*, and all of them can appeal to the piece itself for support. Mythological or racist, psychoanalytical or eschatological, every facet is reflected in the piece, and those that cannot be made to fit are simply dismissed as examples of the 'irreconcilable contradictions' that are said to typify all Wagner's works. Only in the case of the official Bayreuth reading does nothing fit: the Schopenhauerian Christian interpretation canonized by Cosima has led to such a multiplicity of contradictions that one has to conclude either that the work's message concerning the true faith is not amenable to logical thought or that Wagner simply took leave of his senses towards the end of his life.

His infallible widow naturally derived her dogma from the Master himself. After all, he had supplied his own interpretation of the prelude to *Parsifal* that was the answer to a maiden's prayer. As the spiritual columns on which the work was built, it cited the phrase from Paul's First Letter to the Corinthians about faith, hope and charity, all three of which were treated in the prelude, albeit in the order charity (or love), faith and hope. At the outset, according to Wagner, we find the words from the Communion, 'Take this my body, take this my blood', repeated 'in faint whispers by angelic voices', after which faith declares itself 'firmly and stoutly'. The famous dove then appears, and faith fills the whole world with its force. An interlude expressive of 'terrible sinful remorse' is followed by the hope of ultimate redemption. Cosima and the Grail community could be well pleased.

But they overlooked the fact that this text was geared to the intellectual grasp of the man who had commissioned it: Wagner wrote it in November 1880 for Ludwig II, whose propensity for mystical piety was matched only by his sense of religious contrition, with the result that the complex ideas of the original were transposed down to a level accessible to the king. Ludwig was in any case not interested in any deeper meaning. At the private performance that was arranged for him in Munich under Wagner's own direction he immediately insisted on hearing the prelude again, after which he demanded the 'overture to *Lohengrin* by way of a comparison', as though it were a concert of family favourites.[179]

The truth of the matter is that the *Parsifal* prelude is only superficially connected with Schopenhauer or Christianity. Rather, it expresses within the narrowest confines its composer's philosophy of love. According to Nietzsche, this hypnotically solemn piece reveals not only an understanding that 'cuts through the soul like a knife' but also 'a sense of empathy with all that is seen and judged there', prompting the apostate disciple to ask 'whether a painter had ever painted so melancholy a gaze of love?'[180]

The so-called Love Feast motif with which the prelude begins in so strange a way, rising up from unfathomable depths, had a completely different meaning for Wagner from the one that is normally associated with it, inasmuch as the floating solemnity of the melody to which the words 'Take this my blood, take this my body, for the sake of our love' rise up expresses the whole self-sacrifice of love. Like the God of the beginning and like his human embodiment in Jesus, the lover gives himself wholly to the Other, whether it be the world or his beloved, without the least certainty that he will rediscover himself in it.

This voluntary self-sacrifice expresses the unfathomable nature of the divine beginning into which the melody in Wagner's prelude sinks back in its expectancy. In making his offer, the lover asks an inscrutable question similar to the one found at the start of the prelude to *Tristan und Isolde*. He yearns for an answer but is unable to demand one. The same was true of Wagner, who interpreted the motif in a wholly personal way. In November 1877, after sketching the prelude, he wrote it out on a separate sheet of paper, adding the note 'd'en haut du Temple du St. Gral' and then sending it off to Judith Gautier. 'Take this my body, take this my blood in remembrance of me.'[181]

Judith's reply to this confession of Wagner's love was destroyed in Bayreuth, but what he hoped to receive from her is preserved in the prelude: the poet's words plunge deep into the feminine element of the music, where they are reborn in transfiguring radiance. The same melody rises up like a transfigured echo from the shimmering carpet of sound that expresses anxious expectancy, then, pulsating like the vision of the Grail in *Lohengrin*, breaking out in an otherworldly light that fills the whole of the world.

Once this confession of love has sunk back in turn into the uncertainty of the beginning, the familiar strains of the Dresden Amen rise up from the silence. The tension has finally been broken, and the lovers who have been moving towards each other can merge at last. The fact that this signals a creative new beginning is revealed by the dove winging down 'from the gentlest heights' and recalling its marriage-broking mission in one of the drafts of *Die Meistersinger*.

Redeemed mankind is greeted by a trombone chorale that is equally reminiscent of *Die Meistersinger*, conjuring up God's kingdom of love in an unprecedented vision of sound that surpasses the magic of the *Lohengrin* prelude, only to be followed by a sudden plunge into the abyss, as the earlier Utopian vision gives way to the drama's true prelude, above which, according to Wagner, a crucified corpse towers up. A muted timpani roll and a tremolando in the lower strings usher in a funereal mood and a presentiment of death. As once before, darkness shrouds the world in its sable garment.

Yet again we hear the phrase 'Take this my blood', but this time as the hopeless lament of a human sacrifice bleeding to death before our eyes. As Wagner explained to King Ludwig, it was 'the sacred sweat of fear on the Mount of

Olives, the godly pain of suffering of Golgotha' that finds expression in these sounds, in which love is wholly enshrouded in darkness. There follows no conciliatory cadence but only the anguished chord of a dominant seventh that remains unresolved and unredeemed.

The tragedy begins and, with it, its manifold interpretations, each new attempt at exegesis refuting another, and each new production on stage reducing the 'illusory splendour' of its predecessor to 'mourning and ruins', much as Klingsor's bag of tricks is destroyed by Parsifal's spear. The work's message has remained obscure, its ending as baffling as its opening, all more recent interpretations leading to ultimate obfuscation.

Yet Wagner's Bühnenweihfestspiel can be understood, albeit not from a single perspective. Rather, we need to approach it from the various trajectories along which Wagner's own life and thought developed. Within the work, his unresolved private mythology rubs shoulders with his desperate nationalism, which is itself bound up with his hatred of all things Jewish, while his belief in creative love is grafted onto Wolfram's legendary history of the Grail. While Wagner suffered from his unrequited passion for Judith as though from an open wound, he was also filled with the certainty that with his marriage and his festival theatre he had created a prison for himself. The end of the work was left intentionally ambiguous: 'Redemption to the Redeemer.'

As early as 1845, when he first read 'Wolfram's strange yet so intimately familiar poem' in Marienbad, Wagner must have been struck by the parallels with his own life. As with his earlier summer breaks, all of which had led to moments of self-discovery in the mines of the past, he encountered long-familiar archetypes in *Parzival*. Appropriately enough in the context of Marienbad, the melancholy Grail king Anfortas suffers from a secret wound and takes the waters, rather as Wagner's stepfather Ludwig Geyer had done. Redemption can come only from the hero who on the tangled pathways of his journey through life is purified, ceasing to be a foolish lad and becoming Grail king.

The hero not only redeems the ailing ruler but, central to the miraculous tale, frees the castle of the Grail from the spell that paralyzes it. The mysterious Communion that takes place here reminded Wagner of his oratorio *Das Liebesmahl der Apostel*, which he had celebrated in the Frauenkirche in Dresden. The drama now unfolds between the domed church in the Saxon capital, the health resort in Bohemia and a wonderful garden of the kind that Geyer had once owned. And it is a drama in which nothing less than the world's salvation is at stake.

The action certainly seems to begin in an ideal world in the idyllic setting of the woods surrounding Marienbad. The motif associated with Holy

Communion rings out on the trombones, before dying away through the clearing beside the lake, and members of the Grail community then kneel in prayer to the strains of the Dresden Amen. As dawn breaks, a holiday atmosphere develops, the members of the community living here like one big family, close to nature, cut off from the world and protected by the castle and by the Grail's blessing. But the three principal members of this family, who enter the clearing one after the other, are now scarcely recognizable as such, for horror and disfigurement have infiltrated the community, albeit unnoticed by the outside world.

Another name for the spell that lies on the world of the Grail is 'guilt', a guilt as mysterious as that which, according to Wagner, Geyer 'thought he had to atone for'. The female 'servant' of the Grail is the first to set foot on stage. Bowed down by guilt, she is followed by the Grail's guardian, whom a psychological burden fetters to his sickbed. Next comes the hero himself, caught in flagrante delicto. Only later does it emerge that all three characters are from the same family, even though they have introduced themselves independently, for the subtle affinity between their motifs makes it plain that we are dealing here with a son and his parents.

A shared sense of guilt binds them to each other – not because they are all in thrall to Schopenhauer's world will or because they have violated God's commandments but because they have sinned against each other and thus against themselves. Not only have the adversary and the wicked mother sinned against the son, the latter is guilty of trespassing against them in turn. Only in this way can the son see through the family entanglements and destroy them with a flash of insight as though they were some Gordian knot.

Things have not always been bad. Before 'degeneration' set in, Wagner explained to Ludwig II in 1880, the divine race of humans had 'reached its true apogee'.[182] As in *The Wibelungs*, an archetypal monarch ruled the world, which was entrusted to him as a treasure. Following its loss, the myth changed, and the symbol of ownership passed into that of pure blood. The Grail was born. Whereas the descendants of the first race of men longed for its healing power and Frederick Barbarossa travelled in vain to the Holy Land in search of it, Wagner was able to find it in Wolfram's *Parzival*. In a castle, inaccessible to the rest of mankind, it nurtured the new race of kings around whom noble knights foregathered, providing them with celestial food and every year re-enacting the miracle of creation, an act announced by a dove that descended from Heaven.

But this soteriological community was soon torn apart, when its ruling monarch, renamed Amfortas, sustained an incurable wound, so that, no longer the lord of 'the most victorious race', he is reduced to 'the slave of his sickness'. His groans and outbursts of despair provide a graphic illustration of the tragic dilemma in which he finds himself. Here the explanation offered by Gurnemanz, who acts as our guide to the world of the Grail, fails to go far enough. If the king's illness was really the result of a lack of chastity that drove him into the arms of a 'terribly beautiful woman', this would hardly have been tragic, for the violation of any vow of chastity that he may have sworn would presuppose a kind of order that would have been restored by his punishment.

But the wound is the least of his worries. Not even the all-knowing Gurnemanz could know what Wagner had told Mathilde Wesendonck in 1859 – namely, that Amfortas, as an intensified reincarnation of the fatally wounded Tristan, bears not only a 'spear wound but also, no doubt, another wound – in his heart', a wound that makes him long for death as the 'ultimate solace', just as his hapless forebear once longed to die.[183] This can mean only that Amfortas has been seized by the same insatiable yearning as the Dutchman, Tannhäuser and the composer of *Parsifal*. It is not the violation of some law that has reduced Amfortas to the level of a slave but the collapse of the whole world of laws that he represents. A single embrace has reduced the whole apparently solid structure to no more than a pile of rubble. On the ruins of his own world, Amfortas longs for the love that is denied to him for ever.

As a result, it is not only Tristan who returns in the guise of the hapless Amfortas, but Wotan, too. In the *Ring*, the god had built Valhalla to rule the world, an edifice comparable with the Castle of the Grail, only for him to realize that well-regulated government rules out the selfless love to which the whole of creation owes its existence. And so Wotan despaired of a world in which he was forced to forgo love, recognizing his own features in Alberich's reflection – Alberich who cursed love in order to inherit the earth. In *Parsifal* this demon is called Klingsor, and he too uses a mirror to ensnare Amfortas's doomed world.

Enter Kundry, the exotically dressed female messenger of the Grail, wearing Eve's snakeskin belt and revealing a brusqueness that suggests there is no room for feminine nature within the strictly regulated world in which she finds herself. The servile stance that she adopts as a 'restlessly timid maid' is, of course, a mask. In fact she does not even belong to the present, which is circumscribed by time and place, but can bridge any distance through flight. Needless to say, the 'Grail's commandments' that are derived from the Bible do not apply to her, but as Gurnemanz assures the Squires, she hopes that through her assistance she may 'atone for guilt from a former life'. Even so, she remains a pagan, laughing as she confirms the threat that she poses: 'I never do good.'

Even when she offers the patient imported Arabian balm, she immediately dampens his hopes with her brusque 'What use will it be?' This may relate to the fact that, by her own admission, she never helps, but it may also apply to the medicine itself, a medicine that we may well suppose to be Wagner's tried and tested opium, which is not really intended to have healing properties. Or is she alluding to an embarrassing aspect of Amfortas's illness which, unsuited to the operatic stage, is left unmentioned by Gurnemanz in his Ciceronian guise? It is clear from Wolfram that the spear mutilated Amfortas's genitals.[184] Like Wotan, he had turned against himself: in both cases, the spear of their manhood was broken by their own weapon.

And this is precisely what his alter ego, Klingsor, had intended when – if we may believe Gurnemanz – he had inflicted on himself a wound that mirrors Amfortas's. 'I'll now destroy his line', love's demonic foe boasts in the 1877 draft. When Wolzogen related the word 'line' – in German 'Stamm' – to Amfortas and the Grail knights, Wagner immediately corrected his 'error'.[185] For what is at stake in this struggle is not the community and its property but the propagation of Titurel's proto-race. Who will continue his line? Who will inherit the world and ensure its regeneration? Who can become the new proto-king and father new proto-kings? Or bring about their definitive downfall?

As his name suggests, Amfortas is powerless (the word is thought to derive from Latin 'infirmitas') and so he is unable to perpetuate the line, leaving only his grey-haired progenitor Titurel to carry out this function. His race seems destined to die out with his son, unless an heir can be found. Although this son and heir is related not to the Grail but to Wagner, his blood will serve the purpose that the traditional progenitors are prevented from fulfilling. Parsifal now appears, an interloper like the Wälsungs, not even aware of his own name and, like Siegfried, evidently in search of the meaning of fear. Whereas his wildness and closeness to nature, immediately noticed by Gurnemanz, betray his affinity with Kundry, his relationship with Amfortas as yet remains unclear.

Unless, that is, we are to see in Parsifal's sporting achievement in shooting down a swan in flight more than merely the crime against animals that the Grail brotherhood bewails so vociferously. Their revulsion and indignation, movingly depicted by Wagner the animal lover, greet the poor sinner who has no inkling of what he has done with his arrow. Possibly not even Gurnemanz fully suspects, for all that he gives Parsifal a sound dressing-down. For the swan comes from the same direction as its murderer. The king, reports one of the knights, had just greeted it 'as a good omen', but with their low strings and timpani roll, the sounds to which Wagner set these words suggest interment and the horror of death.

The swan whose 'invisible soul', to quote Wagner,[186] is conjured up by the orchestra conceals within it another creature. Just as the Greek god Zeus assumed a cygneous guise in *Tannhäuser* and the progenitor of the swan-maidens plumed himself with another's feathers in *Lohengrin*, so the swan continued to symbolize the father figure for the son of Ludwig Geyer. Now he had violently broken free. Although one of the legends associated with the Buddha tells of such an incident, the immediate source may be found, rather, in Apel's *Der Freischütz*, where the hero shoots down a vulture hovering over the forest, so that it 'falls bleeding to the ground'. This bird conceals within it the satanic enemy Samiel who is ultimately to rob him of his lover and his inheritance.

In Wolfram's romance, too, the guileless Parzival is guilty, like Oedipus, of patricide, becoming enmeshed in the toils of his own guilt by running through an unknown knight with his spear. Wagner was fully aware of the similarity between these events inasmuch as he draws a direct comparison between Parsifal's action and Amfortas's sufferings. Like Oedipus, Wagner's hero, when questioned by Gurnemanz, does not know his own name. Moreover, he assures his interrogator that he made his weapon only 'to chase the wild eagles from the forest'. No doubt they had threatened his relationship with his mother, as in Wagner's dream of the vulture.

This too is reflected in Wagner's libretto, for the king, hoping that his reproductive powers may be restored, interprets the 'wild swan' as a 'good omen' because the male came 'looking for its mate' in order to couple with it. His words are underscored by the sweet strains of *Lohengrin*. Amfortas has scarcely noted the symbolism of this scene when Parsifal appears. In order to point up the symbolic identity of Amfortas and the fatally wounded bird, Gurnemanz orders the Squires to bear the king away at the same time as they remove the dead bird, which they lift up 'reverentially' as though it were the king on his sickbed.

The hero has no sooner got rid of his father than he discovers from Kundry that his mother, too, is dead but that she had asked to be remembered to him. Kundry's cynicism is such that Parsifal would happily strangle her, but it is doubly justified, for he is indeed guilty of causing his mother's death, her heart having been broken in her grief at the loss of her son. Moreover, she is not dead. For Parsifal's ordeal consists in the fact that it leads him not away from his past, but back to it. Much the same must have happened to Wagner in Marienbad, where his mother and stepfather, thoughts of whom he had apparently long since suppressed, were reborn as archetypes. 'Guilt' is only another word for the realization that the world that one thought had been overcome is a perpetual, ever-present nightmare.

And so the hero meets his parents Amfortas and Kundry – whom Wagner once compared to the fallen couple of Adam and Eve[187] – on the banks of the Grail castle's lake, after which he returns to his forgotten homeland. Although it lies not far from Marienbad, it was necessary in terms of the action on stage to leave behind empirical reality while the scene changes and the Transformation Music rings out.

Gurnemanz has prefaced this move with the mysterious remark that 'here time becomes space', a phrase that has led commentators to speculate that in some way we witness the miracle of a change of dimension from the temporal to the spatial. But space is something we can experience only through our idea of time, just as time can be depicted only by three-dimensional means. In other words, the phrase must mean that the world of our outward experience has come to an end here. As Lohengrin has already revealed, no road leads into the heart of the Castle of the Grail that the characters are about to enter, as this world lies at the very heart of human consciousness.

Or in our memories. Transported by the strains of the Transformation Music into a state of ecstasy that renders us clairvoyant, we witness the miracle of a world being born, while Wagner's life passes us by in a solemnly melancholy march. The heavy strokes of the bells in which we may hear the four syllables of his name mark a homecoming that takes him back to the origins of his existence,[188] but also to his 'guilt'. Like Hoffmann's Elis entering the miraculous world of the mine, Parsifal sets foot in the Temple of the Grail where, according to the 1865 prose draft, he is greeted by 'wondrous sounds' and the gentle tolling of 'crystalline bells' descending from a 'high cathedral-like cupola'. Wagner's hero stands there 'enchanted'. Presumably the composer had experienced a comparable musical wonder in the Frauenkirche in Dresden.

As with *Das Liebesmahl der Apostel* in Dresden in 1843, Wagner arranged his Grail choruses on three separate levels in his onstage cathedral, allowing their sounds to complement each other like the harmony of the spheres. Once again we hear the local Amen and the hovering dove is invoked. A divine service is announced, but who is the God who is being worshipped? And which religion is celebrating its bizarre Mass here? The temple knights approach with monklike mien and take up their places at dining tables more secular than sacred in character. From the other side a shrine is brought in, covered with a purple cloth that is no doubt made of satin, followed by the ailing king on his litter. Behind the baldachin beneath which Amfortas's couch is placed rests the first king, Titurel, in a darkened niche, making him look like a statue upon his own tomb.

When viewed objectively, this scene resembles nothing so much as the symbolic representation of a family group. The children receive food and drink without having to worry about it themselves, a reward, as it were, for behaving themselves. For they willingly obey their father's divine commandments, just as they honour their unapproachable mother, who is embodied in the Grail, worshipping her for her goodness and her readiness to sacrifice her life to theirs. More brothers and sisters arrive, thanks to the heavenly miracle, with splendid regularity, without any need to change the perfect edifice of the community over which the figure of the grandfather towers. To the small child, time seems like a space defined by the sublime figures of its parents, while the Temple of the Grail appears as the very first Paradise, in perpetual harmony with itself.

This, however, is only the first step on the road to understanding. Wagner himself compared *Parsifal* to the Eleusinian Mysteries,[189] which, as we know, concerned the procreation of life, rather than its beginnings. As an amateur classical philologist, Wagner knew that the secret cult of Dionysus, the god of ecstasy, and Persephone, the goddess of the underworld, was devoted to sex. The Greeks, Wagner remarked in the context of *Parsifal*, had been 'wise to confine the mysteries to initiates',[190] for the sacred reproductive organs, hidden between covers in the cavernous sacral space, were revealed at the ecstatic climax of these mysteries. The suspicion that the Grail symbolizes the female sexual organ is suggested by the God-fearing Gurnemanz himself when he speaks of the 'sacred votive vessel' of the Grail and the 'lance' that belongs with it as objects associated with the 'divine blood' of the Saviour. Taken together, Gurnemanz explains, they are 'Zeugengüter', literally 'objects that can be used as evidence', but the verb 'zeugen' also means 'to beget'. It is the task of these objects, after all, to beget new life.

Against this mysterious background, Parsifal's entry into the Temple of the Grail no longer seems like a return to the Church of Our Lady but a penetration of the female body. Indeed, the account of his journey there can be interpreted without difficulty as a description of the female anatomy. The impenetrable forest suddenly recedes and in the bare rock 'a large entrance' opens up 'between two enormously powerful pillars'. Thus we read in Wagner's Bayreuth stage direction.[191] After Parsifal has penetrated the opening, he is 'surrounded' by the gateway that leads via a rising corridor to a vast hall that 'opens up at the top into a high arched cupola'.

Here in the maternal belly, where so many heroes have lost their way, stands the shrine containing the Grail whose vessel regularly bleeds. In conversation with Cosima, Wagner praised the 'sanctity' of the 'mother's womb', explicitly including Goethe in his praise for having recognized its 'divine' nature.[192] Although the Grail receives annual visits from the dove of the Holy Ghost, the paternal king has at his disposal a 'sacred spear' of his own that is independent of the dove whose enchantment is associated with its celestial fertility. As Parsifal announces at the end of the work, this spear strives 'in yearning for the kindred wellspring' of the Grail. And by this point in the drama, redemption is at hand: the vessel has finally been revealed, and the spear, now held erect, may perform its function at the culmination of the mystery. This too may be felt by many observers to represent the 'Redemption of the Redeemer'.

Yet this occurs only at the end of a long and painful process that resembles the history of the world in miniature. In the beginning, there are sensational scenes in the Temple of the Grail, where all hungrily await the unveiling of the vessel as demanded by the ancient grey-haired king, whose Commendatore-like voice rings out from his funereal niche. But the guardian is on his guard and will no longer uncover the Grail, for the revelation of the mystery merely brings home to him the dilemma in which he finds himself: he longs to die, but the Grail restores him, instead, to a life that has become an infinitely protracted death.

The father who no longer wants to be a father is now given a chance to put his trauma into words, for there follows a desperate outburst in which Amfortas blames himself for all that has happened, recalling the dying Tristan's self-reproach, before he sinks back, unconscious, like his predecessor. The raging pain of the spear wound, he tells the congregation, is as nothing beside the 'hellish anguish' caused by the sight of the 'most sacred relic': the vessel of the Grail gives his fellow knights sustenance and apparently also immortality, but to him it brings only the opposite.

Although Amfortas attempts to account for his torment mystically and physically as part of a process of repression in which the blood of Christ flows from the Grail into his heart and forces out his own poor sinner's blood through the scab, it seems clear from his choice of words that it is something different that causes his longing and, with it, makes his blood keep oozing out. As soon as the Grail is uncovered, he feels 'convulsed by the most blissful pleasure's pain', a feeling synonymous with the experience of sexual delight denied to his fellow knights.

His hellish torment consists in the fact that the excitement caused by the sight of the womb 'glowing red' can no longer find release, partly because of the wound which, bleeding freely, attests to his lack of procreative powers, but even more because the woman for whom he yearns is perpetually denied him. 'The hot sinful blood', he analyzes himself with startling clarity, 'forever oozes anew from the wellspring of desire, a desire which, alas, no atonement can ever assuage.' In saying this, he is evidently alluding to the sexual ambiguity of the expression 'seine Lust büssen', which in German means not only 'to atone for one's pleasure' in a moral sense, but also 'to gratify one's desires'. Wagner was naturally aware of this ambiguity. Having set the Grail king's 'impassioned ejaculation' to music, he noted drily that he had 'stopped Amfortas's mouth'.[193]

Although this may explain the 'hypochondria' of Wagner's world-weary stepfather, it still leaves much unsaid about the complexities of the process associated with the Communion. After all, the sexual love and its failure on which the Grail king is fixated represent only one aspect of creation. Within a world defined by time and space, all that finds expression as a sense of yearning for the beloved and an all-powerful desire to procreate merely repeats the event in the first creation to which the world of time and space owes its existence.

God's desire to rediscover himself in his own ground reflects the man's desire to unite with a woman. Whereas Schelling had symbolized the prototypical act of love as a ray of light falling into the darkness of nature and stirring nature into life, Wagner had given this graphic expression in his writings on art and especially in his philosophy of love as set forth in the *Ring*. For humankind in general and for Schopenhauer in particular, sexual love was no more than a simple instinct designed to perpetuate life, but for Wagner it revealed the creative essence of the divine. The universe owed its existence to the loving union of God and his own antithesis, just as the light of the sun created nature out of universal night.

And it is in this that the actual miracle of the Grail consists, a miracle that takes place in spite of Amfortas's initial refusal to reveal it. Scarcely has it been uncovered when a 'blinding ray of light descends on the vessel from above', causing it to glow, just as the gold had once done in the Rhine, and to shine 'increasingly brightly in radiant crimson'. In order to illustrate this mystic union of masculine light and feminine matter, Wagner has the anguished Amfortas explain in his exquisite torment that 'The ray of light sinks down on the hallowed object', whereupon 'the mantle falls' and 'the votive vessel's godly contents glow with radiant might'.

But Amfortas's account contains a telltale association, for 'the mantle falls' is a direct quotation from Novalis's well-known 'Hymn to the Night', which the poet devotes to an Eleusinian love feast. 'We sink upon night's altar on the softest couch', Novalis writes, anticipating the pleasures of the mystery to come. 'The mantle falls, and kindled by the warming press, the sweetest sacrifice's fire glows in all its purity.'

But the glowing Grail may be differently interpreted, for behind the dithyrambic hyperbole produced by Amfortas's obsession lies a universally familiar phenomenon. 'On one occasion', Glasenapp recalled Wagner 'expressing his lively objection to all that was superficially miraculous about the events portrayed on stage: even the blinding ray of light that falls on the Grail from above should not be interpreted as a supernatural phenomenon without considerable reservations, but may be imagined as the light of the sun, having reached its highest point in the midday sky, shining down on the sacred vessel through the opening in the cupola above which it now stands'.[194]

This fructifying glance, through which both nature and humanity acquire life, represents one aspect of the act of procreation, the other being symbolized by the receptive vessel of the Grail, with the result that Wagner equates the shaft of sunlight with the sacred spear. In terms of its 'conceptual origins', the spear, he told Glasenapp, was 'clearly the sunbeam that had been lost to nature in winter's night of suffering'. At the end of the Communion service, Parsifal must therefore set out in search of the lost solar spear and 'by bringing it back as the god of spring'. In this way the circle is complete and a link is forged between Parsifal as the new saviour and Siegfried as the old solar hero.

Like that of the first act, the world of the second act, which is soon to overwhelm Parsifal with delights that he has never known before, dates back to Wagner's days in Dresden. It was the 'demonic abyss of the theatre' that cast its spell of make-believe on people in order to alienate them from their godlike nature. Among the principal attractions of this Fata Morgana of false happiness is the woman who wanders through the Grail's purlieus as a penitent before taking on the part of the demonic seductress.

The long-suffering Amfortas reappears, too, but this time in the more active role of the miscreant who uses a willing Venus to ensnare like-minded individuals in the trap that had proved his own downfall as Grail king. If by the end of his life Wagner knew his stepfather only as an incurable invalid, the latter had earlier been a dangerous trickster who stole from others, including Wagner's true father, robbing them of their wives, inheritances and lives. And this is precisely what he now plans for the guileless Parsifal, who soon turns up in search of 'evidence'.

Wagner had already encountered the literary prototype of this adversary while working on *Tannhäuser*. The inhabitant of the magic castle – a fantastical replica of the Castle of the Grail – takes his name from the satanic black magician in Hoffmann's tale of the Wartburg Song Contest. In 1845 Wagner's colleague at the theatre in Dresden, Karl Gutzkow, had drawn his attention to the figure of 'Master Klingsohr', criticizing him for his failure to include him in *Tannhäuser*: 'You'd have a powerful bass role à la Bertram in *Robert le diable*,' advised the dramaturge, 'and in terms of the plot there'd be a demonic representative to work on Tannhäuser in dramatic form.'[195]

Gutzkow would not live to see how seriously Wagner took his advice, for Klingsor resembles not only Hoffmann's black magician but also, and in equal measure, Meyerbeer's devil Bertram. Indeed, he even acquires some of the characteristics of Wagner's hated and now dead rival himself. Like Meyerbeer, the impotent Klingsor creates a deceptive world of empty effects, exploiting their sensual and erotic appeal in his attempt to gain control over others. Love of the purely human is as unfamiliar to him as it was to Wagner's stepfather Geyer. As we know, it was only by the skin of his teeth that Wagner escaped the snares of these father figures, who had both tried to drag him down to hell much as Bertram destroys his son Robert. But in *Parsifal* Wagner finally broke with fathers of every description.

Thanks to his skills as a designer, the charlatan Klingsor has conjured up a wonderful fairy garden in the wilderness, tempting every passing hero with a sea of highly perfumed flowers. In much the same way, Parsifal, whose creator likewise had a weakness for such artificial floral paradises, is powerfully attracted to this world of tropical voluptuousness. His experience here is similar to that of his ancestor, Elis, in Hoffmann's *Die Bergwerke zu Falun*, who discovers a garden full of astonishing flowers deep in the bowels of the earth. On closer inspection they turn out to be 'countless graceful virginal figures who hold him enfolded in their dazzling white arms', while 'sweet harmonies' ring out 'beneath the broad vault' and an 'indescribable feeling of pain and pleasure' fills the young man's heart.

Klingsor, too, can provide such venereal trickery: like Hoffmann's, his flowers prove to be alive and are filled with a quite shameless love of life. Presumably Wagner recalled Schopenhauer's remark that flowers openly expose their private parts. As teasing and alluring as the Rhinedaughters and just as scantily clad – this time in petals – they crowd around Parsifal, for all the world as though the young Richard had wandered into his sisters' bedroom just as they were dressing for the day. In their childlike but emphatically voluptuous way they pretend that they want to play and even to 'blossom' for him. Singing, they flatter him with their 'loving labours', which they barely understand but which their master requires them to perform.

As Wagner suggested in his covert compliment to Judith Gautier, they behave like the 'flowers of evil' that Baudelaire had dedicated to her father. Just as Geyer spoilt Wagner's sisters, so Klingsor has turned these women into seductive coquettes, a process of corruption that began while they were still children – this much seems clear from their ambiguous admission that 'in the spring our master plucks us'. But as with their theatrical sisters, their artificial charms are short-lived, for in the autumn they 'fade and die'. It was at precisely this point, at the 'lovely diminuendo on "We fade and die away"', that a 'warm and heart-felt cry of "Bravo! Bravo!"' was heard coming from Wagner's box at perform-ances of *Parsifal*. 'It really was Wagner's voice.'[196]

The siren sounds of these girls, with their rapidly fading charms, take us back to Wagner's family in Dresden. Indeed, the work's whole musical atmosphere developed, plantlike, from the tempting calls of their fragrant blooms. Accord-ing to Egon Voss, one of the leading authorities on Wagner, their languishing call 'Komm! Holder Knabe!' ('Come! Lovely boy!') is directly related to the Dresden Amen through its 'ascending second', with the result that 'the worlds of the Grail and Klingsor, although antithetical in terms of the subject and libretto, are musically very close, not to say identical'.[197]

That Geyer used the charms of Wagner's sexually dependent sisters to 'catch' the young composer is also suggested by Meyerbeer's *Robert le diable*, where the demonic Bertram lures the hero into the Cemetery of Saint Rosalie and the nuns – 'once heaven's daughters, now doomed to live in hell' – rise up from their graves to perform their famous ballet. As lightly clad as Klingsor's flowers, they finally cast aside their veils and, in keeping with Master Bertram's wishes, bring ruin upon the hero. At the climax of their seductive revels, the lustful abbess herself appears, nestling up to Robert and leaving him 'drunk with love' and incapable of resisting her advances. A kiss seals his downfall.

Wagner had already expressed his indignation at Meyerbeer's frivolous ballet and was determined to show his own mastery with his Flowermaidens' Bac-chanal. To friends he described it 'jokingly as his latest "ballet"'.[198] The entry of Meyerbeer's Mother Superior also appears in Wagner's version of the scene, although he may, of course, have had an additional source in mind here. In the mines at Falun the 'sombre countenance of a powerful woman' had appeared before Elis in the midst of the voluptuous flowers, whereupon 'a gentle voice had called his name as though in disconsolate grief'. According to Hoffmann, it was 'the voice of his mother'.

Hitherto resistant to seduction, Parsifal, too, hears this voice calling his name as though in disconsolate grief. It issues from a woman who needs only to wave her hand for the assembled flowers, loose-living and flighty, to withdraw. With her, a note of seriousness is restored to the proceedings. For only the audience knows what leads up to her appearance, in which respect we have the advan-tage over her victim, Parsifal. Casting a 'powerfully enchanting spell', Klingsor has conjured her up just as Wotan conjured up Erda and Bertram the sisters of mercy. The man who has killed off love in himself has power over the woman who compulsively kills others and herself with her love.

Although Klingsor calls her Kundry like the grovelling messenger of the Grail, she is actually more like the love goddess who was the ruin of Tannhäuser. 'In fact,' Wagner noted in the presence of Cosima, who must have wondered whom he was addressing, 'she should really lie there naked like a Titian Venus.'[199] In short, his feminine ideal – a mixture of Wilhelmine Schröder-Devrient and Judith Gautier – was reborn in Klingsor's magic castle, but very much against her will, for Klingsor forces her to seduce the very man whom she hopes may yet redeem her.

Her past history justifies her master's optimism, for the names that he uses to invoke this 'nameless' creature are all those of women who have been the ruin of men. As 'Rose of Hell', she draws the unwary into the abyss with her perfume; as the valkyrie Gunddryggia, she foments war between men just as the treacherous Helen once did; and as Herodias, she was guilty of causing the death of John the Baptist. But it is not in this capacity that Klingsor rouses the archetype of the seductively destructive mother. According to the eighteenth-century poet Christian Fürchtegott Gellert, whom Wagner held in high regard, 'Herodias, the Holy Writ reveals, broke faith with him who was her lawful spouse and at his brother's side pursued a love that any heathen surely would have shunned.'

It was precisely this that was Wagner's secret reproach to his mother, who bore a number of equally puzzling names, just as it was to all the other women who subsequently entered his life. And as Parsifal learns to his cost, these rose-skinned Lolitas are also traitors who have no difficulty changing their affections from their favourite knights to Parsifal himself as soon as he defeats them in combat. If Wagner commented in rehearsal that 'each of them must be a Donna Anna',[200] he was thinking less of the daughter of Mozart's Commendatore, as Porges assumed, than of the naïvely unfaithful Lady Anne in Shakespeare's *Richard III*, a figure who had once reminded him of Cosima.

The fact that through her betrayal both Amfortas and the entire family of the Grail are lost is the result, she believes, of a curse that has dogged her every move for two millennia or more, just as it hounded Ahasuerus. Like Judas who betrayed his Saviour, she had felt only scorn for his sacrifice, or to be more exact, she had rejected the loving glance that had caught her eye just as the divine ray of light had fallen into the night of nature. Whereas Alberich had seized the radiant gold and stolen it out of self-interest, Kundry had shut herself off from the light of God's sun and thrown back at him the piercing contempt of her own independence.

Her repentance comes too late. She has placed self-willed independence above self-sacrifice, thereby betraying not only her Saviour but also the essence of all creation, and as a result she is prevented from uniting with the whole, abandoned henceforth to the hellish fires of her own self-will. Redemption, she knows very well, can come from love alone. But each time she hopes to meet God's gaze in a man, she encounters not the willingness for self-sacrifice that would have offered even her the possibility of loving self-abandon, but the lustful egoism of natural desire. And so, one after another, she has abandoned, betrayed and sold each of her lovers in turn to their more powerful rivals.

Now it is Parsifal's turn. As his mother – and this is another of Kundry's incarnations – she knows of course how he may be tamed. With an immature lad like Parsifal there can be no talk of love, still less of self-sacrifice, and so she transports him back to a time when he knew only tenderness in his life and immediately awakens in him a desire for the mother who transferred her love to him following the death of his father. Now it is easy for her to channel his state of emotional shock into one of physical desire and turn him into an instrument of betrayal, with no will of his own. She even has the audacity to offer to teach him the facts of life and to tell him about the 'love' to which he ultimately owes his own life, beginning her course of instruction with his mother's 'last greeting', which she imparts in the form of a 'first kiss'. It is a lingering kiss.

Perhaps 'kiss' is not the right word, for Parsifal discovers physical love, melting into the body of the naked Venus. For a moment that lasts an eternity he merges with another being. What is all in a day's work for a professional like Kundry, who, according to Wagner, 'has already experienced Isolde's love-death a hundred times over in her various reincarnations',[201] is a novel experience for the novice. This 'first kiss of love', Wagner explained, brings with it 'a premonition of death'.[202] The pleasing aspect of ecstasy – its ability to break down barriers – is turned into the horror of loss of self. Whether he merely kisses the woman he loves or enters her completely, his union with the body that bore him is synonymous with his becoming one with the ground from which he grew up. In other words, he dies.

And he knows it. The ecstatic union with the ground and with nature and the primal will does not have to lead to destruction but could also, in Wagner's view, be turned into a state of somnambulistic clairvoyance. Our consciousness, entirely thrown back on itself, sees in an inner vision the essence of existence. This is how Michelangelo's *Last Judgement* had been revealed to the ecstatic Cosima, and according to 'Heroism and Christianity', exactly the same is true of the hero whose consciousness, 'in answer to the cravings of the will, rises to that clear-sightedness that casts its own light back upon the will'.[203] But within this light glows the divine spark of the first creation, and so the morning of self-consciousness now dawns, emerging as though by a miracle from the night of non-being.

And it is this that saves his life. For his pleasurable descent into Kundry's body leads, as Amfortas discovers to his cost, to the abyss of unassuaged desire, which is itself a living death. Accursed as she is, Kundry no longer harbours any illusions about her chances of being redeemed, with the result that she is prepared to hand even Parsifal over to the demonic Klingsor to be killed. She is the traitor, and the hero whom she holds in her embrace is her guileless victim. This was the trauma that Wagner associated with his childhood, the wound that would never close. For disinheritance and rejection were preceded by the betrayal first of his actual father's love and then of his own.

Parsifal has to right this wrong. He wakes up from his night of love before it devours him. Instead of disappearing in the lightless unity of the ground, he realizes in a moment of clear-sightedness that everything is one. The 'pure fool', to quote Wagner's oracular pronouncement, becomes 'wise through pity'. He quite literally sees the light, glimpsing before him the womb of the woman that corresponds to the open wound from which the Grail king suffers. In turn, Parsifal's own body suffers the torment felt by Amfortas at being separated from what he bears in *his* own body. He feels it as a 'terrible longing' directed at himself. A feeling that seems like insatiable desire for the other person is in fact a longing for himself, for nature and for inwardly divided creation. This leap of understanding finds expression in a penetrating scream which, according to Wagner, had once figured at the start of all Greek tragedy.

A second vision now rises up above this layer of his understanding. Parsifal sees himself back in the Temple of the Grail, following events there uncomprehendingly and 'dully'. But now their meaning is revealed to him just as the crimson chalice has been revealed. The bloody inner disunity that typifies the human condition and that Parsifal has seen before him in the sufferings of the Grail king now gleams, redeemed, in the Grail. The separation of male and female that had led to the unbearable torments of love is reconciled in the act of procreation, in the union of the light with its fertile ground. In this way, the Grail symbolizes the miracle of the first creation, a miracle betrayed by the desire of the ground. And it is this that constitutes the 'Saviour's lament' that Parsifal hears in his inner ear. Like the vessel itself, nature, too, was violated, and its voice called on Parsifal: 'Redeem and rescue me from hands defiled by guilt!'

At the time of Wagner's obsession with 'regeneration', this voice assumed a certain stridency. By the end of his life, he believed that he had found the cause of the world's disunity in the 'corruption of the blood'. If the blood of Jesus pulsed with pure humanity, the sap of a corrupted life courses through the temptress's veins, and this in turn has entered Amfortas's system as a result of intimate contact. Inasmuch as the propagation of the first Aryan kingship lies in his hands, or rather in his spear, the future of the pure race has been compromised by this blood mixture and the ancestral weapon has fallen into his adversary's hands.

By resisting temptation and rescuing the shaft from impure hands, Parsifal purifies the blood that pours from the Grail. After this curious reading had finally found favour with Wagner himself, his followers mindlessly repeated it, echoing it so enthusiastically that it soon took hold.[204]

But it was not Parsifal's vision. Wagner's Marienbad hero became a saviour not because he restored racial purity but because he healed the breach that affected the whole of creation. It was not in Gobineau's Bayreuth but in Geyer's Dresden that Wagner felt for himself the terrible power that seemed to him more powerful than divine love and that had shaken the world's foundations since the beginning of human life or at least since the dawn of conscious thought. It was the sympathy that is distorted as greed, the insatiable drive of the self that raises itself in triumph over man's initial state of concord.

This basic instinct finds its clearest expression – and this lies at the heart of Parsifal's insight – in the division between the sexes, who come together for brief moments of ecstasy, only to relapse into the torments of desire as a result of the inevitable betrayal of their love. The 'sexual urge', Wagner remarked on one occasion, was a 'unique and mighty force',[205] but what was so 'terrible' about it was that this force was a 'source of torment'.[206] It mimicked the unity that it destroyed in reality.

Parsifal finds the solution. For Wagner, it was not even new but lay in a love that had nothing to do with the sort of love that was preached from church pulpits or that was kindled by the difference between the sexes. As long ago as 1854 Wagner had told August Röckel that the true redemption of humankind lay in the 'union of man and woman', by which he meant not their periodic couplings but the fusion of their opposites.

Only when 'the "I" is subsumed by the "you"', only in the 'union of man and woman does the true human being exist and only through love, then, do man and woman become human'.[207] In *Tannhäuser, Tristan und Isolde* and the *Ring*, this had seemed possible only through a love-death because the world did not yet seem ripe for a life of love, but this great leap forward in human evolution is anticipated by the Utopian message of *Parsifal*.

The hero has scarcely fathomed the true nature of the love that rests on the self-deception of existence when the phantasmagoria created by the deceitful

Klingsor collapses in on itself and his imitation of nature is replaced by the real thing: the matinal meadow on the banks of the Grail Lake. With the return of the liberator of the solar spear to the starting point of his epistemological process, spring returns and wakens creation from its deathlike slumber. Now that Parsifal has freed his own inner nature from its misconception of itself, the external world of nature, too, is redeemed. Strictly speaking, this world is no longer 'outside' him, and herein lies the enchantment of the Good Friday Music.

Together with the seductive flowers whose meadow can once again 'laugh' in childish delight, Kundry herself is redeemed. The question is how. Many writers have argued that this comes about when she is turned into Mary Magdalene, who anoints the new saviour with her perfumed balm and dries his feet with her hair. Or is it the result of her baptism, which she receives at the hands of the anointed Parsifal, causing her to burst into tears? Or is it because of her death, when she gazes into Parsifal's eyes and sinks down 'lifeless' at his feet, thereby fulfilling the prophecy of the 'downfall' – 'Untergang' – of all Jews?

All of these points are true in part, yet they fail to go to the heart of the matter. Just as the wound can be healed only by the spear that dealt it, so the love of the beginning, having lost its way, can be made whole again only through love. In short, the transformed relationship between Parsifal and Kundry in the final act becomes the true secret of the mystery play that is *Parsifal*. This final act, Wagner told Cosima, begins on a note of the 'darkest hopelessness and disconsolation', recalling the Valhalla of *Götterdämmerung*. The World Ash from whose trunk the spear was torn dries out and dies. In the prelude to the third act we hear the 'lament of an extinguished star', a lament continued in Kundry's nightmarish groans.[208]

But a new beginning already lies in the 'thorny hedge' in which Gurnemanz finds the penitent Kundry. For not only had the 'Jew in the Thornbush' been caught in such a hedge; the solar hero's hallowed bride, Brünnhilde, had fallen asleep behind a similarly protective wall. Wagner himself drew attention to the parallel between the *Ring* and *Parsifal* when he claimed that he 'could call the third act of *Parsifal Sleeping Beauty* because she is found in a thornbush'.[209] And the man who will wake her is already approaching. If Kundry is once again lying in a wintery 'sleep of death', as the well-informed Gurnemanz observes, then the hero announces himself as the god of spring, just as Dionysus had once appeared to Persephone.

Parsifal's new role in the Grail community is unambiguously defined. Even while working on *Lohengrin*, Wagner had stressed that, unlike the monkish brethren, the Grail king had the task of propagating the species. And in his report on the 1882 production of *Parsifal*, Wagner continued to emphasize that as the 'head of his race' the king was set apart from the others 'by the mystical importance of the function reserved for him alone',[210] a function that consisted not only in revealing the Grail but also – and Wagner preferred to draw a discreet veil of silence over this – in inseminating it with the spear. As early as 1845, while he was taking the waters in Marienbad, Wagner had decided that this could be achieved only with a 'pure woman so that his august race can be perpetuated for ever, unadulterated'.[211]

And so when Parsifal prays ostentatiously before the spear, which is 'embedded upright' in the ground, causing Gurnemanz to 'cry out in his ecstasy', as Wagner explained to Ludwig,[212] he is issuing a concrete claim. As the only female in the drama, Kundry alone can be considered for his blessing. And this too Wagner had already adumbrated in his 1877 draft, in which Parsifal promises: 'I shall love you and redeem you if you show me the way to Anfortas!'[213]

That he means to keep his word, even though, like Venus, she has led him astray, is made clear by the music. As Egon Voss has shown, there are numerous suggestive quotations of the music associated with the goddess in *Tannhäuser*, as well as the 'Tristan' chord and its resolution, which appears 'three times in succession'. This, Voss comments, hardly squares with the religious ceremonies taking place on stage: 'Who can say exactly what this means? All that we can say for certain is that the relationship between Parsifal and Kundry is still characterized by eroticism and desire even in the third act.'[214]

But before the two are united in an act that brings 'Redemption to the Redeemer', there is one final, climactic build-up of horror that can trace its origins back to Dresden. Once again the scene changes to the very heart of human consciousness and once again Wagner's name rings out in the language of the bells. A funeral march guides the hero through the dark corridors of memory, where not only Geyer and Weber were borne to their final resting places but where it is clear from the desperate cries of grief for the mother, love too has been interred. Now only death holds sway in the family.

This funeral march, whose hammer blows contain an echo of Siegfried's dirge, was occasioned by a death that preceded all other misfortunes. Wagner had not experienced it for himself in his infancy, but his nightmare now caught up with him in the Temple of the Grail. With Titurel, the first Grail king had died in the person of the good father, Friedrich. At the same time, Wagner exposes his murderers, for the head of the family has died only because the ailing Amfortas has barred him from seeing the Grail. Now Wagner saw himself standing 'with Amfortas before Titurel's uncovered body'.[215] Klingsor's action in wresting Amfortas's lover from him is mirrored by the crime committed by Amfortas against the first king. For Amfortas and Klingsor are one and the same, masks of the actor Geyer, which is why the Grail's ailing guardian pleads for the death that his alter ego has already suffered in the fairy-tale garden.

But things turn out differently, for Parsifal's hour has now struck. His spear erect, he confronts the congregation of mourners in order to have himself proclaimed their new king. He loses no time in proving himself the saviour who robs death of its sting, using his spear to close Amfortas's wound. There follows a genuine resurrection of the flesh as Titurel's body rises up from its coffin and gives his paternal blessing to his true son Parsifal. And the Grail, which had once sprung from 'the human heart's unmortifiable longing for love',[216] now stands open again, as radiant as of old, with its light 'shedding a halo over all' – thus the stage direction in the printed libretto.

Is it really over all? The penitent Kundry has stood to one side, saying nothing but shyly observing her hero's miraculous deeds. Countless times she has turned up in history as the embodiment of insidious sexual desire only to sink back down, unredeemed, into a deathly sleep. For two thousand years she has waited for this moment. And once again she has a chance to gaze into the eyes of a man who has overcome the world of egoism and who in spite of that feels love.

That he is indeed a man is shown by his spear, which reacts to the Grail's proximity: 'The tip of the spear glows red', reads Wagner's stage direction from 1882.[217] And Kundry, who is no longer Kundry but only a loving woman, finally meets his gaze while 'sinking slowly lifeless to the ground before Parsifal'.

Thus the great lover dies, gazing into the eyes of her lover, just as Brünnhilde had once done. The 'sound of annihilation in the timpani', noted Cosima, already seemed to have marked her end. This, Wagner went on to explain, was the 'annihilation of the whole being, of every earthly desire'.[218] But it is very much this qualification that defines true love, the love that begins beyond desire, just as it had done for Prakriti and Ananda.

And so Kundry dies so that, undivided, ever united and without end, she may be one with her lover. The evil mother has gone, returning as the self-sacrificing sister who gives herself to her brother. Their union is blessed by the dove that descends from the dome, hovering over the couple with its message of glad tidings.

Thus Titian's earthly Venus is transformed at the end into Titian's heavenly Assunta in whose features Wagner discovered both the 'pain of the mother giving birth and the ecstasy of love'. Only in her, Wagner realized in Venice in 1882, was 'this unique and mighty force in the whole of nature, the sex drive, freed of all desire, the will enraptured and redeemed from itself'. Thus transformed, the Assunta was left with only one 'desire: to create the Saviour'.[219]

Chronicle of a Death Foretold

Wagner's death in Venice on 13 February 1883 saved him from having to sit through the celebrations that would have been held throughout Europe to mark his seventieth birthday on 22 May. These celebrations would have been the greatest triumph of his life, although they would no doubt have inspired only embittered comments on his part, as did all the other acts of recognition that he lived to see in the final years of his life. His dream remained unfulfilled. All that he had created in Bayreuth to the astonishment of the wider world struck him as being 'absurd'.[220] His model life at Cosima's side left him feeling stifled. In the year that witnessed the first performances of *Parsifal*, finally bringing him his breakthrough and, for the first time in his life, a profit of almost 150,000 marks, he longed to die.

At least he spoke of death with increasing frequency. When death finally came, surprising everyone apart from Cosima, to whom he had announced it with almost obsessive persistency, a life whose artistic creations had risen into the light from the endless ocean of harmony was snuffed out on a note of strident disharmony. As in the prelude to *Parsifal*, the discord remained unresolved and unredeemed. Wagner said nothing more, leaving neither a will nor any famous last words. When he collapsed for the final time, it was not 'My Cosima' that he said but 'My watch'. For a while, his widow was dumbstruck, but it then became clear that she would have the final word and would continue to do so for almost half a century.

Wagner's death at the age of sixty-nine was not preordained. Life was no longer a source of 'contentment', and so the thought of death became a favourite topic of conversation. Anyone who did not know him and who failed to see that death plays a vital, life-giving role in his works was bound to misunderstand him. Observers who did not have the notion of a Wagnerian lovedeath at the back of their minds were likely to think of him as tired of life. But Wagner remained a child throughout the whole of his life, and his obsession with death and destruction resembled nothing so much as a child's desperate attempts to draw attention to itself and encourage others to heed it. Cosima by contrast seems to have heard only the wish, and having made it her duty in life to serve her husband in everything, she obliged Wagner in this as in everything else.

In doing so she was not alone. Wagner's death, which he himself predicted, was brought on by the combined actions of his doctors and his wife. When it finally came, they offered him no help. With the exception of his servant Betty Bürkel, Wagner died alone and no longer had anything to say to his wife when she finally arrived. If we are to speak of guilt – and the fact that Wagner made this his lifelong theme entitles us to do so – then the lion's share of that guilt undoubtedly belongs to Cosima.

Unlike his doctors, who resorted to abdominal massages and faith healing, she was always at hand. Only when it was too late, or rather when she herself, who should have known better, had provoked the decisive attack, did she sit herself down at the piano and play a piece by Liszt: the then thirteen-year-old Siegfried always remembered the day of his father's death as the one on which he heard his mother playing the piano for the very first time in his life.

In the years leading up to Wagner's death, the couple, independently of the ebb and flow of their affections, had developed forces that strained in opposite directions. Wagner regarded the Bayreuth enterprise as a failure because it perpetuated the very type of operatic theatre that he most despised. Even the town itself struck him as a mistake. When Paul von Joukowsky refused to believe this in the light of the festival's international success, Wagner declared shortly before his death: 'You laughed when I said that I am the unhappiest of men for having built my home in a blasted climate like this, and you thought it was just a joke; but I meant it.'[221] Just to be on the safe side, he took out a whole year's lease on the rooms in Venice where he died.

Cosima by contrast had blossomed in Bayreuth. Like Minna three decades earlier, she derived the exaggerated opinion that she had of herself from their booming joint enterprise. Her life's goal had been achieved and she could now look down on Liszt and the hated Carolyne. The highest rung on the ladder of social success remained her assumption of power in the Festspielhaus, a possibility that Wagner himself did not even consider. Only under his own direction, he stressed, could he envisage his 'Bayreuth creation'. 'But this will perish,' he confided to Angelo Neumann only months before he died, 'and it will do so with my death, for who will continue it in the spirit in which I intended remains unknown and unknowable to me.'[222]

Cosima thought differently, but as long as her husband was alive she wisely kept this knowledge to herself. The enterprise was just beginning to prosper, and plans to follow up the *Ring* and *Parsifal* with productions of Wagner's other works held out the prospect of gratifying financial gains. There were no royalties to pay, the artists' demands were modest, and Ludwig the Generous 'placed the orchestra and chorus of My Court Theatre at the disposal of the Bayreuth enterprise for two months every year from 1882'. It was precisely at this point that Wagner collapsed, with the result that this intoxicating prospect was endangered by the very man who had opened it up.

This fundamental disagreement was no secret in the family. 'The thirteenth of February 1883', Siegfried wrote in his memoirs with extraordinary matter-of-factness, 'brought a great change in our lives. My father had, to use the popular expression, lived from hand to mouth. . . . There was no invested fortune, only what my mother had brought to the marriage. During the years that followed it was a question of slowly establishing a fortune.'[223] Strange though it may seem, the Wagners found it easier to amass a fortune without the head of the family. Cosima's main concern was to ensure that the son who was dear to her heart should have a golden future, which she hoped to share with him. In fact, he survived her by only four months.

Wagner was always conscious of the power that he allowed Cosima to have over him. Perhaps he even needed the abrasive tension that it involved because it prevented him from ever taking any pleasure anything. The daily scenes of domestic strife were as much a part of this as was the slave-driver about whose 'coldness and disappearance' he regularly dreamt. Unfortunately, his nerves suffered in the process, so that his health, too, was undermined. After one nightmare, he joked with reference to Goethe's 'Prelude in the Theatre' from *Faust*: 'You're coming with me, fast as thought can tell/ From heaven through the world and down to hell.'[224]

Of course he had to complete the final stage of the journey on his own. His chronic gastrointestinal problems proved the principal source of his physical torments, and it was especially unfortunate that he seemed particularly fond of the very types of food that triggered his much-feared 'abdominal diableries'.[225] But it was neither his stomach pains nor the frequent bouts of diarrhoea alternating with constipation that were the real source of his ill humour. Rather, this consisted in an excessive build-up of gas that made itself felt through stomach pains and even more painful symptoms. As early as 1868 he had complained about these 'terrible convulsions caused by flatulence' that plagued him for the most part during the night.[226] They continued to affect him right up to the end of his life, not least on account of an over-acidic diet.

Of course, flatulence was not the cause of Wagner's death, but according to his doctor in Venice, Friedrich Keppler, it contributed to it in no small way. 'Painful disruptions to the action of the heart' were caused, he believed, by 'a massive build-up of gas in the stomach and intestines' and by 'a reflex of the stomach nerves on the heart nerves, finally precipitating the disaster through the rupture of the right ventricle'.[227] It was not a nice death. But how did Keppler know this? His findings were evidently not based on a post mortem examination but were noted down only when the body was embalmed, with the result that more recent specialists have called his results into question.

Presumably Wagner's heart did not rupture, as Keppler supposed, but was asphyxiated. His patient had been suffering for years from coronary insufficiency, leading to a narrowing of the thoracic cavity and a reduction in the blood supply to the coronary arteries. In turn, this is now believed to have led to angina pectoris, the typical symptoms of which – a feeling of tightness, difficulty in breathing and chest pains – coincide exactly with Wagner's complaints.[228] He himself thought that he was suffering from a weak heart, but his family doctor in Bayreuth, Carl Landgraf, emphatically rejected this, inclining rather towards indigestion or rheumatism. Even an expert consulted by Wagner, Professor Wilhelm Olivier Leube of the University of Erlangen, insisted that his organs were 'completely healthy' after examining him in October 1881: his 'troubles' were merely the result of his abdominal complaint.

Leube accordingly prescribed a diet that has been described by two recent writers on the subject as 'unsuited, if not actually harmful, to a patient suffering from coronary disease'.[229] Landgraf and Keppler meanwhile contributed unwittingly to their patient's incorrect treatment, Landgraf recommending the consumption of large quantities of meat washed down with 'fine sparkling wine', while Keppler, who had signally failed to diagnose Wagner's coronary illness, attempted to ease his convulsions by means of valerian drops and cold abdominal massages, evidently a kind of sitz bath involving friction.

Wagner was particularly pleased to be prescribed champagne, so much so that during the rehearsals for *Parsifal* in 1882 the horn player Franz Strauss – by no means a fan of Wagner's – was struck by the Master's inebriated state. 'He drinks so much, and strong liquor at that,' he wrote to his wife from Bayreuth, 'that he is permanently intoxicated. Recently he was so tight at a rehearsal that he almost fell into the pit.'[230]

Their incorrect diagnosis notwithstanding, Wagner's doctors did at least recognize that his condition was being made worse by agitation and stress. Wagner himself had noted in 1867 in a letter to his Viennese doctor, Josef Standhartner, with whom he was on friendly terms: 'After every extreme annoyance, every tormenting worry, I invariably feel exactly the same deterioration in my condition', leading to 'this endless chronic stomach catarrh, or whatever you want to call it'.[231]

Even the lackadaisical Landgraf reminded Wagner's factotum, Bernhard Schnappauf, of the danger of overexcitement. 'He should be protected at all costs from any kind of emotional excitement', he wrote to Schnappauf in 1881, when the composer and his entourage, including the barber whose medical advice he valued, were wintering in Palermo. 'Violent anger could have the worst possible consequences.' This, Landgraf added, had already been made clear to Cosima. 'I have recently written once again to Frau Wagner, therefore, and taken the opportunity to draw her attention to these concerns and warn her, at least, against all physical and mental exertions.' Above all, he went on, it was important to be aware of the 'possible causes of these attacks'.[232]

Wagner was in the picture. On the morning of his death he told his servant: 'I must be careful today.'[233] Keppler later thought that 'emotional excitement' had brought on his death. 'The actual attack that brought such an abrupt end to the Master's life', he explained, '*must* have had a similar cause.' No doubt he had good reasons for underlining the word 'must'.

Wagner had first visited Venice in 1858 while working on *Tristan und Isolde* and had immediately been overcome by a sense of foreboding: the appearance of a gondola filled him with 'genuine' terror, and when he stepped beneath the black awning, he felt 'emphatically' that he was 'taking part in a funeral procession during an epidemic',[234] a fear that continued to haunt him throughout his journey along the Grand Canal.

A quarter of a century later he was able to afford the luxury of two full-time gondoliers who plied him back and forth along the city's canals. Together with his family, domestic tutors and servants, he moved into the Palazzo Vendramin-Calergi on 18 September 1882, occupying a suite of rooms on the mezzanine floor – according to different accounts, the number of rooms varied from fifteen to twenty-eight. Liszt counted eighteen. The annual rent was six thousand francs. The furniture was in the style of Louis XVI, but Wagner added his own personal touch with the fabrics and perfumes he had brought with him. In one room, the scent of beeswax candles was mixed with attar of roses rising from satin flowers, and a chiaroscuro light entered through five blue curtains whose different shades, from the deepest cobalt to a delicate forget-me-not, allowed the level of brightness to be effortlessly controlled. Wagner called this room his 'Blue Grotto'.[235]

There was also a secret rose cabinet in Venice, and when Joukowsky entered it unobserved, he was reminded of 'Klingsor's magic garden thought up by Wagner when high on hashish'. There were pale pink satin wall hangings everywhere, all of them decorated with bunches of fragrant roses, and, lit by candles in an altar chandelier, there was also a grand piano entirely covered in champagne-coloured silk as Wagner could not bear the gondola-black of the wood. A polar bear rug and an image of the Madonna added a touch of contrast.

Hidden behind red silk curtains was a cupboard containing Wagner's most hallowed possessions: expensive fur-lined brocade and silk coats ranging in colour 'from pitch-black to violet and bottle-green, and from crimson and orange to pure white', which he wore depending on his mood. He called them 'Brabant', 'Cornwall' and 'Franconia', no doubt allusions to the scenes where his operas are set.[236] According to Cosima, a green velvet jacket called 'Rembrandt' made him look like Figaro,[237] and even his dyed silver hair shimmered with a green light.

But the perfumes intended to bring balm to Wagner's senses soon evaporated when his adversary arrived on 19 November. 'Half Franciscan, half gypsy' was Wagner's description of Franz Liszt, who stayed with his daughter at the composer's palazzo, remaining until 13 January 1883. The relationship between the three of them was unchanged, as Cosima should have known. Not only was the abbé possessed of a demonic mutability, he also had one of Geyer's special peculiarities that Wagner particularly abhorred. Wagner should by rights have been grateful to him not only for rescuing him financially but for a whole series of artistic borrowings culminating in the Communion theme from *Parsifal*. Above all, he should have been grateful for Cosima, who was officially synonymous with Wagner's whole happiness. So why did he hate him?

Not even Wagner himself could answer this question, although he kept finding new reasons for his loathing. He felt inhibited, for example, by Liszt's colonization of several rooms in his palazzo, one of which commanded a wonderful view of the canal. He was also put out by Liszt's habit of donning a black cassock and going to early Mass every morning. And he found it unsettling that, unlike himself, Liszt led an active social life in the city, even seeking to entice away his daughter and her children. The old man's refusal to stick to regular mealtimes even gave rise to outbursts of anger on Wagner's part. His nights became more disturbed, leading to nightmares and finally to breathing difficulties. On one occasion when Liszt spirited his daughter away on a series of visits, Wagner mixed up his tablets, before washing them down with opium. In spite of this, Cosima noted that her husband's 'agitation continues to mount'.[238]

Wagner was already exhausted by the summer's festival and time and again had sighed: 'Ah! If only I were dead!'[239] He had barely begun to recover – there had been virtually no guests or inquisitive visitors – when the idyll was ruined for him. Each of Liszt's characteristics provoked his displeasure. A habitual gambler, he invited the Wagners to join him at his card table every evening, causing Wagner to pun that he had got whist, not Liszt. He also worked himself up into a rage over the abbé's alcohol problem, which could be kept in check only by means of cognac, beer or Marsala. And his fury was compounded by the fact that by constantly trying to mediate between them, Cosima seemed to be betraying Wagner to her father. When she defended the latter by insisting that he drank only 'Marsala with water', her husband flew off the handle. No doubt she thought she was 'virtue itself'! On another occasion, he said – 'only partly in fun', as she ruefully noted – that she 'hated' him.[240]

But more than anything, it was Liszt's piano playing that annoyed him, as there was nothing he could do in return. The legendary pianist was naturally fully aware of the state that his son-in-law was in. The funeral gondolas gliding past his window on their way to the cemetery island of San Michele inspired him to compose two elegies that he called *La lugubre gondola I* and *II*, so that in the echoing rooms of the Palazzo Vendramin Wagner was forced to listen to the genesis of the piano pieces that were soon to mourn his own passing.[241]

He also passed comment on them, complaining to Cosima about their sense-lessness and venting his anger at them 'keenly and in great detail'. The torture continued the next day, this time prompting him to speak 'brusquely' of Liszt's 'burgeoning madness' as a musician. His other thoughts on his father-in-law's 'dissonances' were subsequently obliterated in ink in Cosima's diaries. During one 'terrible night' just before Christmas, he exclaimed 'I hate all pianists – they are my Antichrist!' – a comical comment aimed both at Liszt and Bülow and carefully calculated to offend the cleric's daughter.[242] It was at precisely this time that Liszt was completing *La lugubre gondola*.

Six weeks later Wagner himself was ferried away in a gondola. He lay in a bronze sarcophagus decorated with lions' heads, a touch that would surely have delighted him. A glass window allowed his embalmed face to be seen. His widow wore the key to the coffin round her neck. A fleet of gondolas made the journey to the main station, where a funeral carriage, draped in black, was already waiting, with a saloon car for the family immediately behind it. The veiled Cosima lay down on a couch, beside the sofa on which Wagner had died. The palazzo was quickly emptied, the rose cabinet and all the wall hangings destroyed. There was a general movement towards Germany, with only the servant Betty Bürkel remaining behind.

Two months later a veritable flotilla of funeral gondolas approached the building in which Wagner had died. At its centre was the city's gondola of state, draped with black crêpe and accommodating the whole of the orchestra that was part of Angelo's Neumann's touring *Ring*. As far as the eye could see, the canal was covered with gondolas filled with a silent throng of mourners, when suddenly, as they reached the Palazzo Vendramin, the orchestra broke into the strains of Siegfried's Funeral March and all present, whether in boats or on dry land, removed their hats. There followed thunderous applause that echoed back and forth from palazzo to palazzo. Wagner would no doubt have cracked a joke at all this.

One person was missing from the burial in Bayreuth, and that was Franz Liszt, whom Cosima had not invited and who learnt of his son-in-law's death from the newspaper. His offer to stand by his daughter in her time of need was turned down by her daughter Daniela. For three years Cosima broke off all contact with her father, ignoring all his attempts at reconciliation and refusing even to receive him at the 1883 festival. What had caused this remarkable change of attitude? According to Liszt's biographer, Alan Walker, there are no convincing reasons for it.

But perhaps the question has been wrongly put. The breach with her father, whom she allegedly loved so much, can presumably be explained once we know why she loved him in the first place. It is beyond doubt, after all, that he had abandoned her as a child and that he spent the rest of his life under the thumb of the woman whom Cosima hated more than anyone else in the world. And Cosima never forgot anything. Did she love him, then, only because it was useful for her to do so – and only as long as it remained so? It seems to have been her affair with Wagner that caused her to intensify her relationship with her father as he offered himself as her trump card in a game of poker that was all about power.

It was with considerable skill that she played off the cosmopolitan Liszt off against the provincial Wagner, whose paralyzing jealousy made him putty in her hands. She needed a father figure not to puff herself up but in order to belittle her husband. As though realizing this for himself, he once told her that her father had called her a 'serpent'. When she asked him what he meant by this, Wagner explained: 'Something is done to a person, something that suddenly strikes at the heart and leaves them no chance of recovery.'[243]

Following Wagner's death from heart failure, Cosima took over the running of the festival. Although she had agreed with Wagner that they would die together, she settled instead for cutting off her hair. While the Wagnerian community assumed that she was hovering between life and death, an assumption she was happy to encourage, she was taking over Wagner's functions one by one. While still in Venice, she appointed the banker Adolf von Groß to act as her children's guardian, and later that same month she enquired after preparations for that summer's performances of *Parsifal*. Following her successful début as the festival's new director, she decided that a further festival would be held in 1884.

Wagner had never said a single word to authorize her actions, but she nevertheless took over the running of Bayreuth and, much to the bemusement of the artistes, 'improved' his production of *Parsifal*, while introducing a note of lugubrious solemnity to the musical side of things. She referred to the Master only allusively, 'as though Wagner had never walked on earth in human form'.[244] From then on, it was she who determined what Wagner had been. Whereas he had once called the shots, people now danced to her tune. The dream of her own Versailles had at last come true, and she reigned over it all as a veiled Sun Queen.

With Wagner dead, her father was no longer of any use to her and so she dropped him. Not until 1886 did she turn up unannounced in Weimar in order to persuade the now seventy-four-year-old abbé to attend the forthcoming festival. His presence, she assured him, was 'vital' if the venture was to survive.[245] But when he arrived in Bayreuth on 21 July, his health undermined by incipient pneumonia, his daughter had no time for him and he was lodged not at Wahnfried but with a local family who took in guests. His condition continued to worsen, but the insouciant Dr Landgraf certified him as fit to attend the performances and thus to drum up trade for Bayreuth.

On Cosima's orders, Landgraf then prescribed morphine for his cough, after which the now feverish Liszt had to drag himself to performances of *Parsifal* and *Tristan und Isolde*. But after that he was allowed to retire to his bed, from which he was never to rise again. Wagner's family neglected their gravely ill grandfather, leaving female students and friends to take turns in keeping a bedside vigil.

While Cosima played the part of the solicitous daughter at festival receptions, she refused to allow his nurses to enter his room, claiming that she wanted to look after her father in person but merely 'putting on an act'.[246] The truth of the matter is that she was anxious to isolate Liszt from his circle of friends during his final days. Since Wagner's death, it was said, 'a numbness' had taken hold of her that prevented her 'from showing any sympathy, any inner emotion of whatever kind it might be. One sees only a marmoreal countenance with an exaggeratedly Lisztian profile'.[247] Liszt died alone. His friends had to wait outside.

Like Wagner, he too was seized by heart spasms at whose 'terrible force he uttered the groaning cries that resounded throughout the house and echoed far around'.[248] From the deathlike state that followed these attacks he was restored to life by massages until he finally fell into a coma, at which point the Wagner family betook themselves back to Wahnfried for a reception from which Cosima returned only in the middle of the night.

Liszt's breathing soon became weaker and his doctors had to bend over him to ascertain signs of life. He was then given two injections – presumably camphor – in the region of the heart, a procedure not without its dangers, for they would have been fatal if they had punctured the heart. Liszt's body was then convulsed by violent spasms, rising up and falling back again, after which he was pronounced dead. According to Lina Ramann, four people were present at his death: Cosima, Carl Landgraf, a doctor from Erlangen and 'a surgeon by the name of Schnappauf who busied himself with the injections'.[249]

Cosima thought it only right and proper not to disrupt the festival. Observers noted an 'almost ostentatious lack of concern'. She had to attend a reception for the crown prince and was unable, therefore, to be present at the Requiem Mass for her father, at which Bruckner played the organ, improvising on the Communion theme from *Parsifal*.

'Liszt suffered a cruel and tormented end,' writes Alan Walker in his biography of the composer. 'His death remains a standing indictment against those who were in a position to ease his last moments.'[250] The same could also be said of Wagner. His death came quickly, lasting only a few hours, although it is conceivable that under the annihilating force of the spasms caused by his heart attack, he was no longer conscious of any sense of time and that the pain, having become space, as it were, seemed to stretch out into timeless eternity.

Assuming that Cosima did not subsequently play with the facts in bringing her diary up to date, a possibility that cannot be ruled out, Wagner sensed that his end was approaching and did so, moreover, well before his final death throes set in. It was as though, surrounded by a comprehensive lack of understanding, he summoned up that familiar world from which he had once emerged, with figures from his earlier life appearing before his mind's eye during the final days of his life. He listened to Klärchen's death scene from *Egmont*, a scene that he associated with Rosalie; and he sang the scene from *Don Giovanni* in which the Commendatore arrives to drag the hero down to hell. He also sang about the recruit Stiefel, who is hanged for deserting the army out of his longing for his mother; and he sang about the joker Harlequin who, as the song puts it, 'has to die'. Cosima heard and noted all this, but failed to understand it.

In his dreams he saw Wilhelmine Schröder-Devrient and 'all my little women', although he declined to name names. He was even reminded of a poem by Gellert from his childhood, a poem about the death of the dog Phylax 'Who loyally on house and yard/ Through many a night kept watchful guard'. Out of a sense of duty he called Cosima Phylax, 'and how happily', she wrote, 'I accept that name'.[251] Evidently she did not know the poem, for Phylax was a miserly cur who not even in death revealed his buried treasures. 'O vanity's great burden!/ To live a squalid life/ And die a painful death, / One seeks to gain possessions!' Three days later, the sight of Venice's palazzi provoked the outburst: 'That is property! The root of all evil.'²⁵² And Wagner praised Wilhelm Heinse, in whose *Ardinghello und die glückseeligen Inseln* all property is abolished. Cosima, whose thoughts were on accumulating property, forbore to comment on this.

Time and again, Johanna Rosine appeared before him, not as a traitress but as a beloved ideal. To his astonishment, he saw her in his dreams as 'youthfully charming' and 'very elegantly dressed', such as he had never consciously known her. Glasenapp reports that he spoke a great deal about his mother, although, if so, Cosima chose not to record it.

The image of a painfully missed first love he rediscovered in the fairytale about Undine, which in turn reminded him of his model, E. T. A. Hoffmann. In the course of the evenings leading up to his death, he read Fouqué's version of the story to his family. This is the tale of the water sprite who yearns, like dark nature, for the divine light in order to unite in a love-death with the lover who redeems and then betrays her and whom she then draws down into the darkness with her. On reading the related story of Melusine in 1866, Wagner had written to Cosima: 'It breaks my heart!'²⁵³

Joukowsky recalled that 'Wagner was deeply moved by the poetry of this watery world and the next day reported that he had dreamt about it all night',²⁵⁴ but Cosima's diaries make no mention of this. Instead, she reports how, lying awake in her bedroom, she heard Wagner talking to himself in a loud voice. When she went to see what was the matter, he explained that he had, of course, been talking to her in his thoughts. After a lengthy embrace, he had then said to her: 'Once every five thousand years it succeeds!' He was alluding to the redemption of these water sprites being a rare occurrence, whereas Cosima assumed he was talking about their love. Glasenapp's claim that Wagner went on to ask, 'Might you too be one of them?' is dismissed even by Gregor-Dellin as a 'brazen and shameless invention'.

The last thing that Wagner was thinking of was Cosima, whom he regarded, like Minna, as entirely like Fricka in character. Rather, he had in mind a creature from a wholly different world, a creature thirsting for redemption and at the same time belonging to another generation. Wagner illustrated his longing by playing a passage from *Das Rheingold* on the piano: 'Falsch und feig ist, was oben sich freut' – 'False and fated is all that rejoices above' – Cosima noted in her diary, misquoting as usual, and failing to notice that she herself must have been the butt of Wagner's quotation. After all, she was fond of basking in the light of Valhalla and looking down from 'above', whereas Wagner preferred to face the opposite direction, where, in the words of the grieving Rhinedaughters, all was 'trusting and true'. 'I am well disposed towards them,' Wagner added, anxious to avoid any misunderstanding, 'to these subservient creatures of the deep, these creatures of longing.'[255] Cosima's diaries break off with this sad confession of Wagner's.

But this was not the end of the argument that poisoned the atmosphere between them. For Cosima knew the subservient creature of whom Wagner spoke. Her name was Carrie Pringle. The curly-haired English soprano had appeared at Wahnfried in August 1881, when her audition pieces had included Agathe's aria from *Der Freischütz*, with which she had struck a particularly sensitive chord with Wagner. He immediately had her sing other numbers from the opera, including the duet and trio, good-humouredly commenting on them and apparently put in the best of moods by the young singer. Thanks to Carrie, he was clearly in his element. So grateful was he that he signed her up as one of the solo Flowermaidens for the following year's world première of *Parsifal*.

It was a good choice. By then, Carrie was under contract to La Scala, Milan, and when Judith Gautier turned up for the festival with a companion, it was only natural that Carrie should step into Judith's shoes. If not a proper replacement, she was at least able to offer some compensation. After extensive individual rehearsals with the Master, her appearances on stage, surrounded by her fellow Flowermaidens, proved one of the highlights of the festival. With mounting suspicion, Cosima watched as Wagner chose to sit with the Flowers, joking with them and even inviting them to dine with him. In general, he was 'completely against Bayreuth' and even thought of selling his Bühnenweihfestspiel and accompanying theatre to the Jewish impresario Angelo Neumann,[256] but Carrie seems to have restored his love of life. 'In my powerlessness,' wrote Cosima, without giving any more details, 'I call on God who reveals Himself to the humble.'

Were there any revelations, as there had been in the past? Cosima kept a note of Wagner's inexplicable absences, as well as his inappropriate shouts of 'Bravo', to which he felt moved as though at a performance of an Italian opera. Being too exhausted to sit through the work in its entirety, he listened only to the 'whole of the Flower Scene because its consummate execution invariably revives him'. As Cosima notes, her husband's spontaneous applause was 'hissed' by the rest of the congregation-like audience. A number of biographers even report that she gave Wagner 'black looks',[257] while Gregor-Dellin asserts that Carrie fell over a tripwire when coming on stage and disappeared down a trap that had suddenly opened up in front of her, slightly injuring herself, so that she had to be taken home in a carriage to her lodgings near Wahnfried.

Following Carrie's departure, Wagner grew increasingly depressed and his coronary illness worsened. He told Cosima that he 'wanted to die'. In September, well after the festival had ended, he expressed his 'longing for the Flowermaidens',[258] and shortly afterwards dreamt of being treated like a stranger at a reception at Wahnfried. The sense of unease continued to haunt him in Venice. He felt inhibited by Cosima's routine, a feeling that found expression in a sense of physical oppressiveness. Shortly before his death he decided on the spur of the moment to take Siegfried to some town or other in northern Italy, where he hoped to find a change of air. 'I believe', Glasenapp reports him as saying, 'that it will help my frame of mind to escape for a few days from the monotony of my life here.' But persistent rain that was driven on ahead of the scirocco and that began on 11 February meant that the trip was postponed.

Perhaps it was at this point, too, that the letter arrived from Carrie Pringle, announcing her visit to Venice. Milan was not too far away, and the solo Flowermaiden may well have felt a desire to see her Master. Was it perhaps because of this that Wagner dreamt he had received letters from two women that he did not dare to open out of his fear of Cosima's jealousy? Yet for Wagner the atmosphere brightened, the monotony of his life was interrupted, and all he had to do was to inform Cosima. And, as he told his servant on the morning of his death, to 'be careful'.

There followed an almighty row. Neither Cosima's diaries nor Glasenapp's biography refer to it, but it is vouched for by Wagner's first daughter, whom her mother later repudiated in order to ensure the inheritance for Siegfried and his heirs. Isolde recalled that her father's fatal heart attack had been preceded by an 'extremely violent scene between her parents',[259] in the course of which Cosima stipulated that Carrie was not to set foot in the Palazzo Vendramin. Wagner conceded defeat, paralyzed by the tragic dilemma of this new ban on love. But this time he did not have the strength to sustain it.

Out of fear of his mother he had repeatedly had to abandon his lovers from Jessie to Mathilde and finally the beautiful Judith. Again and again his longed-for union with the 'you' had been destroyed, together with his self-confidence. And now it was here again, the sense of humiliation caused by a woman stronger than he was. In a final desperate attempt to avoid the inevitable and gain control of his trauma, he returned to his desk.

While the rest of the family ate lunch, Wagner collected his thoughts for his final essay in his Blue Grotto, continuing to work away at a piece on 'The Feminine in the Human' that had been inspired by E. T. A. Hoffmann's

Serapionsbrüder.[260] Once again he explored the theme of the 'purely human' that could arise, he believed, only through love, not from 'conventional marriages'.[261] In the calculated abuse of marriage lay 'the reason for our decline to a level beneath that of the animal kingdom'.

But not even the generic law of sexuality, to which women were particularly subject, offered humanity a future. Ultimate redemption could be achieved only through loving union, in which the woman, in thrall to nature, was subsumed by the man, who was guided by intellect, thereby ending the fatal division between the sexes. But the actual process of liberation, from the 'rebirths' of a figure like Kundry to physical union and the real act of redemption in the process of parturition, was inevitably accompanied by convulsive spasms.

Already in the grip of his final fatal heart attack, Wagner formulated this as follows: 'Yet the process of woman's emancipation takes place only to the accompaniment of ecstatic convulsions.' Just before the pen slipped from his fingers, he then wrote down the two words that had defined the whole of his life and that were not to release their hold on him even at the moment of his death: 'Love – tragedy.'

But the final notes that reached his ears as he fought for air were the music of Liszt. Cosima played Schubert's *Lob der Tränen* in an arrangement by her father that she had learnt as a piano pupil in Paris.[262] At the same time, she wept and looked at Siegfried with 'a completely rapt expression' in her eyes. To her husband, the piece must have seemed like one final attempt to humiliate him.

Wagner removed his velvet beret to die. Only his chambermaid, Betty Bürkel, Vreneli's successor, was with him. According to Glasenapp, she was waiting in the Rose Room next door. Betty was so small that she had to stand on a footstool in order to place her master's ironed beret on his head. It now lay before him on his desk, and, his arms pressed against his breast, he started to groan.

Shortly afterwards an Italian newspaper is said to have voiced the suspicion that Betty Bürkel was in the Master's secret cabinet, but not because Cosima had posted her there for safety's sake. According to Cosima's own biographer, Richard Du Moulin Eckart, Keppler, too, was involved in an 'indiscreet communication that emanated from Venice'.[263] Was it about Carrie? Or Betty?

Whatever the answer, it was Betty who came to Cosima, 'distraught and trembling', whereupon the latter rushed to Wagner's room, followed by his manservant Georg. They found him convulsed with pain. According to the account subsequently given to King Ludwig, Wagner 'was struggling for breath in a violent spasm'.[264] He had previously taken 'some strong medicine', probably opium, but this had had no perceptible effect. He also declined the 'beneficial warm compresses' that Cosima offered, but merely continued to groan. Then his watch fell from his hand, and it was for this that he called with his final words. He twice shrugged his shoulders as though in helpless despair. And then he stopped breathing.

The tragedy was barely over before a farce began. Keppler arrived and felt for Wagner's pulse, but it had already ceased beating. In spite of this, he exclaimed in a loud voice, 'We've not yet lost all hope', and after Georg had loosened Wagner's clothing, he injected him with an alcohol-based liquid, then began to massage him, rubbing and pummelling the body, but without success.

Cosima clung to Wagner's knees. A 'pale twilight fell through the pink curtains', Joukowsky wrote to Liszt, 'and cast a gentle light on the pale and much loved face'. Peace had come to him at last, and only 'his delicate mouth remained half open, as though he were gasping for breath'.[265] By the following day Cosima was already wearing her dead husband's velvet beret.[266]

The tale had an unhappy ending for Betty and Carrie, too. While the whole of Wagner's entourage followed his bronze coffin with its lions' heads back to Bayreuth, Betty Bürkel had to remain behind in the empty palazzo and ensure that, in Cosima's words, 'no personal memento fell into others' hands'. And with that, Wagner's chambermaid disappears from history.

The fate suffered by the final ray of sunlight in his life was no better. When Carrie Pringle reported for duty for the 1883 performances of *Parsifal*, she found herself persona non grata. Although the staging and casting were to remain – at least for the time being – as the Master had ordained, Wagner's favourite singer, the Flowermaiden Carrie, was fired by Cosima's instrument, Hermann Levi, on account of her 'artistic incompetence and ill-mannered behaviour'.[267]

Wagner was laid to rest directly behind his house, where his dogs had already been buried. Even in death Cosima was not to let him out of her sight.

Notes

Preface

1. Ernest Newman, *The Life of Richard Wagner*, 4 vols. (New York 1933–46), ii.598.
2. Émile Ollivier, *Marie-Magdeleine: Récit de jeunesse* (Paris 1897), 21.
3. Newman, *The Life of Richard Wagner* (note 1), iv.33.
4. Cosima Wagner, *Die Tagebücher*, ed. Martin Gregor-Dellin and Dietrich Mack, 2 vols. (Munich 1976–7), ii.156 (7 Aug. 1878).
5. Felix Weingartner, *Lebenserinnerungen*, 2 vols. (Zurich 2/1928–9), i.261.
6. John Deathridge and Egon Voss, 'Wagnerforschung – *Und weiter nichts?? Weiter nichts??* Zur Einführung in das *Wagner-Werk-Verzeichnis*', *Wagnerliteratur – Wagnerforschung: Bericht über das Wagner-Symposium München 1983*, ed. Carl Dahlhaus and Egon Voss (Mainz 1985), 184.
7. Carl Maria Cornelius, *Peter Cornelius: Der Wort- und Tondichter*, 2 vols. (Regensburg 1925), ii.250.
8. Joachim Köhler, *Wagners Hitler: Der Prophet und sein Vollstrecker* (Munich 1997); trans. Ronald Taylor as *Wagner's Hitler: The Prophet and His Disciple* (Cambridge 2000).
9. Gottfried Wagner, *Wer nicht mit dem Wolf heult* (Cologne 1997), 84 and 140; trans. Della Couling as *He Who Does Not Howl with the Wolf* (London 1998), 72 and 118. In this context, Wagner's great-grandson speaks of 'fawning courtiers'.

Chapter 1

1. Volker L. Sigismund, 'Ein unbehauster Prinz: Constantin von Sachsen-Weimar (1758–1793). Der Bruder des Herzogs Carl August – Eine biographische Skizze', *Ortsvereinigung Hamburg der Goethe-Gesellschaft in Weimar, 1984–5*, 5–30. Sigismund writes that Johanna Rosine 'disguised her relationship with the prince in such a way that it came to be rumoured that Constantin was Wagner's grandfather'. As late as 1938, the Bayreuthian biographer Friedrich Herzfeld could still write that Constantin was 'probably' Johanna Rosine's 'actual father. At least Wagner himself believed that he was descended from Constantin'; see Friedrich Herzfeld, *Minna Planer und ihre Ehe mit Richard Wagner* (Leipzig 1938), 34. A similar line was taken by another member of the Wahnfried inner sanctum, Max von Millenkovich-Morold, who claimed that 'there was a tradition in Wagner's family that Prince Constantin was Johanna's natural father'; see Max von Millenkovich-Morold, *Dreigestirn: Wagner–Liszt–Bülow* (Leipzig 1940), 10.

2. Esther Drusche, *Richard Wagner* (Leipzig 1987), plate 5; also reproduced in the present volume.

3. Carl Friedrich Glasenapp, *Das Leben Richard Wagners*, 6 vols. (Leipzig 1905–11), i.78.

4. *König Ludwig II. und Richard Wagner: Briefwechsel*, ed. Otto Strobel, 5 vols. (Karlsruhe 1936–9), i.300 (letter from Wagner to Ludwig of 16 Feb. 1866).

5. Houston Stewart Chamberlain, *Briefe*, 2 vols. (Munich 1928), i.227 (letter to Hellmundt of 12 Dec. 1913).

6. Richard Wagner, *Briefe: Die Sammlung Burrell*, ed. John N. Burk (Frankfurt am Main 1953), 652; trans. Hans Abraham and others as *Letters of Richard Wagner: The Burrell Collection* (London 1951), 505 (Natalie Bilz-Planer's handwritten notes on Ferdinand Praeger's *Wagner, wie ich ihn kannte*).

7. Klaus Günzel, *E. T. A. Hoffmann: Leben und Werk in Briefen, Selbstzeugnissen und Zeitdokumenten* (Düsseldorf 1979), 245.

8. Friedrich Schnapp, *Der Musiker E. T. A. Hoffmann: Ein Dokumentenband* (Hildesheim 1981), 295.

9. Cosima Wagner, *Die Tagebücher*, ed. Martin Gregor-Dellin and Dietrich Mack, 2 vols. (Munich 1976–7), i.818 (15 May 1874).

10. Glasenapp, *Das Leben Richard Wagners* (note 3), i.490.

11. E. T. A. Hoffmann, *Autobiographische, musikalische und vermischte Schriften*, ed. Martin Hürlimann (Zurich 1946), 168; the letter of 27 Dec. 1814 is addressed to the *Undine* poet Friedrich de la Motte Fouqué.

12. Cosima Wagner, *Die Tagebücher* (note 9), ii.191 (5 Oct. 1878).

13. Carl Maria von Weber, *Mein vielgeliebter Muks: Hundert Briefe Carl Maria von Webers an Caroline Brandt aus den Jahren 1814–1817* (Berlin 1986), 499 (letter of 10 Oct. 1817).

14. *Allgemeines Lexikon der bildenden Künstler von der Antike bis zur Gegenwart*, ed. Ulrich Thieme and Felix Becker, 37 vols. (Leipzig R1999), xiii.509.

15. Carl Friedrich Glasenapp, 'Annalen zur Familien- und Jugendgeschichte Richard Wagners', *Richard Wagner-Jahrbuch*, ed. Joseph Kürschner (Stuttgart 1886), 19–71, esp. 38.

16. Julius Kapp and Hans Jachmann, *Richard Wagner und seine erste 'Elisabeth' Johanna Jachmann-Wagner* (Berlin 1927), 18–19.

17. *Richard Wagners Briefe*, ed. Wilhelm Altmann, 2 vols. (Leipzig 1925), ii.308 (letter to Cäcilie Avenarius of 14 Jan. 1870).

18. Cosima Wagner, *Die Tagebücher* (note 9), ii.272 (26 Dec. 1878).

19. Glasenapp, *Das Leben Richard Wagners* (note 3), i.107.

20. Richard Wagner, *Mein Leben*, ed. Eike Middell, 2 vols. (Leipzig 1986), i.9; trans. Andrew Gray as *My Life* (Cambridge 1983), 4.

21. Wagner, *Briefe: Die Sammlung Burrell* (note 6), 100; Engl. trans. (*Letters of Richard Wagner*), 68 (letter from Wagner to Minna Planer of 23 June 1836).

22. Wagner, *Briefe: Die Sammlung Burrell* (note 6), 26; Engl. trans. (*Letters of Richard Wagner*), 12 (letter from Natalie Bilz-Planer to Mary Burrell of 11 Dec. 1890–16 Feb. 1891).

23. Cosima Wagner, *Die Tagebücher* (note 9), ii.425 (14 Oct. 1879).

24. Ibid., ii.530 (8 May 1880).

25. Richard Wagner, *Sämtliche Briefe*, ed. Gertrud Strobel, Werner Wolf, Werner Breig and others (Leipzig 1967–2000 and Wiesbaden 1999–), i.95 ('Autobiographical Sketch').

26. *Richard Wagner an Minna Wagner*, ed. Hans von Wolzogen, 2 vols. (Berlin and Leipzig 1908), ii.123 (letter of 25 July 1859).

27. Cosima Wagner, *Die Tagebücher* (note 9), i.714 (13 Aug. 1873).

28. Ibid., ii.424 (12 Oct. 1879).

29. Ibid., i.410 (5 July 1871).

30. Ibid., i.199 (15 Feb. 1870).

31. Glasenapp, 'Annalen zur Familien- und Jugendgeschichte Richard Wagners' (note 15), 46.

32. Glasenapp, *Das Leben Richard Wagners* (note 3), i.74.

33. Wagner, *Mein Leben* (note 20), i.14; Engl. trans. (*My Life*), 9.

34. Cosima Wagner, *Die Tagebücher* (note 9), ii.305 (16 Feb. 1879).

35. Ibid., ii.476 (15 Jan. 1880).

36. Wagner, *Briefe: Die Sammlung Burrell* (note 6), 29; Engl. trans. (*Letters of Richard Wagner*), 14.

37. Richard Wagner, *Gesammelte Schriften und Dichtungen*, 10 vols. (Leipzig 4/1907), ix.216–17; trans. William Ashton Ellis as *Richard Wagner's Prose Works*, 8 vols. (London 1892–9, R1993–5), v.215. (Extracts from Wagner's prose works have been newly translated for the present volume. References to Ashton Ellis's translation are included merely as a guide.) In order to express his contempt for coarse actors, Wagner pursues this bottle metaphor in his article: the actor is poured into a bottle before being served to the audience by the playwright. First, however, the actor has to be 'carefully bottled, neatly labelled and placed in the repository'. Thus the dangerous bottle of half a century earlier has ended up back on the shelf again. If Wagner continued to belabour this somewhat arcane image, it is because he was recalling another symbolic context: the curious idea of capturing the actor in a bottle and placing him in a 'repository' is first found in E. T. A. Hoffmann's short story *Der goldene Topf*, which was one of Wagner's favourite texts. Here the evil magician Lindhorst punishes people by turning them into bottles and placing them on a bookshelf or in a repository. Wagner knew this story almost by heart, having been introduced to it by his Uncle Adolf, and so he also knew that the sorcerer Lindhorst was particularly fond of turning himself into a vulture.

38. Cosima Wagner, *Die Tagebücher* (note 9), i.782 (17 Jan. 1874). Shortly afterwards, Wagner dreamt that he had lost his hat and that 'all manner of children's hats' had been brought to him in its place, all to the sound of mocking laughter.

39. Friedrich Nietzsche, *Sämtliche Werke: Kritische Studienausgabe*, ed. Giorgio Colli and Mazzino Montinari, 15 vols. (Munich 1980), vi.41; trans. Walter Kaufmann as *Basic Writings of Nietzsche* (New York 1968), 638 (*The Case of Wagner*). This passing comment by the author of the polemical *Der Fall Wagner* acquired additional weight by virtue of the fact that as editor of the first privately printed edition of *My Life* he was fully familiar with the details of Wagner's life.

40. Martin Gregor-Dellin, *Richard Wagner: Sein Leben, sein Werk, sein Jahrhundert* (Munich 1980), 34; trans. J. Maxwell Brownjohn as *Richard Wagner: His Life, His Work, His Century* (London 1983), 17.

41. Glasenapp, *Das Leben Richard Wagners* (note 3), i.75.

42. Wagner, *Gesammelte Schriften* (note 37), viii.81–3; Engl. trans. (*Richard Wagner's Prose Works*), iv.91–3.

43. Cosima Wagner, *Die Tagebücher* (note 9), i.799 (5 March 1874).

44. Richard Wagner, *Das Braune Buch: Tagebuchaufzeichnungen 1865 bis 1882*, ed. Joachim Bergfeld (Zurich 1975), 108; trans. George Bird as *The Diary of Richard Wagner: The Brown Book 1865–1882* (London 1980), 91 (20 Sept. 1867).

45. Wagner, *Das Braune Buch* (note 44), 189–91; Engl. trans. (*The Diary of Richard Wagner*), 158–60. The original

editor Joachim Bergfeld was so shocked by the 'unpretentiousness, crudity and foolishness' of this draft that he attempted to defend Wagner by pointing out, no less comically, that the comedy 'is not on the same high level as Wagner's normal achievements'. (This apologia was excised from George Bird's English translation.)

46. Cosima Wagner, *Die Tagebücher* (note 9), ii.684 (6 Feb. 1881).

47. Ernest Newman, *The Life of Richard Wagner*, 4 vols. (New York 1933–46), i.27.

48. Glasenapp, 'Annalen zur Familien- und Jugendgeschichte Richard Wagners' (note 15), 70.

49. Wagner, *Das Braune Buch* (note 44), 64; Engl. trans. (*The Diary of Richard Wagner*), 56 (29 August 1865); Parzival's astonishment at the 'unutterable charm' of Klingsor's magic garden 'is mingled with an eerie feeling of anxiety, hesitation and horror'.

50. Cosima Wagner, *Die Tagebücher* (note 9), ii.1044 (11 Nov. 1882). Wagner mentions Mignon in his *Beethoven* essay of 1870. That same year he complained to Cosima about the way in which 'Mignon's death is passed over' (23 June 1870).

51. Glasenapp, *Das Leben Richard Wagners* (note 3), i.76–7.

52. Cosima Wagner, *Die Tagebücher* (note 9), i.205 (5 March 1870).

53. Glasenapp, *Das Leben Richard Wagners* (note 3), i.249.

54. Wagner, *Sämtliche Briefe* (note 25), ii.335 (letter to Cäcilie Avenarius of 22 Oct. 1843).

55. Ibid., i.142 (letter to Rosalie Wagner of 11 Dec. 1833).

56. Cosima Wagner, *Die Tagebücher* (note 9), i.805 (27 March 1874).

57. Ibid., i.888 (15 Jan. 1875).

58. Ibid., ii.437 (4 Nov. 1879).

59. Ibid., ii.326 (4 April 1879).

60. Glasenapp, *Das Leben Richard Wagners* (note 3), i.97.

61. Wagner, *Sämtliche Briefe* (note 25), i.95 ('Autobiographical Sketch').

62. Wagner, *Mein Leben* (note 20), i.18; Engl. trans. (*My Life*), 13.

63. Wagner, *Mein Leben* (note 20), i.45; Engl. trans. (*My Life*), 36.

64. Cosima Wagner, *Die Tagebücher* (note 9), i.94 (12 May 1869).

65. Wagner, *Gesammelte Schriften* (note 37), i.207–11; Engl. trans. (*Richard Wagner's Prose Works*), vii.167–70.

66. John Warrack, *Carl Maria von Weber* (London 1968), 212.

67. Cosima Wagner, *Die Tagebücher* (note 9), i.321 (7 Dec. 1870).

68. Curt von Westernhagen, *Richard Wagner: Sein Werk, sein Wesen, seine Welt* (Zurich 1956), 380.

69. Carl Maria von Weber, *Kunstansichten: Ausgewählte Schriften*, ed. Karl Laux (Leipzig 1975), 216; trans. Martin Cooper as *Carl Maria von Weber: Writings on Music*, ed. John Warrack (Cambridge 1981), 292.

70. Glasenapp, 'Annalen zur Familien- und Jugendgeschichte Richard Wagners' (note 15), 49.

71. Wagner, *Mein Leben* (note 20), i.22; Engl. trans. (*My Life*), 16.

72. Wagner, *Mein Leben* (note 20), i.27; Engl. trans. (*My Life*), 20.

73. Wagner, *Sämtliche Briefe* (note 25), i.96 ('Autobiographical Sketch').

74. Cosima Wagner, *Die Tagebücher* (note 9), i.828 (15 June 1874).

75. Published for the first time in *Die Programmhefte der Bayreuther Festspiele 1988*, vii (*Die Meistersinger von Nürnberg*), 95–207.

76. Glasenapp, *Das Leben Richard Wagners* (note 3), i.105.

77. *Cosima Wagner und Ludwig II. von Bayern: Briefe*, ed. Martha Schad (Bergisch Gladbach 1996), 204 (letter from Cosima von Bülow to Ludwig of 7 April 1866).

78. Cosima Wagner, *Die Tagebücher* (note 9), i.193 (31 Jan. 1870).

79. Wagner, *Gesammelte Schriften* (note

37), iv.21; Engl. trans. (*Richard Wagner's Prose Works*), ii.140–1.

80. Wagner, *Sämtliche Briefe* (note 25), i.97 ('Autobiographical Sketch').

81. Glasenapp, *Das Leben Richard Wagners* (note 3), i.123.

82. A. Löhn-Siegel, 'Richard Wagner auf der Nikolaischule in Leipzig (1829)', *Richard Wagner-Jahrbuch*, ed. Joseph Kürschner (Stuttgart 1886), 72–3.

83. Wagner, *Sämtliche Briefe* (note 25), ix.228–31 (letter to Mathilde Wesendonck of 7 April 1858).

84. Eugen Segnitz, *Richard Wagner und Leipzig (1813–1833)* (Leipzig 1901), 44; 'The reader will note the remarkable fact that both the Gretchen songs are in the same key, and the even more remarkable fact that all the numbers are in the same metre [as Berlioz's].'

85. Walter Lange, *Richard Wagner und seine Vaterstadt Leipzig* (Leipzig 1921), 52.

86. Wagner, *Gesammelte Schriften* (note 37), ix.45; Engl. trans. (*Richard Wagner's Prose Works*), v.40 ('Reminiscences of Auber').

87. Wagner, *Gesammelte Schriften* (note 37), ix.295; Engl. trans. (*Richard Wagner's Prose Works*), v.292 ('To Friedrich Nietzsche').

88. Wagner, *Gesammelte Schriften und Dichtungen* (note 37), iv.58–64; Engl. trans. (*Richard Wagner's Prose Works*), ii.184–9 (*Opera und Drama*).

89. Karl-Heinz Kröplin, *Richard Wagner 1813–1883: Eine Chronik* (Leipzig 1987), 32.

90. Cosima Wagner, *Die Tagebücher* (note 9), i.141 (16 Aug. 1869).

91. Wagner, *Sämtliche Briefe* (note 25), i.130 (letter to Theodor Apel of 12 Oct. 1832).

92. Julius Kapp, *Richard Wagner und die Frauen* (Berlin 1951), 24.

93. Wagner, *Sämtliche Briefe* (note 25), i.134 (letter to Theodor Apel of 16 Dec. 1832 to 3 Jan. 1833).

94. Wagner, *Mein Leben* (note 20), i.81;

95. Engl. trans. (*My Life*), 66. Wagner, *Sämtliche Briefe* (note 25), i.100 ('Autobiographical Sketch').

96. Ibid., i.118 (letter to Breitkopf & Härtel of 5 Aug. 1831).

97. Cosima Wagner, *Die Tagebücher* (note 9), i.963 (6 Jan. 1876).

Chapter 2

1. Richard Wagner, *Sämtliche Briefe*, ed. Gertrud Strobel, Werner Wolf, Werner Breig and others (Leipzig 1967–2000 and Wiesbaden 1999–), i.140 (letter to Rosalie Wagner of 11 Dec. 1833).

2. Richard Wagner, *Sämtliche Schriften und Dichtungen*, ed. Richard Sternfeld, 16 vols. (Leipzig 1911–14), xii.11; trans. William Ashton Ellis as *Richard Wagner's Prose Works*, 8 vols. (London 1892–9, R1993–5), viii.66 ('Pasticcio').

3. Wagner, *Sämtliche Briefe* (note 1), i.97 ('Autobiographical Sketch').

4. Carl Friedrich Glasenapp, *Das Leben Richard Wagners*, 6 vols. (Leipzig 1905–11), vi.130.

5. Wagner, *Sämtliche Schriften* (note 2), xii.1; Engl. trans. (*Richard Wagner's Prose Works*), viii.55 ('German Opera').

6. Cosima Wagner, *Die Tagebücher*, ed. Martin Gregor-Dellin and Dietrich Mack, 2 vols. (Munich 1976–7), ii.1112 (12 Feb. 1883).

7. The importance of these 'outlawed' early works for Wagner has been emphasized in particular by Joachim Kaiser, *Leben mit Wagner* (Munich 1990), 39.

8. Egon Voss, '*Wagner und kein Ende*': *Betrachtungen und Studien* (Zurich 1996), 26: 'In this way Ada is linked both to Gretchen and to Wagner's favourite sister.'

9. John Deathridge and Carl Dahlhaus, *The New Grove Wagner* (London 1984), 12.

10. Richard Wagner, *Mein Leben*, ed. Eike Middell, 2 vols. (Leipzig 1986), i.98;

trans. Andrew Gray as *My Life* (Cambridge 1983), 81: 'a short review in which I literally poured out my contempt for *Euryanthe*'.

11. Wagner, *Sämtliche Briefe* (note 1), i.101 ('Autobiographical Sketch').

12. Wagner, *Mein Leben* (note 10), i.100; Engl. trans. (*My Life*), 83.

13. Deathridge and Dahlhaus, *The New Grove Wagner* (note 9), 15.

14. The Dresden Amen was sung at both Protestant and Catholic services; see Richard Wagner, *Sämtliche Werke*, xvi ('Chorwerke'), ed. Reinhard Kapp (Mainz 1993), 34–5.

15. *The Wagner Compendium*, ed. Barry Millington (London 1992), 310.

16. Wagner, *Sämtliche Briefe* (note 1), i.172 (letter to Theodor Apel of 7 Dec. 1834).

17. Werner Otto, *Richard Wagner: Ein Lebens- und Charakterbild in Dokumenten und zeitgenössischen Darstellungen* (Berlin 1990), 24.

18. Wagner, *Mein Leben* (note 10), i.106; Engl. trans. (*My Life*), 89.

19. Cosima Wagner, *Die Tagebücher* (note 6), ii.1094 (18 Jan. 1883).

20. Wagner, *Sämtliche Briefe* (note 1), i.295 (letter to Minna Planer of 8 June 1836).

21. Cosima Wagner, *Die Tagebücher* (note 6), i.807 (1 April 1874).

22. Wagner, *Sämtliche Briefe* (note 1), i.223 (letter to Theodor Apel of 2 Oct. 1835).

23. Ibid., i.291 (letter to Minna Planer of 6 June 1836).

24. Émile Ollivier, *Marie-Magdeleine: Récit de jeunesse* (Paris 1897), 26; Ollivier was Cosima's brother-in-law.

25. Wagner, *Sämtliche Briefe* (note 1), xi.89–91 (letter to Minna Wagner of 18 May 1859).

26. Friedrich Herzfeld, *Minna Planer und ihre Ehe mit Richard Wagner* (Leipzig 1938), 41.

27. Wagner, *Mein Leben* (note 10), ii.60; Engl. trans. (*My Life*), 499.

28. Wagner, *Sämtliche Schriften* (note 2), xii.4; Engl. trans. (*Richard Wagner's Prose Works*), viii.58 ('German Opera').

29. Wagner, *Sämtliche Schriften* (note 2), xii.17 ('Dramatic Singing').

30. *König Ludwig II. und Richard Wagner: Briefwechsel*, ed. Otto Strobel, 5 vols. (Karlsruhe 1936–9), i.89 (letter from Wagner to Ludwig of 28 April 1865).

31. Richard Wagner, *Gesammelte Schriften und Dichtungen*, 10 vols. (Leipzig 4/1907), ix.221; Engl. trans. (*Richard Wagner's Prose Works*) (note 2), v.219 (*On Actors and Singers*).

32. *The Memoirs of Hector Berlioz*, ed. and trans. David Cairns (London 1977), 303 and 326.

33. Glasenapp, *Das Leben Richard Wagners* (note 4), i.497.

34. Cosima Wagner, *Die Tagebücher* (note 6), ii.67 (23 March 1878).

35. Wagner, *Mein Leben* (note 10), i.117; Engl. trans. (*My Life*), 98.

36. Wagner, *Sämtliche Schriften* (note 2), xii.14 ('From Magdeburg').

37. Wagner, *Sämtliche Briefe* (note 1), i.274 (letter to Robert Schumann of 28 May 1836).

38. Dieter Borchmeyer, 'Richard Wagner und die Französische Revolution', *Die Programmhefte der Bayreuther Festspiele 1990*, vi (*Götterdämmerung*), 1–25, esp. 17; trans. Stewart Spencer as 'Wagner and the French Revolution', 37–56, esp. 50.

39. Wagner, *Sämtliche Briefe* (note 1), i.314 (letter to Minna Planer of 22 June 1836).

40. Ibid., ii.587 (letter to Johann Kittl of 4 Jan. 1848).

41. Wagner, *Sämtliche Schriften* (note 2), xi.177.

42. Richard Wagner, *Briefe: Die Sammlung Burrell*, ed. John N. Burk (Frankfurt am Main 1953), 107; trans. Hans Abraham and others as *Letters of Richard Wagner: The Burrell Collection* (London 1951), 74 (Natalie Bilz-Planer's reminiscences).

43. Julius Kapp, *Richard Wagner und die Frauen* (Berlin 1951), 53.

44. Cosima Wagner, *Die Tagebücher* (note 6), ii.149 (29 July 1878).

45. Wagner, *Sämtliche Briefe* (note 1), i.83 ('The Red Pocketbook').

46. Martin Gregor-Dellin, *Richard Wagner: Sein Leben, sein Werk, sein Jahrhundert* (Munich 1980), 133; trans. J. Maxwell Brownjohn as *Richard Wagner: His Life, His Work, His Century* (London 1983), 86.

47. Wagner, *Sämtliche Briefe* (note 1), i.507 (letter to Joseph Tichatschek of 6 or 7 Sept. 1841).

48. Richard Wagner, *Sämtliche Werke*, xxiii ('Dokumente und Texte zu "Rienzi, der Letzte der Tribunen"'), ed. Reinhard Strohm (Mainz 1976), 137 (prose draft).

49. Wagner, *Sämtliche Briefe* (note 1), i.588 (letter to Ferdinand Heine of late Jan. 1842).

50. Wagner, *Gesammelte Schriften* (note 31) vii.119; Engl. trans. (*Richard Wagner's Prose Works*), iii.327 ('*Zukunftsmusik*').

51. Cosima Wagner, *Die Tagebücher* (note 6), i.496 (3 March 1872).

52. Richard Wagner, *Dichtungen und Schriften: Jubiläumsausgabe*, ed. Dieter Borchmeyer, 10 vols. (Frankfurt am Main 1983), x.219 (Afterword to vol. i).

53. Carl Maria von Weber, *Kunstansichten: Ausgewählte Schriften*, ed. Karl Laux (Leipzig 1975), 130; the work in question was *Alimelek*. (This review was not included in John Warrack's 1981 English edition of Weber's writings.)

54. Ernest Newman, *The Life of Richard Wagner*, 4 vols. (New York 1933–46), i.215.

55. Robert W. Gutman, *Richard Wagner: The Man, His Mind, and His Music* (London 1968), 57.

56. Richard Wagner, *Briefe an Hans von Bülow* (Jena 1916), 184 (letter of 6 Sept. 1862).

57. Richard Wagner, *Das Braune Buch: Tagebuchaufzeichnungen 1865 bis 1882*, ed. Joachim Bergfeld (Zurich 1975), 97; trans. George Bird as *The Diary of Richard Wagner: The Brown Book 1865–1882* (London 1980), 82 (12 Nov. 1865).

58. Wagner, *Sämtliche Briefe* (note 1), iv.250 (letter to Hans von Bülow of 17 Jan. 1852).

59. Ibid., iv.402 (letter to Theodor Uhlig of 2 July 1852); for further examples, see *König Ludwig II. und Richard Wagner: Briefwechsel* (note 30), ii.227 (letter from Wagner to Ludwig of 28 May 1868).

60. Hans von Wolzogen, *Bayreuth* (Leipzig n.d.), 3 (unattributed quotation).

61. Édouard Schuré, *Richard Wagner: Son œuvre et son idée* (Paris 1906), liii.

62. Otto, *Richard Wagner: Ein Lebens- und Charakterbild* (note 17), 36.

63. Wagner, *Mein Leben* (note 10), ii.85; Engl. trans. (*My Life*), 520–1.

64. Otto, *Richard Wagner: Ein Lebens- und Charakterbild* (note 17), 143.

65. Hanjo Kesting, *Das Pumpgenie: Richard Wagner und das Geld* (Frankfurt am Main 1988); see also Stewart Spencer, 'Wagner Behind Bars?', *Wagner*, xix (1998), 95–102.

66. Wagner, *Gesammelte Schriften* (note 31), iv.260; Engl. trans. (*Richard Wagner's Prose Works*), 1.302 (*A Communication to My Friends*).

67. Deathridge and Dahlhaus, *The New Grove Wagner* (note 9), 19–20.

68. Ibid., 20–21. Wagner later admitted to Edward Dannreuther that he had made a 'minute study' of Berlioz's instrumentation 'as early as 1840'.

69. Wagner, *Gesammelte Schriften* (note 31), iv. 262; Engl. trans. (*Richard Wagner's Prose Works*), i.304 (*A Communication to My Friends*).

70. Wagner, *Sämtliche Briefe* (note 1), i.106 ('Autobiographical Sketch').

71. Heinz Becker, *Der Fall Heine–Meyer-*

beer: Neue Dokumente revidieren ein Geschichtsurteil (Berlin 1958), 21.

72. Carl Friedrich Glasenapp, 'Annalen zur Familien- und Jugendgeschichte Richard Wagners', *Richard Wagner-Jahrbuch*, ed. Joseph Kürschner (Stuttgart 1886), 19–71, esp. 61.

73. Eric Werner, *Mendelssohn: A New Image of the Composer and His Age*, trans. Dika Newlin (London 1963), 186.

74. Jürgen Rehm, *Zur Musikrezeption im vormärzlichen Berlin* (Studien zur Musikwissenschaft, ii) (Zurich 1983), 135.

75. Giacomo Meyerbeer, *Briefwechsel und Tagebücher*, ed. Heinz Becker, Gudrun Becker and Sabine Henze-Döhring (Berlin 1970–), iii.133 (letter to Minna Meyerbeer of 15 June 1838).

76. Wagner, *Sämtliche Briefe* (note 1), i.168 (letter to Theodor Apel of 27 Oct. 1834).

77. Wagner, *Sämtliche Schriften* (note 2), xii.67–8; Engl. trans. (*Richard Wagner's Prose Works*), viii.111 ('Letter from Paris, 23 Feb. 1841').

78. Wendelin Weißheimer, *Erlebnisse mit Richard Wagner, Franz Liszt und vielen anderen Zeitgenossen nebst deren Briefen* (Stuttgart and Leipzig 1898), 93.

79. Wagner, *Sämtliche Briefe* (note 1), i.378 (letter to Giacomo Meyerbeer of 18 Jan. 1840).

80. Ibid., i.388 (letter to Giacomo Meyerbeer of 3 May 1840).

81. Ibid., i.397 (letter to Giacomo Meyerbeer of 4 June 1840).

82. *Giacomo Meyerbeer: Weltbürger der Musik*, ed. Heinz and Gudrun Becker (Wiesbaden 1991), 35.

83. Eduard Hanslick, 'G. Meyerbeer, Zur hundertsten Wiederkehr seines Geburtstages, 5. September 1891' quoted in Meyerbeer, *Briefwechsel und Tagebücher* (note 75), iv.557: 'But this candid admission was immediately followed by a torrent of abuse directed at Meyerbeer's music, which

he described as no more than a "grotesque caricature".'

84. Cosima Wagner, *Die Tagebücher* (note 6), i.577 (26 Sept. 1872).

85. Wagner, *Sämtliche Briefe* (note 1), i.576 (letter to Robert Schumann of 5 Jan. 1842).

86. Ibid., ii.539 (letter to Eduard Hanslick of 1 Jan. 1847). In the same letter, Wagner adds that he has every reason to 'value' Meyerbeer as a 'kind and sympathetic man' (ii.538).

87. Wagner, *Gesammelte Schriften* (note 31), v.87; Engl. trans. (*Richard Wagner's Prose Works*), iii.126 ('Reminiscences of Spontini'). This opening section of Wagner's article, berating Meyerbeer as a plagiarist, originally appeared as an obituary of Spontini in the Zurich *Eidgenössische Zeitung* on 25 Jan. 1851.

88. Wagner, *Gesammelte Schriften* (note 31), iii.300; Engl. trans. (*Richard Wagner's Prose Works*), ii.94 (*Opera and Drama*).

89. Wagner, *Sämtliche Briefe* (note 1), iii.545 (letter to Franz Liszt of 18 April 1851).

90. Glasenapp, *Das Leben Richard Wagners* (note 4), i.340.

91. Wagner, *Sämtliche Briefe* (note 1), ii.223 (letter to Robert Schumann of 25 Feb. 1843).

92. Ibid., iii.546 (letter to Franz Liszt of 18 April 1851).

93. Otto, *Richard Wagner: Ein Lebens- und Charakterbild* (note 17), 43.

94. Fritz Mende, *Heinrich Heine: Chronik seines Lebens und Werkes* (Berlin 1981), 175.

95. Wagner, *Sämtliche Schriften* (note 2), xii.101–3; Engl. trans. (*Richard Wagner's Prose Works*), viii.147–8 ('Letter from Paris, 6 July 1841').

96. Lina Ramann, *Lisztiana: Erinnerungen an Franz Liszt in Tagebuchblättern, Briefen und Dokumenten aus den Jahren 1873–1886/87*, ed. Arthur Seidl and Friedrich Schnapp (Mainz 1983),

80. Liszt reports that Heine had previously tried a similar trick on him, and that it was only when he refused to accede that Heine's 'attacks' on him began.

97. Becker, *Der Fall Heine–Meyerbeer* (note 71), 41. In his letter to Meyerbeer of 6 April 1835, Heine writes: 'You will see that I shall use it [the sum of 500 francs] in an extremely useful way, one that will be highly beneficial in its consequences. Our needs are once again of a common kind.' Nor did he omit to add: 'If I don't get it straightaway, it will be of no use.'

98. Meyerbeer, *Briefwechsel und Tagebücher* (note 75), iv.29 (diary entry of 19 Feb. 1846).

99. Ollivier, *Marie-Magdeleine* (note 24), 26.

100. *Begegnungen mit Heine: Berichte der Zeitgenossen*, ed. Michael Werner (Hamburg 1973), 514.

101. Heinrich Heine, *Sämtliche Schriften*, ed. Karl Pörnbacher (Berlin 1989), 272; the reference is in a poem called 'Die Menge tut es'.

102. Michael Mann, *Heinrich Heines Musikkritiken* (Hamburg 1971), 105.

103. Heine, *Sämtliche Schriften* (note 101), xi.300; the lampoon is titled 'Der Wanzerich'. When Meyerbeer heard that his tormentor had died, he wrote in his diary: 'May he rest in peace. I forgive him with all my heart'; quoted by Becker, *Der Fall Heine–Meyerbeer* (note 71), 125.

104. Wagner, *Sämtliche Briefe* (note 1), xi.62 (letter to Minna Wagner of 2 May 1859).

105. Heine, *Sämtliche Schriften* (note 101), vi.1020. From the original French version of 'De l'Allemagne' of 1835.

106. Heinrich Heine, *Sämtliche Schriften*, ed. Klaus Briegleb, 6 vols. (Munich 1968 76), iv.454.

107. Cosima Wagner, *Die Tagebücher* (note 6), ii.675 (25 Jan. 1881); on looking through the draft, Heine pointed out

that Erik was Senta's 'amant', not her 'amateur'.

108. Glasenapp, *Das Leben Richard Wagners* (note 4), i.363.

109. Wagner, *Sämtliche Briefe* (note 1), v.122 (letter to Theodor Uhlig of 27 Nov. 1852).

110. John Deathridge, 'Richard Wagners Kompositionen zu Goethes "Faust"', *Jahrbuch der Bayerischen Staatsoper*, v (1982), 90–9, esp. 99.

111. Richard Wagner, *Der fliegende Holländer: Texte, Materialien, Kommentare*, ed. Attila Csampai and Dietmar Holland (Reinbek 1982), 75.

112. Heine, *Sämtliche Schriften* (note 101), ix.443 ('Lutetia', Part Two).

113. Wagner, *Gesammelte Schriften* (note 31), iv.323; Engl. trans. (*Richard Wagner's Prose Works*), i.370 (*A Communication to My Friends*).

114. Wagner, *Sämtliche Briefe* (note 1), i.109 ('Autobiographical Sketch').

115. Wagner, *Gesammelte Schriften* (note 31), v.176–7; Engl. trans. (*Richard Wagner's Prose Works*), iii.228–9 ('Overture to *Der fliegende Holländer*').

116. Wagner, *Gesammelte Schriften* (note 31), v.163; Engl. trans. (*Richard Wagner's Prose Works*), iii.211 ('Remarks on Performing *Der fliegende Holländer*').

117. Wagner, *Gesammelte Schriften* (note 31), v.176–7; Engl. trans. (*Richard Wagner's Prose Works*), iii.228–9 ('Overture to *Der fliegende Holländer*').

118. Wagner, *Gesammelte Schriften* (note 31), iv.264; Engl. trans. (*Richard Wagner's Prose Works*), i.305–6 (*A Communication to My Friends*).

119. This was also how Wagner regarded the whole nature of acting: only when painting was transformed into living sculpture, he wrote in *The Artwork of the Future*, and 'stepped down onto the tragic stage' like a portrait 'of canvas and plaster' would

the art of the 'true dramatic performer' come alive. Painting seeks in vain to reproduce real life by 'heaping up the most abundant means', but the actor can achieve this by 'carrying it out in his own person'; see Wagner, *Gesammelte Schriften* (note 31), iii.147; Engl. trans. (*Richard Wagner's Prose Works*), i.181.

120. Otto, *Richard Wagner: Ein Lebens- und Charakterbild* (note 17), 47.

Chapter 3

1. Cosima Wagner, *Die Tagebücher*, ed. Martin Gregor-Dellin and Dietrich Mack, 2 vols. (Munich 1976–7), i.416 (18 July 1871).

2. Richard Wagner, *Sämtliche Briefe*, ed. Gertrud Strobel, Werner Wolf, Werner Breig and others (Leipzig 1967–2000 and Wiesbaden 1999–), ii.114 (letter to Gottfried Engelbert Anders of 14 June 1842). Wagner's piano reduction of Donizetti's *La favorite* was dedicated to Meyerbeer.

3. Richard Wagner, *Gesammelte Schriften und Dichtungen*, 10 vols. (Leipzig 4/1907), i.168; trans. William Ashton Ellis as *Richard Wagner's Prose Works*, 8 vols. (London 1892–9, R1993–5), vii.109 ('The Virtuoso and the Artist').

4. Cosima Wagner, *Die Tagebücher* (note 1), i.1076 (11 Oct. 1877) and ii.168 (3 Sept. 1878).

5. Werner Otto, *Richard Wagner: Ein Lebens- und Charakterbild in Dokumenten und zeitgenössischen Darstellungen* (Berlin 1990), 53 (report by the Dresden costume designer Ferdinand Heine).

6. Wagner, *Sämtliche Briefe* (note 2), ii.167 (letter to Eduard and Cäcilie Avenarius of 21 Oct. 1842).

7. Ibid., ii.156 (letter to Eduard and Cäcilie Avenarius of 11 Sept. 1842).

8. Richard Wagner, *Mein Leben*, ed. Eike Middell. 2 vols. (Leipzig 1986), i.374 and i.478; trans. Andrew Gray as *My Life*

(Cambridge 1983), 325 and 418. In the first of these passages, the poet Berthold Auerbach is said to have looked 'extraordinarily common and dirty', while in the second the music publisher Gemmy Brandus is described as 'unspeakably dirty' as a person.

9. Wagner, *Mein Leben* (note 8), i.300; Engl. trans. (*My Life*), 260.

10. '. . . *der Welt noch den Tannhäuser schuldig.' Richard Wagner: Tannhäuser und der Sängerkrieg auf Wartburg*, ed. Irene Erfen (Regensburg 1999), 129.

11. Wagner, *Sämtliche Briefe* (note 2), ii.250 (letter to Robert Schumann of 12 May 1843).

12. Wagner, *Gesammelte Schriften* (note 3), iv.272; Engl. trans. (*Richard Wagner's Prose Works*), i.315 (*A Communication to My Friends*).

13. Wagner, *Sämtliche Briefe* (note 2), iv.316 (letter to Gustav Schmidt of 18 March 1852).

14. Wagner, *Gesammelte Schriften* (note 3), v.177–9; Engl. trans. (*Richard Wagner's Prose Works*), iii.229–31 ('Overture to *Tannhäuser*').

15. Wagner, *Sämtliche Briefe* (note 2), iv.319 (letter to Theodor Uhlig of 20 March 1852).

16. Cosima Wagner, *Die Tagebücher* (note 1), ii.1098 (23 Jan. 1883).

17. Richard Wagner, 'Der Venusberg', *Die Programmhefte der Bayreuther Festspiele 1985*, i (*Tannhäuser*), 1–19.

18. Richard Wagner, *Sämtliche Schriften und Dichtungen*, ed. Richard Sternfeld, 16 vols. (Leipzig 1911–14), xi.414–18.

19. Ibid., xi.419.

20. Helmut Kirchmeyer, *Das zeitgenössische Wagner-Bild* (Regensburg 1967), ii.652 (*Neue Zeitschrift für Musik*, 4 Nov. 1845).

21. Wagner, *Sämtliche Briefe* (note 2), iv.376–7 (letter to Franz Liszt of 29 May 1852).

22. Wagner, *Gesammelte Schriften* (note 3), v.138; Engl. trans. (*Richard*

Wagner's Prose Works), iii.184 (*On Performing 'Tannhäuser'*).

23. Wagner, *Sämtliche Briefe* (note 2), ii.435 (letter to Karl Gaillard of 5 June 1845).

24. Karl Gutzkow, *Rückblicke auf mein Leben* (Berlin 1875), 319.

25. Wagner, *Sämtliche Briefe* (note 2), ii.252 (letter to Albert Wagner of 17 May 1843).

26. Ibid., v.106 (letter to Luise Brockhaus of 11 Nov. 1852).

27. Ibid., iii.506 (letter to Hermann Brockhaus of 2 Feb. 1851).

28. Richard Wagner, *Sämtliche Werke*, xvi ('Chorwerke'), ed. Reinhard Kapp (Mainz 1993), 30: 'It is unclear for what purpose the article was written.'

29. Ibid., xvi.171.

30. Wagner, *Sämtliche Briefe* (note 2), ii.297 (letter to Cäcilie Avenarius of 13 July 1843).

31. Ibid., ii.298 (letter to Cäcilie Avenarius of 13 July 1843).

32. John Warrack, *Carl Maria von Weber* (London 1968), 346.

33. Ibid., 154.

34. Cosima Wagner, *Die Tagebücher* (note 1), ii.191 (6 Oct. 1878).

35. Wagner, *Gesammelte Schriften* (note 3), ii.35; Engl. trans. (*Richard Wagner's Prose Works*), v.235 ('Speech at Weber's Last Resting Place').

36. Ferdinand Praeger, *Wagner As I Knew Him* (London 1892), 121. This letter is of questionable authenticity.

37. Otto, *Richard Wagner: Ein Lebens- und Charakterbild* (note 5), 63.

38. Wagner, *Sämtliche Briefe* (note 2), ii.228 (letter to Ernst Benedikt Kietz of 6 April 1843).

39. Martin Gregor-Dellin, *Richard Wagner: Sein Leben, sein Werk, sein Jahrhundert* (Munich 1980), 182; trans. J. Maxwell Brownjohn as *Richard Wagner: His Life, His Work, His Century* (London 1983), 120.

40. Cosima Wagner, *Die Tagebücher* (note 1), i.177 (9 Dec. 1869): 'With such a

person, with that terrifying talent, there was only one possible compensation, sensuousness, without which she would never have been able to bear it'.

41. Wagner, *Gesammelte Schriften* (note 3), iv.276–9; Engl. trans. (*Richard Wagner's Prose Works*), i.320–3 (*A Communication to My Friends*).

42. Cosima Wagner, *Die Tagebücher* (note 1), ii.1111 (11 Feb. 1883).

43. Wagner, *Gesammelte Schriften* (note 3), iv.254; Engl. trans. (*Richard Wagner's Prose Works*), i.294 (*A Communication to My Friends*).

44. Julius Kapp and Hans Jachmann, *Richard Wagner und seine erste 'Elisabeth' Johanna Jachmann-Wagner* (Berlin 1927), 44.

45. Wagner, *Sämtliche Briefe* (note 2), iii.309 (letter to Franziska Wagner of 4 June 1850).

46. Ibid., v.76 (letter to Franziska Wagner of 13 Oct. 1852).

47. Gunhild Oberzaucher-Schüller, Marion Linhardt and Thomas Steinert, *Meyerbeer–Wagner* (Vienna 1998), 223.

48. Heinrich Eduard Jacob, *Felix Mendelssohn and His Times*, trans. Richard and Clara Winston (London 1963), 204; the source of this quotation (wrongly given by Jacob) is Hans von Wolzogen, *Erinnerungen an Richard Wagner* (Leipzig n.d.), 31.

49. Cosima Wagner, *Die Tagebücher* (note 1), i.176 (7 Dec. 1869).

50. Wagner, *Sämtliche Briefe* (note 2), ii.179 (letter to Felix Mendelssohn of 17 Nov. 1842).

51. Wagner, *Sämtliche Schriften* (note 18), xii.147 ('The Oratorio *Saint Paul*').

52. Eric Werner, *Felix Mendelssohn Bartholdy: Leben und Werk in neuer Sicht* (Zurich 1980), 370.

53. Cosima Wagner, *Die Tagebücher* (note 1), ii.293 (18 and 19 Jan. 1879).

54. Richard Wagner, *Briefe: Die Sammlung Burrell*, ed. John N. Burk (Frankfurt am Main 1953), 651; trans. Hans

Abraham and others as *Letters of Richard Wagner: The Burrell Collection* (London 1951), 505 (Natalie Bilz-Planer's undated notes on Ferdinand Praeger's *Wagner, wie ich ihn kannte*). Wagner's attitude may be attributable to Mendelssohn's tendency to take tempi substantially faster. Wagner called it 'disfiguring haste'.

55. Wagner, *Sämtliche Briefe* (note 2), ii.355 (letter to Felix Mendelssohn of 10 Jan. 1844).

56. Cosima Wagner, *Die Tagebücher* (note 1), ii.692 (15 Feb. 1881).

57. Ibid., i.1091 (2 Dec. 1877).

58. Ibid., i.123 (6 July 1869).

59. Ibid., ii.696 (19 Feb. 1881).

60. Wagner, *Gesammelte Schriften* (note 3), v.201; Engl. trans. (*Richard Wagner's Prose Works*), iii.141 ('Reminiscences of Spontini').

61. Eric Werner, *Mendelssohn: A New Image of the Composer and His Age*, trans. Dika Newlin (London 1963), 433.

62. Wagner, *Gesammelte Schriften* (note 3), iii.230; Engl. trans. (*Richard Wagner's Prose Works*), ii.16 (*Opera and Drama*).

63. Cosima Wagner, *Die Tagebücher* (note 1), ii.692 (15 Feb. 1881).

64. Wagner, *Mein Leben* (note 8), i.348; Engl. trans. (*My Life*), 302.

65. Wagner, *Sämtliche Briefe* (note 2), ii.446 (letter to Albert Wagner of 4 Aug. 1845).

66. Wagner, *Gesammelte Schriften* (note 3), v.179–81; Engl. trans. (*Richard Wagner's Prose Works*), iii.231–3 ('Prelude to *Lohengrin*').

67. Wagner, *Gesammelte Schriften* (note 3), iv.289–90; Engl. trans. (*Richard Wagner's Prose Works*), i.333–5 (*A Communication to My Friends*).

68. Cosima Wagner, *Die Tagebücher* (note 1), i.343 (19 Jan. 1871).

69. Richard Wagner, *Lohengrin*, ed. Michael von Soden (Frankfurt am Main 1980), 137 (prose draft).

70. Wagner, *Sämtliche Briefe* (note 2), v.458 (letter to Ferdinand Heine of 31 Oct. 1853).

71. Cosima Wagner, *Die Tagebücher* (note 1), ii.685 (8 Feb. 1881) and ii.794 (12 Sept. 1881).

72. Wagner, *Lohengrin* (note 69), 162 (instructions for staging *Lohengrin* included with a letter to Franz Liszt of 2 July 1850).

73. Cosima Wagner, *Die Tagebücher* (note 1), ii.163 (18 Aug. 1878), ii.184 (27 Sept. 1878) and ii.872 (14 Jan. 1882).

74. Wagner, *Gesammelte Schriften* (note 3), iv.301; Engl. trans. (*Richard Wagner's Prose Works*), i.346–7 (*A Communication to My Friends*).

75. Wagner, *Lohengrin* (note 69), 156 (prose draft).

76. Cosima Wagner, *Die Tagebücher* (note 1), ii.782 (17 Aug. 1881).

77. *Handwörterbuch des deutschen Aberglaubens*, ed. Hanns Bächtold-Stäubli, 10 vols. (Berlin R1987), i.318: 'The mandrake comes from the urine or sperm of a hanged thief.' In Friedrich de la Motte Fouqué's *Geschichte vom Galgenmännlein*, the mandrake is described as a 'little black devil' that is 'locked in a glass vessel'. 'Anyone who owns one of these may receive from it all the pleasures that he may demand of life, but especially an immeasurable amount of money. At the same time the mandrake claims the soul of its owner for its master Lucifer.'

78. Wagner, *Sämtliche Briefe* (note 2), ii.513–14 (letter to Hermann Franck of 30 May 1846).

79. Ibid., ii.512 (letter to Hermann Franck of 30 May 1846).

80. Ibid., iv.273–4 (letter to Franz Liszt of 30 Jan. 1852).

81. Cosima Wagner, *Die Tagebücher* (note 1), ii.619 (11 Nov. 1880).

82. Wagner, *Lohengrin* (note 69), 170.

83. Wagner, *Gesammelte Schriften* (note 3), iv.302; Engl. trans. (*Richard*

Wagner's Prose Works), i.347 (*A Communication to My Friends*).

84. Wagner, *Sämtliche Schriften* (note 18), xii.246–7; Engl. trans. (*Richard Wagner's Prose Works*) (note 3), viii.233–4 ('Revolution').

85. Eduard Devrient, *Aus seinen Tagebüchern*, ed. Rolf Kabel, 2 vols. (Weimar 1964), i.422 (14 March 1848).

86. Gregor-Dellin, *Richard Wagner* (note 39), 239; Eng. trans. (*Richard Wagner*), 150.

87. Devrient, *Aus seinen Tagebüchern* (note 85), i.441 (14 July 1848) and i.451 (21 Oct. 1848).

88. Wagner, *Sämtliche Schriften* (note 18), xii.224; Engl. trans. (*Richard Wagner's Prose Works*), iv.140 ('How Do Republican Aspirations Stand in Relation to the Monarchy?').

89. 'Wagner, der 48er-Revolutionär', *Richard Wagner: Wie antisemitisch darf ein Künstler sein?*, ed. Heinz-Klaus Metzger and Rainer Riehn (Munich 1981), 77; this letter to Friedrich August II of 21 June 1848 is not included in the *Sämtliche Briefe*.

90. Wagner, *Sämtliche Schriften* (note 18), xii.418.

91. Ibid., xii.245–50; Engl. trans. (*Richard Wagner's Prose Works*), viii.232–7 ('Revolution').

92. Joachim Köhler, *Wagners Hitler: Der Prophet und sein Vollstrecker* (Munich 1997), 52; trans. Ronald Taylor as *Wagner's Hitler: The Prophet and His Disciple* (Cambridge 2000), 38–9.

93. Wagner, *Gesammelte Schriften* (note 3), ii.63; Engl. trans. (*Richard Wagner's Prose Works*), vii.254 ('Beethoven's Ninth Symphony').

94. Karl-Heinz Kröplin, *Richard Wagner 1813–1883: Eine Chronik* (Leipzig 1987), 57.

95. Wagner, *Sämtliche Briefe* (note 2), ii.578 (letter to Ernst Kossak of 23 Nov. 1847).

96. Eduard Hanslick, *Aus meinem Leben*, 2 vols. (Berlin 1894), i.134–5.

97. Wagner, *Mein Leben* (note 8), i.441; Engl. trans. (*My Life*), 384.

98. Gregor-Dellin, *Richard Wagner* (note 39), 208; Engl. trans. (*Richard Wagner*), 134–5.

99. Köhler, *Wagners Hitler* (note 92), 62; Engl. trans. (*Wagner's Hitler*), 45.

100. Woldemar Lippert, *Richard Wagners Verbannung und Rückkehr 1849–1862* (Dresden 1927), facsimile facing p. 22; this facsimile was not included in Paul England's English translation *Wagner in Exile 1849–62* (London 1930). An objective account of this period became possible only with Lippert's publication of most of, if not all, the relevant documents.

101. Devrient, *Aus seinen Tagebüchern* (note 85), i.489 (19 May 1849).

102. *Das alte Dresden: Bilder und Dokumente aus zwei Jahrhunderten*, ed Erich Haenel and Eugen Kalkschmidt (Bindlach R1995), 387.

103. William Ashton Ellis, *1849: A Vindication* (London 1892).

104. Ernest Newman, *The Life of Richard Wagner*, 4 vols. (New York 1933–46), ii.80: 'In view of the close association of herself and her father with Wagner during the Zürich period it is not improbable that the information came from Wagner himself.'

105. Bernd Kramer, *'Laßt uns die Schwerter ziehen, damit die Kette bricht ... ': Michael Bakunin, Richard Wagner und andere während der Dresdner Mai-Revolution 1849* (Berlin 1999), 107. Kramer is useful in supplementing Lippert with a number of important details about Wagner's involvement in the uprising.

106. Richard Wagner, *Das Braune Buch: Tagebuchaufzeichnungen 1865 bis 1882*, ed. Joachim Bergfeld (Zurich 1975), 114; trans. George Bird as *The Diary of Richard Wagner: The Brown Book 1865–1882* (London 1980), 96 (Annals for 1849).

107. Wagner, *Sämtliche Schriften* (note 18),

xii.481 ('Fragments of an "Achilles" Drama', 1849).

108. Kramer, 'Laßt uns die Schwerter ziehen' (note 105), 59.

109. Ibid., 64.

110. Das alte Dresden (note 102), 387.

111. Newman, The Life of Richard Wagner (note 104), ii.93.

112. Kramer, 'Laßt uns die Schwerter ziehen' (note 105), 73.

113. Wagner, Das Braune Buch (note 106), 115; Engl. trans. (The Diary of Richard Wagner), 97 (Annals for 1849).

114. Gustav Adolph Kietz, Richard Wagner in den Jahren 1842–1849 und 1873–1875 (Dresden 1907), 49.

115. Lippert, Richard Wagners Verbannung (note 100), 210; Engl. trans. (Wagner in Exile), 188.

116. Wagner, Sämtliche Schriften (note 18), xii.363.

117. Kramer, 'Laßt uns die Schwerter ziehen' (note 105), 54.

118. Das alte Dresden (note 102), 363.

119. König Ludwig II. und Richard Wagner: Briefwechsel, ed. Otto Strobel, 5 vols. (Karlsruhe 1936–9), iv.177 (letter from Wagner to August Röckel of 29 Jan. 1867).

120. Lippert, Richard Wagners Verbannung (note 100), 239; Engl. trans. (Wagner in Exile), 202.

121. Wagner, Sämtliche Briefe (note 2), ii.664 (letter to Eduard Devrient of 17 May 1849).

122. Wagner, Sämtliche Briefe (note 2), ii.654 (letter to Minna Wagner of 14 May 1849).

Chapter 4

1. Richard Wagner, Sämtliche Briefe, ed. Gertrud Strobel, Werner Wolf, Werner Breig and others (Leipzig 1967–2000 and Wiesbaden 1999–), ii.668 (letter to Eduard Devrient of 17 May 1849).

2. Wagner, Sämtliche Briefe (note 1), iii.147 (letter to Ferdinand Heine of 19 Nov. 1849).

3. Martin Gregor-Dellin, Richard Wagner: Sein Leben, sein Werk, sein Jahrhundert (Munich 1980), 283; trans. J. Maxwell Brownjohn as Richard Wagner: His Life, His Work, His Century (London 1983), 186.

4. Richard Wagner, Mein Leben, ed. Eike Middell, 2 vols. (Leipzig 1986), i.483; trans. Andrew Gray as My Life (Cambridge 1983), 422.

5. Werner Otto, Richard Wagner: Ein Lebens- und Charakterbild in Dokumenten und zeitgenössischen Darstellungen (Berlin 1990), 125.

6. Wagner, Sämtliche Briefe (note 1), iii.274 (letter to Theodor Uhlig of 15 April 1850).

7. Richard Wagner, Briefe: Die Sammlung Burrell, ed. John N. Burk (Frankfurt am Main 1953), 545; trans. Hans Abraham and others as Letters of Richard Wagner: The Burrell Collection (London 1951), 412–13 (letter from Wagner to Minna Wagner of 4 July 1863).

8. Wagner, Sämtliche Briefe (note 1), iii.274 (letter to Theodor Uhlig of 15 April 1850).

9. Ibid., iii.218 (letter to Franz Liszt of 6 Feb. 1850).

10. Ibid., iii.273 (letter to Theodor Uhlig of 15 April 1850).

11. Wagner, Briefe: Die Sammlung Burrell (note 7), 416; Engl. trans. (Letters of Richard Wagner), 310 (undated description of Wagner's appearance in Zurich dictated to Lermonda Burrell by Natalie Bilz-Planer).

12. Wagner, Sämtliche Briefe (note 1), iii.262 (letter to Emilie Ritter of 26 March 1850).

13. Ibid., iii.337 (letter to Minna Wagner of late June 1850).

14. Ibid.

15. Ibid., iii.321 (letter to Julie Ritter of 26–7 June 1850).

16. Ibid., iii.271 (letter to Mikhail Bakunin and August Röckel of March 1850).

17. Wagner, *Mein Leben* (note 4), i.501; Engl. trans. (*My Life*), 439.

18. Wagner, *Briefe: Die Sammlung Burrell* (note 7), 393; Engl. trans. (*Letters of Richard Wagner*), 292–3 (letter from Ann Taylor to Minna Wagner of 8 May 1850).

19. Wagner, *Sämtliche Briefe* (note 1), iii.348 (letter to Ernst Benedikt Kietz of 7 July 1850).

20. Ibid., iii.319 (letter to Julie Ritter of 26–7 June 1850).

21. Ibid., iii.257 (letter to Minna Wagner of 17 March 1850).

22. Ibid., iii.348 (letter to Ernst Benedikt Kietz of 7 July 1850).

23. Ibid., iii.275 (letter to Theodor Uhlig of 15 April 1850).

24. Ibid., iii.321 (letter to Julie Ritter of 26–7 June 1850).

25. Ibid., iii.330 (letter to Julie Ritter of 26–7 June 1850).

26. Richard Wagner, *Sämtliche Schriften und Dichtungen*, ed. Richard Sternfeld, 16 vols. (Leipzig 1911–14), xi.232.

27. Richard Wagner, *Gesammelte Schriften und Dichtungen*, 10 vols. (Leipzig 4/1907), iv.271; trans. William Ashton Ellis as *Richard Wagner's Prose Works*, 8 vols. (London 1892–9, R1993–5), i.314 (*A Communication to My Friends*).

28. Wagner, *Sämtliche Schriften* (note 26), xii.225; Engl. trans. (*Richard Wagner's Prose Works*) (note 27), iv.141 ('How Do Republican Aspirations Stand in Relation to the Monarchy?')

29. Wagner, *Sämtliche Schriften* (note 26), xi.271 ('Friedrich I.'). This parallel had already occurred to Ernest Newman, *The Life of Richard Wagner*, 4 vols. (New York 1933–46), ii.23.

30. Carl Wilhelm Göttling, *Nibelungen und Gibelinen* (Rudolstadt 1816), 29: '"Nibelungs" is undoubtedly the older form of "Waiblings" or "Ghibellines".' Wagner was familiar with the writings of the Jena scholar. The dating of *The Wibelungs* is problematical, but the present writer is persuaded to accept the date of 1848 by the detailed analysis of the work by Petra-Hildegard Wilberg, *Richard Wagners mythische Welt: Versuch wider den Historismus* (Freiburg 1996).

31. Gregor-Dellin, *Richard Wagner* (note 3), 246; Engl. trans. (*Richard Wagner*), 155; see also Peter Wapnewski, *Der traurige Gott: Richard Wagner in seinen Helden* (Munich 1978), 118.

32. Wagner, *Gesammelte Schriften* (note 27), iv.314; Engl. trans. (*Richard Wagner's Prose Works*), i.360 (*A Communication to My Friends*).

33. Wagner, *Gesammelte Schriften* (note 27), ii.115; Engl. trans. (*Richard Wagner's Prose Works*), vii.259 (*The Wibelungs*).

34. Eduard Devrient, *Aus seinen Tagebüchern*, ed. Rolf Kabel, 2 vols. (Weimar 1964), i.470 (22 Feb. 1849).

35. Wagner, *Gesammelte Schriften* (note 27), ii.144; Engl. trans. (*Richard Wagner's Prose Works*), vii.287 (*The Wibelungs*).

36. This too is something that Wagner could have learnt from Göttling, who in 1816 had written that 'the Holy Grail is the transfigured Nibelung hoard'; see Göttling, *Nibelungen und Gibelinen* (note 30), 8.

37. Wagner, *Sämtliche Schriften* (note 26), xii.229.

38. Friedrich Nietzsche, *Sämtliche Werke: Kritische Studienausgabe*, ed. Giorgio Colli and Mazzino Montinari, 15 vols. (Munich 1980), i.485 ('Richard Wagner in Bayreuth'), v.185 (*Beyond Good and Evil*) and vi.36 (*The Case of Wagner*); trans. R. J. Hollingdale as *Untimely Meditations* (Cambridge 1983), 236 ('Richard Wagner in Bayreuth') and trans. Walter Kaufmann in *Basic Writings of Nietzsche* (New York 1968), 369 (*Beyond Good and Evil*) and 634 (*The Case of Wagner*).

39. Cosima Wagner, *Die Tagebücher*, ed.

Martin Gregor-Dellin and Dietrich Mack, 2 vols. (Munich 1976–7), i.216 (3 April 1870).

40. Wagner, *Mein Leben* (note 4), i.66; Engl. trans. (*My Life*), 54.

41. Wagner, *Sämtliche Briefe* (note 1), iii.266 (letter to Theodor Uhlig of 26 March 1850).

42. Wagner, *Sämtliche Briefe* (note 1), x.243 (letter to Mathilde Wesendonck of 19 Jan. 1859).

43. Ibid., iv.187 (letter to Franz Liszt of 20 Nov. 1851).

44. Wagner, *Gesammelte Schriften* (note 27), vii.88; Engl. trans. (*Richard Wagner's Prose Works*), iii.296 ('*Zukunftsmusik*').

45. Cosima Wagner, *Die Tagebücher* (note 39), i.111 (17 June 1869).

46. Egon Voss, *Richard Wagner: Dokumentarbiographie* (Mainz 1982), 307; trans. P. R. J. Ford and Mary Whittall as *Wagner: A Documentary Study* (London 1975), 167.

47. Wagner, *Sämtliche Briefe* (note 1), vi.298 (letter to Franz Liszt of 16 [?] Dec. 1854) and vi.347 (letter to August Röckel of 5 Feb. 1855).

48. Wagner, *Gesammelte Schriften* (note 27), iii.3; Engl. trans. (*Richard Wagner's Prose Works*), i.25 ('Introduction to *Art and Revolution*').

49. Wagner, *Sämtliche Schriften* (note 26), xi.299; Engl. trans. (*Richard Wagner's Prose Works*), viii.313 (*Jesus of Nazareth*).

50. *Unterhaltungen mit Bakunin*, ed. Arthur Lehning (Nördlingen 1987), 170 (letter from Georg Herwegh to Ludwig Feuerbach of 3 Dec. 1851).

51. Wagner, *Gesammelte Schriften* (note 27), iii.144; Engl. trans. (*Richard Wagner's Prose Works*), i.177 (*The Artwork of the Future*).

52. Wagner, *Sämtliche Briefe* (note 1), iii.104 (letter to Otto Wigand of 4 Aug. 1849).

53. Wagner, *Mein Leben* (note 4), i.394; Engl. trans. (*My Life*), 342.

54. Wagner, *Gesammelte Schriften* (note 27), iii.35; Engl. trans. (*Richard Wagner's Prose Works*), i.58 (*Art and Revolution*).

55. Wagner, *Mein Leben* (note 4), i.27; Engl. trans. (*My Life*), 20.

56. *Fünfzehn Briefe Richard Wagners mit Erinnerungen und Erläuterungen von Eliza Wille geb. Sloman* (Munich and Berlin 1935), 34. Like Carolyne von Sayn-Wittgenstein, Eliza Wille later recognized Wagner's Mary Magdalene in Kundry in *Parsifal*.

57. Wagner, *Sämtliche Schriften* (note 26), xi.299; Engl. trans. (*Richard Wagner's Prose Works*), viii.313 (*Jesus of Nazareth*).

58. Wagner, *Gesammelte Schriften* (note 27), iv.332; Engl. trans. (*Richard Wagner's Prose Works*), i.380 (*A Communication to My Friends*).

59. Gregor-Dellin, *Richard Wagner* (note 3), 313; Engl. trans. (*Richard Wagner*), 209.

60. Jürgen Kühnel, 'Wagners Schriften', *Richard-Wagner-Handbuch*, ed. Ulrich Müller and Peter Wapnewski (Stuttgart 1986), 471–588, esp. 521; trans. Simon Nye as 'The Prose Writings', *Wagner Handbook*, ed. John Deathridge (Cambridge, Mass., 1992), 565–651, esp. 597.

61. Dieter Borchmeyer, 'Richard Wagner und der Antisemitismus', *Richard-Wagner-Handbuch* (note 60), 137–61, esp. 147; trans. Stewart Spencer as 'The Question of Anti-Semitism', *Wagner Handbook*, 166–85, esp. 174.

62. Wagner, *Gesammelte Schriften* (note 27), iii.67–8; Engl. trans. (*Richard Wagner's Prose Works*), i.96 (*The Artwork of the Future*).

63. Wagner, *Gesammelte Schriften* (note 27), iii.48; Engl. trans. (*Richard Wagner's Prose Works*), i.75 (*The Artwork of the Future*).

64. Wagner, *Gesammelte Schriften* (note 27), iii.50; Engl. trans. (*Richard Wagner's Prose Works*), i.77 (*The Art-*

work of the Future).

65. Wagner, *Gesammelte Schriften* (note 27), iii.54; Engl. trans. (*Richard Wagner's Prose Works*), i.81 (*The Artwork of the Future*).

66. Only the young Adolf Hitler could work up any enthusiasm for the idea of setting Wagner's discarded heroic opera, but as his friend August Kubizek reports, the future Führer's plans foundered on his total lack of any knowledge of music.

67. Wagner, *Sämtliche Briefe* (note 1), v.233 (letter to Franz Liszt of 30 March 1853).

68. Cosima Wagner, *Die Tagebücher* (note 39), ii.424 (11 Oct. 1879).

69. Wagner, *Mein Leben* (note 4), ii.23; Engl. trans. (*My Life*), 467.

70. Wagner, *Gesammelte Schriften* (note 27), viii.242; Engl. trans. (*Richard Wagner's Prose Works*), iii.103 ('Some Explanations Concerning "Jews in Music"').

71. Wagner, *Sämtliche Briefe* (note 1), vi.194 (letter to Hans von Bülow of 29 July 1854).

72. Cosima Wagner, *Die Tagebücher* (note 39), i.722 (4 Sept. 1873).

73. Wagner, *Sämtliche Briefe* (note 1), iii.544 (letter to Franz Liszt of 18 April 1851).

74. Robert Schumann, *Schriften über Musik und Musiker*, ed. Josef Häusler (Stuttgart 1982), 132; trans. Henry Pleasants as *The Musical World of Robert Schumann* (London 1965), 139–40 ('The Huguenots').

75. *Die Hegelsche Linke*, ed. Heinz and Ingrid Pepperle (Leipzig 1985), 324.

76. Wagner, *Gesammelte Schriften* (note 27), v.69; Engl. trans. (*Richard Wagner's Prose Works*), iii.82 ('Jews in Music'). The 1850 version of the essay is reproduced by Tibor Kneif in *Die Kunst und die Revolution* (Munich 1975), esp. 53.

77. Borchmeyer, 'Richard Wagner und der Antisemitismus' (note 61), 147;

78. Wagner, *Gesammelte Schriften* (note 27), iv.54; Engl. trans. (*Richard Wagner's Prose Works*), ii.180 (*Opera and Drama*).

79. Johann Christian Lobe, 'Das Judenthum in der Musik', *Consonanzen und Dissonanzen* (Leipzig 1869), 17.

80. Richard Wagner, *Oper und Drama*, ed. Klaus Kropfinger (Stuttgart 1984), 449.

81. Wagner, *Sämtliche Briefe* (note 1), iii.522 (letter to Theodor Uhlig of 10 March 1851).

82. Rainer Franke, *Richard Wagners Zürcher Kunstschriften* (Hamburg 1983), 69.

83. Wagner, *Gesammelte Schriften* (note 27), iii.306; Engl. trans. (*Richard Wagner's Prose Works*), ii.101 (*Opera and Drama*).

84. Martin Gregor-Dellin and Michael von Soden, *Hermes Handlexikon: Richard Wagner* (Düsseldorf 1983), 152; a similar line is taken by Dieter Borchmeyer in his afterword to Richard Wagner, *Dichtungen und Schriften*, 10 vols. (Frankfurt am Main 1983), x.311.

85. Cosima Wagner, *Die Tagebücher* (note 39), ii.160 (15 Aug. 1878).

86. Wagner, *Sämtliche Briefe* (note 1), iii.467 (letter to Franz Liszt of 25 Nov. 1850).

87. Ibid., iii.477 (letter to Theodor Uhlig of 12 Dec. 1850).

88. Wagner, *Gesammelte Schriften* (note 27), iv.65; Engl. trans. (*Richard Wagner's Prose Works*), ii.192 (*Opera and Drama*).

89. Wagner, *Gesammelte Schriften* (note 27), iv.200; Engl. trans. (*Richard Wagner's Prose Works*), ii.346 (*Opera and Drama*).

90. Wagner, *Gesammelte Schriften* (note 27), iv.147; Engl. trans. (*Richard Wagner's Prose Works*), ii.286 (*Opera and Drama*).

91. Friedrich Wilhelm Joseph Schelling,

Engl. trans. ('The Question of Anti-Semitism'), 174.

Über das Wesen der menschlichen Freiheit (Stuttgart 1964), 72; trans. Priscilla Hayden-Roy as 'Philosophical Investigations into the Essence of Human Freedom and Related Matters', *Philosophy of German Idealism*, ed. Ernst Behler (New York 1987), 231. (Schelling's text was first published in 1809.)

92. Manfred Frank, 'Weltgeschichte aus der Sage', *Bayreuther Festspiele 1994* (Bayreuth 1994), 36. Frank acknowledges Schelling's influence on Wagner but believes that it was limited to his *Philosophy of Mythology*.

93. Carl Friedrich Glasenapp, *Das Leben Richard Wagners*, 6 vols. (Leipzig 1905–11), vi.230.

94. Schelling, *Über das Wesen der menschlichen Freiheit* (note 91), 133; Engl. trans. ('Philosophical Investigations'), 280.

95. Friedrich Wilhelm Joseph Schelling, *Schriften von 1813–1830* (Darmstadt 1976), 213.

96. Schelling, *Schriften von 1813–1830* (note 95), 183.

97. Wagner, *Sämtliche Briefe* (note 1), iv.335 (letter to Julie Ritter of 4 April 1852).

98. *Richard Wagner in Zürich: Materialien zu Aufenthalt und Wirken*, ed. Werner G. Zimmermann (Zurich 1986), 15.

99. Wagner, *Sämtliche Briefe* (note 1), v.495 (letter to Franz Liszt of 15 Jan. 1854).

100. Ibid., v.95 (letter to Franz Liszt of 9 Nov. 1852).

101. Ibid., v.186 (letter to Franz Liszt of 11 Feb. 1853).

102. Ibid., v.498 (letter to Franz Liszt of 15 Jan. 1854).

103. Ibid., iv.192 (letter to Franz Liszt of 20 Nov. 1851).

104. Ibid., iii.276 (letter to Minna Wagner of 16 April 1850).

105. Wagner, *Mein Leben* (note 4), ii.22; Engl. trans. (*My Life*), 465.

106. Wagner, *Sämtliche Briefe* (note 1),

vii.329 (letter to Julie Ritter of 29 Dec. 1855).

107. Wagner, *Mein Leben* (note 4), ii.99; Engl. trans. (*My Life*), 533.

108. Wagner, *Sämtliche Briefe* (note 1), iv.455 (letter to Ernst Benedikt Kietz of 7 Sept. 1852).

109. Richard Wagner, *Das Braune Buch: Tagebuchaufzeichnungen 1865 bis 1882*, ed. Joachim Bergfeld (Zurich 1975), 122; trans. George Bird as *The Diary of Richard Wagner: The Brown Book 1865–1882* (London 1980), 103 (Annals for 1853).

110. Wagner, *Sämtliche Briefe* (note 1), x.127 (letter to Anton Pusinelli of 1 Nov. 1858). Wagner wrote to Lindemann himself on 9 April 1854 to report that things had 'sorted themselves out quite nicely' with Minna following her opium therapy. She was 'able to sleep again, with the result that her nerves are calmer and she feels stronger'; see ibid., vi.106.

111. Ibid., vi.73 (letter to August Röckel of 25–6 Jan. 1854).

112. Wagner, *Sämtliche Briefe* (note 1), xi.314–15 (letter to Mathilde Wesendonck of 23 Oct. 1859).

113. Ibid., iv.482 (letter to Franz Brendel of 4 Feb. 1852).

114. Wagner, *Mein Leben* (note 4), ii.67; Engl. trans. (*My Life*), 505.

115. Paula Rehberg, *Franz Liszt: Die Geschichte seines Schaffens und Wirkens* (Zurich 1961), 271.

116. *Franz Liszt in seinen Briefen*, ed. Hans Rudolf Jung (Berlin 1987), 173 (letter to Hans von Bülow of 21 Oct. 1859).

117. August Wilhelm Ambros, *Bunte Blätter* (Leipzig 1872), 60, quoted from Franz Liszt, *Sämtliche Schriften*, iv (*Lohengrin und Tannhäuser*), ed. Rainer Kleinertz (Wiesbaden 1989), 275.

118. *Franz Liszt–Richard Wagner: Briefwechsel*, ed. Hanjo Kesting (Frankfurt am Main 1988), 29.

119. Wagner, *Gesammelte Schriften* (note 27), iv.340; Engl. trans. (*Richard*

Wagner's Prose Works), i.388 (*A Communication to My Friends*).

120. Wagner, *Sämtliche Briefe* (note 1), v.497 (letter to Franz Liszt of 15 Jan. 1854).

121. Ibid., iii.543 (letter to Franz Liszt of 18 April 1851).

122. Wagner, *Das Braune Buch* (note 109), 84; Engl. trans. (*The Diary of Richard Wagner*), 72.

123. Cosima Wagner, *Die Tagebücher* (note 39), ii.883 (2 Feb. 1882).

124. Ibid., i.509 (11 April 1872).

125. Wagner, *Gesammelte Schriften* (note 27), v.191; Engl. trans. (*Richard Wagner's Prose Works*), iii.247 ('Franz Liszt's Symphonic Poems').

126. Glasenapp, *Das Leben Richard Wagners* (note 93), vi.134.

127. Wagner, *Sämtliche Briefe* (note 1), viii.120 (letter to Franz Liszt of 20 July 1856).

128. Ibid., xi.178–9 (letter to Marie Wittgenstein of 8 August 1859).

129. Ibid., vi.123 (letter to Franz Liszt of 2 May 1854).

130. Ibid., ix.178 (letter to Marie Wittgenstein of 8 Feb. 1858).

Chapter 5

1. Richard Wagner, *Sämtliche Briefe*, ed. Gertrud Strobel, Werner Wolf, Werner Breig and others (Leipzig 1967–2000 and Wiesbaden 1999–), v.495 (letter to Franz Liszt of 15 Jan. 1854).

2. Ibid., v.97 (letter to Franz Liszt of 9 Nov. 1852).

3. Ibid., iv.175 (letter to Theodor Uhlig of 12 Nov. 1851).

4. Ibid., v.189 (letter to Franz Liszt of 11 Feb. 1853).

5. Ibid., v.118 (letter to Theodor Uhlig of 18 Nov. 1852).

6. Wagner, *Sämtliche Briefe* (note 1), iv.175 (letter to Theodor Uhlig of 12 Nov. 1851).

7. Wagner, *Sämtliche Briefe* (note 1), iv.385 (letter to Theodor Uhlig of 31

May 1852).

8. *König Ludwig II. und Richard Wagner: Briefwechsel*, ed. Otto Strobel, 5 vols. (Karlsruhe 1936–9), iii.208 (letter from Wagner to Ludwig II of 17 May 1881).

9. Cosima Wagner, *Die Tagebücher*, ed. Martin Gregor-Dellin and Dietrich Mack, 2 vols. (Munich 1976–7), ii.692 (15 Feb. 1881).

10. Udo Bermbach, 'Die Destruktion der Institutionen: Zum politischen Gehalt des "Ring"', *In den Trümmern der eignen Welt: Richard Wagners 'Der Ring des Nibelungen'*, ed. Udo Bermbach (Berlin and Hamburg 1989), 136.

11. Cosima Wagner, *Die Tagebücher* (note 9), i.129 (17 July 1869).

12. Richard Wagner, *Gesammelte Schriften und Dichtungen*, 10 vols. (Leipzig 4/1907), vii.129; trans. William Ashton Ellis as *Richard Wagner's Prose Works*, 8 vols. (London 1892–9, R1993–5), iii.337 ('Zukunftsmusik').

13. Wagner, *Gesammelte Schriften* (note 12), ix.300; Engl. trans. (*Richard Wagner's Prose Works*), v.297 ('To Friedrich Nietzsche').

14. Cosima Wagner, *Die Tagebücher* (note 9), ii.1113 (12 Feb. 1883).

15. Richard Wagner, *Skizzen und Entwürfe zur Ring-Dichtung*, ed. Otto Strobel (Munich 1930), 203.

16. Ibid., 239.

17. Ibid., 44.

18. Carl Friedrich Glasenapp, *Das Leben Richard Wagners*, 6 vols. (Leipzig 1905–11), vi.71.

19. Cosima Wagner, *Die Tagebücher* (note 9), i.493 (23 Feb. 1872).

20. Wagner, *Sämtliche Briefe* (note 1), vi.249 (letter to Franz Liszt of 7 [?] Oct. 1854).

21. Peter Wapnewski, *Weißt du wie das wird? Richard Wagner: Der Ring des Nibelungen* (Munich 1995), 227.

22. *Nietzsche und Wagner: Stationen einer epochalen Begegnung*, ed. Dieter

Borchmeyer and Jörg Salaquarda (Frankfurt 1994), 296.

23. Wagner, *Sämtliche Briefe* (note 1), vi.68 (letter to August Röckel of 25–6 Jan. 1854).

24. Curt von Westernhagen, *Die Entstehung des 'Ring'* (Zurich 1973), 59; trans. Arnold and Mary Whittall as *The Forging of the 'Ring': Richard Wagner's Composition Sketches for 'Der Ring des Nibelungen'* (Cambridge 1976), 42.

25. Wagner, *Sämtliche Briefe* (note 1), vi.42 (letter to Hans von Bülow of 16 Jan. 1854).

26. Richard Wagner, *Sämtliche Schriften und Dichtungen*, ed. Richard Sternfeld, 16 vols. (Leipzig 1911–14), xii.223; Engl. trans. (*Richard Wagner's Prose Works*) (note 12), iv.139 ('How Do Republican Aspirations Stand in Relation to the Monarchy?').

27. Max Koch, 'Männerlist größer als Frauenlist', *Richard Wagner-Jahrbuch*, ed. Ludwig Frankenstein, iv (Berlin 1912), 134. In a birthday play dating from 1818, Geyer placed the following words in the mouth of his stepson Julius: 'If ever I appear as a goldsmith, I'll help to place my parents on a sound footing.'

28. Wagner, *Gesammelte Schriften* (note 12), x.113; Engl. trans. (*Richard Wagner's Prose Works*), vi.106 ('A Retrospective Glance at the 1876 Festival').

29. Wagner, *Gesammelte Schriften* (note 12), viii.258; Engl. trans. (*Richard Wagner's Prose Works*), iii.120 ('Some Explanations Concerning "Jews in Music"').

30. Wagner, *Sämtliche Briefe* (note 1), v.118 (letter to Theodor Uhlig of 18 Nov. 1852).

31. Ibid., v.463 (letter to Franz Liszt of 14 [?] Nov. 1853).

32. Cosima Wagner, *Die Tagebücher* (note 9), i.940 (6 Oct. 1875).

33. Wagner, *Sämtliche Briefe* (note 1),

34. Wagner, *Gesammelte Schriften* (note 12), vi.266; Engl. trans. (*Richard Wagner's Prose Works*), iii.266 ('Epilogue to the "Nibelung's Ring"').

35. Wagner, *Sämtliche Briefe* (note 1), iv.187 (letter to Franz Liszt of 20 Nov. 1851).

36. Wagner, *Skizzen und Entwürfe zur Ring-Dichtung* (note 15), 201–2.

37. *Isländische Heldenromane*, ed. Felix Niedner (= Thule-Sammlung, xxi) (Jena 1923), 42.

38. Robert von Hornstein, *Memoiren* (Munich 1908), 108–9.

39. Wagner, *Skizzen und Entwürfe zur Ring-Dichtung* (note 15), 212.

40. Cosima Wagner, *Die Tagebücher* (note 9), i.543 (2 July 1872).

41. Wagner, *Sämtliche Briefe* (note 1), vi.286 (letter to Carolyne Sayn-Wittgenstein of Nov. 1854).

42. Ibid., vii.283 (letter to Franz Liszt of 3 Oct. 1855).

43. Ibid., vi.286 (letter to Carolyne Sayn-Wittgenstein of Nov. 1854).

44. Wagner, *Sämtliche Schriften* (note 26), xii.283 ('Achilleus').

45. Wagner, *Skizzen und Entwürfe zur Ring-Dichtung* (note 15), 245.

46. Cosima Wagner, *Die Tagebücher* (note 9), ii.295 (23 Jan. 1879).

47. Wagner, *Sämtliche Schriften* (note 26), xvi.172 ('Programme Note to *Die Walküre*').

48. Camille Saint-Saëns, *Harmonie et mélodie* (Paris n.d.), 85.

49. Wagner, *Gesammelte Schriften* (note 12), x.74; Engl. trans. (*Richard Wagner's Prose Works*), vi.66 ('Public and Popularity').

50. Wagner, *Sämtliche Briefe* (note 1), iv.47 (letter to Ferdinand von Ziegesar of 10 May 1851).

51. Ibid.: Siegfried's characteristics 'cannot, of course, be taken from the *Nibelungenlied*'.

52. Ibid., iv.43 (letter to Theodor Uhlig of

10 May 1851) and iv.94 (letter to August Röckel of 24 Aug. 1851).

53. Cosima Wagner, *Die Tagebücher* (note 9), i.87 (19 April 1869).

54. Wagner, *Gesammelte Schriften* (note 12), iv.328; Engl. trans. (*Richard Wagner's Prose Works*), i.375 (*A Communication to My Friends*).

55. Cosima Wagner, *Die Tagebücher* (note 9), ii.1056 (23 Nov. 1882).

56. Wagner, *Skizzen und Entwürfe zur Ring-Dichtung* (note 15), 116.

57. Wagner, *Sämtliche Schriften* (note 26), xii.244; Engl. trans. (*Richard Wagner's Prose Works*), viii.230 ('Man and Existing Society').

58. Glasenapp, *Das Leben Richard Wagners* (note 18), v.189.

59. Wagner, *Sämtliche Briefe* (note 1), iii.60 (letter to Minna Wagner of 29–30 May 1849).

60. Wagner, *Skizzen und Entwürfe zur Ring-Dichtung* (note 15), 99.

61. Glasenapp, *Das Leben Richard Wagners* (note 18), iii.382.

62. Ibid., v.189.

63. Wagner, *Skizzen und Entwürfe zur Ring-Dichtung* (note 15), 73.

64. Ibid., 117.

65. Wagner, *Sämtliche Briefe* (note 1), vi.69 (letter to August Röckel of 25–6 Jan. 1854).

66. Wagner, *Sämtliche Schriften* (note 26), xi.288; Engl. trans. (*Richard Wagner's Prose Works*), viii.300 (*Jesus of Nazareth*).

67. Wagner, *Sämtliche Briefe* (note 1), vi.69 (letter to August Röckel of 25–6 Jan. 1854).

68. *Richard Wagner an Mathilde Maier (1862–1878)*, ed. Hans Scholz (Leipzig 1930), 53 (letter of 15 Jan. 1863).

69. Peter Wapnewski, *Der traurige Gott: Richard Wagner in seinen Helden* (Munich 1978), 186.

70. Wagner, *Sämtliche Briefe* (note 1), viii.348–9 (letter to Hans von Bülow of 15 June 1857).

71. Ibid., viii.354 and 356 (letter to Franz Liszt of 28 June 1857).

72. Cosima Wagner, *Die Tagebücher* (note 9), i.206 (6 March 1870).

73. Richard Wagner, *Sämtliche Werke*, xxix/1 ('Dokumente zur Entstehungsgeschichte des Bühnenfestspiels "Der Ring des Nibelungen"'), ed. Werner Breig and Hartmut Fladt (Mainz 1976), 165.

74. Westernhagen, *Die Entstehung des 'Ring'* (note 24), 187; Engl. trans. (*The Forging of the 'Ring'*), 156.

75. *König Ludwig II. und Richard Wagner: Briefwechsel* (note 8), ii.257 (letter from Wagner to Ludwig of 23–4 Feb. 1869).

76. Ibid.

77. Wagner, *Sämtliche Schriften* (note 26), xvi.85 ('Preface to an Edition of *Siegfried's Tod* Planned for 1850').

78. *König Ludwig II. und Richard Wagner: Briefwechsel* (note 8), ii.258 (letter from Wagner to Ludwig of 23–4 Feb. 1869).

79. Wagner, *Sämtliche Briefe* (note 1), vi.69 (letter to August Röckel of 25–6 Jan. 1854).

80. Cosima Wagner, *Die Tagebücher* (note 9), ii.1026 (17 Oct. 1882).

81. Wagner, *Sämtliche Briefe* (note 1), vi.64 (letter to August Röckel of 25–6 Jan. 1854).

82. Cosima Wagner, *Die Tagebücher* (note 9), i.140 (15 Aug. 1869).

83. Egon Voss, *Studien zur Instrumentation Richard Wagners* (Regensburg 1970), 218.

84. Cosima Wagner, *Die Tagebücher* (note 9), i.317 (26 Nov. 1870).

85. Wagner, *Skizzen und Entwürfe zur Ring-Dichtung* (note 15), 26.

86. Wagner, *Sämtliche Briefe* (note 1), iv.131 (letter to Theodor Uhlig written between 7 and 11 Oct. 1851).

87. Ibid., vi.68 (letter to August Röckel of 25–6 Jan. 1854).

88. Wagner, *Gesammelte Schriften* (note 12), iv.53; Engl. trans. (*Richard Wagner's Prose Works*), ii.178 (*Opera and Drama*).

89. *König Ludwig II. und Richard Wagner: Briefwechsel* (note 8), ii.307 (letter from Wagner to Ludwig of 5 May 1870).

90. Cosima Wagner, *Die Tagebücher* (note 9), i.190 (21 Jan. 1870).

91. Ibid., i.703 (4 July 1873).

92. Ibid., i.753 (18 Nov. 1873).

93. Ibid.

94. Wagner, *Gesammelte Schriften* (note 12), ii.158; Engl. trans. (*Richard Wagner's Prose Works*), vii.302 ('The Nibelung Myth: As Draft for a Drama').

95. Westernhagen, *Die Entstehung des 'Ring'* (note 24), 228; Engl. trans. (*The Forging of the 'Ring'*), 191.

96. Curt von Westernhagen, *Wagner* (Zurich 1979), 452; trans. Mary Whittall as *Wagner* (Cambridge 1978), 479.

97. Hans von Wolzogen, *Führer durch die Musik zu Richard Wagners Festspiel Der Ring des Nibelungen* (Leipzig n.d.), 81.

98. Cosima Wagner, *Die Tagebücher* (note 9), i.409 (4 July 1871).

99. Westernhagen, *Wagner* (note 96), 412; Engl. trans. (*Wagner*), 438.

100. Wagner, *Gesammelte Schriften* (note 12), x.114; Engl. trans. (*Richard Wagner's Prose Works*), vi.106 ('A Retrospective Glance at the 1876 Festival').

101. Cosima Wagner, *Die Tagebücher* (note 9), i.411 (7 July 1871).

102. Ludwig Strecker, *Richard Wagner als Verlagsgefährte* (Mainz 1951), 134.

103. Cosima Wagner, *Die Tagebücher* (note 9), i.493 (23 Feb. 1872).

104. Ibid., ii.294 (19 Jan. 1879) ('Siegfried's scene with the Norns').

105. Ibid., i.435 (6 Sept. 1871).

106. Eliza Wille, *Erinnerungen an Richard Wagner* (Munich 1935), 63.

107. Cosima Wagner, *Die Tagebücher* (note 9), i.753 (18 Nov. 1873).

108. Wagner's decision not to set Brünnhilde's words of wisdom led Nietzsche to speculate that the composer had betrayed his own concept. By the same token, the three different versions of the ending prompted Hans Mayer to conclude that not only did Wagner's philosophy change, but so too did the meaning of the *Ring*. But the different versions are only apparently contradictory, and Wagner's explanation is entirely convincing; see Hans Mayer, *Richard Wagner in Selbstzeugnissen und Bilddokumenten* (Hamburg 1959), 147.

109. Wagner, *Gesammelte Schriften* (note 12), vi.255.

110. Cosima Wagner, *Die Tagebücher* (note 9), i.552 (23 July 1872).

111. The published text of Cosima Wagner's diary entry for 23 July 1872 contains an unfortunate error, whereby 'Heldin' ('heroine') has been mistranscribed as 'Helden' ('heroes'); see Stewart Spencer, 'A Wagnerian Footnote', *Wagner*, iv (1983), 90.

Chapter 6

1. Richard Wagner, *Sämtliche Briefe*, ed. Gertrud Strobel, Werner Wolf, Werner Breig and others (Leipzig 1967–2000 and Wiesbaden 1999–), ix.231 (letter to Mathilde Wesendonck of 7 April 1858).

2. Carl Friedrich Glasenapp, *Das Leben Richard Wagners*, 6 vols. (Leipzig 1905–11), ii.486.

3. Cosima Wagner, *Die Tagebücher*, ed. Martin Gregor-Dellin and Dietrich Mack, 2 vols. (Munich 1976–7), i.275 (22 Aug. 1870).

4. Ibid., i.353 (9 Feb. 1871).

5. Ibid., i.508 (5 April 1872).

6. Ibid., i.653 (14 March 1873).

7. Ibid., i.531 (7 June 1872).

8. Richard Wagner, *Mein Leben*, ed. Eike Middell, 2 vols. (Leipzig 1986), ii.121; trans. Andrew Gray as *My Life* (Cambridge 1983), 552.

9. *Cosima Wagner und Ludwig II. von Bayern: Briefe*, ed. Martha Schad (Bergisch Gladbach 1996), 431 (letter from

Cosima von Bülow to Ludwig of 29 Sept. 1867).

10. *Richard Wagner in Zürich: Materialien zu Aufenthalt und Wirken*, ed. Werner G. Zimmermann (Zurich 1986), 67.

11. Egon Voss, *Richard Wagner und die Instrumentalmusik: Wagners symphonischer Ehrgeiz* (Wilhelmshaven 1977), 89.

12. Cosima Wagner, *Die Tagebücher* (note 3), i.1069 (30 Aug. 1877).

13. Wilhelm Kienzl, *Meine Lebenswanderung* (Stuttgart 1926), 212.

14. *Richard Wagner in Zürich* (note 10), 11 (the source of this malicious comment was Bertha Roner-Lipka).

15. *Richard Wagner an Mathilde Wesendonk: Tagebuchblätter und Briefe 1853–1871*, ed. Wolfgang Golther (Berlin 1904), vii. The Wesendoncks' son changed his name to 'Wesendonk' around the turn of the century, resulting in a state of confusion that has bedevilled writings on Wagner ever since.

16. Julius Kapp, *Richard Wagner und die Frauen* (Berlin 1951), 119.

17. Richard Wagner, *Briefe: Die Sammlung Burrell*, ed. John N. Burk (Frankfurt am Main 1953), 499; trans. Hans Abraham and others as *Letters of Richard Wagner: The Burrell Collection* (London 1951), 376 (letter from Minna Wagner to an unidentified correspondent of 23 April [1859?]).

18. Wagner, *Sämtliche Briefe* (note 1), ix.228 (letter to Mathilde Wesendonck of 7 April 1858).

19. Ibid., x.31 (letter to Clara Wolfram of 20 Aug. 1858).

20. Wagner, *Briefe: Die Sammlung Burrell* (note 17), 675; Engl. trans. (*Letters of Richard Wagner*), 528 (letter from Natalie Bilz-Planer to Mary Burrell of 2 March 1891).

21. Wagner, *Sämtliche Briefe* (note 1), vii.87 (letter to Otto Wesendonck of 5 April 1855).

22. Friedrich Herzfeld, *Minna Planer und ihre Ehe mit Richard Wagner* (Leipzig

1938), 270.

23. Kienzl, *Meine Lebenswanderung* (note 13), 212.

24. Franz W. Beidler, *Cosima Wagner-Liszt: Der Weg zum Wagner-Mythos*, ed. Dieter Borchmeyer (Bielefeld 1997), 133.

25. Wagner, *Sämtliche Briefe* (note 1), xi.197 (letter to Mathilde Wesendonck of 24 Aug. 1859).

26. Ibid., ix.229 (letter to Mathilde Wesendonck of 7 April 1858).

27. Eduard Devrient, *Aus seinen Tagebüchern*, ed. Rolf Kabel, 2 vols. (Weimar 1964), ii.288 and 301 (29 Sept. 1858 and 6 Feb. 1859).

28. *Richard Wagner an Mathilde Wesendonck* (note 15), 33 (diary entry of 17 Aug. 1858).

29. Advertisement dated 19 Aug. 1858 in the *Tagblatt der Stadt Zürich*, quoted by Werner Otto, *Richard Wagner: Ein Lebens- und Charakterbild in Dokumenten und zeitgenössischen Darstellungen* (Berlin 1990), 198–9.

30. *Richard Wagner an Mathilde Wesendonck* (note 15), 48 (diary entry of 29 Sept. 1858).

31. Glasenapp, *Das Leben Richard Wagners* (note 2), iii.199.

32. Mathilde Wesendonck, 'Erinnerungen', *Allgemeine Musik-Zeitung*, xxiii/7 (14 Feb. 1896), 93. The date given here (1852) is presumably the result of a lapse of memory and has been tacitly corrected in most later editions of these reminiscences.

33. Wagner, *Sämtliche Briefe* (note 1), vi.348 (letter to August Röckel of 5 Feb. 1855).

34. Ibid., vi.298 (letter to Franz Liszt of 16 [?] Dec. 1854).

35. Ibid., viii.153 (letter to August Röckel of 23 Aug. 1856).

36. Houston Stewart Chamberlain, *Richard Wagner* (Munich 1901), 192.

37. Richard Wagner, *Dichtungen und Schriften: Jubiläumsausgabe*, ed. Dieter Borchmeyer, 10 vols. (Frank-

furt am Main 1983), x.261 (Afterword to vol. iii).

38. Arthur Schopenhauer, *Gesammelte Briefe*, ed. Arthur Hübscher (Bonn 1978), 343. Wagner knew this passage, later commenting 'It's not nice.' See Glasenapp, *Das Leben Richard Wagners* (note 2), vi.63.

39. Otto, *Richard Wagner: Ein Lebens- und Charakterbild* (note 29), 169.

40. Wagner, *Sämtliche Briefe* (note 1), vii.127 (letter to August Röckel of April 1855).

41. Glasenapp, *Das Leben Richard Wagners* (note 2), vi.63.

42. Wagner, *Mein Leben* (note 8), ii.152; Engl. trans. (*My Life*), 579.

43. Richard Wagner, *Sämtliche Briefe* (note 1), x.211 (letter to Mathilde Wesendonck of Dec. 1858).

44. Ibid., x.208 (letter to Arthur Schopenhauer of Dec. 1858).

45. Richard Wagner, *Sämtliche Schriften und Dichtungen*, ed. Richard Sternfeld, 16 vols. (Leipzig 1911–14), xii.337–8; trans. by William Ashton Ellis as *Richard Wagner's Prose Works*, 8 vols. (London 1892–9, R1993–5), viii.390–1 ('Metaphysics, Ethics and Art').

46. *Richard Wagner an Mathilde Wesendonck* (note 15), 80 (diary entry of 1 Dec. 1858).

47. Wagner, *Sämtliche Briefe* (note 1), x.243 (letter to Mathilde Wesendonck of 19 Jan. 1859).

48. Ibid., vi.347 (letter to August Röckel of 5 Feb. 1855).

49. Letter from Jakob Sulzer to Mathilde Wesendonck of Aug. 1887, reproduced in Otto, *Richard Wagner: Ein Lebens- und Charakterbild* (note 29), 193.

50. Wagner, *Sämtliche Briefe* (note 1), vii.126 and 129 (letter to August Röckel of April 1855).

51. Ibid., vi.298 (letter to Franz Liszt of 16 [?] Dec. 1854).

52. Peter Wapnewski, 'Die Oper Richard Wagners als Dichtung', *Richard-Wagner-Handbuch*, ed. Ulrich Müller and Peter Wapnewski (Stuttgart 1986), 223–352, esp. 311; trans. Peter Palmer as 'The Operas as Literary Works', *Wagner Handbook*, ed. John Deathridge (Cambridge, Mass., 1992), 3–95, esp. 69.

53. Wagner, *Sämtliche Briefe* (note 1), ix.246 (letter to Marie Wittgenstein written before 28 April 1858).

54. Cosima Wagner, *Die Tagebücher* (note 3), i.728 (15 Sept. 1873).

55. Wagner, *Sämtliche Schriften* (note 45), xii.346.

56. Richard Wagner, *Gesammelte Schriften und Dichtungen*, 10 vols. (Leipzig 4/1907), vii.122–3; Eng. trans. (*Richard Wagner's Prose Works*) (note 45), iii.330–1 ('Zukunftsmusik').

57. Wagner, *Sämtliche Schriften* (note 45), xii.346–7.

58. Bernard Shaw, *The Perfect Wagnerite* (London 1898), 74.

59. Wagner, *Sämtliche Schriften* (note 45), xi.329.

60. Cosima Wagner, *Die Tagebücher* (note 3), ii.1079 (23 Dec. 1882).

61. Ibid., ii.942 (10 May 1882).

62. Martin Gregor-Dellin, *Richard Wagner: Sein Leben, sein Werk, sein Jahrhundert* (Munich 1980), 424; this passage was omitted from the 1983 English translation.

63. Wagner, *Sämtliche Schriften* (note 45), xi.334.

64. Cosima Wagner, *Die Tagebücher* (note 3), ii.67 (23 March 1878).

65. Kienzl, *Meine Lebenswanderung* (note 13), 212.

66. Joachim Kaiser, *Leben mit Wagner* (Munich 1990), 115.

67. Cosima Wagner, *Die Tagebücher* (note 3), ii.997 (31 Aug. 1882).

68. Wagner, *Gesammelte Schriften* (note 56), viii.180; Engl. trans. (*Richard Wagner's Prose Works*), iv.230 ('My Recollections of Ludwig Schnorr von Carolsfeld').

69. Wagner, *Sämtliche Briefe* (note 1), xi.58 (letter to Mathilde Wesendonck

of April 1859).

70. Ibid.

71. Wagner, *Sämtliche Schriften* (note 45), xii.347.

72. Cosima Wagner, *Die Tagebücher* (note 3), ii.1029 (22 Oct. 1882).

73. Glasenapp, *Das Leben Richard Wagners* (note 2), vi.5; see also Cosima Wagner, *Die Tagebücher* (note 3), ii.938 (25 April 1882).

74. Cosima Wagner, *Die Tagebücher* (note 3), ii.634 (8 Dec. 1880).

75. Ibid.

76. Ibid., ii.612 (17 Oct. 1880).

77. Ibid., ii.938 (25 April 1882).

78. Wagner, *Mein Leben* (note 8), ii.251; Engl. trans. (*My Life*), 667.

79. *Richard Wagners Briefwechsel mit B. Schott's Söhne*, ed. Wilhelm Altmann (Mainz 1911), 26 (letter to Franz Schott of 20 Nov. 1861).

80. Wagner, *Sämtliche Briefe* (note 1), xii.239 (letter to Mathilde Wesendonck of 10 Aug. 1860).

81. Otto, *Richard Wagner: Ein Lebens- und Charakterbild* (note 29), 218; the detailed description is that of Wagner's interior designer in Paris, Clemens Mathieu.

82. Kapp, *Richard Wagner und die Frauen* (note 16), 183.

83. Ibid., 179.

84. Wagner, *Mein Leben* (note 8), ii.206; Engl. trans. (*My Life*), 627.

85. Egon Voss, *Richard Wagner: Dokumentarbiographie* (Mainz 1982), 368; trans. P. R. J. Ford and Mary Whittall as *Wagner: A Documentary Study* (London 1975), 190 and 192.

86. Glasenapp, *Das Leben Richard Wagners* (note 2), iii.245.

87. Cosima Wagner, *Die Tagebücher* (note 3), i.272 (18 Aug. 1870): 'R. would like to write to Bismarck to ask him to shoot down Paris.'

88. Glasenapp, *Das Leben Richard Wagners* (note 2), iii.313.

89. Devrient, *Aus seinen Tagebüchern* (note 27), ii.382 (8 May 1861). The

90. Glasenapp, *Das Leben Richard Wagners* (note 2), iii.420.

91. John Deathridge and Carl Dahlhaus, *The New Grove Wagner* (London 1984), 46.

92. Julius Kapp, *Richard Wagner* (Berlin 1929), 119.

93. *Richard Wagner an Mathilde Maier (1862–1878)*, ed. Hans Scholz (Leipzig 1930), 132 (letter of 21 Nov. 1863).

94. Carl Maria Cornelius, *Peter Cornelius: Der Wort- und Tondichter*, 2 vols. (Regensburg 1925), i.350.

95. Kapp, *Richard Wagner und die Frauen* (note 16), 228.

96. Lilli Lehmann, *Mein Weg* (Leipzig 2/1920), 102; trans. Alice Benedict Seligman as *My Path through Life* (New York 1914), 61.

97. Eduard Hanslick, *Aus meinem Leben*, 2 vols. (Berlin 1894), ii.9.

98. Glasenapp, *Das Leben Richard Wagners* (note 2), ii.440.

99. Richard Wagner, *Briefe*, ed. Hanjo Kesting (Munich 1983), 483 (letter to Marie Völkl of 6 Dec. 1863).

100. Richard Wagner, *Das Braune Buch: Tagebuchaufzeichnungen 1865 bis 1882*, ed. Joachim Bergfeld (Zurich 1975), 94; trans. George Bird as *The Diary of Richard Wagner: The Brown Book 1865–1882* (London 1980), 79 (26 Oct. 1865).

101. Glasenapp, *Das Leben Richard Wagners* (note 2), i.505.

102. Cosima Wagner, *Die Tagebücher* (note 3), i.42 (24 Jan. 1869).

103. Ludwig Kusche, *Richard Wagner und die Putzmacherin oder Die Macht der Verleumdung* (Wilhelmshaven 1967), 30.

104. Kapp, *Richard Wagner und die Frauen* (note 16), 261.

105. Cornelius, *Peter Cornelius* (note 94), ii.403.

106. Wagner, *Briefe* (note 99), 488 (letter to

Peter Cornelius of 8 April 1864).

107. Marie Fürstin zu Hohenlohe, *Erinnerungen an Richard Wagner* (Weimar 1938), 14.

108. *Hans von Bülows Leben dargestellt aus seinen Briefen*, ed. Marie von Bülow (Leipzig 1921), 140.

109. Alan Walker, *Franz Liszt*, 3 vols. (London 1983–97), ii.549.

110. Wagner, *Sämtliche Briefe* (note 1), xiv. 281 (letter to Hans von Bülow of 6 Oct. 1862 [wrongly dated 6 Sept. 1862 by Wagner and his first editor]).

111. Cosima Wagner, *Die Tagebücher* (note 3), i.824 (1 June 1874).

112. Ibid., ii.485 (29 Jan. 1880).

113. Wagner, *Sämtliche Briefe* (note 1), ix.165 (letter to Minna Wagner of 29 Jan. 1858).

114. Joachim Köhler, *Friedrich Nietzsche und Cosima Wagner: Die Schule der Unterwerfung* (Berlin 1996), 28; trans. Ronald Taylor as *Nietzsche and Wagner: A Lesson in Subjugation* (New Haven and London 1998), 21.

115. Lina Ramann, *Lisztiana: Erinnerungen an Franz Liszt in Tagebuchblättern, Briefen und Dokumenten aus den Jahren 1873–1886/87*, ed. Arthur Seidl and Friedrich Schnapp (Mainz 1983), 114.

116. Walker, *Franz Liszt* (note 109), ii.465.

117. Herzfeld, *Minna Planer und ihre Ehe* (note 22), 288–9.

118. Manfred Eger, 'Der Briefwechsel Richard und Cosima Wagner: Geschichte und Relikte einer vernichteten Korrespondenz', *Die Programmhefte der Bayreuther Festspiele 1979*, iv (*Das Rheingold*), 115. Eger attempts to reconstruct the lost correspondence between Cosima and Wagner on the basis of a handful of surviving fragments. See also Cosima Wagner, *Die Tagebücher* (note 3), i.873 (entry of 3 Dec. 1874 referring back to 28 Nov. 1874): 'We recall our first union eleven years ago.'

119. Wagner, *Mein Leben* (note 8), ii.321; Engl. trans. (*My Life*), 729.

120. Erich Kuby, *Richard Wagner & Co.* (Hamburg 1963), 109.

121. Wagner, *Sämtliche Briefe* (note 1), x.73 (letter to Franz Liszt of 27 Sept. 1858).

122. Kapp, *Richard Wagner und die Frauen* (note 16), 186.

123. Romain Rolland, 'Vier Tage in Bayreuth', *Sinn und Form* (Potsdam 1955, R1988), 46.

124. Wendelin Weißheimer, *Erlebnisse mit Richard Wagner, Franz Liszt und vielen anderen Zeitgenossen nebst deren Briefen* (Stuttgart and Leipzig 1898), 307.

125. Letter from Martin Plüddemann to Ludwig Schemann of 25 Feb. 1896, quoted by Hans Mayer, *Richard Wagner in Bayreuth 1876–1976* (Frankfurt 1976), 56.

126. Ludwig Strecker, *Richard Wagner als Verlagsgefährte* (Mainz 1951), 209.

127. Cosima Wagner, *Die Tagebücher* (note 3), i.33 (15 Jan. 1869).

128. Otto, *Richard Wagner: Ein Lebens- und Charakterbild* (note 29), 570. The description is that of the Austrian composer Wilhelm Kienzl.

129. Eliza Wille, *Erinnerungen an Richard Wagner* (Munich 1935), 85.

130. Beidler, *Cosima Wagner-Liszt* (note 24), 217.

131. Ibid., 229.

132. Wille, *Erinnerungen* (note 129), 63.

133. Cornelius, *Peter Cornelius* (note 94), ii.63.

134. Engelbert Humperdinck, *Briefe und Tagebücher*, ed. Hans-Josef Irmen (Cologne 1975–), ii.41.

135. Walker, *Franz Liszt* (note 109), iii.92.

136. *Cosima Wagner und Ludwig II. von Bayern: Briefe* (note 9), 38 (letter from Cosima von Bülow to Ludwig of 19 Sept. 1865).

137. Wagner, *Das Braune Buch* (note 100), 75; Engl. trans. (*The Diary of Richard Wagner*), 65 (1 Sept. 1865).

Chapter 7

1. Richard Wagner, *Das Braune Buch: Tagebuchaufzeichnungen 1865 bis 1882*, ed. Joachim Bergfeld (Zurich 1975), 98; trans. by George Bird as *The Diary of Richard Wagner: The Brown Book 1865–1882* (London 1980), 82 (13 Nov. 1865).

2. Wagner, *Das Braune Buch* (note 1), 42; Engl. trans. (*The Diary of Richard Wagner*), 38 (18 Aug. 1865).

3. Carl Maria Cornelius, *Peter Cornelius: Der Wort- und Tondichter*, 2 vols. (Regensburg 1925), ii.250.

4. Wagner, *Das Braune Buch* (note 1), 30; Engl. trans. (*The Diary of Richard Wagner*), 29 (10 Aug. 1865).

5. Cosima Wagner, *Die Tagebücher*, ed. Martin Gregor-Dellin and Dietrich Mack, 2 vols. (Munich 1976–7), ii.335 (22 March 1879).

6. The exception is Peter Wapnewski: 'How farfetched the love affairs were is an open question'; see Peter Wapnewski, 'Die Oper Richard Wagners als Dichtung', *Richard-Wagner-Handbuch*, ed. Ulrich Muller and Peter Wapnewski (Stuttgart 1986), 223–352, esp. 332; trans. Peter Palmer as 'The Operas as Literary Works', *Wagner Handbook*, ed. John Deathridge (Cambridge, Mass., 1992), 3–95, esp. 84.

7. *König Ludwig II. und Richard Wagner: Briefwechsel*, ed. Otto Strobel, 5 vols (Karlsruhe 1936–9), i.171 (letter from Wagner to Ludwig of 7 Sept. 1865).

8. Ibid., i.204 (letter from Wagner to Ludwig of 4 Nov. 1865).

9. Cosima Wagner, *Die Tagebücher* (note 5), ii.199 (15 Oct. 1878).

10. Ibid., i.129 (16 July 1869).

11. Ibid., i.167 (5 Nov. 1869).

12. *Cosima Wagner und Ludwig II. von Bayern: Briefe*, ed. Martha Schad (Bergisch Gladbach 1996), 200 (Wagner's marginal addition to Ludwig's letter to Cosima von Bülow of 5 April 1866).

13. Ibid., 208 (Wagner's marginal addition to Ludwig's letter to Cosima von Bülow of 12 April 1866).

14. *König Ludwig II. und Richard Wagner: Briefwechsel* (note 7), iv.134 (letter from Wagner to Constantin Frantz of 19 March 1866).

15. Ibid., iv.69 (letter from Wagner to August Röckel of 15 July 1865).

16. Ibid., ii.106 (telegram from Ludwig to Wagner of 30 Nov. 1866).

17. Verena Naegele, *Parsifals Mission: Der Einfluß Richard Wagners auf Ludwig II. und seine Politik* (Cologne 1995), 179.

18. Ibid., 220.

19. Ibid., 231.

20. *König Ludwig II. und Richard Wagner: Briefwechsel* (note 7), iv.19 (diary entry of 21 Sept. 1865).

21. Frithjof Haas, *Zwischen Brahms und Wagner: Der Dirigent Hermann Levi* (Zurich 1995), 250.

22. *König Ludwig II. und Richard Wagner: Briefwechsel* (note 7), iii.226 (letter from Ludwig to Wagner of 11 Oct. 1881).

23. Ibid., iii.233 (letter from Ludwig to Wagner of 24 Jan. 1882).

24. Joachim Köhler, *Friedrich Nietzsche und Cosima Wagner: Die Schule der Unterwerfung* (Berlin 1996); trans. Ronald Taylor as *Nietzsche and Wagner: A Lesson in Subjugation* (New Haven and London 1998).

25. *König Ludwig II. und Richard Wagner: Briefwechsel* (note 7), i.224 (letter from Wagner to Ludwig of 25 Nov. 1865).

26. *Cosima Wagner und Ludwig II. von Bayern: Briefe* (note 12), 65 (letter from Cosima von Bülow to Ludwig of 1 Dec. 1865).

27. Cornelius, *Peter Cornelius* (note 3), ii.88.

28. *König Ludwig II. und Richard Wagner: Briefwechsel* (note 7), i.233 (letter from Ludwig to Wagner of 3 Dec. 1865).

29. Ibid., i.235 (letter from Wagner to Ludwig of 6 Dec. 1865).

30. Peter Glowasz, *Auf den Spuren des Märchenkönigs* (Berlin 1988), 404.

31. Walter Beck, *Richard Wagner: Neue Dokumente zur Biographie* (Tutzing 1988), 139 (letter to Karl Eckert of 7 May 1864).

32. Egon Voss, *Richard Wagner: Dokumentarbiographie* (Mainz 1982), 419; trans. P. R. J. Ford and Mary Whittall as *Wagner: A Documentary Study* (London 1975), 213.

33. Wagner, *Das Braune Buch* (note 1), 144; Engl. trans. (*The Diary of Richard Wagner*), 121.

34. Eduard Stemplinger, *Richard Wagner in München 1864–1870: Legende und Wirklichkeit* (Munich 1933), 39.

35. *Cosima Wagner und Ludwig II. von Bayern: Briefe* (note 12), 110 (letter from Cosima von Bülow to Ludwig II of 9 Jan. 1866).

36. *König Ludwig II. und Richard Wagner: Briefwechsel* (note 7), iv.125 (telegram from Wagner to Cosima von Bülow of 20 Jan. 1866).

37. Cosima Wagner, *Die Tagebücher* (note 5), i.276 (24 Aug. 1870).

38. *Cosima Wagner und Ludwig II. von Bayern: Briefe* (note 12), 82, 88 and 106 (letters from Cosima von Bülow to Ludwig of 30 Dec. 1865, 1 Jan. 1866 and 9 Jan. 1866).

39. Ibid., 118 and 122 (letter from Cosima von Bülow to Ludwig of 18 Jan. 1866 and from Ludwig to Cosima von Bülow of 19 Jan. 1866).

40. *König Ludwig II. und Richard Wagner: Briefwechsel* (note 7), iv.188 (telegrams from Wagner to Cosima von Bülow and from Cosima von Bülow to Wagner of 19 May 1867). In an attempt to tone down the affair, Martin Gregor-Dellin quotes only the last two phrases: 'Take note of my last wish, I shan't write again.' The threat to break things off did not square with his image of the relationship between Wagner and Cosima.

41. *König Ludwig II. und Richard Wagner: Briefwechsel* (note 7), v.80 (telegram from Cosima von Bülow to Wagner of 27 Oct. 1868).

42. Peter Wapnewski, *Der traurige Gott: Richard Wagner in seinen Helden* (Munich 1978), 101: 'It is extremely unfortunate that he dictated his memoirs to Cosima, as this meant that from the outset information was glossed over and suppressed as a matter of principle.'

43. Cosima Wagner, *Die Tagebücher* (note 5), i.559 (9 Aug. 1872).

44. Richard Wagner, *Gesammelte Schriften und Dichtungen*, 10 vols. (Leipzig 4/1907), iv.284; trans. William Ashton Ellis as *Richard Wagner's Prose Works*, 8 vols. (London 1892–9, R1993–5), i.329 (*A Communication to My Friends*).

45. Richard Wagner, *Gesammelte Schriften und Dichtungen*, ed. Wolfgang Golther, 10 vols. (Berlin 1913), x.104.

46. Richard Wagner, *Sämtliche Schriften und Dichtungen*, ed. Richard Sternfeld, 16 vols. (Leipzig 1911–14), xi.345–6.

47. Ibid., xi.353.

48. Richard Wagner, *Die Meistersinger von Nürnberg*, ed. Michael von Soden (Frankfurt 1983), 190.

49. Richard Wagner, *Sämtliche Briefe*, ed. Gertrud Strobel, Werner Wolf, Werner Breig and others (Leipzig 1967–2000 and Wiesbaden 1999–), x.384 (letter to Mathilde Wesendonck of 25 March 1859).

50. Ibid., ii.538 (letter to Eduard Hanslick of 1 Jan. 1847).

51. Wagner, *Gesammelte Schriften* (note 44), viii.252; Engl. trans. (*Richard Wagner's Prose Works*), iii.113 ('Some Explanations Concerning "Jews in Music"').

52. Richard Wagner, *Mein Leben*, ed. Eike Middell, 2 vols. (Leipzig 1986), ii.292;

trans. Andrew Gray as *My Life* (Cambridge 1983), 704.

53. Writing in the 1996 Bayreuth *Festspielführer*, Dieter Borchmeyer sought to free Walther's original, if politically incorrect, allusion from its Grimmian associations, but in doing so he failed to notice that Wagner himself lived and breathed the spirit of the Grimms, never more so than when he was working on the drafts of *Lohengrin* and *Die Meistersinger* in Marienbad in 1845. Borchmeyer advances the same untenable argument in *Drama and the World of Richard Wagner*, trans. Daphne Ellis (Princeton 2004), 196–211. Even Thomas Mann spoke of 'Beckmesser the Jew in the Thornbush'; see Thomas Mann, *Wagner und unsere Zeit*, ed. Erika Mann (Frankfurt 1983), 168; trans. Allan Blunden as *Pro and contra Wagner* (London 1985), 210 (letter to Emil Preetorius of 6 Dec. 1949); see also Joachim Köhler, *Wagners Hitler: Der Prophet und sein Vollstrecker* (Munich 1997), 368; trans. Ronald Taylor as *Wagner's Hitler: The Prophet and His Disciple* (Cambridge 2000), 258.

54. Richard Wagner, *Briefe 1830–1883*, ed. Werner Otto (Berlin 1986), 309 (letter to Gustav Hölzel of 22 Jan. 1868). Wagner had no time for the popular practice of casting a sympathetic baritone in the part of Beckmesser. He demanded a 'high tessitura' of the kind that a bass can equally well encompass 'as long as he finds the speaking tone that I need: in no circumstances can my purpose be served by a normal baritone voice, because everything would then acquire a false, sentimental character'.

55. *König Ludwig II. und Richard Wagner: Briefwechsel* (note 7), ii.130 (letter from Wagner to Ludwig of 15 July 1878).

56. *Richard et Cosima Wagner: Lettres à Judith Gautier*, ed. Léon Guichard (Paris 1964), 40 (letter from Wagner to Judith Gautier of early Nov. 1868).

57. Ibid., 41 (letter from Wagner to Judith Gautier of early Nov. 1868).

58. *Cosima Wagner und Ludwig II. von Bayern: Briefe* (note 12), 353 (letter from Cosima von Bülow to Ludwig of 31 Jan. 1867). A facsimile of this passage in Wagner's hand was reproduced in the 1933 Bayreuth *Festspielführer* (facing p.160), with Beckmesser's garbled version of the lines entered directly over Walther's original.

59. Otto Strobel, '"Morgenlich leuchtend in rosigem Schein": Wie Walthers "Preislied" entstand', *Bayreuther Festspielführer 1933*, ed. Otto Strobel (Bayreuth 1933), 148–60, esp. 152.

60. *Cosima Wagner und Ludwig II. von Bayern: Briefe* (note 12), 348 (letter from Cosima von Bülow to Ludwig of 31 Jan. 1867). According to Cosima, 'The second poem is the interpretation of the dream, and a more focused image of it, it is the Mastersong on the subject of the dream.'

61. Ibid.

62. Curt von Westernhagen, *Richard Wagner: Sein Werk, sein Wesen, sein Welt* (Zurich 1956), 325–6.

63. *König Ludwig II. und Richard Wagner: Briefwechsel* (note 7), iv.8 (diary entry of 15 Sept. 1865).

64. Ibid., iv.21 (diary entry of 22 Sept. 1865).

65. Wagner, *Gesammelte Schriften* (note 44), viii.38; Engl. trans. (*Richard Wagner's Prose Works*), iv.45 (*German Art and German Politics*).

66. Köhler, *Friedrich Nietzsche und Cosima Wagner* (note 24); Engl. trans. (*Nietzsche and Wagner*).

67. Friedrich Nietzsche, *Sämtliche Briefe: Kritische Studienausgabe*, ed. Giorgio Colli and Mazzino Montinari, 8 vols. (Munich 1986), ii.340 (letter to Erwin Rohde of 9 Nov. 1868).

68. Ibid., iii.52 (letter to Erwin Rohde of 3 Sept. 1869).

69. Dieter Borchmeyer, 'Richard Wagner und Nietzsche', *Richard-Wagner-Handbuch*, (note 6), 114; trans. by Michael Tanner as 'Wagner and Nietzsche', *Wagner Handbook*, 327.

70. Cosima Wagner, *Die Tagebücher* (note 5), ii.253 (9 Dec. 1878).

71. Ernest Newman, *The Life of Richard Wagner*, 4 vols. (New York 1933–46), iv.607.

72. Wagner, *Sämtliche Briefe* (note 49), xiv.43 (letter to Peter Cornelius of 9 Jan. 1862).

73. *Richard Wagner an Mathilde Maier (1862–1878)*, ed. Hans Scholz (Leipzig 1930), 197 (letter of 29 Jan. 1865).

74. Wagner, *Sämtliche Briefe* (note 49), iv.383 (letter to Theodor Uhlig of 31 May 1852).

75. Cosima Wagner, *Die Tagebücher* (note 5), i.786 (28 Jan. 1874).

76. Ibid., i.415 (18 and 20 July 1871).

77. Friedrich Nietzsche, *Sämtliche Werke: Kritische Studienausgabe*, ed. Giorgio Colli and Mazzino Montinari, 15 vols. (Munich 1980), vi.16; trans. Walter Kaufmann as *Basic Writings of Nietzsche* (New York 1968), 616 (*The Case of Wagner*).

78. Nietzsche, *Sämtliche Werke* (note 77), xi.579.

79. Cornelius, *Peter Cornelius* (note 3), ii.12.

80. *König Ludwig II. und Richard Wagner: Briefwechsel* (note 7), i.110 (letter from Wagner to Ludwig of 25 June 1865).

81. Nietzsche, *Sämtliche Briefe* (note 67), viii.604 (draft of letter to Cosima Wagner, probably dating from early Sept. 1888).

82. Nietzsche, *Sämtliche Werke* (note 77), xiii.16.

83. *Nietzsche und Wagner: Stationen einer epochalen Begegnung*, ed. Dieter Borchmeyer und Jörg Salaquarda (Frankfurt 1994), 63 (letter from Wagner to Nietzsche of 1 March 1870).

84. Ibid., 69 (letter from Wagner to Nietzsche of 16 March 1870).

85. Newman, *The Life of Richard Wagner* (note 71), iii.284. Newman is punning on the phrase 'Cherchez la femme'.

86. *Nietzsche und Wagner* (note 83), 37 (letter from Wagner to Nietzsche of 19 Dec. 1869).

87. Nietzsche, *Sämtliche Briefe* (note 67), iii.38 (letter to Gustav Krug of 4 Aug. 1869).

88. Nietzsche, *Sämtliche Werke* (note 77), xiv.101.

89. Ibid., xiv.52.

90. *Nietzsche und Wagner* (note 83), 42 (letter from Cosima von Bülow to Nietzsche of 17 Jan. 1870).

91. Cosima Wagner, *Die Tagebücher* (note 5), i.375 (5 April 1871).

92. Wagner, *Sämtliche Briefe* (note 49), iii.365 (letter to Theodor Uhlig of 27 July 1850).

93. Nietzsche, *Sämtliche Werke* (note 77), vii.500.

94. Köhler, *Friedrich Nietzsche und Cosima Wagner* (note 24), 106; Engl. trans. (*Nietzsche and Wagner*), 93.

95. *Nietzsche und Wagner* (note 83), 237 (letter from Cosima Wagner to Nietzsche of 20 March 1874).

96. Nietzsche, *Sämtliche Werke* (note 77), xi.689.

97. Ibid., i.25 and 42; Engl. trans. (*Basic Writings of Nietzsche*), 33 and 47 (*The Birth of Tragedy*).

98. Wagner, *Gesammelte Schriften* (note 44), ix.74–5; Engl. trans. (*Richard Wagner's Prose Works*), v.74 (*Beethoven*).

99. Wagner, *Gesammelte Schriften* (note 45), ix.197; Engl. trans. (*Richard Wagner's Prose Works*), v.196 (*On Actors and Singers*).

100. Wagner, *Gesammelte Schriften* (note 44), ix.121; Engl. trans. (*Richard Wagner's Prose Works*), v.121 (*Beethoven*).

101. Nietzsche, *Sämtliche Werke* (note 77), i.23; Engl. trans. (*Basic Writings of Nietzsche*), 31 (*The Birth of Tragedy*).

102. Joachim Köhler, *Zarathustras Geheimnis: Friedrich Nietzsche und seine ver-*

schlüsselte Botschaft (Nördlingen 1989); trans. Ronald Taylor as *Zarathustra's Secret: The Interior Life of Friedrich Nietzsche* (New Haven 2002).

103. *Nietzsche und Wagner* (note 83), 152 and 155 (letters from Wagner to Nietzsche of early Jan. 1872 and 18 Jan. 1872).

104. Cosima Wagner, *Die Tagebücher* (note 5), ii.92 (9 May 1878).

105. Peter Wapnewski, 'Nietzsche und Wagner: Stationen einer Beziehung', *Nietzsche-Studien*, xviii (1989), 412.

106. *Nietzsche und Wagner* (note 83), 1309.

107. Nietzsche, *Sämtliche Werke* (note 77), i.441; trans. R. J. Hollingdale as *Untimely Meditations* (Cambridge 1983), 205 ('Richard Wagner in Bayreuth').

108. Nietzsche, *Sämtliche Werke* (note 77), i.510; Engl. trans. (*Untimely Meditations*), 254 ('Richard Wagner in Bayreuth').

109. Cosima Wagner, *Die Tagebücher* (note 5), i.1012 (1 Nov. 1876).

110. Richard Du Moulin Eckart, *Cosima Wagner: Ein Lebens- und Charakterbild*, 2 vols. (Berlin 1929–31), i.842.

111. Elisabeth Förster-Nietzsche, *Wagner und Nietzsche zur Zeit ihrer Freundschaft* (Munich 1915), 264; trans. Caroline V. Kerr as *The Nietzsche–Wagner Correspondence* (London 1922), 294.

112. Werner Ross, *Der ängstliche Adler* (Stuttgart 1980), 480.

113. Nietzsche, *Sämtliche Werke* (note 77), xv.71.

114. Otto Strobel, 'Michael Georg Conrad zum Gedächtnis', *Bayreuther Festspielführer 1928*, ed. Paul Pretzsch (Bayreuth 1928), 192.

115. Köhler, *Friedrich Nietzsche und Cosima Wagner* (note 24), 156; Engl. trans. (*Nietzsche and Wagner*), 139.

116. Nietzsche, *Sämtliche Briefe* (note 67), vi.335 (letter to Malwida von Meysenbug of 21 Feb. 1883).

117. Ibid., vi.337 (letter to Franz Overbeck of 22 Feb. 1883).

118. Ibid., vi.405 (letter to Ida Overbeck of mid-July 1883).

119. Nietzsche, *Sämtliche Werke* (note 77), viii.506 and 512.

120. Ibid., viii.365.

121. Eugen Kretzer, 'Erinnerungen an Dr. Otto Eiser', *Begegnungen mit Nietzsche*, ed. Sander L. Gilman (Bonn 1981), 345. (This passage was not included in the English-language edition of Gilman's anthology, *Conversations with Nietzsche* [Oxford 1987].)

122. Westernhagen, *Richard Wagner* (note 62), 527.

123. Cosima Wagner, *Die Tagebücher* (note 5), ii.130 (3 July 1878).

124. Ibid., ii.153 (2 Aug. 1878).

125. Ibid., ii.1211–12 (3 and 4 Feb. 1883).

126. Nietzsche, *Sämtliche Werke* (note 77), vi.17; Engl. trans. (*Basic Writings of Nietzsche*), 616 (*The Case of Wagner*).

127. Pia Daniela Volz, *Nietzsche im Labyrinth seiner Krankheit* (Würzburg 1990), 397.

128. Cosima Wagner, *Die Tagebücher* (note 5), i.872 (21 Nov. 1874).

129. John Deathridge and Carl Dahlhaus, *The New Grove Wagner* (London 1984), 56.

130. Cosima Wagner, *Die Tagebücher* (note 5), i.126 (11 July 1869).

131. Ibid., i.310 (8 Nov. 1870).

132. Ibid., i.693 (10 June 1873).

133. Ibid., i.99 (27 May 1869).

134. Ibid., i.137 (6 Aug. 1869).

135. Ibid., i.955 (27 Dec. 1875).

136. Ibid., i.395 (6 June 1871).

137. Ibid., i.695 (16 June 1873).

138. Ibid., i.787 (28 Jan. 1874).

139. Ibid., ii.127 (29 June 1878).

140. Cosima Wagner, *Das zweite Leben*, ed. Dietrich Mack (Munich 1980), 329 (letter to Hugo von Tschudi of 11 March 1893).

141. Ludwig Strecker, *Richard Wagner als Verlagsgefährte* (Mainz 1951), 280.

142. *Nietzsche und Wagner* (note 83), 280 (letter from Wagner to Nietzsche of 23

May 1876).

143. Wagner, *Sämtliche Briefe* (note 49), iii.404 (letter to Ernst Benedikt Kietz of 14 Sept. 1850).

144. Ibid., iii.426 (letter to Theodor Uhlig of 20 Sept. 1850).

145. Ibid., iv.176 (letter to Theodor Uhlig of 12 Nov. 1851).

146. Wagner, *Gesammelte Schriften* (note 44), iv.343; Engl. trans. (*Richard Wagner's Prose Works*), i.391 (*A Communication to My Friends*).

147. Carl Friedrich Glasenapp, *Das Leben Richard Wagners*, 6 vols. (Leipzig 1905–11), iii.467. Wagner apparently made the remark to August Lesimple in Zurich.

148. Wagner, *Gesammelte Schriften* (note 44), vi.279; Engl. trans. (*Richard Wagner's Prose Works*), iii.280 ('Preface to the *Ring* Poem').

149. Stemplinger, *Richard Wagner in München* (note 34), 80.

150. Cosima Wagner, *Die Tagebücher* (note 5), i.758 (29 Dec. 1873).

151. Ibid., i.602 (25 Nov. 1872).

152. Wagner, *Gesammelte Schriften* (note 44), ix.338; Engl. trans. (*Richard Wagner's Prose Works*), v.335 ('The Festival Theatre at Bayreuth').

153. Cosima Wagner, *Die Tagebücher* (note 5), i.202 (25 Feb. 1870).

154. *Nietzsche und Wagner* (note 83), 191 (letter from Wagner to Nietzsche of 25 June 1872).

155. Martin Gregor-Dellin, *Richard Wagner: Sein Leben, sein Werk, sein Jahrhundert* (Munich 1980), 719. (This passage was not included in J. Maxwell Brownjohn's 1983 translation.)

156. Cosima Wagner, *Die Tagebücher* (note 5), i.390 (21 May 1871).

157. Ibid., i.827 (9 June 1874).

158. *Nietzsche und Wagner* (note 83), 268 (letter from Wagner to Nietzsche of 18 Feb. 1875).

159. Glasenapp, *Das Leben Richard Wagners* (note 147), v.286.

160. Wagner, *Gesammelte Schriften* (note 44), x.105; Engl. trans. (*Richard Wagner's Prose Works*), vi.98 ('A Retrospective Glance at the 1876 Festival').

161. Deathridge and Dahlhaus, *The New Grove Wagner* (note 129), 60.

162. *König Ludwig II. und Richard Wagner: Briefwechsel* (note 7), iii.146 and 158 (letters from Wagner to Ludwig of 9 Feb. 1879 and 25 Aug. 1879).

163. Cosima Wagner, *Die Tagebücher* (note 5), i.1011 (29 Oct. 1876).

164. Ibid., i.1034 (26 March 1877).

165. Ibid., i.1013 (5 Nov. 1876).

166. Ibid., ii.144 (23 July 1878).

167. Glasenapp, *Das Leben Richard Wagners* (note 147), v.308.

168. Cosima Wagner, *Die Tagebücher* (note 5), i.996 (26 July 1876).

Chapter 8

1. Cosima Wagner, *Die Tagebücher*, ed. Martin Gregor-Dellin and Dietrich Mack, 2 vols. (Munich 1976–7), i.364 (27 Feb. 1871).

2. Ibid., ii.127 (26 June 1878).

3. Ibid., ii.655 (1 Jan. 1881).

4. Ibid., ii.515 (3 April 1880).

5. Ibid., i.369 (13 March 1871).

6. Ibid., i.577 (26 Sept. 1872).

7. Ibid., i.662 (28 March 1873).

8. Sophie Rützow, *Richard Wagner und Bayreuth: Ausschnitte und Erinnerungen* (Munich 1943), 150.

9. Richard Du Moulin Eckart, *Wahnfried* (Leipzig 1925), 13. The 'Pleiades' was the 'coat of arms chosen by the Master. Through thick and thin he remained true to this constellation, which had always shone down on his life and to which he had often gazed up in times of adversity and yearning.'

10. Cosima Wagner, *Die Tagebücher* (note 1), i.469 (20 Dec. 1871).

11. Ibid., ii.485 (29 Jan. 1880).

12. Ibid., i.840 (24 July 1874).

13. Ibid., ii.125 (27 June 1878).

14. Ibid., ii.726 (12 April 1881).

15. Ibid., i.701 (1 July 1873).
16. Ibid., i.412 (11 July 1871).
17. Ibid., i.941 (9 Oct. 1875).
18. Ibid., i.757 (28 Nov. 1873).
19. Ibid., ii.902 (3 March 1882).
20. Ibid., i.318 (30 Nov. 1870).
21. Ibid., ii.886 (5 Feb. 1882).
22. Ibid., i.796 (1 March 1874).
23. Ibid., ii.1048 (15 Nov. 1882).
24. Ibid., ii.209 (25 Oct. 1878).
25. Ibid., ii.587 (27 Aug. 1880).
26. Ibid., i.757 (28 Nov. 1873).
27. Ibid., i.817 (9 May 1874).
28. Ibid., i.819 (14 May 1874).
29. Ibid., i.827 (11 June 1874).
30. Ibid., ii.322 (26 March 1879).
31. Ibid., ii.714 (20 March 1881).
32. Ibid., i.782 (17 Jan. 1874).
33. Ibid., ii.227 (12 Nov. 1878).
34. Ibid., ii.680 (31 Jan. 1881).
35. Ibid., ii.701 (26 Feb. 1881).
36. Ibid., i.263 (2 Aug. 1870).
37. Ibid., ii.609 (5 Oct. 1880).
38. Ibid., ii.803 (5 Oct. 1881).
39. Ibid., ii.62 (17 March 1878).
40. Ibid., ii.174 (11 Sept. 1878).
41. Ibid., ii.287 (10 Jan. 1879).
42. Ibid., ii.967 (22 June 1882).
43. Ibid., ii.837 (2 Dec. 1881). The sentence drawing a parallel between the two women was inked over by an unknown hand in an attempt to render it illegible.
44. Ibid., ii.1013 (2 Oct. 1882).
45. Ibid., i.968 (7 Feb. 1876).
46. Ibid., ii.596 (7 Sept. 1880).
47. Ibid., i.1009 (21 Oct. 1876).
48. Ibid., i.820 (15 May 1874).
49. Ibid., ii.46 (15 Feb. 1878).
50. Ibid., ii.611 (14 Oct. 1880).
51. Ibid., i.835 (8 July 1874).
52. Ibid., i.289 (25 Sept. 1870).
53. Ibid., i.495 (28 Feb. 1872).
54. Ibid., i.815 (7 May 1874).
55. Ibid., ii.35 (10 Jan. 1878).
56. Ibid., ii.134 (9 July 1878).
57. Ibid., ii.697 (19 Feb. 1881).
58. Annette Hein, 'Es ist viel "Hitler" in Wagner': Rassismus und antisemitische Deutschtumsideologie in den Bayreuther Blättern (1878–1938) (Tübingen 1996), 42.
59. Jürgen Kühnel, 'Wagners Schriften', Richard-Wagner-Handbuch, ed. Ulrich Müller and Peter Wapnewski (Stuttgart 1986), 471–588, esp. 554; trans. Simon Nye as 'The Prose Writings', Wagner Handbook, ed. John Deathridge (Cambridge, Mass., 1992), 565–651, esp. 617.
60. Cosima Wagner, Die Tagebücher (note 1), ii.882 (30 Jan. 1882).
61. Ibid., ii.954 (5 June 1882).
62. Ibid., ii.728 (17 April 1881).
63. Carl Friedrich Glasenapp, Das Leben Richard Wagners, 6 vols. (Leipzig 1905–11), vi.647.
64. Ibid., vi.731.
65. Cosima Wagner, Die Tagebücher (note 1), ii.1054 (22 Dec. 1882).
66. Cosima Wagner, Die Tagebücher (note 1), ii.731 (26 April 1881): the doctor regretted 'that R. consumes so much'.
67. Glasenapp, Das Leben Richard Wagners (note 63), iv.235; see also Cosima Wagner, Die Tagebücher (note 1), ii.401 (1 Sept. 1879).
68. Friedrich Nietzsche, Sämtliche Werke: Kritische Studienausgabe, ed. Giorgio Colli and Mazzino Montinari, 15 vols. (Munich 1980), xii.399.
69. Richard Wagner, Gesammelte Schriften und Dichtungen, 10 vols. (Leipzig 4/1907), x.249; trans. William Ashton Ellis as Richard Wagner's Prose Works, 8 vols. (London 1892–9, R1993–5), vi.249 ('Religion and Art').
70. Dieter Borchmeyer, 'Richard Wagner und der Antisemitismus', Richard-Wagner-Handbuch (note 59), 137–61, esp. 158; trans. Stewart Spencer as 'The Question of Anti-Semitism', Wagner Handbook, 166–85, esp. 183.
71. Martin Gregor-Dellin, Richard Wagner: Sein Leben, sein Werk, sein Jahrhundert (Munich 1980), 796; trans. J. Maxwell Brownjohn as Richard Wagner: His Life, His Work,

His Century (London 1983), 487.

72. Wagner, *Gesammelte Schriften* (note 69), x.218–19; Engl. trans. (*Richard Wagner's Prose Works*), vi.220 ('Religion and Art').

73. Wagner, *Gesammelte Schriften* (note 69), x.32; Engl. trans. (*Richard Wagner's Prose Works*), vi.35 ('Introduction to the Year 1880').

74. Wagner, *Gesammelte Schriften und Dichtungen* (note 69), x.227; Engl. trans. (*Richard Wagner's Prose Works*), vi.228 ('Religion and Art').

75. Wagner, *Gesammelte Schriften* (note 69), x.254; Engl. trans. (*Richard Wagner's Prose Works*), vi.254 ('What Use Is This Knowledge?').

76. Wagner, *Gesammelte Schriften* (note 69), x.229; Engl. trans. (*Richard Wagner's Prose Works*), vi.230 ('Religion and Art').

77. Wagner, *Gesammelte Schriften* (note 69), x.87; Engl. trans. (*Richard Wagner's Prose Works*), vi.79 ('Public and Popularity').

78. Wagner, *Gesammelte Schriften* (note 69), x.86; Engl. trans. (*Richard Wagner's Prose Works*), vi.77 ('Public and Popularity').

79. Glasenapp, *Das Leben Richard Wagners* (note 63), vi.307.

80. Wagner, *Gesammelte Schriften* (note 69), x.214; Engl. trans. (*Richard Wagner's Prose Works*), vi.215–16 ('Religion and Art').

81. Wagner, *Gesammelte Schriften* (note 69), x.260; Engl. trans. (*Richard Wagner's Prose Works*), vi.260 ('What Use Is This Knowledge?').

82. Wagner, *Gesammelte Schriften* (note 69), x.245; Engl. trans. (*Richard Wagner's Prose Works*), vi.244–5 ('Religion and Art').

83. Wagner, *Gesammelte Schriften* (note 69), x.282; Engl. trans. (*Richard Wagner's Prose Works*), vi.282 ('Heroism and Christianity').

84. Ludwig Feuerbach, *Das Wesen des Christentums* (Stuttgart 1969), 354; trans. George Eliot as *The Essence of Christianity* (New York 1989), 236.

85. Cosima Wagner, *Die Tagebücher* (note 1), ii.883 (2 Feb. 1882).

86. Ibid., ii.1042 (8 Nov. 1882).

87. Ibid., ii.424 (11 Oct. 1879).

88. Wagner, *Gesammelte Schriften* (note 69), x.264; Engl. trans. (*Richard Wagner's Prose Works*), vi.264–5 ('Know Yourself').

89. Cosima Wagner, *Die Tagebücher* (note 1), ii.888 (9 Feb. 1882).

90. Wagner, *Gesammelte Schriften* (note 69), x.224; Engl. trans. (*Richard Wagner's Prose Works*), vi.225 ('Religion and Art').

91. Wagner, *Gesammelte Schriften* (note 69), x.231; Engl. trans. (*Richard Wagner's Prose Works*), vi.232 ('Religion and Art').

92. Wagner, *Gesammelte Schriften* (note 69), x.284; Engl. trans. (*Richard Wagner's Prose Works*), vi.284 ('Heroism and Christianity').

93. Wagner, *Gesammelte Schriften* (note 69), x.203; Engl. trans. (*Richard Wagner's Prose Works*), vi.203 ('Open Letter to Herr Ernst von Weber').

94. Wagner, *Gesammelte Schriften* (note 69), x.44; Engl. trans. (*Richard Wagner's Prose Works*), iv.159 ('What Is German?').

95. Wagner, *Gesammelte Schriften* (note 69), x.274; Engl. trans. (*Richard Wagner's Prose Works*), vi.273–4 ('Know Yourself').

96. Angelo Neumann, *Erinnerungen an Richard Wagner* (Leipzig 1907), 139; trans. Edith Livermore as *Personal Recollections of Wagner* (London 1909), 132.

97. Cosima Wagner, *Die Tagebücher* (note 1), ii.148 (28 July 1878).

98. Ibid., ii.688 (10 Feb. 1881).

99. Ibid., ii.766 (20 July 1881).

100. Curt von Westernhagen, *Wagner* (Zurich 1979), 10; this passage does not appear in Mary Whittall's English translation (Cambridge 1978).

101. Gregor-Dellin, *Richard Wagner* (note 71), 733; Engl. trans. (*Richard Wagner*), 443.

102. Hans-Joachim Bauer, *Richard Wagner: Sein Leben und Wirken, oder Die Gefühlwerdung der Vernunft* (Frankfurt 1995), 386.

103. *Die Briefe Richard Wagners an Judith Gautier*, ed. Willi Schuh (Zurich and Leipzig 1936), 83.

104. *Richard et Cosima Wagner: Lettres à Judith Gautier*, ed. Léon Guichard (Paris 1964), 41 (letter of early Nov. 1868).

105. *Lettres à Judith Gautier* (note 104), 83 (letter of 24 Dec. 1877).

106. Edmond and Jules de Goncourt, *Journal*, ed. Robert Ricatte, 3 vols. (Paris 1989), i.791 (27 March 1862), i.855 (31 Aug. 1862), i.987 (17 July 1863) and ii.561 (28 Dec. 1873).

107. Judith Gautier, *Wagner at Home*, trans. Effie Dunreith Massie (New York 1911), 63.

108. Cosima Wagner, *Die Tagebücher* (note 1), i.129 (16 July 1869).

109. Joanna Richardson, *Judith Gautier: A Biography* (London 1986), xvi.

110. Cosima Wagner, *Die Tagebücher* (note 1), i.132 (27 July 1869).

111. Ibid., i.142 (21 Aug. 1869).

112. Ibid., i.134 (30 July 1869).

113. Ibid., i.132 (27 July 1869).

114. *Lettres à Judith Gautier* (note 104), 93 (letter of 22 Jan. 1878).

115. Ibid., 47 (letter of 6 Nov. 1869).

116. *König Ludwig II. und Richard Wagner: Briefwechsel*, ed. Otto Strobel, 5 vols. (Karlsruhe 1936–9), v.227 (letter from Wagner to Reinhard Schäfer of 5 Sept. 1869).

117. *Die Briefe Richard Wagners an Judith Gautier* (note 103), 134.

118. Cosima Wagner, *Die Tagebücher* (note 1), i.272 (18 Aug. 1870).

119. *Lettres à Judith Gautier* (note 104), 56 (letter of 12 Dec. 1873).

120. Ibid., 59 (letter written between 25 and 29 Sept. 1876).

121. Ibid., 57 (letter of 2 Sept. 1876).

122. Cosima Wagner, *Die Tagebücher* (note 1), ii.687 (9 Feb. 1881).

123. *Lettres à Judith Gautier* (note 104), 58 (letter of Sept. 1876).

124. Ibid., 63 (letter of 18 Nov. 1877).

125. Gregor-Dellin, *Richard Wagner* (note 71), 733; Engl. trans. (*Richard Wagner*), 443.

126. *Lettres à Judith Gautier* (note 104), 59 (letter written between 25 and 29 Sept. 1876) and 63 (18 Nov. 1877).

127. Judith Gautier, *Auprès de Richard Wagner: Souvenirs (1861–1882)* (Paris 1943), 231.

128. *Lettres à Judith Gautier* (note 104), 74–5 (letter of 9 Dec. 1877).

129. Ernest Newman, *The Life of Richard Wagner*, 4 vols. (New York 1933–46), iv.605.

130. *Lettres à Judith Gautier* (note 104), 65 (letter of 20 Nov. 1877).

131. Ibid., 76 (letter of 11 or 12 Dec. 1877).

132. Ibid., 93 (letter of 27 Jan. 1878).

133. Ibid., 79 (letter of 18 Dec. 1877).

134. Ibid., 76 (letter of 11 or 12 Dec. 1877).

135. Ibid., 82 (letter of 24 Dec. 1877).

136. Ibid., 65–6 (letter of 22 Nov. 1877).

137. Ibid., 64 (letter of 20 Nov. 1877).

138. Richard Wagner, *Briefe: Die Sammlung Burrell*, ed. John N. Burk (Frankfurt am Main 1953), 576; trans. Hans Abraham and others as *Letters of Richard Wagner: The Burrell Collection* (London 1951), 436. The woman was called Susanne Weinert: she was engaged only briefly at Wahnfried during the winter of 1875–6.

139. Hans von Wolzogen, *Lebensbilder* (Regensburg 1923), 87.

140. *Lettres à Judith Gautier* (note 104), 57–8. Guichard's dating of this letter – September 1876 – is problematical. The editors of the new *Wagner Briefe Verzeichnis* (Wiesbaden 1998) are almost certainly right to accept Schuh's dating of May 1877.

141. *Lettres à Judith Gautier* (note 104), 76 (letter of 11 or 12 Dec. 1877).

142. Ibid., 65 (letter of 20 Nov. 1877).
143. Ibid., 60 (letter of 1 Oct. 1877).
144. Ibid., 84 (letter of 24 Dec. 1877).
145. Cosima Wagner, *Die Tagebücher* (note 1), i.1100 (27 Dec. 1877).
146. Ibid., i.1100 (26 Dec. 1877).
147. Ibid., ii.433 (29 Oct. 1879).
148. *Lettres à Judith Gautier* (note 104), 87 (letter of 4 Jan. 1878).
149. Ibid., 96 (letter of 15 Feb. 1878).
150. Cosima Wagner, *Die Tagebücher* (note 1), ii.64 (19 March 1878).
151. Ibid., ii.62 (17 March 1878).
152. Werner Otto, *Richard Wagner: Ein Lebens- und Charakterbild in Dokumenten und zeitgenössischen Darstellungen* (Berlin 1990), 610. The eyewitness was the Austrian journalist and industrialist Friedrich Eckstein. Houston Stewart Chamberlain also heard these strange words of Wagner's, as well as his final remark: 'Unless you all go mad, our aim will not be achieved'; quoted by Rützow, *Richard Wagner und Bayreuth* (note 8), 189.
153. *Lettres à Judith Gautier* (note 104), 66 (letter of 22 Nov. 1877).
154. Rützow, *Richard Wagner und Bayreuth* (note 8), 150.
155. Ibid., 186.
156. Richard Wagner, *Mein Leben*, ed. Eike Middell, 2 vols. (Leipzig 1986), i.27; trans. Andrew Gray as *My Life* (Cambridge 1983), 20.
157. Wagner, *Gesammelte Schriften* (note 69), ix.80; Engl. trans. (*Richard Wagner's Prose Works*), v.79 (*Beethoven*).
158. Glasenapp, *Das Leben Richard Wagners* (note 63), vi.255.
159. Ibid., vi.38.
160. Ibid., vi.311.
161. Adelheid von Schorn, *Zwei Menschenalter* (Berlin 1901), 426 and 460.
162. Richard Wagner, *Tristan und Isolde. Programmheft zur Neuinszenierung*, ed. Klaus Schultz (Munich 1980), 30. The entry comes from a small brown

pocketbook now lodged in the National Archives in Bayreuth.
163. Glasenapp, *Das Leben Richard Wagners* (note 63), vi.119.
164. Ibid.
165. Richard Wagner, *Sämtliche Schriften und Dichtungen*, ed. Richard Sternfeld, 16 vols. (Leipzig 1911–14), xi.325; Eng. trans. (*Richard Wagner's Prose Works*) (note 69), viii.385 (*The Victors*).
166. Glasenapp, *Das Leben Richard Wagners* (note 63), iii.119.
167. Wolfgang Osthoff, 'Richard Wagners Buddha-Projekt "Die Sieger"', *Archiv für Musikwissenschaft*, lx (1983), 189–211, esp. 198.
168. Heinrich Porges, *Die Bühnenproben zu den Bayreuther Festspielen 1876* (Leipzig 1896), 29; trans. by Robert L. Jacobs as *Wagner Rehearsing the 'Ring'* (Cambridge 1983), 103.
169. Cosima Wagner, *Die Tagebücher* (note 1), ii.224–5 (10 and 11 Nov. 1878).
170. Richard Du Moulin Eckart, *Cosima Wagner: Ein Lebens- und Charakterbild*, 2 vols. (Berlin 1929–31), ii.312.
171. Cosima Wagner, *Die Tagebücher* (note 1), ii.335 (22 April 1879).
172. *König Ludwig II. und Richard Wagner: Briefwechsel* (note 116), i.83 (letter from Wagner to Ludwig of 14 April 1865).
173. Ibid., iii.148 (letter from Wagner to Ludwig of 9 Feb. 1879).
174. Richard Wagner, *Sämtliche Briefe*, ed. Gertrud Strobel, Werner Wolf, Werner Breig and others (Leipzig 1967–2000 and Wiesbaden 1999–), xi.104–5 (letter to Mathilde Wesendonck of 30 May 1859).
175. Richard Wagner, *Das Braune Buch: Tagebuchaufzeichnungen 1865 bis 1882*, ed. Joachim Bergfeld (Zurich 1975), 53; trans. George Bird as *The Diary of Richard Wagner: The Brown Book 1865–1882* (London 1980), 46. Wagner initially spelt the name 'Anfortas' but changed it to 'Amfortas' in 1877, at the

same time shifting the stress to the second syllable.

176. Wagner, *Das Braune Buch* (note 175), 77; Engl. trans. (*The Diary of Richard Wagner*), 66 (2 Sept. 1865).

177. Wagner, *Das Braune Buch* (note 175), 70; Engl. trans. (*The Diary of Richard Wagner*), 61.

178. Cosima Wagner, *Die Tagebücher* (note 1), ii.1108 (6 Feb. 1883): 'I am like Othello, the day's long task is done.'

179. Otto, *Richard Wagner: Ein Lebens- und Charakterbild* (note 152), 483.

180. Friedrich Nietzsche, *Sämtliche Briefe: Kritische Studienausgabe*, ed. Giorgio Colli and Mazzino Montinari, 8 vols. (Munich 1986), viii.13 (letter to Heinrich Köselitz of 21 Jan. 1887).

181. *Lettres à Judith Gautier* (note 104), 62 (letter of 9 Nov. 1877).

182. *König Ludwig II. und Richard Wagner: Briefwechsel* (note 116), iii.174 (letter from Wagner to Ludwig of 31 March 1880).

183. Wagner, *Sämtliche Briefe* (note 174), xi.104 (letter to Mathilde Wesendonck of 30 May 1859).

184. Peter Wapnewski, *Der traurige Gott: Richard Wagner in seinen Helden* (Munich 1978), 220: 'His genital equipment is destroyed by the poisoned weapon and is now nothing but a single horrifying festering frostbitten wound.'

185. Cosima Wagner, *Die Tagebücher* (note 1), ii.768 (25 July 1881).

186. Richard Wagner, *Sämtliche Werke*, xxx ('Dokumente zur Entstehung und ersten Aufführung des Bühnenweihfestspiels Parsifal'), ed. Martin Geck and Egon Voss (Mainz 1970), 176.

187. *König Ludwig II. und Richard Wagner: Briefwechsel* (note 116), i.174 (letter from Wagner to Ludwig of 7 Sept. 1865).

188. By way of a joke, Wagner occasionally gave autographs notated in a similar way. Liszt's biographer Alan Walker thinks that the sound of the bells symbolized the relationship between the two men in the eyes of the Hungarian composer, who worked the motif into his own piano piece *Am Grabe Richard Wagners*; see Alan Walker, *Franz Liszt*, 3 vols. (London 1983–96), iii.432.

189. Newman, *The Life of Richard Wagner* (note 129), iv.612.

190. Cosima Wagner, *Die Tagebücher* (note 1), i.586 (29 Oct. 1872).

191. Wagner, *Sämtliche Werke* (note 186), 144. Noted down after the performances in July 1882.

192. Cosima Wagner, *Die Tagebücher* (note 1), ii.673 (23 Jan. 1881).

193. Glasenapp, *Das Leben Richard Wagners* (note 63), vi.45.

194. Ibid., vi.12.

195. Karl Gutzkow, *Rückblicke auf mein Leben* (Berlin 1875), 319.

196. Felix Weingartner, *Lebenserinnerungen*, 2 vols. (Zurich 2/1928–9), i.133; translated from the first edition by Marguerite Wolff as *Buffets and Rewards: A Musician's Reminiscences* (London 1937), 77.

197. Egon Voss, 'Die Möglichkeit der Klage in der Wonne: Skizze zur Charakterisierung der *Parsifal*-Musik', '*Wagner und kein Ende*': *Betrachtungen und Studien* (Zurich 1996), 222–33, esp. 227.

198. Hans von Wolzogen, *Wagner und seine Werke* (Regensburg 1924), 247.

199. Cosima Wagner, *Die Tagebücher* (note 1), ii.657 (4 Jan. 1881).

200. Wagner, *Sämtliche Werke* (note 186), 195.

201. Cosima Wagner, *Die Tagebücher* (note 1), ii.1002 (14 Sept. 1882).

202. Ibid., i.177 (8 Dec. 1869).

203. Wagner, *Gesammelte Schriften* (note 69), x.277; Engl. trans. (*Richard Wagner's Prose Works*), vi.277 ('Heroism and Christianity').

204. Joachim Köhler, *Wagners Hitler: Der Prophet und sein Vollstrecker* (Munich 1987), 164; trans. Ronald Taylor as *Wagner's Hitler: The Prophet and His*

Disciple (Cambridge 2000), 115.

205. Cosima Wagner, *Die Tagebücher* (note 1), ii.938 (25 April 1882).

206. Wagner, *Sämtliche Werke* (note 186), 203. Wagner's stage direction for *Parsifal*, noted down by Heinrich Porges.

207. Wagner, *Sämtliche Briefe* (note 174), vi.63 (letter to August Röckel of 25–6 Jan. 1854).

208. Cosima Wagner, *Die Tagebücher* (note 1), ii.214 (31 Oct. 1878).

209. Ibid., ii.219 (5 Nov. 1878).

210. Wagner, *Gesammelte Schriften* (note 69), x.304; Engl. trans. (*Richard Wagner's Prose Works*), vi.309 ('The Stage Consecration Festival in Bayreuth in 1882').

211. Richard Wagner, *Lohengrin*, ed. Michael von Soden (Frankfurt am Main 1980), 156.

212. *König Ludwig II. und Richard Wagner: Briefwechsel* (note 116), iii.141 (letter from Wagner to Ludwig of 29 Dec. 1878).

213. Wagner, *Sämtliche Werke* (note 186), 84.

214. Voss, 'Die Möglichkeit der Klage' (note 197), 232.

215. *König Ludwig II. und Richard Wagner: Briefwechsel* (note 116), iii.149 (letter from Wagner to Ludwig of 27 March 1879).

216. Wagner, *Gesammelte Schriften* (note 69), v.179; Engl. trans. (*Richard Wagner's Prose Works*), iii.231 ('Prelude to *Lohengrin*').

217. Wagner, *Sämtliche Werke* (note 186), 154.

218. Cosima Wagner, *Die Tagebücher* (note 1), ii.303 (3 Feb. 1879).

219. Glasenapp, *Das Leben Richard Wagners* (note 63), vi.591; see also Cosima Wagner *Die Tagebücher* (note 1), ii. 938 (25 April 1882).

220. Cosima Wagner, *Die Tagebücher* (note 1), ii.1110 (9 Feb. 1883): 'Finally he loudly complains that he has built Wahnfried, the festival too strikes him as absurd.'

221. Glasenapp, *Das Leben Richard Wagners* (note 63), vi.762.

222. Neumann, *Erinnerungen an Richard Wagner* (note 96), 260; Engl. trans. (*Personal Recollections*), 250.

223. Siegfried Wagner, *Erinnerungen* (Stuttgart 1923), 43.

224. Cosima Wagner, *Die Tagebücher* (note 1), ii.623 (21 Nov. 1880).

225. Rützow, *Richard Wagner und Bayreuth* (note 8), 196.

226. Joachim Thiery and Dietrich Seidel, '"Ich behage mir nicht": Richard Wagner und seine Ärzte', *Münchener Medizinische Wochenschrift*, cxxxvi (1994), 40; trans. Stewart Spencer as '"I Feel Only Discontent": Wagner and His Doctors', *Wagner*, xvi (1995), 3–22, esp. 14.

227. Henry Perl, *Richard Wagner in Venedig: Mosaikbilder aus seinen letzten Lebenstagen* (Augsburg 1883), vii.

228. Thiery und Seidel, '"Ich behage mir nicht"' (note 226), 43; Engl. trans. ('"I Feel Only Discontent"'), 21.

229. Thiery und Seidel, '"Ich behage mir nicht"' (note 226), 44; Engl. trans. ('"I Feel Only Discontent"'), 20.

230. Willi Schuh, *Richard Strauss: Jugend und frühe Meisterjahre 1864–1898* (Zurich 1976), 19; trans. Mary Whittall as *Richard Strauss: A Chronicle of the Early Years 1864–1898* (Cambridge 1982), 6.

231. Thiery and Seidel, '"Ich behage mir nicht"' (note 226), 41; Engl. trans. ('"I Feel Only Discontent"'), 13.

232. Thiery and Seidel, '"Ich behage mir nicht"' (note 226), 45; Engl. trans. ('"I Feel Only Discontent"'), 19–20.

233. Glasenapp, *Das Leben Richard Wagners* (note 63), vi.773.

234. Wagner, *Mein Leben* (note 156), ii.144; Engl. trans. (*My Life*), 572–3.

235. Cosima Wagner, *Die Tagebücher* (note 1), ii.1099 (24 Jan. 1883).

236. Joachim von Kürenberg, *Carneval der Einsamen: Richard Wagners Tod in*

Venedig (Hamburg 1947). Although Kürenberg was a novelist, he spoke to many eyewitnesses, all of whose accounts are entirely trustworthy.

237. Cosima Wagner, *Die Tagebücher* (note 1), ii.1026 (17 Oct. 1882).

238. Ibid., ii.1054 (22 Nov. 1882).

239. Ibid., ii.1014 (3 Oct. 1882).

240. Ibid., ii.1074 (19 Dec. 1882).

241. Walker, *Franz Liszt* (note 188), iii.426. It struck Walker as a 'quixotic thought' that Wagner might have heard his own elegy. One could also describe it as eerie.

242. Cosima Wagner, *Die Tagebücher* (note 1), ii.1076 (20 Dec. 1882).

243. Ibid., i.834 (5 July 1874).

244. Weingartner, *Lebenserinnerungen* (note 196), i.261; this passage was added to the second edition and is therefore not included in the 1937 English translation.

245. Walker, *Franz Liszt* (note 188), iii.503.

246. Ibid., iii.514.

247. Lina Ramann, *Lisztiana: Erinnerungen an Franz Liszt in Tagebuchblättern, Briefen und Dokumenten aus den Jahren 1873–1886/87*, ed. Arthur Seidl and Friedrich Schnapp (Mainz 1983), 372.

248. Ibid., 375.

249. Ibid., 376.

250. Walker, *Franz Liszt* (note 188), iii.509.

251. Cosima Wagner, *Die Tagebücher* (note 1), ii.1104 (31 Jan. 1883).

252. Ibid., ii.1107 (5 Feb. 1883).

253. *König Ludwig II. und Richard Wagner: Briefwechsel* (note 116), v.150 (letter from Wagner to Cosima von Bülow of 17 April 1866).

254. Glasenapp, *Das Leben Richard Wagners* (note 63), vi.769.

255. Cosima Wagner, *Die Tagebücher* (note 1), ii.1113 (12 Feb. 1883).

256. Ibid., ii.989 (11 Aug. 1882).

257. Peter P. Pachl, *Siegfried Wagner: Genie im Schatten* (Munich 1988), 63.

258. Cosima Wagner, *Die Tagebücher* (note 1), ii.999 (6 Sept. 1882).

259. Westernhagen, *Wagner* (note 100), 568; this passage was not included in the 1978 English translation but formed the basis of Westernhagen's article 'Wagner's Last Day', *Musical Times*, cxx (1979), 395–7.

260. Cosima Wagner, *Die Tagebücher* (note 1), ii.939 (26 April 1882).

261. Wagner, *Sämtliche Schriften* (note 165), xii.343; Engl. trans. (*Richard Wagner's Prose Works*), viii.396 ('On the Feminine in the Human').

262. Walker, *Franz Liszt* (note 188), ii.435.

263. Du Moulin Eckart, *Cosima Wagner* (note 170), ii.10.

264. Detta and Michael Petzet, *Die Richard Wagner-Buhne König Ludwigs II.* (Munich 1970), 286 (letter from Ludwig Bürkel to Ludwig II of 20 Feb. 1883).

265. Glasenapp, *Das Leben Richard Wagners* (note 63), vi.775.

266. Petzet and Petzet, *Die Richard Wagner-Bühne* (note 264), 287.

267. Frithjof Haas, *Zwischen Brahms und Wagner: Der Dirigent Hermann Levi* (Zurich 1995), 281. Of the six solo Flowermaidens, Carrie Pringle was the only one not to be invited back in 1883.

Index

WITHDRAWN